WEBSTER'S NEW WORLD™

COMPUTER DICTIONARY

10TH EDITION

By Bryan Pfaffenberger, Ph.D.

WILEY

Wiley Publishing, Inc.

Webster's New World™ Computer Dictionary, 10th Edition

Copyright © 2003 by Wiley Publishing, Inc., Indianapolis, Indiana

Published by Wiley Publishing, Inc., Indianapolis, Indiana
Published simultaneously in Canada

For general information on our other products and services or to obtain technical support please contact our Customer Care Department within the U.S. at 800-762-2974, outside the U.S. at 317-572-3993 or fax 317-572-4002.

Wiley also publishes its books in a variety of electronic formats. Some content that appears in print may not be available in electronic books.

Library of Congress Cataloging-in-Publication Data is available from the publisher.

ISBN 0-7645-2478-X

Manufactured in the United States of America

5   4   3   2

Dedication

For Suzanne, always

— BP

Acknowledgments

No work of this scope could have been undertaken without a great deal of help, and this book is no exception. I'd like to express very special thanks to the crew at Wiley Publishing, Inc. in Indianapolis, including acquisitions editor Roxane Cerda and production editor M. Faunette Johnston. This is an especially talented and diligent pair, and they've helped me bring to fruition the most comprehensive revision that this work has ever received. Ultimately, though, the responsibility for any errors or omissions you might find is mine and mine alone, so please address your ire to me (bp@virginia.edu); you may very well find your contribution reflected in the next edition of this work!

About the author

Bryan Pfaffenberger is Associate Professor of Technology, Culture, and Communication at the University of Virginia. An expert in explaining complex information technology to the public, he is the author of more than 75 books on every aspect of computer and Internet technology.

Trademarks

All terms in this book that are known to be trademarks or service marks have been appropriately capitalized. Wiley Publishing, Inc. cannot attest to the accuracy of this information. Use of a term in this book should not be regarded as affecting the validity of any trademark or service mark.

Introduction

We live in a computerized society—and, increasingly, knowledge of computer terminology paves the way to personal and professional advancement.

- Commerce on the Internet may have taken a hit in the stock market slump of 2001, but it's back and bigger than ever. Most experts believe that e-commerce has taken its rightful place as a mainstay of the world economy. If you want to be part of this, you'll need to know why *strong authentication* is necessary, how to tell the difference between a *digital signature* and a *certificate,* and why *cookies* are needed to implement virtual *shopping carts*.

- Computer knowledge and expertise bring big payoffs in the job market. In today's job market, though, yesterday's computer skills won't pay off. You'll be wise to know the difference between *Java* and *Javascript,* why *virtual private networks (VPN)* are replacing *leased lines,* and whether *HTML* or *XML* represents the best choice for encoding content on a Web page.

- Currently, the Internet is available in well over half of all U.S. households. A major impetus is electronic mail, which is increasingly a favorite method of staying in touch with others. Unless you want to be left in the dark, you'll be wise to know what people are talking about when they begin that litany of acronyms: *S/MIME, POP, IMAP, X.509, LDAP,* and many more. You'd also better know how to handle *attachments,* which may—all too often—contain *computer viruses* that could wipe out all the data on your computer's hard drive.

- Buying a computer is your ticket to better performance in school and a better job after graduation. If you're thinking about purchasing a computer, or upgrading an existing one, you'll need to choose between such obscure things as *DDR-SDRAM, Rambus DRAM memory, G4, Athlon,* and *Pentium 4 processors*. If your head's spinning, welcome to the club.

This book can help. Offering thousands of definitions in every area of computer and Internet technology, this book defines terms in clear, plain English. What's more, it goes beyond merely defining the terms; you'll find additional background information that will prove invaluable in understanding *why* a particular term is important and *how* it relates to others.

You can use this book as a learning tool by following the extensive cross-references. You've probably heard about *Linux,* an operating system that's distributed on *open source software* principles. Start tracking down the cross-references in these articles, and you'll learn a great deal about the nature of the open source software movement, which many people believe is capable of posing a serious challenge to the commercial software industry.

Special features help make this book easier to use. Some words have more than one sense; if so, their definitions are numbered. Where pronunciation isn't obvious, you'll learn how to pronounce the word. (*Cache,* for example, is pronounced "cash.")

Bryan Pfaffenberger
Charlottesville, Virginia

& (Ampersand) In Unix and Unix-like operating system shells, a symbol appended to a command to force the job to function in the background. See *Linux, shell, Unix*.

* (Asterisk) Commonly used in file specifications as a wildcard character denoting zero to an infinite number of characters. See *wildcard*.

@ (Pronounced at.) In an e-mail address, a symbol used to separate the user name from the name of the computer on which the user's mailbox is stored (for example, frodo@bagend.org).

@ function (Pronounced at function.) See *built-in function*.

^ (Caret symbol) See *caret*.

= (Equals sign) In programming languages, a notation that is commonly used to indicate the assignment of a value to a variable.

! (Exclamation point, pronounced bang.) In programming languages, a notation that commonly indicates a logical NOT operator. See *Boolean operator*.

? (Question mark) Commonly used in file specifications as a wildcard denoting any single character. See *wildcard*.

. (Pronounced star-dot-star.) Commonly used in file specifications to match all available files. See *wildcard*.

> (Right angle bracket or greater-than symbol) **1.** In e-mail, a symbol used at the beginning of a line of text to designate quoted text (text copied from a received message). **2.** In Unix and Unix-like operating system shells, a redirection operator that is used to send the output of a command to a second command. See *Linux, shell, Unix*. **3.** In spreadsheet and other programs that enable users to specify logical formulas, a logical operator meaning "greater than."

< (Left angle bracket or less-than symbol) **1.** In Unix and Linux shells, a redirection operator that is used to route the input of a file to a specified command. See *Linux, shell, Unix*. **2.** In spreadsheet and other programs that enable users to specify logical formulas, a logical operator meaning "less than."

| (Vertical bar character) In operating system shells such as bash, signifies a pipe. See *pipe, shell, Unix*.

/ (Forward slash) **1.** In Unix and Linux shells and file utilities, a character used to denote the root directory (the top-level directory) or, in path names that include one or more directory names, to separate the parts of a directory path. Internet standards (such as FTP and HTTP) also adhere to this convention for describing directory and path names. **2.** In MS-DOS and Microsoft Windows, a character used to preface switches (command options) when these are typed at the command prompt.

// (Two forward slashes) On the Internet, a separator within a Uniform Resource Identifier (URI) that separates the name of the protocol (such as http: or ftp:) from the domain name (for example, http://www.virginia.edu). See *URI*.

** (Backslash) **1. In MS-DOS and Microsoft Windows, a character used to denote the root directory (the top-level directory) or, in path names that include one or more directory names, to separate the parts of a directory path. **2.** In Unix shells, a notation indicating that the following single character should be taken literally by the shell and not processed as a special character.

**** (Two backslashes) In Windows networking, a separator that precedes the name of a computer. See *Common Internet File System (CIFS), Server Message Block (SMB) Protocol*.

' (Single quote) In Unix shells, a quotation character that indicates to the shell that the following characters (up to the next single quote) should be taken literally and not processed as special characters. See *"*, *Linux, shell, Unix*.

" (Double quote) In Unix and Linux shells, a quotation character that indicates to the shell that the following characters (up to the next double quote) should be taken literally and not processed as special characters See *Linux, shell, Unix*.

$0.02 In e-mail, Usenet, instant messaging, and Internet Relay Chat (IRC), a shorthand expression for the expression "This is just my two cents' worth."

0.13 micron technology The most advanced semiconductor chip fabrication technology in actual use for production at this writing; it is capable of miniaturizing the switching components of processing chips (called gates) to approximately one-eighth of a micron (one millionth of a meter). See *microprocessor, submicron technology*.

0.18 micron technology A submicron processor fabricating technology capable of miniaturizing the basic switching components of processing chips (called gates) to approximately one-fifth of a micron (one-millionth of a meter). See *submicron technology*.

1NF In relational database normalization, the first level of normalization, in which each field in a table is sufficiently distinguished so that it contains different types of information. See *normalization*.

2NF In relational database normalization, the second level of normalization, in which it is ascertained that the data in one field is not derived from the data in a second field. See *normalization*.

3-D Abbreviation for three dimensions or three-dimensional.

3-D graph A business or scientific chart that depicts information using three axes: width (x-axis), height (y-axis), and depth (z-axis).

3-D graphics The display of objects and scenes with sufficient height, width, and depth information to produce the illusion of a realistic, three-dimensional scene. To portray such images, the viewing software uses a coordinate system capable of representing any point as the intersection of three axes (x, y, and z).

3-D rendering Transforming graphic images by adding shading and light sources so that they appear to be three-dimensional.

3NF In relational database normalization, the third level of normalization, in which it is ascertained that the database contains no duplicate information. See *normalization*.

3.5-inch floppy disk A floppy disk that is enclosed in a hard plastic case with a sliding metal access door. High-density 3½-inch disks, capable of storing 1.44MB, are most common. Older, double-density disks hold 720K, while new, somewhat rare 3.5-inch disks store 2.88MB. Macintosh 3.5-inch disks hold either 800K (double density) or 1.4MB (high density).

4nf In relational database normalization, the fourth level of normalization, in which independent facts that are stored in one table, even though they have multiple values, are stored in separate tables. See *normalization*.

5.25-inch disk An obsolete type of floppy disk, enclosed in a flexible plastic shell. The most widely used type of floppy disk before 1987, 5.25-inch disks have been replaced by 3.5-inch disks. The term "floppy disk" derives from the flexible packaging used for 5.25-inch disks and their predecessor, 8.5-inch floppy disks.

8-bit color A color depth of 8 bits, which enables the display of up to 256 colors. See *16-bit color, 24-bit color, 32-bit color*.

8-bit microprocessor A microprocessor that can handle only 1 byte (8 bits) of data at a time. The Intel 8088, used in the first IBM personal computers, is an 8-bit microprocessor and has an internal data bus 8 bits wide. See *16-, 32-, 64-bit microprocessor*.

8-bit video adapter A color video adapter that can display 256 colors simultaneously.

8-VSB A standard developed by the Advanced Television Systems Committee (ATSC) for broadcast high definition digital television (HDTV) in the U.S. and other conforming countries. The standard supports the transmission of up to 19.38 Mbps of data in a single channel. Although approved by the U.S. Federal Communications Commission (FCC), the standard is controversial due to the high potential for multipath interference in urban areas. See *HDTV.*

8.3 file name format The standard MS-DOS file name format, which restricts file name length to a maximum of eight characters for the file name and three characters for the optional extension (for example, autoexec.bat). See *file name.*

10BASE-2 A specification for an Ethernet local area network (LAN) capable of transmitting 10Mb of data per second via thin coaxial cables with a maximum length of 185 meters. Also known as Thin Ethernet. The standard is part of the IEEE 802.3 specification. See *Ethernet.*

10BASE-5 A specification for an Ethernet local area network (LAN) capable of transmitting 10Mb of data per second via thick coaxial cables with a maximum length of 500 meters. Also known as Thick Ethernet. The standard is part of the IEEE 802.3 specification. See *Ethernet.*

10BASE-F A specification for an Ethernet local area network (LAN) capable of transmitting 10Mb of data per second via fiber optic cable. The standard is part of the IEEE 802.3 specification. See *Ethernet.*

10BASE-T A specification for an Ethernet local area network (LAN) capable of transmitting 10Mb of data per second via twisted-pair wiring. The standard is part of the IEEE 802.3 specification. See *Ethernet.*

10-Gigabit Ethernet An Ethernet specification for networks capable of transmitting 10 Gb of data per second over fiber optic cable; transmissions are full duplex, which eliminates the need for collision detection protocols. This standard is expected to expand the range of Ethernet applications from local area networks to metropolitan area networks (MAN) and wide area networks (WAN). See *collision, Ethernet, fiber optic.*

16-bit application In Microsoft Windows, an application that is designed to use the 16-bit processing mode of Intel microprocessors. Most 16-bit Windows applications were designed to run with Microsoft Windows 3.1. The more recent consumer versions of Microsoft Windows, including Windows 95, Windows 98, and Windows Me, are hybrid 16/32-bit operating systems that are capable of running 16-bit applications as well as newer 32-bit applications, which take full advantage of Intel's 32-bit microprocessors. See *32-bit application.*

16-bit color A color depth of 16 bits, which enables the display of up to 65,536 colors. See *8-bit color, 24-bit color, color depth.*

16-bit microprocessor A microprocessor that can handle 2 bytes of data at a time, making it significantly faster than the even more obsolete 8-bit microprocessor. The Intel 8086 and Intel 80286 are 16-bit microprocessors. See *external data bus, internal data bus, register.*

16-bit operating system An operating system that employs a microprocessor's 16-bit processing mode, in which 2 bytes of data can be processed simultaneously. Microsoft Windows 3.1 is a 16-bit operating system. See *32-bit operating system.*

16-bit sound card A sound card capable of processing and reproducing sounds and music recorded with 16-bit resolution, the resolution of the Compact Disc-Digital Audio (CD-DA) standard. Most 16-bit sound boards also can process sounds recorded at resolutions lower than 16 bits.

24-bit color   A color depth of 24 bits, which enables the display of more than 16 million colors simultaneously. With a video adapter and monitor capable of processing and displaying 24-bit color, users can view beautiful, photographic-quality images at high resolutions. Displaying 24-bit color in resolutions higher than standard VGA (640 × 480) requires 2MB or more of video memory. See *color depth, resolution.*

30-pin SIMM   A small rectangular circuit board containing memory chips, designed to fit into a 30-pin SIMM slot on a motherboard. Although obsolete, these chips can still be used in modern 72-pin SIMM slots by purchasing a 30-to-72-pin SIMM converter, an accessory that modifies the 30-pin SIMM socket. See *SIMM.*

30-pin SIMM slot   A socket, usually on the motherboard, for 30-pin SIMMs. Such SIMMs are obsolete and have been replaced by 72-pin versions on modern motherboards. See *72-pin SIMM slot.*

32-bit application   A program designed to take full advantage of the processing capabilities of 32-bit microprocessors, which can handle 4 bytes of data at a time. These applications require 32-bit operating systems. See *16-bit application, 32-bit operating system.*

32-bit color   Nominally, a color depth of 32 bits; in practice, 32-bit color refers to the use of 24-bit color depth with the addition of 8 bits that are used for three-dimensional rendering or transparency information. See *color depth.*

32-bit microprocessor   A microprocessor that can handle 4 bytes (32 bits) of data at a time, making it much faster than 16-bit microprocessors. 32-bit microprocessors such as the Intel 486 and Intel 386DX have internal data buses 32 bits wide that connect to 32-bit external data buses; the Intel 386SX, an obsolete 32-bit microprocessor, is a compromise design that connects to a less expensive 16-bit external data bus. See *16-bit microprocessor, 64-bit microprocessor.*

32-bit operating system   An operating system that takes full advantage of the 32-bit microprocessors, which can perform operations on 4 bytes (32 bits) of information at a time. Among the many advantages of 32-bit operating systems is their capability to set up a flat address space, in which the operating system can map out the available memory without restrictions imposed by segmentation. Microsoft Windows NT, Windows 2000, Windows XP, Linux, and Unix are true 32-bit operating systems; Microsoft Windows 95, 98, and Me are hybrids, retaining some 16-bit code so that users can continue to run their Windows 3.1 applications. See *16-bit operating system, 64-bit operating system.*

32-bit video adapter   An obsolete type of video adapter with a graphics coprocessor that is capable of processing 32 bits of data at a time. 32-bit video adapters cannot handle the high resolutions that make Microsoft Windows 95/98 easy to use, and they are too slow for most modern graphics tasks. 64-bit video adapters and 128-bit video adapters have replaced 32-bit video adapters. See *video adapter.*

64-bit microprocessor   A microprocessor that can handle 8 bytes (64 bits) of data at the same time. A full 64-bit microprocessor (such as Intel's Itanium and Sun's UltraSPARC) features 64-bit internal and external data buses, bringing impressive gains in input/output (I/O) performance, and is capable of working with 64-bit operating systems such as Windows XP 64-Bit Edition. Although Intel Pentium microprocessors have a 64-bit internal data bus, they only have a 32-bit external bus; they are designed to work with 32-bit operating systems such as Microsoft Windows 95, 98, and NT, and are therefore not true 64-bit microprocessors. See *32-bit microprocessor, Alpha, Itanium.*

64-bit operating system   An operating system that is capable of taking full advantage of a 64-bit microprocessor's data-processing capabilities. Examples include Microsoft's Windows XP 64-Bit Edition,

Sun's Solaris 9, and a version of Linux that is designed to work with the 64-bit Alpha processor. Relatively little software is currently available for 64-bit operating systems, which are mainly used for engineering and science applications, but it is likely that 64-bit Web servers will become more common as Internet usage increases. See *16-bit operating system, 32-bit operating system, Alpha, Itanium, Linux, Unix*.

64-bit video adapter   A video adapter with a graphics co-processor that is capable of processing 64 bits of data at a time.

72-pin SIMM   A small rectangular circuit board containing memory chips that is designed to be inserted into a 72-pin SIMM slot. On many Pentium systems, SIMMs must be upgraded two at a time because each SIMM makes available only half of the required 64-bit memory path. 72-pin SIMMS are still used in many computers, but the latest RAM standard in PCs is becoming the SDRAM DIMM. See *DDR-SDRAM*.

72-pin SIMM slot   A socket, usually on the motherboard, for 72-pin SIMMs. These slots enable users to increase memory capacity by inserting 72-pin SIMMs.

80x8   The generic designation of early Intel microprocessors. See *Intel 8086, Intel 8088*.

84-key keyboard   See *AT keyboard*.

100% column graph   A column graph that resembles a pie graph in that each "slice" of the column displays the relative percentage of that data item compared to the total. See *stacked column graph*.

100% Pure Java   A certification from JavaSoft, the Sun Microsystems venture founded to promote the Java programming language, that a given Java product conforms to the current cross-platform Java specification, contained in the current Java development kit (JDK), and will therefore execute on any platform for which a Java interpreter has been developed. The 100% Pure Java program is intended to protect Java's "write-once, run anywhere" philosophy against proprietary versions of the language, which could contain extensions that would restrict Java programs to execution on a single platform. See *Java*.

100BASE-FX   A specification for a Fast Ethernet (100Base-T) local area network (LAN) capable of data transfer rates of 100 Mbps over fiber optic cable. The standard is part of the IEEE 802.3 specification. See *Ethernet, fiber optics*.

100BASE-T   A specification for an Ethernet local area network (LAN) capable of transmitting 100Mb of data per second over a variety of transmission media. The standard is part of the 802.3 specification. Synonymous with Fast Ethernet. See *CAT-5, Ethernet, twisted-pair*.

100VG-AnyLAN   A local area network (LAN) standard capable of data transfer rates over doubled CAT-3 twisted-pair wires; such networks can carry token ring as well as Ethernet data. The "VG" in the standard's name stands for "voice grade," a reference to the fact that CAT-3 twisted-pair wiring is normally used for voice but not for high-speed data transfer.

101-key keyboard   See *extended keyboard*.

104-key keyboard   A keyboard that contains three additional keys besides the ones on the 101-key (enhanced) keyboard. The additional keys vary by manufacturer. The Microsoft Natural keyboard, for example, contains extra keys that perform special functions in Windows 95 and 98. Gateway 2000, a leading computer manufacturer, also has a 104-key keyboard, with the additional keys used for programming keyboard macros. See *extended keyboard*.

108-key Apple Pro keyboard   See *Apple Pro Keyboard*.

128-bit domestic-level encryption   A level of encryption used for secure Web sites and e-mail that uses an encryption bit length of 128 bits. This bit length prevents the message from being intercepted and decoded, but current U.S. export regulations prevent U.S. companies from exporting software that incorporates this strong level of encryption. See *encryption*.

128-bit video adapter A video adapter with an internal data bus 128 bits wide, making it the fastest kind of video adapter available for personal computer monitors today. A 128-bit video adapter can significantly speed up graphics-intensive tasks such as computer-aided design (CAD) and animation.

216 browser-safe color palette A palette of 216 colors that look approximately the same on Macintosh and Windows displays. The use of other colors may lead to unpredictable results.

4GL See *fourth generation programming language*.

401—Unauthorized An error code generated by Web servers. This message indicates that the site is password-protected and the wrong user name or password was provided.

403—Forbidden An error code generated by Web servers. This message indicates that the requested resource cannot be supplied to the Internet address you are currently using.

404—Not Found **1.** An error code generated by Web servers. This message indicates that the requested resource cannot be found. Often, these messages result from a typographical error (for example, typing "index.htm" when the actual file name is "index.html"). **2.** In computer slang, a person who is daydreaming or not paying attention.

765 A chip that controls the flow of data and instructions between the central processing unit (CPU) and the floppy disk drive. Because it is easily programmed with BIOS instructions, the 765 has been used in personal computers for many years.

680x0 See *Motorola 680x0*.

6845 A video controller chip that has appeared on or that has been simulated on all video adapters since IBM's early-1980s MDA standard. Video drivers can program the 6845's registers and define the characteristics of the video signal the 6845 sends to the screen.

802.11g See *IEEE 802.11g*.

8250 The UART chip found on the original IBM Personal Computer, the IBM Personal Computer XT, and compatible machines. Now obsolete, the 8250 will experience overrun errors if used with modern machines because it cannot handle the fast data transfers they demand.

16450 The UART chip found on IBM Personal Computer AT machines and compatibles. The 16450 can handle faster modems than its predecessor, the 8250, but is technically inferior to the newer 16550 because of its tendency to cause overrun errors under fast data-transfer conditions. A 16550 UART is needed for today's high-speed modems. See *16550, UART*.

16550 The UART chip found on fast, modern computer systems. As the state-of-the-art UART, the 16550 has a much larger storage buffer than the obsolete 8250 and 16450, making it less prone to overrun errors. See *16450, UART*.

A

AAMOF Abbreviation for "as a matter of fact." Commonly used on Internet Relay Chat (IRC), e-mail, and Usenet. See *abbrev.*

abandon To clear a document, spreadsheet, or other work from the screen—and therefore from memory—without saving it to a floppy or hard disk. The work is irretrievably lost. See *save.*

abbrev Abbreviation for abbreviation. To cut down on unneeded typing, abbrevs are commonly used in text-based communication services such as Internet Relay Chat (IRC), chat rooms, e-mail, and Usenet. Examples include AFK (as far as I know), BRB (be right back), and YMMV (your mileage may vary).

A-BONE An Asian Internet backbone network that enables users throughout East and South Asia to connect without requiring an intermediary connection through Europe or North America. See *backbone.*

abort To cancel a program, command, or procedure while in progress. One can often abort a procedure manually, or a procedure may abort by itself because of a bug in the program, a power failure, or another unexpected cause.

A-B roll editing In multimedia, a method for creating a master edited video sequence by directing selected portions of video signals from two video sources (VCRs or camcorders) to a destination recording device, usually a VCR.

absolute address In a program, a method of specifying a memory location that uses the location's physical address. An alternative method uses an expression to calculate the address.

absolute cell reference A spreadsheet cell reference that does not adjust when one copies or moves a formula. An absolute cell reference includes a symbol such as ($) before the column letter ($A6) or the row number (A$6), or both (A6), that locks the indicated cell reference so that it does not change when formulas are copied. See *relative cell reference.*

absolute link In an HTML document, a hyperlink that fully and precisely specifies the file location of the referenced remote document. An absolute link specifies the protocol (such as http:// or ftp://) as well as the name of the computer and the location of the referenced file within the computer's directory structure. See *relative URL (RELURL).*

absolute path In a hierarchical file system, such as NTFS or Unix, a path statement that includes all the information necessary to locate the file relative to the root directory. See *NTFS, path statement, relative path.*

absolute URL On the Web, a uniform resource locator (URL) that fully specifies the resource's location on the Internet. See *relative URL (RELURL).*

absolute value The positive value of a number, regardless of its sign (positive or negative). The absolute value of −357, for example, is 357. In Microsoft Excel and many other spreadsheet programs, the @ABS built-in function returns the absolute value of a number.

abstract class In object-oriented programming, a class that that has no other function besides providing inheritance; no instances are created from it. Typically, abstract classes are incomplete; the missing features are added by various sub-classes. See *class, object-oriented programming.*

abstraction In object-oriented programming, one of the seven fundamental principles of the object model.

Abstract Syntax Notation One (ASN.1) An international standard that specifies how varying types of data can be coded so that applications can recognize which type of data they are dealing with. The rules that express how this coding should be done are called Basic Encoding Rules (BER). Examples of data types include telephone numbers and bibliographic citations. The standard is a key part of the Open Systems Interconnection (OSI) protocol suite but has had relatively little impact on other networking standards, with the exception of e-mail protocols such as X.400 and X.500. See *Basic Encoding Rules (BER), OSI Protocol Suite.*

AC-3 An audio file compression and file encoding standard developed by Dolby Laboratories that enables the compression of up to six channels of digital audio into a compact data stream.

AC adapter An accessory that modifies ordinary household electrical current so that it can be used with an accessory that requires a different voltage, such as computer speakers or a portable computer.

ACAP See *Application Configuration Access Protocol.*

Accelerated Graphics Port See *AGP.*

accelerator board A circuit board designed to speed up some function of a computer. A graphics accelerator board, for example, contains a microprocessor that relieves the central processing unit (CPU) of many video chores, enabling it to get to other work sooner.

accelerator key See *shortcut key.*

accent A mark that forms one of the special characters of many languages. Some examples include: ç (cedilla), ` (grave), ˆ (macron), and ˜ (tilde). Accented characters are included in most font sets, and some application programs include commands or keystrokes that insert accented characters for the user. See *compose sequence, extended character set.*

Acceptable Use Policy See *AUP.*

acceptance test A final demonstration of a new software or hardware product that illustrates the product's capabilities and special features. When companies or other entities hire systems analysts or other computer consultants to do work for them, the acceptance test serves to show that the consultants have satisfied their contract obligations.

access **1.** The right or ability to gain entry to a computer system and make use of its resources. **2.** On a computer system, to open or retrieve any kind of data or document. **3.** To retrieve data or program instructions from a hard or floppy disk drive or from a computer connected to another computer by a network or a modem.

Access See *Microsoft Access.*

access arm See *head arm.*

access charge In telecommunications, a fee levied by a communications company for the use of its network. To reach customers, long-distance telephone companies must pay local telephone companies an access charge.

access code An identification number or password used to gain access to a computer system. See *password, security.*

access control In a network, a means of ensuring the system's security by demanding that users supply some means of identifying themselves, such as a login name and password. The most secure authentication systems require the user to know something (such as a password) and have something (such as a smartcard). See *authentication.*

access control list (ACL) In a network, a database that lists the valid users of the systems and the level of network access that they have been granted.

access denied An error message indicating that a file cannot be opened or modified. This message often means that the file is in use by another application or user.

access hole See *head access aperture.*

accessibility The degree to which a given technology, including hardware and software, is deliberately designed so that it may be used conveniently with limited vision, hearing, or dexterity.

accessible software Software that is designed to be easily and conveniently used by people with limited vision, hearing, or dexterity.

accessor/interrogator In object-oriented programming, a type of method that enables other objects to obtain information about the object's state. See *method, object-oriented programming.*

accessory slot See *expansion slot.*

access point In an IEEE 802.11 wireless LAN, a central station that is analogous to an Ethernet hub. All of the clients' communications travel through the access point. Among the services provided by the access point are automatic IP configuration by means of DHCP and Internet connectivity. See *DHCP, hub, IEEE 802.11, wireless LAN.*

access privileges On a network, the extent of a user's ability to use and modify directories, files, and programs located on other computers in the network. See *LAN.*

access provider See *ISP.*

access rights In a computer network, the privileges possessed by a user or group of users to use resources on a given computer. Some users may have no access rights to a given resource. Guest users are often granted read-only rights; authenticated users are given full read/write and execute rights to the resources in their own directories. The term *execute right* refers to the ability to start a program and run it. See *read-only, read/write.*

access time The amount of time that lapses between a request for information from a device and the delivery of that information. Access times apply to disks and to random access memory (RAM).

account In a network, a contractual agreement between the user and the service provider. In return for network access, the user agrees to abide by the service provider's regulations and, in some cases, to pay a fee.

accounting package A program or group of programs intended to help a business owner automate a firm's accounting procedures. Though accounting packages have grown easier to use recently, they still often require a level of accounting expertise and tedious data entry. See *integrated accounting package, modular accounting package.*

accumulator A register in a central processing unit (CPU) that holds values to be used later in a computation. Computer multiplication, for example, frequently is done by a series of additions; an accumulator holds the intermediate values until the process is completed.

accuracy A statement of how correct a measurement is. Accuracy is different from precision, which describes the number of decimal places to which a measurement is computed.

ACK **1.** Commonly used abbreviation for the acknowledge character (ASCII code 006) in the standard ASCII character set. **2.** Commonly used abbreviation for the acknowledgment message used in handshaking operations between two communication devices, such as modems.

ACL See *access control list.*

ACM See *Association for Computing Machinery.*

ACPI Acronym for Advanced Configuration and Power Interface. A power management scheme that enables compatible operating systems to allocate power to the system as efficiently as possible by shutting down power-consuming resources, such as the display and hard drive, after a specified period of disuse. This is particularly useful for conserving battery life on laptops. In order for ACPI to function properly, your operating system and BIOS must support it. ACPI is designed to replace the Advanced Power Management (APM) standard. See *Advanced Power Management.*

ACPI hardware Computer hardware that is compatible with the Advanced Configuration and Power Interface (ACPI) standard. See *ACPI*.

Acrobat See *PDF*.

acronym A new word made from the first letters or other important letters in a descriptive phrase, used to help people remember technical phrases. For example, RAM is an acronym for random access memory. To pronounce acronyms, spell out the letters unless the acronym contains enough vowels to make it pronounceable as a word (as in BASIC and SIMM). See *abbrev*.

ACT See *contact management program*.

active addressing In portable computers, a type of LCD screen that provides better performance than passive-matrix LCD screens, but without the expense of active-matrix LCD screens. See *active matrix display*.

active area In a spreadsheet document, such as a Lotus 1-2-3 or Microsoft Excel worksheet, the area bounded by cell A1 and the lowest rightmost cell containing data.

active attack In computer security, an attack based on altering information in the computer system so that an intrusion is possible. See *passive attack*.

active cell In a spreadsheet, the cell in which the cell pointer is located. Synonymous with current cell.

Active Channel A standard for push media content delivery on the Web. Developed by Microsoft Corporation, Active Channel enables Web authors to use the Channel Definition Format (CDF), an XML-based markup language, to specify subscription settings. These settings are automatically detected by Active Channel-compatible browsers. See *push media*.

active configuration The current configuration of a modem, usually employing an initialization string. The active configuration supersedes the factory configuration

and remains in effect until one turns off the modem or reboots the computer. See *initialization string*.

active database In database management, the database file in use and present in random access memory (RAM).

Active Desktop In Microsoft Windows, a user interface technology that enables users to place Web content (including Web pages, ActiveX controls, Java applets, or DHTML scripts) on the desktop (background) of their displays. Active Desktop requires the installation of Microsoft Internet Explorer v. 4.0 or later. Once added to the desktop, the Active Desktop item can be sized, positioned, or removed.

Active Desktop item In Microsoft Windows, an object (such as a Web page or an ActiveX control) that the user has placed on the desktop. See *Active Desktop*.

Active Directory In Microsoft Windows 2000 and Windows Server 2003, a directory service that provides centrally administered authentication, application serving, and user registration services for a distributed networking environment.

active file The document that appears onscreen when working with an application program. Some programs can have more than one file open at once, but only one of those can be active at a time.

active hub See *repeater*.

active index In database management systems (DBMSs), the index file being used to determine the order in which data records are displayed.

active matrix display A full-color LCD (liquid crystal display) in which each of the screen's pixels is controlled by its own transistor. Active matrix displays offer higher resolution, contrast, and vertical refresh rate than cheaper passive matrix displays. Although active matrix displays are most commonly found on laptops, the technology has matured sufficiently so that larger active matrix displays have now appeared for desktop systems. Most active matrix displays use thin-film transistor (TFT) technology. See *passive matrix display, thin-film transistor.*

active monitoring   In online banking, a security measure in which a security team constantly monitors the system that holds account information for the telltale signs of unauthorized access.

ActiveMovie   In digital video, an application programming interface (API) developed by Microsoft Corporation that supports streaming video in MPEG, AVI, and other formats. Incorporated into the latest versions of Microsoft Internet Explorer and the consumer versions of Microsoft Windows (including Microsoft Windows Me), ActiveMovie is rivaled by Apple Computer's QuickTime format. See *application program interface (API), AVI, MPEG, QuickTime.*

active partition   On a computer hard disk, the partition that is used to start the computer. Synonymous with boot sector.

active sensing   In multimedia, an error-checking process that MIDI devices use to determine whether they are still receiving a signal. If the device detects that no signal is being received, it turns off all musical notes.

Active Server   Generic term for the various server-side technologies developed by Microsoft Corporation for use with Microsoft Windows NT Server and Windows 2000. These technologies include scripting languages such as VBScript, programming interface standards such as Active Server Page (ASP), and component object models such as COM and COM+. Using these technologies, developers can create server-based applications such as workflow automation, e-commerce, and interactive online databases. See *Active Server Page (ASP), COM, COM+, Microsoft Windows 2000, Microsoft Windows Server 2003, VBScript.*

Active Server Page (ASP)   A standard, developed by Microsoft, for incorporating server-side script programming in a Web page. Such scripts can perform actions such as accessing information stored in a database. ASP resembles CGI in its functionality, but it relies on VBScript or JavaScript and employs the ActiveX scripting engine to read the scripts. Predecessor to ASP.NET. See *ASP.NET, CGI, JavaScript, VBScript.*

active termination   A means of ending a chain of SCSI devices. Active termination is noted for its capability of reducing electrical interference in a long string of SCSI devices. See *forced perfect termination, passive termination.*

active window   In a program or operating system that displays multiple windows, the window in which the cursor is located and where text appears if one starts typing. Only one window can be active at a time. See *windowing environment.*

ActiveX   An Internet-enabled version of Microsoft Corporation's object linking and embedding (OLE) technology, which enables applications to communicate with each other by means of messages passed with the aid of the computer's operating system. The previous version was called Component Object Model (COM). ActiveX adds features designed to enable the distribution of executable programs, called controls, via the Internet. To use these controls, a computer must be running Microsoft Windows or an OLE-enabled version of Mac OS. Unlike Java applets, which run in a protected memory region that isolates the code from the computer's file system, ActiveX controls can directly affect files. For this reason, ActiveX controls are packaged with digitally signed certificates, which prove that the program emanates from a respectable software publisher (and will therefore presumably not do nasty things to one's computer). ActiveX has been renamed and incorporated into Microsoft's .Net strategy. See *ActiveX control, Java, .Net, virus.*

ActiveX control   An executable program that is designed to be distributed in Microsoft's ActiveX packaging, which includes digitally signed certificates. To execute ActiveX controls, the user must be running a Web browser that supports ActiveX, as well as an operating system (Microsoft Windows or an OLE-enabled version of Mac OS) that supports Microsoft's Object Linking and Embedding (OLE) technology for interprocess communication. See *Authenticode, .Net.*

activity light On the front panel of a computer's case, a small colored light that flickers when a hard disk drive is reading or writing data.

actual parameter In computer programming, the values passed to a function by means of a parameter passing convention. These values replace the logical parameters (placeholders) defined within the function. See *parameter.*

actuator See *head actuator.*

AD See *administrative domain.*

Ada A high-level programming language developed by the U.S. Department of Defense (DoD) and required by the DoD for all military programming applications. Ada uses the principles of structured programming, including the use of program modules that can be compiled separately. Ada programs are designed to be highly readable so that they are easy to maintain. Recent versions include ADA++, an object-oriented version of ADA, and ADA 95, the most recent version. See *compiler, high-level programming language, Modula-2, object-oriented programming, Pascal, structured programming.*

adapter **1.** In general, any component that enables two physically dissimilar systems to function together smoothly. **2.** A circuit board that plugs into an expansion slot in a computer to give the computer additional capabilities. Popular adapters for personal computers include video adapters that produce video output, memory expansion boards, internal modems, and sound boards. Synonymous with card and expansion board. **3.** An electrical transformer or voltage converter that enables a computer or peripheral to work with a source of electrical power that differs from its specifications.

adapter segment See *upper memory area (UMA).*

adaptive answering In modems, a feature that enables a fax modem to determine whether an incoming call contains a fax or computer data and then to pass control to the appropriate program.

adaptive bridge In a local area network (LAN), a bridge device that connects two physically separate network segments; an adaptive bridge can be programmed to detect and direct specified network addresses so that they are routed as efficiently as possible. See *bridge, LAN, router.*

adaptive compression A capability of advanced data compression software that selects the optimum compression algorithm based on an analysis of the data to be compressed and its intended uses. See *algorithm, compression.*

Adaptive Differential Pulse Code Modulation (ADPCM) In multimedia, a method of digital waveform compression in which the difference between successive samples (rather than their actual values) is encoded. Using ADPCM, the quantity of audio information that can be stored on a single CD-ROM increases from 1 hour to about 16 hours while maintaining or improving fidelity. ADPCM is the storage technique used by CD-ROM/XA certificate authority (CA) and Compact Disc-Interactive (CD-I) disks.

adaptive equalization In modems, a technique used to find the optimum data transfer rate for a given telephone connection. If both modems are equipped with adaptive equalization capabilities, they cooperate to adjust the data transfer rate to the physical capabilities of the connection; these capabilities may change during the session as noise rises and falls. See *modem.*

ADB See *Apple Desktop Bus.*

ad click rate In Web advertising, the frequency with which users click on banner or other advertisements embedded within the page. See *banner ad.*

A/D converter See *analog-to-digital converter.*

add-in program An accessory or utility program designed to work with and extend the capabilities of an application program. Add-in programs can be created by other software developers or can be included with the application, such as the auditors, file viewers, and "what-if" programs included in many spreadsheet programs. Often used interchangeably with plug-in.

address **1.** The precise location of some type of resource (such as a file, a website, or storage space) in a computer system or network. See *memory address.* **2.** In e-mail, an e-mail address. **3.** In the Internet, the location of a host on the network. See *IP address.*

addressability A measure of monitor performance. Addressability describes the number of positions on the display at which a monitor's electron guns can be pointed. Dot pitch, resolution, and refresh rate are more important specifications of monitor performance.

address book In an e-mail program, a utility that enables users to store and retrieve e-mail addresses and other contact information.

address bus An internal electronic channel from the microprocessor to the RAM, along which the addresses of memory storage locations are transmitted. Like a post office box, each memory location has a distinct number or address; the address bus provides the means by which the microprocessor can access the contents of every location in memory.

addressing In microprocessor architecture, the method used to determine how the operand of an instruction is stored temporarily for processing purposes. For example, a common method is to store operands in a register. See *operand, register.*

address mask See *subnet mask.*

address resolution In a local area network (LAN) that is connected to the Internet, the automated process by which the LAN address of each workstation is converted into an IP address. The translation is needed because the Internet and LANs handle workstation addresses in different ways. Programs based on the Address Resolution Protocol (ARP) handle the translation.

Address Resolution Protocol (ARP) An Internet standard that assigns IP addresses to the network interface cards (NIC) of workstations on a local area network (LAN).

address space The total amount of RAM memory that can be addressed (theoretically) by a given processor. In practice, motherboards impose limitations on the maximum amount of memory that can be physically installed on a computer.

ad-hoc network A local area network (LAN) that is created for some temporary purpose. Ad-hoc networks typically use wireless or infrared media.

ADI See *Apple Desktop Interface.*

adjacency operator In database searching, an operator (typically abbreviated ADJ) that enables the searcher to specify that records should not be retrieved unless the terms linked by the operator are next to each other. For example, the query "Hale ADJ Bopp" rejects a record unless these two terms are adjacent to one another. See *proximity operator.*

admin Abbreviation for administrator. In IT departments, a person who possesses the privileges granted to a network or system administrator, such as the ability to create or delete user accounts and passwords.

adminisphere The levels of management above a technical position that are capable of affecting, positively or negatively, the work done in the technical department.

administrative domain In a network created with Internet technology, a named zone of the network (a domain) that contains equipment operated by a company or some other organization, such as a university.

Apple Computer's administrative domain is apple.com. See *domain*.

administrator The person who is responsible for installing, maintaining, and troubleshooting a specific computer system (system administrator) or network segment (network administrator).

ad network On the World Wide Web, a commercial service that uses cookies to track user's movements and browsing preferences through all of the network's participating sites. This information is used to present the user with advertisements tailored to the user's interest.

Adobe Acrobat A cross-platform document distribution program created by Adobe Systems. With Adobe Acrobat, a document publisher can create a file in Adobe's Portable Document Format (PDF) format. This file can be read on any computer system that can run an Adobe Acrobat reader program. Versions of the reader are available for most popular operating systems, including Windows, Macintosh, and Unix.

Adobe Acrobat Reader A freely distributed program used to view Adobe Acrobat files.

Adobe FrameMaker See *desktop publishing software*.

Adobe Illustrator See *vector graphics*.

Adobe PageMaker See *desktop publishing software*.

Adobe PageMill See *WYSIWYG HTML editor*.

Adobe PhotoShop See *image-editing software*.

Adobe PostScript See *PostScript*.

Adobe Systems A software publisher, headquartered in San Jose, California, that focuses on desktop publishing software and related technologies, such as portable document formats, graphics imaging and illustration, World Wide Web publishing software, printer description languages, and display technologies. See *PostScript*.

Adobe Type Manager (ATM) A font utility that enables Windows and Macintosh users to display PostScript Type 1 fonts onscreen. The program is available in Windows and Macintosh versions. See *PostScript font, TrueType*.

ADPCM See *Adaptive Differential Pulse Code Modulation*.

ADSL Acronym for Asymmetric Digital Subscriber Line. Invented by AT&T and adopted by ANSI as standard T1.413 in 1995. Like all DSL broadband technologies, ADSL enables a standard telephone line (copper twisted-pair) to simultaneously carry voice and data. It replaces ISDN and is a competitor to cable modem service. ADSL bandwidth is divided into three channels: voice/fax; downstream data, which is anything your computer receives; and upstream data, also called "duplex," which is anything your computer sends. ADSL is asymmetric because downstream data speed (384 Kbps to 6.1 Mbps) is much faster than upstream data speed (16 Kbps to 832 Kbps). Asymmetric bandwidth is ideal for Internet access because users typically download much more information than they upload. ADSL's other advantages include: it is always on (you don't need to "dial up" to the Internet), it works over existing telephone lines, you can talk on the phone and surf the Internet at the same time, and it offers increased security. The actual performance you receive from ADSL depends on many factors. First, the type of service offered in your area: Full Rate ADSL (the standard), RADSL (a non-standard version), VDSL (the fastest service available, with speeds up to 26Mbps; typically installed on college campuses and business parks), and G.lite (the slowest but least expensive). Second, your distance from the nearest ADSL switching station; like any electronic signal, it is strongest near the source and weakens with distance. If you are more than 3 miles from an ADSL switching station, you will not be able to receive service. Third, the type of ADSL modem you use. Fourth, the gauge, length, and quality of the phone lines between the switching station and your home or business. ADSL service can be obtained from your telephone company and some Internet Service Providers. See also *ADSL modem, DSL, G.lite.*

ADSL modem A digital modem designed for use with an Asymmetric Digital Subscriber Line (ADSL) connection. These modems are only available from telephone companies and ISPs, due to the fact that they must be highly customized to work with the specific ADSL network they will operate on. See *ADSL, digital modem.*

Advanced Configuration and Power Interface See *ACPI.*

Advanced Encryption Standard See *AES.*

Advanced Interactive Executive (AIX) An IBM version of the Unix operating system. AIX runs on PS/2 computers equipped with the Intel 80386 microprocessor, IBM workstations, minicomputers, mainframes, and supercomputers. See *Linux, Unix.*

Advanced Micro Devices (AMD) A manufacturer of microprocessors and other integrated circuits. Based in Sunnyvale, California, AMD markets Intel-compatible microprocessors that are typically less expensive than their counterparts.

Advanced Power Management (APM) A power-saving feature that shuts off power to the monitor or other display device after a predetermined period of inactivity. Replaced by the ACPI standard. See also *ACPI.*

Advanced Research Projects Agency (ARPA) An agency of the U.S. Department of Defense (DoD), now called Defense Advanced Research Projects Agency (DARPA), and a major source of funding for important computer innovations. In the late 1960s and early 1970s, ARPA funded the development of the ARPANET, the Internet's predecessor, and the TCP/IP protocols, which have since provided the foundation for the emergence

of a wide area network (WAN) of global proportions. See *ARPANET, Internet.*

Advanced Run-Length Limited (ARLL) A method of storing and retrieving information on a hard disk that increases the density of Run-Length Limited (RLL) storage by more than 25 percent and that offers a faster data transfer rate (9 Mbps). See *data-encoding scheme.*

Advanced SCSI Programming Interface (ASPI) A standard that states how SCSI devices work with each other and the rest of the computer system.

advanced setup options Options in the BIOS setup program that let the user choose PCI interrupts, port addresses, and hard disk setup options. Can also refer generically to setup options in some application installation programs. See *BIOS.*

Advanced Streaming Format See *ASF.*

Advanced Technology Attachment Packet Interface See *ATAPI.*

advertisement In a computer file system, a file name that refers to data that is not actually physically present on the computer; the file is accessible via network connections.

AES Acronym for Advanced Encryption Standard. An encryption algorithm adopted by U.S. government agencies for use with sensitive but unclassified documents. Intended to replace the obsolete DES standard, AES is a symmetric key encryption algorithm that supports key sizes of up to 256 bits. See *DES, symmetric key encryption algorithm.*

AFAIK Abbreviation for "as far as I know." Commonly used abbreviation on Internet Relay Chat (IRC), chat rooms, e-mail, and Usenet. See *abbrev.*

AFIPS Acronym for American Federation of Information Processing Societies. Founded in 1961, this organization was one of the earliest professional societies for professionals in the computer and data processing industries. The Federation on Computing in the United States (FOCUS) succeeded AFIPS in 1990.

AFK Abbreviation for "away from keyboard." Commonly used on Internet Relay Chat (IRC) and chat rooms. See *abbrev.*

AFM Acronym for audio frequency modulation, an analog record/playback standard for audio that is widely used in consumer audio devices such as cassette decks and VHS video cameras and recorders. AFM's drawbacks include limited dynamic range and limited frequency response.

AfterStep A window manager for the X Window System that emulates the look and feel of the NeXT graphical user interface. A popular feature is the wharf, which enables users to create application launchers without editing configuration files. See *X Window System.*

agate A 5.5-point type size often used in newspaper classified advertisements and financial tables.

agent **1.** A program specifically designed to interact with a server and access data on the user's behalf. Synonymous with client. **2.** An automatic program that is designed to operate on the user's behalf, performing a specific function in the background. When the agent has achieved its goal, it reports to the user. In the future, agents may roam the world's computer networks, looking for information and reporting only when the information has been retrieved.

aggregate function In database management programs, a command that performs arithmetic operations on the values in a specific field in all the records within a database, or in one view of the database.

aggregate operator In a database management program, a command that tells the program to perform an aggregate function.

aglet Abbreviation of agile applet. In Java, a small, self-contained agent that can

function autonomously on a computer network, even to the extent of moving to an available computer if the current system is about to be shut down. See *agent, applet, Java.*

AGP A port specification developed by Intel Corporation to support high-speed, high-resolution graphics, including 3-D graphics. AGP provides a direct connection between an AGP-compatible video card and the computer's chipset, thus enabling AGP to transcend the 133 Mbps limitations of the PCI. The earliest AGP standard (now called 1X AGP) transfers data (theoretically) at 264 Mbps. More recent standards include 2X AGP (528 Mbps), 4X AGP (1056 Mbps), and 8X AGP (2.1 Gbps). An AGP video card can only be used with a motherboard that has an AGP-compatible chipset and an AGP slot.

AI See *artificial intelligence.*

AIFF An 8-bit monaural sound file format developed by Apple Computer for storing digitized sounds. The format is also widely found on Silicon Graphics workstations and is often encountered on the Internet. See *wave sound.*

AirPort An Apple implementation of the IEEE 802.11b Wireless LAN standard. Designed for Macintosh computers, AirPort technology includes the AirPort base station and AirPort adapters for Macintosh desktop systems and PowerBook portables. AirPort is fully compatible with the 802.11b (Wi-Fi) standard and is certified to work in cross-platform 802.11b networks. To prevent intruders from intercepting network data, AirPort includes 128-bit encryption. See *IEEE 802.11b.*

alert box In a graphical user interface (GUI), a dialog box that appears onscreen to warn that the command given may result in lost work or other errors, or that explains why an action cannot be completed. Alert boxes remain onscreen until the user takes some action—usually clicking an OK button or choosing Yes or No—to remove the box or cancel the operation.

algorithm **1.** A mathematical or logical procedure for solving a problem. An algorithm is a recipe for finding the right answer to a difficult problem by breaking down the problem into simple steps. **2.** In data compression, the standard used to compress or decompress the data.

algorithmic art In computer art and music, the use of an unfolding mathematical procedure as a means of artistic expression.

alias **1.** A secondary or symbolic name for a file, a collection of data, a computer user, or a computer device. **2.** In a spreadsheet, a range name, such as Income, is an alias for a range, such as A3–K3. **3.** In networks, group aliases provide a handy way to send e-mail to two or more people simultaneously.

aliasing In graphics, the undesirable jagged or stair-stepped appearance of diagonal lines in computer-generated images. A low-resolution monitor causes aliasing. Bitmapped characters also have aliasing, especially when they are enlarged. See *anti-aliasing.*

alignment **1.** The placement of hard and floppy disk drive read/write heads over the disk tracks they must read and write. **2.** In desktop publishing it is synonymous with justification.

allocate To reserve sufficient memory for a program's operation.

allocation table See *FAT.*

all points addressable (APA) graphic See *bitmapped graphic.*

Alpha **1.** A RISC-based microprocessor, developed by Digital Equipment Corporation (DEC) and now marketed by Compaq, that can process 64 bits of data at a time. **2.** A workstation, marketed by Compaq, that uses the Alpha microprocessor. **3.** An early version of a program that is generally so buggy that it is tested in-house prior to more widespread beta tests. See *beta, microprocessor, RISC.*

alpha build In Web publishing, a preliminary version of a website that is submitted to clients for approval before serious coding begins.

alphanumeric characters Characters available on a keyboard, including uppercase and lowercase letters A through Z, numbers 0 through 9, punctuation marks, and symbols that can be entered from the keyboard, such as (and ★. See *ASCII character set, ANSI, extended character set.*

alpha test The first stage in the testing of computer products before they are released for public use. Alpha tests are usually conducted by the hardware manufacturer or software publisher. Later tests, called beta tests, are conducted by selected users. See *alpha, beta.*

AltaVista See *search engine.*

Alt key On IBM PC–compatible keyboards, a key used in combination with other keys to select commands from the menu or as shortcut keys to execute commands. In WordPerfect, for example, pressing Alt+F2 begins a search-and-replace operation. In Windows programs, the Alt key activates the menu system via the keyboard. See *Control key (Ctrl), Shift key.*

ALU See *arithmetic-logic unit.*

always on **1.** In an online or Internet connection, a connection that does not require the user to wait for a dial-up procedure to complete before online data becomes available. Always-on services include the various types of Digital Subscriber Line (DSL) service, such as ADSL. **2.** In an operating system, a design feature than enables system administration and maintenance operations to take place, including the installation of new software and recovery from application crashes, without rebooting the system. See *ADSL, DSL.*

AMD See *Advanced Micro Devices.*

American National Standards Institute See *ANSI.*

American Standard Code for Information Interchange See *ASCII character set.*

America Online (AOL) The largest online service (with millions of subscribers), headquartered in Vienna, Virginia. Offering a mix of news, sports, chat rooms, e-mail, computer support, Internet access, and fee-based services, AOL targets new computer users. Also produces AIM (AOL Instant Messenger), a popular and free Internet chat client.

Amiga A personal computer originally developed by Commodore in 1985 and sold until the company's bankruptcy in 1994. Designed from the beginning as a multimedia workstation, the Amiga is highly esteemed for its graphics and video capabilities. The computer's special-purpose hardware is optimized for these applications. Since Commodore's bankruptcy, the rights to the Amiga's hardware design, operating system, and applications have changed hands numerous times; a Gateway 2000-owned subsidiary, Amiga Inc., hopes to market new Amiga models successfully.

Amiga persecution complex Hacker slang for users of a computer that has performed poorly in the marketplace due to what these users perceive as a massive and cynical conspiracy, the aim of which is to replace superior technology with inferior technology.

AMP Acronym for asynchronous multiprocessing (also called asymmetric multiprocessing). An operating system feature that enables a single processing unit to perform two dissimilar server functions, such as file management versus input/output operations, at a high rate of efficiency. See *symmetric multiprocessing (SMP).*

amper In hacker slang, an abbreviation for ampersand.

ampersand The character *&,* sometimes used in place of the English word *and.* The ampersand was originally a ligature of *et,* which is Latin for *and.* The ampersand is used as an operator in spreadsheet programs to include text in a formula.

amplitude In analog technologies, the maximum distance that an oscillating wave travels from a mean (average) point; the greater the amplitude, the stronger the wave. See *frequency, phase.*

anacronym An acronym (a word formed from the first letters of a phrase) that is so well established in common usage that the phrase itself is seldom known (examples are radar and scuba). Many computer terms (such as ASCII and SCSI) are well on their way to becoming anacronyms, which is why this dictionary defines such terms at the acronym rather than the spelled-out phrase.

analog Based on continuously varying values or voltages. For example, a speedometer is an analog device that shows changes in speed using a needle indicator that can move over an infinite range of speeds up to the maximum limit of the vehicle. Analog techniques also are used for the reproduction of music in standard LP records and audio cassettes. See *digital.*

analog cellular phone A first-generation cellular phone technology that supports voice only, except where service providers offer simultaneous Cellular Digital Packet Data (CDPD) service. See *CDPD, digital cellular phone.*

analog computer A computer used to measure conditions that change constantly, such as temperature, heartbeat, or atmospheric pressure. Analog computation is used widely in laboratory settings to monitor ongoing, continuous changes and to record these changes in charts or graphs. See *analog, digital computer.*

analog device A peripheral that handles information in continuous and infinitely variable quantities, such as a mercury thermometer. The opposite is a digital device, such as a digital watch, which samples data at a set frequency and, at its most basic level, can only distinguish between 1 and 0, or on and off. See *analog.*

analogical reasoning   A form of analysis in which the dynamics of something in the real world—such as the aerodynamics of a proposed airplane—are understood by building a model and exploring its behavior. One of the computer's greatest contributions has been to lower the cost (and increase the convenience) of analogical reasoning. See *model*.

analog modem   The most common kind of modem available today. Analog modems (unlike digital modems) are designed to communicate over plain old telephone service (POTS) lines. An analog modem converts a computer's digital data to an analog sound and sends it over the phone lines to another modem, which in turn converts the data back to digital form. See *digital modem*.

analog monitor   A monitor that accepts a continuously varied video signal and that consequently can display a continuous range of colors. Video Graphics Array (VGA) monitors are analog monitors. See *digital monitor.*

analog-to-digital   conversion   A process in which the magnitude of an analog signal at a particular moment in time is converted into a digital representation, which is called a sample. See *analog, analog-to-digital converter (A/D converter), digital, sample.*

analog-to-digital converter (A/D converter)   An adapter that allows a digital computer to accept analog input, such as that from laboratory instruments. Analog-to-digital converters are frequently used when monitoring temperature, movement, and other conditions that vary continuously. Such devices employ analog-to-digital conversion. See *analog, analog-to-digital conversion, digital.*

analog transmission   A communications scheme that uses a continuous signal varied by amplification. See *broadband, digital transmission.*

analysis   A method of discovery in which a situation is broken down to its component parts, and the parts are studied to try to understand how they affect one another. In personal computing, a common form of analysis is sensitivity testing, or "what-if" analysis, using a spreadsheet program. In sensitivity testing, the user alters the variables in a formula to see how changing each variable affects the outcome of the calculation.

analytical graphics   The preparation of charts and graphs to aid in the understanding and interpretation of data. The graphs available with spreadsheet programs fall into this category because they are useful for clarifying trends in worksheet numbers.

anamorphic   Also called 16x9, 16:9, Anamorphic Scope, anamorphic widescreen, enhanced, and widescreen. In DVD technology, a process for preserving a movie's entire image and rich detail by compressing it horizontally during the DVD printing process. The stored image is actually a distortion of the original one, hence the term *anamorphic*. The movie image is uncompressed when viewed, though the entire image will only be visible on a widescreen television, HDTV, or DTV. Modern films are created for a movie theatre screen format using a range of aspect ratios from 1.85:1 (Academy Flat) to 2.35:1 (Anamorphic Scope, CinemaScope, and Panavision). A standard television, however, has an aspect ratio of 1.33:1, also denoted as 4x3. In the past, several techniques were used to transfer movies to DVD for viewing on a standard television, but these techniques resulted in a loss of image clarity and detail (letterboxing), or in deleting parts of the image itself. In many respects, the resulting DVD did not contain the entire movie. The anamorphic process results in a DVD that preserves the film's entire image in full detail.

anchor   In hypertext, a word, phrase, or image—usually demarcated by color, underlining, or both—that provides the gateway to another resource. Some hyperlinks also have a destination anchor, a specific point at which the link traversal ends. See *fragment identifier.*

anchor cell In a spreadsheet program, the cell in a range in which the cell pointer is located.

anchored graphic A graph or picture fixed in an absolute position on the page rather than attached to specific text. See *floating graphic, wrap-around type.*

AND 1. In Boolean logic, an operator that specifies that a statement is true only if both of its arguments are true. **2.** In computer database searching, a query operator that retrieves a record only if the record contains both of the terms linked with AND. (For example, the query "computers AND internet" retrieves a term only if a record contains both of these terms.) Boolean operators are capitalized by convention; they are not acronyms. See *NOT, OR.*

Andrew File System (AFS) A network-based file system that makes external resources available on a by-request basis. AFS enables a client/server architecture for file sharing that includes strong authentication and file survivability (designated volumes are automatically replicated on two or more separate physical devices). AFS was developed at Carnegie-Mellon University (CMU).

angle bracket The less-than (<) or greater-than (>) characters found on the standard ASCII keyboard, when used in place of parentheses to enclose a string of characters (for example, <NAME>).

angry fruit salad Slang for a poorly designed user interface or Web page that uses too many bright colors.

animated GIF A GIF file that contains multiple images, enabling graphic designers to create simple, effective animations that require little storage space. When an application displays the multiple images in a looping sequence, the result is an animation, albeit a rather jerky one. Because most Web browsers can download and play the enclosed graphic images in a sequence without requiring helper applications or plug-ins, the use of GIF animations has become widespread in Web publishing. GIF animations require software that supports the GIF89a standard. See *GIF, GIF89a.*

animation Creating the illusion of movement by saving a series of images that show slight changes in the position of the displayed objects, and then displaying these images back fast enough that the eye perceives smooth movement. The illusion is convincing only if the frame rate (the number of frames displayed per second) is sufficiently fast to trick the eye into seeing continuous motion. See *animated GIF, cell animation.*

annotation An explanatory note or comment inserted into a document. With some application programs, one can insert an annotation as an icon that, when clicked by the person who reads the document, opens a separate window containing the note. Users of personal computers equipped with sound boards and microphones can add voice annotations to their documents in some programs.

anonymous Originating from a concealed or unknown source. See *anonymous post, anonymous remailer.*

anonymous FTP An FTP (File Transfer Protocol)–based service that allows any user to download files from the Internet. When logging on to an anonymous FTP server, use "anonymous" as and the user name, and use your e-mail address as the password. See *FTP.*

anonymous post In Usenet, an article that has been posted through an anonymous remailer so that the identity of the person posting the article is impossible to determine. See *article, post, Usenet.*

anonymous remailer An Internet mailing service that strips an e-mail message of its originating header information so that its origin cannot be easily determined. True anonymous remailers retain absolutely no information regarding the messages they relay; they should be distinguished from pseudoanonymous remailers, which retain origin information to facilitate replies to the message's originator. See *pseudoanonymous remailer.*

ANSI Acronym for American National Standards Institute. A private, non-profit technical standards organization that is composed of industry and university representatives. ANSI is the sole official U.S. representative and member of the International Organization for Standardization (ISO), which develops international technical standards. Founded in 1918, ANSI seeks to enhance U.S. global competitiveness and the American quality of life by promoting and facilitating voluntary consensus standards and associated conformity assessment procedures. The organization's headquarters are in Washington, D.C.

ANSI graphics A set of cursor-control codes, developed by the American National Standards Institute (ANSI), that enables the display of graphics and colors on a remote computer's monitor.

ANSI/ISO C++ A standardized version of the C++ programming language, developed by a committee affiliated with the American National Standards Institute (ANSI) and the International Organization for Standardization (ISO). The standard is widely perceived to be needed to eliminate incompatibilities introduced by publishers of proprietary C++ compilers.

ANSI screen control A set of standards developed by the American National Standards Institute (ANSI) to control the display of information on computer screens and to enable ANSI graphics. See *ANSI.SYS*.

ANSI.SYS In MS-DOS, a configuration file containing instructions needed to display ANSI graphics and to control cursor location, line wrapping, and the behavior of the keyboard, following the recommendations of the American National Standards Institute (ANSI).

answer mode See *auto-dial/auto-answer modem*.

answer/originate The capability of a communications device, such as a modem, to receive (answer) and send (originate) messages.

anti-aliasing The automatic removal or reduction of stair-step distortions (aliasing) in a computer-generated graphic image. This is accomplished by filling the jagged edges with gray or a color to make the aliasing less noticeable. Unfortunately, the result is often a fuzzy display. See *aliasing*.

anticipatory paging A method of increasing the speed of virtual memory operations in which the operating system attempts to predict which memory pages will be needed in advance of their actual demand from applications. See *demand paging*.

anti-glare Any procedure or treatment used to reduce the reflection of outside light sources on a monitor, ranging from repositioning the monitor in relation to windows to coating the display with a light-damping chemical. Chemical anti-glare treatments can reduce the brightness of a display.

antistatic mat A mat or pad placed on or near a computer device. The mat absorbs static electricity, which can damage semiconductor devices if the devices are not properly grounded.

antitrust A legal statute that regulates the marketplace tactics of firms that have obtained a monopoly in a given market. Antitrust laws strive to benefit the public by ensuring that markets remain competitive, which keeps prices down and encourages competitors to invest in new technologies. See *monopoly*.

antivirus program A utility designed to check for and remove computer viruses from a computer system. Most antivirus programs detect a virus in two ways: first, by searching every file on the system in an attempt to match thousands of virus "signature" code fragments; second, by monitoring the system in order to detect the malicious activities of viruses that were not detected by the first technique. See *virus*.

anycast In Internet Protocol (IPv6), to send a signal to the nearest of several receivers in a group. See *broadcast, multicast, unicast.*

AOL　See *America Online.*

Apache　A popular, open-source Web server that currently powers more than half of all websites. Originally developed by programmers who were using a Web server daemon called httpd, developed at the National Center for Supercomputing Applications (NCSA). These programmers fixed errors in httpd and modified it by releasing a series of software patches. Over time, they had created a more sophisticated Web server, which they called Apache because it was "a patchy" version of httpd. These programmers went on to found The Apache Software Foundation, which creates a wide range of open source software and tools. Apache has grown into an exceptionally powerful Web server that offers a host of advanced features, including SSL security and Web scripting integration. Versions are available for Unix (including Linux) and for 32-bit Microsoft Windows server operating systems, including Windows NT Server, Windows 2000 Server, and Windows XP Server. Apache's popularity has been fueled by the rapid penetration of Linux into the lower-end Wintel-based server market, formerly the exclusive domain of Windows NT. An additional reason for Apache's popularity is the program's excellent reputation for security; when security holes appear, the community quickly develops solutions that are immediately available on the Internet. See *open source software (OSS), Web server.*

APA graphic　See *bitmapped graphic.*

aperture grille　The equivalent of a shadow mask in Sony Trinitron monitors and monitors of similar design. Aperture grilles use vertical wires to direct electron beams to phosphors of a particular color. Slot pitch and screen pitch are the Trinitron equivalent of dot pitch, so compare monitors on those specifications.

API　See *application program interface.*

APL　Acronym for A Programming Language, a high-level programming language well suited for scientific and mathematical applications. APL uses Greek letters and requires a display device that can display these letters. Previously used only on IBM mainframes, the language is now available for IBM PC–compatible computers.

A-Plus　A certification program developed by the Computing Technology Industry Association. Designed for entry-level service technicians, the program is based on a two-part examination that covers core knowledge as well as Microsoft Windows.

APM　See *Advanced Power Management.*

app　Common slang expression for application or applet.

append　To add data at the end of a file or a database. In database management, for example, to append a record is to add a new record after all existing records.

Apple Desktop Bus (ADB)　An interface for connecting keyboards, mouse devices, trackballs, and other input devices to Macintosh computers. These computers come with an ADB serial port capable of a maximum data transfer rate of 4.5 Kbps. It is possible to connect up to 16 devices to one ADB port, with each additional device daisy-chained to the previous device. See *asynchronous communication.*

Apple Desktop Interface (ADI)　A set of user interface guidelines, developed by Apple Computer and published by Addison-Wesley, intended to ensure that the appearance and operation of all Macintosh applications are similar.

Apple File Exchange　A utility program provided with each Macintosh computer that allows Macs equipped with suitable floppy disk drives to exchange data with IBM PC–compatible computers.

Apple Pro keyboard　The standard keyboard for the Macintosh, which replaces the extended keyboard. This 108-key keyboard includes alphanumeric keys, cursor control keys, 15 programmable function keys, and a key for ejecting CDs and DVDs.

AppleShare   A file server utility for AppleTalk networks. AppleShare transforms any Macintosh on the network into a dedicated file server; the server's hard disk icon appears on every network user's desktop.

applet   1. A small to medium-sized computer program that provides a specific function, such as emulating a calculator. **2.** In Java, a miniprogram embedded in a Web document that, when downloaded, is executed by the browser. Both of the leading browsers (Netscape Communicator and Microsoft Internet Explorer) can execute Java applets. See *Java applet, Java application.*

AppleTalk   A local area network (LAN) standard developed by Apple Computer. AppleTalk can link as many as 32 Macintosh computers, IBM PC–compatible computers, and peripherals such as laser printers. Every Macintosh computer has an AppleTalk port; the only hardware required for an AppleTalk network is a set of LocalTalk connectors and ordinary telephone wire for cables (called twisted-pair cable). AppleTalk networks are simple and inexpensive but quite slow; they are capable of transmitting only up to 230 Kbps. EtherTalk, in contrast, is capable of speeds of up to 10 million bps. See *EtherTalk.*

appliance server   A network server program that enables non-programmers to make data and documents available to others without requiring advanced technical expertise.

application   A program that enables a user to do something useful with the computer, such as writing or accounting (as opposed to utilities, programs that help the user maintain the computer).

application binary interface (ABI)   A set of communications standards that specifies how a binary executable file should interface with computer hardware.

Application Configuration Access Protocol (ACAP)   A proposed Internet standard that transfers crucial user configuration settings (including address books, bookmarks, and options choices) to an Internet-accessible file. Because these settings are stored on the network instead of the user's computer, they are accessible no matter which computer is being used. ACAP will greatly benefit anyone who accesses the Internet from more than one computer.

application control menu   See *control menu.*

application development system   A coordinated set of program development tools, typically including a full-screen editor; a programming language with a compiler, linker, and debugger; and an extensive library of ready-to-use program modules. The use of an application development system lets experienced users develop a standalone application more easily than writing a program using a language such as C++ or COBOL.

application heap   In the Macintosh computer architecture, the base memory, the area of memory set aside for user programs.

application icon   In a graphical user interface (GUI), an onscreen graphic representation of a minimized program. The icon appears on the taskbar to remind the user that the application is still present in memory. Double-clicking the application re-displays the program. See *minimize.*

application layer   In the Open System Interconnection (OSI) reference model of computer network architecture, the first or topmost of seven layers, in which the data is presented to the user. At this layer, protocols are needed to ensure that products made by different manufacturers can work together. For example, every e-mail program should use the same protocols for sending and receiving e-mail. When the data is ready to be sent to the network, it is passed down the protocol stack to the next layer, the presentation layer. See *layer, OSI Reference Model, protocol stack.*

application-level encryption In a computer network, the implementation of encryption by individual applications rather than at the operating system or network level. Web browsers typically implement encryption at this level.

application program See *application.*

application program interface (API)
1. A set of standards or conventions by which programs can call specific operating system or network services. **2.** In Web servers, the standards or conventions that enable a hyperlink to originate a call to a program that is external to the server See *CGI, ISAPI, NSAPI.*

application shortcut key In Microsoft Windows, a shortcut key assigned to launch or bring an application to the foreground. Application shortcut keys are also available in applications such as DESQview and PC Tools Desktop to launch and switch among programs.

application software Programs that perform specific tasks (such as word processing or database management), in contrast to system software (which maintains and organizes the computer system), and utilities, which help to maintain and organize the system.

application window In a graphical user interface (GUI), an application's main window, containing a title bar, the application's menu bar, and a work area. The work area can contain one or more document windows. See *window.*

A Programming Language See *APL.*

aptent An Internet-accessible resource that combines a computer application (ap) with Web-based textual and graphic content (tent). The term aptly describes many of the Web's most popular destinations and features, including search engines, discussion sites, and guest books.

arbitrator In a computer operating system, a program module that handles peripherals' competing demands for the processing unit's resources and allocates hardware resources among the various devices.

architecture **1.** The overall conceptual design and design philosophy of a hardware device or computer system or network. **2.** The specific configuration of hardware and software that determines the capabilities of a computer system or computer network.

archival backup A backup procedure in which a backup utility backs up all files on the hard disk by copying them to floppy disks, tape, or some other backup medium. See *incremental backup.*

archive **1.** An infrequently accessed but comprehensive collection of data. **2.** A file designed for space-efficient storage or distribution that contains two or more original files. In Unix, the most popular archive program is tar, which lacks compression capabilities. In Microsoft Windows, WinZip is the most popular archiving and compression program, while StuffIt holds this place among Macintosh users. See *extraction.*

archive attribute In MS-DOS and Microsoft Windows file systems, a hidden code, stored with a file's directory entry, that indicates whether the file has been changed since it was last copied using XCOPY or a backup utility.

archive bit A file attribute that is used to indicate whether the file has been backed up. If so, the archive bit is set to 1. If the file has been altered since it was last backed up, or if the file has never been backed up, the archive bit is set to 0. Backup software is designed to clear the archive bit (that is, set the bit to 0) when full backups and incremental backups are performed. When a differential backup is performed, the archive bit is not cleared. See *backup, differential backup, full backup, incremental backup.*

archive site An Internet-accessible computer that serves as a repository for a large or complete collection of data, such as all the messages exchanged on a mailing list or newsgroup. Synonymous with FTP site because archive sites are frequently accessed by FTP programs.

ARCnet A popular local area network (LAN) originally developed by Datapoint Corporation for IBM PC–compatible computers and now available from several vendors. ARCnet interface cards are inexpensive and easily installed. ARCnet networks use a star topology, a token-passing protocol, and coaxial or twisted-pair cable. The network can transmit data at speeds of 2.5MB per second. See *network topology, NIC.*

area graph A line graph in which the area below the line is filled in to emphasize the change in volume from one time period to the next. The x-axis (categories axis) is the horizontal axis, and the y-axis (value axis) is the vertical axis.

areal density The tightness with which data can be packed onto a hard disk or floppy disk. Both the smoothness of the disk surface and the nature of the recording medium affect areal density, which is expressed in megabits per square inch (Mb/in^2). Areal densities of between $100Mb/in^2$ and $200Mb/in^2$ are typical for modern hard disks.

argument 1. In a programming statement that calls a routine, a value or option that provides data for the routine to process or that tells the routine which option to use when processing this data. For example, if the statement calls a routine that rounds numbers, the argument tells the routine how many decimal places to use. This term is often used synonymously with parameter, but in some usages the term parameter is used to refer to nonoptional values that are subject to change. **2.** In command-line interfaces and applications that employ typed commands (such as spreadsheets), a value or option that modifies how the command is carried out. See *parameter, switch.*

argument separator In spreadsheet programs and programming languages, a comma or other punctuation mark that sets off one argument from another in a command.

Arial A sans serif TrueType font developed by Microsoft Corporation and distributed with its products. Arial closely resembles Helvetica. See *Helvetica, TrueType.*

arithmetic-logic unit (ALU) The portion of the central processing unit (CPU) that makes all the decisions for the microprocessor, based on the mathematical computations and logic functions it performs.

arithmetic operation One of the two groups of operations performed by the arithmetic-logic unit (ALU). The arithmetic operations include addition, subtraction, multiplication, and division.

arithmetic operator A symbol that tells a program the arithmetic operation to perform, such as addition, subtraction, multiplication, and division. In most computer programs, addition is represented by a plus sign (+), subtraction by a hyphen or minus sign (–), multiplication by an asterisk (*), division by a slash (/), and exponent by a caret (^). See *Boolean operator, relational operator.*

ARLL See *Advanced Run-Length Limited.*

ARP See *Address Resolution Protocol.*

ARPA See *Advanced Research Projects Agency.*

ARPANET A wide area network (WAN) created in 1969 with funding from the Advanced Research Projects Agency (ARPA). Undergoing constant research and development in the early to mid-1970s, ARPANET served as the testbed for the development of TCP/IP (the protocols that make the Internet possible). Initially, the ARPANET was available only to government research institutes and to universities holding Department of Defense (DoD) research contracts. In 1983, ARPANET was divided into a high-security military network (Milnet) and an ARPANET that was recast as a research and development network, supervised by the National Science Foundation (NSF). NSF constructed a new TCP/IP-based network backbone called NSFnet and decommissioned the remnants of ARPANET in 1990.

array 1. In a high-level programming language, a compound data type consisting of a single-dimensional or multidimensional table that the program treats as one data item. Any information in the array can be referenced by naming the array and the location of the item in the array. See *compound data type, data type.* **2.** In hard disks, a collection of hard drives that have been linked together to provide a large amount of auxiliary storage. See *RAID.*

arrow keys See *cursor-movement keys.*

article In Usenet, a contribution that an individual has written and posted to one or more newsgroups. There are two kinds of articles: original articles on new subjects, and follow-up posts.

article selector In Usenet, a newsreader feature in which the newsreader groups and displays the articles that are currently available for reading. Threaded newsreaders automatically sort the articles in such a way that one can see the thread of discussion; an article is followed immediately by all its follow-up articles. See *follow-up post, thread.*

artifact In computer technology, unintended, meaningless, and undesirable data that result from processing operations. Examples of artifacts include the visual or audible distortions introduced by the use of lossy compression at high compression ratios. See *compression ratio, lossy compression.*

artificial intelligence (AI) A computer science field that tries to improve computers by endowing them with some of the characteristics associated with human intelligence, such as the capability to understand natural language and to reason under conditions of uncertainty. See *expert system, Turing Test.*

artificial life A scientific research area devoted to the creation and study of

computer simulations of living organisms. Computer viruses have forced a renewal of the debate on the definition of life. Besides forcing us to re-examine our definition of life, artificial life research may create more effective technology. By applying artificial life concepts to real-life problems, we can program computer-generated solutions to compete for survival based on their capability to perform a desired task well.

arts A new top-level domain (TLD) name for the Internet, added in 1998, that is designed for Web sites featuring cultural and entertainment activities. See *domain name, gTLD-MoU, top-level domain (TLD).*

AS See *autonomous system.*

ascender In typography, the portion of the lowercase letters *b, d, f, h, k, l,* and *t* that rises above the height of the letter *x.* The height of the ascender varies in different typefaces. See *descender.*

ascending order A sort in which items are arranged from smallest to largest (1, 2, 3) or from first to last (a, b, c). Ascending order is the default sort order for virtually all applications that perform sorting operations. See *descending sort.*

ASCII (Pronounced *AS-kee.*) Acronym for American Standard Code for Information Interchange. See *ASCII character set, extended character set.*

ASCII art A simple picture made by using the standard (ASCII) characters available on the computer keyboard. ASCII art requires fixed spacing and looks best with a monospaced font, which assigns the same amount of space to each character. Some e-mail users like to include ASCII art in their signatures, but the art may look garbled if readers display mail messages using proportionally spaced fonts. See *smiley.*

asciibetical order Slang term for data sorted in ASCII sort order. See *ASCII sort order.*

ASCII character set A standard character set consisting of 96 uppercase and lowercase letters, plus 32 nonprinting

control characters, each of which is numbered to achieve uniformity among
different computer devices. Based on a 7-
bit coding scheme, the ASCII character set
dates from the 1960s and is incapable of
representing the character sets of most non-
English languages. Most modern computers
use an extended character set containing
accented, technical, and illustrative characters. However, these character sets are
proprietary and partially incompatible with
each other; for example, the IBM PC's
extended character set differs from the one
employed by the Macintosh. To avoid these
problems on the Internet, Web browsers use
the ISO Latin-1 character set encoding. See
ANSI, extended character set.

ASCII file　A file that contains only characters drawn from the ASCII character set.
No special formatting (such as boldface or
underlining) is in an ASCII file. See *ASCII
character set, binary file.*

ASCII sort order　A sort order determined by the sequence used to number the
characters in the standard ASCII character
set. Words or lines that begin with spaces or
punctuation come first, followed by those
beginning with numbers. Next come words
or lines that begin with uppercase letters *A*
through *Z*, followed by those that begin
with lowercase letters *a* through *z*. Note
that this sort order violates most publication style guidelines. See *dictionary sort.*

ASCII transfer　A file transfer protocol
that employs no error-correction protocol
or flow control. ASCII transfers are less
efficient than binary protocols such as
XMODEM, but they are the only type of
transfer some older computers—particularly
mainframes—support. See *binary transfer.*

ASF　Acronym for Advanced Streaming
Format. A Microsoft-developed format for
streaming audio, graphics, and video data
via the Internet See *streaming audio, streaming video.*

ASIC　Acronym for application-specific
integrated circuit. A specialized integrated
circuit (IC) that is designed for a specific

application, such as decoding streaming
video.

A-size paper　As defined by the
American National Standards Institute
(ANSI), a page that is 8.5 by 11 inches (210
by 297 millimeters) in size.

ASM　The MS-DOS file name extension
usually attached to a file containing assembly language source code. See *Association for
Systems Management.*

ASN　See *autonomous system number.*

ASN.1　See *Abstract Syntax Notation One.*

ASP　See *Active Server Page, Association of
Shareware Professionals.*

AspectJ　An aspect-oriented programming language developed by researchers at
Xerox Corporation's Palo Alto Research
Center (PARC) and currently managed by
Eclipse.org. AspectJ is exclusively designed
for use with the Java programming language. See *aspect-oriented programming.*

aspect-oriented programming (AOP)
A new approach to object-oriented programming　developed by researchers at
Xerox Corporation's Palo Alto Research
Center (PARC). AOP solves problems created by object-oriented programming's
emphasis on modularity, in which programs
are self-contained units called objects. AOP
introduces the capability to specify code
that cuts across object categories, thus
removing the need for individual objects to
reinvent the wheel for systemic concerns
such as memory utilization and networking
standards.

aspect ratio　In graphics, the ratio of the
width of an image to its height. When
changing the size of a graphic, maintaining
the width-to-height ratio is important to
avoid distortions.

ASPI　See *Advanced SCSI Programming
Interface.*

ASP.NET　An updated version of
Microsoft's Active Server Page (ASP) specification that enables Web authors to embed

compiled code from a variety of programming languages in Web pages; this code is used to retrieve data from a relational database and incorporate the retrieved data into the Web page. The standard fully separates the programming code from the content, enabling authors to focus on Web page design without the distraction of embedded code. The standard is part of Microsoft's .NET initiative. The ASP.NET standard is not downwardly compatible with previous versions of ASP. See *Active Server Page (ASP), relational database, .NET.*

assemble edit   In digital video, an editing technique in which content with signal characteristics that vary from the rest of the content is added at the end of the video. See *auto-assembly, insert edit.*

assembler   A program that transforms an assembly language program into machine code so that the computer can execute the program. See *assembly language, machine language.*

assembly language   A low-level programming language in which each program statement corresponds to an instruction that the microprocessor can carry out. Assembly languages are procedural languages. They tell the computer what to do in precise detail, requiring as many as two dozen lines of code to add two numbers. Assembly language programs are difficult and tedious to write. On the other hand, assembly language code is compact, processes quickly, and, when assembled, is more efficient than a compiled program written in a high-level language such as C. See *BASIC, C, compiler, Pascal.*

assign   To give a value to a named variable.

assigned number   In the Internet, a value associated with a specific protocol that is controlled by the Internet Assigned Numbers Authority (IANA). An example of an assigned number is the port number assigned to a specific network service, such as Usenet or Internet Relay Chat (IRC).

assignment   The process of storing a value in a named variable.

assignment operator   In programming, a symbol that enables the programmer to assign a value to a variable. This is usually an equals sign (=) and appears in an assignment statement.

assignment statement   In programming, a program statement that places a value into a variable. In BASIC, for example, the statement LET A=10 places the value 10 into the variable A. See *assignment operator.*

assistive technology   A technology that helps people with limited vision, hearing, or dexterity to use the computer comfortably and productively. See *accessibility.*

associated document   A file linked at the system level with the application that created it or that knows how to read its data type. In the Mac OS, association is automatic because applications record their identity in a new file's resource fork. In Windows, association is based on three-letter file extensions; for example, doc files can be associated with Microsoft Word. Users or setup programs can change the association between an application and an extension.

Association for Computing Machinery (ACM)   The oldest professional society for computer experts. ACM was founded in 1947 and sponsors conferences, journals, book publishing, and student groups at colleges and universities. The ACM is known for its annual Computer Science Conference and its ethical code, to which all members are expected to adhere. A popular feature of the organization is its numerous Special Interest Groups (SIGS), which facilitate communication among ACM members with shared interests. With more than 80,000 members, ACM is the leading professional society in computing and is an influential source of leadership on computing issues of broad public concern.

Association for Information Systems (AIS)   A professional organization that was founded in 1994 to serve as the premier international society for university-related information system specialists.

Association for Systems Management (ASM) A professional society for systems analysts and other computer professionals. The ASM has chapters in most cities and offers many short courses in systems analysis and other information systems topics. The ASM was formerly known as the Systems and Procedures Association (SPA).

Association for Women in Computing (AWC) A professional society dedicated to the advancement of women in computer-related fields. The organization strives to promote professional growth through networking and the society's professional programs, which include career awareness workshops. Founded in 1978, AWC is currently headquartered in San Francisco, California, and has numerous state and local chapters.

Association of Shareware Professionals (ASP) A professional society for authors and marketers of user-supported software (shareware) that is devoted to strengthening the future of shareware as an alternative to commercial software. The organization's members subscribe to a respected code of ethics. Founded in 1987, the organization is currently headquartered in Muskegan, Minnesota.

asterisk In DOS, the wildcard symbol (*) that stands for one or more characters; contrast this with the question mark (?) wildcard, which stands for only one character. An asterisk is also the arithmetic symbol for multiplication. See *arithmetic operator, wildcard.*

astonisher See *bang character.*

asymmetrical compression A compression algorithm that requires significantly more processing capability to compress data than to decompress it. Asymmetrical compression algorithms are beneficially employed over networks and the Internet, where servers are likely to have more processing power available than the clients that receive and decompress the data.

asymmetric digital subscriber line (ADSL) See *ADSL, ADSL modem, cable modem, G.lite.*

asymmetric key cryptography See *public key cryptography.*

asynchronous Not kept in time (synchrony) by the pulses of a system clock or some other timing device. See *asynchronous communication.*

asynchronous communication A method of data communication in which the transmission of bits of data is not synchronized by a clock signal but is accomplished by sending the bits one after another, with a start bit and a stop bit to mark the beginning and end, respectively, of each data unit. Telephone lines can be used for asynchronous communication. See *baud rate, modem, synchronous communication, UART.*

ATA See *IDE.*

ATA-2 See *Enhanced IDE (EIDE).*

ATA-3 An experimental standard for attaching many different recording media, such as disk drives and tape drives, to a PC. ATA-3 is capable of transferring data at a rate of 30 Mbps.

ATA flash memory A PC card (PCMCIA card) containing solid-state flash memory circuits that present themselves to the computer as if they were a standard ATA (IDE) hard drive. ATA flash memory cards are used in digital camera, notebook computers, and other devices where storage capacity must be balanced against weight and portability. See *CompactFlash (CF), flash memory, SmartMedia.*

ATA packet interface See *ATAPI.*

ATAPI Acronym for Advanced Technology Attachment packet interface. A standard that makes it very easy to connect a CD-ROM drive to an Enhanced IDE host adapter.

AT Attachment (ATA) See *IDE.*

AT bus The 16-bit expansion bus used in the IBM Personal Computer AT, as distinguished from the 8-bit bus of the original IBM Personal Computer and the 32-bit bus of computers using the Intel 80386 and Intel 486 microprocessors. Most 80386 and 486 machines contain AT-compatible expansion slots for backward compatibility. See *local bus, Micro Channel Bus.*

AT case A type of computer case designed to hold an AT form factor motherboard. See *ATX case.*

AT command set See *Hayes command set.*

AT form factor A motherboard designed to fit in an AT case. On an AT form factor motherboard, the expansion slots run parallel to the narrow side of the board. See *ATX form factor.*

Athlon A high-performance 32-bit microprocessor line created by Advanced Micro Devices (AMD) to compete with Intel's Pentium III and Pentium 4 microprocessors. Initial models offered high clock speeds—the Athlon was the world's first commercially offered gigabit processor—at the expense of overall performance, in that they lacked sufficient support for on-die L2 cache memories. Manufactured with AMD's new in-house .18 micron technologies, current models offer higher clock speeds and up to 256K of on-die L2 cache.

Athlon XP An enhanced version of the AMD Athlon processor that is intended to compete with Intel's top-of-the-line Pentium 4 processors. The chip supports Intel's latest 3D instructions, MP3 compression, and DVD playback. Note that AMD's model-naming system is not intended to reflect a chip's clock speed; for example, the Athlon XP 2800+ runs at a clock speed of 2.25 GHz.

AT keyboard An obsolete 84-key keyboard introduced with the IBM Personal Computer AT in response to complaints about the original IBM Personal Computer keyboard, which used a layout different from that of office typewriters. Most PCs come equipped with a 104-key keyboard. See *keyboard layout.*

ATM 1. Acronym for Asynchronous Transfer Mode. A network architecture that divides messages into fixed-size units (called cells) of small size (53 bytes) and that establishes a switched connection between the originating and receiving stations. Network speed, determined partly by the speed of the switching devices, is as high as 622 Mbps. The advantage of breaking all transmissions into small-sized cells is that the network can transmit voice, audio, and computer data over a single line without any single type of data dominating the transmission. ATM's connection-oriented design differs from the Internet's connectionless design; unlike the Internet, ATM enables service providers to bill by network usage and is capable of very high transmission speeds. For these reasons, ATM is often touted as a potential architecture for the Information Superhighway. **2.** Acronym for Adobe Type Manager. See *Adobe Type Manager.*

at sign The symbol (@) used to distinguish between the mailbox name and the computer name in e-mail addresses. An address such as frodo@bagend.com is read "Frodo at bagend dot com."

Attached Resource Computer Network See *ARCnet.*

attachment In e-mail, a binary file, such as a program or a compressed word processing document, that has been attached to an e-mail message. The content of the file does not appear within the e-mail message itself. Instead the content is encoded following the specifications of the MIME standard or older encoding standards called BinHex or uuencode. To include an attached document with an e-mail message, both the sender and the receiver must have e-mail programs that are capable of working with the same encoding format. MIME is the most widely used format. Note that many computer viruses propagate by means of executable files, or Microsoft Office files containing destructive macros, that are attached to e-mail messages. Never open an attachment from an unknown correspondent. See *e-mail, executable program, macro, Microsoft Office, MIME, uuencode, virus.*

attachment encoding The encoding format used to attach a binary file to an e-mail message. See *BinHex, MIME, uuencode.*

Attachment Unit Interface See *AUI.*

attenuation The loss of signal strength when cables exceed the maximum length stated in the network's specifications. Attenuation prevents successful data communications. One can use a device called a repeater to extend a network's cable range.

attribute **1.** In many word processing and graphics programs, a character emphasis, such as boldface and italic, and other characteristics, such as typeface and type size. **2.** In MS-DOS and Microsoft Windows, information about a file that indicates whether the file is a read-only file, a hidden file, or a system file. **3.** In HTML, an optional or required setting that controls specific characteristics of an element and that enables authors to specify values for these characteristics. See *archive attribute, file attribute.*

ATX case A computer case designed to hold an ATX form factor motherboard. See *AT case, ATX form factor.*

ATX form factor A motherboard design created by chipmaker Intel that provides better accessibility to motherboard components, better cooling, more full-size expansion slots, and a more convenient layout for system upgrades than the AT form factor. In an ATX form factor motherboard, the expansion slots run parallel to the wide edge of the board.

AU **1.** Abbreviation for audio. An 8-bit monaural sound file format that is widely used on Unix workstations, including Sun and NeXT machines for storing digitized wave sounds. The format employs an advanced storage technique that enables 14-bit sounds to be stored in only 8 bits of data, with minimal loss. **2.** In the Internet's domain name system, an abbreviation for Australia.

audible feedback The capacity of a keyboard to generate sounds each time a key is pressed. Audible feedback makes it easier for some people to determine when a key has been depressed sufficiently for a character to be generated onscreen. See *tactile feedback.*

audio codec See *codec.*

audio compression See *compression.*

audio effects board In digital video, an audio mixer that can be used to adjust the video's audio characteristics.

audio file In computers and computer-based reproduction systems, such as audio compact discs, sound described by taking many thousands of samples of the sound each second and recording the sound's waveform as a discrete value.

audio frequency modulation See *AFM.*

audio mixer An electronic device or computer program that can combine multiple streams of audio data into a single stream.

audio monitor Any speaker, but especially a speaker mounted on a modem, that lets one hear what is happening on the telephone line. A busy signal can be heard, for example, or the hissing sound of two modems establishing a carrier.

Audio-Video Interleave See *AVI.*

audit trail In an accounting package, any program feature that automatically keeps a record of transactions so that one can backtrack to find the origin of specific figures that appear on reports.

AUI Acronym for Attachment Unit Interface. On Ethernet local area networks (LAN), a standard that specifies how network cables are connected to network interface cards (NIC).

AUP Acronym for Acceptable Use Policy. An Internet service provider (ISP) policy that indicates which types of uses are permissible. Some services sharply restrict commercial use.

authenticate To establish the identity of a person accessing a computer network. See *authentication, log on, password, strong authentication.*

authentication In a network, the process by which the system attempts to ensure that the person logging on is the same person to whom the account was issued. The sole means of authentication in some networks is the demand for a password, even though password-based authentication is known to have several serious security flaws. See *CHAP, PAP.*

Authenticode A Microsoft-developed security technology that provides a "wrapper" for downloaded software. Authenticode "wrappers" enable the user to determine the identify of the software's author and to determine whether the software has been tampered with.

authoring In multimedia, the process of preparing a presentation. This involves not only writing the text, but also preparing the sound, graphic, and video components.

authoring language A computer-assisted instruction (CAI) application that provides tools for creating instructional or presentation software. For example, a popular authoring language for Macintosh computers is HyperCard, provided free with every Macintosh computer. Using HyperCard, educators can develop instructional programs quickly and easily.

authoring tools In multimedia, application programs that enable the user to blend audio files, video, and animation with text and traditional graphics. The leading commercial authoring tool is Macromedia Director.

authoritative Official and superior to other, competing directives. In a data restore procedure, for example, the authoritative backup set will replace existing data.

auto-answer mode In a modem, a user-selectable mode that automatically answers incoming calls. This mode is switched off by default in most modem's default configuration since most users employ their modems only for originating calls.

auto-assembly In digital video, a type of assemble edit in which the editing proceeds automatically based on a previously specified edit decision list (EDL). See *assemble edit, edit decision list (EDL).*

AutoCAD A computer-assisted design and drafting (CAD) program, created by AutoDesk, that is widely used in professional engineering and architectural settings.

auto-dial/auto-answer modem A modem that can generate tones to dial the receiving computer and that can answer a ringing telephone to establish a connection when a call is received.

autodial modem See *auto-dial/auto-answer modem.*

AUTOEXEC.BAT In MS-DOS, a batch file containing instructions that DOS executes when the system is started. AUTOEXEC.BAT files commonly include PATH statements that tell DOS where to find application programs and the commands to install a mouse or to operate a printer. All this information must be provided at the start of every operating session; AUTOEXEC.BAT does the task for the user. See *CONFIG.SYS, path, path statement.*

autologon A feature of communications programs that lets one automate the process of logging on to an online service.

automagically Performed by means of a process that is too complex to be explained in the context in which this word is used or by a process that appears quite simple to the user but in fact is accomplished by extremely complex, hidden procedures.

automatic backup An application program feature that saves a document automatically at a period the user specifies, such as every 5 or 10 minutes. After a power outage or system crash, the user can retrieve the last automatic backup file when he or she restarts the application. This feature can help to avoid catastrophic work losses. Also called autosave.

automatic emulation switching In printers, the capability to change printer control languages without human intervention. Printers with automatic emulation switching sense the language, such as PostScript or PCL6, used by incoming documents and adjust automatically.

automatic font downloading The transfer of downloadable fonts from the hard disk to the printer by a utility program as the fonts are needed to complete a printing job.

automatic head parking A hard disk feature that moves the read/write head over the landing zone—preventing a head crash—whenever power is shut off.

automatic hyphenation See *hyphenation*.

automatic mode switching In video adapters, the automatic detection and adjustment of a video adapter's internal circuitry to the video output of a program on an IBM PC–compatible computer. Most Video Graphics Array (VGA) adapters, for example, switch to adjust to Color Graphics Array (CGA), Monochrome Display Adapter (MDA), Extended Graphics Array (EGA), or VGA output from applications.

automatic name recognition In databases and Web search engines, a feature that automatically detects that a keyword supplied for a search is a person's name and restricts the search to capitalized names.

automatic network switching A feature of departmental laser printers and workgroup printers that allows them to serve several different kinds of computers and several different kinds of networks. A printer equipped with automatic network switching can receive data from Ethernet, AppleTalk, or TCP/IP networks and print it without human attention. See *automatic emulation switching*.

automatic recalculation In a spreadsheet, a mode in which cell values are recalculated every time any cell changes in the worksheet. Automatic recalculation can be switched to manual calculation while one is entering data into a large spreadsheet if recalculation takes a long time. See *background recalculation, manual recalculation*.

automatic speed sensing A modem feature that lets the modem automatically determine the maximum speed at which a connection can be made. Performed during the handshaking period at the beginning of a call, this enables modems with automatic speed sensing to fall back to the fastest speed that the two connected modems—and line conditions—can support. See *fall back, handshaking*.

automation The replacement of human skill by automatic machine operations. Word processing software is an example of the potential of automation. These programs automate tasks as simple as centering text and as complex as sorting a mailing list into ZIP code order.

autonomous system (AS) In Internet network topology, a collection of routers under the control of a single administrative authority. Within an autonomous system, an administrator can create and name new subdomains, and assign IP addresses and domain names to workstations on the network.

autonomous system number (ASN) In an autonomous system, an IP address that has been assigned by an automatic protocol to one of the workstations on the network.

AutoPlay A Microsoft-initiated standard for CD-ROMs. When an AutoPlay disc is inserted into a CD-ROM drive, Microsoft Windows searches for an AutoRun file on the CD, and if found, begins executing it automatically.

autorepeat key A key that repeatedly enters a character as long as it is held down.

autosave   See *automatic backup.*

autosizing   A monitor feature that allows a monitor to size an image to fit the display, regardless of its resolution. Autosizing monitors maintain the aspect ratio of an image but enlarge or reduce it to fit in the space available.

autostart routine   A set of instructions contained in read-only memory (ROM) that tells the computer how to proceed when one switches on the power. See *BIOS, Power-On Self-Test (POST).*

AutoText   See *glossary.*

autotrace   In a graphics program, such as Adobe Illustrator, a command that transforms an imported bit-mapped graphic into an object-oriented graphic. Object-oriented graphics print at the printer's maximum resolution (up to 300 dots per inch for laser printers). Using the autotrace tool, one can transform low-resolution graphics into art that prints at a higher resolution.

A/UX   Apple Computer's version of the Unix operating system.

AUX   In MS-DOS, an abbreviation for the auxiliary port, the communications (COM) port that DOS uses by default (usually COM1).

auxiliary battery   A backup battery designed for use with a portable computer. Some notebook computers automatically switch to the auxiliary battery, if available, when the primary battery reaches a predetermined drain level.

auxiliary speakers   Two or more stereo speakers that connect to the sound board and that allow one to hear their output. Auxiliary speakers replace a computer's onboard speaker and are usually magnetically shielded to prevent interference with the monitor.

auxiliary storage   See *secondary storage.*

AV   Acronym for audiovisual. This term refers generically to any analog or digital technology that combines sounds and graphics or sounds and video.

availability   One of four basic measures of system dependability (the others are reliability, safety, and security). Availability measures the capacity of a computer system or network to respond to requests for use of its resources. A highly available system has 24/7 availability (24 hours per day, 7 days per week). See *reliability, safety, security.*

avatar   A graphical representation of a person that appears on the computer screen in an interactive game or communication system. The avatar's appearance, actions, and words are controlled by the person whom the avatar represents.

average access time   See *access time.*

average latency   See *latency.*

average seek time   See *seek time.*

AVI   Acronym for Audio-Video Interleave. A file format for storing audio and video information developed by Microsoft Corporation and specifically designed for recording and playback on Microsoft Windows systems. The AVI format can produce near-CD-quality stereo, as well as videos with an associated sound track, but AVI files consume large amounts of file space relative to other audio and video file formats. See *ASF, MPEG, QuickTime.*

AWC   See *Association for Women in Computing.*

awk   A programming language designed for the manipulation of textual data. It is available on most Unix and Unix-like systems.

axis   In computer graphics, a line that serves as a reference baseline for plotting data points. Business charts such as line and bar graphs typically have two axes: the x-axis (horizontal axis) and y-axis (vertical axis). Three-dimensional graphics employ a third reference line, the y-axis, to indicate depth. See *x-axis, y-axis, z-axis.*

B **1.** Abbreviation for byte (8 bits). **2.** An experimental programming language created at AT&T's Bell Laboratories in 1970; also a predecessor to C.

baby AT The form factor used by most PC motherboards prior to the introduction of the current standard, the ATX form factor. It is slightly smaller (8.5" by 13") than the original AT form factor (12" by 13"), which was introduced with the IBM Personal Computer AT in 1984. See *AT form factor, ATX form factor, form factor.*

baby AT case A computer case and power supply unit that will accommodate a baby AT motherboard. See *baby AT.*

backbone In a wide area network (WAN) or a TCP/IP-based network such as the public Internet, a high-speed, high-capacity medium that is designed to transfer data over hundreds or thousands of miles. A variety of physical media is used for backbone services, including microwave relay, satellites, and dedicated telephone lines. See *Internet, WAN.*

backbone site In Usenet's telephone-based store-and-forward network, a site that is centrally located on the article distribution network. See *UUCP.*

back door A means of gaining access to a computer program or computer system without having to go through the normal security and authentication procedures. Programmers may create back doors to speed development work, but they create a significant security risk if left in the code after its release.

back end The portion of a program that handles the processing tasks that the program is designed to perform, but in such a way that it is not apparent to the user. In a local area network (LAN) with client/server architecture, the back-end application may be stored on the file server, while front-end programs handle the user interface on each workstation. See *front end.*

back-end processor A processing unit (such as a microprocessor) that is dedicated to perform a back-end task, such as processing complex graphics images. See *back end.*

background In computers that can do more than one task at a time, the environment in which self-running tasks (such as printing a document or downloading a file) are carried out behind the scenes while the user works actively with an application in the foreground. In computers that lack multitasking capabilities, background tasks are carried out during brief pauses in the execution of the system's primary (foreground) tasks.

background application In a multitasking operating system, any application that is inactive. See *foreground application.*

background communication Data communication, such as downloading a file from an online service, that takes place in the background while the user concentrates on another application in the foreground. See *multitasking.*

background noise See *noise.*

background pagination See *pagination.*

background printing The printing of a document in the background while some other task is actively being performed in the foreground. Background printing is particularly useful for those who frequently print long documents or use a slow printer. With background printing, work can continue while the document prints. See *background, multitasking, print queue, print spooler.*

background recalculation In spreadsheet programs, an option that causes the program to perform recalculations in the background while one continues to work in the spreadsheet.

background tasks In a multitasking operating system, the operations occurring in the background (such as printing, sorting a large collection of data, or searching a database) while one works in another program in the foreground. See *multitasking*.

backlighting A display design that involves shining light at an LCD (liquid crystal display) from behind, increasing the contrast between light and dark pixels. Although backlighting increases power consumption, it makes LCDs much more readable in bright-light conditions, such as those outdoors. See *LCD (liquid crystal display)*.

backlit display A display design that incorporates backlighting. See *backlighting*.

backoff The time delay (often selected randomly) initiated by a network workstation when the computer attempts to send data to the network but experiences a collision. At the conclusion of the backoff period, the computer attempts to retransmit the data. A random backoff ensures that the colliding workstations will not attempt to retransmit simultaneously. See *collision*.

BackOffice See *Microsoft BackOffice*.

BackOrifice A Trojan horse program that relies on tricking users to get them to install the software on a Microsoft Windows system; once the software is installed, intruders can use it to perform read, write, and execute operations on the system with the same privileges as the user who installed the software. See *Trojan horse*.

backplane A circuit board that contains plugs designed for specific components. In personal computers, the term is synonymous with motherboard. Originally, the term described a main circuit board mounted vertically at the rear of the case.

back quote The left single-quote character on the standard ASCII keyboard (`); also called the grave accent.

back-side bus In the Intel-developed Dual Independent Bus (DIB) package for microprocessors, the bus that connects the processing unit to the L2 cache unit. See *DIB*.

backside cache In Power Macintosh computers, an L2 cache (secondary cache) that is mounted on the back of the cartridge containing the microprocessor.

backslash The backward-slanting slash character on the standard ASCII keyboard (\); also known as the reverse slash.

backspace A key used to delete the character to the left of the cursor's position, or the act of moving one space to the left by using the backspace or cursor-movement keys.

back up **1.** To make a duplicate or archival copy of one or more files on a computer system. **2.** To restore a previous configuration in case a more recent one proves to be unstable.

backup A duplicate, archival copy of some or all of the files on a computer system. Regular backup procedures are required for successful use of a hard disk system. See *archival backup, full backup, incremental backup*.

backup and recovery A data maintenance procedure available in advanced database management systems that enables the database to be restored to the last known stable state after a catastrophic software or hardware error has rendered the data unusable. This process resembles the backup and recovery procedures used for other types of computer data, except that a transaction log is used to monitor each step of the data recovery process. See *database management system (DBMS)*.

backup domain controller (BDC) In a Microsoft network, a computer configured as a domain controller that maintains a frequently backed-up version of the domain's directory database; the system can step in to provide domain controller functions if the primary domain controller becomes unavailable.

backup file A copy of a file created as a safety precaution in case anything happens to the original.

backup medium A storage medium that is suitable for data backup purposes, such as a tape drive.

backup set A named and dated collection of backup files that has been stored on a backup medium. See *backup file, backup medium.*

backup type The data archiving method that is chosen for backing up one or more files for archival purposes. Backup types include full backup (a backup of the entire hard disk), differential backup (a backup of only the files that have been changed since the last full or incremental backup, but not those that have changed since the last differential backup), and incremental backup (a backup of only those files that have changed since the last full or incremental backup). See *full backup, incremental backup.*

backup utility A utility program designed to back up program and data files from a hard disk to a backup medium such as a floppy disk or a tape drive. Backup utility programs include commands to schedule regular backups, to back up only selected directories or files, and to restore all or only a few files from a backup set. Backup utilities can implement a full range of backup types. See *backup type.*

Backus-Naur Form (BNF) A set of rules for describing the organization of a program without actually writing instructions in any particular programming language. BNF is useful for teaching programming concepts and for comparing procedures written in different languages.

backward chaining In expert systems, a commonly used method of drawing inferences from IF/THEN rules. A backward-chaining system starts with a question such as "How much is this property worth?" and searches through the system's rules to determine which ones allow the system to solve the problem and what additional data must be provided. A backward-chaining expert system asks questions of users, engaging them in a dialogue. See *forward chaining, knowledge base.*

backward-compatible Compatible with earlier versions of a program or earlier models of a computer. Synonymous with downward-compatible.

backward search In a database, spreadsheet, or word processor document, a search that begins at the cursor's location and proceeds backward toward the beginning of a database or document (rather than searching forward to the end).

bad break An unattractive formatting flaw caused by breaking a line or a page in violation of typography guidelines. A bad line break may occur when hyphens are used incorrectly (or not used in such a way that line lengths are uneven or the space between words in proportionately spaced text are too large). See *bad page break.*

bad page break In a document or spreadsheet, a soft page break that divides text at an inappropriate location. Headings can be left dangling at the bottom of pages (widows), data tables can be split, and single lines of text (orphans) can be left at the top of pages. A common flaw in documents produced on computers, bad page breaks can be caught by a final, careful review of the document using the program's print preview command or with widow/orphan protection features in some software. See *block protection, soft page break.*

bad sector An area of a floppy or hard disk that will not reliably record data. Many brand-new hard disks have a few bad sectors as a result of manufacturing defects. The operating system locks these sectors out of reading and writing operations as it formats the disk so that the disk is usable as though the bad sectors do not exist. In addition, bad sectors may develop as the disk is being used, requiring the use of a disk utility program to identify these sectors and lock them out of storage operations. See *bad track table.*

bad track A hard disk or floppy disk track that contains a bad sector. Marked as unusable in the file allocation table (FAT), bad tracks are harmless unless Track 0 is bad, in which case the disk must be replaced. See *bad sector, bad track table.*

bad track table   A document attached to or packaged with a hard disk that lists the bad sectors of the disk. Almost every hard disk comes off the assembly line with some defects. During the low-level format, these defective areas of the disk are locked out so that system software cannot use them. See *bad sector, bad track.*

BAK   The file name extension usually attached to a file containing backup data. Many programs assign the BAK extension to the old version of a file any time the file is modified. For example, when one edits AUTOEXEC.BAT and saves changes, the previous version is saved to AUTOEXEC.BAK and the previous AUTOEXEC.BAK is overwritten.

ball bat   In Unix, a common slang term for an exclamation point (!). Also called a bang character or an astonisher. See *bang path.*

balloon help   In the MacOS, an optional help feature that displays cartoon balloons containing an explanation of an onscreen feature (such as an icon or part of a window) when the user positions the mouse over it.

band-stepper actuator   In a disk drive, a mechanism, incorporating a stepping motor and a track (a band), that positions the read/write head of a hard disk over a track. Band-stepper actuators are not as common as servo-voice coil actuators on today's hard disks. See *servo-voice coil actuator.*

bandwidth   **1.** In analog communications, the difference between the lowest and the highest frequencies that can be accommodated in a given communication channel. Designed for the human voice, telephones offer a bandwidth of only 3,000 Hz. In comparison, high-fidelity music reproduction equipment offers a bandwidth that encompasses the bandwidth of human hearing (20 Hz to 18,000 Hz). **2.** In digital communications, the amount of data that can be transmitted via a given communications channel (such as a computer network) in a given unit of time (generally 1 second). For digital devices, bandwidth is measured in bits per second (bps).

bandwidth on demand   In telecommunications, a voice and data service that is capable of expanding the amount of available bandwidth as traffic increases.

bang   **1.** In programming, a common slang term for an exclamation point (!). **2.** In HTML, a common slang term for a forward slash (/), especially when telling someone a URL "Go to www-dot-Microsoft-dot-com-bang-search-dot-html." See *HTML.*

bang character   Unix slang for an exclamation point (!). Also called ball bat or astonisher. See *bang path.*

bang path   In UUCP, an e-mail address that specifies the location of a specific computer on a UUCP-based network. The address is called a bang path because the various units of the address are separated by exclamation points (bang characters). See *UUCP.*

bank switching   A way of expanding memory beyond an operating system or microprocessor's address limitations by switching rapidly between two banks of memory. See *EMS, expanded memory.*

banner ad   On a Web page, a box running across the page that is often used to contain advertisements. The banner generally contains a link to the advertiser's Web site. Web-based advertising services can track the number of times users click the banner, generating statistics that enable advertisers to judge whether the advertising fees are worth paying.

bar code   A printed pattern of wide and narrow vertical bars used to represent numerical codes in machine-readable form. Computers equipped with bar code readers and special software can interpret bar codes. Supermarkets use bar codes conforming to the Universal Product Code (UPC) to identify products and ring up prices, while the U.S. Postal Service uses POSTNET bar codes to make ZIP codes machine-readable. The latest versions of word processing programs, such as WordPerfect and Microsoft Word, include options to print POSTNET bar codes on envelopes.

bar code reader   An input device that scans bar codes and, with special software, converts the bar code into readable data. See *bar code.*

bar graph   In presentation graphics, a graph that plots data using horizontal bars. Commonly used to show the values of unrelated items, such as the sales figures for several unrelated products. The x-axis (categories axis) is the vertical axis, and the y-axis (value axis) is the horizontal axis. Often confused with a column graph, which uses vertical bars, a bar graph is best for conveying quantities, while a column graph is best for conveying changes over time. See *area graph, column graph, line graph, paired bar graph.*

base   The number of digits available for use in a given numbering system. Binary numbers, which are a base 2 numbering system, employ only two digits, 0 and 1. Synonymous with radix. See *binary number, decimal notation, hexadecimal notation.*

base 2   A numbering system that employs only two digits. The binary numbering system used in computers is a base 2 numbering system. See *base.*

base 8   A numbering system that employs eight digits. The hexadecimal numbering system used by computer programmers is a base 8 system. See *base, hexadecimal notation, hexadecimal number.*

base 10   A numbering system that employs 10 digits. The familiar decimal numbering system people use every day is a base 10 numbering system. See *base, decimal number.*

base 60   A numbering system that employs 60 digits. Believed to have its origins in ancient Babylon, the numbering system that is today widely used for keeping time is a base 60 numbering system.

base 64   A data encoding method that converts a binary file into plain ASCII text that can be transmitted via the Internet and other computer networks. For example, the MIME standard uses base 64. See *ASCII, binary file, MIME.*

base address   In a computer memory, a portion of the memory address that remains constant and provides a reference point from which the address of additional memory locations can be calculated. The base address is accompanied by an offset that specifies how far from the base address a specific memory location is positioned. See *address.*

baseband   In local area networks (LANs), a communications method in which the information-bearing signal is placed directly on the cable in digital form without modulation. Because many baseband networks can use twisted-pair (ordinary telephone) cables, they are cheaper to install than some broadband networks that require coaxial cable. However, a baseband system is limited in its geographic extent and provides only one channel of communication at a time. Most personal computer local area networks are baseband networks. See *broadband.*

base font   The default font (typeface, size, and attributes) for a document. It is possible to make some of the text in the document a different size or typeface, or to apply different attributes such as bold or italic, but text for which changes are not specified will appear in the base font. In most word processing programs, one can choose a default base font for all documents or for just the document being edited.

base-level synthesizer   In multimedia, the minimum capabilities of a music synthesizer required by the Multimedia Personal Computer (MPC) specifications. In the MPC-3 specification, a base-level synthesizer must be capable of playing at least 16 simultaneous notes on melodic instruments and 6 simultaneous notes on three percussion instruments. See *extended-level synthesizer, MIDI.*

baseline In typography, the lowest point that characters reach (excluding descenders). For example, the baseline of a line of text is the bottom of letters such as *a* and *x*, excluding the lowest points of *p* and *q*, which have descenders. See *ascender, descender.*

baseline test A test performed before any changes are made to the system. Changes are then made and tested one at a time, and the results are compared to the baseline test.

base memory See *conventional memory.*

bash Acronym for Bourne-Again Shell. In Linux and other Unix-like operating systems, a text-only command shell that facilitates communication between users and the operating system's kernel. The default shell in most Linux distributions, bash is POSIX-compliant and offers convenient tools for editing the command line. Based on the Bourne shell (sh), bash was developed by the Free Software Foundation. See *csh, ksh, Linux, POSIX, sh, shell.*

BASIC Acronym for Beginner's All-Purpose Symbolic Instruction Code. An easy-to-use high-level programming language developed in 1964 for instructional purposes. Initially, BASIC was criticized for encouraging poor program structure due to the use of goto statements and the lack of control structures. Newer versions, such as Visual Basic, incorporate the principles of structured programming and some of the features of object-oriented programming (OOP). See *BASICA, spaghetti code, Visual Basic.*

BASICA An interpreter for the Microsoft BASIC programming language that was supplied on the MS-DOS disk provided with IBM-manufactured personal computers.

Basic Encoding Rules (BER) The set of standardized rules for encoding data according to the Abstract Syntax Notation One (ASN.1) protocol. The purpose of these rules is to encode all data in such a way that BER-compatible applications can immediately recognize which type of data the encoding contains. BER is not widely used.

basic input/output system (BIOS) See *BIOS.*

Basic Rate Interface See *BRI.*

BAT The MS-DOS file name extension attached to a batch file. See *AUTOEXEC.BAT.*

batch file A file containing a series of MS-DOS commands executed one after the other, as though one had typed them. The mandatory .BAT file extension causes COMMAND.COM to process the file one line at a time. Batch files are useful when one needs to type the same series of MS-DOS commands repeatedly. Almost all DOS and Windows users have an AUTOEXEC.BAT file, a batch file that MS-DOS loads at the start of every operating session.

batch processing A mode of computer operation in which program instructions are executed one after the other without user intervention. Batch processing efficiently uses computer resources but is less convenient than interactive processing, in which one sees the results of his or her commands onscreen so that he or she can correct errors and make necessary adjustments before completing the operation.

battery pack A rechargeable battery that supplies power to a computer, usually a portable computer, when external (main) power is not available. The least expensive battery packs use nickel-cadmium (NiCad) batteries, which have two significant drawbacks: They are prone to becoming incapable of accepting a full charge, and they are extremely toxic because of their cadmium content. More expensive but of greater popularity are nickel metal hydride (NiMH) and lithium-ion battery packs, which provide increased capacity without either drawback. See *auxiliary battery.*

baud A variation or change in a signal in a communications channel. See *baud rate, bits per second (bps).*

baud rate The maximum number of changes that can occur per second in the electrical state of a communications circuit. Under RS-232C communications protocols, 300 baud is likely to equal 300 bits per second (bps), but at higher baud rates, the number of bits per second transmitted is usually twice the baud rate because 2 bits of data can be sent with each change. Therefore, the transfer rate of modems, for example, is usually stated in bps. See *modem, RS-232C.*

bay See *drive bay.*

BBS Acronym for Bulletin Board Service. A small-scale online service, usually set up by a personal computer hobbyist for the enjoyment of other hobbyists, and based on a single personal computer that is accessed by means of direct-dial modem links. A typical BBS includes topically oriented discussion groups, file downloading, and games. The Internet's explosive popularity has all but eliminated the use of BBSs, most of which have either ceased to exist or have made their resources accessible by means of direct Internet connections.

BCC See *blind carbon copy.*

BCD See *binary-coded decimal.*

B channel In ISDN, a digital communications channel that operates over the twisted-pair wiring common in homes and offices. The B channel can carry digitized voice or data at a transfer rate of 56 Kbps or 64 Kbps. The least expensive ISDN service, Basic Rate Interface (BRI), offers one or two B channels, while the higher-end Primary Rate Interface (PRI) offers 32. See *ISDN.*

bean A reusable object, created with the Java programming language and in conformity to Sun's 100 percent Pure Java specifications, that is packaged according to the JavaBeans specifications. A bean differs from a Java applet in that it has persistence (it remains on the user's system after execution). Additionally, beans are capable of communicating and exchanging data with other JavaBeans by means of interprocess communication. In this sense, a JavaBean is similar to an ActiveX control, but with a very important exception: Unlike ActiveX controls, which execute only on computers that support object linking and embedding (OLE) at the operating system level, a bean will execute on any computer platform that is capable of running a Java interpreter. Users will find that beans seamlessly add functionality to beans-aware applications, while developers can quickly create applications by combining bean components. See *Java, Java applet, JavaBeans.*

bed In multimedia, the instrumental or choral music that provides the enveloping background for a presentation.

BEDO DRAM Acronym for burst EDO (extended data out) DRAM (dynamic random access memory). A type of dynamic RAM memory chip that can send and receive data at the same time. See *random access memory (RAM).*

Beginner's All-Purpose Symbolic Instruction Code See *BASIC.*

behavior In object-oriented programming, a type of method made publicly available by an object; an object's behaviors include all the methods that can be used to obtain information about or from the object (accessors/interrogators) as well as all the methods that can be used to manipulate or alter the object (manipulators/mutators). See *accessor/interrogator, manipulators/mutators, method, object-oriented programming.*

Bell 103A In the United States, an obsolete modulation protocol for computer modems governing sending and receiving data at a speed of 300 bps. See *ITU-TSS, modem, modulation protocol.*

Bell 212A In the United States, an obsolete modulation protocol for computer modems governing sending and receiving data at a speed of 1200 bps. See *ITU-TSS, modem, modulation protocol.*

Bell Operating Company (BOC) See *Regional Bell Operating Companies (RBOC).*

bells and whistles Slang term for advanced features that are of interest only to specialized users. See *plain vanilla*.

benchmark A standard measurement, determined by a benchmark program, that is used to test the performance of different brands of equipment. See *benchmark program*.

benchmark program A utility program used to measure a computer's processing speed and component performance so that its overall performance can be compared to that of other computers running the same program. See *cache memory*, *throughput*.

BeOS An operating system for Macintosh computers and Intel-based, created by Be, Inc., which is led by ex-Apple executive Jean-Louis Gassée. Designed from the ground up as an entirely new operating system, BeOS does not interface with applications by means of time-consuming procedural calls, but rather by means of an elegantly designed object-oriented interface. The operating system is highly multithreaded and supports parallel processors. BeOS is targeted to high-end multimedia developers who need these features to create compelling, high-resolution multimedia presentations. See *MacOS*.

Beowulf An inexpensive supercomputer created by clustering off-the-shelf personal computer components linked by a high-speed network and powered by Linux; each of the networked computers executes a portion of a program in parallel. The term originated with the Beowulf Project at NASA's Goddard Space flight Center. See *clustering*, *Linux*, *Piranha*.

BER See *Basic Encoding Rules*.

Berkeley Internet Name Daemon See *BIND*.

Berkeley Software Distribution See *BSD*.

beta In software testing, a preliminary version of a program that is widely distributed before commercial release to users who test the program by operating it under realistic conditions. See *alpha*, *alpha test*, *beta site*, *beta test*, *beta version*.

beta build In Web publishing, a preliminary version of a Web site that contains most or all of the final content and that is submitted to the client for final approval. See *alpha build*.

beta site The company, university department, or individual authorized to beta-test software. When developing a program or a version of an existing program, a company chooses out-of-house beta sites where the program is subjected to demanding, heavy-duty usage. This process reveals the program's remaining bugs and shortcomings before it is officially released. See *beta software*.

beta test The second stage in the testing of computer software, after alpha test but before commercial release. Beta tests are at beta sites. Also used as a verb, as in "The software is ready to be beta-tested."

beta version In software testing, a preliminary version of a program that is widely distributed before commercial release to users who test the program by operating it under realistic conditions. See *alpha*, *alpha test*, *beta site*, *beta test*.

Bézier curve (Pronounced *BEH-zee-ay*.) A mathematically generated line that can take the form of nonuniform curves; named after its inventor, the French mathematician Pierre Bézier A Bézier curve is constructed with a minimum of four points: two anchor points that define the beginning and end of the curved line, and two midpoints (called control handles) which influence the shape of the line but do not normally lie on the path of the line. In graphics applications, dragging the control handles (shown as small boxes onscreen) manipulates the complexity and shape of the curve.

b-frame In digital video formats that use interframe compression, such as MPEG video, a frame that records the changes that occur between the preceding frame and the next frame. Because this information is recorded in both directions, MPEG videos can be played in reverse. See *i-frame, interframe compression, MPEG, p-frame.*

BGP Acronym for Border Gateway Protocol. An Internet protocol that defines the routing of Internet data between an autonomous system (AS) and the wider Internet. This protocol replaces the older Exterior Gateway Protocol.

bibliographic retrieval service An online information service that specializes in maintaining huge computerized indexes to scholarly, scientific, medical, and technical literature. The two leading information firms are BRS Information Technologies (Latham, New York) and DIALOG Information Services (Menlo Park, California). Serving mainly corporate and institutional customers, these companies charge fees that average more than $1 per minute. Personal computer users can access, at substantially lower rates, special menu-driven night and weekend versions of these services, BRS/After Dark and Knowledge Index.

bidirectional parallel port A parallel port, capable of both sending and receiving detailed messages, that can transfer data much faster than a standard parallel port. In its standard IEEE 1284, the Institute of Electrical and Electronics Engineers (IEEE) established the technical rules governing bidirectional parallel ports. Both the enhanced parallel port (EPP) and the extended capabilities port (ECP) conform to IEEE 1284, and one of the two standards—probably the ECP, experts say—will replace the standard parallel port in the next few years. See *ECP, EPP.*

bidirectional printing Printing by means of a bidirectional parallel port, which enables bidirectional communication between the printer and the operating system. With bidirectional printing, detailed error messages appear when the printer malfunctions. See *bidirectional parallel port.*

biff A Unix utility program that notifies users of incoming mail.

Big Blue Nickname for IBM, which uses blue as its corporate color.

big-endian A philosophical orientation toward computer system and network design that favors putting the most significant (largest) digit first in numerical encoding schemes. The contrasting orientation, little-endian, favors putting the most significant digit last. Because it cannot be proven that either orientation is more efficient, the dispute between big-endians and little-endians classically exemplifies the pointless holy war, in which the various positions taken are based on irreducible pseudoreligious principles rather than reason. The terms derive from Jonathan Swift's *Gulliver's Travels*, which depicts Lilliputian wars concerning whether boiled eggs should be opened at the big end or the little end. See *little-endian.*

big iron Slang term for mainframe.

bin Common abbreviation for binary file.

binaries Two or more binary files.

binary **1.** A system with two possible states, such as a home electrical circuit (on or off). **2.** Abbreviation of binary notation.

binary-coded decimal (BCD) A method of coding long decimal numbers so that they can be processed with great precision in a computer. Each decimal digit is encoded using a 4-bit binary number.

binary-compatible In microprocessors, a high degree of compatibility such that a given microprocessor is capable of running software designed for another company's central processing unit (CPU). In software, a program will run on any microprocessor with which it is binary-compatible. See *microprocessor.*

binary file A file containing data or program instructions in a computer-readable format. Binary files are typically not readable onscreen. The opposite of a binary file is an ASCII file.

binary newsgroup In Usenet, a newsgroup in which the articles contain (or are supposed to contain) binary files, such as sounds, graphics, or movies. These files have been encoded with uuencode, a program that transforms a binary file into coded ASCII characters so that it can be transferred via the Internet. See *Usenet*.

binary notation A method of representing numbers that employs a base (radix) of 2; therefore, there are only two possible values (0 and 1). Binary notation strongly differs from the notation systems people prefer; these have bases of 10 (decimal numbers), 12 (measurements in feet and inches), or 60 (minutes and hours). Still, binary notation shares one characteristic in common with more familiar notation systems: it is a positional notation system with place values. In decimal notation, each position represents an order of magnitude ($1 = 10^0$ $10 = 10^1$, $100 = 10^2$, and so on). The same is true of decimal notation, except that the orders of magnitude are squares of 2, not 10 ($0 = 2^0$, 10 [2 in decimal] $= 2^1$, 100 [4 in decimal] $= 2^2$, 1000 [8 in decimal] $= 2^3$, and so on). Binary notation is preferred for computers for precision and economy. Building an electronic circuit that can detect the difference between two states (high current and low current, or 0 and 1) is easy and inexpensive; building a circuit that detects the difference among 10 states (0 through 9) is much more difficult and expensive. The word *bit* derives from the phrase BInary digiT. See *base, base 2, decimal notation*.

binary number One of two possible numbers (0 and 1) in binary notation. See *binary notation, decimal notation*.

binary search A search algorithm that avoids a slow search through hundreds or thousands of records by starting in the middle of a sorted database and determining whether the desired record is above or below the midpoint. Having reduced the number of records to be searched by 50 percent, the search proceeds to the middle of the remaining records and so on, until the desired record is found. See *algorithm*.

binary transfer 1. In general data communications, a file transfer protocol that allows users to transfer binary files to and from a remote computer using terminal software. **2.** In FTP, a file download or upload that preserves binary files intact (unlike an ASCII transfer).

Binary Tree Predictive Coding (BTPC) A compression method for still graphics that performs both lossless compression and lossy compression, and that is particularly effective for the computer transmission and presentation of photographs.

bind In computer programming, to associate two objects or values.

BIND Acronym for Berkeley Internet Name Daemon. A domain name server (also called a DNS server) for Unix-like operating systems. Originally developed as part of the Berkeley Software Distribution (BSD), BIND is available with most versions of Unix and Linux. See *BSD, DNS server, Linux, Unix*.

binder Before the invention of thin-film magnetic media, the adhesive that held a recording medium on the surface of a hard disk. Binder was mixed with the medium (and sometimes a lubricant, too) and was applied to the substrate by sputtering or some other means.

binding offset In word processing and desktop publishing (DTP), a gap left on one side of a printed page to allow room for binding the document. Binding offset is used only for documents printed or reproduced on both sides of the page (duplex printing); the text is shifted to the left on verso (left, even-numbered) pages and to the right on recto (right, odd-numbered) pages. See *desktop publishing (DTP)*.

BinHex A protocol for encoding binary files so that the coded file contains nothing but the standard ASCII characters and, therefore, can be transferred to other computers via the Internet. The receiving computer must decode the file using BinHex-capable decoding software.

BinHex is especially popular among Macintosh users because the encoded files can preserve the unusual Macintosh file format, in which files contain two forks (a data fork and a resource fork). Note that BinHex is not a compression technique and that a BinHexed file may actually be longer than the source file. For this reason, BinHexed files are generally compressed after they are encoded using the Macintosh standard compression program, StuffIt. See *ASCII character set.*

bioinformatics   A scientific field devoted to the development of database software specially designed to enhance biological research. Bioinformatics researchers combine academic backgrounds in molecular biology and computer science.

biological feedback device   A device that translates eye movements, body movements, and even brain waves into computer input.

biometric authentication   A method of authentication that requires a biological scan of some sort, such as a retinal scan or voice recognition.

BIOS   Acronym for Basic Input/Output System. A set of programs encoded in read-only memory (ROM) in IBM PC–compatible computers. These programs handle startup operations such as the Power-On Self-Test (POST) and low-level control for hardware, such as disk drives, keyboard, and monitor. Popular brands of BIOS chips on motherboards sold today include Phoenix Technologies and American Megatrends, Inc. Some system components have their own BIOS chip, whose instructions are also read into the PC's memory at startup. The BIOS on a hard disk controller, for example, stores a table of tracks and sectors on the drive. Computer manufacturers occasionally release BIOS upgrades to fix errors in a computer's operation and to make the system compatible with new types of hardware and technologies. Great care must be taken, however, when upgrading your BIOS; follow your manufacturer's instructions.

B-ISDN   See *Broadband ISDN.*

bit   The basic unit of information in a binary numbering system (BInary digiT). The electronic circuitry in computers detects the difference between two states (high current and low current) and represents these states as one of the two numbers in a binary system: 1 or 0. These basic high/low, either/or, yes/no units of information are called bits. Because building a reliable circuit that tells the difference between a 1 and a 0 is easy and inexpensive, computers are accurate in their internal processing capabilities, typically making fewer than one internal error in every 100 billion processing operations. Eight bits comprise 1 byte, or octet.

bit depth   In a scanner, the length (expressed in bits) of the storage unit used to store information about the scanned image. The greater the bit depth, the better the scanner's resolution. A common bit depth for a home-quality scanner is 30 bits.

bit length   In encryption, the length (expressed in bits) of the key used to encode and decode the text data. The greater the bit length, the stronger (less breakable) the encryption.

bit map   The representation of a video image stored in a computer's memory as a set of bits. Each picture element (pixel), corresponding to a tiny dot onscreen, is controlled by an on or off code stored as a bit (1 for on, or 0 for off) for black-and-white displays. Color and shades of gray require more information. The bit map is a grid of rows and columns of the 1s and 0s that the computer translates into pixels to display onscreen. See *bitmapped graphic, block graphics.*

bitmapped font   A screen or printer font in which each character is composed of a pattern of dots. To display or print bitmapped fonts, the computer or printer must keep a full representation of each character in memory. When referring to bit-mapped fonts, the term font should be taken literally as a complete set of characters of a given typeface, weight, posture, and type size. For example, if one wanted to use Palatino (Roman) 12 and Palatino Italic 14, he or she must load two complete sets of characters into memory. Bit-mapped fonts cannot be scaled up or down without introducing grotesque staircase distortions, called aliasing. See *anti-aliasing, outline font*.

bitmapped graphic A graphic image formed by a pattern of pixels and limited in resolution to the maximum resolution of the display or printer on which it is displayed. Bitmapped graphics are produced by paint programs. Considered inferior to vector graphics for most applications, bitmapped graphics may have aliasing caused by the square shape of pixels. See *aliasing, Encapsulated PostScript (EPS) file, object-oriented graphic, vector graphics*.

BITNET A wide area network (WAN) that, at its peak, linked mainframe computer systems at approximately 2,500 universities and research institutions in North America, Europe, and Japan. BITNET (an acronym for Because It's Time Network) does not use the TCP/IP protocols but can exchange e-mail with the Internet. BITNET was operated by the Corporation for Research and Educational Networking (CREN), with headquarters in Washington, D.C. To become a member of the network, an organization was required to pay for a leased line that connected to the nearest existing BITNET site. Faced with competition from the Internet, BITNET ceased operations in January, 1997. A lasting contribution of BITNET was its mailing list software, called LISTSERV (now known as ListProc), which is still available and is one of the most widely used mailing list servers in Unix computing. See *mailing list, Unix*.

bits per inch (bpi) In magnetic media, such as backup tape drives or disk drives, a measurement of the medium's recording density.

bits per second (bps) In asynchronous communications, a measurement of a Data

Communication Equipment (DCE) component's maximum data transfer rate. In personal computing, bps rates frequently are used to measure the performance of modems and serial ports. The bps rates are enumerated incrementally: 110 bps, 150 bps, 300 bps, 600 bps, 1200 bps, 2400 bps, 4800 bps, 9600 bps, 14400 bps, 19200 bps, 38400 bps, 57600 bps, and 115200 bps. Note that modem data transfer rates are often (and incorrectly) described as baud rates rather than bit per second (bps) rates. See *asynchronous communication, baud rate, Data Communications Equipment (DCE), modem*.

bit stream In synchronous communications, a continuous flow of data in which bits flow through a single communication channel. In order to distinguish internal data units, such as bytes, start bits and stop bits are used. See *asynchronous communication, start bit, stop bit, synchronous communication*.

black letter In typography, a family of typefaces derived from German handwriting of the medieval era. Black letter typefaces often are called Fraktur (after the Latin word *fractus*, meaning "broken") because the medieval scribes who created this design lifted their pens from the line to form the next character, fracturing the continuous flow of handwriting.

black-write technique See *print engine*.

blank cell In a spreadsheet program, a cell that contains no values, labels, or formatting different from the worksheet's default formatting.

bleed In desktop publishing, a photograph, text box, or other page-design element that extends to the edge of the page, such as the thumb tab index at the edge of this page. This usually is not possible in laser printing because most laser printers cannot print in a ⅛-inch strip around the page's perimeter. Bleeds are usually achieved by positioning the image so that it extends beyond the page edge, printing the image on larger paper, and then cutting the paper to the correct size. This ensures that the image extends to the actual edge of the final page.

bleed capability   The capability of a printer to print bleeds.

blessed folder   On the Macintosh, the System Folder, which is automatically searched by programs that are looking for needed files. This folder contains the configuration files (called Preferences) as well as other support files that are needed by installed applications.

blind carbon copy (BCC)   In e-mail, a copy of a message that is sent to one or more persons without the knowledge of the recipient. Also called blind courtesy copy.

blind certificate   In electronic commerce, a digital certificate that contains no information about the user to whom it is issued. Blind certificates are used in applications in which the user's identity is unimportant (such as cash transactions) or needs to be disguised (such as anonymous communications).

bloat   The unwarranted and inefficient multiplication of software features, which are added in an attempt to make a program more marketable. Synonymous with feature creep.

bloatware   Software that consumes an inordinately large amount of storage and memory space, thanks to bloat. See *bloat, fatware.*

BLOB   Acronym for binary large object. In computer databases, a large multimedia file that must be stored and handled in a special way so that its resources remain available.

block   **1.** A unit of information that is processed or transferred. The unit may vary in size. **2.** In modems, a unit of information passed from one computer to another is a block. For example, when using XMO-DEM, a file transfer protocol, 128 bytes are considered a block. Under MS-DOS, a

block transferred to or from a disk drive is 512 bytes in size. **3.** In word processing, a unit of text that one marks so that a block operation can be used to move, copy, or otherwise affect that text.

block cipher   In symmetric encryption, an encryption method that encrypts data in fixed-size blocks that have the same size as the unit of unencrypted data. See *symmetric key encryption algorithm.*

block definition   See *selection.*

block device   A storage or memory device that is capable of working with data in groups of bytes (blocks) rather than one bit at a time. See *character device.*

block graphics   On IBM PC–compatible computers, graphics formed onscreen by graphics characters in the ASCII extended character set. The graphics characters in the ASCII extended character set are suitable for creating and shading rectangles but not for fine detail. Because the block graphics characters are handled the same way as ordinary characters, the computer can display block graphics considerably faster than bit-mapped graphics. See *ASCII art.*

block move   An editing technique in word processing in which a marked block of text is cut from one location and inserted in another. Synonymous with cut and paste.

block operation   The act of transferring a block of information from one area to another. In word processing, an editing or formatting operation, such as copying, deleting, moving, or underlining, performed on a marked block of text. See *block move.*

block protection   In word processing and page-layout programs, a command that prevents the insertion of a soft page break in a specific block of text, preventing a bad page break.

block size   The size of an individual piece of data transmitted by a file transfer protocol or error-correction protocol over a modem. XMODEM uses a block size of 128 bytes, for example.

blog   See *Weblog.*

Blowfish   A symmetric encryption algorithm that is designed to be used in place of the significantly slower DES or IDEA algorithms Developed in 1993 by Bruce Schneier of Counterpane Internet Security, Inc., it can use encryption keys of variable length (from 32 to 448 bits). Blowfish is patent-free and freely available for implementation without licensing fees.

Blue Book   **1.** The first of the four official references for the PostScript display language. **2.** Commonly used name for one of three official references on the SmallTalk programming language. **3.** The standards issued by the International Telecommunications Union (ITU) in 1988 describing a number of important e-mail and fax protocols. See *X.400.*

blue screen of death   Slang phrase to describe the error message that appears when Microsoft Windows encounters a potentially fatal error condition. The screen has a blue background.

Bluetooth   A digital packet radio service, operating at 2.4 GHz and with a range of about 30 feet, that enables compatible wireless devices to exchange data at transfer rates of up to 1 Mbps (the maximum transfer rate for full duplex operation is 432 Kbps). Bluetooth capability is enabled in a device by means of an embedded Bluetooth chip and supporting software. Although Bluetooth is slower than competing Wireless LAN technologies such as IEEE 802.11a and IEEE 802.11b, the Bluetooth chip enables Bluetooth networking to be built into a wide range of devices—even small devices such as cellular phones and personal digital assistants (PDA)—at low cost. Bluetooth can be used to implement a personal area network (PAN) at low cost. See *IEEE 802.11a, IEEE 802.11b, PDA, personal area network (PAN), wireless LAN.*

blurb   In desktop publishing, a brief explanatory subheading that is set below or next to a headline.

BMP   **1.** An extension indicating that the file contains a Windows-compatible bitmapped graphic. **2.** A graphics format used by Windows for background graphics and icons, as well as and by many graphics creation and editing programs.

BNC connector   In an Ethernet network, a male connector mounted at each end of a length of coaxial cable.

BNF   See *Backus-Naur Form.*

board   An electronic printed circuit board. Boards that are designed to press into expansion slots are also called adapters or cards.

body type   The font (usually 8- to 12-point) used to set paragraphs of text, distinguished from the font used to set headings, captions, and other typographical elements. Serif typefaces, such as Century, Garamond, and Times Roman, are preferred over sans serif typefaces for body type because they are more legible. See *display type, font.*

boilerplate   A block of text that is reused in letters, memos, or reports. See *template.*

bold   See *boldface.*

boldface   A character emphasis visibly darker and heavier in weight than normal type. Each entry word in this dictionary is in boldface type.

bomb   **1.** To crash. **2.** To impede someone's e-mail access by filling his inbox with hundreds or even thousands of unwanted messages. **3.** In the Macintosh, a most unwelcome icon that signifies that the computer has crashed. **4.** Abbreviation for logic bomb. See *logic bomb.*

bookmark (noun)   A named and saved location within a document or network. Synonymous with favorite. See *favorite.*

bookmark (verb)   To record the location of a desired Web page or passage in a word processing document so that the user can easily return to it later.

booksize PC   A small desktop computer system, roughly the size of a 4" wide three-binder notebook, that offers most of the performance of a larger system. Booksize PCs use motherboards conforming to the microATX or NLX form factors to save space. See *microATX NLX*.

book weight   A typeface that is darker and heavier than most typefaces, but not as dark and heavy as boldface. Book weight fonts are used to set lengthy sections of text so that they are easy to read and produce a pleasing gray tone on the page. See *weight*.

Boolean data type   In programming, a data type that has only two possible values: true or false. See *data type*.

Boolean logic   A branch of mathematics, founded by nineteenth-century English logician George Boole (1815–1864), in which all operations produce one of two alternative values: true or false. Boole's work remained obscure until the rise of digital computing based on binary numbers, which have just two values: 1 and 0. Boolean logic is used to design computing circuits. It provides the conceptual foundation for computer searches using Boolean operators. See *Boolean operator*.

Boolean operator   A word, generally typed in capital letters, that indicates how search terms should be combined in a Boolean search. Synonymous with logical operator. See *Boolean logic*.

Boolean search   A search that involves the use of Boolean operators (AND, OR,

and NOT). In a Boolean search, these operators are used to refine the scope of the search. The AND and NOT operators narrow the scope of the search, while the OR operator broadens it. See *Boolean operator*.

boot   **1.** To initiate an automated routine that clears the memory, loads the operating system, and prepares the computer for use. Included in the computer's read-only memory (ROM) is the Power-On Self-Test (POST), which executes when the power is switched on (a cold boot). After a system crash or lockup occurs, one usually must boot the computer again, or reboot, by pressing the Reset button or a key combination such as Ctrl+Alt+Del (IBM PCs and compatibles) or Ctrl+Command+Start (Macintoshes) (a warm boot). The term is derived from the expression "pulling oneself up by the bootstraps." **2.** The process of starting the computer (cold boot) or restarting without turning off the power (warm boot). See *cold boot, Power-On Self-Test (POST), warm boot.* **3.** To terminate a user's online connection, as in "to give the boot to." See *boot off.*

boot disk   A floppy disk that contains a minimal version of the operating system sufficient restore access to hard disk files after a major operating system failure. Synonymous with emergency disk.

boot drive   A disk drive that is configured so that the computer starts by reading boot information from this drive. Synonymous with boot volume. See *boot*.

boot failure   A serious computer malfunction in which the computer is unable to start, as it normally does, by reading boot

Boolean Operators

If one links two search terms with:	The search retrieves:
AND ("Chardonnay AND Zinfandel")	Only those records or documents that contain both of these terms.
OR ("Chardonnay OR Zinfandel")	Any record or document that contains either of these terms.
NOT ("Chardonnay NOT Zinfandel")	Any record or document that contains "Chardonnay," except those that also contain "Zinfandel.".

information from the boot drive. A boot failure may indicate a hard disk failure or data corruption in the boot sector. See *boot, boot sector.*

boot off Slang for getting disconnected from an online service or Internet connection, either by someone in authority for violation of the rules, by a malicious person using a boot program, or by a bad telephone connection causing one or both modems to disconnect. See *boot program.*

BOOTP Acronym for Bootstrap Protocol, an Internet protocol that enables workstations on a local area network to find their IP address dynamically.

boot program Illegal but widely available software that can be used to disconnect users from any network or Internet service; particularly popular in chat rooms. Simple boot programs work by sending an overload of data to your application, causing it to lock up.

boot sector The first track on a hard or floppy disk (track 0). During the boot process, read-only memory (ROM) tells the computer to read the first block of data on this track and to load whatever program is found there. If system files are found, they direct the computer to load MS-DOS.

boot sector virus A computer virus that infects the crucial boot sector of a disk so that it is loaded into the computer's memory at the beginning of every operating session. A boot virus will subsequently infect any additional disks that are inserted into the system.

boot sequence The order in which a computer's BIOS searches disk drives for operating system files. Unless programmed otherwise, most personal computers look for the operating system on the floppy drive, and then the hard drive, and finally a CD-ROM.

bootstrap loader A program stored in the computer's read-only memory (ROM) that enables the computer to begin operating when the power is first switched on.

Bootstrap Protocol See *BOOTP.*

boot volume See *boot disk.*

Border Gateway Protocol See *BGP.*

bot **1.** In chat services such as Yahoo!, multiuser dungeons (MUDs), and Internet Relay Chat (IRC), a character whose onscreen actions stem from a program rather than a real person. The term is an abbreviated form of robot. The most famous of all bots, Julia, inhabits a MUD called LambdaMoo and has tricked thousands into thinking that she is a real human being. On IRC, bots are often used for mischievous purposes and are not allowed on many servers. See *MOO.* **2.** In Internet searching, an automated search agent that explores the Internet autonomously and reports back to the user when the search conditions have been successfully fulfilled.

bottom weighting In digital cameras, an automated exposure control method that employs matrix metering (measuring only part of the image captured by the camera's lens or viewfinder). In bottom weighting, preference is given to the lower portion of the image. Bottom weighting produces better outdoor portraits than other matrix metering technologies, which may favor the sky and underexpose the subject. See *digital camera, matrix metering.*

bounce In e-mail, to come back marked as undeliverable. See *bounce message.*

bounce message An e-mail message informing the user that an e-mail message could not be delivered to its intended recipient. The failure may be due to an incorrectly typed e-mail address, an expired account, or a network problem.

boundary test In Y2K readiness testing, a test that examines how a program performs within a specified date range.

Bourne Shell See *sh.*

bowl In typography, the curved strokes that enclose or partially enclose a blank space, called the counter, that is part of a letter, such as the blank space in the letter *a* or *c.*

box **1.** Common slang term for a computer of a particular type (a "Wintel box" or a "Unix box"). **2.** Abbreviation of dialog box. **3.** A border around a paragraph or graphic in a word processing or desktop publishing document. See *Wintel.*

bozo Derogatory slang term for a computer-illiterate, uneducated, stupid, or boorish person.

bozo filter An e-mail or newsgroup filter that prevents messages from specified individuals from appearing in a user's list of new messages. See *filter.*

bpi See *bits per inch.*

bps Acronym for bits per second, a fundamental measurement of transmission speed of digital data in a communications channel. Rapid gains in transmission speed necessitate the following: Kbps (kilobits per second), Mbps (megabits per second), and Gbps (gigabits per second).

brace The left ({) or right (}) curved bracket character on the standard keyboard. Synonymous with curly brace. See *angle bracket, bracket.*

bracket The left ([) or right (]) bracket character on the standard keyboard. See *angle bracket, brace, curly brace.*

Braille output device An output device that prints computer output in raised Braille letters, which can be read by people with severely limited or no vision.

brain-damaged Designed with a serious and possibly fatal flaw (slang). A brain-damaged program may behave erratically or may not enable certain operations that one would expect software of that type to perform.

branch **1.** In a tree structure, a subordinate line off the tree that leads to a leaf. **2.** In a hierarchical file system, one or more subdirectories located within a directory. **3.** In programming, a type of control structure that routes program execution to a subroutine. See *control structure, hierarchical file system, tree structure.*

branch control structure In programming, a control structure that tells a program to branch to a subroutine only if a specified condition is met. If a program detects that a vital data file has been irretrievably corrupted, for example, the program branches to display a message that says something like, "The file you want to open is corrupted." Synonymous with selection. See *IF/THEN/ELSE.*

branch prediction An educated guessing method employed by microprocessors that use superscalar architecture. By looking at a program and predicting how a true/false test will turn out, a microprocessor that employs branch prediction can get ready to execute the code that follows a certain test outcome. The Pentium microprocessor employs branch prediction and guesses correctly 90 percent of the time.

break A user-initiated signal that interrupts processing or receiving data. See *Control+Break.*

break-out box A testing device inserted into a communications cable or between a serial port and a serial cable that allows each signal to be tested separately.

breakpoint A location in a program where it pauses to let the user decide what to do next.

BRI Acronym for Basic Rate Interface. In ISDN, the basic digital telephone and data service that is designed for residences. BRI offers two 56 Kbps or 64 Kbps channels for voice, graphics, and data, plus one 16,000bps channel for signaling purposes. With Multilink PPP, Windows combines the two B channels, creating an Internet connection at 112 Kbps or 128 Kbps. If one is using an ISDN adapter that has analog (POTS) telephone ports, he or she can connect a telephone and fax machine to the circuit, and the Internet connection will automatically drop down to one B channel to accommodate incoming or outgoing telephone calls.

bridge In local area networks (LANs), a device that allows two adjacent networks to exchange data. The bridge examines each broadcasted message and determines whether the message should be routed to the current network or forwarded to the adjacent network. See *brouter, router.*

brightness **1.** A monitor control that regulates the strength of electron beams striking the rear of a cathode ray tube (CRT) display. A high brightness setting increases the strength of the beams and makes the onscreen image brighter, while a low brightness setting weakens the beams and dims the image. LCD and other types of displays have similar controls that have the same effects. **2.** In the HSV color scheme, one of three fundamental characteristics (the others are saturation and value) that can fully specify a color displayed on a computer monitor. Brightness refers to the intensity of the light source.

broadband In networks, an analog communications method characterized by high bandwidth. The signal usually is split, or multiplexed, to provide multiple communications channels. Because a computer's signals are digital signals, they must be transformed by a process called modulation before they can be conveyed over an analog signal network. A modem at each end of a network cable performs this task. Broadband communications can extend over great distances and operate at extremely high speeds. Common broadband technologies include ADSL, cable, and DSL. See *baseband.*

Broadband ISDN (B-ISDN) A high-bandwidth digital telephone standard for transmitting up to 1.5 Mbps over fiber-optic cables. See *BRI, ISDN.*

broadcast To make a signal available to any receiver tuned to the correct channel. See *anycast, multicast, unicast.*

broadcast fax A fax sent to multiple recipients. Many fax programs are capable of dialing each fax recipient and delivering the fax automatically with a single command.

broadcast message In a network, a message to all system users that appears when they log on to the system. For example, broadcast messages are used to inform users when the system will be shut down for maintenance.

broadcast network A computer network architecture in which all data packets are sent to all of the devices attached to the network. A workstation must therefore determine which of the packets are addressed to it. An example of a broadcast network is the Ethernet local area network (LAN). See *Ethernet, LAN.*

broken Not working or disabled. In beta software, some features are deliberately disabled because they do not function correctly yet.

broken link On the World Wide Web, a hyperlink that refers to a resource (such as a sound or a Web page) that is unavailable, usually because it has been moved or deleted. Synonymous with stale link.

brouter In computer networking, a device that combines the characteristics of a bridge (which connects two local area networks that use the same networking protocol) and a router (which connects dissimilar networks). A brouter is needed when one of the connected networks contains a connection to the external Internet; a bridge alone would not provide the routing services necessary so that both of the connected networks could have external Internet access. See *bridge, router.*

brownout A period of low-voltage electrical power caused by unusually heavy demand, such as that created by summertime air-conditioner use. Brownouts can cause computers to operate erratically or to crash, either of which can result in data loss. If brownouts frequently cause a computer to crash, the user may need to buy a line-interactive uninterruptible power supply to continue using the computer safely.

browse **1.** To look for information by manually looking through a series of storage locations. **2.** To look for information on the World Wide Web (WWW) by jumping from hyperlink to hyperlink.

browse mode In a database management program, a mode in which data records are displayed in columns for quick onscreen review. Generally, one cannot modify data while in the browse mode. See *edit mode.*

browser A program that enables the user to navigate the World Wide Web (WWW). The two leading browsers are Netscape Navigator and Microsoft Internet Explorer. A browser serves as the client for Web and other types of Internet servers. Browsers have become the interface of choice most types of data accessible by means of networks based on Internet technology. Synonymous with Web browser. See *light client.*

browse view In a database, a way of viewing records one by one.

browsing In hypertext, an information-seeking method that involves manually searching through linked documents. On the World Wide Web (WWW), browsing is rarely effective for finding information on a specific topic (better results are obtained by using subject trees and search engines), but browsing may lead to serendipitous discoveries. Also referred to as surfing. See *search engine, subject tree.*

brush script In typography, a typeface design that simulates script drawn with a brush or broad-pointed pen.

brute force In programming, a crude technique for solving a difficult problem by repeating a simple procedure many times. Computer spell-checkers use a brute-force technique. They do not really check spelling; they merely compare all the words in a document to a dictionary of correctly spelled words.

BSD Acronym for Berkeley Software Distribution. A version of the Unix operating system that was independently developed by University of California, Berkeley computer science faculty and graduate students, as well as participants in a widespread open source development project called the Berkeley Software Distribution (BSD). AT&T, where Unix originated, helped to initiate BSD Unix by providing the source code to Berkeley and other university researchers; subsequently, it participated in BSD Unix development and incorporated BSD Unix innovations into what would later become its commercial version of Unix, called System V. In the early 1980s, a version of BSD was released that incorporated the TCP/IP (Internet) protocols; the subsequent free distribution of this version of BSD Unix to colleges and universities laid the foundation for the Internet's subsequent explosive growth. Today, BSD code is commercially distributed by BSDI, Inc. It is also available in several open source distributions, including FreeBSD, NetBSD, and OpenBSD. In addition, some commercial operating systems incorporate BSD code, including Microsoft Windows NT, Microsoft Windows 2000, and Mac OS X. See *FreeBSD, open source software (OSS), TCP/IP, Unix.*

BSD license A software license developed by University of California attorneys to govern the distribution of BSD Unix. The license states that Berkeley-originated code can be freely redistributed, and even incorporated into commercial products, as long as the Berkeley copyright is included and acknowledged. See *General Public License (GPL).*

B-size paper A page that measures 11 by 17 inches, as specified by the American National Standards Institute (ANSI). See *A-size paper.*

B-size printer A printer capable of printing on B-size (11-by-17-inch) and smaller paper.

BSS Mode See *infrastructure mode.*

BTPC See *Binary Tree Predictive Coding.*

BTW In online conferences, an abbreviation for "by the way."

bubble-jet printer A variation on the inkjet printer concept that uses heating elements instead of piezoelectric crystals to shoot ink from nozzles.

bubble memory A type of memory that employs materials that can be magnetized in only one direction. When a magnetic field is applied at right angles to the plane of magnetization, the materials form a tiny circle (a "bubble"). The resulting differences between the properly magnetized and bubbled areas can be used to represent digital data. Bubble memory is nonvolatile (that is, it does not lose its contents when the power is turned off) and is sometimes used in portable computers to store data between operating sessions. However, it is considerably slower than competing nonvolatile memory technologies, such as EEPROM, and flash erasable programmable read-only memory.

buckyball toner In computer printers, a toner made of large molecules of a synthetic carbon called buckminsterfullerene, named after engineer Buckminster Fuller (designer of the Geodesic Dome). Buckyball toner is easier to control than toner made of other types of carbon, and it is frequently used in today's printers.

buddy list A popular Internet service, also known as instant messaging (IM), that informs a user when his or her buddies are online. To develop a buddy list, one must install a buddy list application such as ICQ, Yahoo! Messenger, or AOL Instant Messenger. (The people on the buddy list must also use the same software.) When someone on a user's list is online and starts their buddy list application, the user is notified, and can exchange messages with his or her buddy via text chatting, voice, computer-to-phone calls, and web camera. See *instant messenger.*

buffer A unit of memory given the task of holding information temporarily, especially while waiting for slower components to catch up.

buffer overflow A system error that results from a faulty program, which writes more data to a buffer than the memory unit can accommodate. See *buffer.*

bug A programming error that causes a program or a computer system to perform erratically, produce incorrect results, or crash. The term bug was coined when a real insect was discovered to have fouled up one of the circuits of the first electronic digital computer, the ENIAC. In contrast, a hardware problem is called a glitch.

bug fix release A maintenance release of a computer program that is intended to repair a bug. Instead of a bug fix release, a publisher may release a patch, which modifies the original program's code to eliminate the bug.

build number A number that a software publisher sequentially assigns to each of the hundreds or thousands of compiled versions that are created in the life of a program. Sometimes software publishers make a program's build number available to users (for example, users can view Internet Explorer's build number by choosing About Internet Explorer from the Help menu). Build numbers may provide more accurate information about the program's currency than version numbers See *version.*

build or buy decision In the development of information systems, the choice of building a new system within the organization or purchasing it from an outside vendor.

built-in Included in the most basic functions of a computer program or programming language.

built-in font A printer font encoded permanently in the printer's read-only memory (ROM). All printers offer at least one built-in font (also called a resident font). See *cartridge font, downloadable font, screen font.*

built-in function In a spreadsheet program, a ready-to-use formula that performs mathematical, statistical, trigonometric, financial, and other calculations. A built-in function begins with a special symbol (usually @ or =) followed by a keyword, such as AVG or SUM, that describes the formula's purpose. Most built-in functions require one or more arguments enclosed in parentheses and separated by an argument separator such as a colon or comma. Also called @ function.

built-in pointing device In portable computers, a trackball or pointing stick that is built into the computer's case in a fixed position. See *clip-on pointing device, freestanding pointing device, mouse, snap-on pointing device.*

bulk storage Devices used to store massive amounts of computer data, including clusters of hard drives, optical disks, and magnetic tape. Synonymous with mass storage. See *secondary storage.*

bullet In typography, a dot, square, triangle, or some other symbol that is used to set off items in a bulleted list. Often used with a hanging indentation format, bullets are appropriate when listing items whose content is roughly equal in emphasis or significance. See *bulleted list, hanging indent.*

bulleted list 1. A list of text items (words, sentences, paragraphs, etc.), each of which begins with a bullet. 2. In presentation graphics, a text chart that lists a series of ideas or items of equal weight, each of which is set off with bullets. See *bullet.*

Bulletin Board System See *BBS.*

bulletproof Capable, because of high fault tolerance, of resisting external interference and recovering from situations that would crash other programs. Synonymous with robust. See *fault tolerance.*

bundled software Software included with a computer system as part of the system's total price. Also, several programs that are packaged and sold together. See *software suite.*

burn To record data on a writable optical disc, such as a CD-R, CD-RW, DVD-R, DVD-RW, or DVD-RAM disk. See *CD-R, CD-RW, DVD-R, DVD-RAM, DVD-RW.*

burn-in 1. A test period used to determine whether new electronic equipment is serviceable. Semiconductor components, such as memory chips and microprocessors, tend to fail either in the first few hours of

operation or late in their lives. Responsible computer retailers, therefore, run systems continuously for 24 to 48 hours before releasing the systems to customers. 2. A ghost image that is permanently etched on the screens of older monitors (synonymous with ghosting) that have seen prolonged use displaying the same onscreen image. See *screen saver.*

burn rate In high-tech start-up firms, a slang term for the rate at which the company is exhausting its venture capital prior to generating positive cash flow.

burst A temporary, high-speed data transfer mode that, under certain or ideal conditions, can transfer data at significantly higher data transfer rates than the rate normally achieved with a nonburst technology. For example, memory chips can be designed so that, under certain circumstances, a processor can write quickly to a matrix of memory locations without having to address each of these locations individually. See *data transfer rate.*

burst EDO RAM A high-speed version of extended data out random access memory (EDO RAM) that improves read and write times significantly by eliminating wait states, or computer clock cycles that are wasted while memory operations take place. Although burst EDO RAM is faster than EDO RAM, both have been replaced in the PC market with even faster technologies, including DDR-SDRAM and RDRAM. See *DDR-SDRAM, DRAM, FPM, random access memory (RAM), RDRAM.*

bus An internal electrical pathway along which signals are sent from one part of the computer to another. Personal computers have a processor bus design with several pathways: The internal data bus sends data back and forth between the memory and the microprocessor. The address bus identifies which memory location data will be sent to or retrieved from. The control bus carries the control unit's signals. An extension of the data bus, called the expansion bus, connects the computer's expansion slots to the processor. The data, address, and expansion buses are wired in parallel rows so that all the bits being sent can travel simultaneously, like cars side by side on a 16- or 32-lane freeway. See *address bus, control bus, data bus, expansion bus.*

bus architecture   The overall design of a bus, especially as it affects the compatibility of expansion boards. See *bus, EISA, ISA, Micro Channel Architecture (MCA), PCI.*

business audio   A category of inexpensive sound hardware that supports sounds useful in business applications, such as putting background music into presentations, adding voice annotations to word processing documents, and voice-checking spreadsheets. Business audio hardware is not suitable for applications requiring high-fidelity reproduction of music.

business process patent   In the United States, a form of patent protection that legally applies to business processes (methods of doing business) to the extent that they involve novel uses of computers or computer networking technology. Enabled by a controversial 1996 U.S. district court decision that was sustained on appeal to the U.S. Supreme Court, business process patents are often criticized for enabling firms with little technological creativity to obtain what amounts to a state-sponsored monopoly in emerging areas of electronic commerce. See *intellectual property (IP), patent, software patent.*

Business Software Alliance (BSA)   A consortium of software publishers, founded in 1988, that seeks to reduce software piracy. The BSA does so by means of public education, lobbying efforts to increase protection for intellectual property, and lawsuits against copyright infringers.

bus master   A program that directs the flow of information on a computer motherboard's input/output (I/O) bus. See *bus.*

bus mouse   A mouse connected to the computer through an adapter card inserted into an available expansion slot. See *serial mouse.*

bus network   In local area networks (LANs), a decentralized network topology (used by AppleTalk and Ethernet, for example). In a bus network, a single connecting line (the bus) is shared by a number of nodes, including workstations, shared peripherals, and file servers. Each node in the network has a unique address, and its reception circuitry monitors the bus for messages being sent to the node, ignoring all other messages.

button   In graphical user interfaces (GUIs), a graphical component resembling a push button that can be clicked on with the mouse to execute a command, choose an option, or open a dialog box. See *Cancel button, default button, OK button, pushbutton, radio button.*

button bar   See *icon bar, toolbar.*

byline   In desktop publishing, the author's name (often including organizational affiliation and address) positioned directly after the article's title.

byte   Eight contiguous bits, the fundamental data unit of personal computers. Storing the equivalent of one character, the byte is also the basic unit of measurement for computer storage. Because computer architecture is based (for the most part) on binary numbers, bytes are counted in powers of 2. Many members of the Internet community prefer to call groups of 8 bits octets. The terms kilo (in kilobyte, abbreviated as K or KB) and mega (in megabyte, abbreviated as M or MB) are used to count bytes but are misleading; they derive from decimal (base 10) numbers. A kilobyte actually is 1,024 bytes, and a megabyte is 1,048,576 bytes. Many computer scientists criticize these terms, but the terms give those who think in decimal numbers a convenient handle on the measurement of memory. See *kilobyte (K), megabyte (MB).*

bytecode   A compiled Java program, with the extension .class, that can be executed by a Java virtual machine. Unlike ordinary compiled languages, which produce machine language suitable for execution on a particular brand of computer, Java compilers produce an intermediary format, called bytecode, which can be executed on any computer capable of running a bytecode interpreter (such as a Java-compatible browser). However, because bytecode is interpreted, Java applications execute more slowly than programs written for a specific type of computer (although not as slowly as true interpreted code). See *Java*.

bytecode compiler A compiler that outputs a program in bytecode rather than machine code. See *bytecode, compiler, Java*.

bytecode interpreter An interpreter that translates bytecode on-the-fly (while the program is executing). See *bytecode, interpreter, TrueType*.

bzip2 A patent-free file compression and archiving program developed for Linux and other Unix-like operating systems. The program uses the LZ77 compression algorithm. See *gzip, Lempel-Ziv compression algorithm, tar, zip*.

C A high-level programming language widely used for professional programming and preferred by most major software publishers. A general-purpose procedural language, C combines the virtues of high-level programming languages with the efficiency of an assembly language. Many commercial applications are written in C or C++. Because the programmer can embed instructions that directly reach the bit-by-bit representation of data inside the central processing unit (CPU), compiled C programs run significantly faster than programs written in other high-level programming languages. C programs are highly portable, being easily and quickly rewritten to run on a new computer as long as the target environment has a C compiler. See *C++, high-level programming language, Java, Visual Basic.*

C: In IBM PC–compatible personal computers, the default letter assigned to the first hard disk. See *disk drive, drive designator.*

C# (Pronounced *C-sharp.*) An object-oriented programming language, developed by Microsoft Corporation, that combines the sophistication of C++ with Visual Basic's ease of use. By making extensive use of the Simple Object Access Protocol (SOAP), C# offers a high degree of code reusability in that developers will be able to incorporate programming objects without having to write additional code. The language closely resembles Java. C# is one of several components of Microsoft's .NET initiative. See *ASP.NET, C++, Java, object-oriented programming, .NET, SOAP, Visual Basic.*

C++ A high-level programming language developed by Bjarne Stroustrup at AT&T's Bell Laboratories. Combining all the advantages of the C language with those of object-oriented programming, C++ has been adopted as the standard

in-house programming language by several major software vendors, including Apple Computer. See *object-oriented programming*

CA See *certificate authority.*

cabinet file A Microsoft-developed compressed file format that is used to store installation files.

cable modem A device that enables a computer to access the Internet by means of a cable TV connection. Cable modems typically connect to a computer through an Ethernet network card or USB port. Cable TV service offers several advantages over telephone-based Internet access technologies (such as dial-up and ADSL). Most importantly, cable TV uses a broadband, coaxial cable which is inherently capable of carrying higher speed data than telephone wiring. Cable services typically have data rates of 1.5 to 3Mbps in both directions (uploading and downloading). Cable modems are also relatively easy to configure and can be purchased at retail stores—ADSL modems cannot. Cable modems also allow you to watch television and surf the Internet simultaneously. One disadvantage to cable Internet service is that bandwidth is distributed to "neighborhoods"; if too many people in a cable neighborhood are simultaneously accessing the Interenet, each person's access speed will sufferr. This may be largely mitigated by DOCSIS 2.0, a new cable network specification adopted by ITU that is expected to make cable Internet access six times faster. See *ADSL modem, dial-up modem.*

cable select (CSEL) A feature of Plug and Play (PnP) IDE/TAA hard disk drives that enables them to automatically determine whether the drive being installed should be configured as a master or slave. See *IDE, master, Plug and Play (PnP), slave.*

cache (Pronounced *cash*) **1.** A storage area that keeps frequently accessed data or program instructions readily available so that the computer does not retrieve them repeatedly from slow storage. Caches improve performance by storing data or instructions in faster sections of memory and by using efficient design to increase the likelihood that the data needed next is in the cache. See *buffer, cache memory.* **2.** In a browser, a section of the hard drive that is set aside for storing recently accessed Web pages. When one revisits one of these pages, the browser retrieves the page from the cache rather than the network, bringing about a considerable improvement in apparent retrieval speed.

cache controller A chip, such as the Intel 82385, that manages the retrieval, storage, and delivery of data to and from cache memory or a hard disk. When data or instructions are requested by the central processing unit (CPU), the cache controller intercepts the request and handles the delivery from random access memory (RAM). The cache controller then determines where in the cache to store a copy of the just-delivered data, when to fetch data or code from adjacent addresses in RAM in case it is needed next, where in the cache to store this new data, and which data to discard if the cache is full. The cache controller also keeps an up-to-date table of the addresses of everything it is holding. Despite the magnitude of these duties and the small amount of memory actually used (32K to 256K), a well-designed cache controller can predict and have stored in the cache what the CPU needs next with an accuracy greater than 95 percent.

cache hit A successful request for data from cache memory; the data is present in the cache and does not have to be retrieved from the considerably slower main memory circuits. Can also refer to a successful reloading of a cached Web page in a Web browser. See *cache miss, hit rate.*

cache memory A small unit (typically ranging in size from a few kilobytes to 256K or 512K) of ultra-fast memory that is used to store recently accessed or frequently accessed data so that the microprocessor does not have to retrieve this data from slower memory circuits. Cache memory that is built directly into the microprocessor's circuits is

called primary cache or L1 cache. Cache memory contained on an external circuit is called secondary cache or L2 cache.

cache miss An unsuccessful request for data from cache memory; the data is not present in the cache and must be retrieved from the considerably slower main memory circuits. See *cache hit, hit rate.*

cache poisoning A type of computer attack that involves the deliberate corruption of cached Internet domain name system (DNS) server data; the attack may succeed in directing network access requests to a rogue server.

cache settings Options in the setup program that enable or disable a motherboard's secondary cache. Sometimes disabling the secondary cache will make a game designed for a slow computer easier to play on a computer that would otherwise run it fast enough to make it unplayable. Can also refer to the settings in a Web browser that control the way Web pages are cached. See *cache.*

CAD See *computer-aided design.*

CAD/CAM Acronym for computer-assisted design/computer-assisted manufacturing. The direct linkage of computer-aided design (CAD) output with computer-controlled manufacturing tools that enables rapid prototyping of electronic designs into physical objects.

CADD See *computer-aided design and drafting.*

caddy A tray, usually plastic, into which a CD-ROM is inserted before it is placed in certain CD-ROM drives. Caddies prevent fingerprints from getting on the disk surface, but it can be a hassle to load and unload caddies every time the user wishes to change CD-ROMs. See *CD-ROM drive.*

CAE See *computer-aided engineering.*

CAI See *computer-assisted instruction.*

calculated field In a database management program, a data field that contains the results of calculations performed on other fields. Synonymous with derived field. See *database management*.

Caldera OpenLinux See *Linux distribution*.

call In programming, a statement that transfers program execution to a subroutine or procedure. When the subroutine or procedure is complete, program execution returns to the command following the call statement. Also, a statement that invokes a library routine. See *programming*, *statement*, *subroutine*.

callback In computer security, an authentication method used by some dial-up computer services. When logging on, the system notes the caller's user ID and password and then hangs up. The system then calls back at a previously specified number and enables the connection. This procedure protects the system against an intruder who obtains a user ID and password and attempts unauthorized access from an unauthorized telephone number. However, it prevents access to the system unless the caller is logging on from the correct location. See *authentication*.

call center A high-volume, computer-based communication center, used by large organizations and mail order firms. Outgoing call centers are typically used by telemarketers, while in-bound centers are used for customer support. Call centers typically offer a combination of telephone, online chat, e-mail, and Web access.

caller ID A telephone company service that, with compatible equipment, displays the caller's number and name when the phone rings. Increasingly, voice-capable modems and ISDN terminal adapters incorporate caller ID features.

Call for Votes (CFV) In the standard Usenet newsgroups, a voting procedure that controls the creation of new newsgroups. Following a period of discussion, the Call for Votes is posted to the newsgroup news.announce.newgroups. See *Usenet*.

callout In desktop publishing (DTP), items of text that name parts of an illustration, usually with a line or arrow pointing to the part of the illustration that the text describes.

call waiting A service provided by the telephone company that lets someone put one call on hold while he or she answers another. This feature can wreak havoc with modem communications, so many users disable call waiting before dialing a number with the modem. (Entering ★70 and a comma before the phone number to be dialed by the communications program is a common method of disabling call waiting.)

cam See *webcam*.

camcorder In digital video, an analog or digital device that can record audio and video simultaneously.

camera-ready copy A finished, printed manuscript or illustration ready to be photographed by a printing company for reproduction. See *desktop publishing (DTP)*.

campus-wide information system (CWIS) An information system that provides students, faculty, staff, and the public with all the information pertinent to a large college or university, including registration information, events, faculty and staff telephone numbers, and access to the library catalog. Most CWISs use Web technology.

cancelbot In Usenet, a program that can hunt down a given individual's posts and remove them from the network. Cancelbots, such as the one used by the storied Cancelmoose, are frequently wielded against spammers (those who post unwanted messages to dozens or even hundreds of newsgroups), but they have also been used to try to silence unwanted opinion.

Cancel button An option in a graphical user interface (GUI) dialog box that one uses to cancel a command and return to the active document. Equivalent to pressing Esc.

canonical Conforming to canonical form. See *canonical form*.

canonical form In mathematics and programming, an expression that conforms to established principles learned only through practice, apprenticeship, and interaction with experts.

canonical name In the Internet, the official name of an Internet host, as opposed to its aliases.

cap height In typography, the height of capital letters, measured in points, from the baseline. See *baseline*.

CAPI Acronym for computer-assisted personal interviewing. The use of the computer or the Internet to administer questionnaires to individuals. CAPI software enables the results to be processed automatically.

Caps Lock key A toggle key that locks the keyboard so that one can enter uppercase letters without pressing the Shift key. While in uppercase mode, most keyboards have a light that illuminates; many programs also display a message, such as CAPS LOCK or CAPS. The Caps Lock key has no effect on the number and punctuation keys.

caption In desktop publishing (DTP), a descriptive phrase that identifies a figure, such as a photograph, illustration, or graph.

capture **1.** To record an ongoing communications session in a file that can be viewed or analyzed later. **2.** In computer graphics, to copy all or part of an image on-screen and convert it to a graphics file format to insert in a document or save on a disk.

carbon copy (CC) In e-mail, a copy of a message that is sent to one or more specified recipients in a way that enables all the recipients, including the user or users to whom the message was addressed, to see who received carbon copies. See *blind carbon copy (BCC)*.

card A rectangular circuit board that is designed to be inserted into a suitable receptacle on another circuit board; for example, a graphics accelerator card that is inserted into a slot on a computer's motherboard. See *adapter, circuit board, expansion slot*.

cardinal number **1.** A number used to count (such as "4" or "1,211" rather than one used to indicate sequence, such as "first," second," etc.) **2.** In mathematics, the total number of units in a set. See *ordinal number*.

caret A symbol (^) commonly found over the 6 key on computer keyboards. In spreadsheet programs, the caret is the symbol for exponent, or "to the power of." Caret also can be used to stand for the Ctrl key in computer documentation, as in "Press ^C."

carpal tunnel syndrome A type of repetitive stress injury (RSI) caused by repeated compression of the medial nerve within the carpal tunnel, an opening into the hand formed by the bones of the wrist and certain hand ligaments. Symptoms begin with numbness in the medial nerve's distribution area (the palm, the thumb, and the first three digits, but not the little finger) so that it might feel like the whole hand is asleep. This may be followed by severe pain that travels up the arm and that could result in severe incapacitation, including an inability to bring the thumb into opposition with the hand. Therapy may include improved workstation ergonomics, the use of a brace, cortisone injections, vitamin B_6 therapy, or surgery. See *ergonomics*.

carpet bomb See *spam*.

carriage return A standard ASCII control character that tells the printer to move to the left margin. In DOS and Windows text files, a line ends with a line feed character as well as a carriage return character, and most printers are set up to work with these files. Unix text files end with a line feed character only, which may result in laddered text (the printer starts a new line but does not move to the left margin). See *laddered text, line feed*.

carrier detect signal   A signal sent from the modem to the rest of the computer to indicate that a connection has been made and that the carrier tone has been established. The carrier detect (CD) light on external modems will illuminate when the carrier detect signal is sent.

carrier sense multiple access with collision detection   See *CSMA/CD*.

carrier signal   In data communications, a continuous signal that can be modulated (altered or varied) to convey data. In amplitude modulation (AM), the volume (amplitude) of the carrier signal is varied to correspond with the input signal; in frequency modulation (FM), the frequency of the carrier signal is varied to accomplish the same result.

Cartesian coordinate system   A method created by seventeenth-century French mathematician René Descartes for locating a point in a two-dimensional space by defining a vertical axis and a horizontal axis. A mouse uses the Cartesian coordinate system to locate the pointer on-screen. In some graphics applications, one can display the pointer's coordinates so that it can be positioned precisely.

cartridge   A removable module containing data storage media such as magnetic tape or disks. In printers, a removable module that expands the printer's memory, or that contains fonts, ink, or toner. See *cartridge font*.

cartridge font   A printer font supplied in the form of a read-only memory (ROM) cartridge that plugs into a receptacle on Hewlett-Packard LaserJet laser printers and clones. Unlike downloadable fonts, a cartridge font is immediately available to the printer and does not consume space in the printer's random access memory (RAM), which can be used up quickly when printing documents loaded with graphics. The popular cartridges contain multiple fonts, often more than 100. Cartridge fonts have fallen out of vogue due to the ready availability of scalable TrueType fonts in Microsoft Windows.

CAS 1   In SDRAM memory, a very fast memory chip that introduces a CAS latency of only one clock cycle between the registration of a memory read command and the availability of the first unit of memory output. See *CAS latency*.

CAS 2   In SDRAM memory, a fast memory chip that introduces a CAS latency of two clock cycles between the registration of a memory read command and the availability of the first unit of memory output. See *CAS latency*.

CAS 3   In SDRAM memory, a slower but less expensive memory chip that introduces a CAS latency of three clock cycles between the registration of a memory read command and the availability of the first unit of memory output. See *CAS latency*.

cascading menu   A menu system in which selecting a command on a pulldown menu causes another menu to appear, or cascade, next to the selected command. The presence of a cascading menu is usually indicated by a triangle at the right edge of the menu. Synonymous with submenu.

Cascading Style Sheet   See *CSS*.

cascading windows   In a graphical user interface (GUI), two or more windows displayed so that they overlap. This mode is convenient because the title bar and an edge of all the other open windows are visible. See *overlaid windows, tiled windows*.

case   **1.** The metal cabinet of a computer that contains the motherboard, adapters, and any internal components, such as disk drives. There are several types of cases, but the most basic distinction is between desktop cases, which lie flat, and tower cases, which stand vertically. Cases typically are sold with a power supply installed. **2.** In typography, a property that determines the shape and size of a particular letter in the alphabet. In the English language, for instance, the first letter of the alphabet can be written in both upper-case (A) and lower-case (a). Alphabets that employ both upper- and lower-case letters are called bicameral, and alphabets that employ only one case are called unicameral. Bicameral alphabets often employ a third case, called title case, to capitalize the first letters of appropriate words in titles and headings; for instance "The Decline and Fall of the Roman Empire." See *AT case, mini-AT case, mini-tower case.*

case control structure   In structured programming, a logical construction of programming commands that contains a set of possible conditions, and instructions that are executed if those conditions are true.

case-insensitive   In a search, ignoring the difference between uppercase and lowercase letters. See *case-sensitive.*

case-insensitive search   A search in which a program ignores the pattern of uppercase and lowercase letters. A case-insensitive search for "Carter" would match any of the following: cArter, CARTER, carter, and carTER. See *case-sensitive search.*

case-sensitive   Distinguishing between upper- and lowercase letters. See *case-insensitive.*

case-sensitive search   A search in which a program tries to match the exact pattern of uppercase and lowercase letters. A case-sensitive search for "Porter," for example, matches Porter but not these: PORTER, porter, or porTer. See *case-insensitive search.*

CAS latency   In SDRAM memory, the delay (measured in clock cycles) between the registration of a memory read command and the availability of the first unit of memory output. The lower the CAS number, the faster the SDRAM operates.

Castanet   A push medium developed by Marimba that enables computer users to "tune" to Java software delivery channels. When updated versions of a program become available, the software is automatically downloaded and installed without the user's involvement. See *Java, push media.*

cast-based animation   In multimedia, an animation method in which each object

in a production is treated as an individual graphic image (a cast member). One can manipulate each cast member individually by means of a script.

Cat 1   Abbreviation for Category 1. Standard telephone wiring used in plain old telephone service (POTS) that follows ANSI/EIA/TIA standards. The oldest and least expensive type of twisted-pair copper cable, CAT-1 was designed to carry voice only, but in ideal circumstances can transmit digital data at less than 1 Mbps, which is sufficient for Basic Rate ISDN and G.Lite ADSL. See *ADSL, G.Lite, ISDN, twisted pair.*

Cat 2   Abbreviation for Category 2. A twisted pair quality standard that ensures data transfer rates of up to 4 Mbps. See *twisted pair.*

Cat 3   Abbreviation for Category 3. A twisted pair quality standard that ensures a maximum data rate of 16 Mbps, which is sufficient for 10Base-T Ethernet service. In 2001, the FCC mandated that all new telephone wiring in U.S. homes must be Cat 3. See *Ethernet, twisted pair.*

Cat 4   Abbreviation for Category 4. A twisted pair quality standard that ensures a maximum data rate of 20 Mbps. Cat 4 cable is sufficient for use with IBM token ring LANs. See *twisted pair.*

Cat 5   Abbreviation for Category 5. A twisted pair quality standard that ensures a maximum data rate of 100 Mbps, which is sufficient for wiring workstations to gigabit Ethernet systems. See *gigabit Ethernet, twisted pair.*

Cat 5e   Abbreviation for Category 5e. An enhanced version of the CAT 5 twisted pair quality standard that enables a maximum data rate of 1000 Mbps (1 Gbps). See *Cat 5, twisted pair.*

Cat 6   Abbreviation for Category 6. A twisted pair quality standard that enables data rates of 1000Mbps (1Gbps). Although Cat 6 data rates are similar to Cat 5e, Cat 6 is more efficient in reducing line noise and errors. However, no network transmission standards presently require Cat 6 cabling, so its future is uncertain. See *twisted pair.*

Cat 7 Abbreviation for Category 7; also called Class F. An emerging standard that is not backwards compatible with other Category cabling. Unlikely to be widely adopted.

catalog In database management, a list of related database files grouped together so that they can be easily distinguished from others. All relational database management systems can work with more than one file at a time. Frequently, the results of relational operations (such as a join) produce a new file. Also, one creates several indexes and other files that support the application. A catalog helps to track all these related files in a unit.

catatonic Incapable of responding. A catatonic program has probably crashed; a catatonic network connection may eventually produce a timed-out message. See *crash, freeze.*

catch up In Usenet, a command commonly implemented in newsreaders that marks all the current articles in a newsgroup as read, even if one has not actually read them.

cathode ray tube (CRT) In a monitor, a vacuum tube that uses an electron gun (cathode) to emit a beam of electrons that illuminates phosphors on-screen as the beam sweeps across the screen repeatedly. The monitor is often called a CRT. The same technology is used in television sets.

CATV Acronym for community antenna television, but commonly used as if the term is synonymous with cable television.

CAV See *constant angular velocity.*

CBT See *computer-based training.*

CC See *courtesy copy.*

CCITT Acronym for Comité Consultatif International Téléphonique et Télégraphique. A defunct international

organization that designed standards for analog and digital communications involving modems, computer networks, and fax machines. For computer users, CCITT's most important role lay in the establishment of international standards for modem connectivity, the famous "V-dot" standards (such as V.32bis and V.34). The CCITT has been replaced by the International Telecommunications Union-Telecommunications Standards Section (ITU-TSS). See *ITU-TSS.*

CCP See *Certified Computer Programmer.*

CCYY A date format in which two digits are used to indicate the century (CC) and two additional digits are used to represent the year (for example, 2004).

CD Acronym for compact disc. A read-only optical disc format capable of providing up to 72 minutes of audio. Employing discs 4.75 inches in diameter, the CD format was originally designed for consumer audio but has since been adapted for read/only (CD-ROM) and read/write (CD-R, CD-RW) audio and data storage. A CD encodes information digitally by means of tiny pits and smooth areas on the disc's internal surface; in CD-ROM, CD-R, and CD-RW drives, the encoded data is detected by means of a laser beam. See *CD-R, CD-ROM, CD-RW.*

CD-DA See *Compact Disc-Digital Audio.*

CDEV See *control panel device.*

CDF Acronym for Channel Definition Format. A Microsoft-originated markup language, created with XML, that enables Web authors to specify subscription information and to create a channel that can be detected by Microsoft Internet Explorer (version 4.0 and higher).

CD-I See *Compact Disc-Interactive.*

CDMA Acronym for Code Division Multiple Access. One of two major protocols for digital cellular telephony (the other is TDMA). Unlike TDMA, which gives each phone a unique slice of time in which it may transmit or receive without competition from other users on the same channel, CDMA encodes each caller's signals across the full range of available frequencies; the signals are decoded and separated when they are received. In theory, CDMA allows more simultaneous users than TDMA. Capable of operating at 800 MHz or 1900 MHz, TDMA enables Personal Communication Services (PCS), such as paging, text-based Internet access by means of the Wireless Applications Protocol (WAP), and voice mail, when operating at the higher frequency. Initial versions of CDMA services offer point-to-point (circuit-switched) data transfer rates of 14.4 Kbps. US carriers include Sprint PCS and Verizon. Synonymous with spread spectrum and full spectrum. See *digital cellular phone, TDMA, WAP.*

CDP   See *Certified Data Processor.*

CDPD   Acronym for Cellular Digital Packet Data. A data standard that can be used to transmit computer data (at slow data transfer rates) over analog cellular hones. See *analog cellular phone.*

CD-R   Acronym for compact disc-recordable. An optical disc format capable of storing up to 80 minutes of audio or 700MB of data. Unlike CD-RW discs, CR-R discs can be recorded one time only. A CD-R or CD-RW drive is required to record music or write computer data to a CD-R disc. These discs are inexpensive and are widely used to back up computer data. To create CD-R discs that consumer electronic equipment can play, audio-capable CD-R discs are required; these are more expensive that data-only CD-R discs. See *CD, CD-RW.*

CD-R drive   A read/write-capable storage device that is capable of reading audio tracks and computer data from CD, CD-R, CD-ROM, and CD-RW discs; however, the drive can record only on CD-R discs, which can be recorded only once. See *CD, CD-R, CD-ROM, CD-RW, CD-RW drive.*

CD-ROM   Acronym for compact disc-read only memory, a read-only optical storage technology that uses compact discs. CD-ROMs can store up to 700MB of data in the most commonly used format. CD-ROM technology was originally used for encyclopedias, dictionaries, and software libraries, but now these discs often are used in multimedia applications and for software distribution. To access the data on a CD-ROM, one needs a CD-ROM drive.

CD-ROM changer   A machine that will robotically load any of up to 100 CD-ROMs into a CD-ROM disc drive. Synonymous with jukebox, a CD-ROM changer usually requires about 5 seconds to locate and load a requested disk.

CD-ROM drive   A read-only disk drive designed to read the data encoded on CD-ROMs and to transfer this data to a computer. Unlike audio compact disc players, CD-ROM drives contain circuitry optimized to locate data at high speeds; audio CD players need to locate only the beginning of audio tracks, which they play sequentially. CD-ROM drives retrieve data much more slowly than computer disk drives. The speed of CD-ROM drives is typically expressed as a multiple of the original CD-ROM specification, which called for a data transfer rate of 150K per second; typical drives today function at speeds of 16 or 24 times the original standard (indicated as 16x or 24x) or more; with software enhancement, one drive's manufacturer claims 100x performance.

CD-ROM interface   A feature of a sound board that allows the connection of a CD-ROM disc drive directly to the sound board, thereby easing installation and enabling a person to send audio from a CD-ROM disc directly to the sound circuitry, without taxing the rest of the computer.

CD-ROM player   Same as CD-ROM drive.

CD-ROM/SD   See   *CD-ROM/Super Density.*

CD-ROM/Super Density (CD-ROM/SD) A little-used standard for packing up to 9.6GB onto a CD-ROM. The CD-ROM/SD standard uses both sides of disks and is not compatible with any mass-produced CD-ROM drives. See *MMCD*.

CD-ROM/XA A CD-ROM drive that conforms to the CD-ROM/eXtended Architecture standard, created by a consortium of media and computer firms (including Microsoft, Sony, and Phillips). This standard enables CD-ROM discs to combine music and data.

CD-RW Acronym for compact-disc-read/write. An optical disc format that enables CD-RW drives to erase existing data and to write new data repeatedly. In contrast, CD-R discs can be recorded only once. CD-RW discs are more expensive than CD-R discs and require a CD-RW drive for recording purposes; these drives are more expensive than CD-R drives. See *CD, CD-R, CD-R drive, CD-RW drive.*

CD-RW drive A read/write-capable storage medium that can write repeatedly to CD-RW discs. See *CD-RW.*

Celeron See *Intel Celeron.*

cell **1.** In a spreadsheet or table, a rectangle formed by the intersection of a row and column in which the user enters information in the form of text (a label) or numbers (a value). **2.** In Asynchronous Transfer Mode (ATM) networking, a small unit of data that has been broken up for efficient transmission. Synonymous with packet.

cell address In a spreadsheet, a letter and number combination that identifies a cell's location on the worksheet by column and row (A3, B9, C2, and so on). If one refers to a cell in a formula, the cell address is called the cell reference.

cell animation An animation technique in which a background painting is held in place while a series of transparent sheets of celluloid-containing objects are placed over the background painting, producing the illusion of movement. Cell animation is

much easier than drawing a new background for every frame in the animation sequence.

cell cursor See *cell pointer.*

cell definition The actual contents of a cell in a spreadsheet, as displayed on the entry line. If one places a formula in a cell, the program displays the result of the calculation rather than the formula itself.

cell format In a spreadsheet, the way the program displays the contents of cells. Label formats include aligning the text on the left, right, or center. Numeric formats include currency, percent, comma placement, decimal places, and date and time display. The font and font size are changeable, and values and labels can be made bold and italic. See *current cell, global format, graphics spreadsheet, label alignment, range format.*

cell pointer In spreadsheet programs, the rectangular highlight that indicates the current cell. When one enters data in the spreadsheet, it is recorded in the current cell.

cell protection In a spreadsheet program, a format applied to a cell, a range of cells, or an entire file that prevents alteration of the contents of protected cells.

cell reference In a spreadsheet formula, the address of the cell that contains a value needed to solve the formula. When used in a formula, a cell reference tells the program to go to the named cell (such as B1) and use the value in that cell to perform the calculation. A cell reference can refer to a cell containing a formula, which may contain its own cell references to other cells, which can themselves contain formulas. A change made to any constant in such a worksheet affects intermediate values and, ultimately, the bottom line. See *recalculation method.*

Cellular Digital Packet Data See *CDPD.*

center weighting In digital cameras, an automated exposure control method that employs matrix metering (measuring only part of the image captured by the camera's lens or viewfinder). In center weighting, preference is given to the central portion of the image, the most likely location of the photograph's subject. See *bottom weighting, digital camera, matrix metering*.

central mass storage   See *file server*.

central office   See *CO*.

central processing unit (CPU)   A computer's "brains," the CPU contains the arithmetic-logic unit (ALU), which performs calculations; and the control unit, which retrieves instructions from memory, takes calculations from the ALU, and then executes the instructions. The ALU, control unit, and many other support devices are wholly contained on a chip called the microprocessor; the computer's primary memory is elsewhere on the motherboard. *CPU* is often used interchangeably with *processor* and *microprocessor*.

Centre Universitaire d'Informatique (CUI)   A unit of the University of Geneva, located in Geneva, Switzerland, that has played a leading role in the development of the World Wide Web (WWW).

Centronics interface   The original parallel port of IBM PC–compatible computers, named after the company that designed a predecessor to this interface standard. See *parallel port*.

Centronics port   See *parallel port*.

century   A unit of time spanning 100 years and encompassing the years numbered 1 to 100. Technically, the twenty-first century began January 1, 2001.

century byte   In a CCYY date, the portion of the data that indicates the century. See *CCYY*.

CERN   Acronym for Organisation Européenne pour la Recherche Nucléaire (European Laboratory for Particle Physics). A research center based in Geneva, Switzerland, for advanced physics research. CERN is the birthplace of the World Wide Web (WWW), which the center's computer

staff began in 1989 as a collaborative network for high-energy physicists.

CERT   Acronym for Computer Emergency Response Team. An Internet security task force that is designed to detect and respond rapidly to Internet security threats. Formed by the Defense Advanced Research Project Agency (DARPA) in 1988 in response to the infamous Internet Worm, CERT monitors Internet security and alerts system administrators concerning the activities of computer crackers and computer virus authors. See *Internet worm*.

certificate   Synonymous with digital certificate. An encrypted and digitally signed attachment to an e-mail message or downloaded file that attests that the received data really comes from its claimed source and has not been altered while it was en route. A certificate is virtually impossible to fake. To be considered valid, however, the certificate should be digitally signed by a certificate authority (CA), an independent agency that uses some type of identity-checking procedure (such as viewing a driver's license) prior to signing the certificate. See *personal certificate, public key cryptography*.

certificate authority (CA)   A company that verifies the identity of individuals and issues certificates attesting to the veracity of this identity. To obtain a certificate, an individual may be asked to show identification, such as a driver's license. See *personal certificate*.

certificate revocation list (CRL)   A list maintained by a certificate authority (CA) that identifies certificates that have been revoked for some reason (such as violation of service agreements or non-payment of required fees). See *certificate authority (CA)*.

certification   An endorsement of professional competence that is awarded on successful completion of a rigorous test.

certified   Guaranteed by the manufacturer to accurately hold a certain quantity of data. For example, a disk might be certified for 1.44MB of data.

Certified Computer Programmer (CCP) A person who has earned a Certificate in Computer Programming from the Institute for Certification of Computer Professionals (ICCP). CCPs must pass an examination in programming rules and concepts. CCP certification is considered equivalent to Certified Public Accountant status for accountants, although it is rarely an employment requirement.

Certified Data Processor (CDP) A person who has earned a Certificate in Data Processing from the Institute for Certification of Computer Professionals (ICCP). CDPs must pass an examination in hardware, software, programming, and systems analysis. CDP certification is considered equivalent to Certified Public Accountant status for accountants, although it is rarely an employment requirement.

CF See *CompactFlash.*

cfm Acronym for cubic feet per minute. A basic unit of airflow measurement for fans; the higher the measurement, the more air is moved by the unit. This unit of measurement is used to describe the cooling capacity of fans attached to microprocessors and computer power supplies.

CFML See *ColdFusion Markup Language.*

CFV See *Call for Votes.*

CGI Acronym for Common Gateway Interface. A standard that describes how Web servers should access external programs so that this data is returned to the user in the form of an automatically generated Web page. CGI programs, called scripts, come into play when a Web user fills out an on-screen form; the form generates output that is handled by the script, which brings other programs into play as necessary. These may include a database search engine or a mailer program. Common applications of CGI include providing a means for users to type and mail feedback, enabling database searches, and creating gateways to other Internet services that are

not directly accessible through the Web. See *PHP, scripting language, Web server.*

CGM See *Computer Graphics Metafile.*

chad In punched card data storage systems, the small pieces of waste that are produced by the keypunching equipment. Some keypunch machines, such as voting machines, may not record data correctly if the chad reservoir is not cleaned periodically; the accumulated chad prevents the equipment from fully detaching the chad from the card.

chaining A relaying operation in which e-mail messages are routed through several anonymous remailers to destroy any possibility of back-tracking the message's path. See *anonymous remailer.*

chain printing The printing of separate files as a unit by placing commands at the end of the first file to direct the program to continue printing the second file, and so on. Full-featured word processing programs, such as Microsoft Word, allow chained printing with continuous pagination and, in some cases, the generation of a complete table of contents and index for the linked files. See *master document.*

Challenge-Handshake Authentication Protocol See *CHAP.*

chamfer In desktop publishing (DTP) and presentation graphics, a beveled edge between two intersecting lines.

channel 1. On Internet Relay Chat (IRC), a named, topically focused forum where one can chat in real time with other computers. Synonymous with chat room. **2.** In push media, a named link to a network-based transmitter to which a user can tune. See *Internet Relay Chat (IRC), push media.*

channel access In local area networks (LANs), the method used to gain access to the data communication channel that links the computers. Three common methods are contention, polling, and token passing.

Channel Definition Format　See *CDF*.

channel op (CHOP)　On Internet Relay Chat (IRC), a person who possesses op (operator) privileges, including the right to kick unruly users out of the channel.

Channel Service Unit/Data Service Unit (CSU/DSU)　A data communications device that connects a digital T1 line to an Ethernet network. This equipment is generally provided by the data communications service provider when a T1 line is leased. See *Ethernet, leased line, T1*.

CHAP　Acronym for Challenge-Handshake Authentication Protocol. In Internet dial-up services that use the Point-to-Point Protocol (PPP), a standard that prevents hackers from intercepting passwords. CHAP is used to verify the identity of the person logging on by using a three-way handshake. After the link is established, the service provider's computer sends a "challenge" message to the user's computer, which must then consult a "secret" stored on the user's computer, as well as on the service providers computer, but that is never sent over the network. The user's computer then performs a calculation using the challenge as well as the secret. If the result does not match the service provider's calculation, the connection is terminated. This authentication method provides a very high degree of protection against previous password-based authentication measures and is more secure than its predecessor, the Password Authentication Protocol (PAP). See *PAP, PPP*.

character　Any letter, number, punctuation mark, or symbol that one can produce on-screen by pressing a key on the keyboard, or (for certain little-used characters) a key combination. A character uses 1 byte of memory.

character-based program　A program that relies on the ASCII and extended ASCII character sets that includes block graphics to create its screens and display the text one enters. See *what-you-see-is-what-you-get (WYSIWYG)*.

character device　A computer peripheral (such as a serial printer or modem) that works with data in a bit stream (one bit after the other) rather than a group of bytes (a block). See *bit stream, block device*.

character generator (CG)　In digital video, a device that generates text that can be incorporated into videos for such purposes as titling and subtitles (translations).

character graphics　See *block graphics*.

character-mapped display　A method of displaying characters in which a special section of memory is set aside to represent the displayed image; programs generate a display by inserting characters into the memory-based representation of the screen. Therefore, the whole screen—not just one line—remains active, and the user or the program can modify characters anywhere on-screen. See *teletype (TTY) display*.

character mode　A display mode in which the computer displays only those characters contained in its built-in character set. Synonymous with text mode. See *character view, graphics mode*.

character set　The fixed set of keyboard codes that a particular computer system uses. See *ASCII character set, code page, extended character set*.

characters per inch (cpi)　The number of characters that fit in an inch of type of a given font. Standard sizes drawn from typewriting are pica (10 cpi) and elite (12 cpi). Nontypewriter fonts are measured in points.

characters per second (cps)　A measurement of the speed of a modem (although modem speed is most often measured in bits per second [bps]), an impact printer, or an inkjet printer.

character string　See *string*.

character view　In some MS-DOS application programs, a mode in which the program switches the display adapter circuitry to character mode; also called draft mode by some programs. In character mode, the computer can display only those characters contained in the computer's built-in character set. See *character mode, graphics view.*

charge-coupled device (CCD) A device used in a scanner or digital camera to convert light into electrical signals readable by the computer. A scanner's horizontal resolution is determined by the number of CCDs it packs into a row—usually 300 dpi (dots per inch), but 600 to 1200 dpi in some high-end scanners.

chart A representation of data in pictorial form. Charts make it easier to discern the significance of data and identify trends. Also called graph. See *presentation graphics.*

chat In an online service, Web-based chat service, or Internet Relay Chat (IRC), to converse with other computer users by exchanging typed lines of text in a real-time conversation.

chat room In an online service, a named, topically focused forum or conference for online, real-time chatting. Unlike IRC channels, chat rooms may be supervised, and antisocial actions (such as the use of profanity) can result in expulsion.

chatterbot In Internet Relay Chat (IRC) and online chat rooms, a program that engages users in conversation and mimics the behavior of a human interlocutor. For example, the program includes typing errors and speed variations that make the program's output appear as if it were being typed by a person. See *bot, Internet Relay Chat (IRC).*

check box In a graphical user interface (GUI) dialog box, a square box that one chooses to toggle an option on or off. When the option is turned on, an X or a check mark appears in the check box. A check box can appear alone or with other check boxes in a list of items. Unlike radio buttons, more than one check box can be selected at once. See *graphical user interface (GUI).*

checksum An acronym for SUMmation CHECK. In data communications, an error-checking technique in which the number of bits in a unit of data is summed, transmitted along with the data, and checked by the receiving computer. If the sum differs, an error probably occurred in transmission, and the transmission is repeated.

child A subcategory. In a hierarchical file system, a subdirectory is a child of the parent directory. See *hierarchical file system.*

child directory In a hierarchical file system, a directory inside another directory. See *hierarchical file system.*

child process A utility program or subroutine that executes under the control of a controlling program, called a parent process. See *process.*

Children's Internet Protection Act (CIPA) A U.S. Federal law, enacted in 2000, that requires all schools and libraries that receive Federal funds to install and use Internet filters to block access to sites containing material deemed "harmful to minors." The law is controversial because Internet filtering programs have been shown to block many sites that do not contain indecent or obscene material (for example, sites providing information concerning homosexuality or abortion). See *filtering software.*

chip A miniaturized electronic circuit mass-produced on a tiny wafer of silicon. Chips are made out of semiconducting materials and duplicate the function of several transistors and other electronic components. The first integrated circuits contained only a few components, but the same manufacturing techniques can now generate 16 million components on a chip smaller than a fingertip. Today's leading microprocessors sell for less than $1,000 but easily surpass the performance of million-dollar mainframe processors of 30 years ago. The achievement of chip-manufacturing technology has enabled the diffusion of computer technology throughout society. See *microprocessor.*

chipset   The collection of chips that work together to perform a function, such as helping a microprocessor access memory or update a display. The chips that comprise a chip set must be designed to work together and are mounted on a single circuit board, such as the motherboard.

choose   In a program that uses menus and dialog boxes, the process of picking an option that begins an action.

Chooser   A Macintosh desktop accessory (DA) supplied by Apple Computer with the Macintosh operating system, Mac OS. The Chooser governs the selection of printer and network drivers, the programs that control communication with the printer and local area network (LAN). The Chooser displays the icons of the printer and network drivers installed in the System Folder.

CHOP   See *channel op.*

chord   In desktop publishing and presentation graphics, a straight line that connects the end points of an arc.

chroma   A dimension of color description that specifies the strength, or degree of saturation, of the dominant color. Chroma thus combines hue and saturation in a single measurement. See *saturation.*

chroma corrector   In digital video and computer graphics, a device or program that automatically detects and corrects chroma problems, such as oversaturated color. See *chroma.*

chrominance   In digital video and computer graphics, the color characteristics of the video or image as opposed to its luminance (brightness). See *luminance.*

CICA   See *Center for Innovative Computer Applications.*

CIDR   Acronym for Classless Interdomain Routing. A method of allocating Internet addresses that greatly increases the number of available IP addresses. CIDR provides for Internet addressing roughly the same capability that area codes provide for long-distance telephony; CIDR enables the uses of prefixes that designate a specific network gateway. The next-generation Internet protocol (IPv6) will provide virtually unlimited IP addresses, but CIDR has effectively solved the problems created by class-based IP addressing. See *Class A network, Class B network, Class C network, IP address, IPv6.*

cipher   A method used to encrypt text so that it cannot be read by anyone who does not know the exact cipher that was used. Simple ciphers work by realigning the alphabet (for example, the ROT-13 cipher rotates the letters of the alphabet thirteen letters to the right). For high security encryption, ciphers employ a key (a mathematical formula) and an encryption algorithm (a complex, step-by-step procedure for applying the key to the unencrypted text). See *encryption, encryption algorithm, key.*

ciphertext   In cryptography, a message that has been encrypted so that it can be read only by the intended recipient, who possesses the key needed to decode the message. See *encryption.*

CIRC   See *circular reference.*

circuit board   A flat plastic board on which electrically conductive circuits are laminated. Synonymous with printed circuit board. See *adapter, card, motherboard.*

circuit-switching network   A type of wide area network (WAN), epitomized by the world telephone system, in which the originating and receiving stations are linked by a single, physical circuit, created by complex switching mechanisms. The connection is maintained until the communication is finished. See *packet-switching network.*

circular reference   In a spreadsheet, an error condition caused by two or more formulas that refer to one another. A circular reference occurs, for example, when the formula +B5 is placed in cell A1, and the formula +A1 is placed in cell B5.

Spreadsheet programs usually have a command that displays a screen that includes a list of the cells containing circular references. Circular references do not always result in errors. They can be used deliberately, for example, to create an iterative function in a worksheet: Each recalculation increases the values of the two formulas.

CIS Acronym for computer information system. A computer system in which all the components are designed to work together. Can also refer to a college degree in Computer Information Systems.

CISC See *complex instruction set computer.*

clari In Usenet, an alternative hierarchy that includes dozens of read-only newsgroups containing wire service articles— the same ones that will appear in today's newspapers. These wire services include United Press International (UPI), Newsbytes, and TechWire.

Claris FileMaker Pro See *relational database management system (RDBMS).*

Claris Home Page See *WYSIWYG HTML editor.*

class In object-oriented programming, a template for building objects that all have the same properties (variables) and methods (functions). The class is used to declare the property names and the methods that will be shared by all the objects created from the class. See *method, object-oriented programming, property.*

Class 1 A standard for fax modems that describes the way in which the Hayes command set is modified to send faxes. Unlike Class 2 fax modems, Class 1 fax modems leave most of the tasks relating to digitizing images and preparing faxes for transmission to the software, which is perfectly fine in most computers.

Class 2 A standard for fax modems that describes the way in which the Hayes command set is modified to send faxes. Class 2 fax modems handle most of the fax-preparation tasks that Class 1 fax modems leave to software, which makes Class 2 modems

very expensive. Class 2 is not a true industry standard, so one is better off buying a Class 1 fax modem.

Class A certification A Federal Communications Commission (FCC) certification that a given make and model of computer meets the FCC's Class A limits for radio frequency interference (RFI), which are designed for commercial and industrial environments.

Class A network On the Internet, a participating network that is allocated up to 16,777,215 distinct Internet addresses (called IP addresses). Current Internet addressing limitations define a maximum of 128 Class A networks. See *Class B network, Class C network, IP address.*

class-based language In object-oriented programming, a programming language that enables the programmer to create abstract templates, called classes. A class describes the properties and methods to be shared by all the instances of the class (objects) and also provides a mechanism for creating new objects. See *class, method, object-oriented programming, property.*

Class B certification A Federal Communications Commission (FCC) certification that a given make and model of computer meets the FCC's Class B limits for radio frequency interference (RFI), which are designed for homes and home offices. Class B standards are tougher than Class A standards and are designed to protect radio and television reception in residential neighborhoods from excessive RFI generated by computer usage. Class B computers are also shielded more heavily from external interference.

Class B network On the Internet, a participating network that is allocated up to 65,535 distinct Internet addresses (called IP addresses). Current Internet addressing limitations define a maximum of 16,384 Class B networks. This method of allocating IP addresses threatened to create a shortage of available IP addresses because many organizations need more than the 256 addresses allowed in a Class C network but far fewer than 65,535 addresses; thus, most Class B addresses are wasted. This problem has been temporarily solved by means of the CIDR addressing protocol on Internet backbone networks, and it will be permanently solved by IPv6, the next-generation IP protocol, which will introduce a 128-bit address space. See *CIDR, Class A network, Class C network, IP address, IPv6.*

Class C network   On the Internet, a participating network that is allocated up to 256 distinct Internet addresses (called IP addresses). Current Internet addressing limitations define a maximum of 2,097,152 Class C networks. See *Class A network, Class B network, IP address.*

clean management   In a Y2K readiness program, a management program in which any new system components (including hardware peripherals, programs, or network components) are tested for Y2K compliance before being added to a Y2K-compliant system. See *Y2K.*

clear   To remove data from a document, cell, or field. In the Microsoft Windows and Macintosh environments, the Clear command (Edit menu) completely wipes out the selection, as opposed to Cut, which removes the selection to the Clipboard (from which one can retrieve the selection, if he or she later discovers that he or she deleted it by mistake).

cleartext   In cryptography, a message that is transmitted without any encryption so that it can be easily intercepted and read while it is en route. A major security drawback of the Internet is that, with most password authentication schemes, passwords are transmitted in cleartext. See *ciphertext.*

Clear to Send/Ready to Send   See *CTS/RTS.*

ClearType   A screen font technology designed by Microsoft for LCD (flat panel) displays. When supported by the necessary ClearType system software (included with Microsoft Windows XP and subsequent versions of Microsoft's operating systems), ClearType fonts appear as sharp as printed text. The technology takes advantage of the fact that, in an LCD display, each pixel that appears to be black is in fact composed of three subpixel-sized vertical strands, corresponding to the three primary colors. Previous screen font technologies assumed that pixels have no internal structure, so their on-screen font-smoothing techniques reduce sharpness. Based on a model of the human visual system, ClearType adjusts the brightness and color balance of each pixel to achieve what amounts to sub-pixel font smoothing. The result is significantly sharper and more readable text. See *LCD, Microsoft Windows XP, pixel, screen font.*

CLEC   Acronym for competitive local exchange carrier. In U.S. telephony, a local exchange carrier (LEC) that is now permitted (thanks to the U.S. 1996 Telecommunications Act) to compete in local telephone markets with the incumbent local exchange carrier (ILEC), the company that possessed a monopoly in that market prior to the passage of the 1996 reforms. See *ILEC, LEC.*

click   To press and quickly release a mouse button. When no button is specified on Windows systems, the left button is assumed. One frequently sees this term in instructions such as "Click the Bold check box in the Fonts dialog box." For users of IBM-compatible PCs, this instruction means, "Move the mouse pointer so that its tip touches the Bold check box, and then click the left mouse button." See *double-click, Shift+click.*

click and brick   A strategy in which a Web retail site is paired with a chain of local retail stores. This enables customers to view and order products on the Web site, but pick up the merchandise at the store. Any merchandise exchanges or returns can also be handled at the store. Customers often prefer click and brick because they can shop at their leisure on the Web site, ensure their local store has exactly what they want before going there, avoid shipping costs and delays, and receive better customer support. See *e-commerce.*

client **1.** In an Internet service, a program that can communicate with a server located on the Internet to exchange data of a certain type. A Web browser is a client for accessing information available on Web servers. **2.** In a client/server network, a program that is designed to request information from a server. See *client/server, heavy client, light client.* **3.** In Object Linking and Embedding (OLE), an application that includes data in another application, called the server application. See *client application.*

client application In Object Linking and Embedding (OLE), an application in which one can create a linked object or embed an object. See *server application.*

client/server A design model for applications running on a network, in which the bulk of the back-end processing, such as performing a physical search of a database, takes place on a server. The front-end processing, which involves communicating with the user, is handled by smaller programs (called clients) that are distributed to the client workstations. See *heavy client, LAN, light client, WAN.*

clip A portion of a video, especially one that has been digitized using a video capture board. See *video capture board.*

clip art A collection of graphics, stored on disk and available for use in a desktop publishing or presentation graphics program. The term is derived from a graphics design tradition in which packages of printed clip art were sold in books and actually clipped out by layout artists to enhance newsletters, brochures, and presentation graphics. Most page layout or presentation graphics programs can read graphics file formats used by clip art collections available on disk.

Clipboard In a graphical user interface (GUI), a temporary storage area in memory where material cut or copied from a document is stored until one pastes the material elsewhere.

clip-on pointing device A trackball that clips on the side or front of a portable computer. These devices have fallen in popularity because modern notebook computers have built-in pointing devices such as touchpads or pointing sticks. See *freestanding pointing device, mouse, snap-on pointing device.*

Clipper Chip A U.S. government-backed encryption technology, housed on a semiconductor that would have been manufactured in massive quantities that would provide private individuals with the means to encrypt their messages. However, the Clipper Chip includes a back door that would enable law enforcement agencies to eavesdrop on the message. To do so, law enforcement personnel would have to obtain a warrant, which is now required to eavesdrop on telephone communications. Privacy advocates fear that the government would abuse its power, eavesdropping on conversations without having obtained the proper certification, while law enforcement personnel fear that encryption technologies will prevent the detection of terrorist and drug-dealing activity. The Clipper Chip proposal was seriously derailed after a researcher proved that its encryption scheme was not reliable, but U.S. government security agencies continue to make similar proposals. See *back door, encryption, key escrow.*

clock An electronic circuit that generates evenly spaced pulses at speeds of millions of hertz (Hz). The pulses are used to synchronize the flow of information through the computer's internal communication channels. Most computers also contain a separate circuit that tracks the time of day, but this has nothing to do with the system clock's function. Synonymous with system clock. See *clock/calendar board, clock speed.*

clock/calendar board An adapter that includes a battery-powered clock for tracking the time and date. These were popular on the earliest PCs, which were not otherwise capable of remembering the date and time when turned off.

clock cycle   The time between two ticks of a computer's system clock. A typical personal computer goes through millions or even billions of clock cycles each second.

clock-doubled   Operating twice as fast as the system clock. A 50 MHz 486DX2 operates on a motherboard with a 25 MHz system clock, for example, and completes internal microprocessor operations faster than a 25 MHz 486DX on the same motherboard. A clock-doubled chip, though, does nothing to speed up operations outside the microprocessor. Clock doubling, tripling, and even quadrupling were popular with 486–class microprocessor systems but are not used in Pentiums and newer systems. See *clock-quadrupled, clock-tripled.*

clock-quadrupled   Operating close to four times as fast as the system clock. A 133 MHz 486 processor operates on a motherboard with a 33 MHz system clock. See *clock-doubled, clock-tripled.*

clock speed   The speed of the internal clock of a microprocessor that sets the pace—measured in megahertz (MHz)—at which operations proceed within the computer's internal processing circuitry. Higher clock speeds bring noticeable gains in microprocessor-intensive tasks, such as recalculating a spreadsheet, but this is not the only feature that determines performance. The system's bus speed, and the speed of its memory, contribute dramatically to the overall performance of the computer. Disk-intensive operations proceed slowly, regardless of clock speed, if hard and floppy disks are sluggish. When comparing clock speeds, do not compare dissimilar processors; for example, a G3 running at 300 MHz is faster than a Pentium II running at 300 MHz.

clock-tripled   Operating three times as fast as the system clock. Clock-tripled microprocessors perform internal microprocessor functions faster than clock–doubled or standard microprocessors but do nothing to speed up the rest of the system. See *clock-doubled, clock-quadrupled.*

clone   A functional copy of a hardware device, such as a personal computer, that runs the software and uses all the peripherals intended for the IBM Personal Computer. Can also refer to a generic knock-off of a popular program, such as the shareware product As Easy As, which reads Lotus 1-2-3 files and includes most of the common Lotus 1-2-3 features.

close   In a program that can display more than one document window, to exit a file and remove its window from the display.

close box   In a graphical user interface (GUI), a box on the title bar of a window that is used to close the window. In Windows, the close box has an X on it.

closed bus system   A design in which the computer's data bus does not contain receptacles and is not easily upgraded by users. See *open bus system.*

closed-loop actuator   A mechanism that moves the read/write head of a hard disk and then sends messages to the hard disk controller confirming its location. Because the read/write head can be positioned with greater accuracy over the recording medium, closed-loop actuators improve areal density.

cloud   In computer networking, a section of the network through which precise data routes need not be defined because routers handle this task.

cluster   On a floppy or hard disk, the basic unit of data storage. A cluster includes two or more sectors.

clustering   A method of solving computationally intensive problems by linking two or more off-the-shelf personal computers in a high-speed local area network (LAN), and devising software that solves the problem quickly by dividing the processing tasks among the networked computers. Using clustering, an inexpensive alternative to a supercomputer can be created even by modestly funded orginzations. See *Beowulf, Piranha, supercomputer.*

CLV See *constant linear velocity*.

CMOS Acronym for Complementary Metal-Oxide Semiconductor. The dominant chip fabrication technology in the semiconductor industry. With CMOS technology, semiconducting materials are "doped" with impurities, which conduct current when they are charged; however, this process produces heat. The faster CMOS devices run, the hotter they become; this fact places a limitation on the clock speed CMOS-based processors can achieve. See *silicon on insulator (SOI)*.

CMOS reset jumper A jumper on the motherboard that, when moved, clears the user-defined setup options from the BIOS setup program, restoring the BIOS settings to the factory defaults. The CMOS reset jumper is useful if poor setup option selections render a computer incapable of starting.

CMYK color model A color model that makes all colors from combinations of cyan, magenta, yellow, and black. The CMYK model supports device-independent color better than the RGB (red, green, blue) and HSB (hue, saturation, brightness) models and supports the Pantone Matching System (PMS). See *color model, HSB color model, RGB color model*.

CO Acronym for central office. In telephony, the office that houses the central switching circuitry. This office's location is important to Digital Subscriber Line (DSL) users because DSL service is generally available only within a sharply circumscribed geographic area, with a radius of 2 or 3 miles from the central office. See *DSL*.

coated paper Specially treated paper that enhances the output of color printers. Some inkjet printers require coated paper specially designed for inkjets when printing photographs or other artwork at the highest resolution. See *consumables*.

coaxial cable In local area networks (LANs), a high-bandwidth connecting cable in which an insulated wire runs through the middle of the cable. Surrounding the insulated wire is a second wire made of solid or woven metal. Coaxial cable is much more expensive than twisted-pair cable (ordinary telephone wire) but can carry more data. Coaxial cables are used mostly in broadband applications like cable television. See *twisted-pair wiring*.

COBOL A high-level programming language specially designed for business applications. Short for COmmon Business Oriented Language, COBOL is a compiled language that was released in 1964 and that was the first language to use the data record as a principal data structure. Because COBOL is designed to store, retrieve, and process corporate accounting information and to automate functions, such as inventory control, billing, and payroll, the language quickly became the language of choice in businesses. COBOL is the most widely used programming language in corporate mainframe environments. Versions of COBOL are available for personal computers, but business applications for personal computers are more frequently created and maintained in C or Xbase. See *high-level programming language*.

cobot A robotic device that works with human beings in a shared workspace. Cobots can be used to constrain human movements to acceptable parameters and may have promise in safety-critical or hazardous applications such as surgery or nuclear power plant maintenance.

CODASYL See *Conference on Data-Systems Languages*.

code 1. Instructions written in a computer programming language. See *object code, source code*. 2. To express a problem-solving algorithm in a programming language. Also a synonym of source code.

code-and-fix In programming, an early method of program development in which the programmer first created a program and subsequently tried to correct its shortcomings.

codec In multimedia, an algorithm that compresses audio, video, or graphics files for efficient storage or transmission, and then decompresses them for playback purposes. Codec is an abbreviation of compression/decompression. Codecs can be implemented as software, hardware, or a combination of both. Popular media players, such as the Windows Media Player and Apple's QuickTime use an array of codecs to play music and video. See *lossless compression, lossy compression.*

Code Division Multiple Access See *CDMA.*

code of conduct A professional organization's rules specifying the ethical responsibilities of the organization's members.

code page In MS-DOS, a table of 256 codes for an IBM PC–compatible computer's character set. The two kinds of code pages are classed as follows: hardware code page, which is the character set built into the computer's ROM; and prepared code page, which is a disk-based character set one can use to override the hardware code page.

code reuse A software engineering goal based on the philosophy that there is no need to reinvent the wheel. Code reuse focuses on the creation and perfection of internally cohesive but loosely coupled program modules or objects which can be accessed as needed by several other program components or incorporated into new programs as the need arises. See *modular programming, module, object, software engineering.*

codes See *hidden codes.*

code snippet One or more lines of source code embedded in a user-defined menu option or button. The instructions define what the button or option does.

coercivity A measure (in Oersteds) of the strength of the magnetic field required to alter the direction of magnetization in magnetic tape or disks.

cold boot Starting a computer by turning on the system's power switch. See *boot, warm boot.*

ColdFusion A Web site development program that enables Web developers to store portions of Web pages, called piece parts, in a database; following the markup embedded in a Web page, the server retrieves the piece parts from the database and assembles the Web page on the fly. Developed by Macromedia, ColdFusion employs a proprietary declarative markup language called ColdFusion Markup Language (CFML).

ColdFusion Markup Language (CFML) A proprietary markup language developed by Macromedia for use with its ColdFusion software. Combining components of HTML and XML, CFML enables Web developers to embed server instructions in Web pages. These instructions tell the server how to assemble a Web page on the fly using components of Web pages, called piece parts, that are stored in a database.

cold link A method of copying information from one document (the source document) to another (the target document) so that a link is created. Cold links are distinguished from hot links in that cold links are not automatically updated; one must update them manually with a command that opens the source document, reads the information, and recopies the information if it has changed. See *DDE, hot link, Inter-Application Communication (IAC).*

collaboratory In scientific networking, a shared workspace, including shared scientific databases, facilities for teleconferencing, and network-accessible facilities for collaborative experimentation. See *federated database, Grand Challenge.*

collapse When creating an outline or viewing a directory tree (such as in the Windows Explorer), the process of hiding all the outline levels or subdirectories below the selected outline heading or directory.

collate To organize the pages of a print-out when more than one copy is printed. With collation, one complete copy of a document is printed before the next copy begins, and so on.

collating sequence See *sort order.*

collection A compound data type that represents all the available units of data in a certain logical or physical location; for example, the names of all the files currently present in a certain disk directory constitute a collection. In an object-oriented programming language, a collection includes all of an object's data as well as the functions (behaviors) required to make use of that data. See *data type, object-oriented programming.*

collision In local area networks (LANs), a garbled transmission that results when two or more workstations transmit to the same network cable at exactly the same time. Networks have means of preventing collisions. See *backoff.*

color 1. A specific degree of hue, saturation, and brightness generated by a computer video display. 2. In typography, the visual appearance of a black-and-white printed page, which should be perceived by the eye as an even shade of gray. Defects, such as rivers, bad breaks, poor character spacing, or uneven line spacing, disrupt this even appearance. To maintain good color, use consistent word spacing, avoid widows and orphans, use kerning as necessary (especially for display type), and avoid hyphen ladders (two or more rows ending in hyphens). See *brightness, saturation.*

color depth In video adapters, monitors, scanners, and other graphics devices, the maximum number of colors that can be simultaneously displayed on-screen. Color depth is a function of the number of bits used to store each distinct color. See *video adapter, video standard.*

Color Graphics Adapter See *CGA.*

color inkjet printer An inkjet printer that can generate color output. Some color inkjet printers create all colors from cyan,

Color Depth

Bit length	Number of colors
1	2
2	4
4	16
8	256
16	65,536
24	16,777,215
32	16,777,215 plus 8 bits to indicate the transparency of each pixel.

magenta, and yellow inks, but better ones use black ink, too, to fully conform with the CMYK model. See *CMYK color model, inkjet printer.*

color laser printer A laser printer that can generate output that includes color but that (for now, anyway) cannot match the output quality of thermal wax transfer, dye sublimation, or thermal dye transfer printers. Color laser printers are less expensive, are faster, and have lower consumables costs than other color-capable printers, but they are more expensive than monochrome laser printers.

color model A method of specifying the exact color assigned to a given pixel on the computer screen. Three popular color models exist: the HSB model, which describes colors in terms of hue, saturation, and brightness; the RGB model, which describes colors in terms of the intensity of the primary colors (red, green, and blue); and the CMYK model, which describes colors in terms of the intensity of colors that remove primary color information from the eye's perception (cyan, magenta, and yellow). See *CMYK color model, HSB color model, Pantone Matching System (PMS), RGB color model.*

color monitor A display device that can display an image in multiple colors, unlike a monochrome monitor that displays one color on a black or white background.

color scanner A scanner that records colors as well as shades of gray. Color scanners are distinguished from one another mainly by their color depth. See *color depth*.

color separation The separation of a multicolor graphic into several layers of color, with each layer corresponding to one of the colors that will be printed when a professional printer reproduces the graphic. See *Pantone Matching System (PMS)*.

column **1.** In character-based video displays, a vertical one-character-wide line down the screen. **2.** In a spreadsheet, a vertical block of cells usually identified by a unique alphabetical letter. **3.** In a database management program, the terms column and field are sometimes used synonymously. **4.** In word processing and desktop publishing, a rectangle of text that is arranged vertically on the page along with one or more additional columns.

column graph In analytical and presentation graphics, a graph with vertical columns. Column graphs are commonly used to show the values of items as they vary at precise intervals over a period of time. The x-axis (category axis) is the horizontal axis, and the y-axis (value axis) is the vertical axis. Such graphs are often called bar graphs, but technically speaking, bar graphs have horizontal bars.

column indicator In word processing programs, such as Microsoft Word, a message in the status bar that shows the current horizontal position of the cursor on the screen.

column text chart In presentation graphics, a chart showing related items as side-by-side columns of text.

column–wise recalculation In spreadsheet programs, a recalculation order that calculates all the values in column A before moving to column B, and so on.

.com On the Internet, a top-level domain name that is assigned to a corporation or business. Top-level domain names come last in a given Internet computer's domain name (such as www.apple.com).

COM **1.** In MS-DOS, a device name that refers to the serial ports available in a computer. A computer can have up to four COM ports, designated as COM1, COM2, COM3, and COM4. **2.** Acronym for Component Object Model. A standard developed by Microsoft Corporation that enables properly prepared objects to exchange data with each other, even if the objects have been created with varying programming languages. COM requires that the computer's operating system be equipped with OLE, which is fully implemented (at present) only on Microsoft Windows systems. COM was replaced by COM+ and then .NET. See *ActiveX, CORBA, DCOM, .NET, OLE*.

COM+ A set of middleware services developed by Microsoft Corporation for its Windows 2000 client and server products. Based on extensions of the Microsoft Transaction Server (MTS) and Component Object Model (COM), COM+ provides improved security, transaction management, more efficient object requests, and centralized application management. COM+ is slated to be replaced by Microsoft's .NET architecture, which will employ the Internet as the staging ground for providing a wide variety of network services. See *.NET*.

combination chart See *overlay chart*.

combinatorial explosion A barrier to the solution of a problem that occurs when the possibilities that must be computed are too numerous. See *artificial intelligence (AI)*.

COMDEX Acronym for Computer Dealers Exhibition. A huge computer-industry trade show at which hardware manufacturers and software publishers display their wares for customers, the computer press, and each other.

Comité Consultatif International Téléphonique et Télégraphique See *CCITT*.

comma-delimited file See *tab-separated file*.

command A user-initiated signal given to a program that initiates, terminates, or otherwise controls the execution of a specific operation. In command-driven programs, one types the command statement and its associated syntax and presses Enter. In a menu-driven program, one chooses a command from an on-screen menu.

command button In graphical user interfaces (GUIs), a pushbutton in a dialog box that initiates an action, such as carrying out a command with the options chosen, canceling a command, or displaying another dialog box. One can quickly choose the default button just by pressing Return (for Macintoshes) or Enter (for Windows systems).

COMMAND.COM In MS-DOS, a file that contains the command interpreter. This file must be present on the startup disk for MS-DOS to run.

command-driven program A system, utility, or application program that requires one to type command statements, with the correct syntax and nomenclature, to use the program's features. See *graphical user interface (GUI)*, *menu-driven program*.

Command key On Macintosh keyboards, a control key that is frequently used in combination with alphabetical keys to provide keyboard shortcuts for menu options. See *Control key (Ctrl)*.

command line An area where commands are typed in a command-line user interface.

command mode A modem mode in which the modem takes instructions from other parts of the computer, such as the keyboard, instead of transmitting everything over the phone line. For example, in command mode one could issue an instruction for the modem to lower the volume of its speaker or to dial a number. Communications programs usually handle the distinction between command mode and communications mode.

command processor The part of an operating system that accepts input from the user and displays prompts and messages, such as confirmation and error messages. Also referred to as the command interpreter. See *COMMAND.COM*.

comma-separated Delimited by commas so that the separated data can be imported into a spreadsheet or some other program. See *comma-separated values (CSV)*, *tab separated*.

comma-separated values (CSV) A table of values that have been delimited using commas so that the data can be easily imported into a spreadsheet or some other program.

comment 1. A feature in some business applications that allows users to attach nonprinting notations to comment on parts of a document. See *REM*, *remark*. 2. In programming, lines of text that explain the function of the surrounding code. Comments are for documentation purposes and are not executed as the program runs.

comment out In programming, to place a symbol (such as a semicolon) or a command at the beginning of a line that marks the line as documentation. The compiler or interpreter ignores any lines preceded with this symbol. The characters used to comment out a line vary among programming languages. In batch files, synonymous with REM out. See *batch file*.

commercial software Copyrighted software that must be paid for before it can be used. In general, commercial software is not actually sold; the software publisher retains ownership. Customers are not purchasing the software, but rather certain rights to *use* the software. These rights are specified in a contractual agreement called a software license, such as the End-User License Agreements (EULA) included with mass-market software. Typically, such licenses permit the user to install the software on one computer only. See *EULA*, *freeware*, *open source software (OSS)*, *shareware*, *secondary user rights*, *site license*, *software license*, *volume purchasing agreement*.

committed information rate (CIR) A minimum data transfer rate that is guaranteed to be available at all times from a frame relay service provider. See *frame relay*.

Common Gateway Interface See *CGI*.

Common Internet File System (CIFS) The public version of the Windows networking standard, formerly known as the Server Message Block (SMB) Protocol. The CIFS standard is maintained by an independent international standards organization (X/Open) and has been proposed to the Internet Engineering Task Force (IETF) as an Internet standard. See *Internet Engineering Task Force (IETF), Samba, Server Message Block (SMB) Protocol.*

Common Object Request Broker Architecture See *CORBA*.

Communications Decency Act (CDA) A U.S. federal law, enacted in 1996 as part of the Telecommunications Act of 1996 and signed by President Clinton, that prohibited the publication of indecent material on the Internet in such a way that it could be accessed by a minor. Indecent material includes words or images that refer directly or explicitly to sexual or excretory acts. This and other provisions of the CDA were overturned by a Supreme Court decision that held the Act's provisions to represent an unconstitutional restraint on free speech.

communications mode A modem mode in which everything sent to the modem, such as text from the keyboard, is put onto the telephone line. See *command mode*.

communications parameters In telecommunications and serial printing, the settings (parameters) that customize serial communications for the hardware one is contacting. See *baud rate, communications protocol, full-duplex, half-duplex, parameter, parity bit, stop bit.*

communications program An application that turns a computer into a terminal for transmitting data to and receiving data from distant computers through the telephone system.

communications protocol The standards that govern the transfer of information among computers on a network or using telecommunications. The computers involved in the communication must have the same settings and follow the same standards to avoid errors.

communications settings See *communications parameters, communications protocol.*

comp Abbreviation for composite. In desktop publishing (DTP), a complete mock-up of a page layout design, showing what the final printed page will look like.

compact disc See *CD*.

Compact Disc-Digital Audio (CD-DA) The sort of CD-ROM one can buy in a record store. Based on an early-1980s standard for recording sounds on compact discs, CD-DA is still one of the most popular music-recording media.

Compact Disc-Interactive (CD-I) A compact disc (CD) standard designed for interactive viewing of audiovisual recordings with a television set and a CD-I player. Designed for education, training, and entertainment, CD-I has been slow to find a market.

CompactFlash (CF) In digital cameras, PDAs, and other devices, a flash memory card technology that enables the device to store up to 128MB of images, music, and other data on a single card. The most recent version, CompactFlash+, enables Compact-Flash memory cards to be used with other types of devices. See *ATA flash memory, digital camera, flash memory card, SmartMedia.*

comparison operator See *relational operator.*

compatibility The capability of a device, program, or adapter to function with or substitute for another make and model of computer, device, or program. Also, the capability of one computer to run the software written to run on another computer. To be truly compatible, a program or device should operate on a given system without changes; all features should operate as intended and run—without changes—all the software that the other computer can run. See *clone*.

competitive local exchange carrier See *CLEC*.

comp hierarchy In Usenet, one of the seven standard newsgroup hierarchies; the comp.* newsgroups deal with all aspects of computing. See *Usenet*.

compiled program A program that has been transformed into machine-readable object code by a compiler. Compiled programs run significantly faster than interpreted programs because the program interacts directly with the microprocessor and does not need to share memory space with the interpreter. See *machine language*.

compiler A program that reads the statements written in a human-readable programming language, such as Pascal or Modula-2, and translates the statements into a machine-readable executable program. See *compiled program*.

Complementary Metal-Oxide Semiconductor See *CMOS*.

complex instruction set computer (CISC) A type of central processing unit (CPU) that can recognize as many as 100 or more instructions, enough to carry out most computations directly. Most microprocessors are CISC chips. The use of reduced instruction set computer (RISC) technology, however, is becoming increasingly common in professional workstations. Apple's G4 processor uses RISC technology.

component 1. A part or module of a program or package. For example, Netscape Messenger is a component of Netscape Communicator. **2.** An object. See *object-oriented programming*.

Component Object Model See *COM*.

component reusability In programming, the capability of creating a program module that can perform a specific task and be used in another program with little or no modification.

component video A video recording and playback technique that employs separate channels for chrominance (hue and saturation) and luminance (brightness). Component video produces higher resolution and better quality images than composite video. See *composite video*, *NTSC*, *PAL*.

compose sequence A series of keystrokes that allows one to enter a character not found on the computer's keyboard. See *ASCII character set*, *extended character set*.

composite See *comp*.

composite color monitor A monitor that accepts a standard video signal that mixes red, green, and blue signals to produce the color image. Display quality is inferior to that of RGB monitors. See *composite video*.

composite video A method for broadcasting video signals in which the red, green, and blue components, as well as horizontal and vertical synchronization signals, are mixed together. Regulated by the U.S. National Television Standards Committee (NTSC), composite video is used for television. Some computers have composite video outputs that use a standard RCA phono plug and cable, such as on the backplane of a hi-fi or stereo system. See *composite color monitor*, *NTSC*, *RGB monitor*.

compound data type In a high-level programming language, a class of data types that enable more than one value to be stored in a variable. Compound data types include arrays, collections, and objects. See *array*, *collection*, *data type*, *object*, *scalar data type*, *value*, *variable*.

compound device In multimedia, a device such as a MIDI sequencer that reproduces sound or other output that one recorded in a specific media file.

compound document In object linking and embedding (OLE), a single file created by two or more applications. When one uses OLE to embed a Microsoft Excel chart into a Microsoft Word document, for example, the resulting file contains the Word text as well as the Excel object. The object contains all the information Excel needs to open the chart for editing. This information results in file sizes considerably larger than normal. See *OpenDoc.*

compress 1. To reduce the size of a file by running a compression program such as PKZIP on it. Used when transferring or archiving large amounts of data. **2.** To change the way a disk stores files with a disk compression utility. **3.** A Unix compression utility that creates files with the *.Z extension. A copyrighted program, compress cannot be freely redistributed, so many Unix users prefer to use the Open Software Foundation's gunzip, which creates compressed files with the *.gz extension.

compressed disk A disk (hard or floppy) that has had its file storage system changed with a disk compression utility so that it can hold more content.

compressed file A file converted by a file compression utility to a special format that minimizes the disk storage space required.

compressed SLIP (CSLIP) An optimized version of the Serial Line Interface Protocol (SLIP), commonly used to connect PCs to the Internet by means of dial-up connections, that includes compression and produces improved throughput. Because of its security shortcomings, Internet service providers (ISPs) prefer to implement dial-up access using the Point-to-Point Protocol (PPP).

compression The reduction of a file's size by means of a compression program. The technique used to reduce the file's size (and to restore the data when the file is decompressed) is called the compression algorithm.

compression algorithm The method used to compress a file and to restore the data when the file is decompressed for use. The two types of compression algorithms are lossless compression and lossy compression. In lossless compression, the compression process allows for the subsequent decompression of the file with no loss of the original data. Lossless compression is used for program and data files. In lossy compression, the compression processes remove some of the data in a way that is not obvious to a person using the data. Lossy compression is used for sounds, graphics, animations, and videos. Many modems offer on-the-fly compression and often use the MNP5 or V.42bis protocols. Most of today's modems are using the v.90 for 56k.

compression ratio A ratio, fraction, or percentage that expresses the difference between the size of an uncompressed file and the size of the file after compression is complete. The higher the compression ratio, the more computational resources are required to compress and decompress the data. Compression ratios are sometimes expressed in qualitative terms, such as "fair," "good," or "excellent"; in general, compression ratios of less than 1:10 are considered fair or good, while compression ratios in excess of 1:10 are considered very good or excellent. With lossy compression, high compression ratios may produce artifacts (visible or audible anomalies that are attributable to the compression process). See *artifact, lossy compression.*

computation The successful execution of an algorithm, which can be a textual search or sort, as well as a calculation.

computationally infeasible Not capable of being solved due to practical constraints, even though a known algorithm exists. With some encryption algorithms, such as DES, it is theoretically possible to crack the code without possessing the key, but doing so would require such an enormous expenditure of computing resources, money, and time. Such an algorithm is considered computationally infeasible, and thus secure.

computationally secure In computer security, an encryption algorithm that is so time-consuming to break that it is considered safe; it would be computationally infeasible to break the algorithm. See *computationally infeasible*.

computer A machine that can follow instructions to alter data in a desirable way and to perform at least some operations without human intervention. Computers represent and manipulate text, graphics, symbols, and music, as well as numbers. See *analog computer, digital computer*.

computer addiction See *computer dependency*.

computer-aided design (CAD) The use of the computer and a CAD program to design a wide range of industrial products, ranging from machine parts to homes. CAD has become a mainstay in a variety of design-related fields, such as architecture, civil engineering, electrical engineering, mechanical engineering, and interior design. CAD applications are graphics- and calculation-intensive, requiring fast microprocessors and high-resolution video displays.

computer-aided design and drafting (CADD) The use of a computer system for industrial design and technical drawing. CADD software closely resembles computer-aided design (CAD) software but has additional features that enable the artist to produce drawings conforming to engineering conventions.

computer-aided engineering (CAE) The application of computer technology to engineering problems, including design, analysis, testing, and maintenance.

computer-assisted design/computer-assisted manufacturing See *CAD/CAM*.

computer-assisted instruction (CAI) The use of programs to perform instructional tasks, such as drill and practice, tutorials, and tests. Unlike human teachers, a CAI program works patiently with bright and slow students alike. Ideally, CAI can use sound, graphics, and on-screen rewards to engage a student in learning with huge payoffs.

computer-assisted manufacturing (CAM) See *CAD/CAM*.

computer-based training (CBT) The use of computer-aided instruction (CAI) techniques to train for specific skills, such as operating a numerically controlled lathe.

Computer Dealers Exhibition See *COMDEX*.

computer dependency A psychological disorder characterized by compulsive and prolonged computer usage. For example, medical authorities in Denmark have reported the case of an 18-year-old who spent up to 16 hours a day with his computer. Doctors found that he was talking to himself in a programming language.

Computer Emergency Response Team See *CERT*.

computer ethics A branch of ethics that is specifically concerned with the use of computer resources. Areas of concern include unauthorized access, computer viruses, unethical behavior toward others on a computer network, and software piracy. See *cracker, hacker, netiquette, spam*.

Computer Fraud and Abuse Act of 1984 A U.S. federal law that criminalizes the abuse of U.S. government computers or networks that cross state boundaries. Fines and/or prison sentences are spelled out for unauthorized access, theft of credit data, and spying with the intent to aid a foreign government.

computer information system See *CIS*.

computer literacy A standard of knowledge and skills regarding computers that is sufficient to prepare an individual for working and living in a computerized society.

computer-mediated communication (CMC) Any communication between or among people that employs computers as a medium. Examples of CMC include chat, e-mail, MUDs, and Usenet.

Computer Professionals for Social Responsibility (CPSR) A nonprofit, public advocacy organization based in Palo Alto, California, that brings together computer scientists, computer educators, and interested citizens who are broadly concerned about the impact of computer technology on human welfare. Issues of CPSR concern include worker health and safety, the impact of computer technology on modern warfare, and civil liberties in the electronic age. The group's activities include educating the public, hosting conferences, creating publications, lobbying, and pursuing litigation.

computer science (CS) A scientific discipline that focuses on the theoretical aspects of improving computers and computer software.

computer-supported cooperative work (CSCW) A collection of applications that supports the information needs of workgroups. This includes electronic mail, videoconferencing, and group scheduling systems.

computer system A complete computer installation—including peripherals, such as hard and floppy disk drives, monitor, mouse, operating system, software, and printer—in which all the components are designed to work with each other.

computer virus See *virus*.

Computer Vision Syndrome See *CVS*.

CON In MS-DOS, the device name for console, which refers to the keyboard and monitor.

concatenation To link together two or more units of information, such as strings or files, so that they form one unit. In spreadsheet programs, concatenation is used to combine text in a formula by placing an ampersand between the formula and the text.

concordance file A file containing the words one wants a word processing program to include in the index that the program constructs.

concurrency In object-oriented programming, one of the seven fundamental principles of the object model. The concurrency principle states that an active object should be clearly differentiated from those that are not active. See *object, object model, object-oriented programming.*

concurrency control In a local area network (LAN) version of an application program, the features built into the program that govern what happens when two or more people try to access the same program feature or data file. Many programs not designed for networks can run on a network and allow more than one person to access a document, but this may result in one person accidentally destroying another person's work. Concurrency control addresses this problem by enabling multiple access, in which such access can occur without losing data, and by restricting multiple access, in which access could result in destroyed work. See *file locking, LAN-aware program, LAN-ignorant program.*

concurrency management See *concurrency control.*

concurrent processing See *multitasking.*

condensed type Type narrowed in width so that more characters can fit into a linear inch. In dot-matrix printers, condensed type usually is set to print 17 characters per inch (cpi). See *pitch.*

Conference on Data-Systems Languages (CODASYL) A professional organization dedicated to improving and standardizing COBOL.

confidentiality In network security, the protection of any type of message from being intercepted or read by anyone other than its intended recipient.

CONFIG.SYS In MS-DOS, an ASCII text file in the root directory that contains configuration commands. MS-DOS consults this file at system startup.

configuration The choices made in setting up a computer system or an application program so that it works properly and meets the user's needs. Newer technologies such as Plug and Play have reduced the amount of configuration a user must perform, but configuring one's system can still be a time-consuming and difficult task.

configuration file A file created by an application program that stores the choices a person makes when he or she installs the program so that the choices are available the next time he or she starts the program.

confirmation message An on-screen message asking one to confirm a potentially destructive action, such as closing a window without saving one's work. See *alert box.*

connect To begin a session with a remote service, such as an Internet service provider (ISP).

connection hijacking An attack in which a cracker seizes control of an ongoing Telnet session. See *cracker, Telnet.*

connection laundering The use of compromised computer systems as a base from which a cracker can launch attacks on additional systems, with little chance of the cracker's actual location being detected.

connectionless Not requiring a direct electronic connection to exchange data. See *connection-oriented, packet-switching network.*

connectionless protocol In wide area networks (WANs), a standard that enables the transmission of data from one computer to another even though no effort is made to determine whether the receiving computer is online or capable of receiving the information. This is the underlying protocol in any packet-switching network, such as the Internet, in which a unit of data is broken down into small-sized packets, each with a header containing the address of the data's intended destination. In the Internet, the connectionless protocol is the Internet Protocol (IP). IP is concerned only with breaking down data into packets for transmission and reassembling the packets after they have been received. A connection-oriented protocol (on the Internet, TCP) works at another level to ensure that all the packets are received. Research on computer networks has disclosed that this design is highly efficient. See *connection-oriented protocol, TCP.*

connection-oriented Requiring a direct electronic connection, by means of switching circuits, to exchange data. See *connectionless, connectionless protocol, packet-switching network.*

connection-oriented protocol In wide area networks (WANs), a standard that establishes a procedure by which two of the computers on the network can establish a physical connection that lasts until they have successfully exchanged data. This is accomplished by means of handshaking, in which the two computers exchange messages that say, in effect, "Okay, I'm ready," "I didn't get that; please resend," and "Got it, bye." On the Internet, the Transmission Control Protocol (TCP) is a connection-oriented protocol; it provides the means by which two Internet-connected computers can enter into communication with each other to ensure the successful transmission of data. By contrast, the Internet Protocol (IP) is a connectionless protocol, which enables the transmission of data without requiring handshaking. See *connectionless protocol.*

connectivity A computer program or device's capability to interoperate with other programs and devices in a networked environment.

connectivity platform A program or utility designed to enhance another program's capability to exchange data with other programs through a local area network (LAN). Oracle for the Macintosh, for example, provides HyperCard with the connectivity required to search for and retrieve information from large corporate databases.

connector conspiracy A computer manufacturer's plot to force its customers to buy its products, which contain bizarre connectors that work only with peripherals made by the same company. Vastly unpopular with users, connector conspiracies nevertheless spring up periodically, fueled by greed.

connect speed The data-transmission rate at which a modem establishes a connection, after performing a handshaking sequence with another modem and determining the amount of line noise. The connect speed may be lower than the modem's top speed See *baud*.

console A terminal, consisting of a monitor and keyboard. In multiuser systems, console is synonymous with terminal, but console also is used in personal computer operating systems to refer to the keyboard and display. See *CON*.

constant **1.** In programming, a symbol representing a fixed value. See *variable*. **2.** In a spreadsheet program, a number one types directly into a cell or place in a formula. See *cell definition*, *key variable*.

constant angular velocity (CAV) In data storage media such as hard and floppy disk drives, a playback technique in which the disk rotates at a constant speed. This technique results in faster data retrieval times as the read/write head nears the spindle; retrieval times slow as the read/write head moves toward the perimeter of the disk. See *constant linear velocity (CLV)*.

constant linear velocity (CLV) In CD-ROM drives, a playback technique that speeds or slows the rotation of the disk to ensure that the velocity of the disk is always constant at the point where the disk is being read. To achieve constant linear velocity, the disk must spin more slowly when reading or writing closer to the spindle. See *constant angular velocity (CAV)*.

construction A phase in the software development life cycle (SDLC) in which the software is written according to the design worked out in the previous phase. Preferred methodologies are those that emphasize code reusability and modularity (such as structured programming or object-oriented programming). See *code reuse*, *modularity*, *object-oriented programming*, *software development life cycle (SDLC)*, *software engineering*, *structured programming*.

consumables The supplies a printer uses up as it operates. Consumables expenses, such those for ink cartridges and paper, can add up quickly. Consumables costs are usually expressed as a cost per page.

contact head In a hard disk, a read/write head that skates on the surface of a platter instead of flying over it. Contact heads offer resistance to head crashes and improved areal density.

contact management program An application program that enables business-people to create directories of their business contacts and to set up contact schedules. Microsoft Outlook is a combination e-mail and contact management program See *personal information manager (PIM)*.

contact manager A program designed to help keep track of contacts by maintaining a list of addresses, phone numbers, and fax numbers. Information is also maintained through the use of a notepad, automatic telephone dialing with a modem, and search and sort capabilities.

container See *compound document*.

contention In local area networks (LANs), a channel access method in which access to the communication channel is based on a first-come, first-served policy. See *CSMA/CD*, *device contention*.

context-sensitive help In an application program, a user-assistance mode that displays documentation relevant to the command, mode, or action one is now performing. Context-sensitive help reduces the time and keystrokes needed to get on-screen help.

context switching Changing from one program to another without exiting either program. See *multiple program loading*.

contiguous Adjacent; placed one next to or after the other. A range of cells in a spreadsheet is often, but not always, made up of contiguous cells. Its opposite is non-contiguous.

continuous paper Paper manufactured in one long strip, with perforations separating the pages so that one can feed the paper into a printer with a tractor-feed mechanism. Synonymous with continuous-feed paper. Also called fanfold paper. The opposite is cut-sheet paper, in which every sheet is a separate piece.

continuous speech recognition The decoding of continuous human speech (without artificial pauses) into transcribed text by means of a computer program.

continuous-tone image Printer output in which colors and shades of gray blend smoothly together, as they would in a chemically printed photograph.

continuous-tone printer A printer that can generate photorealistic output, with smooth gradations between colors or shades of gray.

contrast In monitors, the degree of distinction between dark and light pixels. Most monitors have a contrast control that one can adjust to regulate contrast.

control **1.** In a graphical user interface (GUI), a dialog box feature (such as a check box, radio button, or list box) that allows the user to choose options. **2.** In ActiveX, a downloaded mini-program that adds functionality to a Web page. See *ActiveX, graphical user interface (GUI)*.

Control+Break In MS-DOS, a keyboard command that cancels the execution of a program or command at the next available breakpoint.

control bus A data pathway that has been set aside to carry control instructions from the computer's central processing unit (CPU). See *bus*.

control character See *control code*.

control code In American Standard Code for Information Interchange (ASCII), a code reserved for hardware-control purposes, such as advancing a page on the printer. ASCII has 32 control codes. See *ASCII*.

Control key (Ctrl) In IBM PC–compatible computing, a key frequently pressed in combination with other keys to issue program commands. In Microsoft Word, for example, pressing Ctrl+F calls up the Find dialog box.

controlled vocabulary In database searching, a fixed set of predetermined subject terms that can be used to describe a data record's content unambiguously. The use of controlled vocabulary dramatically increases the precision of information retrieval operations, but coding records with the controlled terms is time-consuming. See *free-text search*.

controller See *floppy disk controller, hard disk controller*.

controller card An adapter that connects hard and floppy disk drives to the computer. Most personal computers today have controllers for four hard and two floppy drives integrated into the motherboard. Controller cards are not needed unless there are more drives to connect.

control menu In Microsoft Windows, a pull-down menu found in all windows and dialog boxes that contains options for managing the active window. The control menu icon, usually a small picture, is on the left end of the title bar. The content of the menu varies, but the menu usually includes commands to move, size, maximize, and minimize windows, as well as to close the current window or switch to another application window or the next document window.

Control Panel In Mac OS and Microsoft Windows, a utility window that lists options for hardware devices, such as the mouse, monitor, and keyboard.

Control Panel device (CDEV) Any Macintosh utility program placed in the System Folder that appears as an option in the Control Panel.

control structure A logical organization for an algorithm that governs the sequence in which program statements are executed. Control statements govern the flow of control in a program by specifying the sequence in which the steps in a program or macro are carried out. Control structures include branch structures that cause a special set of instructions to be executed if a specified situation is encountered; loop structures that execute repeatedly until a condition is fulfilled; and procedure/function structures that set aside distinct program functions or procedures into separate modules, which are invoked from the main program.

control track A separate track of the video that stores synchronization information. See *control track editing*.

control track editing An editing method that uses information recorded on a videotape's control track for synchronization purposes. See *control track*.

control unit A component of the central processing unit (CPU) that obtains program instructions and emits signals to carry them out. See *arithmetic-logic unit (ALU)*.

convenience copier A printer/scanner combination or a fax machine that can be used to make small numbers of photocopies. These usually lack copying options such as image size adjustment, contrast control, and automatic feeders.

conventional memory In any IBM PC–compatible computer, the first 640K of random access memory (RAM). The Intel 8086 and Intel 8088 microprocessors, which were available when the IBM Personal Computer (PC) was designed, could directly use 1MB of random access memory (RAM). The PC's designers decided to make 640K of RAM accessible to programs, reserving the rest of the 1MB memory space for internal system functions. Obsolete with newer operating systems, such as Windows XP, which make the entire range of memory available to all Windows applications, and which automatically configures memory to support older DOS programs.

conventional programming The use of a procedural programming language, such as BASIC, FORTRAN, or assembly language, to code an algorithm in machine-readable form. In conventional programming, the programmer must be concerned with the sequence in which events occur within the computer. Nonprocedural programming languages let the programmer focus on the problem without worrying about the precise procedure the computer must follow to solve the problem. See *declarative programming language*.

convergence **1.** In monitors, the alignment of the red, blue, and green electron guns to create colors on-screen. If these are not perfectly aligned, poor convergence results, causing a decrease in image sharpness and resolution. White areas also tend to show colors around their edges. **2.** In a packet-switching network, an automatic process of network mapping that occurs after a router is switched on. A router is a device, usually a dedicated computer, that reads each incoming packet and determines where to send it next. To do its job correctly, the router needs an accurate map of the networks to which it is directly connected. If this map had to be updated manually, organizations would have to devote a considerable amount of time and human resources to the job. Convergence software enables the router to detect changes to the network, such as the addition or removal of workstations, and to adjust its map automatically. The process is called convergence because it takes a few minutes for the router's map to "converge" to reality (the current state of the network).

conversion utility A program that transforms the file format in which data is stored. For example, Microsoft Word comes with several conversion utilities that can read files created by other word processing programs and then rewrite them using Word's file format.

cookie **1.** In the World Wide Web (WWW), a small text file that the server writes to the user's hard drive. The data in the cookie file enables one Web page to pass information to other pages, thus directly addressing a major shortcoming of the underlying Web protocol, HTTP. Many cookie applications benefit the user—for example, the shopping basket used by many online shopping malls would not function without cookies. However, direct marketing firms are using cookies to compile information about users' browsing habits in ways that have raised grave concerns among privacy advocates. Newer Web browsers, such as Microsoft Internet Explorer 6, enable users to determine when and if cookies can be written to their hard drives. **2.** In Unix, a one- or two-line quotation that can be automatically appended to an outgoing e-mail message.

cooperative multitasking In an operating system, a means of providing the appearance that more than one task (executing process) us running at a time. Cooperative multitasking represents an improvement over multiple program loading, in which more than program can be loaded into memory but only one can execute at a given time. Multitasking creates the impression that two or more programs are actually running simultaneously by switching tasks rapidly. In cooperative multitasking, tasks are designed to give up their control of the CPU to other applications voluntarily. If the application is involved in a lengthy processing operation, however, it cannot yield control until the operation is completed. Users are therefore faced with delays in which they are unable to use the computer until the task is completed. Another drawback of cooperative multitasking is its inability to protect tasks from invading each other's memory space, which causes both processes to cease operating and crashes the system. Early personal computer operating systems, such as Windows 3.1 and Mac OS, used cooperative multitasking; they were superceded by operating systems that use an improved approach to multitasking called preemptive multitasking. See *preemptive multitasking, task.*

cooperative network A wide area network (WAN), such as BITNET or UUCP, in which the costs of participating are borne by the linked organizations. See *research network.*

coprocessor A microprocessor support chip that takes over a specific processing operation, such as handling mathematical computations or displaying images on the video display. See *numeric coprocessor.*

copy **1.** The material—including text, graphic images, pictures, and artwork—to be assembled for printing. **2.** To reproduce part of a document at another location in the same document or in another document. See *Clipboard.*

copy fitting In desktop publishing (DTP), a method used to determine the amount of copy (text) in a specified font that can fit into a given area on a page or in a publication.

copyleft A type of copyright promoted by the Free Software Foundation (FSF) that is intended to promote the distribution of source code. Favoring software users' rights, copyleft insists on the right of licensees to examine, copy, and redistribute a program's source code, as long as they pass on the same rights to others. Although copylefted software is not necessarily free of cost, there is little incentive to sell copylefted software because anyone can redistribute the code. The most prominent copyleft software license is the GNU General Public License (GPL). Companies that sell copylefted software can attract buyers because they offer convenience, service, or support. Copylefted software is also called open source software (OSS). See *Free Software Foundation (FSF), General Public License (GPL), open source software (OSS).*

copy protection Hidden instructions included in a program intended to prevent a person from making unauthorized copies of software. Because most copy-protection schemes impose penalties on legitimate owners of programs, such as forcing them to insert a specially encoded key disk before using a program, most business software publishers have given up using these schemes. Copy protection is still common, however, in recreational and educational software.

copyright A form of intellectual property (IP) protection, in the U.S. and many other countries, that applies to creative works such as books, computer programs, multimedia productions, musical recordings, and motion pictures; a contrasting form of IP protection, patents, applies to inventions. Copyright laws grant exclusive rights to the copyright holder, including the right to duplicate the work for commercial purposes and to prevent the creation of derivative works based on the work's original content. Because copyrights can be transferred, the holder of a copyright is not necessarily the same as the person who created the work. In the United States, copyright privileges are countered by laws that provide rights (such as fair use and first sale) under certain conditions. See *fair use, first sale, patent.*

CORBA Acronym for Common Object Request Broker Architecture. A middleware standard developed by the Object Management Group (OMG) that enables objects to communicate with each other in a computer network, even if the network connects physically dissimilar computers and if the objects are written in varying programming languages. CORBA is part of OMG's Object Management Architecture (OMA). Microsoft offers a competing standard, called COM. See *DCOM, IIOP, middleware, OMA, ORB.*

core dump 1. In mainframe computing, a debugging technique that involves printing out the entire contents of the computer's core, or memory. 2. In slang, the term refers to a person who, when asked a simple question, recites everything he or she remembers about a subject. See *dump.*

Corel A Canadian software publisher, founded in 1985, that won initial success with a CorelDraw, a graphics package. The firm acquired the WordPerfect word processing program, QuattroPro spreadsheet program, and Paradox database program; it offers these (and additional) programs in its WordPerfect Office suite.

CorelDRAW See *illustration software, image-editing software.*

core-logic chip set A collection of integrated circuits that allows a central processing unit (CPU) to work with an external cache, random access memory (RAM), and an expansion bus.

Corel Quattro Pro See *spreadsheet.*

Corel WordPerfect Suite See *office suite.*

corona wire In laser printers, a wire that applies electrostatic charge to paper.

corrupted file A file that contains scrambled and unrecoverable data. Files can become corrupted due to bad sectors (surface flaws on the disk), hard or floppy disk drive controller failures, or software errors.

cost-benefit analysis A projection of the costs and benefits of buying certain equipment or taking certain actions.

cost per page In printers, an estimate of the cost of consumables for each page of output generated. Because consumables can ultimately cost more than the printer, pay attention to cost-per-page figures when shopping for printers. Some high-end color-capable printers have costs per page of $3.00 or more. See *consumables.*

counter 1. In typography, the space fully or partially enclosed by a bowl, the strokes that form a letter, such as the blank space inside the letter *a* or *o*. 2. On a Web page, an indicator that shows how many times the page has been browsed. Used to gauge the popularity of a Web site.

Courier A monospace typeface, commonly included as a built-in font in laser printers. Courier simulates the output of office typewriters. For example, This is Courier type.

courseware Software developed for computer-assisted instruction (CAI) or computer-based training (CBT) applications.

courtesy copy (CC) In e-mail, a copy of an e-mail message that is sent to one or more addresses. These addresses are included in the header information that the message's recipient sees. In a blind carbon copy (BCC), the recipient does not know who, if anyone, has received copies of the message. Also called carbon copy.

cpi See *characters per inch.*

CP/M Abbreviation for Control Program for Microprocessors. An early operating system for personal computers that used the 8-bit Intel 8080 and Zilog Z-80 microprocessors. CP/M was created in the late 1970s as floppy disk drives became available for early personal computers.

CPM See *critical path method.*

cps See *characters per second.*

CPU Widely used to refer to a computer's primary microprocessor. See *central processing unit.*

CPU fan A fan that mounts directly on top of the microprocessor chip (or cartridge) to keep it cool. CPU fans are designed for specific types of CPUs (microprocessors). All electronics generate heat; microprocessors generate enormous amount of heat due to the millions of transistors they have packed tightly together. Without a CPU fan, most microprocessors would burn themselves out in a few minutes. See also *heat sink, liquid cooling.*

cracker A computer hobbyist who enjoys gaining unauthorized access to computer systems; many crackers consider it a game in which the object is to defeat even the most secure computer systems. Although many crackers do little more than leave a "calling card" to prove their victory, some attempt to steal credit card information or destroy data. Whether or not they take malicious actions, all crackers injure legitimate computer users by consuming the time of system administrators and making computer resources more difficult to access. In the press, the term "cracker" is used synonymously with "hacker," but hacking has a completely different meaning and plays a valuable role in computing. See *hacker, hacker ethic, script kiddies.*

crash An abnormal termination of program execution, usually (but not always) resulting in a frozen keyboard or an unstable state. In most cases, one must reboot the computer to recover from a crash.

crawler A program that accesses Web sites and catalogs the site's pages for a search engine's database. Synonymous with spider.

CRC See *cyclic redundancy check.*

creator type In the Macintosh, a four-letter code that identifies the program used to create a document. The code associates the document with the application so that one can start the application by opening the document. See *associated document.*

crippled version A freely distributed version of a program that lacks one or more crucial features, such as printing, that have been deliberately disabled in an attempt to introduce the user to the program in the hope that the user will buy the full version. Synonymous with working model. See *demo.*

crippleware See *crippled version.*

criteria range In a spreadsheet program that includes database functions, the range of cells that contains the conditions, or criteria, one specifies to govern how a search is conducted or how an aggregate function is calculated.

critical date In a Y2K readiness program, the date on which a system may experience problems because of the system's incapability of handling four-digit dates.

critical path method (CPM) In project management, a technique for planning and timing the execution of tasks in which one identifies a critical path—a series of tasks that must be completed in a timely fashion if the entire project is to be completed on time. Project-management software helps project managers identify critical paths.

CRL See *certificate revocation list*.

CRM Acronym for customer relationship management. A computerized customer relationship management system that integrates call centers, integrated databases, and specialized software to provide an improved level of customer service.

cropping A graphics editing operation in which one trims the edges from a graphic to make it fit into a given space or to remove unnecessary parts of the image.

cross-hatching A pattern of parallel and crossed lines added to solid areas in a graph to distinguish one data range from another.

cross-linked files A file-storage error that occurs when the file allocation table (FAT) in DOS and older Windows systems indicates that two files claim the same disk cluster. As with lost clusters, cross-linked files occur when the computer is interrupted (by a crash or a power outage) while it is writing a file. Disk repair utilities such as Microsoft Scandisk can repair cross-linked files.

cross-platform Software that can function on a variety of computer hardware and operating systems (for example, Macintoshes running OS X, PCs running Windows, and Intel-based computers running Linux). Netscape Navigator is a cross-platform browser because versions of the program exist for all three major computing formats, and the program conforms to cross-platform standards, which do not lock users into proprietary standards. Likewise, Java is a cross-platform programming language; you can use Java to write an application that will run on many types of computers.

cross-platform standard A communication standard or protocol that does not require the use of a proprietary operating system or proprietary hardware to function.

cross-post To post a contribution to two or more newsgroups simultaneously. Cross-posting is rarely warranted and is a favorite tactic of spammers, who post unsolicited, unwanted, and off-topic advertisements to hundreds or even thousands of newsgroups at a time. See *netiquette, spam*.

cross-reference In word processing programs, a code name used to refer to material discussed elsewhere in a document. Cross-references, such as "See the discussion of burnishing methods on page 19," are helpful to the reader.

crosstalk In an analog electrical circuit, the interference (such as buzzing or static) created between wires that are too close together. Excessive crosstalk on network cables reduces the amount of data that the cable can carry.

CRT See *cathode ray tube*.

cryptanalysis The science of breaking encrypted messages, both to determine the strength of encryption techniques and to provide the nation with a military advantage. See *cryptography*.

cryptography The science of coding messages so that they cannot be read by any person other than the intended recipient. Cryptography dates back to ancient Rome, but it has always been plagued by the messenger problem: If one wants to send an encrypted message to somebody, then one must also somehow send the key that is needed to decode the message. There is always the threat that the key could be intercepted en route without one's knowing, thus defeating the purpose of encryption. Possibly the most significant event in the history of cryptography is the recent invention of public key cryptography, which completely eliminates the need to send a key via a separate, secure channel, and which enables two people who have never before communicated to exchange virtually unbreakable messages. See *crypt-analysis.*

cryptolope A secure, encrypted container for a message transmitted via a computer network.

csh A text-mode command shell for Unix and Unix-like operating systems that enables programmers to write shell scripts using a scripting language closely resembling C (csh is an acronym for C Shell). See *bash, ksh, sh, shell.*

C Shell See *csh.*

CSLIP See *compressed SLIP.*

CSMA/CD Acronym for carrier sense multiple access with collision detection. In local area networks (LANs), a method used by Ethernet, AppleTalk, and other network protocols for controlling a computer's access to the communication channel. With CSMA/CD, each component of the network (called a node) has an equal right to access the communication channel. If two computers try to access the network at the same time, the network uses a random number to decide which computer gets to use the network first. This channel access method works well with relatively small- to medium-sized networks (two or three dozen nodes). Large networks use alternative channel access methods, such as polling and token passing, to prevent overloading or locking up the system.

CSO name server An Internet-accessible white pages directory that an organization makes available. Listing the names, telephones, and e-mail addresses of all the organization's employees, a CSO name server provides an alternative to the telephone directory. The acronym CSO stands for Computing Service Office (CSO), a unit of the University of Illinois, where the original name server software was developed.

CSS **1.** Acronym for Cascading Style Sheet. A World Wide Web Consortium (W3C) standard for style sheets capable of

indicating presentation formats (such as fonts, font sizes, and paragraph alignment) for HTML elements. Using CSS syntax, Web authors can incorporate style statements using HTML 4.0's style attribute, a separate style area (using the STYLE element) within the document's HEAD element, or a completely separate text file (with the .css extension). The term "cascading" is meant to suggest the various levels of authority; style definitions within the HEAD override external style sheets, while style statements placed within an HTML element override all other style definitions. CSS is currently in its Level 2 specification. **2.** Acronym for Content Scrambling System. An encryption scheme used to scramble the content of DVD video discs so that the content can be viewed only on players equipped with CSS decryption software. CSS is not an anti-piracy scheme; it does nothing to prevent bit-level copying of DVD discs. It is an access control system that enforces DVD region locking and forces the user to watch previews and other commercial content at the beginning of some DVD movies. See *deCSS, DVD region locking.*

CSV See *comma-separated values.*

Ctrl See *Control key.*

Ctrl+Break See *Control+Break.*

CTS/RTS Also called hardware handshaking, a method of flow control used between the modem and the computer in which it is installed. When ready to send data, the computer sends a Request To Send (RTS) signal, to which the modem replies with a Clear To Send (CTS) signal when it is ready to receive data. CTS/RTS prevents the computer from sending more data than the modem can handle.

cumulative trauma disorder (CTD) See *carpal tunnel syndrome, repetitive stress injury (RSI).*

Curie temperature A distinct temperature at which a material's coercivity changes drastically. Magneto-optical disc drives take advantage of the Curie temperature by recording data at high temperatures but storing and reading it at low temperatures, ensuring a long shelf life for the data.

curly brace The brace characters ({) and (}) on the standard keyboard. Synonymous with brace. See *angle bracket, bracket.*

current cell In a spreadsheet program, such as Excel, the cell in which the cell pointer is positioned. Synonymous with active cell.

current cell indicator In a spreadsheet program, such as Excel, a message in the upper-left corner that displays the address of the cell in which the cell pointer is positioned.

current directory The directory that MS-DOS or an application program uses by default to store and retrieve files. Synonymous with default directory

current drive The hard drive, floppy drive, CD-ROM, or other drive that the operating system uses for an operation unless one specifies otherwise. Synonymous with default drive.

cursor An on-screen blinking character that shows where the next character will appear. See *pointer.*

cursor-movement keys The keys that move the cursor on-screen. Synonymous with arrow keys.

curved surface support In computer game programming, a set of programming techniques that enables game designers to represent curved surfaces. Previous techniques restricted game environment display to a matrix of polygons.

CU-SeeMe See *videoconferencing.*

customer relationship management See *CRM.*

customize To select options or preferences that configure a program or system to a user's liking.

cut **1.** To delete selected text, a graphic, or some other object from a document. The cut object is stored temporarily in the Clipboard, from which it can be pasted elsewhere or discarded. **2.** In digital video and multimedia production, the transition from one program source to the next. See *Clipboard.*

cut and paste See *block move.*

cut-sheet feeder A paper-feed mechanism that feeds separate sheets of paper into the printer, where a friction-feed mechanism draws the paper through the printer.

cut-sheet paper Paper in separate sheets, with each sheet unconnected to another. See *continuous paper.*

CVS Acronym for Computer Vision Syndrome. An eyesight disorder that results from focusing closely on a computer screen for long periods of time, such as temporary nearsightedness and blurred vision.

cyber- A prefix, connoting "computer," which is commonly prepended to non-computer words to form neologisms such as cybercafe or cybercash.

cybercafe A coffee shop that offers Internet access.

cybercash See *digital cash.*

cyberphobia An exaggerated and irrational fear of computers. Noted by the psychotherapist Craig Brod and others, cyberphobia stems from the stress individuals encounter as they try to cope with an increasingly computer-driven society. Alert employers that offer training to employees new to computers can help ease employee transition to a computerized work environment.

cyberpunk A genre of science fiction that depicts a dystopian future dominated by worldwide computer networks, battling artificial intelligences, monopoly capitalism, and a world culture as ethnically eclectic as it is politically apathetic and alienated. On this stage are chronicled the exploits of hackers who use hallucinogenic drugs, cyborg implants, and trance states to carry out criminal and heroic missions within the networks' fabulous realms of virtual reality. The originator of the genre is William Gibson in his 1982 book *Neuromancer*, which coined the term cyberspace. Curiously, Gibson knew little about computing when he wrote the book—on a typewriter.

cybersex A form of long-distance eroticism made possible by a real-time computer chat room. To stimulate a virtual partner, one relays a favorite sexual fantasy or describes in vivid terms what he or she would be doing if the person were actually present.

cyberspace The virtual space created by computer systems. One definition of space is "a boundless three-dimensional extent in which objects and events occur and have relative position and direction." In the twentieth century, computer systems are creating a new kind of space that fits the previous definition, called cyberspace. (The prefix "cyber" refers to computers.) Cyberspace can take the form of elaborate virtual reality worlds or relatively simple e-mail. E-mail advocates will readily testify that the ability to communicate with other users located all over the world breaks down social and spatial boundaries in an exhilarating way. See *cyberpunk, Internet, virtual reality (VR)*.

cyclic redundancy check (CRC) An automatic error-checking method used by MS-DOS when writing data to a hard or floppy disk. When MS-DOS later reads data from the disk, the same error check is conducted, and the results of the two checks are compared to make sure that the data has not changed. If one sees an error message such as "CRC ERROR READING DRIVE C," it signals serious problems with the disk. A similar CRC checking procedure also is commonly used by file compression utilities (such as PKZIP) and when transferring files using data communications. See *XMODEM/CRC*.

cylinder In hard and floppy disk drives, a unit of storage consisting of the set of tracks that occupy the same position on opposite sides of the platter. On a double-sided disk, a cylinder includes track 1 of the top and the bottom sides. On hard disks in which several disks are stacked on top of one another, a cylinder consists of track 1 on both sides of all the disks.

cypherpunk A programmer who strongly believes that private citizens possess the right to send a secure, encrypted message to anyone they please and that encryption technology should not be regulated.

DA See *desk accessory.*

DAC Acronym for digital-to-analog converter; a computer chip, or set of chips, that converts digital signals into analog signals. Many devices that contain DAC functionality can also convert analog signals into digital signals; for instance, modems.

daemon (Pronounced *demon* or *daymon.*) A memory-resident program that remains in the background, awaiting an event that triggers a predefined action. For example, the Apache Web server runs a daemon called httpd that listens for Web page requests.

daisy chain A method of connecting together several devices along a bus and managing the signals for each device. Devices that use a SCSI interface, such as a CD-ROM, hard disk, and scanner, can be daisy-chained to one SCSI port. See *daisy chaining.*

daisy chaining In displays, the act of linking several monitors together so that they all show the same thing. Daisy chaining is convenient when large numbers of people must see the output of a computer simultaneously, such as at a convention or trade show. See *daisy chain.*

DARPA See *Defense Advanced Research Projects Agency.*

DASD See *direct access storage device.*

DAT Acronym for Digital Audio Tape. A digital magnetic tape format originally developed for CD-quality audio recording and now used for computer backup tapes. The latest DAT storage format, DDS, specifies storage capacities of up to 24GB.

data Factual information (such as text, numbers, sounds, and images) in a form that can be processed by a computer. Although data is the plural of the Latin word *datum,* the term data is commonly used to represent both singular and plural. In formal contexts (such as university computer science and engineering departments), the plural (data) and the singular (datum) are sometimes distinguished.

data aging In Y2K readiness testing, a method of testing system readiness by changing date values to future dates.

database **1.** A collection of related information about a subject organized in a useful manner that provides a base or foundation for procedures, such as retrieving information, drawing conclusions, and making decisions. Any collection of information that serves these purposes qualifies as a database, even if the information is not stored on a computer. In fact, important predecessors of today's sophisticated business database systems were files kept on index cards and stored in file cabinets. Information usually is divided into data records, each with one or more data fields. See *relational database.* **2.** An application that provides the tools for data retrieval, modification, deletion, and insertion; for instance, Access, MySQL, and Oracle. Such applications also can create a database and produce reports. In personal computing, three kinds of database management programs exist: flat file, relational, and text-oriented. See *flat file database, relational database management system (RDBMS), text-oriented database.*

database design The choice and arrangement of data fields in a database so that fundamental errors (such as data redundancy and repeating fields) are avoided or minimized. See *1NF, 2NF, 3NF, normalization.*

database driver A program that enables a spreadsheet application (such as Excel) to exchange data with database applications (such as Access).

database management Tasks related to creating, maintaining, organizing, and retrieving information from a database. See *data manipulation.*

database management system (DBMS) A group of programs that organize data in a database, providing information storage, organization, and retrieval capacities, sometimes including simultaneous access to multiple databases through a shared field (relational database management). See *flat file database, relational database management system (RDBMS)*.

database structure In databases, a definition of the data records in which information is stored, including the number of data fields; a set of field definitions that specify the type, length, and other characteristics of the data that can be entered in each field; and a list of field names. See *data type*.

data bits The number of bits a computer uses to represent a character of data. When two computers communicate by modem, they must use the same number of data bits—usually eight, but sometimes seven. See *parity, stop bit*.

data bus An internal electronic pathway that enables the microprocessor to exchange data with random access memory (RAM). The width of the data bus, usually 128 or 256 bits, determines how much data can be sent at one time. Synonymous with internal bus. See *expansion bus*.

data communication The transfer of information from one computer to another. The transfer can occur via direct cable connections, as in local area networks (LANs) or over telephone lines using modems. See *telecommunications*.

Data Communications Equipment (DCE) In asynchronous communications, an intermediary device (such as a modem) that enables Data Terminal Equipment (DTE, such as a computer) to establish communication with other DTE devices by means of a telephone line. See *Data Terminal Equipment (DTE), modem*.

data compression See *compression*.

data-compression protocol In modems, a standard for automatically compressing data when it is sent and decompressing data when it is received. With data compression, gains of up to 400 percent in effective transmission speed can be realized. Older modems support V.42bis and MNP-5; newer modems support ITU V.92 and K56flex. See *CCITT, ITU-TTS*.

data deletion In databases, an operation that deletes records according to specified criteria. Many database programs do not actually delete the records in such operations; they merely mark the records so that they are not included in data retrieval operations. Therefore, one usually can restore the deleted records if he or she has made a mistake.

data dependency A situation in which a central processing unit (CPU) using superscalar architecture and multiple pipelines must have the result of one calculation before beginning another. See *false dependency*.

data dictionary In databases, a list of all the database files, indexes, views, and other files relevant to a database application. A data dictionary also can include data structures and any information pertinent to the maintenance of a database.

data diddling A computer crime in which data is modified to conceal the theft or embezzlement.

data-encoding scheme The technique a disk drive controller uses to record bits of data on the magnetic surface of a floppy disk or hard disk. Disk drives are categorized by the data-encoding scheme the drive uses. See *Advanced Run-Length Limited (ARLL), disk drive controller, MFM, Run-Length Limited (RLL)*.

data encrypting key In SSL and other security protocols that begin a secure connection with public key encryption, a symmetric encryption key that is used to encrypt the transmitted data after a secure key exchange has taken place. See *symmetric key encryption algorithm*.

Data Encryption Standard   See *DES*.

data-entry form   In databases, an onscreen form that makes entering and editing data easier by displaying only one data record at a time.

data field   In databases, a space reserved for a specified piece of information in a data record. In a table-oriented database management program, in which all retrieval operations produce a table with rows and columns, data fields are displayed as vertical columns.

data file   A file containing the work created with a program; in contrast, a program file contains instructions for the computer's handling of the data.

data flow diagram   A graphical representation of the flow of data through an information system.

data fork   In the Macintosh file system, the file component that contains the data stored in the file, such as a spreadsheet or word processing document. The other component is the resource fork.

data glove   A device that translates the user's hand and arm movements into computer input. See *virtual reality (VR)*.

datagram   The original Internet term for a data packet.

data independence   In databases, the storage of data in a way that enables one to access that data without knowing exactly where it is located or how it is stored. Newer database applications include command languages, called query languages, that let one phrase questions based on content rather than the data's physical location.

data insertion   In databases, an operation that adds new records to the database. Unlike appending records, however, insertion lets a user add records anywhere in the database.

data integrity   The accuracy, completeness, and internal consistency of the information stored in a database. A good database management program ensures data integrity by making it difficult (or impossible) to accidentally erase or alter data. Relational database management programs help ensure data integrity by eliminating data redundancy.

data interchange format (DIF) file   In spreadsheet applications and some database applications, a standard file format that simplifies importing and exporting data between different spreadsheet programs. Originally developed by Software Arts, the creators of VisiCalc, DIF is supported by Lotus 1-2-3, Microsoft Excel, Corel Quattro Pro, and most other spreadsheet programs.

data link layer   In the Open Systems Interconnect (OSI) Reference Model of computer network architecture, the sixth of seven layers, in which the addressed packets are transformed so that they can be physically conveyed at the physical layer. At this layer, protocols govern the detection and resolution of transmission errors, the conversion of data into a form appropriate for the physical layer that is being used, and the regulation of data to avoid bottlenecks. When the data is ready to be sent over the network, it is transferred to the physical layer, where the data is encapsulated by physical-layer protocols. See *layer, OSI Reference Model, protocol stack*.

data manipulation   In databases, the use of the basic database manipulation operations—data deletion, data insertion, data modification, and data retrieval—to make changes to data records.

data mart   A large database that contains all the data used by one of the divisions of an organization.

data mask   See *field template*.

data mining   In a data warehouse, a discovery method applied to very large collections of data. In contrast to traditional database queries, which phrase search questions using a query language (such as SQL), data mining proceeds by classifying and clustering data, often from a variety of different and even mutually incompatible databases, and then looking for associations.

data modem A modem that can send and receive data but not faxes. See *fax modem*.

data modification In databases, an operation that updates one or more data records according to specified criteria. One uses a query language to specify the criteria for the update. For example, the following statement, written in a simplified form of Structured Query Language (SQL), tells the database application to open the table named "inventory"; for each data record in which the "supplier" data field contains "CC", the value in the "price" data field should be increased by 15 percent.

```
UPDATE inventory.

SET price = price * 1.15.

WHERE supplier = "CC".
```

datapac A type of packet-switching network. Datapac networks use the TCP/IP network protocol.

data privacy In local area networks (LANs), limiting access to a file so that other users in the network cannot display the contents of that file. See *encryption, field privilege, password protection.*

data processing Preparing, storing, or manipulating information.

Data Processing Management Association (DPMA) A professional society specializing in business computing issues for programmers, systems analysts, and managers. DPMA established the Certified Data Processor (CDP) recognition process in the 1960s but later turned the responsibility for certification over to the Institute for Certification of Computer Professionals (ICCP).

data record In databases, a complete unit of related data items stored in named data fields. In a database, a data record is synonymous with a row. A data record contains all the information related to the item the database is tracking. Most programs display data records in two ways: as data-entry forms and as data tables. In a table-oriented relational database management system, the data records are displayed as horizontal rows and each data field is a column.

data redundancy In databases, the repetition of the same data in two or more data records. Generally, users should never enter the same data in two different places within a database; if someone mistypes just one character, the error destroys accurate retrieval because the computer does not know that the two entries are supposed to be the same. Data integrity is a serious issue for any database management system, and careful system design can help reduce redundancy-related problems.

data retrieval In databases, an operation that retrieves information from the database according to the criteria specified in a query. A database application is most useful when one wants to access only a few records, such as all customers whose bills are past due or those who have not been contacted in the last 90 days. By using queries, a person can tell the application to sort the data in many convenient ways. In some programs, the query can specify which fields to display after the matching records are selected.

data series In business and presentation graphics, a collection of values that all pertain to a single subject, such as the third-quarter sales of three products. In spreadsheet programs, a column, row, or block of values that increases or decreases a fixed amount. When creating a data series, one indicates a beginning value, the amount to increase or decrease the value, and an ending value.

data storage capacity The maximum amount of data that can be stored by a storage device, such as a disk drive; measured in bytes. See *bit, byte, exabyte (EB), gigabyte (GB), kilobyte (KB), megabyte (MB), petabyte (PB), terabyte (TB), yottabyte (YB), zettabyte (ZB).*

data storage media Collectively, the technologies used for auxiliary storage of computer data, such as hard drives, optical discs, and magnetic tapes.

data stream In data communications, a flow of undifferentiated data that is transmitted byte after byte.

data striping An important method employed by redundant arrays of inexpensive disks (RAID) in which a single unit of data is distributed across several hard disks, increasing resistance to a failure of one of the drives.

data table In databases, an onscreen view of information in a columnar (two-dimensional) format, with the field names at the top. Most database applications display data tables as the result of sorting or querying operations. In spreadsheet applications, a form of what-if analysis in which a formula is calculated many times using different values for one or two of the arguments in the formula. The results are displayed in a table. See *data-entry form*.

Data Terminal Equipment (DTE) The term used by the specification that defines the standard serial port to describe the computer that is connected to a modem or a fax modem. See *Data Communications Equipment (DCE)*.

data transfer rate In modems, the speed, expressed in bits per second (bps), at which a modem can transfer or is transferring data over a telephone line. In hard disks, the theoretical speed at which a hard disk can transfer data to the rest of the computer. Data transfer rate is established by laboratory tests; throughput is a better indication of how well a hard disk performs. See *connect speed*.

data type **1.** In a high-level programming language, one of several distinct types of data that can be expressed as a value for a variable or constant. Data types fall into two general categories: scalar (single value) and compound (multiple values). Examples of scalar data types are integers, decimal numbers, strings (characters), dates, and Boolean (True/False) data. Examples of compound data types include arrays, collections, and objects. See *array, Boolean data type, collection, compound data type, constant, integer, object, scalar data type, string, value*. **2.** In a database management program, a classification given to a data field that governs the kind of data one can enter, such as character, numeric, date, or logical. See *field template*.

data validation In a database, a method of increasing the validity of data by defining acceptable input ranges for each field in the record.

data warehouse A collection of related databases that have been collected and stored together so that the maximum value can be extracted from them. The basic idea of data warehousing is to gather as much data as possible, in the hope that somehow a meaningful picture will emerge. Data mining techniques enable programmers to collate and extract meaningful data from the warehouse; by means of a technique called drilldown, the data mining software enables data warehouse users to see as much detail or summarization as they need to support decision-making. See *DSS*.

daughterboard A printed circuit board that is designed to attach to another larger circuit board, such as a motherboard or an adapter.

dBASE A relational database management system (RDBMS) for personal computers that was developed with the assistance of U.S. government funding in the 1970s, and subsequently marketed by Ashton-Tate, which was subsequently acquired by Borland International. dBASE is now owned by dBASE, Inc. The dBASE data, query, and file formats became a de facto standard, known as xBASE, that is still implemented in a few commercial database packages, such as Microsoft's Visual FoxPro.

DBMS See *database management system*.

DCE See *Data Communications Equipment*.

DCE speed The speed, measured in bits per second (bps), at which Data Communications Equipment (DCE) devices can communicate over a telephone line.

DCOM Acronym for Distributed Component Object Model. A middleware standard developed by Microsoft that extends the company's OLE-based Component Object Model (COM) to the network level. DCOM was Microsoft's answer to CORBA; Microsoft has since replaced DCOM with .Net. See *CORBA, middleware.*

DDE Acronym for Dynamic Data Exchange. A Microsoft-specified inter-process communication channel (IPC) based on the client/server model through which programs can exchange data and control other applications. To be capable of DDE, programs must conform to Microsoft Corporation's specifications. DDE enables simultaneously running programs to exchange data as the information changes. Through the use of object linking and embedding, which makes using DDE easier, a DDE-capable spreadsheet program can receive real-time data from an online information service, record changes in the price of key stocks and bonds, and recalculate the entire worksheet as the change occurs. DDE was renamed ActiveX, which in turn has become .Net. See *.Net, server application.*

DDR-SDRAM Acronym for double data rate synchronous dynamic random access memory. A type of high-speed RAM for cutting-edge microprocessors that supports data transfers on both margins of a clock cycle. This design effectively doubles the chip's data transfer rate. It is also less expensive and much more popular than its nearest competitor, RDRAM. DDR-II SDRAM is the newest specification, functioning at twice the speed of standard DDR. See *random access memory (RAM), SDRAM.*

DDS Acronym for Digital Data Storage, a tape backup format for digital audio tape (DAT) cartridges.

debug In programming, to detect, locate, and fix errors in a program's source code.

debugger A utility program often included in compilers or interpreters that helps programmers find and fix errors in source code.

debugging The process of locating and correcting errors in a program.

decimal notation The numbering system in use throughout the industrialized world, with a base or radix of 10. See *binary notation, hexadecimal notation, octal notation.*

decimal tab In a word processing or page layout program, a tab stop configured so that values align at the decimal point.

decision support system See *DSS.*

declaration In a high-level programming language, a statement that binds a given value with a constant or that links a variable to a specific memory location or data type.

declarative markup language (DML) In text processing, a markup language—a system of codes for marking the format of a unit of text—that indicates only that a particular unit of text is a certain part of the document, such as an abstract, a title, or an author's name and affiliation. The actual formatting of the document part is left up to another program, called a parser, which displays the marked document and gives each document part a distinctive format (fonts, spacing, and so on). An international standard DML is the Standard Generalized Markup Language (SGML), which was little-known until a subset of SGML, the Hypertext Markup Language (HTML), came into widespread use on the World Wide Web (WWW). HTML is a declarative markup language, and the Web browsers in use by millions today are parsers for HTML.

declarative programming language A programming language that frees the programmer from specifying a sequence of steps the computer must follow to accomplish a task. Instead, programmers using a declarative language create an application by describing a set of facts and relationships that connect some data. The user of the application then writes searches or queries about the data and receives results. For example, Structured Query Language (SQL) allows one to search a database by asking to see a list of records that contain specific information instead of by telling the computer to open the first record, search it, report back, then close the record; move to the second record, open it, report back, close the record; and so forth. Includes such languages as Prolog and Lisp. See *data independence, declarative markup language (DML), expert system, procedural programming language.*

decode To convert an encrypted or encoded file so that it is readable, normal data.

decompress To restore compressed data to its original state. See *compress, extraction.*

decrement To decrease a value. See *increment.*

decryption In cryptography, the decoding of an encrypted message by means of a key. See *encryption.*

deCSS A free Windows utility that breaks the weak DVD encryption and access control scheme called Content Scrambling System (CSS) and enables the user to copy all or part of a DVD to the user's hard disk. It also enables users to evade DVD region locking and skip previews and other commercial content included with DVD releases. Released on the Internet in 1999, deCSS soon became the focus of a major controversy and numerous lawsuits. According to the DVD Copy Control Association (CCA), the industry consortium responsible for the CSS encryption scheme, deCSS was intended to promote the "piracy" of copyrighted DVD content. Claiming "misappropriation of trade secrets," the organization sued more than 500 people in 11 countries for making deCSS available for downloading or providing links to download sites. In Norway, alleged deCSS author Jon Johansen was prosecuted under a Norwegian law that prohibits breaking into another person's locked property to gain access to data. In 2003, a Norwegian court ruled that Norwegians cannot be held criminally liable for breaking into property that they had lawfully purchased. See *CSS, DVD, DVD region locking.*

dedicated e-book reader A portable hardware device that's only purpose is to present electronic book (e-book) text in a highly readable onscreen format. See *e-book.*

dedicated file server In a local area network (LAN), a computer dedicated exclusively to providing services to the users of the network and running the network operating system (NOS). Some file servers can be used for other purposes. In peer-to-peer networks, for example, all the networked computers are potential file servers, although they are being used for standalone applications.

dedicated line A telephone line devoted to data communications that has been specially conditioned and permanently connected. Dedicated lines are often leased lines from regional telephone companies or public data networks (PDNs).

deep link A hyperlink to a page located within a Web site rather than to the Web site's home page.

de facto standard A software or hardware standard, or a communications protocol, that has come into very widespread use, not because any international standards body has ratified it, but rather because the company that makes products using this standard has overwhelmingly dominated the market in a particular sector. In the late 1980s, for example, keyboard commands used by the most popular word processing program, WordStar, were emulated by most other programs. Now, however, Microsoft Word is the de facto standard word processor.

default Automatically configured; set up with a certain predefined value or option, usually because such a setting is likely to be preferred by most users.

default button In graphical user interfaces, such as Microsoft Windows, the highlighted button automatically selected as the most likely choice in a dialog box. One can press Enter to choose this button quickly. See *command button, pushbutton, radio button*.

default directory See *current directory*.

default editor In a Unix system, the text editor (such as emacs or vi) that the system automatically starts when the services of a text editor are needed.

default extension The three-letter extension an application program uses to save and retrieve files unless one overrides the default by specifying another extension. Using the default extension makes retrieving files easier. During retrieval operations, programs that use a default extension display a list of only the files that use their default extension. If a person gives a file a different extension, he or she still can retrieve the file, but must remember the file's name or change the file name entry to *.* so that all files are listed.

default font The font that the printer uses unless told otherwise. Synonymous with initial base font.

default home page In a Web browser, the World Wide Web (WWW) document that appears when one starts the program or clicks the Home button. Most Web browsers are set up to display the browser publisher's home page, but one can easily change this setting so that the browser displays a more useful default home page.

default numeric format In a spreadsheet program, the numeric format that the program uses for all cells unless the user chooses a different one.

default printer The printer that a program automatically uses when told to print. If one changes printers for a single print job, some programs return to the printer designated as the default when the document is closed. Others treat the currently selected printer as the default printer until the user selects another printer.

default setting The settings that a program uses unless one specifies another setting. For example, a word processing program has a default font, and a spreadsheet has a default column width.

default value A value that a program uses when one is not specified. For example, one might set up a currency field in a database that has a default value of 00 unless one enters a different number.

Defense Advanced Research Projects Agency (DARPA) A unit of the U.S. Department of Defense (DoD), the successor to the Advanced Research Projects Agency (ARPA) that played a key role in the development of the ARPANET, the Internet's predecessor. DARPA is one of several U.S. agencies that participate in the High Performance Computing and Communications Program (HPCC).

deflection yoke See *yoke*.

defragmentation A procedure in which all the files on a hard drive are erased and rewritten on the disk so that all parts of each file are written to contiguous sectors. The result is an improvement of up to 75 percent in the drive's speed during retrieval operations. During normal operations, the files on a hard disk eventually become fragmented so that parts of a file are written all over the drive, slowing retrieval operations.

degauss To initiate a monitor's degaussing process. See *degaussing*.

degaussing In a monitor, the process of balancing the monitor's internal magnetic field so that it compensates for the Earth's magnetic field. An internal magnetic field that has not been balanced by degaussing may produce unwanted color distortions. Degaussing is sometimes needed after moving a monitor or after a brownout or power spike.

Delete key (Del) A key that erases the character to the right of the cursor. One uses the backspace and Delete keys to correct mistakes as one types.

delimiter A code, such as a space, tab, or comma, that marks the end of one section of a command and the beginning of another section. Delimiters also are used to separate data into fields and records when one wants to export or import data using a database format. For example, using delimiters makes it easy to export a merge file created using a word processing program or to import data into a spreadsheet program and have lines of data divided logically into columns.

Delphi An easy-to-learn programming language created by Borland International, Inc., to compete with Microsoft Visual Basic. Delphi is an object-oriented programming (OOP) language that is based on an object-oriented version of Pascal. Delphi development suites equip the programmer with libraries of reusable objects as well as a compiler that produces executable programs.

demand paging In virtual memory, a method of moving data from the disk to memory that waits until the required data is needed. See *anticipatory paging*.

demilitarized zone (DMZ) A server that is directly connected to the Internet so that an organization can establish an external Web presence; however, the organization's internal network is hidden behind a firewall that prevents direct access from the outside. See *firewall, server.*

demo An animated presentation or a preview version of a program distributed without charge in an attempt to acquaint potential customers with a program's features. Synonymous with demoware. See *crippled version.*

demodulation In telecommunications, the process of receiving and transforming an analog signal into its digital equivalent so that a computer can use the information. See *modulation.*

demount To remove a disk from a disk drive. See *mount.*

denial-of-service (DoS) attack A form of network vandalism that attempts to make a service (such as a Web site) unavailable to other users, generally by flooding the service with meaningless data or sending information that causes a key service to crash.

density See *areal density.*

departmental laser printer A high-end laser printer designed to serve large groups of people and print 12,000 pages or more each month. Departmental laser printers often feature automatic emulation switching, automatic network switching, bidirectional communication, duplex printing, and remote management.

dependent worksheet In Microsoft Excel, a worksheet that contains a link or reference formula to data in another Excel worksheet, called the source worksheet, on which it depends for the data. More than one worksheet can depend on a single source worksheet. In other spreadsheet programs, such as Lotus 1-2-3 and Corel Quattro Pro, a worksheet containing a link is called a target worksheet. See *external reference formula, source worksheet.*

deprecate In a technical standard, to discourage a former usage. In HTML 4.0, for example, elements and attributes that have presentation (formatting) aspects are deprecated.

derived field See *calculated field.*

DES Acronym for Data Encryption Standard. A controversial IBM-developed encryption technique that was adopted by the U.S. government for nonclassified information and widely used by financial institutions to transfer large sums of money electronically. Critics charge that DES technology was deliberately weakened so that the government would be able to break DES-encoded messages when it chose to do so. DES encryption is quite vulnerable to cryptanalysis, even when performed by amateurs, and its use is no longer recommended See *encryption, encryption algorithm.*

descender The portion of a lowercase letter that hangs below the baseline. Five letters of the English alphabet have descenders: *g, j, p, q,* and *y.* See *ascender.*

descending sort A sort that reverses the normal ascending sort order. Rather than sort A, B, C, D and 1, 2, 3, 4, for example, a descending sort lists D, C, B, A and 4, 3, 2, 1.

descriptor In databases, a word used to classify a data record so that all records containing the word can be retrieved as a group. In a video store's database, for example, the descriptors Adventure, Comedy, Crime, Horror, Mystery, or Science Fiction can be entered in a field called CATEGORY to indicate where the film is shelved in the store. See *identifier, keyword.*

design In the software development life cycle (SDLC), the phase (following requirements analysis) in which functional specifications are translated into a program design. See *software development life cycle (SDLC).*

desk accessory (DA) In a graphical user interface (GUI), a set of utility programs that assist with day-to-day tasks, such as jotting down notes, performing calculations on an onscreen calculator, maintaining a list of names and phone numbers, and displaying an onscreen calendar.

desktop In a graphical user interface (GUI), a representation of one's day-to-day work, as though one were looking at an actual desk with folders full of work to do. In Microsoft Windows, this term refers specifically to the background of the screen, on which windows, icons, and dialog boxes appear.

desktop case A computer case designed to rest on its widest surface, usually on a desk. The monitor often sits on top of it. Compare to a tower case, which stands on end.

desktop computer A personal computer or professional workstation designed to fit on a standard-sized office desk that is equipped with sufficient memory and disk storage to perform business computing tasks. See *portable computer.*

desktop environment The portion of a computer's system software that implements a desktop for computer users. Features of a desktop environment include drag-and-drop, a Clipboard for copying and pasting, customizable backgrounds and screen colors, application launchers, fonts, a graphical file management utility, and accessory programs such as a calendar and calculator. See *windowing environment.*

Desktop Management Interface (DMI) A system for printers developed by the Desktop Management Task Force (DMTF) that warns users when printers need attention, such as when toner runs low, paper jams occur, or paper is exhausted. DMI is expected to supersede the Simple Network Management Protocol (SNMP).

Desktop Management Task Force (DMTF) A consortium of computer equipment manufacturers that has established standards for the Desktop Management Interface (DMI) and Plug and Print.

desktop pattern In graphical user interfaces such as Microsoft Windows, a graphical pattern (called wallpaper) displayed on the desktop (the background "beneath" windows, icons, and dialog boxes).

desktop publishing (DTP) The use of a personal computer as an inexpensive production system for creating typeset-quality text and graphics. Desktop publishing programs often merge text and graphics on the same page and print pages on a high-resolution laser printer or typesetting machine. Desktop publishing software lets one person produce typeset-quality text and graphics with a personal computer, enabling an organization to reduce publication costs by as much as 75 percent.

desktop publishing software Programs designed to transform a computer into a desktop publishing workstation. Leading packages include Adobe FrameMaker, Adobe PageMaker, and QuarkXpress.

desktop video A multimedia application that displays a full-motion video on the computer's display. Without special processing circuitry (a video adapter with special support for decompressing and playing videos at high speed), the result may be a postage-stamp-sized video playing with jerky motion.

destination The record, file, document, or disk to which information is copied or moved, as opposed to the source.

destination document In object linking and embedding (OLE), the document in which one inserts or embeds an object. When one embeds a Microsoft Excel object (such as a chart) into a Microsoft Word file, for example, the Word document is the destination document. See *source document*.

destination file In many DOS commands, the file into which data or program instructions are copied. See *source file*.

development suite A package of utilities that enable programmers to create programs as quickly and effortlessly as possible. Typically included are a compiler, a debugger, a text editor, libraries of useful routines, and tools for such tasks as connecting to databases.

device Any hardware component or peripheral, such as a printer, modem, monitor, or mouse, that can receive and/or send data. Some devices require special software, called a device driver.

device contention The technique that Microsoft Windows uses to handle simultaneous requests from multitasked programs to access devices.

device-dependent Incapable of operating successfully on a certain type of computer system or on a computer that is not equipped with a certain type or brand of peripheral, such as a sound card or modem. For example, some voice-recognition programs require a SoundBlaster-compatible sound card and will not work with other types of sound cards.

device-dependent color A printer or monitor's color palette that does not conform to any established color scheme but that instead results from the device's unique characteristics. Because most printers and monitors generate device-dependent color, it is often difficult to accurately match a color generated by one device with a color generated on another. Device-independent color overcomes this deficiency.

device driver A program that provides the operating system with the information needed for it to work with a specific device, such as a printer.

device independence The capability of a program, operating system, or programming language to work on many types of computers or peripherals. Unix, an operating system for multiuser computer systems, is designed to run on a wide variety of computers, from personal computers to mainframes. PostScript, a page description language for high-quality printing, is used by many printer manufacturers.

device-independent Capable of working correctly on many types of computers or on computers equipped with a wide variety of peripherals.

device-independent color A method of describing colors in a standard way, such as with the Pantone Matching System (PMS), and then modifying output devices, such as printers and monitors, to conform to the standard. Though rare and expensive, device-independent color is far superior to device-dependent color and is essential if one is in the publishing business.

Device Manager In Windows, the utility used to examine and change the configuration of your computer's hardware and device drivers. See *configuration, device driver*.

device name An abbreviation, such as COM2, LPT1, or /dev/eth0, that refers to a peripheral device. Some programs will not function correctly unless the user can identify and supply the device name to which a peripheral (such as a modem) is connected.

device node In Microsoft Windows 95 and 98, an object in the hardware tree that represents a piece of hardware. Synonymous with Plug and Play object.

DHCP Acronym for Dynamic Host Configuration Protocol. An Internet protocol that assigns temporary IP addresses to workstations on a local area network (LAN). When a workstation logs on to the network, the workstation's DHCP client requests a temporary IP number, which is used until the workstation logs off the network. Most Internet users who access the network by means of dialup, ISDN, DSL, or cable connections receive temporary IP numbers by the Internet service provider's DCHP server. See *fixed IP address*.

DHTML Acronym for dynamic HTML. Any of several technologies for adding interactivity to Web pages, including ActiveX, JavaScript, and Java. Unlike previous methods for creating interactive Web pages, such as forms processed with CGI scripts, Dynamic HTML does not require communication with a Web server. Dynamic HTML is supported by the Document Object Model (DOM), a World Wide Consortium (W3C) standard that defines how Web browsers define the properties of Web pages as objects that can be accessed and manipulated by scripts.

diagnostic program A utility program that tests computer hardware and software to determine whether they are operating properly.

dialer program In SLIP and PPP, a program that dials an Internet service provider's number and establishes the connection. A dialer program is unlike a communications program, which transforms a computer into a terminal of a remote computer. Instead, the dialer program establishes the connection that fully integrates a computer into the Internet. Many service providers distribute preconfigured dialer programs that enable users to connect to their service without configuring or programming the dialer; if a person cannot obtain a preconfigured dialer, he or she may have to write his or her own login script, which can be tedious for people who lack programming experience.

dialog Synonymous with dialog box.

dialog box In a graphical user interface (GUI), an onscreen message box that conveys or requests information from the user.

dial-up access A means of connecting to another computer or a network such as the Internet with a modem-equipped computer. Amercia Online is the leading provider of dial-up Internet access for consumers in the United States. See *ISP*.

dial-up IP A dial-up access method that gives one full access to the Internet. By means of dial-up IP (in conjunction with Point-to-Point Protocol [PPP] or Serial Line Internet Protocol [SLIP]), one can use graphical programs such as Netscape Navigator to browse the World Wide Web (WWW) and collect e-mail. See *ISP*.

dial-up modem In contrast to a modem designed for use with a leased line (such as digital cable service), a modem that can dial a telephone number, establish a connection, and close the connection when it is no longer needed. Most personal computer modems are dial-up modems. See *ADSL modem, cable modem*.

DIB 1. Acronym for Dual Independent Bus. An Intel-developed standard for plugging microprocessors into the computer's motherboard. The device contains a data bus (called the front side bus) that connects the processor to the computer's RAM. It also contains a bus called the backside bus that connects the microprocessor to an external L2 cache unit. See *back-side bus, frontside bus*. 2. Acronym for Device

Independent Bitmap. The standard bit-mapped graphics format for Microsoft Windows, DIB stores colors in a format that is independent of the actual output device. The device's driver determines how the colors will be displayed.

dictionary attack   An attack on a computer in which the intruder attempts to guess user passwords by supplying common words found in a dictionary. Many users naively choose such words as passwords, thus creating a potential security hole.

dictionary sort   A sort order that ignores the case of characters as data is rearranged. See *sort*.

DIF   See *data interchange format (DIF) file*.

differential backup   A data backup technique that backs up only those files that have been created or altered since the last full backup was performed. A differential backup does not change the files' archive bit. See *backup, full backup*.

Diffie-Hellman encryption algorithm A public key encryption algorithm that was created by the inventors of public key encryption, and subsequently named after them. A widely used implementation of this algorithm is called El Gamal. See *encryption algorithm, public key encryption*.

digest   **1.** In Usenet, an article that appears in a moderated newsgroup summarizing the posts received by the newsgroup's moderator. **2.** On a mailing list, an e-mail received from the list server containing a copy of every message sent to the mailing list in a given time period.

digicash   See *digital cash*.

digital   Any system in which data is sampled at regular, discrete intervals; opposite of analog systems, in which data is sampled in constant and infinite variation. Digital data is composed of distinct objects, or digits, that represent something in the real world—measurements such as speed, temperature, or time—so that counting, calculations, and other operations can be

performed conveniently. For example, a digital speedometer might register a speed of 66.5 mph. An analog speedometer has a needle that sweeps across the dial, and can, for instance, represent an infinite degree of speeds between 60 and 70 mph. In digital electronic computers, two electrical states correspond to the 1s and 0s of binary numbers, which form the basis of all digital data. See *algorithm, analog, program*.

Digital Audio Tape   See *DAT*.

digital camera   A portable camera incorporating one or more charge-coupled devices (CCDs) that records images in a machine-readable format. Although digital cameras are expensive and generate output of far lesser quality than that of film-based cameras, they eliminate the potentially expensive and time-consuming film-processing and photo-scanning steps involved in getting photos into computer-readable form.

digital cash   A proposed method of ensuring personal privacy in a world in which electronic commerce becomes common. In digital cash commerce, a person who maintains an electronic bank account could make online purchases, which would be debited automatically and transferred to the payee. The transactions would be secure for all three parties concerned—the bank, the payer, and the payee—yet none of these parties, nor any outside investigator, would be able to determine just what has been done with the money. Relying on public key cryptography, this technology alarms government and law enforcement officials, who see it as an open invitation to tax cheats and drug dealers. Although experiments in digital cash infrastructures employing smartcards have met with considerable success in Europe, they have not proven successful in the U.S.

digital cellular phone   A type of cellular phone service that, unlike analog cellular systems, transmits and receives data in an encoded digital format. Digital cellular phones offer better sound, less noise and static, and higher bandwidth, which is important for the increasing number of users who use cellular phones to check e-mail and access Web sites. One factor delaying the acceptance of digital cellular phones is the existence of two competing service standards called CDMA and TDMA. See *analog cellular phone, CDMA, TDMA.*

digital certificate See *certificate.*

digital computer A computer that uses the digits 0 and 1 to represent data and then uses at least partly automatic procedures to perform computations on this information. A digital computer does not have to be electronic; an abacus is a digital computer because it represents information by means of separable units (digits) and because the user can follow a procedural recipe to solve problems. Most of today's computers are digital computers, although analog computers are still used for certain specialized applications (such as real-time data analysis).

digital controls Monitor controls that consist of pushbuttons instead of knobs or dials. Like analog controls, digital controls, can adjust brightness, contrast, and image size.

Digital Data Storage See *DDS.*

digitally signed In e-mail, signed with a certificate that confirms that the person sending the message is actually who he claims to be. See *digital signature.*

digitally signed certificate A certificate to which someone or some organization's digital signature has been affixed as a further corroboration of its authenticity.

Digital Millennium Copyright Act (DMCA) A 1996 U.S. legislative act that defines new procedures for dealing with copyright infringements involving digitized media, including Web content. Before the DMCA's passage, copyright holders had to go to a judge and prove that allegedly purloined content was indeed unlawfully infringed. After the DMCA, a certified letter to the alleged infringer's Internet service provider (ISP) is all that is required to get the allegedly infringing material off the Web. The ISP is required to remove the material; if the ISP refuses, the ISP automatically becomes liable for contributory infringement. After 14 days, the person accused of copyright infringement may request that the material be reinstated, but to do so is to state, in effect, that the person is willing to risk a lawsuit over the matter. Additional controversial provisions of the DMCA include stiff fines and prison sentences for the mere possession of devices or programs capable of disabling digital rights management (DRM) technologies, such as encryption or copy protection. See *copyright, digital rights management (DRM).*

digital modem A communications adapter designed to connect one computer to another digitally. Digital modems are not really modems at all because modulation and demodulation are necessary only for analog connections. Digital modems work with digital telephony standards such as ADSL and ISDN.

digital monitor A monitor that accepts digital output from the display adapter and converts the digital signal to an analog signal. Digital monitors cannot accept input unless the input conforms to a digital standard, such as the IBM Monochrome Display Adapter (MDA), Color Graphics Adapter (CGA), or Enhanced Graphics Adapter (EGA) standards. All these adapters produce digital output but, unlike Video Graphics Array (VGA) and other analog monitors, can display a limited number of colors.

digital rights management (DRM) The practice of protecting intellectual property (IP) that exists in any digital form, such as e-books, graphical images, and CD music. Common DRM concerns include administering copyrights and preventing unlawful use of digital content. Many laws, procedures, and technologies are being developed to protect the owners of intellectual property while allowing for fair use by anyone who purchases it. See *copy protection, trusted system.*

digital signal processor (DSP) A programmable sound-processing circuit used in both modems and sound boards. Sound boards use DSPs to handle a variety of sound resolutions, formats, and sound-altering filters without requiring separate circuits for each one; modems use DSPs to handle several modulation protocols.

digital signature An encrypted, tamper-proof attestation, usually attached to an encrypted e-mail message or a certificate, that the person or authority signing the certificate is confident that the message's originator is actually the person he claims to be.

Digital Subscriber Line See *DSL*.

digital telephony A telephone system based on the use of digital rather than analog transmission techniques. Most private branch exchange (PBX) systems are digital.

digital transmission A data communications technique that passes information encoded as discrete on/off pulses. Digital transmission does not require digital-to-analog converters at each end of the transmission; however, analog transmission is faster and can carry more than one channel at a time.

Digital Versatile Disc See *DVD*.

digital video (DV) A method of representing video content using digital rather than analog storage formats. Although digital video data consumes significantly more storage space than corresponding analog data, digital video enables superior quality because the various components of video content—including sound and the various components of color—can be separately stored with optimal definition. To be of practical use, digital video all but requires on-the-fly compression and decompression, which can be implemented in hardware, software, or both. See *compression*.

Digital Video Disc See *DVD*.

Digital Video Disc–Random Access Memory See *DVD-RAM*.

Digital Video Disc–Read Only Memory See *DVD-ROM*.

Digital Video Interface See *DVI*.

digital zoom In digital cameras, an electronic substitute for an optical zoom lens; image magnification is accomplished by enlarging a portion of the image, but at the expense of decreasing the image's clarity and introducing artifacts (visual distortions) into the resulting file. See *artifact, digital camera*.

digitize The process of transforming analog data into digital form. A scanner converts continuous-tone images into bit-mapped graphics. CD-ROMs contain many digital measurements of the pitch and volume of sound. See *digitizing tablet*.

digitizing tablet In computer-aided design (CAD), a peripheral device, usually measuring 12 by 12 or 12 by 18 inches and ½ inch thick, that is used with a pointing device called a cursor to convert graphics, such as pictures and drawings, into digital data that a computer can process. The location of the cursor on the tablet is sensed magnetically in relation to a wire grid embedded within the tablet, and the position is tracked onscreen. Synonymous with graphics tablet.

digizine A magazine or newsletter published electronically by means of a CD-ROM or Web site.

DIMM Acronym for Dual In-Line Memory Module. A rectangular circuit board that contains memory chips and fits into a receptacle with a 64-bit data bus. Unlike SIMMs (single inline memory modules), which fit into 32-bit receptacles and must be paired to function, DIMMs enable users to upgrade by inserting one module at a time.

dimmed The display of a menu command, icon, or dialog box option in a different color or shade of gray to indicate that the selection is not available. Sometimes called "grayed out."

dingbats Ornamental characters, such as bullets, stars, pointing hands, scissors, and flowers, used to illustrate text. Dingbats originally were used between columns or, more commonly, between paragraphs to provide separation.

diopter correction   In a digital camera, a rotable magnification selector that is designed to compensate for variations in users' visual capabilities.

DIP   **1.** See *document image processing.* **2.** See *dual in-line package, DIP switch.*

DIP switch   One or more toggle switches enclosed in a small plastic housing, called a dual in-line package (DIP). This housing is designed with downward-facing pins so that it can be inserted into a socket on a circuit board or soldered directly to the circuit board. DIP switches are frequently used to provide user-accessible configuration settings for computers, printers, and other electronic devices.

DirecPC   A satellite-based Internet service offered by Hughes Network Systems. The service requires a telephone line for outgoing requests for information, but it can deliver data at download speeds of up to 400 Kbps. This service has recently been upgraded to offer satellite transmission as well.

Direct3D   An application programming interface (API) developed by Microsoft Corporation to support three-dimensional game programming in the Windows environment. Direct3D enables programmers to write generic instructions to hardware devices, such as video cards, without having to know exactly how these devices are wired and configured.

direct access storage device (DASD)   Any storage device, such as a hard disk, that offers random access or direct access to the stored data, in contrast to a sequential access device (such as a tape drive).

direct-connect modem   A modem equipped with a jack like the standard jack found in a telephone wall outlet, both of which accept an RJ-11 plug. The modem can be connected directly to the telephone line using ordinary telephone wire, unlike an acoustic coupler modem designed to cradle a telephone headset.

DirectDraw   An interface standard developed by Intel and subsequently by Microsoft that enables applications to send video instructions directly to the video adapter, bypassing the CPU.

direct-map cache   A means of organizing cache memory by linking it to locations in random access memory (RAM). Although direct-map caches are simpler than other types of caches and are easier to build, they are not as fast as other cache designs. See *full-associative cache, set-associative cache.*

direct memory access   See *DMA.*

direct memory access (DMA) conflict   See *DMA conflict.*

direct memory access (DMA) controller   See *DMA controller.*

Director   A leading authoring tool for creating dynamic content that can be delivered on the Web, CD-ROM, DVD-ROM, or kiosks. Developed by Macromedia, the program can work with Flash animations, photo-quality images, digital video, sounds, 3D images, and text. See *Flash, Macromedia.*

directory   A logical storage unit that enables computer users to group files in named, hierarchically organized folders and subfolders. See *current directory, directory markers, hierarchical file system, parent directory, path name, subdirectory.*

directory markers   In DOS, symbols displayed in a directory table that represent the current directory (.) and the parent directory (.). See *directory, subdirectory.*

directory sorting   The organized display of the files in a directory, sorted by name, extension, or date and time of creation. The Windows Explorer can sort the contents of directories in several ways.

directory title   In Gopher, an item on a Gopher menu that, when accessed, reveals another menu (rather than a document, graphic, or other item).

directory tree A graphical representation of a disk's contents that shows the branching structure of directories and subdirectories. The Microsoft Windows 95 and 98 Windows Explorer, for example, displays a directory tree.

direct-to-drum imaging Hewlett-Packard's design for color laser printers. The print drum in HP Color LaserJets turns four times—once each for cyan, magenta, yellow, and black—and once more to fuse the various toners to the page. With this method, as many as five pages can be printed each minute. See *CMYK color model.*

DirectX An application programming interface (API) developed by Microsoft Corporation for Windows-powered PCs that enables programmers to write multimedia instructions for Windows devices, even if they do not know precisely what kind of device (graphics card or monitor) is installed. See *Direct3D, OpenGL.*

dirty **1.** Full of extraneous signals or noise. A dirty telephone line causes problems when trying to log on with a modem to a distant computer system or BBS. The result can be garbage characters onscreen (in terminal mode) or repeated disconnections. One must log off, hang up, and dial again. **2.** A file that has been changed but has not yet been saved.

dirty power An AC power line that is subject to voltage fluctuations, surges, or other anomalies sufficient to cause problems with computing equipment. A surge suppressor can help prevent the power anomalies from harming a PC.

disable To temporarily disconnect a hardware device or program feature; to make it unavailable for use. One might disable a device in Windows, for example, to keep it from consuming system resources, or one might disable an automatic spell-checker in a word processor to keep it from interrupting one's typing with corrections.

disaster recovery plan A written plan, with detailed instructions, specifying an alternative computing facility to use for emergency processing until a destroyed computer can be replaced.

disconnect To terminate a connection with a server.

discrete speech recognition The prevailing type of computer speech recognition, in which users must speak each word separately and distinctly (with a pause between each) so that the system can accurately transcribe spoken language. Discrete speech recognition is unpleasant and unnatural to use. Continuous speech recognition programs, which transcribe normal (nondiscrete) speech, have been available for certain highly specialized applications in medicine and other professional fields, but only recently have consumer products appeared that make continuous speech recognition more widely available. See *continuous speech recognition.*

disintermediation The process of removing an intermediary, such as a car salesman, by providing a customer with direct access to rich information and warehouse-size selection and stock.

disk See *floppy disk, hard disk.*

disk array See *drive array.*

disk buffer See *cache controller.*

disk cache **1.** In a Web browser, a portion of one's hard drive that has been set aside to store the World Wide Web (WWW) documents one has accessed recently. When one reaccesses these pages, the browser first checks with the server to find out whether the document has been changed; if not, the browser retrieves the document from the disk cache rather than the network, resulting in significantly faster retrieval. Synonymous with cache. **2.** In general personal computing, a portion of random access memory (RAM) set aside to hold data recently retrieved from a disk. Disk caches can significantly speed up a system's performance.

disk capacity   The storage capacity of a floppy disk or hard drive, measured in kilobytes (K), megabytes (MB), or gigabytes (GB).

disk compression utility   A compression utility that operates on all or most of the files of an entire drive, making the drive appear to have as much as two to three times its normal storage capacity. Compression and decompression are performed on-the-fly, which means some loss of performance due to the overhead produced by these operations. See *compression.*

disk drive   A secondary storage device, such as a floppy disk drive or a hard drive. This term usually refers to floppy disk drives. A floppy disk drive is an economical secondary storage medium that uses a removable magnetic disk that can be recorded, erased, and reused repeatedly. Floppy disk drives are too slow to serve as the main data storage for today's personal computers but are needed to copy software and disk-based data onto the system and for backup operations. See *random access, read/write head, secondary storage.*

disk drive controller   The circuitry that controls the physical operations of the floppy disks or hard drives connected to the computer.

diskette   See *floppy disk.*

diskless workstation   In a local area network (LAN), a workstation that has a microprocessor and RAM but lacks its own disk drives. Diskless workstations reduce security risks and ensure compatibility among departments, but they limit speed, flexibility, and originality. See *distributed processing system, personal computer (PC).*

disk operating system   See *operating system (OS).*

disk optimizer   See *defragmentation.*

disk partition   See *partition.*

display   See *monitor.*

display adapter   See *video adapter.*

display card   See *video adapter.*

display font   See *display type.*

display memory   See *video memory.*

display power management signaling (DPMS)   A system in which a specially equipped video adapter sends instructions to a compatible monitor telling it to conserve electricity. The video adapter can tell the monitor to assume any of three levels of power conservation.

display type   A typeface, usually 14 points or larger and differing in style from the body type, used for headings and subheadings. Synonymous with display font.

distance learning   The use of telecommunications (particularly, the Internet) to provide educational outreach programs for students at remote locations.

distributed bulletin board   A collection of computer conferences, called newsgroups, automatically distributed throughout a wide area network (WAN) so that individual postings are available to every user. The conferences are organized by topic, embracing such areas as ecology, politics, current events, music, specific computers and computer programs, and human sexuality. See *follow-up post, Internet, moderated newsgroup, post, thread, unmoderated newsgroup, Usenet.*

distributed object architecture   In computer networks, a design in which programs called object request brokers (ORB) can detect the presence of other objects on the network. An object is a unit of computer code that contains data as well as the procedures, called methods, for performing specific tasks with this data. When a new object is detected, its methods become available for use by other objects, perhaps in ways that were not anticipated by the objects' programmers. See *CORBA, IIOP.*

distributed operating system   An operating system that resides on the network rather than individual workstations. Much operating system research is focused on developing distributed operating systems. See *operating system (OS), Plan 9.*

distributed processing system A computer system designed for multiple users that provides each user with a fully functional computer. In personal computing, distributed processing takes the form of local area networks (LANs), in which the personal computers of the members of a department or organization are linked by high-speed cable connections. Distributed processing offers some advantages over multiuser systems. If the network fails, a person can still work. One also can select software tailored to his or her needs. One can start a distributed processing system with a modest initial investment because he or she needs only two or three workstations and, if desired, a central file server.

distribution   1. In Usenet, the geographic area throughout which one wants his or her post to be distributed. With most systems, a person can choose from world distribution (the default in most systems), his or her country, his or her state, his or her local area, or his or her organization. One must choose a distribution that is appropriate for his or her message, unless he or she really wants a "Dinette Set for Sale in New Jersey" post to be read in Wollongong, Australia. **2.** A list of users to whom one is sending the same e-mail message. **3.** Synonymous with Linux distribution.

distro   Slang term for Linux distribution.

dithering   In color or grayscale printing and displays, the mingling of dots of several colors to produce what appears to be a new color. With dithering, one can combine 256 colors to produce what appears to be a continuously variable color palette, but at the cost of sacrificing resolution; the several colors of dots tend to be mingled in patterns rather than blended well.

DLL   Acronym for dynamic link library. The file name extension attached to a collection of library routines in Microsoft Windows and Windows-compatible applications.

DMA   Acronym for direct memory access. A bus standard that enables compatible devices to access the computer's main memory directly, without the CPU's intervention. The older DMA standard, called third-party DMA, is closely associated with the ISA and is not widely used in newer computer systems. More recent versions, called Ultra DMA, provide superior performance. They are based on a principle called bus mastering, in which the peripheral using the bus becomes its "master," obviating the need for a controller unit. Ultra DMA is also said to use the first-party DMA principle in that it is directly controlled by the active peripheral. See *bus master, DMA channel, DMA conflict, first-party DMA, third-party DMA, Ultra DMA.*

DMA channel   A circuit that enables a peripheral device to access the computer's memory directly instead of going through the processor. Each peripheral must be assigned its own unique DMA channel to avoid a DMA conflict.

DMA conflict   A problem that results when two peripherals try to use the same DMA channel. A DMA conflict usually causes a system crash and can be solved by assigning one of the conflicting peripherals a new DMA channel. See *Plug and Play (PnP).*

DMA controller   A chip that controls the flow of data through the DMA channels. By handling the work of regulating data flow through the channels, the DMA controller frees the microprocessor to do other work.

DMI   See *Desktop Management Interface.*

DMTF   See *Desktop Management Task Force.*

DNS   See *domain name system.*

DNS server   A program that runs on an Internet-connected computer system and provides an automatic translation between domain names (such as watt.seas.virginia. edu) and IP addresses (such as 128.143.7.186). The purpose of this translation process, called resolution, is to enable

Internet users to continue using a familiar name (such as www.yahoo.com) even though the service's numeric IP address may change. Also called name server. See *domain name system (DNS), resolution.*

DNS server attack An attack on an Internet-connected computer running a DNS server. The attacker attempts to exploit flaws in the server's programming that enable the attacker to load the server with erroneous information that can be used to gain entry into a secured system.

dockable toolbar A toolbar that the user can drag from its default location and reposition at other locations within the application's window, or outside the window, if desired.

docking station A cabinet containing disk drives, video circuits, and special receptacles designed to house a portable computer. When the portable is inserted into the docking station, it can function as a desktop PC, complete with external monitor, keyboard, and drives.

DOCSIS Acronym for Data Over Cable Service Interface Specification. A cable modem standard that defines high-speed, two-way Internet service by means of cable TV connections. See *cable modem.*

document A file containing work one has created, such as a business report, a memo, or a worksheet. See *word processing.*

documentation The instructions, tutorials, and reference information that provide the information needed to use a program or computer system effectively. Documentation can appear in printed form or in online help systems.

document-centric In a software suite, a user interface concept in which the end product is more important than the program being used to create various portions of it. Menus and toolbars dynamically and automatically change to those relevant to the type of data being edited.

document-comparison utility A utility program or word processing command that compares two documents created with word processing programs. If the two documents are not identical, the program displays the differences between them, line by line.

document file icon In Microsoft Windows, the icon of a document associated with an application program. One can open the document and launch the application simultaneously just by double-clicking a document file icon.

document format 1. In a word processing program, a set of formatting choices that control the page layout of the entire document. Examples of document formats include margins, headers, footers, page numbers, and columns. 2. The file type of the document—for example, WordPerfect or Word.

document image processing (DIP) A system for the imaging, storage, and retrieval of text-based documents that includes scanning documents, storing the files on optical or magnetic media, and viewing when needed using a monitor, printer, or fax.

document processing The use of computer technology during every stage of the production of documents, such as instruction manuals, handbooks, reports, and proposals. A complete document-processing system includes all the software and hardware needed to create, organize, edit, and print such documents, including generating indexes and tables of contents. See *desktop publishing (DTP), word processing program.*

document type definition See *DTD.*

dog food A beta version of a program that is used internally within the software publishing firm in the hope that such use will disclose further defects.

DOM Acronym for Document Object Model. A World Wide Web Consortium (W3C) standard that specifies how Web browsers make the various objects on a page, such as CSS styles, available to scripts for processing purposes.

domain   In a computer network, a group of computers that are administered as a unit. Network administrators are responsible for all the computers in their domains. On the Internet, this term refers to all the computers that are collectively addressable within one of the four parts of an IP address. For example, the first part of an IP address specifies the number of a computer network. All the computers within this network are part of the same domain. See *domain name.*

domain controller   A server in a Microsoft Windows network that maintains a database of users who are given access rights to the domain. Synonymous with primary domain controller. See *backup domain controller.*

domain name   In the system of domain names used to identify individual Internet computers, a single word or abbreviation that makes up part of a computer's unique name (such as watt.seas.virginia.edu). Reading from left to right, the parts of a domain name go from specific to general; for example, "watt" is a specific computer, one of several RS-6000 minicomputers in service at the School of Engineering and Applied Science (seas) at the University of Virginia (virginia). At the end of the series of domain names is the top-level domain (here, edu), which includes hundreds of colleges and universities throughout the U.S. See *domain name system (DNS).*

domain name system (DNS)   In the Internet, the conceptual system, standards, and names that make up the hierarchical organization of the Internet into named domains.

dongle   A small piece of hardware that plugs into a port, usually to control access to a peripheral or software application. Some very expensive programs use dongles as copy-protection devices—if one does not have the dongle plugged in, the program will not work. Other dongles provide infrared data transfer or network connectivity.

doping   In semiconductor manufacturing, the process of deliberately introducing impurities to create variations in the electrical conductivity of the materials.

DOS   See *MS-DOS, operating system (OS).*

DOS prompt   In MS-DOS, a letter representing the current disk drive followed by the greater-than symbol (>), which together inform the user that the operating system is ready to receive a command. See *prompt.*

dot address   See *IP address.*

dot file   In Unix, a file that has a name preceded by a dot. Such a file normally is not displayed by Unix file-listing utility programs. Dot files are frequently used for user configuration files, such as a file that lists the newsgroups the user regularly consults.

dot-matrix printer   An impact printer that forms text and graphic images by hammering the ends of pins against a ribbon in a pattern (a matrix) of dots. Dot-matrix printers are relatively fast, but their output is generally poor quality because characters are not well-formed. These printers also can be extremely noisy. See *font, impact printer, letter-quality printer, near-letter quality (NLQ) printer.*

dot pitch   In monitors, the diagonal distance from a dot of one color to a dot of the same color. The lower the number, the crisper the image. High-resolution monitors use dot pitches of approximately 0.28 mm or less; the best monitors use dot pitches of 0.25 mm or less.

dot prompt   In dBASE, the prompt, a lone period on an otherwise empty screen, for the command-driven interface of the program.

dots per inch (dpi)   A measure of resolution that states the number of dots that the device can print, scan, or display in a linear inch.

double-click   To click a mouse button twice in rapid succession.

double date rate SDRAM   See *DDR-SDRAM.*

double density A widely used recording technique that packs twice as much data on a floppy or hard disk as on the earlier, single-density standard. See *DS/DD, high density, MFM, Run-Length Limited (RLL), single density.*

Double-Layer Supertwist Nematic See *DSTN.*

double precision In floating point notation, a unit of data storage that is 64 bits in length. See *floating point notation, IEEE 754.*

double-scanned passive matrix See *dual-scan.*

double-sided floppy disk A floppy disk that can store data on both its surfaces. Almost all floppy disks are double-sided, although a few obsolete floppy disks record data on only one side. See *DS/DD, DS/HD.*

double-speed drive Also called 2x drive. A CD-ROM drive that can transfer data at up to 300K per second. Although the maximum data transfer rate of double-speed disk drives is twice that of the first CD-ROM drives, the access times of the two are about equal. Double-speed drives are now nearly obsolete, replaced by much faster drives that operate at 24x to 36x.

DO/WHILE loop In programming, a loop control structure that continues to carry out its function until a condition is satisfied. A DO/WHILE control structure establishes a condition that, if true, causes the program to wait until the test is false and then move to the next instruction. See *loop, sequence control structure, syntax.*

download To transfer data from a network location to the user's computer. The downloading process requires the use of a data transmission protocol (standard) that automatically checks for errors and requests re-transmissions, if necessary. The contrasting process, upload, occurs when data is sent from the user's computer to a network location. Internet file transfers make use of the File Transmission Protocol (FTP). See *error correction, FTP, upload.*

downloadable font A printer font that is transferred from the computer's hard disk to the printer's memory at the time of printing. Often called soft fonts. See *bitmapped font, built-in font, cartridge font, downloading utility, font, font family, outline font, page description language (PDL), PostScript.*

downloading Transferring a copy of a file from a distant computer to a disk in one's computer using data communication links. See *FTP, modem.*

downloading utility A utility program that transfers downloadable fonts from a computer or printer hard disk to a printer's random access memory (RAM). Such a program is not needed in Windows because Windows fonts are sent to the printer automatically.

download manager A utility, designed to work with popular Web browsers, that manages Internet file downloads. Download managers can resume an interrupted download without requiring retransmission of the previously downloaded portion.

downward-compatible See *backward-compatible.*

dpi See *dots per inch.*

DPMA See *Data Processing Management Association.*

DPMS See *display power management signaling.*

drag To move the mouse pointer while holding down a mouse button.

drag-and-drop In Microsoft Windows programs and Macintosh programs running under System 7.5 or higher, a technique that enables one to perform operations on objects by dragging them with the mouse. One can open a document by dragging its icon to an application icon, or one can install icons in folders by dragging icons to them. Many word processing programs feature drag-and-drop editing, which speeds rearrangement of text.

drag-and-drop editing   An editing feature that enables one to perform a block move or copy by highlighting a block of text and then using the mouse to drag the block to its new location. When one releases the mouse button, the text appears in the new location. Some DOS programs, such as WordPerfect 6.0, allow drag-and-drop editing.

DRAM   Acronym for dynamic random access memory. A type of random access memory (RAM) that represents information by using capacitors to store varying levels of electrical charges. Because the capacitors eventually lose their charge, DRAM chips must refresh regularly (hence "dynamic"). DRAM chips are often used on inexpensive video adapter cards to store video information. See *SDRAM, SRAM.*

drawing tools   Graphics capabilities in an application program, such as a command that transforms the cursor into a "pen" for creating object-oriented (vector) graphics. Drawing tools typically include options for creating lines, circles, ovals, polylines, rectangles, and Bézier curves.

draw program   A graphics program that uses vector graphics to produce line art. A draw program stores the components of a drawing, such as lines, circles, and curves, as mathematical formulas rather than as a configuration of bits onscreen, as paint programs do. Unlike images created with paint programs, line art created with a draw program can be sized and scaled without introducing distortions. Draw programs produce output that prints at a printer's maximum resolution. See *paint program.*

Dreamweaver   A WYSIWYG HTML editor, developed by Macromedia, that has become the standard in the Web development industry. Dreamweaver offers a suite of easy-to-use (but powerful) Web development tools that, in contrast to Microsoft's FrontPage, do not introduce built-in biases that serve to restrict the Web page's audience to Internet Explorer users. In addition to its Web page development tools, Dreamweaver offers powerful site management tools. In addition, the program is highly extensible; its commands are implemented by means of JavaScript modules that can be supplemented by users with programming skills. Alternatively, they can be easily installed by downloading Web-accessible extensions. In addition, Dreamweaver includes features that enable Web developers to make full use of Web scripting environments, including JavaScript, ASP, and PHP. Closely and intelligently integrated with Macromedia's Flash (animation) and FireWorks (graphics) applications, Dreamweaver is well established as the Web development environment of choice for industry practitioners. See *Fireworks, Flash, Microsoft FrontPage, WYSIWYG HTML editor.*

drill down   In data mining, a method of data exploration and analysis that involves more detailed examination of the data that produced a summary value or aggregate.

drive   See *disk drive, hard drive.*

drive activity light   A small signal light, often mounted so that it shows through the computer's case, that indicates when a disk drive is in use.

drive array   Group of hard drives organized (often as a Redundant Array of Inexpensive Disks [RAID]) to improve speed and provide protection against data loss. Drive arrays may incorporate data striping schemes. See *data striping, RAID.*

drive bay   A receptacle or opening into which one can install a hard drive or floppy disk drive. Half-height drive bays are common in today's IBM and IBM-compatible personal computers. See *full-height drive bay, half-height drive bay.*

drive designator   In DOS, an argument that specifies the drive to be affected by the command. The command FORMAT B:, for example, tells DOS to format the disk in drive B. The drive designator is B:.

driver   A program designed to operate a specific peripheral such as a monitor or printer. See *device driver.*

drop cap An initial letter of a chapter or paragraph, enlarged and positioned so that the top of the character is even with the top of the first line, and the rest of the character descends into the second and subsequent lines. See *initial*.

drop-down list box An industry-standard interface and graphical user interface (GUI), a list of command options that displays as a single-item text box until one selects the command, which causes a list of options to drop down (or pop up). After "dropping down" the list, the user can choose one of its options. The drop-down list box lets a programmer provide many options without taking up much space onscreen.

dropouts Characters lost in data transmission for some reason. On slower systems, for example, a fast typist may find that some typed characters do not make it into a word processing program's data file; this is caused by an interruption of user input when the program must access the disk for some reason. The user soon learns to pause when the drive activity light comes on.

dropout type In typography, white characters printed on a black background.

drop shadow A shadow placed behind an image, slightly offset horizontally and vertically, creating the illusion that the topmost image has been lifted off the surface of the page.

drunk mouse A mouse with a pointer that seems to jump wildly and irritatingly just as one is about to select something. Many users suspect that this malady is caused by a virus, but its most common cause is dirt in the mouse's inner mechanism.

DS/DD A double-sided disk that uses double-density formatting. Now nearly obsolete.

DS/HD A double-sided disk that uses high-density (HD) formatting. Modern 3 ½-inch disks are usually DS/HD.

D-shell connector The connector from the monitor that plugs into the video adapter. Video Graphics Array (VGA) and Super VGA video adapters use 15-pin D-shell connectors; older video standards use 9-pin D-shell plugs.

DSL Acronym for Digital Subscriber Line. Generic term for a family of digital telephony standards that homes and businesses to connect to the Internet at high speeds by means of regular telephone lines, without interfering with voice calls. The most widely used DSL standard currently is asymmetric digital subscriber line (ADSL), which offers faster downloads than uploads (hence the term "asymmetric"). See *ADSL, G.Lite, HDSL*.

DSMR See *dual-stripe magneto-resistive (DSMR) head*.

DSP See *digital signal processor*.

DSS Acronym for decision support system. A complex program designed to help corporate management discover the data needed to make decisions. To be useful, a DSS must reduce the complexity of the retrieved data so that the overall trends are visibly and accurately available to management.

DSTN Acronym for Double-Layer Supertwist Nematic. A passive matrix display, used mainly in notebook computers, that uses two superimposed LCD (liquid crystal display) layers to improve color rendition. Considered inferior to active matrix.

DSVD Acronym for Digital Simultaneous Voice Video. A protocol for high-speed modems that enables users of two DSVD modems to converse via real-time voice communication while they exchange data. This feature is particularly attractive to computer game players.

DTD Acronym for document type definition. In SGML, a complete definition of a markup language that defines the elements of the document as well as the tags used to identify them. HTML is defined by a standard DTD maintained by the World Wide Web Consortium (W3C).

DTE   See *Data Terminal Equipment*.

DTE speed   The rate, measured in bits per second (bps), at which a Data Terminal Equipment (DTE) device, such as a personal computer, can send data to a Data Communication Equipment (DCE) device such as a modem.

DTP   See *desktop publishing*.

dual-actuator hard disk   A hard disk design that incorporates two read/write heads. Dual-actuator hard disks have better access times than standard hard disks because they have half the latency: A needed bit of data is always less than half a revolution away from one of the heads instead of a full revolution away in a standard hard disk. See *latency, read/write head*.

dual boot system   A computer that enables the user to choose between two operating systems at boot time.

Dual Independent Bus   See *DIB*.

Dual In-Line Memory Module   See *DIMM*.

dual in-line package (DIP)   A standard packaging and mounting device for integrated circuits. DIP is the favored packaging for dynamic random access memory (DRAM) chips, for example. The package, made of hard plastic material, encloses the circuit; the circuit's leads are connected to downward-pointing pins that stick in two parallel rows. The pins are designed to fit securely into a socket; one also can solder them directly to a circuit board. See *single in-line package (SIP)*.

dual-issue processor   Type of central processing unit (CPU) that can process two instructions simultaneously, each in its own pipeline. See *superscalar architecture*.

dual-scan   An improved passive-matrix LCD design in which the display is refreshed twice as fast as standard passive-matrix LCDs (liquid crystal displays).

Although dual-scanned passive-matrix displays have better brightness and contrast than standard passive-matrix displays, they are generally inferior to active-matrix displays. See *DSTN*.

dual-stripe magneto-resistive (DSMR) head   A new read/write head design for hard disks that reduces their sensitivity to interference from the outside environment. DSMR heads have separate portions for reading and writing, and they pack data tightly onto disks.

dual-tone multifrequency (DTMF) tones   The tones generated by a touch-tone telephone during dialing. Most dial-up modems generate DTMF tones as well.

dual y-axis graph   In presentation and analytical graphics, a line or column graph that uses two y-axes (value axes) when comparing two sets of data measured differently.

dumb terminal   See *terminal*.

dump   To transfer the contents of memory to a printer or disk storage. Programmers use memory dumps while debugging programs to see exactly what the computer is doing when the dump occurs. In graphics, a screen dump prints or saves what is currently displayed onscreen. See *core dump, Print Screen (PrtScr), screen dump*.

dumpster diving   A method of gaining unauthorized access into a computer system by finding passwords or other sensitive information in an organization's trash.

duplex   See *full-duplex, half-duplex*.

duplex printing   Printing or reproducing a document on both sides of the page so that the verso (left) and recto (right) pages face each other after the document is bound. See *binding offset*.

duplication station   A printer/scanner combination that can serve as a light-duty photocopier.

Duron A high-performance 32-bit microprocessor line created by Advanced Micro Devices (AMD) to compete with Intel's budget-line Celeron microprocessors. Manufactured using a .18 micron process, the Duron incorporates 25 million transistors, 128K of onboard primary (L1) cache, and clock speeds of up to 1 GHz. See *Athlon*.

DV See *digital video*.

DVD Acronym for Digital Video Disc (also called Digital Versatile Disc). A CD-ROM format capable of storing up to a maximum of 17GB of data; enough for a full-length feature movie. This format is expected to replace current CD-ROM drives in computers, as well as VHS video tapes and laser discs. DVD players are compatible with existing CD-ROMs.

DVD region locking An access control mechanism used in commercial DVD movie discs that specifies the geographical region in which a DVD may be viewed; for example, Region 1 includes the U.S. and Canada, while Region 2 includes Europe and Japan. The scheme is intended to prevent non-North American consumers from viewing DVDs of movies that have not yet been released to theaters in their regions. Some consumer electronic manufacturers sell DVD players that are capable of circumventing region locking. Numerous computer utilities are available that are capable of circumventing region locking mechanisms in DVD-ROM drives. Region locking circumvention may be illegal in some countries, including the U.S. See *deCSS, DVD, DVD-ROM*.

DVD-R Acronym for Digital Video Disc-Recorder. A standard for DVD discs and player/recorder mechanisms that enables users to record in the DVD format. Like CD-R drives, DVD-R drives can record on DVD-R discs only once.

DVD-RAM Acronym for Digital Video Disc–Random Access Memory. A read/write version of the Digital Video Disc (DVD) standard that enables computer users to create DVD-ROM discs containing up to 2.6GB of data.

DVD-ROM Acronym for Digital Video Disc–Read Only Memory. A Digital Video Disc (DVD) format capable of storing up to 4.7GB of data, transferring data at higher speeds, and reading Digital Video Disc and existing CD-ROM discs. Future DVD-ROM drives will offer capacities up to 17GB.

DVD-ROM drive A read-only drive designed to read the data encoded on DVD-ROM discs and to transfer this data to a computer.

DVD-RW Acronym for Digital Video Disc-Read/Write. A standard for DVD discs and player/recorder mechanisms that enables users to record in the DVD format. Like CD-RW drives, DVD-RW drives can record multiple times on the same DVD-RW disc.

DVI Acronym for Digital Video Interface. A standard for digital video adapters and digital monitors that is expected to supplant the current VGA-derived analog standards which are in widespread use, such as SuperVGA (SVGA). By eliminating the processing overhead involved in digital to analog conversion, DVI offers improved performance, higher resolutions (such as 2048 × 1536) and the elimination of artifacts (such as flicker and ghosting) associated with analog display technologies.

Dvorak keyboard An alternative keyboard layout in which 70 percent of the keystrokes take place on the home row (compared to 32 percent with the standard QWERTY layout). According to its proponents, a Dvorak keyboard is easier to learn and faster to use. However, every time one returns to a QWERTY keyboard, he or she must go back to the hunt-and-peck method.

dye sublimation A high-quality color printing process in which tiny heating elements are used to evaporate pigments from a plastic film and fuse them to the paper.

The result is a photographic-quality image with brilliant color and good definition. Dye sublimation printers are expensive, and so is the pigment-bearing film.

dynamic astigmatism control See *dynamic beam forming.*

dynamic bandwidth allocation (DBA) In ISDN, a method of allocating bandwidth on-the-fly so that the line can handle data and voice communications simultaneously. DBA works with the Multilink Point-to-Point Protocol (MPPP) and enables an ISDN user to accept a call on one of the lines even if both are being used to download or upload data. See *BRI, ISDN.*

dynamic beam forming A monitor design that ensures that electron beams are perfectly round when they strike the display, no matter where onscreen the yoke steers them. Without dynamic beam forming, electron beams would be elliptical at the edges of the display—like a flashlight beam striking the ground at an angle—and poor focus would result.

dynamic checking In high-level programming languages, a type checking procedure.

Dynamic Data Exchange See *DDE.*

dynamic HTML See *DHTML.*

dynamic link A method of linking data so that it is shared by two programs. When data is changed in one program, the data is also changed in the other when an update command is used. See *cold link, hot link.*

dynamic link library See *DLL.*

dynamic object A document or portion of a document pasted or inserted into a destination document using object linking and embedding (OLE) techniques. A linked object is automatically updated if one makes changes to the source document. An embedded object includes information to enable one to open the application used to create the object and edit the object. See *embedded object, linked object, OLE.*

dynamic random access memory See *DRAM.*

dynamic range The range of colors a scanner can detect and, along with color depth, one of the main indicators of a scanner's quality. Although any 24-bit scanner can record 16.7 million colors and 265 levels of gray, a 24-bit scanner with a narrow dynamic range could not detect both pale shades of yellow and very dark indigo hues.

dynamic typing In a programming language, a form of type checking in which data types are checked just before the operation is performed. Most interpreted scripting languages, such as JavaScript, are dynamically typed. See *interpreted programming language, JavaScript, type, type checking, typing.*

E

Easter egg A message or animation buried within a program and accessible only through an undocumented procedure. These are inserted by programmers as a joke. Buried in the Macintosh system, for example, is the message "Help! Help! We're being held prisoner in a system software factory!"

EBCDIC (Pronounced *ebb-see-dick*.) Acronym for Extended Binary Coded Decimal Interchange Code. A character set coding scheme that represents 256 standard characters. IBM mainframes use EBCDIC coding; personal computers use ASCII coding. Networks that link personal computers to IBM mainframes must include a translating device to mediate between the two systems.

e-book A book made available in digital form and designed to be read using special e-book software, some of which preserve the book's original layout and design. E-books can be read on a variety of PCs (desktops, notebooks, tablets, and handhelds), PDAs, and dedicated e-book readers using specially designed e-book software, such as Microsoft Reader. E-book market growth is currently hampered by competition among several incompatible file-formatting standards. An emerging open e-book standard, Open eBook (OeB), may encourage further development in this area. See *dedicated e-book reader, OeB.*

ECC Acronym for error checking and correction. A feature of memory chips and motherboards that performs automatic parity checking on parity-enabled memory chips; in contrast to noncorrecting forms of parity checking, the detection of a minor error will not shut down the system.

echoplex A communications protocol in which the receiving station acknowledges and confirms the reception by echoing the message back to the transmitting station. See *full-duplex, half-duplex.*

ECMAScript See *JavaScript.*

e-commerce The use of the Internet for business-to-business and business-to-consumer transactions. E-commerce is made possible by encryption technologies such as SSL (Secure Sockets Layer).

ECP Acronym for Extended Capabilities Port. An improvement on the parallel port that supports two-way communication between the computer and a peripheral device. For example, a scanner can use an ECP to tell the CPU that it has a paper jam and needs attention. The ECP may eventually displace the competing enhanced parallel port (EPP) standard, although many motherboards currently support both standards.

ECPA See *Electronic Communications Privacy Act.*

edge connector The part of an adapter that plugs into an expansion slot.

edgelighting A scheme for shining light at an LCD (liquid crystal display) to improve readability in bright-light conditions. Unlike backlighting, which shines light from behind the LCD, edgelighting relies on shining lights around the borders of an LCD. Edgelighting is considered less effective than backlighting.

EDI Acronym for Electronic Data Interchange. A widely employed standard for the electronic exchange of business documents, such as invoices and purchase orders. The Data Interchange Standards Association (DISA) developed the standard. Using field codes, such as BT for Bill To or ST for Ship To, EDI specifies the format in which data is being transmitted electronically. By ensuring that all EDI-based communications have the same data in the same place, this protocol enables companies to exchange purchase orders and other documents electronically.

edit decision list (EDL) In digital video, a list of editing decisions.

edit mode A program mode that makes correcting text and data easier. In Lotus

1-2-3, for example, pressing F2 displays the contents of a cell in the second line of the control panel, where one can use editing keys to correct errors or add characters. Few programs have special edit modes anymore because they allow editing in their normal modes.

editor   See *text editor.*

EDO RAM   Acronym for Extended Data Output Random Access Memory. A type of dynamic RAM (DRAM), the main memory of the computer, that is significantly faster than conventional DRAM. Many high-end modern computers have abandoned EDO RAM in favor of even faster such as SDRAM (synchronous DRAM) and DDR-SDRAM.

.edu   An Internet domain name denoting a U.S. college or university.

edutainment   Application programs designed to tell the user about a subject but presented in the form of a game that is sufficiently entertaining or challenging to hold the user's interest. A long-time best-selling example of edutainment is the "Microsoft Flight Simulator," which many people buy to play as a game but which many flight schools use as a prelude to flight instruction in the air. Almost as well known is the Carmen Sandiego series of games, including "Where in the World Is Carmen Sandiego?" and "Where in Europe Is Carmen Sandiego?".

EEMS   See *Enhanced Expanded Memory Specification.*

EEPROM   Acronym for Electrical Erasable Programmable Read-Only Memory. A type of read-only memory (ROM) that can be erased and reprogrammed by applying an electrical current to the memory chips and then writing new instructions to them. See *EPROM, flash memory.*

EFF   Acronym for Electronic Frontier Foundation. A nonprofit public advocacy organization dedicated to ensuring the survival of privacy and civil liberties in the computer age. Spurred by an ill-conceived

and heavy-handed Secret Service program that resulted in the seizure of hackers' computer systems throughout the United States, the organization's founders, Mitchell Kapor and John Perry Barlowe, initially contributed to hackers' legal defense funds and have since developed an extensive public education and lobbying program.

effective resolution   The resolution of a printer's output on which resolution enhancement has been performed. For example, some printers print at 600 dpi, but they vary the size of the dots placed on the page to achieve an effective resolution as good as a 1200 dpi printer could produce.

effective transmission rate   The rate at which a modem that uses on-the-fly data compression communicates data to another modem. Data compression ensures that a given amount of data can be communicated at a given speed in a shorter amount of time than uncompressed data, so modems that use on-the-fly compression have higher throughput than modems that do not.

egosurfing   Searching the Web for pages that mention one's name.

EGP   An Internet protocol that defines the routing of Internet data between a local area network and the wider Internet. This protocol has been superceded by the Border Gateway Protocol (BGP). See *BGP.*

EIDE   See *Enhanced IDE.*

EISA   A 32-bit expansion bus design introduced by a consortium of computer makers to counter IBM's proprietary Micro Channel Bus. Unlike the Micro Channel Bus, the EISA bus is downwardly compatible with existing 16-bit peripherals, such as disk drives and display adapters. Once state-of-the-art in personal computing, EISA machines have been eclipsed by the PCI bus. See *PCI.*

EISA-2   An improved version of the EISA expansion bus that can transfer data at 132 Mbps. The earlier EISA standard could transfer data at only 33 Mbps. Like EISA, EISA-2 has been mostly replaced by the

PCI standard, but it remains in some high-end Ethernet servers.

Electrical Erasable Programmable Read-Only Memory See *EEPROM.*

electrocutaneous feedback A primitive method of providing tactile feedback in virtual reality systems by administering a low-voltage shock to the user's skin. The user feels a mild buzz. Varying the voltage and frequency of the current produces variations in the buzz that the user can learn to discriminate.

electron gun A cathode (electron emitter) in the back of a cathode ray tube (CRT) that releases a stream of electrons toward the display. Steered by the yoke, the electrons "paint" an image on the display. Color monitors have three electron guns—red, green, and blue—while monochrome monitors have only one.

electronic book See *e-book.*

Electronic Communications Privacy Act (ECPA) A U.S. federal law enacted in 1986 that prevents U.S. investigative agencies from intercepting e-mail messages or reading such messages that are temporarily stored in interim storage devices (up to 180 days) without first obtaining a warrant. In a major omission that might stem from the legislators' lack of technical knowledge, the act does not prevent such agencies from obtaining and reading copies of e-mail permanently stored in archives. Investigators used this loophole to obtain Oliver North's e-mail messages to other White House officials involved in the Iran-Contra scandal. The act does not prevent any other persons or agencies from intercepting or reading e-mail. See *confidentiality.*

Electronic Data Interchange See *EDI.*

Electronic Frontier Foundation See *EFF.*

electronic mail See *e-mail.*

electronic warfare In information warfare, the use of electronic devices to destroy or damage computer systems.

electrostatic printer A printer that relies on the attraction between oppositely charged particles to draw toner to paper. Laser printers and LED printers are electrostatic printers.

element In HTML, a distinctive component of a document's structure, such as a title, heading, or list. HTML divides elements into two categories: head elements (such as the document's title) and body elements (headings, paragraphs, links, and text).

elevator seeking In hard drives, a way to sort data requests to minimize jumping between tracks. In an elevator-seeking scheme, the drive handles data requests in track order—that is, it gets needed data from inner tracks first and then from the outer tracks. Elevator seeking minimizes access time.

elite A typeface (usually on a typewriter) that prints 12 characters per inch (cpi). The other common typewriter font is pica, which prints at 10 characters per inch. See *pitch.*

em A distance equal to the width of the capital letter *M* in a given typeface.

eMac A mid-line desktop Macintosh computer, based on the G4 processor, that is optimized for multimedia applications. The system includes a built-in 17-inch CRT display, a SuperDrive capable of reading and burning CDs and DVDs, and other features designed to compete effectively with comparably-priced Microsoft Windows XP systems. See *G4, SuperDrive.*

emacs A Unix-based text editor that is sometimes configured as the default editor on Unix systems. Programmed in LISP, emacs is an excellent hacker's tool but can be difficult for users accustomed to user-friendly word processing programs.

e-mail The use of a computer network to send and receive messages. Also called electronic mail. Although transmission is instantaneous or nearly so, the message may not be received until the recipient logs on and receives notice that mail has arrived.

E-mail can be implemented on local area networks (LANs) and on wide area networks (WANs), such as the Internet. E-mail is the most popular Internet application and is well on the way to supplanting first-class mail as the preferred means for transmitting personal and business messages between individuals. To implement e-mail, e-mail clients and e-mail servers are needed. By means of mailing lists, e-mail can be used to send messages to many people at once. See *e-mail address, e-mail client, e-mail server, IMAP, mailing list, MIME, POP-3, SMTP.*

e-mail address   A series of characters that precisely identifies the location of a person's electronic mailbox. On the Internet, e-mail addresses consist of a mailbox name (such as rebecca) followed by an "at" sign (@) and the computer's domain name (as in rebecca@hummer.virginia.edu).

e-mail client   A program or program module that provides e-mail services for computer users, including receiving mail in a locally stored inbox, sending e-mail to other network users, replying to received messages, and storing received messages. The better programs include address books to facilitate message addressing, filters that route low-priority mail into folders, the capability to process and display attachments (binary files such as data files and graphics), and the capability to compose and read messages coded in HTML. Leading e-mail clients include Microsoft Outlook, Microsoft Outlook Express, and Eudora. Synonymous with user agent (UA).

e-mail reflector   A program that enables users to create an electronic mailing list. The program works by copying a received message to every e-mail user who is currently subscribed to the list. Leading programs include Majordomo and ListServ. Synonymous with list server.

e-mail server   A program that performs either or both of the following tasks: sending e-mail messages to their destinations on the network, or receiving incoming mail and storing it until the user logs on and accesses the waiting mail. Many organizations use proprietary e-mail servers such as the Microsoft Outlook server or Lotus cc:Mail; these servers include features such as scheduling and workgroup collaboration. Servers for Internet e-mail conform to the IMAP or POP-3 protocols (for incoming mail) or the SMTP protocol (for outgoing mail). See *IMAP, POP-3, SMTP.*

embed   In object linking and embedding (OLE), to place an object in a document. See *embedded object, link.*

embedded chart   In Microsoft Excel, a chart created within a worksheet rather than as a separate chart sheet.

embedded formatting command   A text formatting command placed directly in the text to be formatted. In some programs, the command does not affect the text's onscreen appearance, which can make the program more difficult to use. In other programs, such as WordPerfect, only a few embedded commands—full justification or a font change—do not change the screen display. Microsoft Windows applications include a graphical display that immediately displays formatting. Synonymous with off-screen formatting. See *hidden codes, onscreen formatting, what-you-see-is-what-you-get (WYSIWYG).*

embedded object   In object linking and embedding (OLE), an object wholly inserted, or embedded, into a destination document created by an application other than that which created the destination document. The object can be text, a chart, a graphic, or sound. See *linked object, OLE.*

em dash   In typography a lengthy dash (equal to the width of the capital letter *M* in a given typeface) that is used to introduce parenthetical remarks. The following sentence contains em dashes: The butler—or someone who knows what the butler knows—must have done it.

emergency disk   A floppy disk that contains a minimal version of the operating system sufficient restore access to hard disk files after a major operating system failure. Synonymous with boot disk.

em fraction A single-character fraction that occupies one em of space and uses a diagonal stroke (/) rather than a piece fraction made from three or more characters (1/4). See *en fraction*.

EMM See *expanded memory manager*.

EMM386.EXE In MS-DOS running on a computer with an 80386 or higher microprocessor and extended memory, an expanded memory emulator that enables DOS applications to use the extended memory as though it were expanded memory (EMS). EMM386.EXE also enables the user to load device drivers and programs into the upper memory area when used along with the DOS=HIGH,UMB and the DEVICE=HIMEM.SYS commands.

emoticon See *smiley*.

emphasis The use of a special type style—such as underlining, italic, bold, or small caps typefaces—to highlight a word or phrase.

EMS Acronym for Expanded Memory Specification. An expanded memory standard that allows the programs that recognize the standard to work with more than 640K RAM under DOS. The LIM EMS Version 4.0 standard, introduced in 1987, supports up to 32MB of expanded memory and lets programs run in expanded memory.

emulation The duplication within a device of another device's functional capability, or a device designed to work exactly like another. In telecommunications, for example, a personal computer emulates a dumb terminal (a terminal without its own microprocessor) for online communication with a distant computer. With printers, lesser-known brands emulate popular models such as Hewlett-Packard's LaserJet line.

emulation sensing See *automatic emulation switching, automatic network switching*.

emulation switching See *automatic emulation switching*.

en In typesetting, a unit of measurement that equals half the width of an em space, which is the width of the capital letter *M* in a typeface. En dashes are used in place of the English words *to* or *through*, as in January 9–January 23 or Pages 63–68. They also are used as minus signs, as in −30 degrees Fahrenheit. See *em dash*.

Encapsulated PostScript (EPS) file A high-resolution graphic image stored in the PostScript page description language. The EPS standard enables users to transfer high-resolution graphics images between applications. One can size EPS images without sacrificing image quality. A major drawback of EPS graphics is that to print them, one usually needs a PostScript-compatible laser printer. A second drawback is that with most application programs, one cannot view the image onscreen unless he or she attaches a screen image to it. To provide an alternative to expensive PostScript printers, developers have created programs such as LaserGo, Inc.'s GoScript that interpret and print EPS files on non-PostScript printers. See *PostScript*.

encapsulation **1.** In computer networks such as the Internet, the process by which transmitted data is altered as it moves down the computer's protocol stack. As each layer's protocols alter the data, it is translated into a form that can be sent out over the network. At the receiving computer, this process is reversed so that the data is restored in such a form that it can be passed to an application and made intelligible to the user. See *OSI Reference Model, TCP/IP*. **2.** In object-oriented programming, one of the seven fundamental principles of the object model. The encapsulation principle states that the details of an object's inner workings (the way in which its data are stored and its behaviors are functionally coded and implemented) should not be available to other objects; instead, the object employs an interface that, by means of a common communication protocol, enables other objects to make use of the object's methods without their having to know anything about how the methods work. The encapsulation principle is based on long experience with complex, sequential programs, in which major errors are likely to occur if functions are accessed in a way that was not predicted when the program was written. See *object, object model, object-oriented programming.*

encryption In cryptography, the process of converting a message into a ciphertext (an encrypted message) by using a key so that the message appears to be nothing but gibberish. However, the intended recipient can apply the key to decrypt and read the message. See *decryption, public key cryptography, rot-13.*

encryption algorithm A procedure for scrambling (encrypting) data so that it cannot be read by anyone other than its intended recipient. The two major types of encryption algorithms are symmetric key encryption algorithms, which require a secure channel to transmit the decoding key to the user, and public key encryption.

encryption engine An encryption program that can perform encryption and decryption services for two or more compatible applications.

End key A key on IBM PC–compatible keyboards with functions that vary from program to program. Frequently, pressing the End key moves the cursor to the end of the line or the bottom of the screen, but the assignment of this key is up to the programmer.

endless loop A fundamental programming error in which the computer is made to cycle in a repeating loop, which cannot be broken without shutting down the computer.

endnote A footnote positioned at the end of a document or section rather than the bottom of a page. Many word processing programs let the user choose between footnotes and endnotes.

end of file See *EOF.*

end of line See *EOL.*

end user The person who uses a computer system and its application programs at home or at work to perform tasks and produce results.

end user license agreement See *EULA.*

Energy Star A U.S. Environmental Protection Agency (EPA) program that seeks to reduce energy waste by encouraging monitor and printer manufacturers to reduce the amount of electricity that their devices require. Energy Star devices typically have a sleep mode that reduces their power consumption when they are not being used. Energy Star devices, identifiable by a blue and green EPA sticker, can save their owners hundreds of dollars in electrical costs each year. See *power management.*

en fraction A single-character fraction that occupies one en of space and uses a horizontal stroke, like this: ½. Contrast to em fractions, which are built with regular-width characters, like this: 1/2.

engine A program that performs services for other applications, such as encryption or file compression.

enhanced 101-key keyboard See *enhanced keyboard.*

Enhanced ATA See *Enhanced IDE (EIDE).*

Enhanced CD A standard created by Microsoft Corporation for audio compact discs. This standard enables audio CD publishers to include digital information on compact discs; for example, a performer could include pictures and video clips on an audio CD that can be displayed on a PC.

Enhanced Expanded Memory Specification (EEMS) A version of the original Lotus-Intel-Microsoft Expanded Memory Specification (LIM EMS) that is enhanced to enable DOS applications to use more than 640K of memory.

Enhanced Graphics Adapter See *EGA*.

Enhanced Graphics Display A color digital monitor designed to work only with an EGA video adapter.

Enhanced IDE (EIDE) An improved version of the IDE disk-interface standard that dictates how hard drives and CD-ROM drives connect to the rest of the computer. The EIDE standard allows hard drives as large as 8.4GB, while IDE supports hard drives no larger than 528MB. Also, the EIDE standard enables one to connect four hard drives to his or her computer rather than two.

enhanced keyboard The modern keyboard standard for PCs. An enhanced keyboard has 101 keys, including a numeric keypad, 12 function keys, and several navigation keys. Largely replaced by the 104-key keyboard.

enhanced parallel port See *EPP*.

enhanced serial port (ESP) A speedy serial port that uses dedicated random access memory (RAM) to move data quickly.

Enhanced System Device Interface See *ESDI*.

enterprise resource planning See *ERP*.

Enter/Return A key that confirms a command, sending the command to the central processing unit (CPU). In word processing, the Enter/Return key starts a new paragraph. Early PC keyboards labeled this key with a hooked left arrow. On more recent AT and enhanced keyboards, the word *Enter* is printed on the key. (The word *Return* appears on Macintosh keyboards.) Most PC-compatible keyboards have an Enter key to the right of the typing area and a second one in the numeric keypad's lower-right corner. These two keys have identical functions in most but not all programs. Synonymous with carriage return.

entity In the Hypertext Markup Language (HTML), a code that represents a non-ASCII character, such as an accented character from a foreign language.

entity relationship diagram See *ERD*.

entry-level system A computer system considered to be the minimal system for using serious computer application programs, such as spreadsheet programs or word processing software. The definition of an entry-level system changes rapidly. Twenty years ago, an entry-level system—incapable of running the latest versions of today's most popular software—had at least one 360K floppy disk drive, a monochrome text monitor, and 256K of random access memory (RAM). Today's entry-level systems have a Pentium III or Pentium 4 microprocessor, a 30GB hard drive, a 17-inch-high resolution monitor, and at least 128MB of RAM.

entry line In a spreadsheet program, a text entry area where the user can type a value or formula. The program does not insert the characters into the current cell until the user presses Enter. The entry line also facilitates editing because formulas do not appear in cells. Synonymous with formula bar.

envelope printer A printer designed specifically to print names, addresses, and U.S. Postal Service POSTNET bar codes on business envelopes. Businesses that use the bar codes receive an attractive discount on postal rates and receive faster and more accurate delivery of their business correspondence. Many laser and inkjet printers can print POSTNET codes. Envelope printers, however, do a better job of handling high-volume printing jobs.

environment The hardware and operating system for application programs, such as the Macintosh environment. In MS-DOS, the environment also is a space in memory reserved for storing variables that applications running on a system can use. See *environment variable*.

environment variable An instruction stored in the computer's memory that makes certain configuration settings or values available to applications.

EOF   Abbreviation for "end of file." This abbreviation is used in scripts and programming languages to denote the physical end of a file.

EOL   Abbreviation for "end of line." A control character that demarcates the end of a line of text in a text file.

EPIC   Acronym for Explicitly Parallel Instruction Computing. A design philosophy that underlies Intel Corporation's 64-bit microprocessors, including the Itanium. In this design philosophy, the compiler is given the task of deciding which instructions should be executed first rather than leaving this task to superscalar processes implemented in processor hardware, such as branch prediction. See *branch prediction, Itanium, RISC, superscalar architecture.*

EPP   Acronym for enhanced parallel port. An improvement on the parallel port, which enables two-way communication. Using an EPP, for example, a printer can tell a microprocessor how much paper or toner remains in its bins. The Extended Capabilities Port (ECP) might eventually replace the EPP, but for now, many motherboards support both standards.

EPP/ECP port   An improved version of the parallel port that supports both the enhanced parallel port (EPP) and Extended Capabilities Port (ECP) standards. EPP/ECP ports can transmit data very fast, as fast as an Ethernet network interface card.

EPROM   Acronym for erasable programmable read-only memory. A read-only memory (ROM) chip that can be programmed and reprogrammed with a special electronic device. EPROM chips are packaged in a clear plastic case so that the contents can be erased using ultraviolet light. The erasability of EPROM chips matters to computer manufacturers, who often find that they need to reprogram ROM chips containing bugs. Programmable read-only memory (PROM) chips, which cannot be reprogrammed, must be discarded when a programming error is discovered.

EPS   See *Encapsulated PostScript (EPS) file.*

equation typesetting   Codes in a word processing document that cause the program to print multiline equations, including mathematical symbols such as integrals and summation signs. The best word processing programs, such as WordPerfect and Microsoft Word, offer what-you-see-is-what-you-get (WYSIWYG) onscreen equation editors, which allow a person see the equation as he or she builds it.

erasable optical disc drive   Also called a floptical. A read/write data storage medium that uses a laser and reflected light to store and retrieve data on an optical disc. Unlike CD-ROM drives and write-once, read-many (WORM) drives, erasable optical disc drives can be used like hard disks: One can write and erase data repeatedly. Storage capacities can exceed 9 GB per disc. They are expensive and much slower than hard drives, however. See *secondary storage.*

erasable programmable read-only memory   See *EPROM.*

e rate   See *vertical refresh rate.*

ERD   Acronym for entity relationship diagram. In the design of information systems, a diagram that shows all the entities (organizations, departments, users, programs, and data) that play roles in the system, as well as the relationships between those entities.

ergonomic keyboard   A keyboard designed to reduce strain on the wrists, which can result in repetitive stress injury (RSI). Some ergonomic keyboards, such as the Microsoft Natural Keyboard, angle keys away from the center, while others put keys in pits into which a naturally curved hand can fit. See *carpal tunnel syndrome, repetitive stress injury (RSI).*

ergonomics   The science of designing machines, tools, computers, and physical work areas so that people find them easy and healthful to use.

ERP Acronym for enterprise resource planning. A computerized business management networking technology that provides on-demand information and process synchronization involving all facets of an enterprise, including planning, supply chain management, manufacturing, sales, and marketing. In the past, corporations developed their own ERP tools, but these projects were expensive and frequently failed to produce a workable system. As a result, a major market has developed for vendors (such as Baan and SAP) of ERP applications.

error **1.** A discrepancy between a value present in a computer system and the true, specified, or theoretically correct value. Errors may be caused by a variety of factors, including system failures, faults, and operator mistakes. **2.** A condition that interrupts the normal execution of a program. If programmers fail to anticipate errors, the results may compromise system dependability. See *error checking, error trapping*. **3.** In engineering, a discrepancy between an actual value and a statistical prediction of that value. See *system error*.

error checking A procedure that examines transmitted, computed, or entered data to ensure that errors are not inadvertently introduced into a computer system. Errors are detected by adding redundant data (such as a parity bit) that can be examined to determine whether the data is likely to be correct. Examples of error-checking procedures are parity tests and cyclic redundancy checks (CRCs). See *cyclic redundancy check (CRC), error, parity, parity checking*.

error condition In a computer system, a state or condition that deviates from the system's intended behavior. For example, if a user attempts to open a file on a disk that is not present on the system, an error condition results. If programmers fail to predict and handle error conditions, the result may adversely affect the system's dependability. See *error handling, error trapping*.

error correction In a computer system, a procedure that substitutes theoretically predicted values in place of incorrect values, as determined by the system's error-checking procedures. For example, audio CDs substitute predicted values if data becomes briefly unavailable for some reason (for example, if the mechanism is subjected to shock or the CD is dirty or scratched). See *error, error checking*.

error-correction protocol In modems, a method for filtering out line noise and repeating transmissions automatically if an error occurs. Error correction requires the use of sending and receiving modems that conform to the same error-correction protocols. When error correction is in use, a reliable link is established. Two widely used error-correcting protocols are MNP-4 and V.42. See *CCITT*.

error handling The way that a program copes with errors, such as the failure to access data on a disk or a user's failure to press the right key. A poorly written program might fail to handle errors at all, leading to a system crash. The best programmers anticipate possible errors and provide information that helps the user solve the problem. See *error trapping*.

error message In application programs, an onscreen message informing one that the program cannot carry out a requested operation.

error trapping An application's capability to recognize an error and perform a predetermined action in response to that error; applications with poor error trapping may crash frequently.

Esc A key that application programs can implement in various ways. In most applications, pressing Esc cancels a command or an operation.

escape ASCII character 27, which is assigned on most computer keyboards to the Esc key. See *Esc*.

escape character In programming, a character (such as a slash mark) that is entered to indicate that the following character should be taken literally.

escape sequence   A series of characters, combining Esc (ASCII value 27) with one or more ASCII characters, that are used to control peripheral devices (such as printers, displays, or modems). The escape sequence can be embedded in a program or, in some cases, directly entered by the user.

ESDI   An acronym for Enhanced System Device Interface. An interface standard for hard disk drives. Drives that use the ESDI standard transfer at 10 to 15 Mbps, which is two to three times as fast as the earlier ST-506/ST-412 interface standard. Faster, more flexible IDE drives have almost totally replaced ESDI drives.

ESP   See *enhanced serial port.*

e-tailing   The use of the Internet to market retail goods, such as books and automobiles.

Ethernet   A local area network (LAN) hardware, communication, and cabling standard originally developed by Xerox Corporation that can link up to 1,024 nodes in a bus network. A high-speed standard using a baseband (single-channel) communication technique, Ethernet provides for a raw data transfer rate of 10 Mbps, with actual throughput in the range of 2 to 3 Mbps. Ethernet uses carrier sense multiple access with collision detection (CSMA/CD) techniques to prevent network failures when two devices try to access the network at the same time. See *AppleTalk, Fast Ethernet.*

EtherTalk   An implementation of Ethernet local area network (LAN) hardware, jointly developed by Apple and 3Com, and designed to work with the AppleShare network operating system. EtherTalk transmits data through coaxial cables at the Ethernet rate of 10 Mbps, in contrast to AppleTalk's rate of 230 Kbps.

e-trading site   On the Internet, an online brokerage that enables investors to buy and sell stocks without a human broker's intervention.

ETX/ACK handshaking   See *handshaking.*

Eudora   See *e-mail client.*

EULA   Acronym for end user license agreement. The most common type of license provided with commercial software. Typically, the license denies ownership of the software because ownership would entail first sale rights under traditional copyright law. (According to the first sale doctrine, a person who purchases a copyrighted work is subsequently free to sell the work to another person.) Additional provisions typically specify that the program can be used only by one person on one computer and that the software publisher accepts no responsibility for losses attributable to the use of the software. See *first sale, shrink-wrap license, UCITA.*

European Laboratory for Particle Physics   See *CERN.*

even parity   In asynchronous communications, an error-checking technique that sets an extra bit (called a parity bit) to 1 if the number of 1 digits in a 1-byte data item adds up to an even number. The parity bit is set to 0 if the number of 1 digits adds up to an odd number. See *odd parity, parity checking.*

event   In an event-driven environment, an action, such as moving the mouse or clicking a mouse button, that generates a message. See *event handler.*

event-driven environment   A program or operating system that normally functions in an idle loop, waiting for events such as a mouse click, keyboard input, or a message from a device to occur. When an event occurs, the program exits the idle loop and executes the program code designed to handle the specific event. This code is called an event handler. After handling the event, the program returns to the idle loop. Microsoft Windows and the Macintosh operating system (Mac OS) are event-driven environments.

event-driven language   A programming language that creates programs that respond to events, such as input, incoming data, or signals received from other applications.

Such programs keep the computer in an idle loop until an event occurs, at which time they execute code that is relevant to the event. See *object-oriented programming.*

event handler In an event-driven environment, a block of program code designed to handle the messages generated when a specific kind of event occurs, such as a mouse click.

exabyte (EB) A unit for measuring data storage capacity that is approximately equal to one quintillion (10^{18}) bytes; it is exactly equal to 1,152,921,504,606,846,976 (2^{60}) bytes or 1,024 petabytes. One exabyte is roughly equal to all the information generated worldwide in a six-month period. See *data storage capacity.*

Excel See *spreadsheet program.*

exception report In a transaction processing system (TPS), a document that alerts someone of unexpected developments, such as high demand for a product.

.EXE In MS-DOS and Windows, a file name extension that indicates that the file is an executable program.

executable Capable of being run on the computer; a script or a program. See *executable program.*

executable file See *executable program.*

executable program A program that is ready to run on a given computer. For a program to be executable, it first must be translated, usually by a compiler, into the machine language of a particular computer.

execute To carry out the instructions in an algorithm or program.

expand 1. In an outlining utility or a graphical file management utility (such as Windows Explorer), to reveal all the subordinate entries below the selected outline heading or directory. In Explorer, for example, one can expand a directory quickly by double-clicking the directory icon, a folder. 2. In file compression, synonymous with decompress.

expandability The capability of a computer system to accommodate more memory, additional disk drives, peripherals, or other devices that enhance its usefulness or performance. Synonymous with upgrade. Thanks to recent expansion bus technologies such as USB and IEEE 1394 (FireWire), most of today's personal computer systems are easily expanded; however, computer shoppers should note that some system upgrades may require physical slots (such as expansion slots or memory slots) on the computer's motherboard. If unused memory slots are not present, for example, the system's memory capacity may not be easily expanded without additional and unnecessary cost. For example, if the system is equipped with two 64 MB memory chips and two memory slots, an upgrade to 256 MB of memory will require discarding the 64 MB chips and installing two 128 MB chips. Expandability is not the same as scalability; a scalable system is able to accommodate more users without unacceptable performance degradation. See *expansion slot, scalability.*

expanded memory In older IBM PCs and compatibles running MS-DOS, a method of using more than 640K of random access memory (RAM). Expanded memory works by paging blocks of data into and out of a fixed location within conventional memory, creating the appearance of a larger memory (but at the sacrifice of overhead due to the processing operations). See *EMM386.EXE, extended memory.*

expanded memory board An adapter that adds expanded memory to an IBM PC–compatible computer. These were common in Intel 80286 computers but were rendered unnecessary by the Intel 80386, which was capable of using extended memory to simulate expanded memory as needed through EMM386.EXE.

expanded memory emulator A utility program for Intel 80386 and Intel 486 computers that uses extended memory to simulate expanded memory to accommodate older programs and the many games that require it. See *EMM386.EXE.*

expanded memory manager (EMM)
A utility program that manages expanded memory in an IBM PC–compatible computer equipped with an expanded memory board. See *EMM386.EXE*.

Expanded Memory Specification (EMS) See *Lotus-Intel-Microsoft Expanded Memory Specification (LIM EMS)*.

expanded type A typeface that places characters farther apart or that makes the characters wider so that there are fewer characters per inch (cpi). See *kerning*.

expansion board See *adapter*.

expansion bus An extension of the computer's data bus and address bus that includes several expansion slots for adapters. Peripheral Component Interconnect (PCI) and Accelerated Graphics Port (AGP) are the most popular expansion bus designs available today. See *Micro Channel Bus*, *motherboard*, *VESA local bus*.

expansion bus bottleneck A phenomenon that occurs when the microprocessor performs far better than the expansion bus and which results in poor overall computer system performance. The expansion bus bottleneck problem has been solved by fast expansion bus standards such as the Peripheral Component Inter-connect (PCI) standard.

expansion card See *adapter*.

expansion slot A receptacle connected to the computer's expansion bus, designed to accept adapters. Motherboards generally have several expansion slots. The slots in today's PCs are usually a combination of PCI and AGP slots.

expect statement In a communication program's login script, a statement that tells the dialer to wait for the service provider's computer to send certain characters (such as "Please type your password").

expert system A program that contains much of the knowledge used by an expert in a specific field and that assists nonexperts

as they try to solve problems. Expert systems contain a knowledge base expressed in a series of IF/THEN rules and an engine capable of drawing inferences from this knowledge base. The system prompts one to supply information needed to assess the situation and come to a conclusion. Most expert systems express conclusions with a confidence factor, ranging from speculation to educated guess to a firm conclusion. See *artificial intelligence (AI)*, *backward chaining*, *forward chaining*, *PROLOG*.

expiration date In Usenet, the date at which a post is set to expire. See *expired article*.

expired article In Usenet, an article that is still listed in the article selector, even though the Usenet system software has deleted the article because it has expired. One cannot read an expired article. See *expiration date*.

expired password A password that has exceeded the time period of its validity, as established by the system administrator.

Explicitly Parallel Instruction Computing See *EPIC*.

exploded pie graph A pie chart in which one or more of the slices is offset slightly (exploded) from the others to emphasize the data represented by the exploded slice. See *pie graph*.

export To save data in a format that another program can read. Most programs can export a document in ASCII format, which almost any program can read and use. When saving a document with a recent version of a word processing program, one can choose a format from a list of dozens. See *import*.

ext2 Abbreviation for Second Extended Filesystem. An advanced hierarchical file system developed for the Linux operating system and installed by default by most Linux distributions. Advanced features include a maximum file system size of 4TB, a maximum file size of 2GB, a maximum file name length of 255 characters, and support for three time/date stamps (date of creation, date of last modification, and date of last access). See *hierarchical file system, Linux*.

ext3 Abbreviation for Third Extended Filesystem. A version of the standard Linux file system, ext2, that incorporates journaled file system technology. See *journaled file system*.

Extended Binary Coded Decimal Interchange Code See *EBCDIC*.

Extended Capabilities Port See *ECP*.

extended character set In IBM PC–compatible computing, a 256-character set stored in a computer's read-only memory (ROM) that includes, in addition to the 128 ASCII character codes, a collection of foreign language, technical, and block graphics characters. The characters with numbers above ASCII code 128 sometimes are referred to as higher-order characters.

eXtended Graphics Array (XGA) A video standard intended to replace the 8514/A standard and to bring 1,024-pixel-by-768-line resolution to IBM and IBM PC–compatible displays. An XGA board equipped with sufficient memory (1MB or more) can display 65,536 colors at its low-resolution mode (640 × 480) and 256 colors at its high-resolution mode (1,024 × 768). For downward compatibility with software that supports earlier standards, XGA boards also support the Video Graphics Array (VGA) standard. See *SXGA, UXGA*

Extended Industry Standard Architecture See *EISA*.

extended keyboard The 101-key keyboard distributed with Macintosh computers, which includes a numeric keypad, up to 15 function keys, and cursor-control keys. It is very similar to the enhanced keyboard available with PCs. Replaced by the Apple Pro keyboard.

extended-level synthesizer A synthesizer that can play a minimum of 16 simultaneous notes on nine melodic instruments and 16 simultaneous notes on eight percussive instruments. See *base-level synthesizer*.

extended memory The random access memory (RAM), if any, above 1MB that usually is installed directly on the motherboard and that is directly accessible to the microprocessor. Windows 95/98 does not make a distinction between the first megabyte of memory and the extended memory; it is all one pool. See *expanded memory*.

extended memory manager A utility program that lets certain MS-DOS programs access extended memory. The programs must be written to conform to the eXtended Memory Specification (XMS) standard. See *conventional memory, HIMEM.SYS*.

eXtended Memory Specification (XMS) A set of standards and an operating environment that enables all programs to access extended memory. XMS requires a utility program known as an extended memory manager, such as HIMEM.SYS (which is provided with DOS 5.0 and higher).

extended VGA See *SVGA*.

extensible Capable of accepting new, user-defined commands.

eXtensible Markup Language See *XML*.

eXtensible Style Language See *XSL*.

extension A three-letter suffix (such as .BMP, .RTF, or .ASM) added to an MS-DOS file name that describes the file's contents. The extension is optional and is separated from the file name by a period.

Exterior Gateway Protocol See *EGP*.

external cache See *secondary cache*.

external command An MS-DOS command that executes a program. The program file must be present in the current drive, directory, or path. FORMAT and

DISKCOPY are examples of external commands. Contrast with internal command.

eXternal CoMmanD (XCMD) In HyperTalk programming, a user-defined command (written in a language such as Pascal or C) that uses built-in Macintosh library routines to perform tasks not normally available within HyperCard. A popular XCMD is ResCopy, which is widely available in public domain or shareware stack-writing utility programs. ResCopy enables a HyperTalk programmer to copy external commands and external resources from one program or stack to another. See *external function (XCFN)*, *ResEdit*.

external data bus A set of communications channels that facilitate communication between a central processing unit (CPU) and other components on the motherboard, including random access memory (RAM).

external function (XCFN) In HyperTalk programming, a program function (written in a language such as Pascal or C) that is external to HyperTalk but that returns values to the program that can be used within the HyperTalk program. For example, Resources, an XCFN widely available in public domain or shareware stack-writing utilities, returns a list of all named resources in a file of a specified type. See *eXternal CoMmanD (XCMD)*.

external hard drive A hard drive equipped with its own case, cables, and power supply. External hard drives usually cost more than internal hard disks of comparable speed and capacity.

external modem A modem with its own case, cables, and power supply, designed to plug into a serial port. See *internal modem*.

external reference formula In Microsoft Excel and other dynamic data exchange (DDE)–capable spreadsheet programs, a formula placed in a cell that creates a link to another spreadsheet.

external table In Lotus 1-2-3, a database created with a database management program (such as dBASE) that 1-2-3 can access directly.

extraction The process of restoring archived files. A file archive contains two or more files that have been stored as a single file for convenience in backup and file transfer operations. See *archive*.

extra-high density floppy disk A nearly obsolete type of floppy disk that requires a special floppy disk drive (equipped with two heads rather than the usual one) and can hold 2.88MB when formatted for MS-DOS.

extranet An intranet (internal TCP/IP network) that has been selectively opened to a firm's suppliers, customers, and strategic allies.

extremely low-frequency (ELF) emission A magnetic field generated by commonly used electrical appliances such as monitors, electric blankets, hair dryers, and food mixers, and extending 1 to 2 meters from the source. ELF fields have caused tissue changes and fetal abnormalities in laboratory test animals and might be related to reproductive anomalies and cancers among frequent users of computers.

eye candy An appealing graphic that is displayed to attract viewers' attention to a computer monitor.

e-zine An Internet-based magazine. Also called a digizine.

F

F2F In e-mail, a common abbrev that means "face to face"—a real-life meeting. See *abbrev.*

fabless Without large-scale fabrication facilities. A fabless chip maker must farm out chip-manufacturing jobs to other companies.

facing pages The two pages of a bound document that face each other when the document is open. See *recto, verso.*

factory configuration The set of operating parameters built into a hardware device. The configuration can be overridden by the user.

failure A type of mishap in which a system component no longer fulfills its intended function. See *mishap.*

failure horizon In Y2K readiness preparation, the time period in which a system failure is predicted to occur.

fair use In U.S. copyright law, an exception to the otherwise exclusive rights of copyright holders to make copies of a copyrighted work. Under the fair use doctrine, copyrighted works may be duplicated for purposes such as criticism, comment, news reporting, and teaching. However, such uses may still constitute copyright infringement if they are clearly commercial and profit-oriented rather than educational or scholarly in nature, if the copied work is designed for entertainment rather than edification, if the extent of copying is substantial (a commonly cited rule of thumb is 5 percent of the original content), or if the duplication adversely affects the market for the copyrighted work. See *copyright.*

fall back In modems, to decrease the data transfer rate to accommodate communication with an older modem or across a dirty line. Some modems also fall forward if line noise conditions improve.

fall forward In modems, to increase the data transfer rate if the quality of a connection improves. Some modems that fall back due to line noise can fall forward again if noise abates.

false dependency In microprocessors that use superscalar architecture, a condition in which the results of two calculations are written to the same register if separate pipelines perform the calculations simultaneously. The more registers a microprocessor has, the fewer false dependencies are likely to occur. See *data dependency, register renaming.*

false drop In a database search, a retrieved record that has nothing to do with the searcher's interests. False drops are an unintended consequence of free-text searching, in which users type keywords in an attempt to retrieve relevant documents. For example, a search for the computer game Quake may retrieve documents relating to a recent earthquake in Japan.

fanfold paper See *continuous paper.*

FAQ Acronym for frequently asked questions. A document containing a list of the questions that are commonly asked by newcomers to a subject. FAQs are available on many Web sites and cover a huge variety of subjects, including many nontechnical ones.

Fast ATA See *Enhanced IDE (EIDE).*

Fast CGI A programming interface for Web servers that markedly improves the server's performance when dealing with CGI script's processing requests. See *CGI.*

Fast Ethernet An Ethernet specification that enables data transmission rates of 100 Mbps. Fast Ethernet networks use the same media access control method that 10Base-T Ethernet networks use (see CSMA/CD) but achieve 10 times the data transmission speed. Fast Ethernets use twisted-pair wiring or fiber-optic cable. Synonymous with 100Base-T. See *Ethernet.*

Fast Page Mode See *FPM.*

Fast SCSI   A SCSI standard that uses an 8-bit data bus and that supports data transfer rates of up to 10 Mbps. See *Fast/Wide SCSI, Ultra SCSI, Ultra/Wide SCSI.*

Fast/Wide SCSI   A SCSI standard that uses a 16-bit data bus and that supports data transfer rates of up to 20 Mbps. See *Fast SCSI, Ultra SCSI, Ultra/Wide SCSI.*

FAT   Acronym for file allocation table. A hidden table of every cluster on a floppy or hard disk. The FAT records how files are stored in distinct—and not necessarily contiguous—clusters. A file allocation table uses a simple method, much like a scavenger hunt, to keep track of data. The directory file stores the address of the file's first cluster. In the FAT entry for the first cluster is the address of the second cluster used to store the file. In the entry for the second cluster is the address of the third cluster, and so on, until the last cluster entry, which contains an end-of-file code. Because this table provides the only means for finding data on a disk, DOS creates and maintains two copies of the FAT in case one is damaged. See *file fragmentation.*

FAT16   A file allocation table (FAT) that restricts the maximum size of a hard drive to 2.1GB; this limitation stems from the use of a 16-bit cluster addressing method. In addition, FAT16 utilizes disk space inefficiently (the smallest allocation unit is a cluster, as large as 32K on a 2.1GB drive) so that a 1-byte file requires an entire cluster. See *FAT32.*

FAT32   A 32-bit file allocation table (FAT) usable with 32-bit operating systems such as Windows 98 and Windows 95 Service Release 2 (OSR2). FAT32 removes the previous 2.1GB limit on hard disk size by employing a 32-bit cluster addressing method; FAT32 can use disks as large as 2TB. In addition, FAT32 improves storage efficiency by using 4K clusters as the smallest allocation unit. See *FAT16, NTFS.*

fatal error   An error in a program that, at best, causes the program to abort and, at worst, causes a crash with loss of data.

Bulletproof programs are supposed to be immune to fatal errors, but they usually are not.

fat client   In client/server networks, a proprietary client application program that consumes a great deal of local and network processing time and that forces data to be captured in proprietary file formats. See *light client, thin client.*

fatware   Software that is so laden with features or that is designed so inefficiently that it monopolizes huge chunks of hard disk space, random access memory (RAM), and microprocessor power. Fatware is one of the undesirable results of creeping featurism.

fault tolerance   The capability of a computer system to cope with internal hardware problems without interrupting the system's performance, often by automatically bringing backup systems online when the system detects a failure. Fault tolerance is indispensable whenever computers are assigned critical functions, such as guiding an aircraft to a safe landing or ensuring a steady flow of medicines to a patient. Fault tolerance also is beneficial for noncritical, everyday applications. See *bulletproof, Microsoft Windows NT.*

fault tree analysis   In testing, a method of discovering potential faults by tracking down every conceivable option in the way the program or hardware can be used.

favorite   In Microsoft Internet Explorer, a saved hyperlink to which the user plans to return. In Netscape Navigator, this is called a bookmark.

fax modem   A circuit board that fits into an expansion slot in a computer, providing many of the features of a fax machine at a lower cost. The fax modem also provides crisper output and convenience, as well as offering the features of a high-speed modem. If a person is traveling or at a remote location, he or she can use a portable computer with a fax board to fax materials to and from any place with a phone. Fax boards send a coded image of a document and receive that image in the form of a file that can then be printed. Before using a fax board to send printed or handwritten material, one must use a scanner or other input device to scan or record the material. See *broadcast fax, modem, scanner.*

fax on demand   An information service in which faxes can be requested by means of a telephone call and automatically are sent to the caller.

fax program   An application that enables one to use a fax modem. Usually, a fax program enables one to compose, send, receive, and print faxes, and also complete one of a variety of fax cover pages included with the program. When a person receives documents that include text, the newest fax programs use optical character recognition (OCR) to convert the faxed image back into text so that he or she can edit the document by using any of the popular word processing programs. See *fax modem.*

fax server   A computer or dedicated device that provides fax capabilities to all the workstations in a local area network (LAN). See *fax modem.*

fax switch   A device that routes incoming telephone calls to the telephone, the modem, or the fax machine, whichever is appropriate. A fax switch can save the cost of extra telephone lines.

FCC   Acronym for Federal Communications Commission. An independent U.S. government agency that is directly responsible to Congress, the FCC was created by the Communications Act of 1934. The FCC's responsibilities include regulating interstate and international communication by radio, television, cable, satellite, and wireless technologies.

FCC certification   An attestation formerly made by the U.S. Federal Communications Commission (FCC) that a given brand and model of a computer meets the agency's limits for radio frequency emissions. There are two certification levels: Class A certification, for computers to be used in industrial and commercial locations (specifically, mainframes and minicomputers); and

Class B certification, for computers to be used in home locations, including home offices. All personal computers are explicitly defined as Class B equipment. See *radio frequency interference (RFI).*

FDD   An acronym for floppy disk drive sometimes used in advertisements.

FDDI   See *Fiber Distributed Data Interface.*

FDHD   An acronym for floppy drive high density. See *high density.*

FDM   See *frequency division multiplexing.*

feathering   Adding an equal amount of space between each line on a page or column to force vertical justification. See *leading.*

feature   A capability of a program. Occasionally, programs contain undocumented features. See *feature creep.*

feature creep   An unfortunate tendency in programming in which software developers add more features in an attempt to keep up with the competition. The result is a program that is difficult to use, has sluggish performance, and takes up too much disk space. See *bloat.*

FED   Acronym for field emission display. A flat-panel display technology that uses a grid of tiny cathodes, a miniature version of the same technology that generates images in standard computer monitors. FED displays combine the image quality of standard displays with the thin, flat-panel space consumption of LCD displays.

Federal   Information   Processing Standard   See *FIPS.*

federated database   In scientific networking, a collaborative database (part of a collaboratory) in which scientists pool their knowledge and discoveries. Federated databases are one proposed solution to the Grand Challenges, problems that are so complex that they far outstrip the capabilities of individual scientists or even individual research institutions to tackle them independently.

female connector A cable terminator and connection device with receptacles designed to accept the pins of a male connector. See *male connector.*

femto- A Metric prefix indicating one quadrillionth, or a millionth of a billionth (10^{15}).

Fetch A popular FTP client for Macintosh Computers developed by Dartmouth College. The program is freeware.

Fiber Distributed Data Interface (FDDI) A standard for creating high-speed computer networks that employ fiber-optic cable. The FDDI specification calls for networks up to 250 km long that can transfer data at speeds of 100 Mbps.

fiber-optic cable A high-speed physical medium that can be used for transmitting data. Constructed from thin fibers of glass, fiber-optic cable guides the light of transmitting lasers without significant loss, despite twists and turns along the way. At the receiving end, optical detectors transform the light into electrical impulses. Fiber optics enable very high-speed networking (the Fiber Distributed Data Interface [FDDI] specification calls for data transfer at speeds of 100 Mbps) but are expensive and difficult to work with. See *coaxial cable, twisted-pair.*

fiber optics A data transmission technology that uses fiber-optic cable to convey information.

Fidonet A set of data exchange standards and procedures that permit privately operated computer bulletin board systems (BBSs) to exchange data, files, and e-mail internationally, using the world telephone system. At an agreed-on time when telephone rates are low, subscribing BBSs send e-mail messages and files to a regional host, which in turn distributes them to other bulletin boards. Responses, or echoes, eventually find their way back to the host bulletin board. A popular Fidonet feature is EchoMail, a set of moderated conferences that cover a variety of popular subjects, such as *Star Trek*, model aircraft, and political issues. See *Internet, WAN.*

field See *data field.*

field-based search In a database or Web search engine, a search that is restricted to a given field in the database. This is one of several methods that can be used to improve recall and precision. See *precision, recall.*

field definition In a database management program, a list of the attributes that define the type of information that one can enter into a data field. The field definition also determines how the field's contents appear onscreen. See *database.*

field emission display See *FED.*

field expansion In Y2K readiness preparation, a data conversion method that expands the size of a data field to a length sufficient to cope with four-character years.

field name In a database management program, a unique name given to a data field. The name should help users identify the field's contents.

field privilege In a database management program, a database definition that establishes what one can do with the contents of a data field in a protected database.

field template In database management programs, a field definition that specifies the kind of data that one can type in the data field. If one tries to type some data into a field that does not match the field template, the program displays an error message. Use field templates as often as possible; they help prevent users from adding inappropriate information to the database. Synonymous with data mask. See *data type.*

FIFO Acronym for first-in, first-out. In computer programming, an approach to handling queued requests that ensures that the oldest request will be the next one processed.

file   A document or other collection of information stored on a disk and identified as a unit by a unique name. When a person saves a file, the disk may scatter the data among dozens or even hundreds of noncontiguous clusters. The file allocation table (FAT) is an index of the order in which those clusters are linked to equal a file. To the user, however, files appear as units on disk directories and are retrieved and copied as units. See *file name, secondary storage.*

file allocation table   See *FAT.*

file attribute   A hidden code stored with a file's directory that contains the file's read-only or archive status and tells whether the file is a system, hidden, or directory file. See *archive attribute, hidden file, locked file, read-only attribute.*

file archiving utility   A utility program that combines two or more files into a single file for storage purposes. See *tar.*

file compression utility   A utility program or that compresses and decompresses infrequently used files so that they take up 40 to 90 percent less room on a hard disk. One uses another utility to decompress a file. Specialty file compression utilities that compress only certain types of files, such as downloadable font files, are also available. These programs usually load a special driver that remains in memory to decompress and recompress the files as needed. Note that file compression and file archiving should be clearly differentiated; some programs (such as WinZip) combine these capabilities. See *archive, bzip2, compressed file, disk compression utility, file archiving utility, gzip, WinZip.*

file conversion utility   A utility program that converts text or graphics files created with one program to the file format used by another program. The best application programs now include a conversion utility that can handle a dozen or more file formats.

file defragmentation   See *defragmentation, file fragmentation.*

file deletion   The process of rendering a file unusable. There are two types of file deletion: physical and logical. Logical deletion makes a file disappear but ensures that it is recoverable. Dragging a file to the Macintosh TrashCan icon or to the Windows 95 or 98 Recycling Bin icon logically deletes it.

file extension   See *extension.*

file format   The patterns and standards that a program uses to store data on disk. Few programs store data in ASCII format. Most use a proprietary file format that other programs cannot read, ensuring that customers continue to use the company's program and enabling programmers to include special features that standard formats might not allow. See *file conversion utility, native file format.*

file fragmentation   The allocation of a file in noncontiguous sectors on a floppy disk or hard drive. Fragmentation occurs because of multiple file deletions and write operations. File fragmentation can seriously reduce disk efficiency because a disk drive's read/write head must travel longer distances to retrieve a file that is scattered all over the disk. Defragmenting can improve disk efficiency by as much as 50 percent by rewriting files so that they are placed in contiguous clusters. See *defragmentation.*

file infector   A type of computer virus that attaches to program files and, when that program is executed, spreads to other program files. See *boot sector virus, macro virus, virus.*

file locking   On a network, a method of concurrency control that ensures the integrity of data. File locking prevents more than one user from accessing and altering a file at the same time. See *LAN.*

file management program   A program that enables users to manage files, directories, and disks by displaying a disk's directory structure and listing existing files. Commands available on the program's menus are used to move and copy files, create directories, and perform other housekeeping tasks that help improve disk performance and protect one's data. Windows Explorer is a popular file management program.

file name   A name assigned to a file when the file is written on a disk. A file name may have as many as three parts: the file name proper, a period, and an extension. Microsoft Windows XP, Linux, and Mac OS X permit 255-characterfile names.. See *flat file system, hierarchical file system.*

file ownership   In a multiuser operating system such as Linux or Microsoft Windows NT, a file attribute that specifies the name of the user who created the file. See *file permissions.*

file permissions   In a multiuser operating system such as Linux or Microsoft Windows XP, a file attribute that specifies varying levels of file access for different types of file owners (individual owners, group owners, and others). Access levels include no access, read-only access, and read/write access. An additional level of access, execute access, is available for executable programs and scripts. Synonymous with permissions.

file server   In a local area network (LAN), a computer that stores on its hard disk the application programs and data files for all the workstations in the network. In a peer-to-peer network, all workstations act as file servers because each workstation can provide files to other workstations. In the more common client/server architecture, a single, high-powered machine with a huge hard disk is set aside to function as the file server for all the workstations (clients) in the network. See *client/server, peer-to-peer network, LAN, network operating system (NOS).*

file sharing   On a computer network, making a file available to other users by modifying the file's access privileges (also called permissions). See *file permissions.*

filespec   A complete statement of a file's location, including a drive letter, pathname,

file name, and extension, such as C:\ REPORTS\REPORT1.

file transfer protocol (ftp)   In asynchronous communications, a standard that ensures the error-free transmission of program and data files through the telephone system. When written in lowercase, ftp refers to any protocol, such as XMODEM, Kermit, or ZMODEM. When uppercase, FTP refers to the Internetprotocol. See *FTP.*

File Transfer Protocol (FTP)   See *FTP.*

file transfer utility   A utility program that transfers files between different hardware platforms.

fill   **1.** In a spreadsheet program, to enter the same text or value (numbers, dates, times, or formulas) or a sequence of values in a worksheet. **2.** In a graphics program, to add color to an outlined geometric shape.

filter   Any software feature or program that functions automatically to screen data. In e-mail, one can use a filter to delete unwanted messages automatically or move certain types of messages to folders one has created. In a graphics program, a filter alters the image in a certain way, such as increasing its contrast or adding a color tint.

filtering software   Any program that filters incoming data in an attempt to eliminate unwanted material. See *Internet filter.*

Finder   A file management program provided by Apple Computer for Macintosh computers. The Finder provides a file management shell for the Macintosh operating system (Mac OS).

FinePrint   A resolution enhancement technology that produces an effective resolution of 600 by 600 dots per inch (dpi) in Apple laser printers. Normally, the resolution is 300 dpi. See *PhotoGrade.*

finger   An Internet utility that enables one to obtain information about a user who has an e-mail address. Normally, this information is limited to the person's full name, job title, and address. However, the user can set up finger to retrieve one or more text files that contain information (such as a resumé) that the user wants to make public.

FIPS Acronym for Federal Information Processing Standard. A standard adopted by the U.S. federal government that is mandatory for all government agencies.

firewall A program or set of programs that serve to disguise an internal network's addresses so that they cannot be directly accessed from the external Internet. To provide external Internet service to internal users, a proxy server is used to make external information requests on behalf of internal users, but without disclosing the IP addresses of the internal user's computers. See *proxy server*.

FireWire A standard (IEEE 1394) established by the Institute of Electrical and Electronic Engineers (IEEE), and subsequently developed by Apple Computer, that lays out specifications for a 400 Mbps port designed for use with peripheral devices. See *IEEE 1394*.

Fireworks A Web graphics development program, created by Macromedia, that offers Web developers an ideal environment for creating Web graphics. The program gathers into one application a variety of graphics manipulation features that formerly required the use of several different programs, such as GIF transparency, image maps, and conversion to Web-safe color palettes. As graphics are developed in the Fireworks development, the program automatically generates dynamic HTML code that can be incorporated into HTML pages for features such as rollovers, dynamic menus, and animations. The program is closely integrated with Macromedia's Flash and Dreamweaver development environments. See *Dreamweaver, Flash*.

firm A new top-level domain (TLD) name for Internet usage, added in 1998, that is designed for the home pages of businesses. See *domain name, gTLD-MoU, top-level domain (TLD)*.

firmware Broadly, the system software stored in a computer's read-only memory (ROM) or elsewhere in the computer's circuitry, such as the BIOS chips in IBM PC–compatible computers. See *flash BIOS*.

FIRST See *Forum of Incident Response and Security Teams*.

first-generation computer The earliest phase of electronic digital computer technology, dating from the mid-1940s to the late 1950s. Huge, power-hungry, and expensive, these computers used vacuum tubes for switching devices. Significant achievements during this period were: the stored program concept, the notion that the program instructions as well as the data could be stored in the computer's memory; the use of binary instead of decimal numbers for processing purposes; and the development of auxiliary storage using magnetic tape drives.

first-generation programming language The earliest programming languages; designed to be easily understood by computers. These languages consist entirely of numbers and are extremely difficult for humans to work with. See *fourth generation programming language, second-generation programming language, third-generation programming language*.

first normal form See *1NF*.

first-party DMA An improved Direct Memory Access (DMA) bus that does not require the intervention of a controller unit or the CPU. In first-party DMA, the bus is taken over and controlled by the peripheral that is using it; it becomes the "master" of the bus. See *bus master, DMA, third-party DMA*.

first sale In U.S. copyright law, a doctrine developed in two centuries of jurisprudence that provides rights to those who have lawfully purchased a copy of a copyrighted work, such as a book. According to the first sale doctrine, the first purchase of a copyrighted work satisfies the financial obligation owed to the copyright holder. After lawfully purchasing a copyrighted work, the user may then lend, give, or sell a copy of the work to any other person without risking a copyright infringement lawsuit. (Such rights do not include copies of the work in a way that would violate fair use guidelines.) In the United States, copyright holders are pressing for legislative changes that would abolish the first sale concept for digitized works. See *Digital Millennium Copyright Act (DMCA)*, *digital rights management (DRM)*, *fair use*, *trusted system*.

fixed disk   Synonymous with hard drive.

fixed-frequency monitor   An analog monitor designed to receive input signals at only one frequency. In contrast, a multiscanning monitor automatically adjusts to match the incoming signal.

fixed IP address   An IP address that a network administrator assigns to a workstation on the network. With a fixed IP address, such a computer can run server programs and make information available to other network users. See *DHCP*.

fixed-length field   In a database management program, a field whose length is set and cannot vary, as opposed to a variable-length field, which can adjust to accommodate entries of different lengths.

fixed numeric format   In spreadsheet programs, a numeric format that rounds values to the number of decimal places that are specified.

fix on failure (FoF)   In Y2K readiness preparation, a policy of repairing problems only after they occur. This approach is not considered wise by most Y2K experts.

F key   See *function key*.

Fkey   A Macintosh utility program that one executes by pressing the Command (⌘) and Shift keys with a number key from 0 to 9, the keys that simulate the function keys on IBM PC–compatible keyboards. The Macintosh System software includes four Fkey utilities; shareware and commercial sources offer additional Fkey utilities (and software for managing them).

flag   A variable that serves as an indicator about the status of a program, a file, or some data. A flag in a database record might be true if the other fields in the record show that a videotape is overdue, for example. Synonymous with file attribute.

flame   **1.** In Usenet and e-mail, a message that contains abusive, threatening, obscene, or inflammatory language. In e-mail, a slang term meaning to lose one's self-control by writing a message that uses derogatory, obscene, or inappropriate language. See *flame bait*, *flame war*, *moderated newsgroup*, *rave*. **2.** To write an abusive, threatening, obscene, or inflammatory e-mail message or Usenet post out of anger.

flame bait   In an unmoderated newsgroup, a posting that contains opinions that prompt flames (abusive remarks and personal attacks) and that may ultimately launch a flame war. Flame-bait topics include abortion, homosexuality, and the desirability of using Microsoft Windows 95/98. True flame bait unintentionally elicits such responses; when such postings are made intentionally, the post is more properly called a troll. See *moderated newsgroup*.

flame war   In newsgroups, listservs, and mailing lists, an unproductive and longrunning debate marked by high emotion and little information. See *flame*, *flame bait*, *unmoderated newsgroup*.

Flash   A scriptable animation framework developed by Macromedia and widely used to implement Web-based animations. The Flash development environment enables Web developers to create eye-catching animations quickly; the scripting capabilities enable programmers to build interactivity and special effects into Flash animations.

flash BIOS   A read-only memory (ROM) chip storing the computer's Basic Input-Output System (BIOS) that one can reprogram with software instead of having to remove the BIOS chip, reprogram it in a special machine, and then replace the chip. With flash BIOS, users can easily update their BIOS chips by obtaining the appropriate software from their computer manufacturer. Great care must be taken when updating BIOS; the manufacturer's directions must be followed precisely. Flash BIOS is made possible by flash erasable programmable read-only memory (flash EPROM).

flash EPROM   A type of read-only memory (ROM) that can be erased by an electrical current and then reprogrammed with new instructions at very high speeds. After the reprogramming occurs, the circuits retain these instructions even if the power is switched off. Flash EPROM is used in flash BIOS as well as modems that are set up so that one can download and install support for new communications protocols as they become available.

flash erasable programmable read-only memory   See *flash EPROM*.

flash memory   A special type of read-only memory (ROM) that enables users to upgrade the information contained in the memory chips. Also called flash BIOS or flash EPROM.

flash memory card   In digital devices such as cameras and PDAs, a unit of flash memory that holds data, such as captured images, music, or text files. Flash memory cards are removable; when one is full, the user can insert an additional card. Subsequently, the data can be downloaded from the card to a desktop computer. The card can then be erased and used again. The two most popular flash memory card technologies are called CompactFlash and SmartMedia. See *CompactFlash (CF)*, *digital camera*, *SmartMedia*.

flat   Lacking elaborate structure. A file system without subdirectories in which one can group files is said to be flat. Such systems have not been used since the earliest days of personal computing.

flat address space   A method of organizing a computer's memory so that the operating system can allocate portions of the memory without restriction. The opposite of a flat address space is the segmented

memory architecture of MS-DOS and Microsoft Windows 3.1, which divides memory into 64K sections (called segments). A flat memory space design is more efficient because the processor does not have to map each memory address to a specific 64K segment, but such a design requires the use of 32-bit memory addresses. Microsoft Windows 95/98, which employs 32-bit memory addresses, creates a flat address space for one's applications.

flatbed scanner   A scanner with a flat scanning area large enough to accommodate a letter-sized page (8½ × 11 inches) or more of material. A sheet feeder to automate scanning multiple-page documents is an available option. See *digitize*.

flat file database   A database application that stores, organizes, and retrieves all its data in a single table. This approach is well-suited for small, simple databases; more complex databases can be built with relational database applications. See *data integrity*, *relational database management system (RDBMS)*.

flat file system   A file system in which each file must have a unique name. Most modern operating systems use a hierarchical file system, in which two or more files can have the same name as long as they are located in different directories. See *hierarchical file system*.

flat-panel display   A thin display screen that uses one of several display technologies, such as active matrix (also known as thin film transistor), field emission display, gas plasma display, LCD (liquid crystal display), or passive matrix. A backlit display makes the display easier to read. Traditionally used in portable computers, flat-panel displays are becoming common for desktop computers and digital televisions.

flat-square monitor   A monitor that is more gently curved than most but really neither flat nor square. Although such monitors have less distortion than most displays, they are not free of spherical distortion, as flat tension-mask monitors are.

flat tension-mask monitor A monitor design that includes an absolutely flat—and, therefore, distortion-free—display. Flat tension-mask monitors are the only truly distortion-free monitors available but are too expensive for most computer users. See *flat-square monitor, vertically flat.*

flexATX A form factor for PC-compatible computers that employs a motherboard slightly smaller than that specified by the microATX form factor; flexATX is a more recent, derivative version of the microATX standard. The flexATX form factor is typically used in low-end systems. See *form factor, microATX.*

flicker A visible distortion that occurs when one scrolls the screen of a monitor that uses a low refresh rate. Also, a visible distortion apparent in light areas on an interlaced monitor. See *interlacing.*

flight simulator A program designed to act like the aircraft on which the pilot is training.

floating graphic A graph or picture that has not been fixed in an absolute position on the page, so it moves up or down on the page as one deletes or inserts text above it. See *anchored graphic.*

floating point notation A method of representing very large or very small numbers in an expression of fixed size that closely resembles scientific notation, in which a number is denoted using a mantissa (a decimal number), a multiplication symbol, the base of the numbering system being used, and an exponent (for example, 1.1×10^8).

In floating point notation, the expression is based on binary numbers; furthermore, the expression is modified by a process called normalization so that the first digit of the mantissa is always 1 (for example, 1.011 [binary] $\times 2^4$ = 22 [decimal]. This number, called the hidden bit, does not have to be stored in memory. Most computers can represent floating point numbers in single precision (32 bit length) or double precision (64 bit length).

Computers equipped with floating point units (FPU) may be able to store these numbers in bit lengths of 80 or more. Floating point notation is standardized by the IEEE 754 standard, which is observed by all save a few special-purpose computer platforms. See *binary notation, double precision, IEEE 754.*

floating-point operations per second See *FLOP.*

floating-point unit (FPU) A portion of a microprocessor that handles operations in which the decimal point moves left and right to allow for very high precision when dealing with very large or very small numbers. An FPU usually makes a microprocessor much faster.

flooding Using automated techniques to overwhelm a computer-based service so that access to the service is impaired or denied. See *denial-of-service (DoS) attack.*

FLOP Acronym for floating-point operations per second. The speed at which a computer can carry out floating-point calculations. Such speeds are often specified in megaflops (millions of operations per second), gigaflops (billions), and teraflops (trillions). See *floating point notation, gigaflop, megaflop, petaflop, teraflop.*

floppy disk A removable and widely used data storage medium that uses a magnetically coated flexible disk of Mylar enclosed in a plastic envelope or case. Software publishers sometimes distribute their applications on floppy disks. At one time, these also were the only medium for data storage for personal computers, but the availability of inexpensive hard drives, recordable optical discs (such as CD-R and DVD-R) has relegated floppy disks to the sidelines. See *double density, head access aperture, high density, read/write head, single-sided disk, write-protect notch.*

floppy disk controller The circuitry responsible for operating a floppy disk drive. Usually based on the 765 controller chip, the floppy disk controller moves the read/write head and operates the spindle motor under directions from the host adapter.

floppy disk drive A mechanism that enables a computer to read and write information on floppy disks. Floppy disk drives come in two sizes—3.5 inch and 5.25 inch—and several densities, to handle a variety of floppy disks. A high-density floppy disk drive can work with both high-density and double-density floppy disks, but a double-density floppy disk drive can use only double-density disks.

floptical disk A removable optical disc the size of a 3.5-inch floppy disk, but with capacities of more than 9 GB.

floptical drive A data storage device that uses laser technology to illuminate optical tracts on a floptical disk. The reflected light is sensed by a photodetector, which generates a signal that allows precise positioning of the read/write heads. The pattern of tracks, created when the disk is manufactured, is extremely compact, making it possible to create 3.5-inch floptical disks the same size as the familiar 3.5-inch floppy disks but capable of storing more than 9 GB of information. Floptical drives manufactured by such companies as Iomega can read and write on standard 3.5-inch floppy disks.

flow A feature that allows text in a page layout to wrap around graphics and to move automatically from column to column (called newspaper columns or snaking columns). Page layout programs and better word processing programs can format text this way.

flow chart A chart that contains symbols referring to computer operations, describing how the program performs. Sometimes written as one word: flowchart.

flow control A method of ensuring that the data device, such as a modem or a computer system, does not overwhelm the receiving device, such as a modem. Software handshaking (also called XON/XOFF handshaking) regulates communications

between two modems. Hardware handshaking (CTS/RTS) regulates data flow between the computer and the modem.

flush To clear or empty. Flushing a printer's random access memory (RAM) by turning it off for a few seconds and then turning it on again may correct certain problems. Flushing a cache in a Web browser erases the record of what sites one has visited.

flush left In word processing, the alignment of text along the left margin, leaving a ragged right margin. See *justification*.

flush right In word processing, aligning text along the right margin, leaving a ragged left margin. Flush-right alignment is seldom used except to create decorative effects or cover pages. See *justification*.

FM synthesis In sound boards that use the MIDI standard, a method of simulating musical instruments that is less costly than wave table synthesis but also of much lower quality. See *wave table synthesis*.

focus In a graphical user interface (GUI), the activation of a window so that it is ready to receive keyboard input. Also called keyboard focus.

folder In the Macintosh Finder and Microsoft Windows desktop, an onscreen representation of a file folder on the desktop and into which one can organize files. Folders are called directories in MS-DOS.

follow-up post In an online newsgroup, a contribution posted in response to a previous posting. Unlike a reply, a follow-up post is public and can be read by everyone in the newsgroup. Follow-up posts form a thread of discussion. See *distributed bulletin board, netiquette, Usenet*.

font One complete collection of letters, punctuation marks, numbers, and special characters with a consistent and identifiable typeface, weight (roman or bold), posture (upright or italic), and type size. The term often is used incorrectly in reference to a typeface or font family. There are two basic font technologies for computers: bitmapped fonts and outlined fonts (also called vectored or scalable fonts) such as Adobe PostScript and Microsoft TrueType. See *book weight*.

font cartridge A plug-in read-only memory (ROM) cartridge (designed to fit into a receptacle on a printer) that contains one or more fonts and that expands the printer's font capabilities. See *cartridge font*.

font downloader See *downloading utility*.

font engine An interpreter that translates mathematically represented outline fonts (scalable fonts) into bitmapped representations for screens and printers. See *Freetype, interpreter, outline font, TrueType*.

font family A set of fonts in several sizes and weights that share the same typeface. A font family can sometimes include several similar typefaces. Arial, Helvetica, and MS Sans Serif are all considered part of the Swiss font family, for example.

font ID conflict In the Macintosh environment, a system error caused by conflicts between the identification numbers assigned to the screen fonts stored in the System Folder. The Macintosh System and many Mac application programs recognize and retrieve fonts by the identification number, not by name. The original Mac operating system lets one assign only 128 unique numbers, so one could inadvertently assemble a repertoire of screen fonts with conflicting numbers, causing printing errors. Beginning with System 6, Macintosh introduced a New Font Numbering Table (NFNT) scheme that lets one assign 16,000 unique numbers, reducing—but not eliminating—the potential for font ID conflicts.

font metric The width and height information for each character in a font. The font metric is stored in a width table.

font smoothing In high-resolution laser printers, the reduction of aliasing and other distortions when text or graphics are printed.

font substitution Substituting an outline font in place of a bitmapped screen font for printing purposes. In the Macintosh environment, the Apple LaserWriter printer driver substitutes the outline fonts Helvetica, Times Roman, and Courier for the screen fonts Geneva, New York, and Monaco.

font utility A utility program, used with early laser printers, that downloaded fonts to the printer's memory so that they could be used to print a document. The functions of font utilities are now built into current operating systems, such as Microsoft Windows 95/98.

foo A textual variable of unknown origin (though there is no shortage of theories) that is frequently used in place of a word or phrase that one is instructed to type (for example, "Type your e-mail account name before the @ sign, as in foo@wibble.com.").

footer In a word processing or page layout program, repetitive material printed at the bottom of the document's pages. See *header*.

footnote In a word processing or page layout program, a reference or note positioned at the bottom of the page. Most word processing programs number footnotes automatically and renumber them if one inserts or deletes a note. The best programs can float lengthy footnotes to the next page so that they take up no more than half the page. See *endnote*.

footprint The amount of space occupied by a computer, printer, monitor, or other piece of equipment on a desk, shelf, or floor.

forced page break A page break inserted by the user; the page always breaks at this location. Synonymous with hard page break.

forced perfect termination Like active termination and passive termination, a way of ending a SCSI daisy chain. Terminating the chain of SCSI devices presents a problem because the terminator may reflect signals, causing errors. Forced perfect termination actively monitors the electrical characteristics of the bus to make sure that no reflection occurs. See *active termination, passive termination, SCSI.*

forecasting   In a spreadsheet program, a method of analysis that projects past trends into the future.

foreground application   In a multitasking operating system, the application that is active. See *background application.*

foreground task   In a computer capable of multitasking, the job that the computer is performing in the active window. In networks and MS-DOS, a foreground task is a job that receives priority status before background tasks are executed. Background printing or calculation, for example, takes place in brief pauses while the foreground task executes. See *background tasks.*

forgery   In Usenet, mailing lists, or e-mail, a message written by someone other than the apparent author. Internet software enables any person with a modicum of technical knowledge to forge messages. See *anonymous remailer.*

forking   In software development, a split that occurs when a several versions of a single application are being actively updated and released. Normally, the software development process is linear: when a new version of an application is released, the developers never modify the older versions. Forking is particularly popular when the new version of an application is based on emerging technology or takes a radically different approach that not all users will want or need. See *open source software (OSS).*

form   **1.** In database programs, an onscreen form that enables users to supply data in the provided data entry areas. **2.** In Hypertext Markup Language (HTML) and World Wide Web (WWW) documents, a set of document features (including fill-in text areas, drop-down list boxes, check boxes, and option buttons) that enable one to interact with a Web page. Not all Web browsers can interact with forms. See *forms-capable browser.*

format   **1.** The organization of information for storage, printing, or displaying. The format of floppy disks and hard disks is the magnetic pattern laid down by the formatting utility. In a document, the format includes margins, the font and alignment used for text, headers, footers, page numbering, and the way that numbers are displayed. **2.** In a database management program, the physical arrangement of field names and data fields in an onscreen data-entry form. See *file format.*

formatting   An operation that establishes a pattern for the display, storage, or printing of data. In operating systems, an operation that prepares a floppy disk for use in a particular computer system by laying down a magnetic pattern. See *format, high-level format, low-level format.*

form factor   **1.** The physical size (usually just height) of a hard disk drive or floppy disk drive. Most modern hard and floppy disks fit into half-height drive bays, but a few high-capacity hard disks require full-height bays. **2.** The size and orientation of a motherboard. See *AT form factor, ATX form factor.*

form feed   A command that forces the printer to eject the current page and start a new page.

form-feed paper   See *continuous paper.*

forms-capable browser   A Web browser that can deal with Hypertext Markup Language (HTML) tags that create onscreen, interactive forms, including fill-in text boxes, option buttons, and drop-down list boxes. Some early Web browsers could not interact with forms; the leading programs, such as Microsoft Internet Explorer and Netscape Navigator, have no trouble with these features.

formula   In a spreadsheet program, a cell definition that defines the relationship between two or more values. In a database management program, an expression that tells the program to perform calculations on numeric data contained in one or more data fields. See *calculated field, precedence.*

formula bar In Microsoft Excel, the bar located below the toolbar, in which one enters or edits formulas and which displays the address of the current cell.

FOR/NEXT loop In programming, a loop control structure that carries out a procedure a specified number of times. For example, a person has a list of 10 items. A FOR/NEXT loop to change each item might read "Set the count to 1. Select to the end of the line. Apply formatting. Move down one line. Then set the count to the previous count plus 1. Keep doing this until the count is equal to 10." See *control structure.*

FORTH A high-level, fourth-generation programming language that offers direct control over hardware devices. Astronomer Charles Moore developed FORTH in 1970 to help him control the equipment at the Kitt Peak National Radio Observatory. FORTH (short for fourth-generation programming language) has been slow to gain acceptance as a general-purpose programming language. Because FORTH accepts user-defined commands, one FORTH programmer's code might be unintelligible to another programmer. FORTH sometimes is preferred for laboratory data acquisition, robotics, machine control, arcade games, automation, patient monitoring, and interfaces with musical devices.

FORTRAN The first compiled high-level programming language. FORTRAN (short for formula translator), which strongly resembles BASIC, enables programmers to describe and solve complex mathematical calculations. Still highly suited to mathematical applications, FORTRAN is widely used in scientific, academic, and technical settings. See *modular programming, Pascal, structured programming.*

forum In an online service, a topically focused discussion group that is supervised by a moderator.

Forum of Incident Response and Security Teams (FIRST) A unit of the Internet Society that coordinates the activities of several Computer Emergency Response Teams (CERTs) worldwide. FIRST's purpose is to bring these teams together to foster cooperation and coordination when security-related incidents occur and to promote the sharing of information concerning the security perils facing the Internet.

forward chaining In expert systems, an inference technique that requires the user to state all the relevant data before processing begins. A forward-chaining system starts with the data and works forward through its rules to determine whether additional data is required and how to draw the inference. See *backward chaining, knowledge base.*

foundation classes In object-oriented programming (OOP), a library of basic routines that programmers can use to handle essential program functions, such as responding to user input, displaying windows on the screen, and interacting with peripherals. See *object-oriented programming.*

fourth-generation computer An electronic digital computer created using very large scale integration (VLSI) technology, including microprocessors. VLSI technology, with origins in the late 1970s, enables computer manufacturers to publish complicated computer circuits in huge quantities; this has led to the phenomenon of ubiquitous computing, in which computers penetrate deeply into virtually every facet of our lives.

fourth-generation programming language A high-level programming language that is very close to human language, so it is easy for programmers to understand but requires many layers of translation for the computer to understand. Examples include FORTH, PROLOG, and the report-generation languages found in some advance database applications. See *first generation programming language, second-generation programming language, third-generation programming language.*

four-way, set-associative cache The set-associative cache design that strikes the best balance between speed and cost control. Four–way, set–associative caches are faster than two–way, set–associative caches and direct–map caches but are also more expensive.

four-year data format In data storage, a date format in which four characters are reserved for the year, thus enabling the system to distinguish between differing centuries. See *Y2K*.

FPM Acronym for fast page mode. A type of dynamic random access memory (DRAM) that divides the memory into pages, which can be directly accessed by the microprocessor and transferred in an entire block. FPM is not sufficiently fast for today's microprocessors and has been superceded by EDO RAM and, more recently, SDRAM. See *EDO RAM*, *random access memory (RAM)*, *SDRAM*.

FPU See *floating-point unit*.

FQDN See *fully qualified domain name*.

fractal geometry The study of a certain type of irregular geometric shapes, in which the shape of internal components is similar to the overall shape. Fractal shapes are common in nature.

fractional T1 A type of Internet connection that does not use all 24 of the 64Kbps channels available in a standard T1 digital telephone line. See *T1*.

FRAD Acronym for Frame Relay Access Device. In a frame relay service, a device that encapsulates outgoing data in frames for transmission on a frame relay network. The same device also de–encapsulates incoming data. See *frame relay*.

fragmentation See *file fragmentation*.

fragment identifier In HTML, a hyperlink that points to a named location within the current document or another document. For example, a hyperlink that points to #CHAP1 will display the document beginning at the point where the anchor named CHAP1 is inserted. The XPointer language, part of the XML language specification, includes more sophisticated ways of linking to selected content within the destination document.

frame **1.** In data communications, a unit (packet) of data that is transmitted via the network. **2.** In desktop publishing (DTP) and word processing, a rectangular area absolutely positioned on the page. The frame can contain text, graphics, or both. **3.** In the World Wide Web (WWW), a section of the window that has been partitioned off to display a separate document. This is done with frame tags. **4.** In animation and video, one of the still images that, when played at a rapid speed (see frame rate), produces the illusion of continuous movement.

frame buffer **1.** A portion of video memory that stores the information used to generate an image onscreen. Usually, the central processing unit (CPU) writes data to the frame buffer; then the video controller reads it, but dual-ported video random access memory (VRAM) allows simultaneous reads and writes. A frame buffer that can handle more information than the display might be used for hardware panning. **2.** In Lotus 1-2-3, the shaded border across the top of the spreadsheet containing the column letters and down the left of the spreadsheet containing the row numbers.

frame grabber In digital video, a utility that can capture a single frame (still image) within a video.

frame rate In animation and video, the number of still images presented per second. The frame rate is measured in frames per second (fps).

frame relay A service provided by telecommunications companies that connects local area networks (LANs) to regional or national backbone networks. Frame relay protocols place data within variably sized units called frames, which can encapsulate data conforming to other protocols (including Ethernet, X.24, and TCP/IP). Physically implemented by means of T1 or T3 digital telephone lines, frame relay creates a permanent virtual circuit (PVC) that can be priced according to the actual volume of transmitted data; frame relay thus frees customers from the fixed cost of a leased line that may have unused capacity. See *FRAD, leased line, permanent virtual circuit (PVC), T1, T3*.

frames   In Web publishing, the division of a Web page into two or more independent sections. This division is achieved by creating a master frames page, which specifies the layout of the frames and the HTML pages to be included by default in each frame. Depending on how the frames are set up, users may be able to scroll and resize each frame independently. Originated by Netscape Communications, Inc., as an extension to the HTML standard, frames are now part of the official HTML 4.0 specification.

frames per second (fps)   The number of still images (frames) that are presented per second in an animation or video. To produce the illusion of continuous movement, an animation or video should display at least 15 fps; roughly 30 fps is required to produce a convincing illusion of smooth motion.

FreeBSD   An open source version of BSD Unix, originally developed for Intel-based computers but increasingly available for additional platforms. Compared to Linux, FreeBSD is claimed to offer superior performance for networking and server applications. See *BSD, Linux, NetBSD*.

free-form text chart   In presentation graphics, a text chart used to handle information difficult to express in lists, such as lengthy explanations, directions, invitations, and certificates.

freenet   A community-based computer service, usually based in a public library, that attempts to make useful resources available to the local citizenry. Such resources include transcripts of city council meetings, access to the local library's card catalog, the names and addresses of community organizations, and, increasingly, access to the Internet. In keeping with the freenet's public-service orientation, access is free or very inexpensive.

free software   Software distributed under the terms of the Free Software Foundation's General Public License (GPL), which means that the user is granted certain freedoms (but not necessarily that the software is available free of charge). See *Free Software Foundation (FSF), General Public License (GPL)*.

Free Software Foundation (FSF)   A nonprofit organization, based in Massachusetts and founded in 1983, that promotes the distribution of software accompanied by freely modifiable source code. To promote this goal, FSF supports a Unix-compatible operating system (called GNU) and system utilities, which are distributed under the terms of the FSF's General Public License (GPL). GPL-licensed software can be freely copied or altered without permission from the copyright holder, as long as subsequent recipients of the software receive the same privileges (access to source code, unrestricted copying, and unrestricted rights to modify the software). A major FSF achievement is the GNU Project, which created—most of the major components of—GPL-licensed version of the Unix operating system. See *copyleft, General Public License (GPL), GNU Project, Hurd, Linux, open source software (OSS)*.

freestanding pointing device   A pointing device, such as a mouse or a trackball, connected to the computer through the serial or mouse port that is not otherwise attached to the computer. See *built-in pointing device, clip-on pointing device*.

free-text search   In a database, a search that begins by supplying one or more keywords, which the search software attempts to match against an inverted file (an index of all the words that appear in all the data records). Although free-text searching is easy to do, the results are often unsatisfactory because the list of retrieved items is likely to contain many false drops (records that do not pertain to the actual search subject). In addition, free-text searches generally achieve poor recall (a measure of the percentage of records that are actually in the database that were retrieved by the search). To improve the results of a free-text search, search restrictions may be needed, including case-sensitive searches, controlled vocabulary, field-based searches, and phrase searches.

Freetype An open source font engine that enables users of Unix and Unix-like operating systems to display TrueType and other fonts onscreen. See *font engine, open source software (OSS), TrueType.*

freeware Copyrighted programs that have been made available without charge for public use. Generally, program authors forbid the resale of such programs for profit. See *open source software (OSS), public domain program, shareware.*

freeze **1.** To stop software development at a point at which the developer judges that the software is sufficiently stable for release. **2.** To stop functioning. Synonymous with crash.

frequency In analog technologies, the number of oscillations (waves) that pass a specific point within the circuit in a given period of time. Frequencies are measured in cycles per second (Hz).

frequency division multiplexing (FDM) In local area networks (LANs), a technique for transmitting two or more signals over one cable by assigning each to its own frequency. Broadband (analog) networks use this technique. See *multiplexing.*

frequency modulation (FM) recording An early, low-density method of recording digital signals on recording media, such as tapes and disks. Synonymous with single-density recording. See *MFM.*

frequency shift keying (FSK) In modems, an obsolete way of communicating data by changing the frequency of the carrier. The Bell 103A protocol employs FSK, but newer data transmission protocols use group coding or trellis-code modulation.

frequently asked questions See *FAQ.*

friction feed A printer paper-feed mechanism that draws individual sheets of paper through the printer by using a plate to exert pressure on the paper. See *cut-sheet feeder, tractor feed.*

fried Burned out; short-circuited.

front end The portion of a program that interacts directly with the user. A front end can also be a separate program that acts as a user-friendly interface for a more difficult environment; for example, Hypertext Markup Language (HTML) has been called a front end for the Internet. A local area network (LAN) might distribute the front end to each workstation so that the user can interact with the back-end application on the file server. See *back end, client/server.*

frontside bus In a dual independent bus (DIB), the physical interface between the processor unit and the computer's data bus. See *back-side bus, DIB.*

FTP Acronym for File Transfer Protocol. An Internet standard for the exchange of files. FTP (uppercase) is a specific set of rules that comprise a file transfer protocol (ftp, note the lowercase letters). To use FTP, one starts an FTP client, an application program that enables one to contact another computer on the Internet and exchange files with it. To gain access to the other computer, one normally must supply a login name and password, after which he or she is given access to the computer's file directory system, and he or she can send (upload) and receive (download) files. An exception is anonymous FTP, which makes a file archive publicly accessible to any Internet user who possesses an FTP client; in response to the authentication prompts, one enters "anonymous" rather than a login name and, as a courtesy, supplies his or her e-mail address as a password. Most Web browsers can function as FTP clients to download files from anonymous FTP file archives. See *anonymous FTP, FTP client, FTP server, FTP site.*

FTP client   A program that is capable of assisting the user in uploading or downloading files from an FTP site. There are many standalone FTP clients, and FTP downloading capabilities are built into Web browsers such as Netscape Navigator.

FTP server   On the Internet, a server program that enables external users to download or upload files from a specified directory or group of directories. In anonymous FTP, the server accepts all external requests for downloads, but uploading or other file operations are generally prohibited.

FTP site   On the Internet, an Internet host running an FTP server that makes a large number of files available for downloading. See *anonymous FTP*.

full-associative cache   A secondary cache design that is superior to the direct-map cache design but inferior to the set-associative cache design. Full-associative caches require the central processing unit (CPU) to search the entire cache for a needed piece of information. See *four-way*, *set-associative cache*.

full backup   A backup of every file on a computer's hard drive. Although extremely tedious, the procedure is necessary for secure computing. Synonymous with global backup. See *incremental backup*.

full bleed   Text or graphics extending from one edge of a page to the other. See *bleed capability*.

full-duplex   An asynchronous communications protocol that allows the communications channel to send and receive signals at the same time. See *communications protocol*, *half-duplex*.

full-height drive bay   A mounting space in the computer's case for a component 3.38 inches tall. Designed to accept an old IBM hard drive, a single full-height drive bay can accept two modern hard disks. See *half-height drive*, *half-height drive bay*.

full justification   See *justification*.

full-motion video   A video presentation that gives the illusion of smooth, continuous action, even though it is actually made up of a series of still pictures. The key to full-motion video is a frame rate fast enough to create the illusion of continuous movement.

full-motion video adapter   A video adapter that can display moving video images (prerecorded or live) in a window that appears on the display. To display video images, one connects the adapter to a videocassette recorder, a laser disk player, or a camcorder. Most full-motion video adapters come with software that enables users to develop a multimedia presentation, complete with wipes, washes, fades, animation, and sound. Full-motion video applications are expected to play a growing role in corporate and professional presentations and training applications.

full-page display   A monitor that can display a full page of text at a time in a portrait rather than landscape orientation. Such monitors have not proven popular in the marketplace and are now difficult to find. A large (21") landscape-oriented monitor can display two full pages of text.

full-screen editor   A word processing utility, often included with application development systems, designed specifically for creating and editing programs. Such utilities include special features for indenting lines of program code, searching for nonstandard characters, and interfacing with program interpreters or compilers. See *line editor*, *programming environment*.

full-travel keyboard   A keyboard on which the keys can be depressed at least ⅛ inch. Full-travel keyboards provide good tactile feedback and enable professional typists to work quickly.

fully formed character printer   A printer, such as a daisywheel printer, that prints one character at a time.

fully qualified domain name (FQDN)   An Internet domain name that contains all the higher-level name components, including the highest level (i.e., com, org, or edu) that allows the domain to be accessed from any location on the Internet; for example, www.seas.virginia.edu is a fully qualified domain name. See *domain name, domain name system (DNS)*.

function **1.** In application programs, a named procedure that is designed to accept one or more supplied values (called arguments or actual parameters); the supplied values replace their corresponding placeholders in the function, which returns a calculated value as a result. For example, the PMT function in Microsoft Excel requires three arguments: rate (interest rate), nper (number of periods financed), and pv (initial principal value):

PMT(rate,nper,pv)

To call the function and supply real values (called actual parameters), the following expression can be used to find the monthly payment for a car loan:

PMT(4.8%/12, 60, $23,170)

2. In programming languages, a separate, named unit of code that performs a specific calculation or procedure. In order to use functions, they must be declared in a special area of the program set aside for this purpose. A function includes placeholders, called logical parameters, that will be replaced by real values (actual parameters) when the function is initiated by means of a function call placed elsewhere in the program. For example, the following pseudocode function adds two numbers and displays the result:

```
add(x, y) {
    sum = x + y;
    print sum;
}
```

The variables within the parentheses (x, y) are the logical parameters that will be replaced with actual parameters when the function is called. Elsewhere in the program, a statement such as the following calls the function and supplies the actual parameters:

add(5,10)

See *actual parameter, function call, parameter, parameter passing convention*.

function call In computer programming, a statement that tells a declared function to begin processing using the supplied data (actual parameters). See *function*.

function key A programmable key — conventionally numbered F1, F2, and so on — that provides special functions, depending on the software that one is using. See *F key*.

fuser wand In laser printers, a heated roller that melts toner onto the page. Dirty fuser wands sometimes cause unwanted vertical stripes on output.

fuzzy logic A branch of logic that involves logical problems to be investigated and solved even though some of the values cannot be specified as absolutely true or absolutely false. Fuzzy logic has been used to implement artificial intelligence and advanced control systems for high-speed railways.

G3 The third generation of Motorola-developed PowerPC processors, called the 750 series. Apple Computer features these processors in its G3 product line. The chip features a high-performance secondary cache located on the processor card (called a backside cache). G3s are fabricated using .27 micron technology and are capable of clock speeds of up to 450 MHz. See *backside cache, PowerPC, secondary cache*.

G4 The fourth generation of Motorola-developed PowerPC RISC processors, called the 74xx series. Apple Computer features these processors in its Power Mac G4 product line. The chip features a vector processing technology that Motorola and IBM call AltiVec, and Apple calls Velocity Engine. AltiVec uses an approach called SIMD (Single Instruction, Multiple Data) to simultaneously perform the same operation on 16 separate pieces of data, effectively increasing the processor's speed. However, software must be rewritten to take advantage of AltiVec. Fabricated with IBM-developed silicon on insulator (SOI) technology, G4 processors are capable of clock speeds of more than 1 GHz. See *PowerPC, silicon on insulator (SOI)*.

G5 The fifth generation of Motorola-developed PowerPC processors, called the 85xx series. The G5 features a redesigned pipeline and symmetric processing (SMP) capabilities. Fabricated with IBM-developed silicon on insulator (SOI) technology, G5 processors are capable of clock speeds of more than 2 GHz. See *pipeline, silicon on insulator (SOI)*.

G5 Messaging Protocol A standard proposed by a consortium of multimedia vendors that seeks to create a common method of encoding fax and e-mail messages so that these messages can be managed seamlessly by a single application.

game port A socket that allows one to connect a joystick, control yoke (a device that simulates an aircraft's control devices), or other game device to a computer. Game ports are often attached to a computer's sound card.

gamut In graphics, the range of colors that a color monitor can display.

garage A special bracket in inkjet printers in which an unused ink cartridge may be stored without the ink drying out. Also, the place the print head goes when it is not in use.

garbage characters In modems, meaningless characters caused by line noise. In printers, meaningless characters caused by line noise, a faulty printer driver, or some other communication problem.

garbage collection A process by which a program goes through random access memory (RAM), decides which information stored there is no longer needed, and deletes it. This process frees system resources so that the computer can run more efficiently and is less likely to crash.

gas plasma display See *plasma display*.

gateway **1.** A means by which users of one computer service or network can access certain kinds of information on a different service or network. This may be achieved by means of hardware devices called bridges, by computer programs that perform the necessary translation, or both. **2.** In networks, a device that connects two dissimilar local area networks (LANs) or that connects a local area network to a wide area network (WAN), a minicomputer, or a mainframe. A gateway has its own microprocessor and memory, and may perform network protocol conversion and bandwidth conversion. See *bridge*.

GB Abbreviation for gigabyte. See *gigabyte*.

Gbps Abbreviation for one billion (one thousand million) bits per second.

GDI See *Graphical Device Interface.*

GDI printer See *Graphical Device Interface (GDI) printer.*

geek Slang expression for a technically oriented person who may prefer spending time with the computer instead of socializing.

general format In most spreadsheet programs, the default numeric format in which all the numbers on either side of the decimal point (up to the farthest number that is not a zero) are displayed, but without commas or currency signs. When a number is too large to display with the current column width, scientific notation is used.

General MIDI (GM) In multimedia, a standard controlled by the MIDI Manufacturers' Association (MMA) that defines a set of 96 standard voices corresponding to traditional musical instruments and an additional set of voices corresponding to nonmelodic percussion instruments. When one uses the standard code numbers from these sets to create a MIDI file, any GM-compatible synthesizer will reproduce the sounds in the file in the intended way. See *MIDI.*

general protection fault (GPF) In an operating system, a computer crash that is caused by one program invading another's memory space. GPF-related crashes are common in older operating systems that implement cooperative multitasking, in which programs must be expertly designed to coexist in the computer's memory. Today's leading operating systems (including Linux, Mac OS X, and Microsoft Windows XP) offer preemptive multitasking, in which the operating system intervenes in memory-space squabbles; these operating systems offer significantly more reliable operation. See *cooperative multitasking, preemptive multitasking, protected mode.*

General Public License (GPL) An open source software (OSS) license developed by the Free Software Foundation (FSF) to promote the distribution of high-quality, free software. Software licensed with GPL is copyrighted, but the license specifically grants licensees the right to copy, examine, and modify the underlying source code, as long as subsequent distributions extend the same privileges to new recipients. The GPL is specifically designed to prevent the recipients of GPL-licensed code from incorporating this code in commercial products or products distributed without source code; in this respect, it contrasts sharply with the license accompanying BSD Unix, which allows firms to incorporate BSD Unix code into commercial products. See *BSD license, Free Software Foundation (FSF), GNU Project, Linux, open source software (OSS).*

general-purpose computer In contrast to a computer that is dedicated to a specific purpose, such as collecting the results of a laboratory experiment, a general-purpose computer is one that is designed to run a variety of applications. The function of a general-purpose computer depends on the specific applications that it runs rather than the configuration of its hardware.

generate To produce something by setting in motion an automatic procedure. For example, after marking the entries and indicating the table, list, and index locations, one can generate a table of contents, a lists of figures, and an index in a word processing program when one chooses the generate command.

genetic algorithm An automated program development environment in which various alternative approaches to solving a problem are introduced; each is allowed to mutate periodically through the introduction of random changes. The various approaches compete in an effort to solve a specific problem. After a period of time, one approach may prove to be clearly superior to the others.

genlock In digital video, a procedure that synchronizes the video signals of dissimilar devices.

geometry   The physical layout of a hard disk's surface, including number of tracks, number of sectors, tracks per sector, and landing zone location. Disk geometry specifications are part of a disk's setup parameters.

geostationary satellite   An Earth-orbiting satellite that is placed in geosynchronous orbit at an altitude of approximately 22,000 miles so that the period of the satellite's orbit is identical to the Earth's rotational speed. Therefore, the satellite is in a fixed position relative to the Earth's surface. Geostationary satellites are used for telecommunications, weather forecasting, and military applications.

ghost   The effect of an image being displayed continuously onscreen. Such images "burn" into the screen phosphors, resulting in a shadowy image. Also the name of a popular backup software from Symantec. See *screen saver.*

GIF   (Pronounced *jiff* or *giff.*) An acronym for Graphics Interchange Format. A graphics file originally developed by CompuServe and widely used to encode and exchange graphics files on the Internet. The bitmapped GIF format employs a patented lossless compression technique (called LZW) that reduces the size of the graphics file. Although GIF graphics are in widespread use, the JPEG format (which uses lossy compression) reduces graphics files to a size roughly one-third the size of a corresponding GIF file, leading to speedier Internet transmission. However, GIF graphics are more efficient than JPEGs if the depicted image contains many areas of solid color. Because GIF graphics rely on a patented compression algorithm, efforts are underway to replace GIFs with PNG graphics, which use public-domain algorithms. See *animated GIF, GIF89a, PNG, software patent.*

GIF89a   A revised version of the CompuServe GIF graphics format, which enables animation, transparent backgrounds, and interleaving. See *animated GIF.*

GIF animation   A GIF89a graphics file that contains more than one image stored using the GIF graphics file format. Also stored in the file is a brief script that indicates the sequence of images and how long to display each image. See *GIF, GIF89a.*

giga-   A prefix indicating one billion.

gigabit   A unit of measurement approximately equal to 1 billion bits (1,073,741,824 bits). Usually used when indicating the amount of data that can be transferred or transmitted per second.

gigabit Ethernet   An Ethernet standard than enables data transfer rates of up to 1 Gbps using optical fiber or copper cable.

gigabyte (GB)   A unit of measurement approximately equal to 1 billion bytes (1,073,741,824 bytes). Used when stating an amount of memory or disk capacity. One gigabyte equals 1,000MB (megabytes).

gigaflop   A measurement of processor speed equal to one billion (10^9) floating point operations per second. See *FLOP, megaflop, teraflop.*

GIGO   Acronym for "garbage in, garbage out," which is usually said in response to fouled-up computer output that is attributable to erroneous input, such as a mistyped command.

glare   Light reflected off the display from an outside source, such as a lamp or a window, and into one's eyes. Glare makes the display hard to read and may cause eye strain or headaches. Several antiglare techniques exist, but the simplest one is to reposition the monitor.

glitch   Slang term for any computer malfunction, but especially one that causes a momentary interruption of service. In general, a glitch is a hardware problem; a software problem is called a bug, but this usage is not consistently observed. See *bug.*

G.lite   An ITU-TSS standard for consumer versions of Asymmetric Digital

Subscriber Line (ADSL). G.lite defines services that can use existing twisted-pair wiring and offers downstream data transfer rates of 384 Kbps to 1.5 Mbps (upstream rates range from 16 Kbps to 128 Kbps). G.lite eliminates the need for a technician to install a splitter, a signal-separating device required by faster versions of ADSL. Also known as Universal ADSL. See *ADSL, DSL, twisted pair.*

global backup   See *full backup.*

global format   In a spreadsheet program, a numeric format or label alignment choice that applies to all cells in the worksheet. With most programs, one can override the global format by defining a format for certain cells.

global kill file   In a Usenet newsreader program, a file containing words, phrases, names, or network addresses that a person has identified as signals of an unwanted message (such as "Make Money Fast"). The program screens incoming articles for these signals and automatically deletes the articles before the person even see them. A global kill file performs this function in all newsgroups, while a newsgroup kill file deletes unwanted messages only in specific newsgroups.

global scope   In programming, available throughout the program. A variable with global scope can be used anywhere in the program. See *scope.*

global variable   In programming, a variable that is recognized throughout the program (that is, it has global scope). See *global scope, scope, variable.*

glossary   In a word processing program, a feature used to store frequently used phrases and boilerplate text for later insertion into documents when needed.

glossy finish   A quality of paper that reflects light harshly. Glossy finish paper is less popular for laser printer use than matte finish paper.

GM   See *General MIDI.*

GMT   Acronym for Greenwich Mean Time. See *UTC.*

GNOME   (Pronounced *guh-NOME.*) Acronym for GNU Network Object Model Environment. A desktop environment for Unix and Unix-like operating systems that requires the X Window System. GNOME is the default desktop in Red Hat Linux 6.0 and later. When used with GNOME-compliant applications, GNOME offers many advanced features, including drag-and-drop, dockable toolbars, and tear-off menus. GNOME is distributed on open source principles and is part of the GNU Project. See *desktop environment, windowing environment, X Window System.*

GNU   Acronym for GNU's Not Unix. An open source version of the Unix operating system created by the Free Software Foundation's GNU Project. See *GNU Project.*

GNU Project   Initiated in 1983 by the Free Software Foundation (FSF), the GNU Project is an ongoing effort to create an open source version of the Unix operating system. Project achievements include an open source version of the Bourne shell (called bash) and an impressive set of file utilities. Work is currently underway to create a kernel for GNU, called hurd. The Linux operating system uses the Linux kernel and many of the utilities created by the GNU Project. See *bash, Free Software Foundation (FSF), GNU, kernel, Linux, open source software (OSS).*

Gnutella   An application and communications protocol for peer-to-peer (p2p) Internet file sharing that bears some similarity to Napster, in that most users employ Gnutella to share MP3 files with other Internet users. Unlike Napster, Gnutella does not require a coordinating enterprise and central server facility, so it is significantly less vulnerable to lawsuits from copyright holders and the organizations, such as the Recording Industry Association of America (RIAA), that represent them. Gnutella networks are ad-hoc communities that form and disband without central coordination. A significant disadvantage of Gnutella's underlying protocols is their inefficiency; network searching and file exchange speeds degrade considerably when Gnutella networks begin to approach the critical mass of users that makes Napster such an attractive resource for locating specific recordings. See *MP3, Napster, p2p.*

Gopher In Unix-based systems linked to the Internet, a menu-based program that helps one find files, programs, definitions, and other resources on specified topics. Gopher was originally developed at the University of Minnesota and was named after the school mascot. Unlike FTP and Archie, Gopher does not require the user to know and use the details of host, directory, and file names. Instead, one browses through menus and presses Enter when he or she finds something interesting. One usually sees another menu with more options until finally selecting an option that displays information. One can then read the information or save it to the disk storage area after retrieving it with anonymous FTP. The World Wide Web (WWW) has made Gopher and other text-based Internet search tools obsolete, although some Gopher servers are still operating.

Gopherspace In Gopher, the enormous computer-based space that is created by the global dissemination of Gopher-accessible resources. A search tool called Veronica enables one to search Gopherspace for directory titles and resources that match supplied keywords.

.gov A domain name denoting a government office or agency.

GPL See *General Public License.*

GPRS Acronym for General Packet Radio Service. A wireless data communication service for cellular telephone systems that enables data transfer rates of up to 114 Kbps.

GPS Acronym for Global Positioning System. A positioning system developed by the U.S. Defense Department that enables users of inexpensive GPS equipment to determine their geographical position within an accuracy of approximately 100 meters. The system uses 24 satellites that have been placed in geosynchronous orbit. Anywhere on Earth, at least four satellites are within a GPS receiver's line of sight; the receiver uses the satellite signals to triangulate its location.

grabber hand In graphics programs and HyperCard, an onscreen image of a hand that one can position with the mouse to move selected units of text or graphics from place to place onscreen.

grab handle In a graphics program, the small black boxes on the periphery of an object. By dragging these handles, the user can move, size, or crop the object.

Grand Challenge An unsolved scientific or engineering problem of such fabulous complexity that no individual researcher or even an individual research institute can hope to tackle it alone. Examples include mapping the human genome or understanding the astrophysics of the Milky Way. Advanced computer networks may help researchers tackle the Grand Challenges by fostering collaboratory research and resource sharing by means of federated databases.

granularity The degree or level of detail available in an information system. A database with high granularity offers highly specific or detailed information.

granularity of allocation The smallest unit of storage space available. The granularity of hard and floppy disks is determined by the size of their clusters; if a disk has a cluster size of 100K, even files smaller than 100K will be assigned an entire cluster.

graph See *chart.*

Graphical Device Interface (GDI) A programming resource (part of a graphical user interface) that enables programmers to generate dialog boxes and other graphical elements in a consistent style. GDIs handle the detail work of drawing such elements onscreen; the programmer needs only to tell the GDI what to draw and where to draw it.

Graphical Device Interface (GDI) printer A printer that has no raster image processor (RIP) and that leaves much of the task of preparing a page for printing to software. GDI printers can be used only with Microsoft Windows. GDI printers tax the often already burdened central processing unit (CPU) and may not be supported by future versions of Windows, so they are probably not a good buy. Synonymous with Windows printer.

graphical user interface (GUI) A design for the part of a program that interacts with the user and that uses icons to represent program features. The Apple Macintosh and Microsoft Windows operating environments are popular GUIs. Having found that people recognize graphic representations faster than they read words or phrases, a Xerox research team designed a user interface with graphic images called icons. GUIs typically work with mousable interfaces with pull-down menus, dialog boxes, check boxes, radio buttons, drop-down list boxes, scrollbars, scroll boxes, and the like. Programs with a GUI require a computer with sufficient speed, power, and memory to display a high-resolution, bitmapped display.

graphics In personal computing, the creation, modification, and printing of pictures, as opposed to text. The two basic types of computer-produced graphics are object-oriented graphics, also called vector graphics, and bitmapped graphics, often called raster graphics. Vector graphics programs, usually called draw programs, store graphic images in the form of mathematical representations that can be sized and scaled without distortion. Vector graphics programs are well suited for architecture, computer-aided design, interior design, and other applications in which precision and scaling capability are more important than artistic effects. Bitmapped graphics programs, often called paint programs, store graphic images in the form of patterns of screen pixels. Unlike draw programs, paint programs can create delicate patterns of shading that convey an artistic touch, but any attempt to resize or scale the graphic may result in unacceptable distortion.

graphics accelerator See *graphics accelerator board*.

graphics accelerator board A video adapter that includes a graphics coprocessor and all the other circuitry normally found on a video adapter. The graphics accelerator handles the graphics processing, freeing the central processing unit (CPU) for other important tasks and thereby dramatically improving a system's capability to run Microsoft Windows and other graphical applications.

graphics adapter See *video adapter*.

graphics board See *video adapter*.

graphics card See *video adapter*.

graphics character In a computer's built-in character set, a character composed of lines, shaded rectangles, or other shapes. One can combine graphics characters to form block graphics: simple images, illustrations, and borders. Some programs called character-based programs use no graphics other than those made up of graphics characters.

graphics coprocessor A microprocessor specially designed to speed the processing and display of high-resolution video images. A graphics accelerator board that includes a graphics coprocessor can speed the display of programs such as Microsoft Windows that use graphical user interfaces (GUIs). Popular graphics coprocessors include the Weitek W5086 and W5186, and S3 Inc.'s 86C911.

graphics file format In a graphics program, the way in which the information needed to display a graphic is arranged and stored on disk.

Graphics Interchange Format See *GIF*.

graphics mode   In video adapters, a display mode in which everything onscreen, including text and graphics, is drawn using pixels instead of characters from the character set. Many adapters also offer a character mode, which runs more quickly because it uses the computer's built-in, ready-made characters instead of composing them individually. Some programs enable the user to switch between a graphics view, which uses graphics mode and accurately shows what printed output will look like, and character view, which is faster than graphics view.

graphics primitive   In an object-oriented graphics program, the most basic unit of graphic expression, such as a line, arc, circle, rectangle, or oval.

graphics scanner   A graphics input device that transforms a picture into an image that can be displayed onscreen.

graphics spreadsheet   A spreadsheet program that displays the worksheet by using bitmapped graphics instead of relying on the computer's built-in character set. Graphics spreadsheets, such as Microsoft Excel and Lotus 1-2-3 for Windows, include desktop publishing tools, such as multiple typefaces, type sizes, rules, and screens (grayed areas). Also, printouts can combine spreadsheets and business graphs on one page. See *what-you-see-is-what-you-get (WYSIWYG)*.

graphics tablet   An input device that allows one to draw with an electronic pen on an electronically sensitive table. The pen's movements are relayed to the screen. See *pen computer*.

graphics view   In some DOS applications, a mode in which the program switches the display circuitry to its graphics mode. In graphics mode, the computer can display bit-mapped graphics. On all except the fastest computers, graphics mode is significantly slower than character mode. Some programs have a fast character view that does not offer the what-you-see-is-what-you-get (WYSIWYG) features of graphics view.

grave accent   See *back quote*.

grave site   Slang for an abandoned Web site that is still accessible to Internet users.

grayscale   In computer graphics, a series of shades from white to black.

grayscale monitor   A monitor (and compatible display adapter) that can display a full range of shades from white to black, but no colors.

grayscale scanner   A scanner that generates monochrome output in levels of gray. The best grayscale scanners can produce output that resembles the tonal range of black-and-white photographs.

greeking   In word processing, pseudo-text, lines, or bars used to fill spaces on the page where real text will later be placed. Graphic artists often use greeking to represent real text so that they can focus on the overall page layout design instead of being distracted by reading the text. Some word processing and page layout programs use a print preview feature that is similar to greeking. See *Greek text*.

Greek text   A block of simulated text or lines used to represent the positioning and point size of text in a designer's composition of a page, used so that the aesthetics of the page design or a particular typeface can be assessed. Greek text most often starts with the words "lorem ipsum dolor", which is actually nonsensical Latin. The text is called, Greek, however, in reference to the famous saying people use when they don't understand something: "It's call Greek to me." See *greeking*.

Green Book   A Philips standard for packing text, sound, and video onto a CD-ROM that is best known as CD-I (Compact Disc-Interactive).

green PC   A computer system designed to operate in an energy-efficient manner. Powerful green PCs typically draw 90 to 130 watts, while standard systems draw 130 to 160 watts. Green PCs also include power-saving modes that dim monitors and stop hard-disk rotation when they are not in use. In sleep mode, green PCs draw between 28 and 36 watts. Electrical efficiency can quickly translate to big monetary savings in offices equipped with hundreds of machines. See *Energy Star.*

Gregorian calendar The standard calendar in widespread use today; a year consists of 365 days with an extra day every leap year (every fourth year). It was first adopted by Pope Gregory XIII in 1582 to replace the Julian calendar.

grounding strap A wrist strap worn when repairing or upgrading computer components. The strap can be connected to an electrical ground to prevent the discharge of static electricity, which can ruin computer components that contain semiconductor chips.

Group 3 The most common standard for fax machines and fax modems, published by the ITU-TSS. The Group 3 specification dictates methods by which a page-long fax can be sent in a minute or less. Several other standards support Group 3, including the V.27ter, V.29, and V.17 standards.

Group 4 A standard for fax transmission designed to work with digital transmission networks such as ISDN. Group 3 will continue to reign until digital communications find their way into more homes and offices.

group coding Like frequency shift keying (FSK), a means used by a modem to transmit data by altering the character of the carrier. Unlike FSK, though, group coding enables the modem to convey more than 1 bit per change in the carrier. Group coding, which is used in most modern modems, uses quadrature modulation and other modulation techniques to modify the carrier.

groupware Programs that increase the cooperation and joint productivity of small groups of co-workers.

GSM Acronym for Global System for Mobile Communications. A version of the Time Division Multiple Access (TDMA) protocol for digital cellular phones that consumes less bandwidth than TDMA while still allowing eight simultaneous calls per device. Capable of transmitting data at rates of up to 9.6 Kbps, GSM is widely used in Europe and Asia, but much less so in the United States. See *TDMA.*

GTK Acronym for GIMP Tool Kit. A set of window widgets (interface controls) for the X Window System that was originally developed for The GIMP, an open source image editing and illustration program for Unix and Unix-like computers. The toolkit has since been broadened for use in developing any type of application, and it provides the basic widget library for the GNOME desktop environment. See *GNOME, X Window System.*

gTLD-MoU Acronym for Generic Top-Level Domain Memorandum of Understanding. An international organization that governs the creation and regulation of top-level domain names for the Internet. In 1998, gTLD-MoU introduced the following new top-level domains: arts, firm, info, nom, rec, shop, and web. See *arts, domain name, firm, info, nom, rec, shop, web.*

guest In a local area network (LAN), an access privilege that enables one to access another computer on the network without having to provide a password.

GUI See *graphical user interface.*

GUID **1.** Acronym for Global Unique Identifier. A unique identification number that Microsoft software automatically assigns to each document a user creates. On a local area network (LAN), this number includes the Ethernet address of the workstation where the document was created. It is therefore possible to use a GUID to determine the authorship of an anonymous document, but this fact was not revealed to users. In response to concerns about user privacy, Microsoft issued a patch for Office 97 that disables the GUID function. See *PSN.* **2.** In Unix and Unix-like operating systems, a file attribute for executable files that gives any user executing the file the privileges assigned to the file's group owner. See *SUID*.

guide In a page layout program, a nonprinting line that appears as a dotted line onscreen, showing the current location of margins, gutters, and other page layout design elements.

GUILE Acronym for GNU's Ubiquitous Intelligent Language for Extension. A program development environment based on the Scheme programming language that includes numerous programming libraries and utilities. GUILE is available for Unix and Unix-like operating systems, including Linux. See *Scheme*.

guru In computing, an expert who can talk about highly technical subjects in an intelligible way (a rare quality) and who does not mind doing so (even rarer).

gutter See *binding offset*.

gzip A Unix compression program, created by the Free Software Foundation (FSF) and free from patent restrictions, that is widely used to compress files on the Internet. Files compressed with gzip have the extension .gz. Based on the Lempel-Ziv (LZ77) algorithm, gzip can decompress files created by several similar compression utilities, including zip (*.zip), compress (*.Z), and pack (*.z). See *file compression utility*, *Lempel-Ziv compression algorithm*.

H

H.323 An ITU-TSS standard that defies standards for real-time Internet telephony as well as audio and videoconferencing via the Internet. Applications that conform to H.323 can work with other H.323-compliant programs, even if they are made by different companies. See *ITU-TSS*.

hack **1.** A clever and original rearrangement of the existing system or network resources that results, as if by magic, in a stunning improvement in system performance (or an equally stunning prank). A hacker is one who uses computers to perform hacks and is not necessarily a computer criminal. See *cracker, hacker ethic, phreaking.* **2.** A quick and dirty job that produces results, but without following any logical or orderly procedure.

hacker Traditionally, a computer enthusiast who enjoys learning everything about a computer system or network and pushing the system to its highest possible level of performance through clever programming. Hackers do not necessarily engage in unauthorized computer access (cracking) or other illegal activities. In the press and popular usage, hackers are often equated with computer criminals, to the consternation of hackers and those with some knowledge of the computer's history. See *black hat, cracker, grey hat, hacker ethic, hacking, white hat.*

hacker ethic A set of moral principles that was common to the first-generation hacker community (roughly 1965–1982), described by Steven Levy in *Hackers* (1984). According to the hacker ethic, all technical information should, in principle, be freely available to all. Therefore, gaining entry to a system to explore data and increase knowledge is never unethical. However, destroying, altering, or moving data in such a way that could cause injury or expense to others is always unethical. In increasingly more states, unauthorized computer access is against the law. See *computer ethics, cracker, cyberpunk, cyberspace, hack, phreaking.*

hacking **1.** An approach to computer programming that emphasizes the playful, creative exploration of the performance limits of computer systems. **2.** An attempt to get a complex program or system working without taking the time to do so in an organized, orderly manner. See *hack, hacker.*

half-duplex An asynchronous communications protocol in which the communications channel can handle only one signal at a time. The two stations alternate their transmissions. Synonymous with local echo. See *communications protocol, full-duplex.*

half-height drive A disk drive half the size of the 3-inch-high drives in the original IBM Personal Computer. Half-height drive bays and drives are standard in today's PCs.

half-height drive bay A mounting space for half-height devices, such as half-height drives in a computer's case. A half-height drive bay is 1.625 inches tall. See *full-height drive bay.*

halftone **1.** In computer graphics, a continuous tone image, such as a photograph, that has been digitized by means of dithering, in which patterns of black and white dots are used to simulate shades of gray. **2.** In printing, a photograph prepared for printing by breaking down the continuous gradations of tones into a series of dots with a special screen or a scanner. Dense patterns of thick dots produce dark shades, and less-dense patterns of smaller dots produce lighter shades. See *dithering, screening, Tagged Image File Format (TIFF).*

Handheld Device Markup Language See *HDML.*

hand-held scanner A scanner that one holds and moves over the material that he or she is scanning. Hand-held scanners are somewhat less expensive than flatbed scanners but often require more than one pass to scan page-size documents. One should avoid hand-held scanners unless he or she plans to scan narrow material, such as newspaper columns. See *flatbed scanner, sheet-fed scanner.*

handle **1.** In programming, a unique number that can be used to access a peripheral device or an object such as a window or file. When programs request access to a resource from the operating system, they receive a handle, which they can then use to access the needed resource. **2.** In a graphics application, the small, black squares around a selected object. One uses these squares to drag, size, or scale the object. Synonymous with grab handle. See *draw program, vector graphics.*

handler A driver, utility program, or subroutine that takes care of a task. Handlers can also be a set of programming instructions attached to a pushbutton. The instructions control what happens when the user selects a button. See *event-driven environment, event-driven language, object-oriented programming.*

handshaking A method for controlling the flow of serial communication between two devices so that one device transmits data only when the other device is ready. In hardware handshaking, a separate wire sends a signal when the receiving device is ready to receive the signal; software handshaking uses special control characters. Devices such as serial printers use hardware handshaking because they are close to one another and can use a special cable. Because the telephone system does not have an extra wire available, the telephone connections that modems use require software handshaking. The two software handshaking techniques are ETX/ACK, which uses the ASCII character Ctrl+C to pause data transmission, and XON/XOFF, which uses Ctrl+S to pause and Ctrl+Q to resume transmission.

handwriting recognition software A program that accepts handwriting as input and converts it into editable computer text.

hang A type of computer crash in which a program initiates an operation but cannot complete it for some reason. The program does not and cannot respond, and it may be necessary to restart the system to continue processing.

hanging indent A paragraph indentation in which the first line is flush with the left margin, but subsequent lines (called turnover lines) are indented.

haptics The use of the sense of touch to provide feedback from computer control devices.

hard Permanent, physically defined, permanently wired, or fixed, as opposed to soft (changeable or subject to redefinition). The printed document is hard because changing the printed document is difficult. A document in the computer's memory is soft because one can still make changes to it. See *hard copy, hard hyphen, hard return, hard space, hard-wired.*

hard boot A system restart initiated by means of pressing the hardware-reset switch or, on computers lacking such a switch, by switching the power off and then back on again. A hard boot may be necessary after a crash so severe that the controls used for the normal restarting procedure (a soft boot) do not work. See *cold boot, soft boot.*

hard copy Printed output, as distinguished from data stored on disk or in memory.

hard disk See *hard drive.*

hard drive A secondary storage medium that uses several rigid disks coated with a magnetically sensitive material and housed together with the recording heads in a hermetically sealed mechanism. Hard drive performance is measured in terms of access time, seek time, rotational speed (measured in revolutions per minute), and data transfer rate. Hard drive interface standards—the means by which hard drives transmit their contents to other parts of a computer—include ST506/ST-412, IDE, EIDE, ESDI, SCSI, and Wide SCSI. IDE and SCSI are most common today. See *disk drive, Enhanced IDE (EIDE), IDE, SCSI.*

hard drive backup program A utility program that backs up hard drive data and programs onto more permanent storage media. See *backup utility.*

hard drive controller The circuitry, usually mounted on the hard drive itself, that controls the spindle motor and the head actuator of a hard disk. Under instructions from the host adapter, the hard drive controller searches for needed information and communicates it to the rest of the computer. IDE hard drive controllers must be configured in different ways, depending on whether they are master or slave drives.

hard drive interface An electronic standard for connecting a hard drive to the computer. See *ESDI, IDE, SCSI*.

hard hyphen In word processing programs, a special hyphen that acts as a regular character so that text cannot word wrap at this hyphen. Synonymous with nonbreaking hyphen. See *soft hyphen*.

hard page break A page break inserted by the user that remains in effect even after the user later adds or deletes text above the break. In contrast, the soft page break inserted by the program moves automatically as one adds and deletes text. Synonymous with forced page break.

hard return In word processing programs, a line break created by pressing the Enter key, as opposed to a soft return, which a program creates automatically at the end of a line. Unlike a soft return, a hard return stays in place when one inserts and deletes text.

hard space In word processing programs, a space specially formatted as a regular character so that the text cannot start a new line, breaking the phrase at the space's location. Hard spaces often are used to keep two-word proper nouns or month and date together on the same line, such as Key Biscayne, [hard space] West Point, and January [hard space] 25.

hardware The electronic components, boards, peripherals, and equipment that make up a computer system; distinguished from the programs (software) that tell these components what to do. See *firmware, software*.

hardware cache A buffer on a disk drive controller or a disk drive. The buffer stores frequently accessed program instructions and data, as well as additional tracks of data that a program might need next. A computer can access required data much more quickly from the hardware cache than from the disk. The data is then delivered as fast as the expansion bus can carry it. Both 32-bit and 16-bit cached disk controller cards are available. See *disk drive controller*.

hardware conflict A computer malfunction caused by two peripheral devices attempting to access the same interrupt line or input/output channel. See *IRQ conflict*.

hardware flow control Physical modem circuits that implement an error-correction protocol, such as MNP4 or V.42. The alternative (found in less expensive modems) is software error control, which requires the computer's central processing unit (CPU) to monitor the data stream for errors.

hardware handshaking In a serial data communications device such as a modem, a method of synchronizing two devices in a communications channel by means of separate physical circuits, which are used to send signals indicating that a device is ready to receive data. Compare software handshaking, in which this task is performed by inserting information into the data stream. See *CTS/RTS*.

hardware MPEG support Circuitry built into a computer to improve MPEG video playback speed and quality.

hardware panning A video adapter feature that enables it to simulate a display larger than the one to which the video adapter is connected. By having extra video memory and being capable of changing the portion of video memory designated as the frame buffer, a video adapter enables one to drag the mouse to the edge of the screen and scroll into other parts of a large "virtual" display.

hardware platform A hardware standard, such as IBM PC–compatible or

Macintosh. devices or programs created for one platform cannot run on others. See *device independence, platform-independent.*

hardware reset Restarting the system by pushing the computer's hardware reset switch. A hardware reset might be necessary after a system crash so severe that one cannot use the keyboard restart command (in DOS, Ctrl+Alt+Del) to restart the computer. See *cold boot, hard boot, soft boot, warm boot.*

hardware reset switch A switch or button, generally located on the front of the computer's case, that initiates a hardware reset (a hard boot). Synonymous with reset button.

hardware sprite A video adapter feature that enables the video adapter to draw a cursor or mouse pointer on the display without having to redraw the entire screen. Hardware sprites, included in all video standards since the late-1980s eXtended Graphics Array (XGA) adapter, make programming easier because programs can move the cursor or pointer with very simple commands.

hardware tree In Microsoft Windows, a graphical representation of the various devices and adapters installed in a computer.

hardware windowing A method of improving video performance, employed by most graphics accelerator boards. A hardware windowing design is particularly well suited to multitasking environments, such as Microsoft Windows, because it keeps track of the screen area (or window) in which each program runs. Besides freeing the central processing unit (CPU) from managing windows, hardware windowing systems enable the graphics accelerator board to work faster because it has to alter only the window in which a change occurs, not the whole screen.

hard-wired Built into the computer's electronic circuits instead of facilitated by program instructions. To improve computer performance, computer designers include

circuits that perform specific functions, such as multiplication or division, at higher speeds. These functions are hard-wired. The term "hard-wired" also refers to the program instructions contained in the computer's read-only memory (ROM) or firmware.

hash **1.** An identifying value produced by performing a numerical operation called a hash function on a data item. The value uniquely identifies the data item but requires far less storage space. For this reason, the computer can search for hash values more quickly than it can search for the longer data items themselves. A hash table associates each hash value with a unique data item. **2.** An identifying value that is used to verify the data integrity of messages transmitted over a computer network. Using a secret algorithm, the sending computer computes the hash value for the message. This value constitutes, in effect, a digital fingerprint for the message because the hash value is uniquely a product of the message's content. In addition, the hashing algorithm cannot be derived from the message content or the hash value. The message and the hash value are then transmitted. The receiving computer, which also knows the secret hash algorithm, performs the same computation on the message. If the resulting hash value does not agree with the value received from the sending computer, then it is proved that the message was altered en route, and the message is discarded. See *one-way hash function.*

hash function In databases, a calculation performed on the key of a data record that produces a value, called a hash value, that uniquely identifies the record. The hash function records the hash value, as well as a pointer to the record's physical location, in a hash table.

hash mark See *hash sign.*

hash sign Common slang expression for the pound symbol (#). Synonymous with hash mark.

hash table In databases, a table of hash values that provides rapid access to data records. The hash values are generated by running a hash function on the keys of each record, such as a person's last name. The hash function uniquely identifies each record, and the hash table includes pointers to each record.

hat Common slang expression for the caret symbol (^).

Hayes command set A standardized set of instructions used to control modems, introduced by Hayes, a pioneering modem manufacturer. Common Hayes commands include the following:

AT	Attention (used to start all commands).
ATDT	Attention, dial-in tone mode.
ATDP	Attention, dial-in pulse mode.
+++	Enter the command mode during the communication session.
ATH	Attention, hang up.

Hayes-compatible modem A modem that recognizes the Hayes command set.

hazard A condition or state in which a mishap (injury, damage, loss, or death) is likely or inevitable if the system is operated in an unsafe manner. In general, such systems involve the use of large and potentially lethal amounts of energy. For example, railways are hazardous because trains develop highly lethal levels kinetic energy. When a hazard is present, safety is obtained by reducing risk (the likelihood that, under the specific conditions in which the system is operated, a severe mishap will occur); for example, risk can be reduced by using procedures or devices that reduce or eliminate the possibility of a mishap. A century of railway operation experience dictates that devices must be installed to ensure that operators obey signaling devices. See *mishap, risk, safety.*

HCI Abbreviation for human-computer interaction. A scientific field focusing on how people interact with computers and how computers can be designed to interact with humans more successfully.

HDD Acronym for hard disk drive. See *hard drive.*

HDML Acronym for Handheld Device Markup Language. A markup language specifically designed for presenting formatted Web content in digital cellular phones, personal digital assistants (PDAs), and other remote digital devices with small screens and limited memory. See *digital cellular phone, PDA, WML.*

HDSL Acronym for High Bit Rate Digital Subscriber Line. A Digital Subscriber Line (DSL) standard that offers up to 2.048 Mbps of Internet connectivity via ordinary telephone lines. HDSL is symmetrical, meaning data speeds for uploading and downloading are identical. Limited to a range of 12,000 feet from the central office (CO), HDSL can be extended by means of repeaters, but at the cost of a diminished data transfer rate. See *ADSL, CO, data transfer rate, DSL.*

HDTV Acronym for High Definition Television. A digital television standard, part of the U.S. Federal Communication Commission's Advanced TV standard, that enables television stations to broadcast high-resolution video with CD-quality sound. To receive HDTV signals, an HDTV-compatible TV is required.

head See *read/write head.*

head access aperture The opening in a floppy disk's shell that enables the read/write head to work with the recording medium. In 3½-inch floppy disks, a sliding metal shutter covers the head access aperture, but 5¼-inch disks expose the head access aperture whenever the disk is out of its protective sleeve.

head actuator In a disk drive, a mechanism that moves the assembly containing the read/write heads across the surface of the disk to the location where data is to be written or read. See *random access, sequential access.*

head arm   In a disk drive, a rigid mechanical rod with a read/write head flexibly connected at one end and attached to a single moving assembly on the other end. Several head arms, one for each side of each platter in a hard disk, are attached to the same assembly so that they can move as a unit. See *hard disk.*

head crash   In a hard disk, the collision of a read/write head with the surface of the disk, generally caused by a sharp jolt to the computer's case and resulting in damage to the disk surface and possibly to the head. Head parking (an automatic feature of most modern operating systems) prevents a head crash when the computer is turned off.

header   1. In word processing, repeated text, such as a page number and a short version of a document's title, that appears at the top of the pages in a document. **2.** In computer networking, the portion of a data packet that precedes the data and provides information about the packet's source and destination. **3.** In e-mail or a Usenet news article, the beginning of a message. The header contains important information about the sender's address, the subject of the message, and other information. **4.** In programming, a preceding line that states the purpose of a program, function, or subroutine.

head-mounted display (HMD)   A stereoscopic set of head-mounted goggles that produces a sensation of three-dimensional space. Head-mounted displays are an integral part of virtual reality systems, in which users feel as though they are exploring a real world that has actually been created within the computer system. See *stereoscopy.*

head parking   Positioning the read/write head over the landing zone to prevent a head crash, in which the head strikes and usually damages the disk surface. Older hard disks required one to issue a command

to park the head before turning off the computers; newer hard disks feature automatic head parking.

head seek time   See *access time.*

head slot   See *head access aperture.*

heap   1. A section of memory that an operating system or application sets aside for storing a certain type of data. **2.** In programming, a list of data that is sorted only partially, but enough so that a given value can be located more quickly than would be the case for a completely unsorted list.

heat sink   A finned metal assembly that sits on top of a hot component, such as a microprocessor, and draws heat out of it, preventing it from overheating. Microprocessors require both a heat sink and CPU fan to keep cool.

heavy client   In a client/server network, a complex client program that is difficult to learn, expensive to maintain, and restricted in its flexibility. See *light client.*

helper application   In a Web browser, a supplementary program that enables the browser to handle multimedia files, such as animations, videos, and sounds. When the browser encounters a file it cannot read, it examines the file's extension. The browser then consults a lookup table that tells it which helper program to start. Users must configure this lookup table manually and make sure that the necessary helper programs are installed. When the helper program starts, it runs as a separate program, unlike plug-ins, which extend the capabilities of the browser and can often display the multimedia data within the browser window. See *plug-in.*

Helvetica   A sans serif typeface frequently used for display type and occasionally for body type. One of the world's most widely used fonts, Helvetica is included in many laser printers as a built-in font. The following are examples of Helvetica type:

ABCDEFGHIJKLMNopqrstuvwxyz1 234567890.

hertz (Hz) A unit of measurement of electrical vibrations; 1 Hz is equal to one cycle per second. See *kilohertz (KHz)*, *megahertz (MHz)*.

heterogeneous network A computer network that includes computers and devices from several manufacturers and that transmits data using more than one communications protocol.

heuristic A method of solving a problem by using rules of thumb acquired from experience. Unlike an algorithm, which is a proven mathematical formula for solving a specific problem, a heuristic cannot guarantee a solution, but it may provide the only way to approach a complex problem. See *expert system, knowledge base.*

Hewlett-Packard Graphics Language (HPGL) A page description language (PDL) and file format for graphics printing with the HP LaserJet line of printers, HP plotters, and high-end inkjet printers, now widely emulated by HP-compatible laser printers. See *Hewlett-Packard Printer Control Language (HPPCL).*

Hewlett-Packard Printer Control Language (HP PCL) The proprietary printer control language (PCL) that Hewlett-Packard introduced in 1984 with the company's first LaserJet printer. Like the Hayes command set in the modem world, HPPCL has become a standard.

hex A commonly used shorthand term for hexadecimal notation (for example, "Here's the mistake. This number should be in hex."). See *hexadecimal notation.*

hexadecimal notation A numbering system that uses a base (radix) of 16. Unlike decimal notation (base 10) or binary notation (base 2), hexadecimal notation uses 16 digits: 0, 1, 2, 3, 4, 5, 6, 7, 8, 9, A, B, C, D, E, and F. Programmers use hexadecimal notation as a convenient way to represent binary notation, which is difficult to read and prone to error when manipulated by humans. The two notational systems are easily translated into one another because

16 is a power of 2. In contrast, decimal numbers are more difficult to translate into binary numbers because its base, 10, is not a power of 2. Because each hexadecimal number can represent 16 quantities, a single hexadecimal number can stand for four binary digits (for example, 1111 [15 in decimal] = F [hexadecimal]). Using hexadecimal notation, a programmer can conveniently represent a byte (such as 01101111) as two consecutive hexadecimal numbers: 0110 (binary) = 6 (hex); 1111 (binary) = F (hex), so that 01101111 = 6F. See *binary notation, byte, decimal notation, octal notation.*

hexadecimal number One of 16 digits in hexadecimal notation: 0, 1, 2, 3, 4, 5, 6, 7, 8, 9, A, B, C, D, E, and F. Note that the first 10 hexadecimal digits are indistinguishable from numbers written in decimal notation; for example, 64 in decimal notation is equal to 40 in hexadecimal notation. To avoid confusion, programming languages typically require the use of a prefix to denote that the following number is in hex. In the C programming language, the prefix is 0x; for example, 0xc9 = 201 in decimal notation. See *hexadecimal notation.*

HFS Acronym for Hierarchical File System. A Macintosh disk storage system, designed for use with hard disks, that enables users to store files within named directories, called folders. HFS replaces an earlier flat file system in which no two files could have the same name. See *flat file system, hierarchical file system.*

HFS+ An updated version of the Macintosh HFS file system, introduced with Mac OS 8.1, that is capable of working with large hard disks. Synonymous with Mac OS Extended Format.

hidden character In word processing, a character formatted with a special style that makes it invisible when printed.

hidden codes The hidden text formatting codes embedded in a document by a word processing program. In most commercial programs, these codes are proprietary, which explains why the files created

Hexadecimal Number

Hexadecimal	Decimal	Binary	Hexadecimal	Decimal	Binary
0	0	00000000	17	11	00010001
1	1	00000001	18	12	00010010
2	2	00000010	19	13	00010011
3	3	00000011	20	14	00010100
4	4	00000100	21	15	00010101
5	5	00000101	22	16	00010110
6	6	00000110	23	17	00010111
7	7	00000111	24	18	00011000
8	8	00001000	25	19	00011001
9	9	00001001	26	1A	00011010
10	A	00001010	27	1B	00011011
11	B	00001011	28	1C	00011100
12	C	00001100	29	1D	00011101
13	D	00001101	30	1E	00011110
14	E	00001110	31	1F	00011111
15	F	00001111	32	20	00100000
16	10	00010000			

by one word processing program cannot be read by another unless a conversion utility is used.

hidden file A file with the hidden attribute set so that when users view a directory, the file name is not displayed. One cannot erase or copy hidden files. See *dot file.*

hierarchical file system In an operating system, a method of organizing files in a tree structure. The topmost level, called the root directory, contains leaves, called subdirectories, that can in turn contain further subdirectories. Two or more files can have the same names as long as they are located within different directories.

hierarchy 1. A method of organizing data so that the most general category is at the top of the list; beneath this category are second-level subcategories, each of which may contain additional subcategories. See *hierarchical file system.* **2.** In Usenet, a category of newsgroups. Within the standard newsgroups, for example, seven hierarchies exist: comp, misc, news, rec, sci, soc, and talk. The term "hierarchies" suggests the way that newsgroups are internally categorized. For example, the rec.* hierarchy includes many newsgroups pertaining to hobbies and recreation; the rec.comics.* hierarchy contains several newsgroups for comic collectors; and the rec.comics.elfquest newsgroup focuses on Wendy and Richard Pini's Elfquest comics. See *local Usenet hierarchy, standard newsgroup hierarchy.* **3.** In object-oriented programming, one of the seven fundamental principles of the object model. According to the hierarchy principle, objects should be grouped in a hierarchical relationship such that parent objects pass their methods and properties to child objects by means of a process called inheritance. See *inheritance, object model, object-oriented programming.*

high bit In a binary number, the most significant bit (msb). This is the leftmost digit in a standard binary number.

High Bit Rate Digital Subscriber Line See *HDSL*.

High Definition Television See *HDTV*.

high density A floppy disk storage technique that uses extremely fine-grained magnetic particles. High-density disks are more expensive to manufacture than double-density disks but can store 1MB or more of information on one 5.25- or 3.5-inch disk. Synonymous with quad density.

high-density disk See *floppy disk*.

High-Density Multimedia CD (HDMMCD) See *MMCD*.

high end An expensive product at the top of a firm's offerings that includes features or capabilities likely to be needed only by the most discriminating users or professionals. See *low end*.

higher-order characters See *extended character set*.

high-level format A formatting operation that creates the boot record, file allocation table (FAT), and root directory on a bootable disk. See *low-level format*.

high-level programming language A programming language such as BASIC or Pascal, which is easier for human-beings to understand than low-level programming languages such as assembly. High-level programming languages use commands such as FOR NEXT or PRINT, enabling programmers to write programs more quickly and easily; however, the program must be translated into assembly language by an interpreter or compiler, resulting in a program that runs more slowly than if it had been originally written in assembly.

highlight **1.** A character, word, text block, or command displayed in reverse video, indicating the current selection. **2.** In

Microsoft Word 97 and later versions, a formatting feature that makes text appear to be highlighted with a transparent color marker.

highlighting The process of marking characters in reverse video onscreen. Synonymous with selection.

high/low/close/open (HLCO) graph In presentation graphics, a line graph in which a stock's high value, low value, closing price, and open price are displayed. The graph aligns the x-axis (categories) horizontally and the y-axis (values) vertically. Another application for a high/low/open/close graph is a record of daily minimum, maximum, and average temperatures. Synonymous with HLCO chart. See *column graph, line graph*.

high memory See *high memory area (HMA)*.

high memory area (HMA) In a DOS computer, the first 64K of extended memory above 1MB. Programs that conform to the eXtended Memory Specification (XMS) can use HMA as a direct extension of conventional memory. In MS-DOS versions 5.0 and higher, most of the portions of DOS that one formerly had to load into conventional memory can be loaded into the high memory area by placing the command DOS = HIGH in the CONFIG.SYS file.

high performance addressing See *HPA*.

high resolution In computer systems, using a sufficient number of pixels in monitors or dots per inch (dpi) when printing to produce well-defined text characters as well as smoothly defined curves in graphic images. The standards for what constitutes high resolution change as technology advances. Currently, a high-resolution video adapter and monitor can display 1,024 pixels horizontally by 768 lines vertically; a high-resolution printer can print at least 300 dpi. See *low resolution*.

high-rez Slang for high resolution.

High Sierra An obsolete standard for encoding data onto CD-ROMs. Although based on High Sierra, the widely used ISO 9660 standard is incompatible with it.

high-speed modem A modem that transfers data at or near the highest possible speed enabled by current modulation protocols (currently 56 Kbps).

High-Speed SDRAM See *HSDRAM.*

HIMEM.SYS An MS-DOS device driver that configures extended memory and the high memory area (HMA) so that programs conforming to the eXtended Memory Standard (XMS) can access it. See *CONFIG.SYS, eXtended Memory Specification (XMS), upper memory area (UMA).*

hint In X Windows, a request for the modification of an object's properties (such as window size) that the window management software will try to fulfill, if possible.

hinting In digital typography, reducing the weight (thickness) of a typeface so that small-sized fonts print without blurring or losing detail on 300 dots per inch (dpi) printers.

histogram A stacked column graph in which one places the columns close together to emphasize differences in the data items within each stack. By stacking data in a column, one emphasizes the contribution that each data item makes to the whole (as in a pie graph). By placing the columns next to each other, one leads the viewer to compare the relative proportions of one data item as it varies from column to column. See *column graph.*

history list In a Web browser, a window that shows all the Web sites that the browser has accessed during a given period, such as the last 30 days.

hit **1.** In database searching, a data record that matches the search criteria. **2.** On the World Wide Web (WWW), an externally originated request for a specific file, such as a graphic or HTML page, by means of the Hypertext Transfer Protocol (HTTP). Servers record the number of hits a Web site receives, but this is not identical to the number of unique individuals who have accessed the site; because many pages contain graphics, Java applets, sounds, and other resources, retrieving one page may require as many as a dozen or more hits. See *cache hit.*

hit rate In cache memory, the percentage of data requests that result in provision of the requested data. If the data has expired from the cache, it must be retrieved from a slower memory unit, such as a disk drive.

HLCO graph See *high/low/close/open graph.*

HMA See *high memory area.*

holy war A protracted and often incendiary debate within the computing community regarding the merits of a particular computer, operating system, or programming style. The term "holy" captures the inflexible and often dogmatic positions that the various participants take in the debate. Famous holy wars include Windows and Macintosh users, and the debate between those who feel that the most significant bit in a unit of represented data should come first (little endian) or last (big endian). See *meme.*

home computer A personal computer specifically designed and marketed for home applications, such as educating children, playing games, balancing a checkbook, paying bills, and controlling lights or appliances.

home directory In Unix, a directory that is assigned to a user to store the user's files, including configuration files. Normally, this is the same as the login directory.

Home key A key on computer keyboards that, in most programs, moves the cursor to the beginning of the line or the top of the screen. However, the assignment of this key is up to the programmer.

home page **1.** In any hypertext system, including the World Wide Web (WWW), a document intended to serve as an initial point of entry to a web of related documents. Also called a welcome page, a home page contains general introductory information, as well as hyperlinks to related resources. A well-designed home page contains internal navigation buttons, which help users find their way among the various documents that the home page makes available. **2.** A central information repository for a given subject. ("This is the home page for owners of Catalina 27 sailing craft.") **3.** The start page that is automatically displayed when one starts a Web browser or clicks the program's Home button. **4.** A personal page listing an individual's contact information, favorite links, and (generally) some information—ranging from cryptic to voluminous—about the individual's perspective on life.

home server In Gopher, the server that the Gopher client program is configured to display automatically when one starts the program.

homophone error A type of spelling error that involves using an incorrect word that sounds the same as the correct word (as in "Two Bee, Oar Knot Too Be"). Although many application programs' spell-checking features fail to find homophone errors, grammar-checking programs usually do find them. Homophone errors are common when using voice-recognition programs to transcribe text. See *speech recognition*.

hook A feature included in a software or hardware product to enable hobbyists and programmers to add their own custom features. For example, Microsoft Word is loaded with hooks that enable experts to create custom dialog boxes, which greatly extends the program's functionality for specific applications. In hardware, an open architecture system might make it easy to design specialized monitoring tools or improved sound capabilities.

hop In a wide area network (WAN), the path data travels from one router to the next. So that the data can reach its destination, several hops may be necessary. This requires processing time, resulting in network latency.

horizontal application A program of such general utility that it can be applied in a wide variety of settings. An example of a horizontal application is a spreadsheet program or a word processing program. See *vertical application*.

horizontal frequency A measure (usually in kilohertz [Khz]) of how fast a monitor draws horizontal lines on its display. Unlike vertical frequency, horizontal frequency does not vary significantly from one monitor to another. Synonymous with horizontal scan rate and line rate.

horizontal market A market that crosses industry sectors. Products developed for horizontal markets, such as word processing programs, are useful for workers in almost any line of work. See *vertical market*.

horizontal retrace The process of the electron beam in a cathode ray tube (CRT) being directed by the yoke from the end of one horizontal scan line to the beginning of the next. Video adapters must allow time for horizontal retrace in preparing the video signal.

horizontal scan rate See *horizontal frequency*.

horizontal scroll bar See *scroll bar/scroll box*.

host **1.** In the Internet, any computer that can function as the beginning and end point of data transfers. An Internet host has a unique Internet address (called an IP address) and a unique domain name. **2.** In networks and telecommunications generally, a server that performs centralized functions, such as making program or data files available to other computers.

host adapter   The adapter that transfers data and instructions back and forth between a hard or floppy disk drive controller and the central processing unit (CPU). Usually an adapter that plugs into the expansion bus, the host adapter complies with a specification such as Integrated Drive Electronics (IDE), Enhanced IDE (EIDE), or Small Computer System Interface (SCSI).

HotBot   See *search engine.*

HotDog   See *HTML editor.*

hot key   A keyboard shortcut that accesses a menu command. A shortcut key, in contrast, gives one direct access to a dialog box or other feature.

hot link   In object linking and embedding (OLE), a method of copying information from one document (the source document) to another (the destination document) so that the target document's information is updated automatically when the source document's information changes. See *cold link.*

hot swapping   Removing or adding a peripheral device while the computer is running. This action is not possible with older peripheral connection standards, with the exception of the PS/2 mouse port. USB and FireWire (also called IEEE 1394) are two peripheral interconnection standards that enable hot swapping. See *FireWire, USB.*

housekeeping   Computer maintenance, including organizing files and directories in a logical manner, running utility programs such as defragmentation utilities and virus checkers, and deleting unneeded files to free up disk space.

HPA   Acronym for high performance addressing. A passive-matrix LCD display technology that provides better images and performance than conventional passive-matrix LCD displays. HPA displays are inferior to the more expensive active-matrix displays found on mid- to high-end notebook computers. See *active matrix display, passive matrix display.*

HP-compatible printer   A printer that responds to the Hewlett-Packard Printer Control Language (HP PCL), which has become the standard for laser printing in the IBM and IBM-compatible computing world.

HPGL   See *Hewlett-Packard Graphics Language.*

HP PCL   See *Hewlett-Packard Printer Control Language.*

HSB color model   A color model in which the color generated by an individual screen pixel is specified by three variables: hue (the color's wavelength), saturation (the purity of the color), and brightness (the relative intensity of energy emitted by the color). See *CMYK color model, color model, RGB color model.*

HSDRAM   Acronym for High-Speed SDRAM. A type of SDARM that is compatible with motherboards with bus speeds of up to 150 Mbps. See *SDRAM.*

HTML   Acronym for Hypertext Markup Language. A markup language for identifying the portions of a document (called elements) so that, when accessed by a program called a Web browser, each portion appears with a distinctive format. HTML is the markup language behind the appearance of documents on the World Wide Web (WWW). HTML is standardized by means of a document type definition (DTD) composed in the Standard Generalized Markup Language (SGML). HTML includes capabilities that enable authors to insert hyperlinks that display another HTML document when clicked. The agency responsible for standardizing HTML is the World Wide Web Consortium (W3C).

HTML 1.0 The original HTML specification, drafted in 1990. Because it contains certain tags that are no longer used, this specification is considered obsolete. Also known as HTML Level 1.

HTML 2.0 A 1994 HTML specification that was developed by the Internet Engineering Task Force (IETF) working committee and formalized as an Internet draft. The major updates from HTML 1.0 are the inclusion of forms and the removal of certain little-used tags. The HTML 2.0 specification does not include many practices, such as tables and the Netscape extensions, that have arisen since its release. Responsibility for the HTML specification subsequently passed to the World Wide Web Consortium (W3C).

HTML 3.0 A proposed HTML specification that would have extended HTML relative to the 2.0 standard. However, this specification did not line up well enough with prevailing Web practice and was never implemented.

HTML 3.2 This version of HTML, adopted as a W3C recommendation in 1996, incorporates many widely used and called-for features, including tables, subscript and superscript characters, text flow around images, Java applets, and style sheets.

HTML 4.01 The most recent (and final) version of HTML, HTML 4.01 is a back-to-basics revision of the popular markup language, which had become cluttered with presentation elements and attributes. The HTML 4.01 specification exists in three versions, called strict, transitional, and frameset. The strict version deprecates all elements and attributes with unnecessary presentation aspects and calls for the use of CSS style sheets to handle presentation aspects. The transitional flavor retains the presentation elements and attributes, and the frameset flavor formalizes the frames tags that have been in widespread use since Netscape introduced them. Note that HTML is being replaced by XHTML, an implementation of the HTML 4.01 tag set in XML. See *XHTML, XML.*

HTML editor A program that provides assistance in preparing documents for the World Wide Web (WWW) using HTML. The simplest HTML editors do not show how a document will appear on the Web, but they do provide automated assistance with HTML coding and display some formats onscreen. The leading packages include site-management features such as multidocument search and replace. Examples include HomeSite and HotDog. See *WYSIWYG HTML editor.*

HTTP The Internet standard that supports the exchange of information on the World Wide Web (WWW). By defining universal resource locators (URLs) and how they can be used to retrieve resources (including not only Web documents but also File Transport Protocol [FTP]–accessible files, Usenet newsgroups, and Gopher menus) anywhere on the Internet, HTTP enables Web authors to embed hyperlinks in Web documents. HTTP defines the process by which a Web client, called a browser, originates a request for information and sends it to a Web server, a program designed to respond to HTTP requests and provide the desired information. HTTP 1.0, in widespread use, has many shortcomings, including an inefficient design and slow performance. A new specification, HTTP 1.1, directly addresses these issues and will result in improved network performance, but servers will have to be updated.

httpd **1.** Acronym for Hypertext Transfer Protocol Daemon. A Web server originally developed at the Swiss Center for Particle Research (CERN) and originally called CERN httpd. Subsequently, httpd was developed at the National Center for Supercomputing Applications (NCSA) for Unix systems; this code formed the basis for the Apache Web server, which is currently dominates the Web server market. **2.** The name of the executable provided with the Apache Web server package. See *Apache, CERN, NCSA.*

HTTPS A variation on the HTTP protocol that provides SSL security for online transactions using the World Wide Web (WWW).

hub   In a local area network (LAN), a device used to create a small-scale network by connecting several computers.

hub ring   The ring of Teflon or plastic in the center of a 5¼-inch floppy disk. The hub ring, which not all disks have, protects the disk from wear caused by contact with the spindle.

Huffman encoding   A data compression technique that takes advantage of the fact that computer data contains many repeated patterns. In place of a pattern, an encoding symbol is created that is much shorter than the lengthier pattern. The shortest encoding symbols are used for the longest patterns of data. This is a lossless compression technique because, when the user decompresses the data, it is fully restored to its exact state prior to compression.

human-computer interaction   See *HCI*.

hung   Not responding to input. See *crash, hang, hung system*.

hung system   A computer that has experienced a system failure and that is no longer processing data, even though the cursor might still be blinking onscreen. The only option in most cases is to restart the system, which means losing any unsaved work.

Hurd   A Unix-like kernel for GNU, a Unix-like operating system created by the GNU Project. See *kernel, GNU Project*.

hyperlink   In a hypertext system, an underlined or otherwise emphasized word or phrase that displays another document when clicked with the mouse.

hypermedia   A hypertext system that employs multimedia resources (graphics, videos, animations, and sounds). The best hypermedia systems employ various media in ways that are more than just window dressing but that materially support the presentation's objective.

hypertext   A method of preparing and publishing text, ideally suited to the computer, in which readers can choose their own paths through the material. To prepare hypertext, one first "chunks" the information into small, manageable units, such as single pages of text. These units are called nodes. One then embeds hyperlinks (also called anchors) in the text. When the reader clicks on a hyperlink, the hypertext software displays a different node. The process of navigating among the nodes linked in this way is called browsing. A collection of nodes that are interconnected by hyperlinks is called a web. The World Wide Web (WWW) is a hypertext system on a global scale. Hypertext applications are particularly useful for working with massive amounts of text, such as encyclopedias and multivolume case law reporters.

Hypertext Markup Language   See *HTML*.

Hypertext Transfer Protocol   See *HTTP*.

hyphenation   In word processing and page layout programs, an automatic operation that hyphenates words at the end of lines, as needed. If one uses it carefully and manually confirms each hyphen, a hyphenation utility can improve a document's appearance, especially when using newspaper columns or large margins. See *hard hyphen, hyphen ladder, soft hyphen*.

hyphen ladder   A formatting flaw caused by the repetition of hyphens at the end of two or more lines in a row. Hyphen ladders distract the eye and disrupt the text's readability. When using automatic hyphenation, one should proofread the results carefully for hyphen ladders. One must adjust word spacing and hyphenation manually, if necessary.

Hz   See *hertz*.

i486 See *Intel 80486.*

IA-32 The instruction set for Intel Corporation's 32-bit microprocessors, ranging from the 386 to the latest versions of the Pentium. To ensure downward compatibility with 32-bit Windows programs, IA-32 preserves a number of design inefficiencies that stem from the design of earlier Intel processors, such as the use of varying bit lengths for instructions, a maximum of eight general purpose registers, and an inefficient floating processing unit (FPU) design. These and other design flaws led to Intel's decision to abandon downward compatibility when the firm introduced its first 64-bit microprocessor, the Itanium, and its new instruction set, IA-64. See *backward-compatible, floating-point unit (FPU), IA-64, instruction set.*

IA-64 The instruction set for Intel Corporation's Itanium, a 64-bit microprocessor. Implementing the EPIC philosophy that the compiler should make decisions about which instruction to execute first, IA-64 abandons many of the inefficient design principles that diminished the performance of Intel's 32-bit processors, which the company kept downwardly compatible with the x86 instruction set. See *EPIC, Itanium.*

IAB See *Internet Architecture Board.*

IAC See *Inter-Application Communication.*

IANA See *Internet Assigned Numbers Authority.*

IAP See *Internet access provider.*

IAPX 80486 See *Intel 80486.*

I-beam pointer In graphical user interfaces (GUI), a type of cursor that is, by definition, positioned between two characters. The cursor is called an "I-beam" because, like a steel girder seen in cross-section, it resembles a capital "I."

IBM Acronym for International Business Machines, the world's largest computer company. Founded in 1911, IBM produced punched-card accounting machines for businesses. In the mid-1950s, the company developed mainframe computers that interfaced with its punched-card tabulating equipment and led the development of a massive business data processing industry. Dominating the mainframe market in the 1960s and 1970s, IBM faced stiff competition from minicomputers in the mid- to late 1970s, and failed to capitalize on the introduction of its influential first personal computer, the IBM PC, which was released in 1981; the result was a series of devastating losses that led some industry observers to question the company's ability to survive. In the 1990s, IBM was restored to profitability by the resurgence of the mainframe computer market and by the firm's new focus on customer service. A revitalized IBM is now asserting leadership in a variety of areas, including semiconductor fabrication, high-powered Web servers that run the Linux operating system on industrial-strength mainframe systems, and its highly regarded line of ThinkPad notebook computers.

IBM 8514 A video adapter for IBM Personal System/2 computers that, with the onboard Video Graphics Array (VGA) circuitry, produces a resolution of 1,024 pixels horizontally and 768 lines vertically. The adapter also contains its own processing circuitry that reduces demand on the central processing unit (CPU). The 8514 replaces the 8514/A and MCGA adapters, which have been discontinued. See *SVGA.*

IBM PC–compatible Capable of running all or almost all the software developed for the IBM Personal Computer; also conforms to industry standards for hardware design so that peripherals—such as monitors and printers—will work properly.

ICCP See *Institute for Certification of Computer Professionals.*

ICMP See *Internet Control Message Protocol.*

icon In a graphical user interface (GUI), an onscreen symbol that represents a program, data file, or some other computer entity or function. Several icons might appear together on an icon bar, an onscreen row of buttons usually placed just above the document window that enables the user to choose frequently accessed menu options without having to use the menus. On each button is an icon that shows the button's function. For example, the Print button might display a tiny picture of a printer.

icon bar In an application, a row of buttons that can be pressed to initiate commands. Synonymous with toolbar.

ICQ (Pronounced *I seek you.*) A popular instant messaging service that informs a user when his or her Internet friends are online. Users can then exchange messages via text chatting. A competing service is America Online's Instant Messenger.

IDE Acronym for Integrated Drive Electronics. A hard drive interface standard for 80286, 80386, 80486, and Pentium computers that offers high performance at low cost. The IDE standard transfers most of the controller electronics to the hard disk assembly. For this reason, the IDE interface can be contained on the computer's motherboard; no controller card or expansion slot is necessary. Superceded by Enhanced Integrated Drive Electronics (EIDE).

IDEA See *International Data Encryption Algorithm.*

identifier In database management, a descriptor used to specify the uniqueness of the information contained in the data record. For example, in a database of travel films, the descriptor "Norway" might appear in a data record for the only travel films that depict scenery from that country.

identity theft A form of fraud in which a thief obtains someone's Social Security number and other personal information, and then uses this information to obtain credit cards fraudulently.

IDSL Acronym for ISDN Digital Subscriber Line. A Digital Subscriber Line (DSL) standard designed to provide Internet data transfer rates of up to 144 Kbps over a digital ISDN telephone line. See *DSL, ISDN.*

IE See *Microsoft Internet Explorer.*

IEEE Acronym for Institute of Electrical and Electronics Engineers (pronounced eye-triple-e). A non-profit, professional organization that is based in the United States but is international in scope, with branches in most countries. Among its members are electrical and electronics engineers, computer scientists, college and university faculty who teach electrical or electronics engineering, and telecommunication industry engineers. Like other leading professional associations, the IEEE publishes peer-reviewed journals, organizes conferences, and develops standards. The IEEE is extremely influential in establishing international standards for emerging computer, electronics, aerospace, and telecommunications technologies.

IEEE 754 A widely observed standard for implementing floating point notation on computer systems. See *floating point notation.*

IEEE 802 A series of telecommunications standards governing local area networks (LANs). Established by the Institute of Electrical and Electronic Engineers (IEEE), the standards include 10Base-2 and 10Base-T cabling, network bridges, and topologies. See *bridge, bus network, Ethernet, fiber optics, star network.*

IEEE 802.11 **1.** A specification for wireless LANs operating at a maximum data rate of 2 Mbps in the 2.4 GHz range. **2.** The family of IEEE Wireless LAN standards based on the original 802.11 specification. See *IEEE 802.11a, IEEE 802.11b, IEEE 802.11g wireless LAN.*

IEEE 802.11a An IEEE standard for wireless LANs. 802.11a has a range of about 20 to 30 feet at the maximum data transfer rate (54 Mbps), though actual rates of

20Mbps are more common; data transfer rates drop by fixed decrements as the receivers are positioned further away from the base station. At 65 feet, the "sweet spot" for IEEE 802.11b (11 Mbps) networks, 802.11a is theoretically capable of as much as 36 Mbps. Because 802.11a signals employ the 5 GHz radio spectrum, its signals are more likely than 802.11b to be blocked by walls and other interior barriers. 802.11a devices are not backwards-compatible with 802.11 devices. An organization called the Wi-Fi Alliance certifies products that fully conform to the 802.11 standards. See *IEEE*

IEEE 802.11b An IEEE standard for wireless LANs. 802.11b networks have a range of about 65 to 100 feet if the maximum data transfer rate (11 Mbps) is desired; as the signal weakens with greater distances from the base unit, the protocol steps down to 5.5 Mbps and finally to 2 Mbps. Capable of penetrating most walls (except thick concrete) at the cost of some range, 802.11b signals employ the 2.4 GHz radio spectrum and uses Carrier Sense Multiple Access with Collision Avoidance (CSMA/CA) to control media access. Networks can be set up in the Ad Hoc Mode, in which all the stations communicate with each other in a peer-to-peer architecture, or an Infrastructure Mode, in which all devices communicate through a central unit called an Access Point. 802.11b devices are backwards-compatible with 802.11 devices. An organization called the Wi-Fi Alliance certifies products that fully conform to the 802.11 standards. Common wireless devices that conform to the 802.11b specification include wireless phones and Bluetooth devices. See *access point, ad hoc network, AirPort, CSMA/CD, IEEE, infrastructure mode, Wi-Fi, Wi-Fi Alliance.*

IEEE 802.11g An amalgam of IEEE 802.11a & b wireless LAN protocols that increases the maximum data transfer rate to 54 Mbps using a 2.4-GHz wireless LAN frequency. Unlike IEEE 802.11a, 802.11g is backwards-compatible with 802.11b networks; some access points can be upgraded to 802.11g with a firmware upgrade. It is expected that many 802.11g devices will be designed to support the entire range of 802.11 specifications. See *access point, IEEE 802.11a, IEEE 802.11b, wireless LAN.*

IEEE 1284 A standard developed by the Institute of Electrical and Electronics Engineers (IEEE) that governs the design of bidirectional parallel ports. Both the enhanced parallel port (EPP) and the extended capabilities port (ECP) are included within the IEEE 1284 specification. See *ECP, EPP.*

IEEE 1394 The generic name for a high-speed serial bus architecture that enables hot swapping, up to 63 daisy-chained devices, and a data transfer rate of up to 400 Mbps. This standard is widely known by Apple Computer's trademarked implementation of the standard, called FireWire, but it is also available (under the IEEE 1394 rubric) on Windows and Linux systems. See *FireWire.*

IEN See *Internet Experiment Notes.*

IEPG See *Internet Engineering and Planning Group.*

IESG See *Internet Engineering Steering Group.*

IETF See *Internet Engineering Task Force.*

i-frame In digital video formats that use interframe compression, such as MPEG video, a reference frame containing information that does not need to be reconstructed or predicted from other frames. See *b-frame, frame, MPEG, p-frame.*

IF/THEN/ELSE In programming, a structure that conducts a test to see whether a condition is true. If the condition is true, then the program branches to one option; if the condition is false, the program branches to another option. With slight variations in the language, IF/THEN/ELSE structures are used when writing macros, as merge codes, as functions in spreadsheet software, and as part of all high-level programming languages.

IIOP Acronym for Internet Inter-ORB Protocol. A protocol that establishes a method by which Web browsers can request objects from Internet-accessible servers. An object is software that includes data as well as the code needed to process that data.

IIS Acronym for Internet Information Server. An FTP, NNTP (Usenet), and Web server developed by Microsoft Corporation and included in the company's Microsoft Windows Server products, such as Microsoft Windows XP Server and Microsoft Windows 2003 Server. Introduced in late 2002, IIS v. 6.0 featured a comprehensive re-write of the underlying code in order to support Microsoft's .NET framework (in particular, the ASP.NET scripting framework); this version is not downwardly compatible with previous versions of IIS. Hampering IIS's marketplace reputation is a steady stream of press reports concerning newly found security holes in the server software. See *Microsoft Windows Server 2003*.

ILEC Acronym for incumbent local exchange carrier. In U.S. telephony, the local telephone company that possessed a monopoly on the local market in 1996, when the United States introduced competition into local telephone markets. See *CLEC*.

ill-behaved Poorly designed, inefficient, wasteful of system resources due to fundamental design errors.

illegal character A character that cannot be used according to the syntax rules of command-driven programs and programming languages. Such characters usually are reserved for a specific program function. With DOS, for example, one cannot assign a file name to a file if the name includes an asterisk (*). The asterisk is reserved for use as a wildcard symbol. Commas, spaces, slashes, and several other punctuation characters also are illegal characters for file names.

illustration software Applications that enable one to create and edit graphical images; illustration software produces vector graphics (as opposed to bitmapped graphics), in which each object in an image can be independently sized and edited. Leading packages include Adobe Illustrator, CorelDRAW, and GIMP. See *image-editing software*.

ILS See *integrated learning system*.

iMac An inexpensive but powerful Macintosh desktop computer, based on the G3 processor, that was introduced in 1998 for use in homes and schools. The system features easy Internet connectivity, a built-in 15-inch CRT monitor, a stylish design, ample memory and hard disk space, FireWire support, Ethernet connectivity, and a built-in modem. See *eMac, G3*.

image-editing software Programs that enable users to manipulate and enhance bit-mapped images, such as those created by scanners or digital cameras. Typical program features include color management, artistic effects, masking tools, and the capability to open and save in a variety of graphics file formats. Some image-editing programs (such as CorelDRAW and GIMP) also include vector graphics capabilities. Leading programs include Adobe PhotoShop, CorelDRAW, GIMP, Microsoft PhotoDraw, and Paint Shop Pro. See *illustration software*.

imagemap In HTML, a graphic that has been coded so that specific regions of the graphic are associated with specific URLs. When the user clicks one of these regions, the browser initiates a hyperlink jump to the associated document or resource.

imagesetter A professional typesetting machine that generates very high-resolution output on photographic paper or film.

imaging model The method of representing output onscreen that is employed by a given application, desktop environment, operating system, or windowing system In a graphical user interface (GUI), for example, the imaging model is for the screen font to closely resemble the way the text is printed.

IMAP Acronym for Internet Message Access Protocol. In Internet e-mail, one of two fundamental protocols (the other is POP3) that governs how and where users store their incoming mail messages. For many users, this standard may prove more convenient than POP3 because all mail is kept in one central location, where it can be organized, archived, and made available from remote locations. IMAP4 is supported by most leading e-mail programs. See *POP-3*.

IMAP4 Acronym for Internet Message Access Protocol Version 4. See *IMAP*.

IMHO In text chatting, an acronym for "in my humble opinion."

impact printer A printer that generates output in a manner similar to typewriters, by actually striking the page with something solid. Daisywheel and dot-matrix printers are impact printers. Impact printers are slow and noisy, but they are inexpensive by printer standards and are necessary for filling out multipart forms. See *laser printer, non-impact printer*.

import To load a file created by one program into a different program. See *export*.

increment To increase a value. See *decrement*.

incremental backup A backup procedure in which the only files that are archived are those that have changed since the last backup procedure. See *archival backup, full backup*.

incremental development In software engineering, a process methodology that emphasizes the virtue of taking small steps toward the goal. In contrast to the waterfall model of software development, in which a working system becomes available only in the latter phases of the project, incremental development begins with a small, working system that is improved and expanded step by step. At each increment, the key phases of the software development life cycle (SDLC), including functional specification, design, implementation, and testing, are reiterated. This approach can cope with the

inevitable changes that result from a client's inability to express system specifications fully at the inception of the project, the shifting fortunes of the various system stakeholders, new business developments that require new or modified features, and technological constraints that emerge only as the system is developed. See *iterative development, software development life cycle (SDLC), software engineering, waterfall model*.

incremental update See *maintenance release*.

indentation The alignment of a paragraph to the right or left of the document margins.

indent style In a programming language, the conventions used to govern the indentation of lines of code. These indentations make it easier to read the code.

Indeo A codec (compression/decompression algorithm) developed by Intel Corporation and used in a variety of video players, including Microsoft Media Player.

independent software vendor See *ISV*.

index 1. In database management programs, a file containing information about the physical location of records in a database file. When searching or sorting the database, the program uses the index rather than the full database. Such operations are faster than sorts or searches performed on the actual database. Synonymous with inverted index. **2.** In word processing programs, an appendix to a document that can be generated to list important words, names, and concepts in alphabetical order, and the page numbers where the terms appear. See *active index, concordance file, sort, sort order*.

indexed sequential access method (ISAM) In hard disks, a method for accessing data on a hard disk that combines sequential access with indexing, resulting in high access speeds overall. Data that is stored sequentially can be directly accessed without consulting the index.

Industry Standard Architecture See *ISA*.

infection The presence of a virus within a computer system or on a disk. The infection may not be obvious to the user; many viruses, for example, remain in the background until a specific time and date, when they display prank messages or erase data. See *Trojan horse, virus, worm*.

infinite loop In programming, a loop in which the condition for terminating is never fulfilled. For example, a loop designed to add 5 to an integer variable until the variable equaled 133.2 would never end — at least, not until a crash occurred or the computer was rebooted.

infix notation In computer programming languages, a syntax preference in which functions or operators are placed between operands (such as a + b or *expression1 | expression2*). See *prefix notation, Reverse Polish Notation (RPN)*.

info A new top-level domain (TLD) name for the Internet, added in 1998, that is designed for Web sites providing information services. See *domain name, gTLD-MoU, top-level domain (TLD)*.

Infobahn A term preferred by some for the so-called Information Superhighway, a high-speed information system that would link homes, schools, and offices with high-bandwidth local delivery systems and backbone systems capable of gigabit-per-second speeds.

information Data—whether in the form of numbers, graphics, or words—that has been organized, systematized, and presented so that the underlying patterns become clear. The temperature, humidity, and wind reports from hundreds of weather stations are data; a computer simulation that shows how this data predicts a strong possibility of tornadoes is information.

information hiding A modular programming technique in which information inside a module remains hidden with respect to other modules.

information kiosk See *kiosk*.

information overload A condition of confusion, stress, and indecision brought about by being inundated with information of variable value.

information service See *BBS, bibliographic retrieval service, online service*.

Information Superhighway An envisioned information infrastructure that will bring broadband computer networking within the reach of homes, schools, and offices (in this context, "broadband" suggests that the minimum connection speed would be at least 1 Mbps). The Internet is not yet an information superhighway; new digital telephone systems such as ADSL, as well as cable modems, are used by only a small percentage of Internet users, and the average speed of the Internet backbone during times of peak usage can be as slow as 50 Kbps.

information system A purposefully designed system that brings data, computers, procedure, and people together to manage the information that is important to an organization's mission.

information technology (IT) A generic term for all aspects of computer, networking, and information systems technology. Most businesses have an IT department.

information warfare A military strategy that targets an opponent's information systems. Synonymous with infowar.

Infoseek See *search engine*.

infowar See *information warfare*.

Infrared Data Association See *IrDA*.

infrared port A port that sends and receives data in the form of infrared radiation (IR), enabling two devices to exchange data without using cables. The technology is similar to that used to control a television set or video recorder using a remote device. Infrared ports can move data at more than 115,000 bps. See *IrDA*.

infrared radiation (IR) A type of electromagnetic radiation that has a wavelength longer than visible light but shorter than microwaves. Objects emitting heat radiate infrared signals, which can be easily detected using specialized equipment. In computing, infrared radiation is used to create short-range communication channels between devices, such as a desktop computer and a personal digital assistant (PDA).

infrastructure mode A method of implementing awireless LAN that employs a central access point in a star network configuration. Synonymous with BSS mode. See *access point, star network, topology, wireless LAN.*

inheritance In object-oriented programming, the capability of newly created objects to take on the properties of existing objects. See *object-oriented programming.*

init 1. Common abbreviation for initiate or initialize. 2. In pre-System 7 Macintoshes, a utility program that executes during a system start or restart, such as SuperClock, which displays the current system date and time in the menu bar, and Adobe Type Manager, which uses outline-font technology to display Adobe screen fonts.

initial In typography, an enlarged letter at the beginning of a chapter or paragraph. Initials set down within the copy are drop caps, and initials raised above the top line of the text are stickup initials.

initial base font The font used by word processing programs for all documents unless one instructs otherwise. The initial base font is part of the printer definition. Whenever a different printer is selected, the initial base font may change. See *base font, default font.*

initialization 1. In modems, the establishment of an active configuration that, in whole or in part, supersedes the factory configuration. By using an initialization string, one can configure the modem to work well with his or her communications program. 2. In disks, the process of formatting a hard disk and floppy disks so that they are ready to store data.

initialization string In modems, a group of AT commands issued to the modem by a communications program at the beginning of a communication session that establishes an active configuration. Initialization strings enable communications programs to work smoothly with a variety of modems, and often a user can choose an initialization string appropriate for his or her modem from a list provided in his or her communications program. See *Hayes command set, initialization.*

initialize To prepare hardware or software to perform a task. A serial port is initialized using the MODE command to set the baud, parity, data, and stop bit values, for example. In some programs, initializing can be setting a counter or variable to zero before running a procedure.

inkjet printer A non-impact printer that forms an image by spraying ink from a matrix of tiny jets. See *bubble-jet printer.*

inline In typography, placed within or directly adjacent to lines of text. See *floating graphic, inline graphic.*

inline graphic A graphic that has been placed so that it appears on the same line with text. In HTML, inline images are defined by the IMG tag, which specifies the source of the graphic, its alignment (top, middle, or bottom), and the text to display if the document is accessed by a text-only browser.

inode In Unix and Unix-like operating systems (including Linux), a basic concept of file system organization in which the file system can contain a predefined number of virtual files, each of which has a precise numerical identifier. Associated with each inode is a set of attributes, including file type, access rights, file ownership, file permissions, timestamps, size, and pointers to the physical data blocks where the file's data is stored. See *ext2, Linux.*

in-order execution In a reduced instruction set computer (RISC) architecture, a method of providing programs with a means of ensuring that specific instructions are carried out in a specified order.

in-place activation   In object linking and embedding (OLE) in Microsoft Windows 95/98, the use of a server application's functions within the client application, without the need to switch to a window containing the server application.

input   Any information entered into a computer.

input device   Any peripheral that assists one in getting data into a computer, such as a keyboard, mouse, trackball, voice recognition system, graphics tablet, or modem.

input/output   See *I/O.*

input/output (I/O) redirection   In DOS and Unix, the routing of a program's output to a file or device, or the routing of a program's input from a file rather than the keyboard. Most DOS commands (such as DIR) send output to the screen, but one can easily redirect a command's output by using the greater-than sign (>). To redirect the output of DIR to the LPT1 (printer) port, for example, one types DIR > lpt1 and presses Enter. To redirect the command's output to a file, one types DIR > dir.txt and presses Enter. In DOS, input redirection is frequently used with filters. See *filter, MS-DOS.*

insert edit   In digital video, an editing method in which new frames are added within the existing video content. See *assemble edit.*

Insert (Ins) key   On IBM PC–compatible keyboards, a programmable key frequently (but not always) used to toggle between insert mode and overtype mode when entering text.

insertion point   In Macintosh and Microsoft Windows applications, the blinking vertical bar that shows the point at which text will appear when one starts typing. The insertion point is similar to the cursor in DOS applications.

insert mode   In word processing programs, a program mode in which inserted text pushes existing text to the right and down. The Insert key is used to toggle between insert and overtype modes.

installation program   A utility program provided with an application that helps one install the program on a hard disk and configure the program so it is usable. Synonymous with setup program.

instantiate   To create an instantiation. See *instantiation.*

instantiation   In object-oriented programming, a process in which an instance of a class (that is, an object) is created from the class template by supplying the needed properties (values). See *class, object, object-oriented programming.*

instant messaging (IM)   Software that detects when a user's friends are online and enables the user to signal them to engage in real-time text or voice chatting. In contrast to most Internet protocols, IM protocols are proprietary and are not interoperabile; the dominant IM players, Microsoft, AOL, and Yahoo!, are (at this writing) using their IM user base to leverage market share in other areas. Still, IM is regarded by many computer experts as the leading edge of an important new dimension of network functionality termed *presence.* See *chat, real time.*

Institute for Certification of Computer Professionals (ICCP)   An organization that sanctions examinations that establish professional competence in various computer fields. The ICCP awards data processing and computer programming certification, making people who pass its examinations Certified Data Processors (CDPs) and Certified Computer Programmers (CCPs). Although ICCP certification is recognized as a professional achievement, it is rarely required for employment or for the awarding of a contract.

Institute of Electrical and Electronic Engineers   See *IEEE.*

instruction In programming, a program statement interpreted or compiled into machine language. See *compiler, interpreter.*

instruction cycle The time it takes a central processing unit (CPU) to carry out one instruction and move on to the next.

instruction mnemonic In assembly language, an abbreviation that represents a machine's instructions, such as ADD or MOVE.

instruction set A list of keywords describing all the actions or operations that a central processing unit (CPU) can perform. See *complex instruction set computer (CISC), RISC.*

Int13h An interface linked to interrupt channel 19 (13h in hexadecimal notation) on Intel-based systems that was widely used on MS-DOS and early Windows systems. Because the Int13h interface imposes a maximum data storage capacity of 8.46 GB, it has been superceded by a new interface called Int13h extension, which enables a maximum data storage capacity of 9.4×10^{21} bytes (equivalent to 9.4 zettabytes, which greatly exceeds the amount of information produced by the entire world annually). See *interrupt, zettabyte.*

integer A whole number, such as 3, 19, and 2,348,039. If a number contains decimal places, the numbers to the left of the decimal point are the integer portion of the number. A rounding error occurs when fractional quantities greater than .5 are ignored in the conversion of quantities to integers.

integer data type In a programming language, a data type assigned to variables that will contain integers (but no other type of data). Typically, an integer can be expressed in decimal, octal, or hexadecimal notation. A given hardware platform can support an enormous range of integers, ranging from approximately −2 billion to +2 billion; integers beyond this range must be represented using floating point notation. See *data type, decimal notation, floating point notation, hexadecimal notation, integer, octal notation, strong typing, weak typing.*

integrated accounting package An accounting package that includes all the major accounting functions: general ledger, accounts payable, accounts receivable, payroll, and inventory. Integrated programs update the general ledger every time an accounts payable or accounts receivable transaction occurs.

integrated circuit (IC) A semiconductor that contains more than one electronic component. An integrated circuit is fabricated on a wafer of silicon. To produce the resistance differentials that produce the effect of separate electronic components, such as transistors, areas of the wafer are differentially mixed with other elements in a procedure called doping. The first ICs offered the equivalent of a few transistors, but improvements in IC design and manufacturing have brought about spectacular improvements in circuit density (today's microprocessors contain as many as 10 million transistors). Synonymous with chip. See *large-scale integration (LSI), small scale integration (SSI), very large scale integration (VLSI).*

Integrated Drive Electronics See *IDE.*

integrated program A program that combines two or more software functions, such as word processing and database management. Microsoft Works and ClarisWorks are examples of integrated programs.

Integrated Services Digital Network See *ISDN.*

integrity A fundamental component of computer security in which data (including transmitted data, such as e-mail) and software are protected from unauthorized modification. See *security.*

Intel The world's largest manufacturer of microprocessors and other semiconductors, based in Santa Clara, California. Founded in 1968, Intel is responsible for a series of key technological innovations in the semiconductor industry, including the first microprocessor. Today, Intel is among the top Fortune 100 corporations; Intel's processors are installed in more than 85 percent of the world's computer systems.

Intel 80x86   Generic name for the family of Intel CISC (complex instruction set computer) microprocessors that dominates the personal computer marketplace. See *Intel 80186, Intel 80286, Intel 80386, Intel 80486, Pentium II, Pentium III, Pentium 4, Pentium Pro*.

Intel 386DX   See *Intel 80386*.

Intel 386SL   A power-conserving variation of the Intel 386SX designed with power-management features for use in portable computers. The 386SL includes a sleep mode that preserves work while using very little electricity during periods of disuse. Like the other 386 microprocessors, the 386SL is now obsolete.

Intel 386SX   A slower but less expensive version of the now-obsolete Intel 80386 microprocessor. The 386SX uses a 16-bit external data bus, compared with the 386DX's 32-bit data pathway. The 386SX can address only 20MB of random access memory (RAM), compared to the 386DX's capability of handling 4GB of RAM.

Intel 486DX   A 32-bit microprocessor that dominated the PC market prior to the introduction of the Pentium. Introduced in 1989, the 486DX offers a significant speed improvement over the Intel 386DX, its predecessor. By using pipelining and an onboard numeric coprocessor, the 486DX can manage 4GB of random access memory (RAM) and 64TB of virtual memory. The two versions of the 486DX operate at clock speeds of 25 MHz and 33 MHz, although clock doubled and clock tripled versions operate at higher clock speeds. See *Intel 486DX2, Intel 486DX4, Intel 486SX*.

Intel 486DX2   An improved version of the Intel 486DX that uses clock-doubling techniques to achieve clock speeds inside the microprocessor of 50 MHz or 66 MHz, while the microprocessor is installed on a motherboard running at half the chip's clock speed (25 MHz or 33 MHz, respectively). Although the performance of the microprocessor far outstrips the performance of the motherboard, good external cache design can minimize the time a clock-doubled microprocessor spends waiting for the motherboard to catch up with it. See *clock-doubled*.

Intel 486DX4   An improved version of the Intel 486DX microprocessor that, by means of clock tripling or quadrupling, operates at clock speeds of 75 MHz or 100 MHz. The 486DX4 boasts a larger internal cache than other 486s, and operates at 3.3 volts instead of 5 volts. See *clock-quadrupled*.

Intel 486SL   A power-saving version of the Intel 486DX microprocessor. Designed for portable computers, the 486SL includes a sleep mode that lets a user stop working and start again later without having to reboot.

Intel 486SX   A 32-bit microprocessor based on the Intel 486DX, but without the 486DX's numeric coprocessor. Designed to be a slower but more affordable alternative to the 486DX, the two versions of the 486SX run at clock speeds of 20 MHz and 25 MHz.

Intel 4004   The first microprocessor, a 4-bit processor released in 1971 that contains the equivalent of 2,300 transistors.

Intel 8080   The 8-bit microprocessor found in the Altair, a popular 1970s microcomputer. The Intel 8080, which runs at a clock speed of 2 MHz, has a 16-bit address bus and can handle a half-million instructions per second. Introduced in 1974, Intel 8080 was obsolete by the early 1980s; however, its odd and error-prone memory addressing architecture continues to influence Intel microprocessor design to this day because Intel is committed to ensuring that its newer microprocessors are downwardly compatible with previous ones.

Intel 8086   A 16-bit microprocessor, introduced in 1978, that was based on the architecture of the Intel 8080 and that retained downward compatibility with code designed for that chip. Because the 8086 can process 2 bytes of data at a time, in contrast to 8-bit processors (which can process only 1 byte of data at a time), it was considerably faster than previous Intel chips. However, the 8086 did not find widespread use due to the high cost and low availability of 16-bit peripherals in the early 1980s.

Intel 8088 Essentially an Intel 8086 with an 8-bit data bus, the 4.77 MHz Intel 8088 was the engine in the earliest IBM personal computers. Although it was a 16-bit microprocessor, the 8088's 8-bit data bus enabled computer manufacturers to use inexpensive, off-the-shelf 8-bit peripherals. Introduced in 1979, the 8088 powered the hugely successful IBM PC, which was introduced in 1981.

Intel 80186 A 32-bit microprocessor, operating at 6 MHz and introduced in 1981, that is functionally very similar to the Intel 8086 (both chips employ a 16-bit internal and external data bus) but that includes additional functions that previously had to be parceled out to expensive support chips, such as timers, DMA channels, and interrupt controllers. Motherboards created with the 80186 could use up to 22 fewer support chips than 8086 motherboards. Because the technically superior Intel 80286 microprocessor appeared shortly after the 80186's introduction, the 80186 saw very little use.

Intel 80286 The now obsolete 16-bit microprocessor that was used in the IBM Personal Computer AT, unveiled in 1984, and compatible computers. Introduced in 1982, the 80286 operates at clock speeds as fast as 20 MHz. The 80286 represents an attempt to overcome the memory-addressing limitations of the previous Intel processors architecture, which was limited to a maximum of 1MB of RAM. By switching from the previous Intel processor-compatible real mode into a new mode, called the protected mode, the chip could use up to 16MB of random access memory (RAM). Unfortunately, the 80286 cannot

switch between these two modes without rebooting, a serious design flaw that led to the 80286's replacement by the Intel 80386.

Intel 80386 A 32-bit microprocessor that helped to launch the Windows era. Thanks to its incorporation of advanced memory management circuitry, the Intel 80386 enables programs to switch from real mode to protected mode without rebooting; in short, the Intel 80386 made protected-mode operating systems and applications possible for the first time. The chip's 32-bit address bus lets it manage as much as 4GB of random access memory (RAM) and 64TB of virtual memory. Various versions of the 80386 run at clock speeds of 16 MHz, 20 MHz, 25 MHz, and 33 MHz. Introduced in 1985, the 80386 was renamed the Intel 386DX when the Intel 386SX (a cheaper version of the microprocessor, with a 16-bit data bus) was introduced.

Intel 80486 A 32-bit microprocessor, released in 1989 and downwardly compatible with the Intel 80386, that incorporates certain design improvements, such as a larger primary cache and a built-in math coprocessor. After Intel found that it could not protect the 80x86 numbering system from use by other semiconductor manufacturers, the company switched to a different numbering scheme; the original 80486 was renamed Intel 486DX. Synonymous with i486 and IAPX 80486.

Intel Celeron A low-end, economy version of Intel's Pentium microprocessor that is designed for entry-level systems. Like the Xeon, the Celeron is a derivative product that is based on Intel's current processor technology. Celeron processors are cheaper than their Pentium counterparts because they include less secondary (L2) cache, lower clock speeds, and a slower data bus. See *clock speed, data bus, Intel Xeon, Pentium, secondary cache.*

Intel Xeon A high-performance version of Intel's Pentium microprocessor that is designed for file servers and workstations.

Like the Celeron, the Xeon is a derivative product that is based on Intel's current processor technology; for example, the Xeon available in early 2003 shares technology with the company's Pentium 4 processor, but includes features to optimize the chip's performance on dual-processor server systems. See *Intel Celeron, Pentium 4.*

Intel Xeon MP A version of Intel's Xeon microprocessor that is designed for use on multiprocessor server systems containing four or more processors. See *multiprocessing, Intel Xeon.*

intellectual property (IP) Generic term for a variety of legal protections for new creative works and inventions. In the United States and internationally, IP protection is provided in the form of copyright (for creative works such as books and musical recordings), trademarks (for corporate names, slogans, and insignia), patents (for inventions), and trade secrets (for knowledge that is essential to maintaining a company's competitive position in a market). See *copyright, patent, trademark, trade secret.*

intelligent hub In a local area network (LAN), a central network connection device that can route as well as forward network data. See *bridge, router, switch.*

Intelligent Transportation System See *ITS.*

Intel Pentium See *Pentium, Pentium II, Pentium III, Pentium 4, Pentium Pro.*

interactive Capable of engaging in a dialogue with the user, generally by means of a text-based interface.

interactive processing A method of displaying the computer's operations on a monitor so that the user can catch and correct errors before the processing operation is completed.

interactive videodisk A computer-assisted instruction (CAI) technology that uses a computer to provide access to up to two hours of video information stored on a videodisk. Videodisks, like CD-ROMs that

came after them, are read-only optical storage media but are designed for the storage and random access retrieval of images, including stills and continuous video. One needs a front-end program to access the videodisk information. With a videodisk of paintings in the National Gallery of Art, the user can demand, "Show me all the Renaissance paintings that depict flowers or gardens," and be led through a series of vivid instructional experiences while retaining complete control.

Inter-Application Communication (IAC) In the Macintosh System 7, a specification for creating hot links and cold links between applications.

interface **1.** The connection between two hardware devices, between two applications, or between different sections of a computer network. **2.** The portion of a program that interacts with the user.

interface standard A set of specifications for the connection between the two hardware devices, such as the drive controller and the drive electronics in a hard disk. Common hard disk interface standards in personal computing include ST506, ESDI, and SCSI. Other standards exist for connections with serial and parallel ports, such as the Centronics interface. See *ST-506/ST-412.*

interframe compression In digital video, a method of compression in which each new frame is specified only by the new information that appears in that frame. The missing information is filled in using data from the previous frame. MPEG videos employ this compression technique. See *b-frame, frame, i-frame, p-frame.*

Interior Gateway Protocol (IGP) An Internet standard (protocol) that governs the routing of data within an autonomous system (AS), a network or group of networks that is under a single administrator's control.

interlaced See *interlacing.*

interlaced GIF   A GIF graphic saved to a special file format (defined by the GIF 89a standard) that enables a graphics program or Web browser to display a rough, out-of-focus version of the graphic immediately. Other page elements, such as text, can appear while the graphic's details are being filled in.

interlaced monitor   A monitor that refreshes every other line of pixels with each pass of the cathode gun. This often results in screen flicker, and almost all monitors now are non-interlaced. See *non-interlaced monitor.*

interlacing   **1.** A method of displaying or transferring information so that the rough contours are sketched out immediately; subsequently, the details are sketched in. **2.** A monitor technology that uses the monitor's electron gun to paint every other line of the screen with the first pass and the remaining lines on the second pass. When most of the screen display is a solid, light-color background, the eye perceives the alternating painted and fading lines as a slight flicker or shimmer. This technique provides higher resolution but at the price of visual comfort. See *interlaced monitor.*

interleaved memory   A method of speeding the retrieval of data from DRAM chips by dividing all the RAM into two or four large banks; sequential bits of data are stored in alternating banks. The microprocessor reads one bank while the other is being refreshed. Naturally, this memory arrangement does not improve speed when the central processing unit (CPU) requests nonsequential bits of data. See *interleave factor, random access memory (RAM).*

interleave factor   The ratio of physical disk sectors on a hard disk that are skipped for every sector actually used for write operations. With an interleave factor of 6:1, a disk writes to a sector, skips six sectors, writes to a sector, and so on. The computer figures out what it needs next and sends the request to the hard drive while the disk is skipping sectors. 80386SX and higher computers operate faster than hard disks, so a

1:1 interleave is standard today. The interleave factor is set by the hard disk manufacturer but can be changed by software capable of performing a low-level format. Synonymous with sector interleave.

interleaving   A method of intentionally slowing down the reading of data from a hard disk to prevent the hard disk from outrunning other parts of the computer system. By placing sectors in nonsequential order, the read/write head has to jump around while collecting data. The interleave factor describes the amount of interleaving employed on a hard disk.

internal cache   A very high-speed cache memory that is built directly into the electronic circuits of a microprocessor, in contrast to an external cache or L2 cache, which requires a separate circuit. Synonymous with onboard cache and primary cache.

internal command   In DOS, a command such as DIR or COPY that is part of COMMAND.COM and therefore is in memory and available whenever the DOS prompt is visible onscreen. See *external command.*

internal data bus   The circuitry on which data moves inside a microprocessor. Internal data bus size is measured in bits; the more bits a bus can handle (the wider it is), the faster it can move data. The internal data bus is independent of the external data bus, which is often half as wide as the internal data bus.

internal font   See *printer font.*

internal hard drive   A storage device designed to fit within a computer or printer's case and to use electricity from the device's power supply. Hard drives are also called fix media, because the media (the physical disk) on which the data is recorded cannot be removed from the drive.

internal modem   A modem designed to fit into the expansion bus of a personal computer. See *external modem.*

internal navigation aid In a series of related World Wide Web (WWW) documents, the hyperlinks or clickable buttons that provide users with a way of navigating through the documents without getting lost. If one sees a Home button on one of the pages in a web, for example, he or she can click it to return to the Web's welcome page. This is different from clicking the browser's Home button, which displays the browser's default home page.

International Business Machines See *IBM*.

International Data Encryption Algorithm (IDEA) An encryption technique that employs a 128-bit key and is considered by most cryptanalysts to be the most secure encryption algorithm available today.

International Organization for Standardization See *ISO*.

International Telecommunications Union-Telecommunications Standards Section See *ITU-TSS*.

International Traffic in Arms Regulation See *ITAR*.

internet A group of local area networks (LANs) that have been connected by means of a common communications protocol and packet redirection devices called routers. From the user's perspective, this group of networks seems as if it is one large network. Note the small "i" — many internets exist besides the Internet, including many TCP/IP-based networks that are not linked to the Internet (the Defense Data Network is a case in point).

Internet An enormous and rapidly growing system of linked computer networks, worldwide in scope, that facilitates data communication services such as remote login, file transfer, electronic mail, the World Wide Web, and newsgroups. Relying on TCP/IP, also called the Internet protocol suite, the Internet assigns every connected computer a unique Internet address, also called an IP address, so that any two connected computers can locate each other on the network and exchange data. The Internet is the largest example in existence of an internet. See *Advanced Research Projects Agency (ARPA)*, *TCP/IP network*, *World Wide Web (WWW)*.

Internet access provider (IAP) A company or consortium that provides high-speed access to the Internet to businesses, universities, nonprofit organizations, and Internet service providers (ISPs), who in turn provide Internet access to individuals. Some IAPs are also ISPs. See *ISP*.

Internet Activities Board (IAB) An organization founded in 1983 that was charged with the development of TCP/IP; its activities have been taken over by the Internet Architecture Board (IAB).

Internet address The unique, 32-bit address assigned to a computer that is connected to the Internet, represented in dotted decimal notation (for example, 128.117.38.5). Synonymous with IP address.

Internet Architecture Board (IAB) A unit of the Internet Society that provides broad-level oversight over the Internet's technical development and that adjudicates technical disputes that occur in the standards-setting process. Among the units that the organization oversees are the Internet Engineering Task Force (IETF), the Internet Research Task Force (IRTF), and the Internet Assigned Numbers Authority (IANA).

Internet Assigned Numbers Authority (IANA) A unit of the Internet Architecture Board (IAB) that supervises the allocation of IP addresses, port addresses, and other numerical standards on the Internet.

Internet Control Message Protocol (ICMP) An extension to the original Internet Protocol that provides much-needed error and congestion control. Using ICMP, for example, routers can tell other routers that a given branch of the network is congested or not responding. ICMP provides an echo function that enables ping applications to determine whether a given host is reachable.

Internet draft   A working document of the Internet Engineering Task Force (IETF), a unit of the Internet Architecture Board (IAB). Internet drafts are unofficial discussion documents meant to be circulated on the Internet and not intended to delineate new standards.

Internet Engineering and Planning Group (IEPG)   A unit of the Internet Society that promotes the technical coordination of day-to-day Internet operations. IEPG is composed of Internet backbone service providers and is not concerned with the development of new standards.

Internet Engineering Steering Group (IESG)   A unit of the Internet Society that reviews proposed standards created by the Internet Engineering Task Force (IETF), in consultation with the Internet Architecture Board (IAB); standards are published in the form of Requests for Comments (RFC).

Internet Engineering Task Force (IETF)   A unit of the Internet Architecture Board (IAB) that is concerned with the immediate technical challenges facing the Internet. The IETF's technical work is done in a number of working groups, which are organized by topics such as security, routing, and network management. Managed by the Internet Engineering Steering Group (IESG), the IETF convenes several meetings per year and publishes its proceedings.

Internet Explorer   See *Microsoft Internet Explorer.*

Internet filter   A program that blocks attempts to access Web sites included in a proprietary database of sites containing material that is objectionable for minors. See *filtering software.*

Internet Inter-ORB Protocol   See *IIOP.*

Internet Message Access Protocol   See *IMAP.*

Internet patent   See *business process patent.*

Internet PCA Registration Authority (IPRA)   A unit of the Internet Society that is devoted to the global implementation of public key cryptography applications on the Internet, both for the purposes of authentication and for privacy.

Internet Protocol (IP)   In TCP/IP, the standard that describes how an Internet-connected computer should break data down into packets for transmission across the network, and how those packets should be addressed so that they arrive at their destination. IP is the connectionless part of the TCP/IP protocols; the Transmission Control Protocol (TCP) specifies how two Internet computers can establish a reliable data link by means of handshaking. See *connectionless protocol, TCP, TCP/IP.*

Internet Relay Chat (IRC)   A real-time, Internet-based chat service in which one can find "live" participants from the world over. Created by Jarkko Oikarinen of Finland in 1988, IRC requires the use of an IRC client program, which displays a list of the current IRC channels. See *chat.*

Internet Research Task Force (IRTF)   A unit of the Internet Architecture Board (IAB) that deals with the long-range challenges facing the Internet, such as the lack of sufficient IP addresses. See *Internet Architecture Board (IAB).*

Internet Server Application Programming Interface   See *ISAPI.*

Internet service provider   See *ISP.*

Internet Society (ISOC)   An international, nonprofit organization headquartered in Reston, Virginia, that seeks to maintain and broaden the Internet's availability. Created in 1992, ISOC is governed by an elected board of trustees. Members include individuals and organizations (including service providers, product providers,

Internet enterprise operators, educational institutions, computer professional organizations, international treaty organizations, and government agencies). The organization sponsors annual conferences and has numerous publication programs. Spearheading the Internet's technical operation and development, the Internet Society coordinates the activities of the Internet Architecture Board (IAB), the Internet Engineering Task Force (IETF), the Internet Engineering Steering Group (IESG), the Internet Engineering and Planning Group (IEPG), the Internet Assigned Numbers Authority (IANA), and the Internet PCA Registration Authority (IPRA).

Internet Worm A rogue program, ostensibly designed as a harmless experiment, that propagated throughout the Internet in 1988, overloading and shutting down thousands of computer systems worldwide. Robert Morris, Jr., the author of the program and at the time a graduate student in computer science at Cornell University, was convicted under the Computer Fraud and Abuse Act of 1986. He was sentenced to three years of probation, 400 hours of community service, and a $10,000 fine. See *worm*.

InterNIC A consortium of two organizations that provide networking information services to the Internet community, under contract to the National Science Foundation (NSF). Currently, AT&T provides directory and database services, while Network Solutions, Inc., provides registration services for new domain names and IP addresses.

interoperability The capability of two or more computer systems to share data and resources, even though they are made by different manufacturers. Interoperability is one of the chief technical achievements of the TCP/IP protocols; using File Transfer Protocol (FTP), for instance, one can use a Macintosh to log on to a Sun workstation and direct that workstation to send a file to him or her via the Internet. In another

example, a U.S. Robotics modem can exchange data with a Zoom modem, as long as both conform to a common standard such as v.32bis.

interpolated resolution A means of improving the output of a scanner by means of a software algorithm. Instead of relying solely on closely spaced charge-coupled devices (CCDs), scanners that use interpolated resolution average the readings of each pair of adjacent CCDs and insert an extra pixel between them. Although a given interpolated resolution is not as good as the same optical resolution, it can cost-effectively improve scan quality.

interpreted Executed line by line from source code rather than from object code created by a compiler. See *interpreted code*, *interpreter*.

interpreted code Program code that requires an interpreter to execute, in contrast to compiled programs, which are executable.

interpreted programming language A programming language, such as JavaScript, that is designed to be translated into executable code "on-the-fly" as the program is executed. An interpreter performs the translation. See *interpreter*, *JavaScript*.

interpreter A translator for a high-level programming language that translates and runs the program at the same time. Interpreters are excellent for learning how to program because, if an error occurs, the interpreter shows the likely place (and sometimes even the cause) of the error. One can correct the problem immediately and execute the program again, learning interactively how to create a successful program. However, interpreted programs run much more slowly than compiled programs. See *compiler*.

interprocess communication (IPC) In a multitasking computing environment, such as Microsoft Windows running in the 386 Enhanced mode, the communication of data or commands from one program to another while both are running, made possible by dynamic data exchange (DDE) specifications. In Microsoft Excel, for example, one can write a DDE command that accesses changing data, such as stock prices, that is being received online in a communications program.

interrupt   A signal to the microprocessor indicating that an event has occurred that requires its attention, or that a peripheral is ready to send or receive data. Processing is halted momentarily so that input/output or other operations can take place. When the operation is finished, processing resumes. See *IRQ*.

interrupt controller   Part of the motherboard's chip set that distributes hardware interrupt request (IRQ) lines. The interrupt controller prevents more than one peripheral device from communicating with the microprocessor at one time.

interrupt handler   A program that executes when an interrupt occurs. Such programs deal with events that are far below the threshold of user perception; for example, they deal with matters as minute as the reception of characters from the keyboard input.

interrupt request   See *IRQ*.

intranet   A computer network designed to meet the internal needs of a single organization or company that is based on Internet technology (TCP/IP). Not necessarily open to the external Internet and almost certainly not accessible from the outside, an intranet enables organizations to make internal resources available using familiar Internet clients, such as Web browsers, newsreaders, and e-mail. Simply by publishing information, such as employee manuals or telephone directories on the Web rather than printed media, companies can realize significant returns on investment (ROI) by creating intranets. An intranet that has been selectively opened to strategic allies (including suppliers,

customers, research labs, and other external allies) is called an extranet.

invention   A new technological artifact (such as a machine, a process, or a new composition of matter) that is based on a new operational principle or a known operational principle that has never before been successfully implemented within the invention's line of technological development. See *technological innovation*.

inverted file   See *inverted index*.

inverted index   In databases, a file containing keys and pointers. Each key uniquely describes a data record, while the pointers tell the program precisely where the record can be physically located in the database. The index is inverted in the sense that it is sorted by the keys, not the pointers. This removes the need to sort the records themselves, which remain (in most systems) in the order they were sequentially added to the database.

invisible file   See *hidden file*.

I/O   Common abbreviation for input/output, the portion of a computer's architecture that deals with the reception and transmission of signals to the computer's peripherals.

I/O adapter   An adapter that plugs into a computer's expansion bus and provides several ports to which peripheral devices may attach. Typically, an I/O adapter provides a bidirectional parallel port, a serial port with a 16550A Universal Asynchronous Receiver/Transmitter (UART), and a game port. Often ports are built into the motherboard and an I/O adapter is not needed.

I/O buffering   A feature of high-end network printers that enables them to print one document while receiving information about another that is to be printed next.

Iomega Corporation   The leading manufacturer of removable drives, including the Jaz drive and ZIP drive. Headquartered in Roy, Utah, Iomega was founded in 1980.

IP A protocol that defines the format of data sent over a packet-switching network. The Internet uses IP, making it the largest packet-switching network in the world. See *packet, packet-switching network, TCP/IP*.

IP address A 32-bit binary number that uniquely and precisely identifies the location of a particular computer on the Internet. Every computer that is directly connected to the Internet must have an IP address. Because binary numbers are so hard to read, IP addresses are given in four-part decimal numbers, each part representing 8 bits of the 32-bit address (for example, 128.143.7.226). Computers that are assigned fixed IP addresses can be configured to run servers, which make information available to other workstations on the network. Most users who access the Internet by means of dial-up, ISDN, DSL, or cable connections receive a session-based, temporary IP address, which is provided by the network's DHCP server. See *fixed IP address, TCP/IP*.

IPC See *interprocess communication*.

IP conflict A name conflict that occurs when two devices on a TCP/IP network are assigned the same IP address. See *IP address, namespace, TCP/IP*.

IP masquerading A local area network (LAN) configuration for Internet access that presents the stream of TCP/IP packets to the external Internet as if they were all coming from a single workstation. Network workstations use IP addresses in one of two reserved address ranges (10.0.0.x or 192.168.0.x). IP masquerading provides a measure of external against attacks from the external Internet because would-be attackers cannot determine internal IP addresses; however, additional security measures (such as a firewall) are still required. See *firewall, IP address, LAN, security, TCP/IP*.

IPng See *IPv6*.

IP number See *Internet address*.

IPRA See *Internet PCA Registration Authority*.

IPv6 The next-generation Internet protocol, also known as IPng, an evolutionary extension of the current Internet protocol suite that is under development by the Internet Engineering Task Force (IETF). IPv6 was originally intended to deal with the coming exhaustion of IP addresses, a serious problem caused by the Internet's rapid growth. However, the development effort has broadened to address a number of deficiencies in the current versions of the fundamental Internet protocols, including security, the lack of support for mobile computing, the need for automatic configuration of network devices, the lack of support for allocating bandwidth to high-priority data transfers, and other shortcomings of the current protocols. An unresolved question is whether the working committee will be able to persuade network equipment suppliers to upgrade to the new protocols.

IPX/SPX The transport protocol used in Novell NetWare networks. Because IPX/SPX is not as easily routed as TCP/IP, it is disappearing, and Novell currently supports TCP/IP as the basic transport protocol for its networking technologies. See *LAN, protocol*.

IR See *infrared radiation*.

IRC See *Internet Relay Chat*.

IrDA Acronym for Infrared Data Association. A non-profit industry consortium that develops standards for network devices that use infrared signals. See *infrared port, infrared radiation (IR)*.

IRQ Abbreviation for interrupt request. In microprocessors, an input line through which peripherals (such as printers or modems) can get the attention of the microprocessor when the device is ready to send or receive data. See *interrupt, IRQ conflict*.

IRQ conflict A problem that results when two peripheral devices have been assigned the same interrupt request (IRQ) line and try to communicate with the microprocessor simultaneously. Assigning a new peripheral an unused IRQ line to prevent an IRQ conflict is usually done by trial and error, but the Plug and Play standard is supposed to eliminate guesswork in installing new adapters. See *IRQ.*

IRTF   See *Internet Research Task Force.*

ISA   A specification for the 16-bit data bus architecture of PC-compatible systems. Introduced in 1984, this architecture has been supplanted by the PCI standard. See *ISA slot, PCI.*

ISAPI   Acronym for Internet Server Application Programming Interface. An application programming interface (API) that enables programmers to include links to computer programs, such as database searches, in Web pages. ISAPI is designed to work with Microsoft's Internet Information Server (IIS). ISAPI provides the same functionality as the Common Gateway Interface (CGI), but with markedly improved functionality and reduced overhead; ISAPI requests make full use of the Windows programming environment, and the called programs remain resident in memory in case they will be needed again. See *application programming interface (API), CGI, IIS.*

ISA slot   A receptacle on the motherboard that accepts peripherals designed to conform to the Industry Standard Architecture (ISA) standard. ISA slots are not as fast as PCI slots, but most motherboard manufacturers offer models with one or two ISA slots for the benefit of users who wish to use legacy expansion boards. See *expansion bus, ISA.*

ISDN   Acronym for Integrated Services Digital Network. A worldwide standard for the delivery of digital telephone and data services to homes, schools, and offices. ISDN services fall into three categories: Basic Rate Interface (BRI), Primary Rate Interface (PRI), and Broadband ISDN (B-ISDN). Designed as the basic option for consumers, Basic Rate Interface offers two 64,000 bps channels for voice, graphics, and data, plus one 16,000 bps channel for signaling purposes. Primary Rate ISDN provides 23 channels with 64,000 bps capacity. Broadband ISDN, still under development, would supply up to 150 million bps of data transmission capacity. See *BRI, Primary Rate Interface (PRI).*

ISDN adapter   An internal or external accessory that enables a computer to connect to remote computer networks or the Internet by means of ISDN. Also (and inaccurately) called an ISDN "modem."

ISDN TA   See *ISDN adapter.*

ISDN terminal adapter   See *ISDN adapter.*

ISO   A Greek word (which means "equal") that stands for the International Organization for Standardization The ISO is a nonprofit organization headquartered in Geneva, Switzerland, that seeks technological and scientific advancement by establishing nonproprietary standards. An umbrella organization for the standards bodies of more than 90 nations, the ISO is responsible for the development of the Open System Interconnect (OSI) Reference Model, a means of conceptualizing computer networks that has proven extremely influential, in addition to many standards that are used throughout the computing world today. In the United States, the ISO is represented by the American National Standards Institute (ANSI). See *ANSI, OSI Reference Model.*

ISO 9000   A quality certification granted by the ISO to corporations that meet exacting specifications for quality control metrics and procedures.

ISO 9660   A standard file system for CD-ROM data that enables the same disc to be read on Macintosh, Unix, and Windows systems. The basic specification limits file names to the 8.3 file name format; the version that includes the Rockridge Extensions enables the use of file names of up to 255 characters.

ISO 10646 The Universal Character Set standard developed by the International Organization for Standards (ISO). See *UCS*.

ISOC See *Internet Society*.

ISO Latin 1 A character set defined by the International Organization for Standardization (ISO). ISO Latin 1 contains the characters needed for most Western European languages and also contains a nonbreaking space, a soft hyphen indicator, 93 graphics characters, and 25 control characters. With certain exceptions, ISO Latin 1 is the default character set used in the Hypertext Markup Language (HTML).

ISP Acronym for Internet service provider. A company that provides Internet accounts and connections to individuals and businesses. Most ISPs offer a range of connection options, ranging from dial-up modem connections to high-speed ISDN and ADSL. Also provided are e-mail, Usenet, and Web hosting. See *Internet access provider (IAP)*.

issue restrictions In a microprocessor with superscalar architecture and multiple pipelines, the set of rules that determines whether two instructions may be processed simultaneously. Generally, the fewer issue restrictions a microprocessor has, the faster it processes instructions. See *data dependency, false dependency*.

ISV Acronym for independent software vendor. A small to medium-sized programming firm that creates special-purpose or custom software.

italic A typeface characteristic, commonly used for emphasis, in which the characters slant to the right. Two words in the following sentence are in italic. See *oblique, Roman*.

Itanium A 64-bit RISC processor developed by Intel Corporation to compete with enterprise-level processors such as Compaq's Alpha. Capable of running 32-bit software only by means of emulation, the Itanium is designed primarily for operating systems and applications that have been specifically designed to take full advantage of the processor's instruction set, which is not downwardly compatible with x86 software. In 2002, Intel introduced the Itanium 2, an upgraded version of the chip, after customers complained that the original Itanium processor failed to meet performance expectations. See *Alpha, EPIC, K8, RISC*.

ITAR Acronym for International Traffic in Arms Regulations. A section of U.S. government regulations enacted under the Export Control Act of 1994 that forbids U.S. individuals or companies from exporting encryption software or utilities that cannot be broken by means of cryptanalysis. The restrictions stem from the concerns of defense experts who are well aware that encryption technologies have played a decisive role in twentieth-century warfare. However, the restricted algorithms are already widely available outside the United States, so—according to computer industry critics of ITAR—the only function of the regulations is to prevent U.S. companies from competing in a lucrative international market for secure business communication. See *encryption*.

iteration The repetition of a command or program statement. See *loop, recursion*.

iterative development In software engineering, a process methodology in which the phases of the software development life cycle (SDLC) are not performed in a step-by-step fixed series; on the contrary, they are repeated numerous times as a small-scale, working system is incrementally developed. This approach can cope with the inevitable changes that result from a client's inability to express system specifications fully at the inception of the project, the shifting fortunes of the various system stakeholders, new business developments that require new or modified features, and technological constraints that emerge only as the system is developed. See *incremental development, software development life cycle (SDLC), software engineering, waterfall model*.

ITS Acronym for Intelligent Transportation System. A system partly funded by the

U.S. government to develop smart streets and smart cars. Such a system can warn travelers of congestion and suggest alternative routes.

ITU-TSS Acronym for International Telecommunications Union-Telecommunications Standards Section. An organization sponsored by the United Nations that sets standards for communications technology. In computers, ITU-TSS standards, such as the widely used V.32bis protocol that governs some high-speed modem communications, enable modems from different manufacturers to communicate with one another. The ITU-TSS is the successor to the Comité Consultatif International Téléphonique et Télégraphique (CCITT).

J

jaggies See *aliasing*.

Java A cross-platform, object-oriented programming language created by Sun Microsystems. Java enables programmers to write software that will execute on any computer capable of running a Java interpreter (which is built into today's leading Web browsers). This is a significant advantage over other programming languages which force the programmer to re-write their software for each processor/operating system combination. Java programs are compiled into applets (small programs that run on a Web browser) or applications (larger, standalone programs), but compiled Java code contains no machine code. Instead, the output of the compiler is byte-code, which can be transmitted via computer networks, including the Internet. A Web browser (or other client) receives the bytecode, interprets it into machine code, and then runs the program. The biggest disadvantage is that Java programs run more slowly than programs that are designed from the beginning with a specific processor in mind. Java has transformed the way software is written, particularly for networks and the Internet, replacing older technologies such as CGI. Java is widely accepted and used in business and Web development. See *bytecode, C++, certificate, compiled program, interpreted programming language, Java applet, Java application, bean, Java Development Kit, Java Virtual Machine*.

Java applet A small program (applet) that is designed for distribution on the World Wide Web (WWW) and for interpretation by a Java-capable Web browser, such as Microsoft Internet Explorer or Netscape Navigator. Java applets execute within the browser window and seamlessly add functionality to Web pages. As a security precaution, applets are restricted from gaining access to the computer's file system. See *Java application*.

Java application A Java program that, unlike a Java applet, executes in its own window and possesses full access to the computer's file system. To run a Java application, the user's computer must be equipped with a standalone Java interpreter, such as the one included with the Java Development Kit (JDK). If Java applications are written in conformity to Sun's 100 percent Pure Java specifications, they will run on any computer that is capable of running a Java interpreter. See *Java applet*.

JavaBeans A component architecture for Java applets and Java applications that enables Java programmers to package Java programs in a container, similar to ActiveX, for increased interoperability with other objects and improved security. Java development environments that conform to the JavaBeans specification enable programmers to create beans, which are reusable Java-based components that are capable of exchanging data with other components. See *bean, Java*.

Java Database Connectivity See *JDBC*.

Java Development Kit (JDK) A package of Java utilities and development tools, created by Sun Microsystems and distributed free of charge, that represents the de facto standard for the Java programming language. The package contains an interpreter that enables users to run Java applications.

Java Native Interface See *JNI*.

JavaScript A scripting language for Web publishing, developed by Netscape Communications, that enables Web authors to embed programming instructions within the HTML text of their Web pages. Note that despite the word "Java" in the language's name, JavaScript is fundamentally different than Java. JavaScript is an interpreted language that executes much more slowly than Java, which is a hybrid compiled/interpreted language; and it requires its own interpreter, which is built into popular Web browsers. JavaScript led to the creation of a standardized language called ECMAScript, published by the European Computer Manufacturing Association (ECMA). Subsequent versions of JavaScript are compliant with the ECMAScript standard. See *JScript*.

JavaScript Style Sheet (JSS) A proprietary extension to the World Wide Web Consortium (W3C) standards, developed by Netscape Communications, for Cascading Style Sheets (CSS). JSS is designed to enable JavaScript programmers to create dynamic effects by including JavaScript instructions in the various style definitions. JSS conflicts with the World Wide Web Consortium's Cascading Style Sheet (CSS) standard and is no longer supported in the versions of Netscape Navigator (beginning with version 5.0). See *style sheet*.

JavaSoft A subsidiary of Sun Microsystems that is responsible for developing and promoting the Java programming language and related products. See *Java*.

Java Virtual Machine A Java interpreter and runtime environment for Java applets and Java applications. This environment is called a virtual machine because, no matter what kind of computer it is running on, it creates a simulated computer that provides the correct platform for executing Java programs. In addition, this approach insulates the computer's file system from rogue applications. Java VMs are available for most computers.

Java VM See *Java Virtual Machine*.

JDBC Acronym for Java Database Connectivity. A JavaSoft-developed application program interface (API) that enables Java programs to interact with any database program that complies with the SQL query language.

JDK See *Java Development Kit*.

JFS See *journaled file system (JFS)*.

Jini A Sun Microsystems-developed architecture that provides, in effect, a Plug-and-Play standard for cross-platform computer networks. Jini-compatible network components, such as printers, storage devices, and other peripherals, will install automatically and declare themselves to a network-based registry of Jini devices, thus freeing computer users from the tedium of maintaining local drivers for such devices.

JIT compiler Acronym for Just in Time compiler. A compiler that receives the byte-code from a Java application or applet and then compiles the bytecode into machine code on-the-fly. Code compiled with a JIT executes much faster than code executed by a non-JIT-enabled Java interpreter, such as the ones built into popular Web browsers.

jitter On a network, an annoying and perceptible variation in the time it takes various workstations to respond to messages—some respond quickly, some respond slowly, and some do not respond at all. Jitter is to be expected when the network cannot ensure fixed latency, the amount of time required for a message to travel from point A to point B in a network. See *latency*.

JNI Acronym for Java Native Interface. An application programming interface (API) for Java that enables programmers to include within Java programs some non-Java code that is native or specific to a particular type of computer system.

job A task for a computer. The word derives from the days when people had to take their programs to a computing department, which assigned a job number to each task to be performed on the organization's mainframe computer. See *mainframe*.

job control language (JCL) In mainframe computing, a programming language that enables programmers to specify batch processing instructions, which the computer then carries out. The abbreviation JCL refers to the job control language used in IBM mainframes.

job queue   A series of tasks automatically executed one after the other by the computer. In mainframe data processing during the 1950s and 1960s, the job queue was literally a queue, or line of people waiting to have their programs run. With interactive, multiuser computing and personal computing, one usually does not need to line up to get his or her work done (although waiting print jobs can still back up at a busy network printer).

join   In a relational database management program, a data retrieval operation in which a new data table is built from data in two or more existing data tables. The following example illustrates how a join works and why join operations are desirable in database applications: For his video store, the owner creates a database table called RENTALS, which lists the rented tapes with the phone number of the person renting the tape and the due date. The owner then creates another database table, called CUSTOMERS, in which he lists the phone number, name, and credit card number of all his customers. To find out whether any customers are more than two weeks late returning a tape, he needs to join information from the two databases. If he wanted to know the title and due date of the movie, as well as the phone number and name of the customer, the following Structured Query Language (SQL) command retrieves the information: SELECT TITLE, DUE_DATE, PHONE_NO, L_NAME, F_NAMEFROM RENTALS, CUSTOMERSWHERE DUE_DATE= <05/07/2004. This command tells the program to display the information contained in the data fields TITLE, DUE_DATE, PHONE_NO, L_NAME, and F_NAME, but only for those records in which the data field DUE_DATE contains a date equal to or earlier than May 7, 2004 The result is

the diagram, below. See *join condition, relationship.*

join condition   In a relational database management program, a statement of how two databases are to be joined together to form a single table. The statement usually specifies a field common to both databases as the condition for joining records. See *join.*

Joint Photographic Experts Group (JPEG)   A committee of computer graphics experts, jointly sponsored by the International Standards Organization (ISO) and the Comité Consultif International de Télégraphique et Téléphonique (CCITT), which developed the JPEG graphics standard.

journaled file system (JFS)   A new file system architecture that ensures the integrity of data stored on a hard disk in the event of an unplanned shutdown, such as one caused by a power outage. A journaled file system maintains a log of all read and write events; this log enables the disk to be restored to its last stable state and additionally allows incompletely written data to be restored to the maximum possible extent. See *ext3.*

joystick   A control device widely used as an alternative to the keyboard for computer games and some professional applications, such as computer-aided design.

JPEG   A graphics format capable of representing up to 16.7 million colors that is ideal for complex pictures of natural, real-world scenes, including photographs, realistic artwork, and paintings. (The format is not well suited to line drawings, text, or simple cartoons.) Developed by the Joint Photographic Experts Group (JPEG), a committee created by two international

Join Diagram

TITLE	DUE_DATE	PHONE_NO	L_NAME	F_NAME
Alien Beings	05/07/2004	499-1234	Jones	Terry
Almost Home	05/05/2004	499-7890	Smith	Jake

standards bodies, the JPEG graphic format employs lossy compression. Exploiting a known property of human vision—namely that small color changes are less noticeable than changes in brightness—JPEG compression is not noticeable unless very high compression ratios are chosen. Typically, JPEG can achieve compression ratios of 10:1 or 20:1 without noticeable degradation in picture quality, a much better compression ratio than that of the Graphics Interchange Format (GIF).

JScript Originally, Microsoft's clone of JavaScript. JScript is now an implementation of the ECMAScript standard, but because it is not completely compatible with JavaScript, JScript is not widely used. See *JavaScript*.

JSS See *JavaScript Style Sheet*.

jukebox A peripheral that allows access to a group of disks. See *CD-ROM changer*.

Julian date As used in computer programming, the number of days that have elapsed since the beginning of the year.

jumper An electrical connector that enables the user to select a particular configuration on a circuit board. The jumper is a small rectangle of plastic with two or three receptacles. One installs a jumper by pushing it down on two or more pins from a selection of many that are sticking up from the circuit board's surface. The placement of the jumper completes the circuit for the desired configuration. See *DIP switch*.

jumper settings The configuration of movable conductors on an adapter. Jumper settings dictate how an adapter interacts with the rest of a system by determining its interrupt request (IRQ) channel, for example. See *jumper*.

jump line A message at the end of part of an article in a newsletter, magazine, or newspaper indicating the page on which the article is continued. Desktop publishing programs include features that make using jump lines for newsletters easier.

justification The alignment of multiple lines of text along the left margin, the right margin, or both margins. The term justification often is used to refer to full justification, or the alignment of text along both margins.

Just in Time compiler See *JIT compiler*.

K Abbreviation for kilobyte (1,024 bytes). See *byte*.

K8 A 64-bit microprocessor developed by Advanced Micro Devices (AMD) to compete with Intel's line of 64-bit microprocessors, initiated by the Itanium. Unlike the Itanium, the K8 is designed to be downwardly compatible with IA-32 (32-bit Windows code) without resorting to the inefficiencies of emulation. See *Athlon, Duron, IA-64, Itanium, IA-32*.

Katmai New Instructions (KNI) A set of microprocessor instructions that implement 3-D graphics capabilities. See *streaming SIMD extensions (SSE)*.

Kb Abbreviation for kilobit (1,024 bits). See *bit*.

KB Alternative abbreviation for kilobyte (1,024 bytes). See *byte*.

Kbps Abbreviation for kilobit per second. See *bits per second (bps)*.

KDE Acronym for the K Desktop Environment. A desktop environment for Linux and other Unix-like operating systems created by a group of largely European volunteers. Designed to remedy the shortcomings of the X Window System, KDE brings a well-designed graphical user interface (GUI) to Unix-like systems, which have not been noted for ease of use. KDE combines the best concepts of the Microsoft Windows and Mac OS interfaces and is designed to transform Linux into a serious contender for desktop applications. Hundreds of KDE-compatible applications are available, including the KDE Office suite, which includes a word processing program (KWord), a spreadsheet (KSpread), a PowerPoint-like presentation graphics program (KPresenter), a vector-graphics-based illustration program (Karbon 14), an image-editing program (Krito), and a flowcharting application similar to Microsoft's Visio package (Kivio). KDE faces competition from a competing project called GNOME; the two projects are working toward interoperability, but progress is slow. See *GNOME, graphical user interface (GUI), Linux, X Window System*.

Kerberos An authentication system for computer networks developed at the Massachusetts Institute of Technology (MIT). Unlike server-based authentication systems, which provide only a single point of authenticated entry to the network, Kerberos enables administration and management of authentication at the network level. Passwords are encrypted to prevent interception en route. Kerberos is widely implemented in Unix-based networks and is the default authentication service for Microsoft's server operating systems. See *authentication*.

Kermit An asynchronous communications protocol that makes the error-free transmission of program files via the telephone system easier. Developed by Columbia University and placed in the public domain, Kermit is used by academic institutions because, unlike XMODEM, Kermit can be implemented on mainframe systems that transmit 7 bits per byte. See *communications protocol*.

kernel In an operating system, the core portions of the program that reside in memory and perform the most essential operating system tasks, such as handling disk input and output operations and managing the internal memory. See *Linux, Unix*.

kerning In desktop publishing, the adjustment of space between certain pairs of characters so that the characters print in an aesthetically pleasing manner.

Kerr effect The tendency of polarized light to shift its orientation slightly when reflected from a magnetized surface. Magneto-optical discs rely on the Kerr effect to read and write data.

key **1.** In cryptography, a complex cipher (such as a mathematical formula) that is paired with an encryption algorithm to encipher the message so that it is unreadable by anyone except the intended recipient (who has the appropriate key to decrypt the message). In symmetric key cryptography, the same key is used to decipher the encrypted text, called ciphertext. Public key cryptography uses two keys: a private key and a public key. A user makes the public key known to others, who use it to encrypt messages; these messages can be decrypted only by the intended recipient of a message, who uses the private key to do so. See *cipher, ciphertext, cryptography, encryption, encryption algorithm, public key cryptography.* **2.** In databases, a unique value that is used to identify a data record. Synonymous with primary key. **3.** A button on a computer keyboard.

key assignments The functions given to specific keys by a computer program. Most of the keys on a personal computer keyboard are fully programmable, meaning that a programmer can use them in different ways. The best programs, however, stick to industry standards when assigning keys to program functions that duplicate functions found in other programs, such as copying and pasting text.

keyboard The most frequently used input device. The keyboard provides a set of alphabetic, numeric, punctuation, symbol, and control keys. When a character key is pressed, a coded input signal is sent to the computer, which echoes the signal by displaying a character onscreen. The 104-key keyboard is standard for PCs, and the 108-key Apple Pro keyboard is standard for the Macintosh. See *104-key keyboard, Apple Pro keyboard, autorepeat key, keyboard layout, toggle key.*

keyboard buffer See *keystroke buffer.*

keyboard layout The arrangement of keys on the computer's keyboard. The standard computer keyboard uses the QWERTY layout that typewriters have used for a century. Because the keyboard's output is fully programmable, other layouts (such as the Dvorak keyboard layout, which is claimed to enable faster typing) are possible. Keyboards can also be designed to suit the needs of users who work in languages other than English. See *Dvorak keyboard.*

key escrow A scheme strongly promoted by U.S. government security agencies that would enable investigators to obtain valid court authorization to obtain the stored decryption key for scrambled messages sent or received by a person who is under investigation. For this scheme to work, an independent agency would have to be established to store every computer user's decryption key so that agents can obtain the key when a judge authorizes them to do so. Critics charge that such an agency would be under strong pressure from government investigators to release keys without a properly executed warrant, and warn that the key escrow agency could become the target of criminals who hope to obtain keys enabling them to intercept financial transactions. See *Clipper Chip, encryption, key recovery.*

key exchange In symmetric key encryption, the confidential exchange of keys via a network connection. To ensure that the key exchange is not monitored by intruders, a secure communication channel is first established by means of public key cryptography. However, public key cryptography is seldom used for the entire confidential session because it is significantly less efficient than symmetric encryption algorithms. See *encryption, encryption algorithm, key, public key cryptography, symmetric key encryption algorithm.*

key frame interpolation Also called keyframing or tweening. In three-dimensional graphics adapters, a combination of hardware and software support that enables an object to appear to move smoothly from one frame (the starting point) to another (the ending point); in fact, only the starting and ending frames are provided. The key frame interpolation technology automatically generates the frames in between (hence the term "tweening").Video adapters that support key frame interpolation produce smoother and more realistic gaming onscreen.

keyframing   See *key frame interpolation*.

key pair   Also called public/private key pair. In public key cryptography, the two keys that are needed to facilitate a confidential exchange: the public key, which is used to encode plaintext messages, and the private key, which is used to decode encrypted messages (ciphertext).To begin using public key cryptography, users employ a public key encryption program to generate the key pair. See *public key cryptography*.

key recovery   A method of providing law enforcement agencies with a means of gaining access to encrypted messages sent or received by persons who are the target of an investigation. of unlocking the key used to encrypt messages so that the message could be read by law enforcement officials conducting a lawful investigation. Key recovery is proposed by law enforcement officials concerned that encryption would prevent surveillance of criminal activities.

key status indicator   An onscreen status message displayed by many application programs that signals which, if any, toggle keys are active on the keyboard. See *Caps Lock key*, *Num Lock key*, *Scroll Lock key*.

keystroke   The physical action of pressing down a key on the keyboard so that a character is entered or a command is initiated.

keystroke buffer   A holding area in memory that is used to save the current keystrokes if one types something while the microprocessor is busy with something else. For example, if a user begins typing while a file is being saved, the characters typed are placed in the keystroke buffer. When it is full (usually the buffer holds 20 characters), a beep is heard each time another key is pressed, indicating that the input is not being accepted. When the microprocessor completes its task, the characters in the buffer are sent to the screen.

key variable   In a spreadsheet program, a constant placed in a cell and referenced throughout the spreadsheet using absolute cell references. See *spreadsheet program*.

keyword   **1.** In programming languages (including macro languages), a word describing an action or operation that the computer can recognize and execute. See *macro*, *programming language*. **2.** In a document summary, one or more words that succinctly describe a document's contents. In the document summary of a letter inquiring about green PCs, a keyword might be "electricity."

keyword search   In a database system, a search that begins by supplying the computer with one or more keywords that describe the topic of a particular search. To retrieve items on North Carolina's Outer Banks, for example, one could type "outer" and "banks." With most systems, Boolean operators can be used to focus or broaden the search. For example, if one types "outer and banks," the system will retrieve only those documents in which both of these words appear. See *keyword*.

KHz   Abbreviation for kilohertz; 1,000 cycles (Hz) per second. See *hertz (Hz)*.

kick   In Internet Relay Chat (IRC), an action undertaken by a channel operator to expel an unwanted user from the channel. Ostensibly, this is to be done only when the user has grossly violated IRC etiquette, but it is sometimes done quite arbitrarily or for the channel operator's amusement. See *boot off*, *Internet Relay Chat (IRC)*.

kill   **1.** To stop an ongoing process, such as a running program. See *break*. **2.** In Usenet newsreaders, to delete an article containing a certain word, name, or origin site so that articles containing this information do not appear subsequently in the article selector. See *article selector*, *global kill file*, *kill file*.

killer app   An application that becomes so indispensable to the way people work that it creates a larger market for the operating systems and platforms for which it is available.

kill file   In a Usenet newsreader, a file that contains a list of subjects or names that a user does not want to appear on the list of messages available for him or her to read. If a user no longer wants to read messages from Edward P. Jerk, he or she can add Ed's name to his or her newsreader's kill file, and Jerk's contributions will be discarded automatically before they reach the user's screen. See *kill, Usenet.*

kilo-   A metric prefix indicating 1,000 (10^3).

kilobit   1,024 bits of information. See *kilobyte (K).*

kilobyte (K)   The basic unit of measurement for computer memory and disk capacity, equal to 1,024 bytes. The prefix "kilo-" suggests 1,000, but the computer world is based on twos, not tens: 210 = 1,024. Because 1 byte is the same as one character in personal computing, 1K of data can contain 1,024 characters (letters, numbers, or punctuation marks).

kilohertz (KHz)   One thousand cycles per second.

kiosk   A publicly accessible computer system that has been set up to allow interactive information browsing. In a kiosk, the computer's operating system has been hidden from view, and the program runs in a full-screen mode, which provides a few simple tools for navigation. See *kiosk mode.*

kiosk mode   In a Web browser, a mode that zooms the program to full screen, permitting its use as an information navigation tool in a kiosk.

kludge   See *kluge.*

kluge   (Pronounced *klooge.*) An improvised, technically inelegant solution to a problem. Also spelled kludge.

knowbot   See *agent.*

knowledge   A set of propositions about the world that can generate additional propositions by means of deduction. For example, one may infer from the following propositions that Sri Lanka is a South Asian country: **1.** Sri Lanka is adjacent to India. **2.** Sri Lanka is a country. **3.** All the countries adjacent to India are in South Asia. Knowledge thus differs from data (unorganized facts) and information (organized facts that are not expressed in a form susceptible to deductive inference) See *data.*

knowledge acquisition   In expert systems, the process of acquiring and systematizing knowledge from experts. A major limitation of current expert system technology is that knowledge engineers must acquire knowledge in a slow and painstaking process, called knowledge representation, that is designed to express the knowledge in terms of computer-readable rules. See *expert system.*

knowledge base   In an expert system, the portion of the program that includes an expert's knowledge, often in IF/THEN rules (for example, "If the tank pressure exceeds 600 pounds per square inch, then sound a warning."). See *expert system.*

knowledge domain   In artificial intelligence (AI), an area of problem-solving expertise. Current artificial intelligence technology works well only in sharply limited knowledge domains, such as the configuration of one manufacturer's computer systems, the repair of a specific robotic system, or investment analysis for a limited collection of securities. See *artificial intelligence (AI).*

knowledge engineer   In expert systems, a specialist who obtains the knowledge possessed by experts on a subject and expresses this knowledge in a form that an expert system can use. See *expert system, knowledge domain.*

knowledge representation   In expert systems, the method used to encode and store the knowledge in a knowledge base. Although several alternative knowledge representation schemes are used, most commercially available expert systems use the production system approach in which knowledge is represented in the form of production rules, which have the following form: IF {condition} THEN {action}. A given rule may have multiple conditions, as in the following example: IF {a person's intraocular pressure is raised} AND {the person has pain in the left quadratic region} THEN {immediate hospitalization is indicated}. See *expert system, knowledge engineer.*

Korn Shell   See *ksh.*

ksh   Abbreviation for Korn Shell. A popular shell (command-line user interface) for the Unix operating system. A command-line interface that is difficult to learn for computer neophytes, the Korn Shell is nevertheless greatly esteemed by experienced computer users due to its programmability and many time-saving shortcuts. See *bash, csh, shell.*

KVM switch   Acronym for keyboard, video, mouse switch. An accessory that enables two or more computers to be controlled using a single keyboard, monitor, and mouse.

L1 cache   See *primary cache.*

L2 cache   See *secondary cache.*

L3 cache   An additional, external secondary cache that is used with microprocessors that incorporate secondary caches within the microprocessor. See *secondary cache.*

L2TP   See *Layer 2 Tunneling Protocol.*

label   **1.** In a spreadsheet program, text entered in a cell. By contrast, a number entered in a cell is a value. **2.** In DOS batch files, a string of characters preceded by a colon that marks the destination of a GOTO command. See *spreadsheet.*

label alignment   In a spreadsheet program, the way labels are aligned in a cell (flush left, centered, flush right, or repeating across the cell). Unless specified otherwise, labels are aligned on the left of the cell. See *label prefix.*

label prefix   In most spreadsheet programs, a punctuation mark at the beginning of a cell entry that tells the program that the entry is a label and that specifies how the program should align the label within the cell. Programs that use prefixes enter the default label prefix—usually an apostrophe (')—when the cell entry begins with a letter.

label printer   A printer designed specifically to print names and addresses on continuous-feed labels.

laddered text   In Unix and Unix-like operating systems, a printing defect caused by the printer's failure to start a new line after executing a line feed. This problem is caused by a basic incompatibility between DOS and Unix text files: DOS text files end with a carriage return and a line feed character, while Unix text files end with a line feed character only. The system administrator can fix this problem by altering a printer configuration file. See *carriage return, line feed.*

LAN   Acronym for local area network. A computer network that uses cables or radio signals to link two or more computers within a geographically limited area (generally one building or a group of buildings). The linked computers are called workstations. LANs are differentiated by their architecture (peer-to-peer or client/server), topology (bus, hierarchical, multipoint, point-to-point, ring, or star), protocols (standards for transferring data among the linked workstations), and media (for instance, coaxial, twisted-pair, and fiber optic). Peer-to-peer LANs are simple to implement using the built-in networking capabilities of computers running Microsoft Windows or Mac OS; such networks enable the linked computers to share expensive peripherals such as laser printers; client/server networks use a LAN server to make centralized resources (such as databases and applications) available to workstation users. Network protocols operate at differing layers; for example, Ethernet is a lower-layer protocol that defines the basic mechanisms by which data enters the network and travels to its destination; Ethernets can work with a variety of higher-level protocols, including AppleTalk, Common Internet File System (CIFS), and TCP/IP. See *AppleTalk, baseband, broadband, bus network, client/server, Ethernet, peer-to-peer network, ring network, star network, wireless LAN.*

LAN-aware program   A version of an application program specifically modified so that the program can function in a local area network (LAN) environment. Network versions of transactional application programs (database management programs) create and maintain shared files. An invoice-processing program, for example, has access to a database of accounts receivable. The network versions of nontransactional programs, such as word processing programs, include file security features to prevent unauthorized users from gaining access to documents. LAN-aware programs boast features such as concurrency control (which manages multiple copies of files) and file locking, and prevents unauthorized users from accessing certain files. LAN-aware programs usually are stored on a file server. See *LAN-ignorant program*.

LAN backup program   A program designed specifically to back up the programs and data stored on a local area network (LAN) file server. The best LAN backup programs automatically back up the file server at scheduled times, without user intervention.

landing zone   Ideally, the only area of a hard disk's surface that actually touches the read/write head. Through a process called head parking, the read/write head moves over the landing zone before the computer is shut off and drifts to rest there. The landing zone, on which no data is encoded, is designed to prevent the read/write head from damaging portions of the disk used to store data.

landscape font   A font in which the characters are oriented toward the long edge of the page. See *portrait font*.

landscape orientation   A page layout in which lines of text are parallel with the long edge of the page. See *portrait orientation*.

LAN-ignorant program   An application program designed for use only as a standalone program and that contains no provisions for use on a network, such as file locking and concurrency control. See *LAN-aware program*.

LAN server   See *client/server, server*.

LAPM   See *Link Access Protocol for Modems*.

laptop computer   A small, portable computer that is light and small enough to hold on one's lap. Small laptop computers, which weigh less than 6 pounds and can fit in a briefcase, are called notebook computers. The smallest portable computers that can emulate all the functions of a desktop computer, weighing about as little as 1.5 pounds, are called subnotebook computers. In practice, this term is often used synonymously

with notebook computer. See *notebook computer*.

large-scale integration (LSI)   In integrated circuit technology, a level of chip fabrication technology that is able to place up to 100,000 transistors on a single chip. See *very large scale integration (VLSI)*.

laser font   See *outline font*.

laser printer   A high-resolution printer that uses a version of the electrostatic reproduction technology of copying machines to fuse text and graphic images to paper. To print a page, the printer's controller circuitry receives the printing instructions from the computer and builds a bitmap of every dot on a page. The controller ensures that the print engine's laser transfers a precise replica of this bit map to a photostatically sensitive drum or belt. Switching on and off rapidly, the beam travels across the drum; as the beam moves, the drum charges the areas exposed to the beam. The charged areas attract toner (electrically charged ink) as the drum rotates past the toner cartridge. An electrically charged wire pulls the toner from the drum onto the paper, and heat rollers fuse the toner to the paper. A second electrically charged wire neutralizes the drum's electrical charge. See *light-emitting diode (LED) printer, resolution*.

latency   **1.** In a computer network, the amount of time required for a message to travel from the sending computer to the receiving computer. This is far from instantaneous in a packet-switching network, given the fact that the message must be read and passed on by several routers before it reaches its destination and results in jitter. **2.** In disk drives, the time required for the portion of the disk containing needed information to rotate under the read/write head. The faster a disk drive spins, the lower its latency.

LaTeX   A page description language that enables a programmer to prepare a page for typesetting.

launch To start a program.

layer **1.** In some illustration and page layout applications, an onscreen sheet on which one can place text or graphics so that they are independent of any text or graphics on other sheets. The layer can be opaque or transparent. **2.** In a computer network, a portion of the total network architecture that is differentiated from other portions because it has a distinctive function, such as preparing data to be transmitted over the network's physical media. Network design is aided by functionally differentiating layers and assigning standards, or protocols, to each. See *OSI Reference Model, protocol stack*. **3.** In version 4 of Netscape Navigator and Netscape Communicator, a means of positioning text or graphics in an absolute location on the page that makes use of Netscape's nonstandard style sheet implementation (JavaScript Style Sheets). Subsequent versions of Netscape Navigator conform to the World Wide Web Consortium's Cascading Style Sheet (CSS) standard, which also specifies a method for absolute positioning. See *CSS, JavaScript Style Sheet (JSS)*.

Layer 2 Tunneling Protocol (L2TP) A standard for "tunneling" (encapsulating) Post Office Protocol (PPP) data so that it can traverse TCP/IP, X.25, frame relay, or ATM networks. The standard combines the Point-to-Point Tunneling Protocol (PPTP) with Layer 2 Forwarding (L2F) technology developed by Cisco Systems. See *ATM, frame relay, PPP, TCP/IP, X.25*.

layout In desktop publishing and word processing, the process of arranging text and graphics on a page. In database management systems, the arrangement of report elements, such as headers and fields, on a printed page.

LBA See *Logical Block Addressing*.

LCD Acronym for Liquid Crystal Display. A low-power display technology used in laptop computers and small, battery-powered electronic devices such as meters, testing equipment, and digital watches. The display device uses rod-shaped crystal molecules that change their orientation when an electrical current flows through them. Some LCD designs use backlit screens to improve readability, but at the cost of drawing more power.

LCD printer A high-quality printer that closely resembles the laser printer in that it electrostatically fuses toner to paper; however, the light source is a matrix of liquid crystal shutters. The shutters open and close to create the pattern of light that falls on the print drum. See *light-emitting diode (LED) printer*.

LCS printer See *liquid crystal shutter (LCS) printer*.

LDAP Acronym for Lightweight Directory Access Protocol. A simplified and TCP/IP-enabled version of the X.500 directory protocol, which defines a method for creating searchable directories of resources available on a network (including people as well as files and programs). Most of the leading e-mail programs and contact managers are compatible with LDAP, which means they can automatically include network-accessible LDAP databases in searches for names and contact information. See *TCP/IP, white pages, X.500*.

ldp See *line printer daemon*.

leader In word processing, a row of dots or dashes that provides a path for the eye to follow across the page. Leaders often are used in tables of contents to lead the reader's eye from the entry to the page number. Most word processing programs let the user define tab stops that insert leaders when the Tab key is pressed.

leading The space between lines of type, measured from baseline to baseline. Synonymous with line spacing. The term originated from letterpress-printing technology, in which lead strips were inserted between lines of type to add spacing between lines.

leading zero The zeros added in front of numeric values so that a number fills up all required spaces in a data field. For example, three leading zeros are in the number 00098.54.

leased line   A permanently connected and conditioned telephone line that provides wide area network (WAN) connectivity to an organization or business. Most leased lines transfer digital data at 56 Kbps.

least significant bit (LSB)   In a binary number, the last or rightmost bit that conveys the least amount of information, given its low place value.

LEC   Acronym for Local Exchange Carrier. A public telephone company that provides local services. LECs are often large companies, such as the regional Bell operating companies that were created from the divestiture of the AT&T monopoly, but the focal point of their local service capabilities is their local exchange system, called the central office (CO). The central office serves homes and businesses within a specific geographic region, such as a portion of a city or county. Local exchanges are connected to neighboring local exchanges by means of local access and transport area (LATA) carriers, as well as to long-distance carriers such as AT&T and Sprint.

LED   See *light-emitting diode.*

LED indicator   See *drive activity light.*

LED printer   See *light-emitting diode (LED) printer.*

left justification   See *justification.*

legacy application   A computer program that was specifically designed for legacy hardware and that continues to be used, despite inefficiencies, a poor user interface, or other shortcomings, because the system is too expensive to replace. See *legacy hardware.*

legacy hardware   Older computers or computer peripherals that do not conform to the standards or performance levels found in newer equipment. For example, an adapter that does not conform to the Plug and Play standard is legacy hardware. In networking, this term strongly connotes hardware that is designed to work with proprietary communication protocols rather than open standards.

legacy system   A computer system consisting of outdated applications and hardware that was developed to solve a specific business problem. Many legacy systems are still in use because they solve the problem well and because replacing them would be too expensive. See *legacy application, legacy hardware.*

legend   An area of a chart or graph that explains what data is being represented by the colors or patterns used in the chart.

Lempel–Ziv compression algorithm   A substitutional compression algorithm that looks for repeated patterns in the data to be compressed, removes the repeated pattern, and inserts a pointer to the first occurrence of the pattern. The resulting compressed file is significantly smaller than the original, but it can be decompressed so that the resulting output file is an exact copy of the original. The original Lempel–Ziv algorithm, LZ77, proposed in 1977, is free from software patents and is implemented by a variety of compression programs. See *bzip2, gzip, LZ78.*

Lempel–Ziv–Welch (LZW) compression algorithm   A patented version of the Lempel–Ziv compression algorithm that was developed in 1984 The patent holder, Unisys, aggressively pursues infringements. The GIF graphics file format, developed by CompuServe, uses LZW compression, as does the Unix compress program. The Portable Network Graphics (PNG) graphics file format uses a different compression technique and is patent-free. See *Lempel–Ziv compression algorithm, PNG, software patent.*

LEO satellite   See *low Earth orbit (LEO) satellite.*

letter-quality printer   A printer that offers fully formed text characters as good as those produced by a high-quality office typewriter.

library A collection of programs kept with a computer system and made available for processing purposes. The term often refers to a collection of library routines written in a given programming language such as C or Pascal.

library routine In programming, a well-tested subroutine, procedure, or function in a given programming language. The library routine handles tasks that all or most programs need, such as reading data from disks. The programmer can draw on this library to develop programs quickly.

ligature In typography, two or more characters designed and cast as a distinct unit for aesthetic reasons, such as æ.

light client In the client/server model of network architecture, traditional client programs were proprietary, complex, and expensive to maintain. By using familiar Web browsers as a universal client for all kinds of servers, network designers can substantially reduce the cost of client maintenance and user training, while at the same time ensuring that the users of differing types of computers will be able to access important data. Synonymous with Web browser. See *heavy client*.

light-emitting diode (LED) A small electronic device made from semiconductor materials. An LED emits light when current flows through it. LEDs are used for small indicator lights, but because they draw more power than LCDs (liquid crystal displays), they rarely are used for computer displays.

light-emitting diode (LED) printer A high-quality printer that closely resembles the laser printer in that it electrostatically fuses toner to paper; however, the light source is a matrix of light-emitting diodes rather than a laser. To create the image, the diodes flash on and off over the rotating print drum. See *LCD printer*.

light pen An input device that uses a light-sensitive stylus so that one can draw onscreen, draw on a graphics tablet, or select items from menus.

Lightweight Directory Access Protocol See *LDAP*.

LIM EMS See *Lotus-Intel-Microsoft Expanded Memory Specification (LIM EMS)*.

line In programming, one program statement. In data communications, a circuit that directly connects two or more electronic devices.

line adapter In data communications, an electronic device that converts signals from one form to another so that one can transmit the signals. A modem is a line adapter that converts the computer's digital signals to analog equivalents so that they can be transmitted using standard telephone lines.

line art In graphics, a drawing that does not contain halftones (shading). Line art can be accurately reproduced by low- to medium-resolution printers that have limited or no halftone printing capability.

line chart See *line graph*.

line editor A primitive word processing utility that is often provided with an operating system as part of its programming environment. Unlike with a full-screen editor, the user can write or edit only one line of program code at a time. See *programming environment*.

line feed A standard ASCII character that tells the printer when to start a new line. See *carriage return, laddered text*.

line graph In presentation and analytical graphics, a graph that uses lines to show the variations of data over time or to show the relationship between two numeric variables. In general, the x-axis (categories) is aligned horizontally, and the y-axis (values) is aligned vertically. A line graph, however, may have two y-axes. See *bar graph, presentation graphics*.

line interactive UPS A type of uninterruptible power supply (UPS) that provides protection from brownouts as well as power failures. A line interactive UPS monitors electrical current from a wall outlet and provides full operating power if the line voltage drops or disappears. See *standby UPS*.

line mode terminal   A terminal that is designed to communicate with the user with one line of text at a time, like an old-fashioned teletype machine (in fact, such terminals are often abbreviated TTY, which stands for "teletype"). When a one-line command is typed, the terminal responds with a one-line conformation or error message. See *network virtual terminal (NVT)*, *Telnet*.

line noise   Interference in a telephone line caused by current fluctuations, poor connections in telephone equipment, crosstalk from adjacent lines, or environmental conditions such as lightning. Line noise may reduce the data transfer rate a modem can sustain or may introduce garbage characters into the data stream.

line printer daemon (lpd)   In Unix and Unix-like operating systems such as Linux, a printing service that implements queued background printing for shared network printers.

liner   The cloth envelope that fits between the recording medium of a floppy disk and its shell. The liner reduces friction and keeps dust off the recording medium.

line rate   See *horizontal frequency*.

line spacing   See *leading*.

link   To establish a connection between two files or data items so that a change in one is reflected by a change in the second. A cold link requires user intervention and action, such as opening both files and using an updating command, to make sure that the change has occurred. A hot link updates automatically. See *hot link*, *OLE*.

Link Access Protocol for Modems (LAPM)   An error-correction protocol included in the V.42 standard. V.42 tries to establish a connection with LAPM but will try MNP4 if it fails. Like other error-correction protocols, LAPM exists to

ensure that data is transmitted accurately and that garbage characters are eliminated.

link checker   In Web publishing, a utility that checks all the hyperlinks used in a site to see whether the destination sites are still available.

linked list   See *list*.

linked object   In object linking and embedding (OLE), a document or portion of a document (an object) created with one application that is inserted into a document created with another application. Linking places a copy of the object, with hidden information about the source of the object, into the destination document. If the source document is changed while the destination document is open, the object in the destination document is automatically updated. If the destination document is not open, the object is updated the next time it is opened. Object linking and embedding are possible only when using OLE-compatible applications on a Microsoft Windows system or on a Macintosh system running System 7. See *embedded object*.

linked pie/column chart   See *linked pie/column graph*.

linked pie/column graph   In presentation graphics, a pie graph paired with a column graph so that the column graph displays the internal distribution of data items in one slice of the pie.

link rot   In Web publishing, the tendency of hyperlinks to become inoperational as the linked sites are renamed, moved, or withdrawn from the Web. Effective Web site administration requires periodic link checking to make sure that the hyperlinks still work. See *link checker*.

Linux   Extremely popular Unix-like operating system, created by Linus Torvalds, that was originally designed to run on Intel-powered PCs. Linux is free, open source software distributed under the terms of the GNU General Public License (GPL). The fundamental component of any Linux operating system is the kernel. Various individuals, groups, and companies create their own versions of the Linux operating system (called distributions) by adding utilities and other programs to the Linux kernel. Linux is now available for Apple computers, Alpha workstations, and additional platforms. Coupled with utilities created by the Free Software Foundation (FSF) and BSD, Linux comprises a functional operating system that is making significant inroads into the lower end of the server market (where it competes directly with Microsoft Windows 2000 Server and Windows Server 2003. The development of GUI desktop environments for Linux, such as GNOME and KDE, led some to predict rising use in the end user market; however, Linux remains challenging to use for those without system administrative or programming experience. See *BSD, Free Software Foundation (FSF), General Public License (GPL), GNOME, KDE, Samba, Unix.*

Linux distribution A collation of Linux software, typically distributed on a CD-ROM, that includes the Linux kernel and all the utilities and accessory programs needed to install and run Linux on a given type of computer. The leading Linux distributions are Caldera OpenLinux, Debian Linux, Mandrake, Red Hat Linux, and SuSE.

liquid cooling A recent trend in PCs, liquid cooling kits are designed to cool the microprocessor; they replace CPU fans and heat sinks. These kits vary widely, but common components include a water block (the housing which surrounds the microprocessor), water pump, hoses, copper radiator, and a fan. Computer cases are also available with liquid cooling built in; these systems also cool the entire PC, including the graphics card, memory, and power supply.

liquid crystal display See *LCD.*

liquid crystal display (LCD) printer See *LCD printer.*

liquid crystal shutter (LCS) printer A printer that uses a light source and a series of shutters and lenses, instead of a laser beam, to create an electrostatic charge on a page. LCS printers may have longer lives than laser printers because they have fewer moving parts.

LISP Abbreviation for List Processor. A high-level programming language, often used for artificial intelligence research, that makes no distinction between the program and the data. This language is considered ideal for manipulating text. One of the oldest programming languages still in use, LISP is a declarative language; the programmer composes lists that declare the relationships among symbolic values. Lists are the fundamental data structure of LISP, and the program performs computations on the symbolic values expressed in those lists. As with other public domain programming languages, however, a number of mutually unintelligible versions of LISP exist. A standardized, fully configured, and widely accepted version is Common LISP. See *interpreter.*

list In programming, a data structure that lists and links each data item with a pointer showing the item's physical location in a database. Using a list, a programmer can organize data in various ways without changing the physical location of the data. For example, the programmer can display a database so that it appears to be sorted in alphabetical order, even though the actual physical data records still are stored in the order in which they were entered.

LISTSERV A commercial mailing list manager, originally developed in 1986 for BITNET mailing lists, that has since been ported to Unix and Microsoft Windows. LISTSERV is marketed by L-Soft International. See *Majordomo.*

literal In programming, a constant, as opposed to a variable.

lithium-ion battery In portable computers, a rechargeable battery technology that offers as much as twice the charge capacity of competing technologies (NiCad and NiMH batteries) with significantly less environmental risk. Lithium-ion batteries currently cost more, but the price differential is expected to decrease as battery factories increase production.

little-endian In computer architecture, a design philosophy that prefers placing the least significant bit at the beginning of a data word. Intel microprocessors and DEC Alpha processors are little-endian; however, most RISC-based systems and Motorola microprocessors are big-endian. See *big-endian.*

live copy/paste See *hot link.*

load To transfer software or data from storage into the computer's random access memory (RAM) so that it will execute.

local area network See *LAN.*

local bus A high-speed bus architecture for IBM-compatible computers that directly links the computer's central processing unit (CPU) with one or more slots on the expansion bus. This direct link means that the signals from an adapter (video or hard disk controller, for example) do not have to travel through the computer's expansion bus, which is significantly slower. Local bus designs enjoyed some prominence in the mid-1990s, but new systems use the Peripheral Component Interconnect (PCI) bus, which offers even better performance. See *VESA local bus.*

local drive In a local area network (LAN), a disk drive that is part of the workstation the user is currently using, as distinguished from a network drive (a drive made available to the user through the network).

locale In Microsoft Windows, the geographical location of a computer. The locale determines the language in which messages appear; the formats for time, date, and money expressions; and the time of day.

local echo See *half-duplex.*

local loop The copper pair wire that connects a home or business to a telephone company switching station. Local loop wires have very low bandwidth and need to

be replaced before implementing high-speed digital telecommunications, such as those provided by the Integrated Services Digital Network (ISDN).

local printer In a local area network (LAN), a printer directly connected to the workstation one is currently using, as distinguished from a network printer (a printer made available to the user through the network).

LocalTalk The physical connectors and cables manufactured by Apple Computer for use in AppleTalk networks.

local Usenet hierarchy In Usenet, a category of newsgroups that is set up for local distribution only, such as within the confines of a company or university. Local newsgroups are not ordinarily accessible outside the organization.

locked file In a local area network (LAN), a file attribute that prevents applications or the user from updating or deleting the file.

lock up See *freeze.*

log A record. In communications programs, a log feature can record everything that appears on the monitor for later review, which can save the user money if he or she is paying a per-minute connection fee.

logarithmic chart See *logarithmic graph.*

logarithmic graph In analytical and presentation graphics, a graph displayed with a y-axis (values) that increases exponentially in powers of 10. On an ordinary y-axis, the 10 is followed by 20, 30, 40, and so on. On a logarithmic scale, however, 10 is followed by 100, 1,000, 10,000, and so on. This makes a logarithmic graph useful when great differences exist in the values of the data being graphed.

logical Having the appearance of and being treated as a real thing, even though it does not exist. See *logical drives, physical drive.*

logical address In virtual memory systems, a memory address that is used to specify a location within a virtual memory space far larger than the system's actual physical memory; the operating system handles the task of translating between the logical addresses and physical memory locations, which include locations outside the computer's random-access memory (RAM). See *physical address, virtual memory.*

Logical Block Addressing (LBA) Part of the Enhanced IDE standard; LBA permits hard disks to store up to 8.4GB of data.

logical drives Sections of a single hard drive that are formatted and assigned a drive letter, each of which is presented to the user as though it were a separate drive. Another way logical drives are created is by substituting a drive letter for a directory. Also, networks typically map directories to drive letters, resulting in logical drives. See *logical, partition, physical drive.*

logical format See *high-level format.*

logical network A network as it appears to the user. In fact, the network could be composed of two or more physical networks, or portions of these, that are linked and coordinated in such a way that they appear to be a unit. One of the most remarkable facts about the Internet is that, even though it links tens of thousands of physically heterogeneous networks, they nevertheless appear to the user to comprise a single, immense network of global proportions.

logical operator See *Boolean operator.*

logic board See *motherboard.*

logic bomb In programming, a form of sabotage in which a programmer inserts code that causes the program to perform a destructive action when some triggering event occurs, such as terminating the programmer's employment.

logic gate An automatic switch incorporated into microprocessors and other chips that tests for certain conditions and that takes certain actions if they are satisfied. Logic gates are at the center of a computer's capability to carry out instructions and solve problems. See *arithmetic-logic unit (ALU).*

login In a computer network, the authentication process in which a user supplies a login name and password.

login ID See *login name.*

login name In a network, a unique name assigned to a user by the system administrator that is used as a means of initial identification. The user must type this name and also his or her password to gain access to the system.

login script In dial-up access, a list of instructions that guides the dialer program through the process of dialing the service provider's number, supplying the user's login name and password, and establishing the connection.

login security An authentication process that requires one to type a password before gaining access to a system.

Logo A high-level programming language well-suited to teaching fundamental programming concepts to children. A special version of LISP, Logo was designed as an educational language to illustrate the concepts of recursion, extensibility, and other concepts of computing, without requiring math skills. The language also provides an environment in which children can develop their reasoning and problem-solving skills, and includes turtle graphics, a teaching aid that involves telling an onscreen turtle how to draw pictures.

log off The process of terminating a connection with a computer system or peripheral device in an orderly way. See *log on.*

log on The process of establishing a connection with or gaining access to a computer system or peripheral device. In MS-DOS, logging on refers to the process of changing to another drive by typing the drive letter and a colon and then pressing Enter. In networks, a user may be required to type a password to log on.

logon file   In a local area network (LAN), a batch file or configuration file that starts the network software and establishes the connection with the network when a user turns on his or her workstation.

lookup function   A procedure in which a program consults stored data listed in a table or file.

lookup table   In a spreadsheet program, data entered in a range of cells and organized so that a lookup function can use the data, for example, to determine the correct tax rate based on annual income.

loop   In programming, a control structure in which a block of instructions repeats until a condition is fulfilled. See *DO/WHILE loop*, *FOR/NEXT loop*.

loopback plug   In serial communications, a diagnostic plug that connects serial inputs to serial outputs so that each circuit in the port can be tested.

loss   **1.** In electronics, the amount (generally measured in decibals) of signal loss that occurs when a circuit or component consumes power without accomplishing useful results. **2.** In computer security, a measure of harm or deprivation resulting from a security compromise. Losses attributable to security breaches can range in severity from a mere annoyance to an outright catastrophe. They include lost business (resources are unavailable); lost customers (customers go to competitors with more secure systems); lost productivity (employees spend too much time securing their systems and coping with breaches); financial losses (intruders manipulate the system to steal money); losses of reputation (damaging confidential data is disclosed to the public); competitive costs (competitors obtain product or strategic plans); and physical losses (resources are destroyed or compromised to the point that they must be destroyed). See *risk*, *security*.

lossless compression   A data compression technique that reduces the size of a file without sacrificing any original data, used by file compression programs to reduce the size of all the program and document files on a hard disk. In lossless compression, the expanded or restored file is an exact replica of the original file before it was compressed; in lossy compression, data is lost in a way imperceptible to humans. Lossless compression is suitable for text and computer code, while lossy compression is good mainly for shrinking audio and graphics files.

lossy compression   A data compression technique in which some data is deliberately discarded to achieve massive reductions in the size of the compressed file. Lossy compression techniques can reduce a file to $\frac{1}{60}$ of its former size (or less), compared to the average of one-third achieved by lossless compression techniques. Lossy compression is used for graphics files in which the loss of data, such as information about some of the graphic's several million colors, is not noticeable. An example is the JPEG compression technique. See *lossless compression*.

lost chain   In MS-DOS, a group of clusters that are connected to each other in the file allocation table (FAT) but that are no longer connected to a specific file.

lost cluster   A cluster that remains on the disk, even though the file allocation table (FAT) contains no record of its link to a file. Lost clusters can occur when the computer is turned off (or the power fails) or tries to perform other operations while a file is being written.

Lotus 1-2-3   See *spreadsheet program*.

Lotus Approach   See *database management program*.

Lotus Domino   See *groupware*.

Lotus-Intel-Microsoft Expanded Memory Specification (LIM EMS)   An expanded memory standard that allows the programs that recognize the standard to work with more than 640K RAM under

DOS. The LIM Version 4.0 standard, introduced in 1987, supports up to 32MB of expanded memory and lets programs run in expanded memory.

Lotus Notes   See *groupware*.

Lotus Organizer   See *personal information manager (PIM)*.

Lotus SmartSuite   See *office suite*.

Lotus Word Pro   See *word processing program*.

low Earth orbit (LEO) satellite   In telecommunications, a satellite that is placed in a low-altitude orbit, just above the Earth's atmosphere. Because LEO satellites are much less expensive to construct and launch than geostationary satellites, they can be positioned in sufficient numbers to provide constant coverage, even though they do not remain in a fixed position relative to the ground. Iridium, a U.S.-based paging service, offers worldwide digital paging and data communications based on its network of LEO satellites.

low end   An inexpensive product at the bottom or near the bottom of a firm's offerings. Low-end products include only a few of the features available in more expensive products and may rely on obsolete or near-obsolete technology to keep costs down.

low-level format   Defining the physical location of magnetic tracks and sectors on a disk. This operation, sometimes called a physical format, is different from the high-level format that establishes the sections where an operating systems's system files are stored and that records the free and in-use areas of the disk.

low-level programming language   In programming, a language—such as machine language or assembly language—that describes exactly the procedures to be carried out by the computer's central processing unit (CPU). Low-level programs consist mostly of numbers and are difficult for human-beings to read, but software written with these languages can run much

faster than software written with high-level programming languages. See *high-level programming language*.

low-power microprocessor   A microprocessor that runs on 3.3 volts of electricity or less. Low-power microprocessors are often used in portable computers to conserve battery power. See *CMOS*.

low resolution   In monitors and printers, a visual definition that results in characters and graphics with jagged edges. The IBM Color Graphics Adapter (CGA) and monitor, for example, can display 640 pixels horizontally but only 200 lines vertically, resulting in poor visual definition. High-resolution monitors and printers produce well-defined characters or smoothly defined curves in graphic images. See *high resolution*.

low-rez   Slang for a technically unsavvy person. Usage: "Our boss is nice enough, but he is kind of low-rez." See *high resolution*.

LPT   In Windows and DOS, a device name that refers to a parallel port to which one can connect parallel printers. See *parallel port*.

LPX   A form factor used in some desktop PCs. Expansion boards are mounted on a riser that is perpendicular to the plane of the motherboard. A more current standard is the NLX form factor. See *form factor, NLX*.

LSB   See *least significant bit*.

LSI   See *large-scale integration*.

luminance   In digital video, the brightness of an image, as opposed to its chrominance (a combination of hue and saturation). See *chrominance*.

LUN   Acronym for Logical Unit Number. In SCSI, a subunit of a SCSI device. With the exception of multidisc CD-ROM players, most SCSI devices do not have such subunits. The LUN number is assigned by the manufacturer and is encoded in the unit's hardware. See *SCSI*.

lurk   To read a newsgroup or mailing list without ever posting a message.

Lycos   See *search engine.*

LYNX   A full-screen, text-only Web browser for Unix computers, created by Lou Montoulli of the University of Kansas. LYNX is a full-featured Web browser, but it cannot display in-line graphics.

LZ77   See *Lempel-Ziv compression algorithm.*

LZ78   A variation on the original Lempel-Ziv compression algorithm that employs a dictionary of repeated data sequences, called phrases, in the data. When phrases occur, they are copied to the dictionary and replaced by an index number corresponding to the phrase's location in the dictionary. This approach provides a greater degree of data compression than is possible with the original Lempel-Ziv compression algorithm, LZ77. See *Lempel-Ziv compression algorithm.*

LZW   See *Lempel-Ziv-Welch compression algorithm (LZW).*

M Abbreviation for megabyte (1,048,576 bytes). Also abbreviated MB.

Mac See *Macintosh*.

MAC See *Media Access Control*.

MacBinary A file transfer protocol (ftp) for Macintosh computers that enables one to store Macintosh files (including icons, graphics, and information about the file, such as creation date) on non-Macintosh computers without losing important information in the resource fork of Macintosh files. Most Macintosh communication programs send and receive files in MacBinary.

Mach A Unix-like microkernel developed by Carnegie-Mellon University and incorporated into several operating systems, including MacOS X. See *MacOS X, microkernel*.

machine code See *machine language*.

machine cycle One complete, four-step process that the computer's processing unit performs for each machine code instruction. An instruction is fetched from memory, decoded so that the processor can generate the correct control signals, and executed by generating the control signals. The results are stored in memory.

machine-dependent The incapability of a given computer program to run on any computer other than the one for which it was designed. See *device-dependent*.

machine language The program instructions that are actually read and acted on by the computer's processing circuitry. Machine language is written in binary numbers and is virtually impossible for humans to read; for this reason, programmers use assembly language or a high-level programming language to write programs, which are then compiled into machine language. In some processors (especially RISC processors), machine language instructions

directly generate control signals that tell the processor which tasks to perform, but a more common design uses microcode, an intermediary, built-in control language, to interpret the machine language instructions. Because machine language takes advantage of the unique characteristics of a given processor, a compiled program written for one processor (or processor family) will not execute on a different processor design. To develop programs for more than one system, it is necessary to use compilers that generate the code needed for each type of processor. Synonymous with machine code. See *assembly language, binary notation, compiler, microcode, RISC*.

machine learning The capacity of a computer program or system to improve its efficiency, speed, or some other aspect of performance based on conclusions drawn from previous experience.

MacHTTP See *Web server*.

Macintosh A line of personal computers created by Apple Computer that were first released in 1984. The Macintosh pioneered the graphical user interface (GUI), which was first developed but never successfully marketed by Xerox Corporation. The Macintosh also pioneered the concept of Plug and Play peripherals, built-in SCSI device support, and built-in local area networking. Early Macs were based on the Motorola 680x0 series of microprocessors; today's Power Macintoshes use Motorola's G4 PowerPC microprocessor (a RISC chip) and a BSD Unix-derived operating system, Mac OS X. Recently, Apple has positioned the Macintosh and related products to compete in the consumer market, stressing easy-to-use digital video and photography capabilities.

Macintosh file system The file storage architecture of the Macintosh computer, in which every file has two components, called forks. The data fork stores data, such as a spreadsheet or word processing document; this component corresponds to the sole contents of files on other computer systems. Unique to the Macintosh is the second component, the resource fork, which contains program icons and information about the program, such as the name of the application that created it. See *BinHex, HFS, HFS+, MacBinary.*

Mac OS The operating system of Macintosh computers, formerly known as the System. Introduced in 1984, Mac OS was strongly influenced by the graphical user interface (GUI) developed at Xerox's Palo Alto Research Center (PARC). Innovative features included QuickDraw (a graphics toolkit for rapid application development), long file names, PostScript laser printing, a built-in SCSI interface, built-in LocalTalk networking, and innovate product design. In the early 1990s, facing competition from Microsoft Windows, Apple released a major upgrade called System 7; unfortunately, System 7 was seriously flawed and did not remedy the operating system's chief deficiency, the lack of preemptive multitasking. With the 2001 introduction of Unix-based Mac OS X, Apple abandoned the remaining vestiges of Mac OS system code. See *cooperative multitasking, LocalTalk, Mac OS X, PostScript, preemptive multitasking, QuickDraw, Xerox PARC.*

Mac OS X The operating system used in Apple Computer's current Macintosh product line. Underlying Mac OS X is a Unix-like operating system, called Darwin, which is based on several open source components (including BSD-Lite, FreeBSD, and Mach, a Carnegie Mellon University–developed microkernel). Surrounding these open source components is a proprietary user interface composed of three components: Quartz (a PDF-based imaging engine with full Unicode support), QuickTime (Apple's multimedia software), and OpenGL (a cross-platform standard for 3D graphics). To increase the Mac's appeal to consumers, Mac OS X includes a spate of built-in features, including an e-mail client, instant messaging, digital photography support, personal information management (PIM) software, and a standards-compliant browser based on the KDE Desktop

Environment's Konquerer project. Macintosh developers can easily translate their software to run natively in the Mac OS X environment. See *BSD, FreeBSD, Mac OS, Mach, microkernel, OpenGL, Quartz, QuickTime.*

MacPaint See *paint program.*

macro A program consisting of recorded keystrokes and an application's command language that, when run within the application, executes the keystrokes and commands to accomplish a task. Macros can automate tedious and often-repeated tasks, such as saving and backing up a file to a floppy, or can create special menus to speed data entry.

Macromedia A San Francisco-based software company that focuses on graphics, animation, and Web development products for the Windows and Macintosh platforms. Many of the firm's products are best sellers in their respective categories. See *ColdFusion, Director, Dreamweaver, Fireworks, Flash.*

macro virus A computer virus that uses the automatic command-execution capabilities of productivity software to spread itself and often to cause harm to computer data. See *virus.*

MacTCP A Macintosh utility program, developed by Apple Computer and included with System 7.5, that provides the TCP support needed to connect Macintoshes to the Internet. A separate communications program is needed to connect via Serial Line Internet Protocol (SLIP) or Point-to-Point Protocol (PPP).

magic cookie Older Unix term for a small unit of data that is passed from one program to another so that the receiving program can perform an operation. See *cookie.*

magnetic disk In data storage, a random access storage medium that is the most popular method for storing and retrieving computer programs and data files. In personal computing, common magnetic disks include 3.5-inch floppy disks, and hard drives of various sizes. The disk is coated with a magnetically sensitive material. Magnetic read/write heads move across the surface of the spinning disk under the disk drive's automatic control to the location of desired information. The information stored on a magnetic disk can be repeatedly erased and rewritten, like any other magnetic storage medium.

magnetic medium   A secondary storage medium that uses magnetic techniques to store and retrieve data on disks or tapes coated with magnetically sensitive materials. Like iron filings on a sheet of waxed paper, these materials are reoriented when a magnetic field passes over them. During write operations, the read/write head emits a magnetic field that orients the magnetic materials on the disk or tape to represent encoded data. During read operations, the read/write head senses the encoded data on the medium.

magnetic tape   See *tape, tape backup unit.*

magneto-optical (MO) cartridge   The removable storage device used in a magneto-optical (MO) drive. MO cartridges are either 5.25 inches across (with capacities up to 5.2 GB) or 3.5 inches across (with capacities up to 2.3 GB). The data on a magneto-optical cartridge is highly stable, unlike the data on floppy and hard drives, which tends to self-erase if the data is not rewritten regularly.

magneto-optical (MO) drive   A data storage device that uses laser technology to heat an extremely small spot on a magneto-optical (MO) cartridge so that the magnetic medium used in the MO disk becomes capable of having its magnetic orientation changed by the read/write head. Although magneto-optical drives are slow (average seek time of 30 ms, compared to about 15 ms for hard drives) and expensive, they are highly suitable for backup storage and for storing large programs or data that is accessed infrequently.

magneto-resistive (MR) head   A technologically advanced kind of read/write head that uses a special metal alloy to improve areal density by packing tracks more tightly; it increases throughput by having separate reading and writing portions. MR heads are often used in hard disks that employ PRML read channel technology.

mail bombing   A form of harassment that involves sending numerous large e-mail messages to a person's electronic mailbox.

mailbox   In e-mail, the storage space that has been set aside to store an individual's e-mail messages.

mailbox name   In an Internet e-mail address, one of the two basic parts of a person's address. The part to the left of the at sign (@) specifies the name of the person's mailbox. To the right of the @ sign is the domain name of the computer that houses the mailbox. A person's mailbox name often is the same as his login name.

mail bridge   A gateway that enables users of one network or online service to exchange e-mail with users of other networks or services.

mail client   See *e-mail client.*

mail exploder   See *mailing list manager.*

mail filter   A filter program or utility within an e-mail program that screens incoming mail and then sorts the mail into folders or directories based on content found in one or more of the message's fields. For example, incoming mail from a mailing list can be directed to a separate folder for later reading so that these messages do not obscure the more important personal mail in the user's inbox. See *kill file.*

mail gateway   A computer that enables two mutually incompatible computer networks to exchange e-mail. America Online users, for example, can exchange e-mail with Internet users by means of a gateway. In some cases, gateways cannot handle attachments.

mailing list An Internet service in which users automatically receive a copy of every e-mail message that is sent to the mail server. Mailing lists are used to carry on group discussions on various topics; for example, a mailing list might discuss computer books or perennial flowers.

mailing list manager A program that enables e-mail users to subscribe to a mailing list, in which all subscribers receive a copy of every message submitted to the list. The list-management software enables the list administrator to maintain list addresses and ensure security. Leading mailing list programs are Majordomo and LISTSERV.

mail merge In word processing programs, a feature that draws information from a database (usually a mailing list) and incorporates it into a form document to create multiple copies of the document. Each copy of the document includes information from one record from the database. The most common application of mail merge is to personalize form letters. Instead of generating "Dear Applicant" letters, one can use a mail-merge utility to generate letters that start, "Dear Mr. Bergman."

mail reflector See *LISTSERV, mailing list manager.*

mail server A program that responds automatically to e-mail messages. Mail server programs exist that enter or remove subscriptions to mailing lists and send information in response to a request.

mailto In HTML, an attribute that enables Web authors to create a link to a person's e-mail address. When the user clicks the mailto link, the browser displays a window for composing an e-mail message to this address.

mail user agent See *e-mail client.*

mainframe Also known colloquially as "big iron." A large, expensive computer

designed to meet the computing needs of a large organization by simultaneously supporting thousands of users. Mainframe computers represent a centralized computing philosophy, as opposed to the distributed computing philosophy of PC-based LANs and the Internet. Originally, the term mainframe referred to the metal cabinet that housed the central processing unit (CPU) of early computers. The term came to be used generally to refer to the large central computers developed in the late 1950s and 1960s to meet the accounting and information-management needs of large organizations. The largest mainframes can handle thousands of dumb terminals and use terabytes of secondary storage. The advent of inexpensive PC-based networks has reduced the popularity of mainframes. See *minicomputer, personal computer (PC), supercomputer, workstation.*

main loop In an event-driven program, the topmost level in the program's control structure. Typically, the main loop waits for user input in the form of a mouse click or a keystroke.

main memory See *random access memory (RAM).*

main program In programming, the part of a program containing the master sequence of instructions, unlike the subroutines, procedures, and functions that the main program calls.

main storage See *random access memory (RAM).*

maintenance programming Altering programs after they have been in use for a while. Maintenance programming may be performed to add features, correct bugs that escaped detection during testing, or update key variables (such as the inflation rate) that change over time.

maintenance release A program revision that corrects a minor bug or makes a minor new feature available, such as a new printer driver. Maintenance releases are usually numbered in tenths (3.2) or hundredths

(2.01) to distinguish them from major program revisions. Synonymous with bug fix release.

Majordomo A popular freeware mailing list manager for Unix computer systems. See *LISTSERV, mailing list manager.*

male connector In cables, a cable terminator and connection device in which the pins protrude from the connector's surface. Male connectors plug into female connectors.

mall On the World Wide Web, a shopping service that provides Web publishing space for business storefronts (Web pages that describe retail or service offerings). Malls typically offer credit-card ordering by means of secure servers and shopping carts, which enable users to select purchases and pay for them all when they are finished shopping.

management information base In a computer network, a database of the various network devices, such as routers, that enables network administrators to detect malfunctions and optimize network performance. See *Simple Network Management Protocol (SNMP).*

management information system (MIS) **1.** A computer system, based on a mainframe, minicomputer, local area network (LAN), or wide area network (WAN), designed to provide business managers with up-to-date information on the organization's performance. **2.** The computer technology department; synonymous with IT. **3.** A degree program offered at universities that emphasizes both technical knowledge and business management skills.

manipulators/mutators In object-oriented programming, a publicly available behavioral method that enables other objects to change the state of the object. See *behavior, method, object-oriented programming.*

man page In Unix, a page of online documentation concerning a given command.

manual recalculation In a spreadsheet program, a recalculation method that suspends the recalculation of values until one issues a command that forces recalculation to take place.

map A representation of data stored in memory.

MAPI See *Messaging Application Program Interface.*

mapping **1.** The process of converting data encoded in one format to another format. In database management, for example, the database index provides a way of mapping the actual data records (which are stored on disk in a fixed order) to the display screen in useful ways. **2.** In a local area network (LAN), mapping refers to assigning drive letters to specific volumes and directories.

markup language In text processing, a system of codes for marking the format of a unit of text that indicates only that a particular unit of text is a certain part of the document, such as an abstract, a title, or an author's name and affiliation. The actual formatting of the document part is left up to another program, called a viewer, which displays the marked document and gives each document part a distinctive format (fonts, spacing, and so on). An international standard language for creating markup languages is the Standard Generalized Markup Language (SGML), which was little-known until an SGML-based markup language, the Hypertext Markup Language (HTML), came into widespread use on the Web. HTML is a markup language, and the Web browsers in use by millions today are viewers for HTML.

marquee **1.** In Web pages, a scrolling banner containing information or advertising. **2.** In Microsoft Excel, a moving dotted line that surrounds a cell or a range of cells that have been cut or copied. **3.** In programs, an initial screen or banner that gives the program and publisher's names.

mask **1.** A pattern of symbols or characters that, when imposed on a data field, limits the kinds of characters that one can type into the field. In a database management program, for example, the mask AZ lets one type any alphabetical character, uppercase or lowercase, but not numbers or other symbols. Synonymous with input mask. **2.** In computer graphics, a pattern that enables a graphic designer to eliminate detail or isolate an image from its background.

massively parallel processing (MPP) A type of parallel processing architecture that employs more than 1,000 microprocessors to tackle an unusually complex scientific or engineering problem. MPP-based computers have supplanted single-processor supercomputers for advanced scientific processing, but they are not useful without supporting architectures (hardware and software) that efficiently allocate programming tasks among the available CPUs. Most MPP-based systems use message parsing architectures, in which each CPU has its own memory and synchronizes with other CPUs by means of communication channels. This approach contrasts with the shared-memory multiprocessors approach used in most PCs equipped with two or more processors; in this architecture, the CPUs communicate by means of a single, shared memory. Also required is an operating system and programs that support parallel processing. See *cluster*, *parallel programming*, *shared memory multiprocessing*.

mass storage See *secondary storage*.

master The first disk in a string of two attached to an IDE host adapter. Although the master disk does not control the slave disk, it interprets commands from the host adapter for it.

master document In word processing, a document that contains commands that tell the program to print additional documents at the commands' locations. The program prints all the documents as though they were one, with consistent running headers/footers and page numbering. See *chain printing*.

master slide In presentation graphics, a template slide that contains a presentation's background and any additional information that will appear on every page of the finished presentation.

masthead In desktop publishing (DTP), the section of a newsletter or magazine that gives the details of its staff, ownership, advertising, subscription prices, and other legal or business information.

math coprocessor A secondary microprocessor that was required for early microprocessors, which did not include special-purpose circuits for processing floating-point instructions. See *numeric coprocessor*.

matrix metering In digital cameras, a form of exposure automation in which the camera determines the exposure by examining light intensity in selected areas of the range finder. Two common approaches to matrix metering are bottom weighting and center weighting. See *bottom weighting*, *center weighting*, *digital camera*.

matte finish A quality of paper that does not reflect light as harshly as a glossy finish. Most users prefer matte finish paper to glossy finish paper because it matches the light-absorbent qualities of laser printer text.

maximize To zoom or enlarge a window so that it fills the screen. See *minimize*.

maximize button In graphical user interfaces, a button that enables the user to maximize a window so that it fills the screen.

maximum RAM The amount of random access memory (RAM) that could possibly be installed on a particular motherboard. Maximum RAM specifications usually are expressed as "expandable-to" statements in advertisements, as in, "The motherboard has 128MB RAM, expandable to 2GB."

maximum transmission unit (MTU) The largest packet that may be transmitted over a packet-switching network.

Mb   Abbreviation for megabit. One million (10^6) bits. Some sources define megabit as 1,048,576 bits (2^{20}), but this is questionable; megabits are generally cited in reference to serial data streams, in which discrete bits are transmitted one at a time and are thus amenable to description using decimal rather than binary numbers. See *bit, Mbps.*

MB   Abbreviation for megabyte (1,048,576 bytes); also abbreviated M.

Mbone   An experimental method of distributing data packets on the Internet in which a server broadcasts data to two or more servers simultaneously. This technique, also called IP multicasting, moves data packets to their multiple destinations in streams rather than packets and is therefore more suitable for real-time audio and video than the standard TCP/IP network. Special routers are required.

Mbps   One million bits per second. See *bits per second (bps), Mb.*

MCA   See *Micro Channel Architecture.*

MCGA   Acronym for MultiColor Graphics Array. A video standard of IBM's Personal System/2. MCGA adds 64 grayscale shades to the Color Graphics Adapter (CGA) standard and provides the Enhanced Graphics Adapter (EGA) standard resolution of 640 pixels by 350 lines, with 16 possible colors.

MCI   See *Media Control Interface.*

MDI   See *multiple document interface.*

mean time between failures   See *MTBF.*

mechanical mouse   Unlike an optical mouse, a mechanical mouse relies on a rubberized ball on the bottom, which turns small metal rollers inside the mouse, to communicate its movements to the central processing unit (CPU). Although mechanical mice may be used almost anywhere, their internal mechanisms tend to get dirty and require cleaning.

mechanicals   In desktop publishing (DTP), the final pages or boards with pasted-up galleys of type and line art, sometimes with acetate or tissue overlays for color separations and notes, which one sends to the offset printer. Mechanicals have been largely replaced by an entirely computerized process of printing in which desktop publishing documents are sent in electronic form to the printer. See *camera-ready copy.*

media   The plural of medium. See *storage medium.*

Media Access Control (MAC)   In a computer network, the layer that controls under what circumstances a workstation can get access to the physical media to originate a message to another workstation. A protocol is needed to prevent data collisions, which occur when two workstations begin broadcasting simultaneously. Ethernet networks use the CSMA/CD access protocol.

Media Control Interface (MCI)   In Microsoft Windows, the multimedia extensions that greatly simplify the task of programming multimedia device functions such as stop, play, and record.

medium   See *storage medium.*

meg   Colloquial term for megabyte.

mega-   Prefix indicating 1 million.

megabyte (MB)   A measurement of storage capacity equal to approximately 1 million bytes (1,048,576 bytes). Also abbreviated M.

megaflop   A measurement of processor speed that equals one million (10^6) floating-point operations per second. See *FLOP, gigaflop, teraflop.*

megahertz (MHz)   A unit of measurement, equal to 1 million electrical vibrations or cycles per second, commonly used to compare the clock speeds of computers.

megapixel   In digital cameras, a commonly used marketing expression that refers (roughly) to the number of millions of discrete image sensors available in a camera's imaging technology (in most cameras, this is a charged-coupled device). The higher a camera's megapixel rating, the richer the detail of its pictures.

membrane keyboard   A flat and inexpensive keyboard covered with a dust- and dirt-proof plastic sheet on which only the two-dimensional outline of computer keys appears. The user presses the plastic sheet and engages a switch hidden beneath. Accurately typing on a membrane keyboard is more difficult, but such keyboards are needed in restaurant kitchens or other locations where users may not have clean hands.

meme   Pronounced "meem." A contagious unit of information (such as an idea, slogan, or fashion) that replicates through communication networks; a successful meme has bait (it promises something) and a hook (it urges people to pass it on to others), An example is the myth that U.S. military forces captured intelligent alien life forms near Roswell, NM in 1947: the meme promises knowledge that the government has denied to the people and inspires believers to pass the word on to others. The Internet provides fertile soil for meme propagation; in 2003, nearly 1 million Internet sites contained the words "Roswell" and "UFO." See *urban legend*.

memory   The computer's primary storage, such as random access memory (RAM), as distinguished from its secondary storage, such as hard drives.

memory address   A code number that specifies a specific location in a computer's random access memory (RAM).

memory cache   See *cache memory*.

memory card   See *flash memory card*.

memory check   Part of the Power-On Self-Test (POST) that verifies that the computer's random access memory (RAM) is properly plugged in and is functioning well. As the computer goes through its boot routine, the user can often see the progress of the memory check on the display. If there is a problem in memory, be sure to record the memory address of the error and give it to a computer repair technician.

memory controller gate array   Alternative term for Multi-color Graphics Array (MCGA), a video standard once used in the low-end models of IBM's Personal System/2 computers.

memory leak   A programming flaw that causes a program to use new portions of memory instead of reusing portions containing data it no longer needs. A program with a memory leak (a common flaw of betas) will consume additional memory as it is used; in the worst case, the program will consume all the available memory and eventually cause the computer to stop operating.

memory management   Collective term for a variety of strategies for ensuring that programs have sufficient available memory to function correctly. See *memory-management program, virtual memory*.

memory-management program   A utility program that increases the apparent size of random access memory (RAM) by making expanded memory, extended memory, or virtual memory available for the execution of programs. Modern operating systems, such as Windows XP, have automatic memory management.

memory management unit (MMU)   In a computer equipped with virtual memory, a chip (integrated circuit) that enables the computer to use a portion of the hard disk as if it were an extension of the computer's random access memory (RAM). See *virtual memory*.

memory map   An arbitrary allocation of portions of a computer's random access memory (RAM), defining which areas the computer can use for specific purposes.

memory protection   See *protected memory*.

memory-resident program See *termi-nate-and-stay-resident (TSR) program*.

Memory Stick A Sony-developed flash memory technology that provides non-volatile memory for a range of portable devices, including digital cameras, MP3 players, personal digital assistants (PDA). A new version of the technology, called Memory Stick Duo, is downwardly compatible with previous Memory Stick readers by means of an adapter. See *flash memory, PDA*.

memory word See *word*.

menu An onscreen display that lists available command choices. See *menu bar, pull-down menu*.

menu bar In a graphical user interface (GUI), a bar stretching across the top of the screen (or the top of a window) that contains the names of available pull-down menus.

menu-driven program A program that provides menus for choosing program options so that the user does not need to memorize commands. See *command-driven program*.

merge printing See *mail merge*.

message queue In Microsoft Windows, a special space in the memory that is set aside to list the messages that applications send each other. Beginning with Microsoft Windows 95/98, each 32-bit application has its own message queue. If one application aborts, the others are not affected.

message transfer agent (MTA) In e-mail, a program that sends e-mail messages to another message transfer agent. On the Internet, the most widely used MTA is sendmail.

Messaging Application Program Interface (MAPI) The Microsoft implementation of an application program interface that provides access to messaging services for developers. MAPI Version 3.2 provides resources to programmers for cross-platform messaging that is independent of the operating system and underlying hardware, and that makes applications mail-aware. MAPI can send messages to and from Vendor Independent Messaging (VIM) programs.

metadata Data that describes other data. For instance, metadata could be used to identify this paragraph of text as a "dictionary definition" and identify the word "metadata" at the beginning of this definition as a "dictionary term." Assigning metadata to data has many advantages, including the ability to return more relevant search results; for instance, a user who wanted to find a definition for the word metadata could indicate the desired type of data, such as "dictionary term" along with the desired keyword "metadata" and only receive search results that are a "dictionary definition." An example of metadata scheme is the World Wide Web Consortium-developed Resource Description Framework (RDF), a symbolic language that enables programmers to develop metadata schemes for a variety of data types. See *RDF*.

meta key In the X Window System, a virtual key that application developers can assign without knowing exactly how the key will be mapped to the workstation's keyboard. On PC keyboards, the meta key is generally mapped to the Alt key.

metal-oxide semiconductor See *MOS*.

metal-oxide varistor (MOV) A device used to protect the computer from abnormally high line voltages. An MOV conducts electrical current only when it exceeds a certain voltage. An MOV in a surge protector conducts electrical current in excess of 350 volts away from the computer. See *surge*.

Metcalfe's Law A prediction formulated by Bob Metcalfe, creator of Ethernet, that the value of a network increases in proportion to the square of the number of people connected to the network.

method In object-oriented programming, the publicly accessible interface to the hidden functional code and data contained within an object. Most objects have three types of methods: constructors, destructors, and behaviors, which include accessors/interrogators as well as manipulators/mutators. See *accessor/interrogator, behavior, manipulators/mutators, object, object-oriented programming, property.*

MFM Acronym for Modified Frequency Modulation. A method of recording digital information on a magnetic medium, such as tapes and disks, by eliminating redundant or blank areas. Because the MFM data-encoding scheme doubles the storage attained under the earlier frequency-modulation (FM) recording technique, MFM recording usually is referred to as double density. MFM often is wrongly used to describe hard disk controllers conforming to the ST-506/ST-412 standard. MFM actually refers to the method used to pack data on the disk and is not synonymous with disk drive interface standards, such as ST-506, Small Computer System Interface (SCSI), or Enhanced Small Device Interface (ESDI). See *Run-Length Limited (RLL).*

MHz Abbreviation for megahertz.

MIB/MI See *Plug and Print.*

micro- Prefix for small. Also a metric prefix indicating one-millionth and an abbreviation (increasingly rare) for microcomputer.

microATX A motherboard form factor developed by Intel for entry-level systems.

Micro Channel Architecture (MCA) The design specifications of IBM's proprietary Micro Channel Bus. An MCA-compatible peripheral is designed to plug directly into a Micro Channel Bus but will not work with other bus architectures.

microcode Program instructions embedded in the internal circuitry of a microprocessor. Microcode makes software programmers' jobs easier because they can remain a step removed from the nitty-gritty details of what physically happens inside a microprocessor, which makes the task of chip designers harder. Because chips equipped with microcodes need extra internal components to translate external instructions into physical actions, they need to be bigger, slower, and more complex than they might otherwise be. See *complex instruction set computer (CISC), RISC.*

Microcom Networking Protocol (MNP) Any of 10 error-correction and data-compression protocols used by modems. MNP 1 is obsolete; MNP 2, MNP 3, and MNP 4 are error-correction protocols used in the V.42 international standard. MNP 5 is an on-the-fly data-compression protocol used by most modern modems, and MNP 6-10 are proprietary communications standards.

microcomputer A computer that uses a microprocessor as its CPU. In the 1980s, microcomputers could be effectively contrasted with minicomputers and mainframes, and typified as inexpensive, single-user systems. However, this is no longer true because minicomputers and even mainframes employ microprocessors. Today, the term microcomputer is rarely used, but when it is, it refers to a desktop computer. See *personal computer (PC), professional workstation.*

microfine toner Special toner for laser and liquid crystal shutter (LCS) printers that consists of finer particles than standard toner, enabling it to render text and graphics with finer detail.

microkernel In Unix and Unix-like operating systems, a kernel that is kept as small as possible by moving functions such as file systems and device drivers to external processes. This design seeks to maximize kernel performance and reliability by reducing the kernel's complexity. See *Mach, Mac OS X, monolithic kernel.*

micron One-millionth of a meter (about 0.0000394 inch).

microphone A device that converts sounds into electrical signals that can be processed by a computer. Microphones can be used to record new system sounds or to add voice annotations to documents. Most PCs require a sound card to be able to accept microphone input. See *sound board.*

microprocessor An integrated circuit that contains the arithmetic-logic unit (ALU), control unit, and usually the floating-point unit (FPU) of a computer's central processing unit (CPU), as well as internal memory registers and other vital circuitry. Fabricated on a small flake of silicon and mass-produced at low cost, microprocessors can contain the equivalent of several million transistors and are unquestionably one of the twentieth century's greatest technological advances. *Microprocessor* is often used interchangeably with *CPU* and *processor.*

microprocessor architecture The overall design concept of a microprocessor. The two top-level architectural options are the complex instruction set computer (CISC) and the reduced instruction set computer (RISC).

Microsoft The world's largest and most successful publisher of operating systems and application programs for personal computers, headquartered in Redmond, Washington. Key products include the company's consumer operating systems (Microsoft Windows XP Home), its corporate workstation and server operating systems (Microsoft Windows 2000 Server and Microsoft Windows Server 2003), its market-leading office suite called Microsoft Office (including Microsoft Word, Excel, PowerPoint, Access, and Microsoft Outlook), and the market-leading Web browser (Microsoft Internet Explorer).

Although Microsoft possesses a monopoly in desktop operating systems and a near-monopoly in the Web browser market, it has not been able to leverage its strong market position into dominance of the Internet, which is still controlled by publicly available, open protocols. The company's .NET initiative is viewed by the firm's critics as an attempt to transform the Internet into a system by which Microsoft clients

communicate with Microsoft servers, thus eliminating Microsoft's competitors from the emerging, highly profitable market for services such as digital music distribution. See *Microsoft Office, Microsoft Windows, .NET, Web Services.*

Microsoft Access An innovative relational database management system (RDMS) that is included with Microsoft Office. The program enables users to construct databases, forms, and queries using visual tools; the capabilities of these tools can be extended with Visual Basic for Applications (VBA). See *Microsoft Office, relational database management system (RDMS), Visual Basic.*

Microsoft BackOffice A package of file server and Web server programs and utilities from Microsoft Corporation designed for Windows NT-based networks. The package includes Microsoft Windows NT Server, Microsoft Internet Information Server, Microsoft FrontPage, and a series of utilities, including Microsoft Exchange Server (enterprise-wide e-mail), Microsoft SQL Server (database searching), Microsoft Proxy Server (enables external Internet access from behind a firewall), Microsoft Systems Management Server (provides centralized management tools for network administrators), and Microsoft SNA Server (integrates existing legacy systems with intranets).

Microsoft BASIC A version of the BASIC programming language, designed for beginners in computing, that was originally developed by Microsoft co-founder Bill Gates for the Altair, the first commercially available microcomputer. Microsoft Visual Basic has supplanted Microsoft BASIC. See *BASIC, Visual Basic.*

Microsoft Excel An innovative spreadsheet program, included with Microsoft Office, that has become the industry standard worldwide. Combining an excellent, graphics-capable spreadsheet with sophisticated analytical capabilities, Excel spans the gamut of spreadsheet applications from initial data analysis to public presentation. See *spreadsheet program*.

Microsoft FrontPage A WYSIWYG HTML editor that is included with Microsoft Office. FrontPage combines an easy-to-use development environment with powerful site-management capabilities. Unlike other Office applications, FrontPage has not dominated the market; developers criticize the many FrontPage features that discourage Web site visitors who do not use Microsoft Internet Explorer. See *Dreamweaver*, *WYSIWYG HTML editor*.

Microsoft Intellimouse An innovative mouse that includes a scrolling wheel positioned between the two mouse buttons. In compatible applications, the wheel can be used to zoom and scroll windows. Requires a PS/2 or USB port. Also available as an optical mouse.

Microsoft Internet Explorer Microsoft's market-leading Web browser. Installed by default with Microsoft's operating systems, Internet Explorer cannot be removed and is initially configured as the system's default browser. Originally developed as an afterthought, the initial versions of Internet Explorer attracted little attention until the release of version 4, which introduced several important World Wide Web Consortium (W3C) innovations (including Cascading Style Sheets [CSS] and XML) to the Web. Still, Internet Explorer 4 reflected Microsoft's "embrace and extend" philosophy with respect to Web standards; the program's implementation of the W3C's Document Object Model (DOM) departed from DOM standards, with the result that developers were subsequently forced to expend a great deal of development time creating alternative, browser-dependent versions of their pages. See *CSS, DOM, Web browser, World Wide Web Consortium (W3C)*.

Microsoft Internet Information Server (IIS) A Web server created by Microsoft Corporation for Microsoft Windows 2000 Server and Windows Server 2003 operating systems. Developed as an alternative to market-leading Unix Web servers such as Apache, IIS enables organizations to build Web services within the Microsoft Windows operating system environment. Included is a built-in search engine for searching documents, management tools, Microsoft FrontPage, and ODBC support for searching external databases. Although IIS is widely implemented, the server has been plagued by security problems. The version of IIS included with Microsoft Windows Server 2003 was comprehensively rewritten in an effort to remedy the server's security problems. See *Apache*.

Microsoft Money A personal finance program that closely resembles the market-leading Quicken. It offers checkbook and credit card management, register reconciliation, interoperability with electronic banking, and a host of financial planning utilities. See *personal finance program, Quicken*.

Microsoft Mouse A mouse and associated software for IBM and IBM PC–compatible personal computers, including IBM's PS/1 and PS/2 computers. Available in PS/2 port version, the Microsoft Mouse uses the mechanical mouse technology that most mouse users favor. See *Microsoft Intellimouse*.

Microsoft Natural Keyboard An ergonomic keyboard developed by Microsoft Corporation that divides the keys into two split panels, which are angled outward so that users' wrists are not bent at an angle when the keyboard is used. This arrangement is believed to reduce the incidence of painful repetitive stress injuries (RSI) such as carpal tunnel syndrome.

Microsoft NetMeeting An innovative Web-based teleconferencing environment developed by Microsoft and widely distributed with Microsoft's operating systems. Closely integrated with Windows, NetMeeting enables conference participants to communicate with voice, text, a graphical whiteboard, and remote display of application windows. See *videoconferencing*.

Microsoft Network See *MSN.*

Microsoft Office The market-leading office suite, which includes Microsoft Word, Microsoft Excel, Microsoft Access, Microsoft PowerPoint, and Microsoft Outlook. See *Microsoft Access, Microsoft Excel, Microsoft Outlook, Microsoft Word, office suite.*

Microsoft Outlook A comprehensive communications platform, included with Microsoft Office, that enables developers to transform Internet-based e-mail into a set of highly interactive communications services (such as work flow management) in an organization. Closely linked to other Windows applications by means of the messaging services built into Microsoft Windows, Outlook creates many opportunities for imaginative application development; however, it exposes organizations to a wide range of security risks that are frequently exploited by virus authors. See *e-mail client.*

Microsoft Outlook Express An easy-to-use e-mail client that is installed by default with all versions of Microsoft Windows; like Internet Explorer, it cannot be easily uninstalled and is automatically configured as the system's default e-mail program. Including a variety of features that users like, including an address book and HTML-compatible e-mail, Outlook Express has nevertheless won an unenviable reputation for its numerous security holes and susceptibility to computer viruses. See *e-mail client.*

Microsoft PowerPoint The market-leading presentation graphics application, included with Microsoft Office. Designed to enable speakers to create eye-catching presentations for a variety of media, including 35mm slides, computer-based presentations, and transparencies, PowerPoint includes animation features that can be easily implemented by users who do not possess programming capabilities. The program's dominance of the market is so extensive that nearly all presentations using visuals are prepared with the program; presenters run the risk of appearing unoriginal unless they take special steps to use custom-designed templates, backgrounds, and colors. See *presentation graphics program.*

Microsoft Project An innovative, easy-to-use project management program that enables users to plan and coordinate complex projects. The software automatically implements critical-path method (CPM) concepts by automatically identifying the tasks that must be completed before others can begin. See *project management program.*

Microsoft Publisher A desktop publishing program, included with Microsoft Office, that is designed for use by non-experts in the desktop publishing field. See *desktop publishing (DTP).*

Microsoft Visual Basic A version of the BASIC programming language that enables programmers to develop functioning Windows applications quickly. Tightly integrated with Microsoft Windows, Visual Basic obviates the need to create the user interface; programmers use built-in tools to create the user interface visually and then attach code to the various onscreen objects. The Professional Edition includes a compiler that creates executable programs that do not require an interpreter. A host of Microsoft and third-party utilities enable programmers to quickly add components, such as database searching or Internet connectivity.

Microsoft Windows Generic name for the various operating systems in the Microsoft Windows family, including Microsoft Windows CE, Microsoft Windows 98, Microsoft Windows Millennium Edition (ME), Microsoft Windows 2000, and Microsoft Windows XP, which are designed to run on Intel-powered hardware. Introduced in 1985, Windows attracted little attention until the 1990 release of Windows 3.0, which was essentially an MS-DOS program that enabled the recently developed 32-bit protected mode of Intel microprocessors. Windows offered many of the graphical user interface (GUI) features that won acclaim for Apple's Macintosh computers; at the same time, it could run on inexpensive Intel hardware. As a significant pool of 32-bit Windows applications developed, Windows emerged as the overwhelmingly dominant operating system for desktop systems worldwide; its market share exceeds 90 percent. Microsoft has been less successful in the server market, where its products face stiff competition from commercial UNIX operating systems, Linux, and FreeBSD. See *FreeBSD, Linux, Microsoft Windows 95, Microsoft Windows 98, Microsoft Windows 2000, Microsoft Windows Millennium Edition (ME), Microsoft Windows XP, Microsoft Windows Server 2003, UNIX.*

Microsoft Windows 3.1   A popular MS-DOS application that switches 80286 and later Intel microprocessors into their protected mode, which breaks the 640KB RAM barrier and enables users to run 32-bit applications. Windows 3.1 was the first version of Windows to persuade skeptical observers that the DOS era was over and that Windows pointed the way to the future. Still, Windows 3.1 lacks many of the features needed to run 32-bit applications in a stable, secure environment; it employs cooperative instead of preemptive multitasking, does not permit multithreading, and earned an unenviable reputation for lack of stability.

Microsoft Windows 3.*x*   A family of programs developed by Microsoft Corporation, including Windows 3.1, Windows 3.11, and Windows for Workgroups 3.1. Although they are often treated like operating systems, these programs are actually MS-DOS applications themselves and are more properly considered operating environments.

Microsoft Windows 95   A hybrid 16/32-bit operating system for Intel microprocessors that takes full advantage of the processing capabilities of Intel 80486 and Pentium microprocessors, while retaining downward compatibility with Windows 3.1 programs. Compared to Microsoft Windows 3.1, Windows 95 offers a redesigned graphical user interface (GUI) that enhances ease of learning as well as day-to-day usability. Additional innovations include long file names, 32-bit disk and file systems, preemptive multitasking, multithreading, improved handling of system resource problems and general protection faults (GPF), and built-in support for the Microsoft Network and the Internet. In addition, it combines 16-bit and 32-bit source code to ensure reliable operation of existing 16-bit applications. Windows 95 is not a true 32-bit operating system (like OS/2 Warp or Microsoft's own Microsoft Windows NT); nevertheless, users appreciate not having to upgrade their applications. For corporate environments, Windows 95 includes built-in network support, offering a consistent interface for accessing network resources on a variety of physical media. To aid in the often arduous task of installing new hardware components, Windows 95 incorporates Plug and Play capabilities, which allow nearly automatic installation and configuration of compatible accessories (such as sound cards and CD-ROM drives).

Microsoft Windows 98   A hybrid 16/32-bit operating system developed for IBM-compatible PCs that was designed as the successor to Windows 95. Windows 98 offers easier Internet connectivity and the availability to work with peripherals that require Universal Serial Bus (USB) or Accelerated Graphics Port (AGP) slots. Like Windows 95, Windows 98 is downwardly compatible with applications developed for Windows 3.*x*. Windows 98's successor is Microsoft Windows 98, Second Edition. See *Microsoft Windows 98, Second Edition; Microsoft Windows 2000; Microsoft Windows Millennium Edition (ME).*

Microsoft Windows 98, Second Edition   A revised version of Microsoft Windows 98 that incorporates a substantial number of bug and security fixes as well as enhanced multimedia support. This operating system was replaced by Microsoft Windows Millennium Edition (ME). See *Microsoft Windows Millennium Edition (ME).*

Microsoft Windows 2000 The next-generation family of Microsoft operating systems, based on Microsoft Windows NT. The workstation version, Microsoft Windows 2000 Professional, offers key features missing from Windows NT Workstation, such as support for Plug and Play devices. Microsoft designates Windows 2000 Professional as the OS of choice for corporate workstation use; consumers and home users are advised to use Windows ME. The server versions (Server, Advanced Server, and Datacenter Server) are designed, respectively, for lower- to higher-demand server installations, including those using up to 16 processors simultaneously. See *Microsoft Windows Millennium Edition (ME)*.

Microsoft Windows CE A 32-bit operating system for hand-held portable computers. Closely resembling the familiar Windows 95/98 but with reduced functionality, Windows CE comes with similarly miniaturized ("pocket") versions of Microsoft Word, Microsoft Excel, and Microsoft Internet Explorer, and is an important factor in the market success of palmtop computers.

Microsoft Windows Millennium Edition (ME) A hybrid 16/32-bit operating system for IBM-compatible PCs that succeeds Windows 98 in Microsoft's OS offerings. Designated as the OS of choice for consumers and home users, Windows ME offers a spate of features designed to unlock the multimedia potential of the Internet, including ActiveMovie support for streaming video and the latest version of Windows Media Player. This operating system has been replaced by Microsoft Windows XP Home Edition, which—for the first time—dispenses with the hybrid (and unstable) 16/32 code base in favor a technology derived from Windows NT and Windows 2000.

Microsoft Windows NT A 32-bit operating system for Intel microprocessors. The official name of the product is Microsoft Windows NT Workstation, to distinguish the client-level program from Windows NT Server, but it is usually referred to as Windows NT. On high-end Pentium systems, Windows NT provides the performance of Unix workstations that cost far more money—without sacrificing compatibility with personal productivity applications. Windows NT is designed for engineers, scientists, statisticians, and other professional or technical workers who carry out processor-intensive tasks. In addition to high-performance Intel processors, Windows NT runs on workstations based on the Alpha and MIPS processors. From Version 4.0, Windows NT boasts a user interface that is identical to the one used on Microsoft Windows 95/98. Microsoft Windows NT Workstation has been replaced by Microsoft Windows 2000 Professional. See *Microsoft Windows 2000*.

Microsoft Windows NT Server A Windows NT-based server for computer networks. Using powerful Intel-based PCs that are capable of matching the performance of many mainframe computer systems, enterprises can create client/server systems using Windows NT at a fraction of the cost of previous solutions. Internet and intranet capabilities are added with Microsoft Internet Information Server, which requires Windows NT Server. Windows NT Server has been replaced by three products in Microsoft's Windows 2000 series: Server (for computers with up to two processors), Advanced Server (up to four processors), and Datacenter Server (up to 16 processors). See *Microsoft Windows 2000*.

Microsoft Windows NT Workstation See *Microsoft Windows NT.*

Microsoft Windows Server 2003 An updated version of Microsoft's Windows Server product line that supports the company's .NET initiative, including the ASP.NET scripting language and XML-based Web services. The product includes four offerings: Web Edition (a low cost, Web-only server that is designed to compete with the Apache Web server), Standard Edition (for departmental and small business use), Enterprise Edition (for medium- and large-sized businesses), and Datacenter Edition (for high-volume applications). See *Apache, ASP.NET, .NET, Web services, XML.*

Microsoft Windows XP A family of related operated systems, all of which share a unified, NT-derived 32-bit code base, that is designed to replace all of Microsoft's operating systems (Windows 95/98/ME, Windows NT, and Windows 2000). Three versions of the product are available: Microsoft Windows XP Home Edition (aimed at home users and consumers), Microsoft Windows XP Professional (aimed at corporate desktop users), and Microsoft Windows XP Server (aimed at the server market).

Microsoft Word A word processing program, included with Microsoft Office, that possesses a commanding dominance in its market. Word was first marketed as an MS-DOS application that, for the first time, enabled users to use the mouse for text selection and editing purposes; however, the MS-DOS versions of the program were unable to unseat the market leader, WordPerfect. As the popularity of Microsoft Windows grew, Word was reborn as a Windows application that equaled or surpassed WordPerfect's feature set while, at the same time, offering a smoother implementation of the new onscreen formatting and font display possibilities of the graphical user interface (GUI). Subsequently, Word took over the market except for a few niche areas, such as legal word processing. Among Word's popular features are user-configurable style sheets and templates, macros, and a host of automated features, including table-of-contents and index generation, revision marks for collaboratively edited documents, on-the-fly spelling and grammar correction, and many more. See *WordPerfect, word processing program.*

micro-to-mainframe The linkage of personal computers to mainframe or mini-computer networks.

middleware In a cross-platform network, programs that serve as intermediaries between clients requesting information and server programs that provide requested data, even though the clients and servers may be running on different computing platforms and were not originally designed to work with each other. A simple example of middleware is a Web server script written according to Common Gateway Interface (CGI) guidelines; the script enables external Web browsers to communicate with programs that can provide such functions as database searching. See *CORBA.*

MIDI Acronym for Musical Instrument Digital Interface. A standard communications protocol for the exchange of information between computers and music synthesizers. MIDI provides tools that many composers and musicians say are becoming almost indispensable. With a synthesizer and a computer equipped with the necessary software and a MIDI port, a musician can transcribe a composition into musical notation by playing the composition at the keyboard. After the music is placed into computer-represented form, virtually every aspect of the digitized sound—pitch, attack, delay time, tempo, and more—can be edited and altered. On the Internet, a major advantage of MIDI is that the exchanged files are text-based and very small. When playing MIDI sounds, best results are obtained with a wave-table synthesis sound card.

MIDI cueing In multimedia, a set of MIDI messages that determines the occurrence of events other than musical notes (such as recording, playing back, or turning on lighting devices).

MIDI file A file containing musical data encoded according to MIDI specifications. In Microsoft Windows 95/98, MIDI files use the extension .MID.

MIDI interface See *MIDI port.*

MIDI port A receptacle that enables one to connect a personal computer directly to a musical synthesizer. See *MIDI.*

MIDI timecode In digital video, a method for timed device control that makes use of the MIDI protocol. See *SMPTE timecode*.

migration A change from an older hardware platform, operating system, or software version to a newer one.

milli- Metric prefix indicating one-thousandth.

million instructions per second See *MIPS*.

millisecond (ms) A unit of measurement equal to one-thousandth of a second; commonly used to specify the access time of hard disk drives.

MIME Acronym for Multipurpose Internet Mail Extensions. An Internet standard that specifies how tools such as e-mail programs and Web browsers can transfer multimedia files (including sounds, graphics, and video) via the Internet. Prior to the development of MIME, all data transferred via the Internet had to be coded in ASCII text. See *uudecode, uuencode*.

MIME encoding In an e-mail message, a method of encoding binary files in conformance with the Multipurpose Internet Mail Extension (MIME) standard. To receive the mail message, the user must be running an e-mail client that is capable of decoding this format. Another commonly used encoding format is uuencode. See *base64*.

MIME type In Multipurpose Internet Mail Extensions (MIME), a code that specifies the content type of a multimedia file. The Internet Assigned Numbers Authority (IANA) controls the naming of MIME types. A Web browser detects MIME types by examining the file's extension; for example, a file with the extension *.mpg or *.mpeg contains an MPEG video.

mini-AT case A desktop (horizontal) case that mounts the motherboard in the same way as the AT-size case but that takes up less space and has fewer expansion slots. See *ATX case, tower case*.

minicomputer A multiuser computer designed to meet the needs of a small company or a department. A minicomputer is more powerful than a personal computer but not as powerful as a mainframe. Typically, about 4 to 100 people use a minicomputer simultaneously.

minimize In a graphical user interface (GUI), to shrink a window so that it collapses to an icon on the desktop. One minimizes a window by clicking the minimize button (the left button in the upper-right corner) or by choosing Minimize from the Control menu. When minimizing an application in Microsoft Windows 95/98, the application appears as an icon on the taskbar.

mini-tower case A vertical case designed to fit into a smaller space than a full-sized tower case. Although they have less space for disk drives and other devices than tower cases, mini-tower cases can have as many expansion slots as desktop cases, even with their smaller footprint. See *AT case, ATX case, mini-AT case*.

MIPS Acronym for million instructions per second. A benchmark method for measuring the rate at which a computer executes microprocessor instructions. A computer capable of 0.5 MIPS, for example, can execute 500,000 instructions per second.

mirror To copy automatically to another storage location.

mirror site An FTP or Web site that is an exact copy of another site; mirror sites are made available for the convenience of users in a specific country or region of a country, or to relieve the traffic load on a very popular site.

MIS See *management information system*.

misc hierarchy In Usenet, one of the standard newsgroup hierarchies, containing newsgroups that do not fit in the other categories (comp, sci, news, rec, soc, and talk). Examples of misc newsgroups include misc.consumers, misc.kids.computers, and misc.writing.

mishap   In safety-critical systems, an event attributable to system errors or failures that involve injury or death to humans, damage or loss to property, environmental degradation, or system losses (such as a fall in stock market prices). A failure occurs when a system component no longer fulfills its intended function; in contrast, an error occurs when an inherent flaw in the system becomes manifest when the system encounters unanticipated conditions. For example, a 1994 Chinook helicopter crash caused 29 deaths. The cause was an error in the engine control system's software rather than an equipment failure. See *error, safety-critical system.*

mission-critical   Vital to an organization's basic function.

mission-critical system   A system that must perform dependably in order for an organization to accomplish its mission. For example, dependable servers are mission-critical systems for online brokerages; loss of use of these systems may cause catastrophic financial losses. System dependability is measured by availability, reliability, safety, and security. See *availability, reliability, safety, security.*

mixed cell reference   In a spreadsheet program, a cell reference in which the column reference is absolute but the row reference is relative ($A9), or in which the row reference is absolute but the column reference is relative (A$9). See *absolute cell reference, cell reference, relative cell reference.*

mixed column/line graph   In presentation and analytical graphics, a graph that displays one data series using columns and another data series using lines. A line graph suggests a trend over time; a column graph groups data items so that they can be compared one to another.

MMCD   Acronym for Multimedia Compact Disc. A proprietary multimedia CD-ROM standard developed by Sony

Corporation that can store up to 3.7GB of multimedia data on a single disc. This proposed standard has been abandoned in favor of industry-wide consensus preferring the Digital Video Disc (DVD) standard.

MMU   See *memory management unit.*

MMX   Acronym for multimedia extensions. A set of instruction set extensions for Intel's Pentium microprocessors that enable direct, high-speed execution of multimedia data, including voice, audio, and video. MMX-enabled systems are capable of executing multimedia programs up to eight times faster than systems equipped with external multimedia processing circuitry, but programs must be specially designed to take advantage of the MMX instructions.

mnemonic   In programming, an abbreviation or word that makes it easier to remember a complex instruction. In assembly language, for example, the mnemonic MOV may stand for an instruction that moves data to a storage location.

MNP   See *Microcom Networking Protocol.*

MNP 4   The most popular modem error-correcting protocol, which filters out line noise and eliminates errors that can occur during the transmission and reception of data via modem. For error correcting to function, both modems—the one sending as well as the one receiving the transmission — must have error-checking capabilities conforming to the same error-correcting protocol.

MNP 5   A data-compression protocol for computer modems that speeds transmissions by compressing (encoding, actually) data on the sending end and decompressing the data on the reception end. If the data is not already compressed, gains in effective transmission speeds of up to 200 percent can be realized. MNP 5 requires that MNP 4 error correction also be available. See *data-compression protocol.*

MO cartridge   See *magneto-optical (MO) cartridge.*

MOD   See *magneto-optical (MO) drive.*

mode   The operating state in which one places a program by choosing among a set of exclusive operating options. Within a given mode, certain commands and keystrokes are available, but one may need to change modes to use other commands or keystrokes.

mode indicator   An onscreen message that displays the program's current operating mode. In Lotus 1-2-3, for example, the mode indicator appears in the upper-right corner of the screen.

model   A simulation of a system that exists in the real world, such as an aircraft fuselage or a business's cash flow. The purpose of constructing a model is to gain a better understanding of the prototype, the system being modeled. By examining or changing the characteristics of the model, one can draw inferences about the prototype's behavior.

modem   A device that converts the digital signals generated by the serial port to the modulated analog signals required for transmission over a telephone line and that, likewise, transforms incoming analog signals to their digital equivalents. The speed at which a modem (short for modulator/demodulator) transmits data is measured in units called bits per second (technically not the same as baud, although the terms are often and erroneously used interchangeably). Modems come in various speeds and use various modulation protocols. The most recent standard, called V.90, enables communication at 56 Kbps. See *ADSL modem, cable modem, digital modem.*

moderated   Supervised by a human being rather than a computer. See *moderated newsgroup.*

moderated newsgroup   In a distributed bulletin board system (BBS), such as Usenet, a topical conference in which one or more moderators screen contributions before the post appears. The moderator's job, often mistaken for censorship, is to ensure that postings adhere to the group's

stated topic. A moderator also may rule out discussion on certain subtopics if postings on such subjects turn out to be flame bait (postings likely to cause an unproductive and bitter debate with low information content).

moderator   In Usenet and mailing lists, a volunteer who takes on the task of screening messages submitted to a moderated newsgroup or moderated mailing list.

Modified Frequency Modulation   See *MFM.*

MO drive   See *magneto-optical (MO) drive.*

Modula-2   A high-level programming language that extends Pascal so that the language can execute program modules independently. Developed in 1980 by computer wizard and Pascal creator Niklaus Wirth, Modula-2 supports the separate compilation of program modules and overcomes many other shortcomings of Pascal. A programmer working as part of a team can write and compile the module he has been assigned and then test the module extensively before integrating it with other modules. Although Modula-2 is increasingly popular as a teaching language at colleges and universities, C++ dominates professional software development. See *modular programming, structured programming.*

modular accounting package   A collection of accounting programs—one for each chief accounting function (general ledger, accounts payable, accounts receivable, payroll, and inventory, for example)—designed to work together, even though they are not integrated into one program. Modular packages require one to follow special procedures to make sure that all the modules work together. These programs have not found a large market in personal computing for two reasons: They rarely mimic the way small-businesses operators keep their books, and they are often hard to use.

modularity   **1.** In computer programming generally, a characteristic or quality of a programming language such that it favors the use of internally cohesive, loosely coupled modules. **2.** In object-oriented programming, one of the seven fundamental principles of the object model. The modularity principle states that a program should be composed of a collection of internally cohesive units, called objects, that can communicate and interoperate with each other without needing information about their internal structure. See *object model, object-oriented programming.*

modular jack   The standard receptacle for the connectors on telephone cable, found both in wall sockets and on modems. Wall sockets built before 1970 may have an incompatible, four-prong connector that can be connected to a RJ-11 plug with an RJA1X adapter. Synonymous with RJ-11 jack.

modular programming   A programming style that breaks down program functions into modules, each of which accomplishes one function and contains all the source code and variables needed to accomplish that function. Modular programming is a solution to the problem of very large programs that are difficult to debug and maintain. By segmenting the program into modules that perform clearly defined functions, one can determine the source of program errors more easily. Object-oriented programming languages, such as SmallTalk and HyperTalk, incorporate modular programming principles.

modulation   The conversion of a digital signal to its analog equivalent, especially for the purposes of transmitting signals using telephone lines and modems. See *demodulation, modem.*

modulation protocol   In modems, the standards used to govern the speed at which a modem sends and receives information over the telephone lines. See *Bell 103A, Bell 212A, CCITT, ITU-TSS.*

module   **1.** In computer programming, a program unit or section that is set aside and differentiated from other sections so that its procedural code can be made available to

more than one component of the program. For example, suppose a program has several components that need to sort data. Instead of placing code for sorting data in each of these components, it is obviously easier to isolate data sorting code in a program module (called a function) that can be called by any program component that needs its services. See *function, modular programming* **2.** In an integrated program, a section of the program that is devoted to one function such as word processing. See *integrated program.*

moiré effect   An optical illusion, perceived as flickering on a monitor, that sometimes occurs when one places high-contrast line patterns (such as cross-hatching in pie graphs) too close to one another. In printed form, the moiré effect appears as geometrical patterns.

monitor   The complete device that produces an onscreen image, including the display and all necessary internal support circuitry. A monitor also is called a video display unit (VDU). See *analog monitor, digital monitor, Enhanced Graphics Display, monochrome monitor, multiscanning monitor.*

monitor program   A program that keeps track of and records the behavior of other programs, often for purposes of tracking bugs. Also, an obsolete synonym for kernel.

monochrome monitor   A monitor that displays one color against a black or white background. Examples include the IBM monochrome monitor that displays green text against a black background, and paper-white Video Graphics Array (VGA) monitors that display black text on a white background. See *paper-white monitor.*

monochrome printer   A printer that can generate output in black, white, and shades of gray, but not color.

monolithic kernel   In Unix and Unix-like operating systems, a kernel design that incorporates functions such as file systems and device drivers into the kernel code. See *microkernel.*

monopoly In U.S. antitrust law, a situation in which a single firm has achieved such overwhelming dominance in a particular market that it is able to exclude new market entrants. By this definition, it is not necessary for a firm to possess 100% of the market before a monopoly can be declared to exist; what matters is the ability to exclude new entrants. Contrary to popular impression, mere possession of a monopoly is not illegal; for example, copyrights and patents are state-guaranteed monopolies of limited duration, and governments sometimes determine that the public's best interest is served by declaring a legal monopoly, which is then carefully regulated to prevent abuses. However, a monopoly is illegal if it was illegally obtained or illegally maintained by the use of illegal, predatory practices, such as price-fixing; moreover, a monopoly violates the law if it uses its market dominance to enter new markets in an anticompetitive manner. In 2001, a U.S. court of appeals affirmed a lower court's finding that Microsoft Corporation, although the company obtained its monopoly in personal computer operating systems legally, subsequently undertook illegal actions to undermine new market entrants. See *antitrust*.

monospace A typeface, such as Courier, in which the width of each character is the same, producing output that looks like typed characters. The following is an example of monospace type: `The width of each character in this typeface is exactly the same.` See *proportional spacing*.

monospaced font See *monospace*.

monthly duty cycle The number of pages a printer is designed to print each month. Personal laser printers can have monthly duty cycles as low as a few hundred pages, while departmental laser printers can have monthly duty cycles in excess of 200,000 pages.

MOO A type of Multi-User Dungeon (MUD) that incorporates a sophisticated, object-oriented programming language, which participants can use to construct their own personalized characters and worlds. See *MUD*.

Moore's Law An observation made in 1965 by Intel co-founder Gordon Moore that chips with approximately twice as much circuit density as their predecessors appear approximately every two years. Although Moore's prediction remains true at this writing, chip designers will inevitably run up against physical limitations that prevent further miniaturization of computer circuits.

morphing Short for metamorphosing; a revolutionary animation technique used to "fill in the blanks" between dissimilar figures so that one seems to melt into another, such as changing a man to a werewolf, a bat to a vampire, or a rock singer to a panther. Morphing, a common film industry special-effects technique, is related closely to another, more prosaic animation technique called tweening (short for "in-between-ing"), which refers to the computer's capability to calculate and draw frames that are intermediate between the key frames hand-drawn by the artist. Morphing is the process of tweening to a different object.

MOS Acronym for metal-oxide semiconductor. A chip based on the conductive and insulative properties of silicon dioxide, aluminum oxide, and other oxidized metals. MOS chips are electrically efficient but must be handled carefully because static electricity can destroy them.

most significant bit (MSB) In a binary number, the bit representing the position of greatest magnitude (normally, this is the left-most bit). See *least significant bit (LSB)*.

motherboard A large circuit board that contains the computer's central processing unit (CPU), microprocessor support chips, random access memory (RAM), and expansion slots. Synonymous with logic board.

Motif A commercial window manager for the X Window System that is a key component of the Common Desktop Environment (CDE). An open source version is called Lesstif. See *X Window System*.

motion capture   An animation technique that involves filming actual actors who are dressed in costumes containing sensors, which record the actors' movements. The resulting action sequences provide a lifelike basis for animation.

motion stabilization   In digital video, an image-processing technology that substantially reduces the wobbling or shaking visible in videos created with a hand-held camcorder. Motion stabilization is built into many camcorders, but it can also be applied in post-processing.

Motorola   A designer and manufacturer of electronic equipment, notably semiconductors, based in Schaumburg, Illinois. Motorola's 680x0 microprocessors were used in early Macintosh computers, and the company collaborated with IBM and Apple to design the PowerPC series of chips (called MPC74xx or G4) that are found in Power Macintoshes.

Motorola 680x0   Any microprocessor in the Motorola 68000 family (including the Motorola 68020, Motorola 68030, and Motorola 68040). These microprocessors powered early Macintosh computers; more recent Power Macintosh computers use the MPC74xx PowerPC processor. See *G4*.

mount   To insert a floppy disk into a floppy disk drive. Installing hardware, such as a motherboard, disk drive, and adapters, is also referred to as mounting.

mousable interface   A user interface that responds to mouse input for such functions as selecting text, choosing commands from menus, and scrolling the screen.

mouse   An input device equipped with one or more control buttons that is housed in a palm-sized case and designed so that one can move it about on the table next to his or her keyboard. As the mouse moves, its circuits relay signals that correspondingly move a pointer onscreen. See *bus mouse,*

Microsoft mouse, optical mouse, PS/2 mouse, serial mouse.

mouse elbow   A painful repetitive stress injury (RSI), similar to tennis elbow, that is produced by lifting one's hand repeatedly to manipulate a mouse.

mouse miles   Slang for time spent at the computer.

mouse port   Also called a PS/2 mouse port, a mouse port that enables one to connect a mouse to the computer without tying up a serial port. A mouse port is a small, round socket into which one plugs a PS/2-compatible mouse. USB ports are quickly replacing PS/2 ports.

MOV   See *metal-oxide varistor.*

moving border   See *marquee.*

Moving Picture Experts Group   See *MPEG.*

Mozilla   **1.** An open-source version of the Netscape Navigator Web browser that is under development by the Mozilla Project. Under the project's agreement with Netscape, project participants can continue to develop Mozilla even as Netscape releases branded versions of Mozilla using the Netscape Navigator name. **2.** An unofficial nickname for Netscape Navigator, which is personified in cartoons as a miniature Godzilla. See *open source software (OSS).*

MP3   Abbreviation for MPEG-I Audio Layer III. An MPEG audio format that produces CD-quality audio with a 12:1 compression ratio.

MPC   Acronym for Multimedia Personal Computer. A standard for multimedia hardware and software jointly developed by the MPC Consortium, which includes Microsoft Corporation, Philips, Tandy, and Zenith Data Systems. Microsoft Windows 3.1 provides the foundation for MPC. The MPC standard assumes an IBM PS/2 or IBM-compatible hardware platform; not surprisingly, Apple Computer has offered a competing standard (QuickTime) for its

Macintosh computer. MPC has been replaced by the MP-3 standard.

MPC-2 Acronym for Multimedia Personal Computer-2. A standard developed by a consortium of computer-industry companies that describes the minimum computer configuration needed to run multimedia applications. The standard calls for a 486SX-25 microprocessor, 8MB of random access memory (RAM), a Video Graphics Array (VGA) monitor, and a double-speed CD-ROM drive.

MPC-3 Acronym for Multimedia Personal Computer-3. A standard developed by a consortium of computer-industry companies that describes the minimum computer configuration needed to run multimedia applications. This standard, the current one, calls for a 75 MHz Pentium processor, 8MB of random access memory (RAM), MPEG video, and a 4X CD-ROM drive.

MPC74xx See *G4*.

MPEG Acronym for Moving Picture Experts Group. A working group of digital video experts that meets regularly under the auspices of the International Standards Organization (ISO) and the International Electrotechnical Commission (IEC) to develop standards for compressed digital audio. See *MPEG video*.

MPEG-I Audio Layer III See *MP3*.

MPEG video A format for the lossy compression of digitized videos and animations developed by the Moving Picture Experts Group (MPEG). The MPEG-1 standard provides a "postage stamp" video resolution of 352 × 240. The MPEG-2 standard provides video resolutions of 720 × 480 and CD-quality stereo sound. A proposed MPEG-3 standard designed for High-Definition Television (HDTV) has been incorporated into MPEG-2.

MPP See *massively parallel processing*.

MPR I An old Swedish standard, outmoded by the more stringent MPR II and TCO standards, for limiting electromagnetic radiation from monitors.

MPR II A standard for monitor radiation developed by Sweden's National Board for Industrial and Technical Development in 1987 and updated in 1990. To meet MPR II standards, a monitor cannot emit more than 250 nanoteslas of electromagnetic radiation at a distance of a half-meter.

MPU 401 The standard that governs the design of the MIDI port, which is used to connect musical instruments to computer sound boards. The MPU 401 standard dictates that the port must have some of its own sound-processing circuitry, lessening the load on the rest of the computer.

MR head See *magneto-resistive (MR) head*.

ms See *millisecond*.

MSB See *most significant bit*.

MS-DOS The standard, single-user operating system of IBM and IBM-compatible computers, introduced in 1981. MS-DOS is a command-line operating system that requires the user to enter commands, arguments, and syntax.

MSN Abbreviation for Microsoft Network. Microsoft's Internet service provider (ISP) and Web portal services. Comparable to AOL's Web portal and Yahoo, MSN offers a Web search engine, news, chat rooms, stock quotes, horoscopes, cartoons, shopping, and other features designed to attract a mass audience. See *America Online (AOL), Yahoo!*.

MTA See *message transfer agent*.

MTBF Acronym for mean time between failures. The statistical average operating time between the start of a component's life and the time of its first electronic or mechanical failure. This figure represents laboratory rather than real-world conditions and may not accurately indicate the longevity of a device in actual use.

MTU See *maximum transmission unit*.

MUD Acronym for Multi-User Dungeon. A MUD is a form of virtual reality designed for network use that offers participants an opportunity to interact with other computer users in real time. Originally developed to support online role-playing games (such as Dungeons & Dragons), MUDs have mostly been replaced by more flexible MOOs.

multicast To send a signal to multiple specific receivers. An electronic mailing list is an example of multicasting. See *anycast*, *broadcast*, *unicast*.

Multicast Backbone (Mbone) An experimental system that can deliver real-time audio and video via the Internet. Capable of one-to-many and many-to-many transmission with low consumption of network resources, Mbone requires special software, which is installed on only a small number of the computers currently connected to the Internet. The Rolling Stones broadcast a concert on the Mbone during their 1994 Voodoo Lounge tour. See *multicast*.

MultiColor Graphics Array See *MCGA*.

multilaunching On a local area network (LAN), the opening of an application program by more than one user at a time.

multilevel sort In database management, a sort operation that uses two or more data fields to determine the order in which data records are arranged. To perform a multilevel sort, one identifies two or more data fields (fields used for ordering records) as sort keys. In a membership database, for example, the primary sort key may be LAST_NAME, so all records are alphabetized by the member's last name. The second sort key, FIRST_NAME, comes into play when two or more records have the same last name. A third sort key, JOIN_DATE, is used when two or more records have the same last name and the same first name. A multilevel sort must be used when one sort key cannot resolve the order of two or more records in a database.

Multilink Point-to-Point Protocol Sometimes abbreviated as Multilink PPP. An Internet standard for ISDN connections between an Internet service provider (ISP) and an ISDN terminal adapter. MP fragments data packets before transmitting them via ISDN lines, greatly improving efficiency and overall throughput.

Multilink PPP See *Multilink Point-to-Point Protocol*.

multimedia A computer-based method of presenting information by using more than one medium of communication, such as text, graphics, and sound, and emphasizing interactivity. In Microsoft Bookshelf, for example, one can see portraits of William Shakespeare, read a list of his works, and follow hyperlinks to related information. Advances in sound and video synchronization enable one to display moving video images within onscreen windows. However, because graphics and sound require so much storage space, a minimal configuration for a multimedia system includes a CD-ROM drive.

Multimedia Compact Disc See *MMCD*.

multimedia extensions Additions to an operating system that allow multimedia software to synchronize graphics and sound. These extensions—called hooks in programmers' slang—enable multimedia software designers to access sound and video capabilities without extensive, nonstandard programming. Apple's QuickTime is a multimedia extension to its System 7 software. Microsoft Windows 95/98 includes the multimedia extensions (called Media Control Interface [MCI]) that were formerly available separately. See *application program interface (API)*, *MMX*.

Multimedia Personal Computer See *MPC*.

Multimedia Personal Computer-2 See *MPC-2*.

Multimedia Personal Computer-3 See *MPC-3*.

multiple document interface (MDI)
In an application program, a user interface that allows the user to have more than one document or worksheet open at once. With its Microsoft Windows 95/98 Application Program Interface (API), Microsoft Corporation discourages the use of MDIs. Instead, Microsoft favors running multiple copies of programs, each with a different document.

multiple matrix skinning An animation technique used in three-dimensional games in which character animation employs two or more skeletal animations in the same frame. To provide a lifelike depiction of a moving character, a "skin" of polygons is stretched around the character's "bones." Video cards that provide hardware support for multiple matrix skinning will provide more lifelike character animations than those that do not.

multiple program loading An operating system that lets a user start more than one program at a time; however, only one of the programs is active at any one time. The user press a key to switch from one program to another. See *context switching*.

multiple selection In a spreadsheet program, a selection of two or more noncontiguous ranges.

multiplex To combine or interleave messages in a communications channel.

multiplexer (mux) A device that merges lower-speed transmissions into one higher-speed channel at one end of the link. Another mux reverses the process at the other end of the link.

multiplexing In local area networks (LANs), the simultaneous transmission of multiple messages in one channel. A network that can multiplex allows more than one computer to access the network simultaneously. Multiplexing increases the cost of a network, however, because multiplexing devices must be included that can mix the signals into a single channel for transmission. See *frequency division multiplexing (FDM), LAN, TDMA*.

multiple zone recording (MZR) A way to pack more data onto hard disks that use constant angular velocity (CAV) recording. MZR drives pack extra data onto their edges, which would otherwise be filled to less than full capacity.

multiprocessing The simultaneous execution of differing portions of a program by a multiprocessor, a computer with more than one central processing unit (CPU). See *parallel processing, symmetric multiprocessing (SMP)*.

multiprocessor A computer that contains more than one central processing unit (CPU). To make use of the additional processors, the computer must be running an operating system or program capable of parallel processing.

Multipurpose Internet Mail Extensions See *MIME*.

multiscan monitor See *multiscanning monitor*.

multiscanning monitor A color monitor that can adjust to a range of input frequencies so that it can work with a variety of display adapters. Multiscanning monitors are often called multisync monitors, but Multisync is a proprietary name of an NEC multiscanning monitor.

multisession PhotoCD A standard for recording PhotoCD information onto a CD-ROM during several different recording sessions. Unlike standard CD-ROM drives, drives that are Multisession PhotoCD-compatible can read information recorded on a disk during several different pressings, an advantage for consumers who do not want to wait until they have taken enough pictures to fill a PhotoCD before having the photos processed but who do not want to waste PhotoCD capacity, either.

multisync monitor See *multiscanning monitor*.

multitasking The execution of more than one task (executing process) at a time on a computer system. Multitasking should not be confused with multiple program loading, in which two or more tasks are present in random access memory (RAM) but only one task is given permission to execute at a time. Unless a computer is equipped with two more processors, only one task can run at a time; however, a multitasking operating system (such as Linux, Windows 2000, Windows XP, and Unix) creates the impression of simultaneous task execution by constantly switching among the various tasks that are competing for system resources. A complete multitasking solution, called preemptive multitasking, involves memory protection, in which programs are prevented from invading each other's memory space. In addition, the operating system should be capable of suspending an unruly program's execution, if necessary. See *cooperative multitasking, preemptive multitasking, protected memory, task.*

multithreaded application   A program that can run two or more threads (independent portions of the program) at the same time. The advantage of dividing a program up into threads is that the operating system can decide which of the threads should get the highest priority for processing. See *preemptive multitasking.*

multithreading   An operating system architecture for rapid program execution in which programs can be divided into several independent execution paths, called threads, which can run simultaneously.

Multithreading operating systems include Microsoft Windows 95/98 and Microsoft Windows XP Professional.

Multi-User Dungeon   See *MUD.*

multiuser system   A computer system that can be used by more than one person to access programs and data at the same time. In a multiuser system, each user is equipped with a terminal. If the system has just one central processing unit, a technique called time-sharing allocates access time to several terminals. Personal computers with advanced microprocessors, such as the Intel 80486, are sufficiently powerful to serve as the nucleus of a multiuser system. Such systems typically are equipped with Unix, OS/2, or Microsoft Windows NT or Windows 2000. See *AppleTalk, Ethernet, file server, LAN, mainframe, minicomputer, NetWare, network operating system (NOS).*

multiword DMA mode 1   The method Enhanced IDE hard disks use to transfer data to the rest of the computer. Multiword DMA mode 1 enables Enhanced IDE drives to transfer data three to four times faster than IDE hard disks.

Musical Instrument Digital Interface   See *MIDI.*

mux   See *multiplexer.*

MZR   See *multiple zone recording.*

n Common mathematical variable for expressing an indeterminate number of items.

nagware Derogatory term for shareware that is programmed to "nag" unregistered users to pay the program's registration fee. Common techniques include presenting a dialog box that increasingly delays the program's execution after it is launched, attention-grabbing reminders, and advertising. After the registration fee is paid, the "nagging" stops. See *shareware*.

naive user A user with little or no previous experience with any type of computer system. See *end user, power user*.

name conflict An error that occurs when two system or network resources have the same name or identification number. For example, a type of name conflict called an IP conflict occurs when the same IP address is given to both. See *IP conflict*.

name server In an Internet-connected local area network (LAN), a computer that provides the domain name system (DNS)—that is, the translation between alphabetical domain names and numerical IP addresses. To establish a connection with an Internet service provider, one needs to know the IP address of the name server.

namespace Within a defined zone (such as a program or a network protocol), a collection of names in which all names are unique and cannot be confused with each other. For example, the uniform resource locator (URL) standard creates a namespace in which it is possible to indicate unambiguously the precise location of a computer resourced on the Internet.

nano- A metric prefix indicating one-billionth.

nanometer (nm) A measurement equal to one-billionth of a meter. A sugar molecule is about one nanometer in diameter.

nanosecond (ns) A unit of time equal to one-billionth of a second. Far beyond the range of human perception, nanoseconds are relevant to computers. An advertisement for 80 ns RAM chips, for example, means that the RAM chips respond to the central processing unit (CPU) within 80 nanoseconds. See *millisecond (ms)*.

nanotechnology 1. In semiconductor technology, the use of fabrication techniques that operate on a level of up to two orders of magnitude smaller than today's technology, which operates on the submicron level. **2.** A branch of engineering, also called molecular manufacturing, which hopes to develop tiny, self-replicating machines that are capable of manipulating atoms and molecules.

Napster Free software that enabled Internet users to share MP3 and other music files on the Internet. Napster was purchased by Bertelsmann AG, and converted into a business. An action in a U.S. Federal court, brought by the leading recording companies, forced Napster to exclude copyrighted material proactively from its systems; subsequently, the company entered bankruptcy, and Bertelsmann closed it down. See *copyright, Digital Millennium Copyright Act (DMCA), Gnutella, MP3*.

NAT Acronym for Network Address Translation. An Internet protocol that enables local area network administrators to use a special, internal set of IP addresses for local computers. These addresses enable local workstations to communicate with each other as well as with the external Internet. See *IP address, IP masquerading*.

National Center for Supercomputing Applications (NCSA) A supercomputer research center, affiliated with the

University of Illinois at Champaign-Urbana, that specializes in scientific visualization. NCSA achieved fame in 1994 as the birthplace of NCSA Mosaic, the first graphical Web browsers.

National Information Infrastructure (NII) A proposed high-speed, high-bandwidth network that can deliver voice, data, and video services throughout the United States. NII will be developed by private firms, cable television, and telephone companies, with minimal government funding.

National Science Foundation (NSF) An independent agency of the U.S. government that seeks to promote the public good through the development of science and engineering. Until 1995, NSF subsidized and coordinated NSFnet, which at one time was the backbone network of the Internet.

National Television Standards Committee See *NTSC*.

native Designed for a particular type of computer.

native application A software program designed to work with a particular type of microprocessor—in other words, a program that is binary-compatible with a particular microprocessor. Non-native applications may run on a given microprocessor with the help of an emulation program, but native applications are almost always significantly faster than non-native applications.

native code See *machine language*.

native compiler In programming, a compiler that is designed to execute on the computer for which it is generating code.

native file format The default file format a program uses to store data on disk. The format is often a proprietary file format. Many popular programs today can retrieve and save data in several formats. See *ASCII*.

natural language A naturally occurring human language, such as Spanish, French, German, or Tamil, as opposed to an artificial language, such as a programming language. In the computer context, this term is often used to describe interfaces in which users can type or speak commands or queries using everyday language. See *fourth-generation programming language*.

natural language processing In artificial intelligence, the use of a computer to decipher or analyze human language.

natural recalculation In a spreadsheet program, a recalculation order that performs worksheet computations in the manner logically dictated by the formulas one places in cells. If the value of a formula depends on references to other cells that contain formulas, the program calculates the other cells first. See *column-wise recalculation*, *optimal recalculation*, *row-wise recalculation*.

navigation In a computer program or network, the process of interacting with the user interface in an effort to find resources or files.

navigation button In a Web browser, a tool on the onscreen toolbar that enables the user to display the previously accessed document (Back), return to the document being displayed when the Back button was clicked (Forward), or return to the current default home page (Home). See *Web browser*.

NCSA See *National Center for Supercomputing Applications*.

near-letter quality (NLQ) printer A dot-matrix printer mode that prints almost typewriter-quality characters. As a result, printing when using this mode is slower than other printing modes.

needle drop In multimedia, a short excerpt from a recorded musical piece that is employed as an element of a new composition. The term "needle" stems from the days of vinyl phonograph needles that could be "dropped" into a specific groove on the record. Synonymous with sampling.

negotiation See *handshaking.*

nested structure A structure in which one control structure is positioned within another. See *DO/WHILE loop.*

nested subtotal In a spreadsheet, a formula that adds several values and that, in turn, is included in a larger formula that adds several subtotals.

.NET A collection of Web services developed by Microsoft Corporation that are intended to reposition the company as a provider of Internet-distributed services, including software maintenance and upgrades and transparent access to one's data, files, and software from any type of device at any location. The .NET architecture is intended to replace Microsoft's Component Object Model (COM) and COM+ middleware architectures with a framework that closely resembles Sun's Java 2 Enterprise platform (J2EE): It relies on a Java-like development language (C#), a Common Language Runtime (CLR) that resembles a Java virtual machine, and a set of protocols for Web-based services, including XML, SOAP, Web Services Description Language (WSDL), and Universal Description, Discovery, and Integration (UDDI). Microsoft's critics fear that the .NET architecture will enable Microsoft to leverage its desktop operating system monopoly into new market areas, such as secure Web authentication for financial transactions and digital music distribution. Such a move would likely violate U.S. antitrust law. See *antitrust, SOAP, UDDI, XML.*

net abuse In Usenet, any action that interferes with peoples' right to use and enjoy Usenet, including flooding newsgroups with unwanted posts (also called spamming), conducting an organized forgery campaign, or carrying out an organized effort to prevent the discussion of an issue. See *flame.*

NetBEUI Acronym for NetBIOS Extended User Interface. A network transport protocol that defines the network layer of Microsoft and IBM local area networks (LANs).

NetBIOS Acronym for Network Basic Input/Output System. An application program interface (API) that provides the support that applications need to send and receive data on an IBM or Microsoft-based local area network (LAN).

NetBSD An open source version of BSD, a Unix-like operating system that is available for Intel-based PCs and certain other platforms. NetBSD is optimized for efficiency in networking and server applications. See *BSD, FreeBSD.*

net god(dess) In Usenet, an individual whose lengthy Usenet experience and savvy online demeanor elevates him or her to heroic status.

netiquette Network etiquette; a set of rules that reflect long-standing experience about getting along harmoniously in the electronic environment (e-mail and newsgroups).

net lag In a packet-switching network, the delay in accessing a document that is caused by latency and other delivery problems.

netnews A collective way of referring to the Usenet newsgroups.

net police In Usenet, a person or group of persons who take upon themselves the enforcement of Usenet traditions and netiquette.

Netscape Application Programming Interface See *NSAPI.*

Netscape Communicator A package of applications developed by Netscape Communications that includes Netscape Navigator (a Web browser), Netscape Composer (a WYSIWYG HTML editing program), voice conferencing, an e-mail client, and a calendaring system. Netscape is now owned by AOL Time Warner See *Netscape Navigator, Web browser.*

Netscape extensions A set of additions to the HTML 2.0 standard that enables Web authors to create documents with tables, frames, and other features not supported by the 2.0 specification. Until competing browsers decided to support Netscape's unilaterally introduced tags, these features could be seen only by Netscape Navigator users. Most of the extensions have been incorporated into HTML Version 3.2, but Netscape (like other browser publishers) has recently introduced new, nonstandard tags that other browsers do not support.

Netscape Navigator A still-popular Web browser that once held a commanding market share until Microsoft used illegal measures to relegate Netscape (as the browser is commonly called) to relative obscurity. In 1998, Netscape initiated an innovative open source project to create a completely new version of Netscape Navigator, to be called Mozilla after Netscape's unofficial mascot (a lizard-like cartoon character). After a lengthy development period, the Mozilla project reached fruition by creating an innovative Web browser that is fully conformant to Web standards, as established by the World Wide Web Consortium (W3C). Under the agreement between the Mozilla project and Netscape, the project can continue Mozilla development while Netscape releases branded versions of the Mozilla browser. AOL Time Warner purchased Netscape and releases the Netscape browser as part of America Online service. See *Mozilla*.

NetWare A network operating system (NOS) manufactured by Novell for local area networks (LANs). NetWare accommodates more than 90 types of network interface cards, 30 network architectures, and several communications protocols. Versions are available for IBM PC–compatibles and Macintosh computers.

network A communications, data exchange, and resource-sharing system created by linking two or more computers and establishing standards, or protocols, so

that they can work together. The three main types of computer networks are local area networks (LANs), metropolitan area networks (WANs), and wide area networks (WANs).

network administrator In local area networks (LANs), the person responsible for maintaining the network and assisting its users.

network architecture The complete set of hardware, software, and cabling standards for a local area network (LAN) design. See *network topology*.

Network Basic Input/Output System See *NetBIOS*.

network drive In a local area network (LAN), a disk drive made available to a user through the network, as distinguished from a drive connected directly to the workstation the user is using.

Network File System   See *NFS*.

Network Information Center See *NIC*.

Network Information Service A local area network (LAN) protocol developed by Sun Microsystems that enables network-wide distribution of user and host name information. It is designed to work with the company's Network File Standard (NFS). The service was formerly known as Yellow Pages.

network interface adapter   See *NIC*.

network interface card   See *NIC*.

network laser printer A laser printer, often with a large monthly duty cycle and remote management features, that is designed to be connected to a network and serve the printing needs of several dozen people. See *automatic network switching*.

network layer In the OSI Reference Model of computer network architecture, the fifth of seven layers, in which packets are addressed so that they can be routed to the correct destination. When the packets have been addressed, they are transferred down to the data link layer, where they are prepared for transmission on the physical network.

Network Neighborhood In Microsoft Windows, a desktop icon that displays the PCs and other resources within the user's workgroup when clicked. With Network Neighborhood, files on other machines can be browsed and accessed just as if they were present on the user's computer.

Network News Transfer Protocol (NNTP) On Usenet, the standard that governs the distribution of Usenet newsgroups via the Internet. See *news server*.

network operating system (NOS) Software that provides local area networking (LAN) capabilities. In today's operating systems, this software is included, so separate NOS packages are not needed.

network operations center (NOC) An administrative and technical coordination office that is responsible for the day-to-day operation of a local, regional, or national Internet backbone service.

network printer In a local area network (LAN), a printer made available to a user through the network, as distinguished from a local printer (a printer connected directly to the workstation a user is using).

network protocol The method used to regulate a workstation's access to a computer network to prevent data collisions. Examples include carrier sense multiple access with collision detection (CSMA/CD) and token passing.

network server See *file server*.

network termination 1 unit (NT-1) In an ISDN system, the device in a subscriber's home or office that is connected between ISDN devices (such as digital modems and digital telephones) and the telephone company's network. Users must usually buy their own NT-1s.

network topology The geometric arrangement of nodes and cable links in a local area network (LAN). Network topologies fall into two categories: centralized and decentralized. In a centralized topology, such as a star network, a central computer controls access to the network. This design ensures data security and central management control over the network's contents and activities. In a decentralized topology, such as a bus network or a ring network, each workstation can access the network independently and establish its own connections with other workstations. See *star network*.

network transport protocol Any of hundreds of communication standards for transmitting data over a specific type of physical network, such as fiber-optic cable.

network virtual terminal (NVT) A generic terminal standard that enables programmers to create applications without having to worry about all the different brands of terminals that are actually in use. The Internet's NVT standard is called Telnet. See *line mode terminal*.

network warfare A form of information warfare characterized by attacks on a society's information infrastructure, such as its banking and telecommunications networks.

neural network (NN) An artificial intelligence technique that mimics the way nerve cells are connected in the human brain. Information is supplied to the neural network to train it to recognize patterns. The result is a program that can make predictions, useful in weather forecasting and stock market software.

newbie In Usenet, a new user who nevertheless makes his presence known, generally by pleading for information that is readily and easily available in FAQs.

news feed In Usenet, a service that enables one to download the day's Usenet articles directly to his or her computer and to upload all the articles contributed by people using his or her computer. Not for personal computer users, a news feed dumps as much as 100MB of Usenet articles per day into the user's system, far more than one person could fruitfully read. A news feed is for organizations that want to set up a Usenet site and that have a computer (usually a minicomputer) with enough storage space to handle the huge influx of articles. Such a computer also has the multiuser capabilities that enable as many as dozens or even hundreds of people to take advantage of Usenet.

newsgroup   In Usenet, a discussion group devoted to a single topic, such as *Star Trek*, model aviation, the books of Ayn Rand, or the music of the Grateful Dead. Users post messages to the group, and those reading the discussion send reply messages to the author individually or post replies that can be read by the group as a whole. The term newsgroup is a misnomer in that the discussions rarely involve "news": the words "discussion group" would be more accurate, but the term newsgroup has taken root. Synonymous with forum. See *FAQ, follow-up post, local Usenet hierarchy, moderated newsgroup, net god(dess), netiquette, thread, unmoderated newsgroup.*

newsgroup reader   See *newsreader.*

newsgroup selector   In a Usenet newsreader, a program mode that presents a list of currently subscribed newsgroups, from which a user can select one to read.

news hierarchy   In Usenet, one of the seven standard newsgroup hierarchies. The news hierarchy is concerned with Usenet itself; the various newsgroups deal with administrative issues, new newsgroups, announcements, and Usenet software. See *local Usenet hierarchy, standard newsgroup hierarchy.*

newspaper columns   A page format in which two or more columns of text are printed vertically on the page so that the text flows down one column and continues at the top of the next. High-end word processing programs such as Microsoft Word and WordPerfect do a good job of producing newspaper columns and can even balance the bottom margin of columns (called balanced newspaper columns) for a professional-looking effect.

newsreader   In Usenet, a client program that enables one to access a Usenet news server, subscribe to Usenet newsgroups, read the articles appearing in these newsgroups, and post his or her own articles or reply by e-mail. Many Web browsers (such as Netscape Navigator) include newsreader functions.

news server   In Usenet, a computer that provides access to newsgroups. To read Usenet newsgroups, one must tell his or her newsreader program or Web browser the domain name of an NNTP server. A person's Internet service provider can provide him or her with the name of this server, if one is available.

Newton   A personal digital assistant, driven by a 32-bit, 20 MHz reduced instruction set computing (RISC) processor with 640K of random access memory (RAM), manufactured by Apple Computer. The Newton includes a date book, address book, and free-form notebook in which one enters data using a stylus or an onscreen keyboard. The handwriting recognition engine can learn a person's writing and improves over time, although recognition is slow. Later models include a keyboard. The Newton is no longer produced. See *pen computer.*

NFS   Acronym for Network File System. A network file access utility, developed by Sun Microsystems and subsequently released to the public as an open standard, that enables users of Unix and Microsoft Windows NT workstations to access files and directories on other computers as if they were physically present on the user's workstation.

nibble   Four bits, half of a byte. Sometimes cutely spelled "nybble."

NIC   1. Acronym for Network Information Center (NIC). A system that contains a repository of Internet-related information, including File Transfer Protocol (FTP) archives of Requests for Comments (RFCs), Internet Drafts, For Your Information (FYI) papers, and other documents, including handbooks on the use of the Internet. There are numerous Network Information Centers, but the official repository of network information is the Defense Data Network NIC (DDN NIC). See *InterNIC.* **2.** Acronym for network interface card. An adapter that lets one connect a network cable to a microcomputer. The card includes encoding and decoding circuitry and a receptacle for a network cable connection. Ethernet network cards are the type most commonly found in PCs.

NiCad Abbreviation for nickel-cadmium, a compound used to create rechargeable batteries. Commonly used in portable computers, NiCads provide the lowest level of battery quality, judged in terms of output power, recharging time, overall longevity, and output time. Cadmium, one of the materials used in NiCad batteries, is highly toxic, and disposal of NiCad batteries poses a serious environment risk. NiCad batteries may demonstrate an undesirable memory effect, in which batteries lose their capacity to take on a full charge if they are not fully discharged before recharging. See *lithium-ion battery, NiMH.*

NII See *National Information Infrastructure.*

NiMH Abbreviation for nickel-metal hydride, a compound used to create rechargeable batteries that do not include toxic substances, as NiCad batteries do. NiMH batteries also offer superior performance, with up to 50 percent longer output time than NiCad batteries. See *lithium-ion battery.*

NIS See *Network Information Service.*

NLQ See *near-letter quality (NLQ) printer.*

NLX A form factor for PC motherboards developed by Intel Corporation. An improved version of the earlier LPX form

factor, it supports current components (such as the latest Pentium processors and memory modules). As in the LPX form factor, expansion cards are mounted on a riser, which is positioned perpendicular to the motherboard plane. This design allows for more compact cases, including booksize PCs. A competing form factor is called microATX. See *booksize PC, form factor, LPX, microATX.*

nn In Usenet, a Unix newsreader created by Kim F. Storm. A threaded newsreader that organizes articles and follow-up articles to show the thread of discussion, nn includes many advanced features but is not particularly easy to use. See *trn.*

NNTP See *Network News Transfer Protocol.*

NNTP server See *news server.*

NOC See *network operations center.*

node In a local area network (LAN), a connection point that can create, receive, or repeat a message. Nodes include repeaters, file servers, and shared peripherals. In common usage, however, the term node is synonymous with workstation. See *network topology.*

noise In data communications, unwanted or random electrical signals on a communications channel, unlike the signal that carries the information a person wants. All communications channels have noise, but if the noise is excessive, data loss can occur and data transfer rates drop. Telephone lines are particularly noisy, requiring the use of communications programs that can perform error-checking operations to make sure that the data being received is not corrupted.

noise reduction A post-processing operation, generally performed by a special-purpose circuit, that is designed to reduce the noise associated with analog recording techniques.

nom A new top-level domain (TLD) name for the Internet, added in 1998, that is designed for Websites created by individuals. See *domain name*, *gTLD-MoU*, *top-level domain (TLD)*.

nonadjacent selection In spreadsheets, a selected range of cells that is separate from another selected range of cells. Nonadjacent selection is useful in formatting operations.

nonbreaking hyphen In word processing, a special hyphen that prevents a line break if reformatting pushes the hyphen to the end of the line. This prevents the program from placing a line break within hyphenated proper nouns (such as A.R. Radcliffe-Brown).

noncontiguous Nonadjacent; not next to one another. See *contiguous*, *nonadjacent selection*.

nondisclosure agreement (NDA) A contract designed to keep sensitive information confidential. Software publishers often establish nondisclosure agreements with their beta test sites so that information about new products is less likely to leak out to competitors.

non-impact printer A printer that forms a text or graphic image by spraying or fusing ink to the page. Non-impact printers include inkjet printers, laser printers, and thermal printers. All non-impact printers are considerably quieter than impact printers, but non-impact printers cannot print multiple copies by using carbon paper.

non-interlaced monitor A monitor that does not use the screen refresh technique called interlacing and, as a result, can display high-resolution images without flickering or streaking.

non parity In asynchronous communications, a communications protocol that disables parity checking and leaves no space for the parity bit.

non-procedural language See *declarative programming language*

non-repudiation In a computer network, a desirable quality of network security such that valid users are never denied access to resources to which they are entitled.

non-transactional application In a local area network (LAN), a program that produces data that one does not need to keep in a shared database for all users to access. Most of the work done with word processing programs, for example, is non-transactional.

non-volatile Not susceptible to memory loss when the power is shut off.

non-volatile memory The memory specially designed to hold information, even when the power is switched off. Read-only memory (ROM) is non-volatile, as are all secondary storage units such as disk drives. See *random access memory (RAM)*, *volatility*.

non-Windows application A DOS application program that does not require Microsoft Windows to run. DOS applications can also be run under Windows. Using Windows 95/98 or Standard or 386 Enhanced modes in Windows 3.1, a person can switch from one non-Windows application to another without closing either program. See *application program interface (API)*.

normalization In relational database management programs, a method of organizing data into separate tables so that no data duplication occurs. The process involves three steps. The first, called First Normal Form (1NF), ensures that each field in a table contains a distinct type of information. The second, Second Normal Form (2NF), ensures that the data in one field cannot be derived from data in another field. The third, Third Normal Form (3NF), ensures that the database contains no duplicate information. The objective of normalization is to make sure that data is recorded in just one place so that editing or modifying the data cannot lead to errors attributable to duplicate data entries. See *1NF*, *2NF*, *3NF*.

Norton AntiVirus See *antivirus program*.

NOS See *network operating system.*

NOT A Boolean operator that can be used to exclude certain documents from a retrieval list. For example, the search expression "sports NOT skiing" retrieves information regarding all sports except skiing.

notebook computer A portable computer that typically weighs less than 7 pounds and that measures about 8 inches by 11 inches by 1½ inches, and that easily fits inside a briefcase. Unlike subnotebook computers, notebook computers can function as a complete replacement for a desktop computer. See *auxiliary battery, battery pack.*

Novell NetWare A network operating system for IBM PCs and compatibles. Current versions of NetWare can use the IPX/SPX, NetBEUI, or TCP/IP transport protocols.

ns See *nanosecond.*

NSAPI Acronym for Netscape Application Programming Interface. An application programming interface (API) for Netscape Web servers that enables programmers to route Web information requests to external programs, such as databases.

NSF See *National Science Foundation.*

NT See *Microsoft Windows NT.*

NT-1 See *network termination 1 unit.*

NTFS Acronym for NT File System, the native file system of Microsoft Windows NT. Compared to FAT32, the file system used in Microsoft's consumer operating systems, NTFS offers advanced features, such as file permissions, transparent encryption and compression, transaction logs, and the capability of creating a virtual volume that spans two or more physical disks.

NTSC Acronym for National Television Standards Committee. A committee that governs physical standards for television broadcasting in the United States and most of Central and South America (but not Europe or Asia). NTSC television uses 525-line frames and displays full frames at 30 frames per second, using two interlaced fields at about 60 frames per second to correspond to the U.S. alternating-current frequency of 60 Hz. Most European and Asian countries use the PAL standard, which is based on their 50 Hz power-line frequencies.

NuBus The expansion bus of early Macintosh and Power Macintosh computers; later Power Macintoshes use the PCI bus. NuBus requires adapters specifically designed for its 96-pin receptacles.

nuke **1.** To erase an entire directory or disk. **2.** In Unix and Unix-like operating systems, to kill or annihilate a running process.

null modem cable A specially configured serial cable that enables a person to connect two computers directly, without mediation by a modem.

null network cable A specially configured network cable that enables a person to connect two computers directly, without mediation by a network hub, router, or other device.

null value In an accounting or database management program, a blank field in which one has never typed a value, as distinguished from a value of zero that one enters deliberately. In some applications, one must distinguish between a null value and a deliberately entered zero; a null value does not affect computations, but a zero does.

number crunching A slang term for calculating, especially with large amounts of data.

numeric coprocessor A microprocessor support chip that performs mathematical computations at speeds up to 100 times faster than the microprocessor alone.

numeric coprocessor socket A push-down socket on the motherboard of many personal computers into which the user or a dealer can mount a numeric coprocessor, such as the Intel 80387. See *numeric coprocessor.*

numeric format   In a spreadsheet program, the way in which the program displays numbers in a cell.

numeric keypad   A group of keys arranged like the keys on an adding machine, usually located to the right of the typing area on a keyboard. The keypad is designed for the rapid touch-typing entry of numerical data.

Num Lock key   A key on a PC keyboard that toggles the numeric keypad between number entry and directional movement (arrow keys). Many modern keyboards have separate arrow keys, making the Num Lock less essential.

NVT   See *network virtual terminal.*

n-way set associative cache   See *set-associative cache.*

nybble   See *nibble.*

object 1. In object-oriented programming (OOP), a self-contained program component that contains properties (data) as well as the methods (procedures) needed to make a certain type of data useful. In class-based languages such as C++ and Java, each object is an instance of a superordinate class, a component that contains abstract declarations of the properties and methods available to all instances of a class. A given object has a private part, used for storing data, that is inaccessible to other objects. It also has a public part, also called an interface, which enables other objects to use its methods. The interface is designed so that external accesses can be performed without knowing the details of how the object stores or manipulates its data. See *class, object model, object-oriented programming.* **2.** In object linking and embedding (OLE), a document or portion of a document that has been pasted into another document using the Paste Link, Paste Special, or Embed Object command. See *dynamic object, OLE, static object.*

object code In programming, the machine-readable instructions created by a compiler or interpreter from source code. See *source code.*

Object Database Connectivity See *ODBC.*

object library In an object-oriented programming language, a collection of reusable objects that programmers can use to build programs quickly. See *object, object-oriented programming.*

object linking and embedding See *OLE.*

Object Management Group (OMG) An industry consortium that is developing standards for computer networks based on a distributed object architecture, in which objects can exchange data on a cross-platform computer network, even if they were written in differing computer programming languages. See *CORBA, Unified Modeling Language (UML).*

object model The principles that form the basis of object-oriented programming. See *abstraction, concurrency, encapsulation, hierarchy, modularity, persistence, typing.*

object-oriented database management system See *OODBMS.*

object-oriented graphic A graphic composed of distinct objects, such as lines, circles, ellipses, and boxes, that one can edit independently. Synonymous with vector graphic.

object-oriented programming A programming method in which a program is conceptualized as an integrated collection of objects, each of which is an instance of a template called a class; in addition, classes are organized into a hierarchy in which lower classes acquire their properties through inheritance. The philosophy of object-oriented programming are expressed by its seven key principles. See *abstraction, concurrency, encapsulation, hierarchy, modularity, persistence, typing.*

object-relational database management system A hybrid approach to database design that blends the concepts of object-oriented database management systems (OODBMS) with traditional relational database management systems. This hybrid design arose out of concerns that OODBMS programs failed to take advantage of the relational database packages' capability to avoid data redundancy. See *OODBMS, relational database management system (RDBMS).*

object request broker See *ORB.*

oblique The italic form of a sans serif typeface.

Occam A parallel programming language that enables programmers to specify how the computer allocates its resources to all currently executing programs. For example, the ! metacharacter command enables the programmer to specify that a given CPU should output data to a communication channel; the ? metacharacter command specifies that another CPU should accept input data from the channel. See *parallel programming*.

OCR   Abbreviation for optical character recognition. A technology (including software and hardware devices) which enables computers to read printed text and to place this text into a text editor or word processing program. Printed text varies in appearance widely; some printed documents are read more successfully than others. An OCR system's performance is judged by the error percentage per 100 words. Even under ideal circumstances, the best systems will make one or two errors per hundred words. Handwritten text is much more difficult to process unless the writer places letters in square boxes so that they are regularly aligned. See *handwriting recognition software*.

octal notation   A numbering system that uses a base (radix) of 8. There are eight octal digits: 0, 1, 2, 3, 4, 5, 6, and 7. Because octal notation's base is one of the squares of 2, a single octal number can take the place of three binary digits (see table). Still, programmers prefer to use hexadecimal notation to denote binary numbers because two hexadecimal numbers can represent a byte, which is composed of eight binary digits. See *binary notation, hexadecimal notation*.

octet   A unit of data exactly 8 bits in length—in other words, a byte. Internet people do not like to use the term byte because some of the computers connected to the Internet use data word lengths other than eight bits. See *word*.

OCX   A control (an executable object) created in conformity to Microsoft's object linking and embedding (OLE) standards. OCX controls are now called ActiveX controls.

ODBC   Acronym for Object Database Connectivity. An application programming interface (API) that enables any ODBC-compatible program to access any ODBC-compatible databases that are present on the local system or network. Using the ODBC Data Source Administrator in Microsoft Windows, users can configure their applications to make use of available ODBC-compatible databases. See *JDBC*.

odd parity   In asynchronous communications, an error-checking protocol in which the parity bit is set to 1 if the number of 1 digits in a 1-byte data item adds up to an odd number. For example, the following byte has five 1s: 01011011. Therefore, the parity bit would be set to 1 in an odd parity-checking scheme. If the parity bit indicates an odd number but the data transmitted actually contains an even number of 1s, the system will report that a transmission error has occurred. See *communications*

Octal Notation

Decimal	Binary	Octal
0	000	0
1	001	1
2	010	2
3	011	3
4	100	4
5	101	5
6	110	6
7	111	7

parameters, communications protocol, even parity, parity checking.

OeB Acronym for Open eBook, an open standard for the presentation of printed media in a highly readable onscreen format. Supported by a consortium of more than 50 e-book vendors, OeB relies on open, public standards, including HTML and XML. The OeB specification is device-independent, which means that OeB-formatted documents can be viewed on any OeB-capable device, including desktop computers, notebook computers, personal digital assistants (PDAs), and dedicated e-book reading devices. See *dedicated e-book reader, e-book, HTML, PDA, XML.*

OEM See *original equipment manufacturer.*

office automation The use of computers and local area networks (LANs) to integrate traditional office activities such as conferencing, writing, filing, calculating, tracking customers and merchandise, and sending and receiving messages.

office suite A package containing several productivity programs (typically a word processing program, a spreadsheet program, a presentation graphics program, and an e-mail client). The leading office suite is Microsoft Office; others include ApplixWare, Corel WordPerfect Office, Lotus SmartSuite, and StarOffice.

offline **1.** Not directly connected with a computer; for example, a device that is not hooked up to a PC is offline or has been switched to offline mode. **2.** In data communications, not connected with another computer; for example, a workstation that has been temporarily or permanently disconnected from a local area network is offline.

offline editing In digital video, a preliminary or demonstration edit that is created with inexpensive videotape copies of the master video. See *online editing.*

off-screen formatting See *embedded formatting command.*

offset See *binding offset.*

OK button A pushbutton one can activate in a dialog box to confirm the current settings and execute the command. If the OK button is highlighted or surrounded by a thick black line, pressing Enter will choose OK.

OLAP Acronym for online analytical processing. In decision support systems (DSS), a method of providing rich, up-to-the-minute data from transaction databases. See *DSS.*

OLE Acronym for Object Linking and Embedding. A set of standards developed by Microsoft Corporation and incorporated into Microsoft Windows and Apple's MacOS that enables users to create dynamic, automatically updated links between documents and also to embed a document created by one application into a document created by another. These standards, updated for Internet use, are now called ActiveX. OLE resembles object-based middleware standards, such as CORBA, but with an important exception: OLE messages are mediated by means of the operating system. As a result, applications developed with OLE components, called controls, cannot execute in a cross-platform environment unless all the linked computer's operating systems can support OLE. Recognizing this point, Microsoft has released the latest version of OLE, called ActiveX, to an independent, nonprofit standards body that seeks to extend OLE support to other operating systems (especially Unix).

OLE client See *client application.*

OLE server See *server application.*

OLTP See *online transaction processing.*

OMA Acronym for Object Management Architecture. A collection of standards and technologies for distributing objects throughout an organization so that they can be retrieved, as needed, from any of the computers on the organization's network. Developed by the Object Management

Group (OMG), the architecture includes several components; the best known of these is the Common Object Broker Request (CORBA). See *CORBA*.

OMG See *Object Management Group.*

onboard Directly contained on a circuit board; contained within.

onboard audio A circuit on the motherboard that simulates a sound board and that is usually adequate only for business audio applications. Onboard audio circuits usually use crude FM synthesis techniques to produce sounds and can be replaced in a desktop computer with a sound board of higher quality.

onboard cache See *internal cache.*

onboard speaker A small speaker located inside the computer's case. Though the onboard speaker can generate crude beeps, buzzes, and honks, it is entirely unsuitable for multimedia applications. A sound board and auxiliary speakers provide much better sound output than the onboard speaker.

one-pass program A program designed to examine a data set one time and one time only; the program completes its job once it reaches the end of the data. An example of a one-pass program is a word processing program's spelling checker (when used to check the entire document).

ones complement A method used to represent negative numbers in binary notation; the method inverts all the bits (0 becomes 1, and 1 becomes 0).

one-shot program A program designed to solve one problem, one time, and never be used again, such as a program designed to compute the trajectory of a test missile. One-shot programs often do not conform to the rules of style and modular programming that govern programs meant to be used repeatedly—in other words, they tend to be cobbled together for one-time use—which presents a problem if a one-shot program becomes widely popular. See *canonical form.*

one-time password A password that is generated by a handheld device, a smart card, or a computer program that enables a user to gain access to a computer network. The password is known to the authenticating network computer because it is running the same password algorithm as the user's device or program. In contrast to reused passwords, one-time passwords provide superior network security. Even if a one-time password is intercepted while it is being transmitted to the authenticated computer, it cannot be subsequently used to gain unauthorized access to the computer network; additionally, it is not possible to derive the underlying password-generating algorithm from an examination of the password itself. Synonymous with token. See *authentication, security.*

one-way hash function A mathematical function that transforms a message of any length into a code of fixed length so that the code is a fingerprint of the original message. However, it is impossible to determine the content of the original message by means of an examination of the code. A one-way hash function can be used to determine whether a message has been altered during transmission over a network; the code is transmitted along with an encrypted message, and the receiving computer performs the same hash function on the message after it is decrypted. If the two codes differ, then the message was corrupted or altered en route. See *hash function.*

one-way synchronization A synchronization method in which the newer files in the source directory are copied to a destination directory; however, newer files in the destination directory are ignored.

online Directly connected with and accessible to a computer or a network, and ready for use. For example, "The printer is online, finally." Or, "We're online again—sorry for the Internet service interruption."

online analytical processing See *OLAP.*

online bank A Web-based banking service that provides almost all the services of real-world banks, including savings and checking accounts, loans, and other standard services. In addition, an online bank offers computer-based services such as register reconciliation, transfer of funds between accounts, and bill payment. Few online-only banks have met with success, owing largely to the difficulty and delay involved in depositing or obtaining funds; far more successful is the "click and brick" strategy, in which local banks extend services by means of a secure Web site. See *click and brick*.

online editing In digital video, the direct editing of the master video content to produce the final, completed version. See *offline editing*.

online help A help utility available onscreen while using a network or an application program.

online service A for-profit firm that makes current news, stock quotes, and other information available to its subscribers by means of dialup connections to public data networks (PDN). America Online (AOL) began as an online service. The rise of the public Internet greatly reduced the market for online services; the leading services (including AOL) reconfigured themselves as Internet service providers (ISP). See *America Online (AOL), ISP*.

online transaction processing (OLTP) In the Internet, the capturing and recording of electronic transaction information (including names, addresses, and credit card numbers) in a database so that all transactions occurring online can be audited and so that the resulting data can be summarized for management purposes.

onscreen formatting In a word processing program, a formatting technique in which formatting commands directly affect the text that is visible onscreen. See *embedded formatting command, what-you-see-is-what-you-get (WYSIWYG)*.

on-the-fly Performed while a process is underway (for example, "The data were generated on-the-fly.").

on-the-fly data compression A method by which data to be sent by modem is packed into a tighter package during transmission rather than beforehand, thereby increasing apparent transmission speed. Protocols such V.42bis and MNP 5 handle on-the-fly data compression.

OO Abbreviation for object-oriented. See *object-oriented programming*.

OODBMS Acronym for object-oriented database management system. A type of database management program that is specifically designed to handle large binary files, such as graphics files, and to enable programmers to devise classification systems for such objects so that they can be organized into classes; by means of inheritance, all the objects within a class will take on the characteristics of that class. See *object-relational database management system*.

OOP See *object-oriented programming*.

op Common abbreviation for operator, as in "channel op" (a channel operator on IRC).

op code Abbreviation of operation code. In machine language, a code that tells the processor to perform a specific operation, such as moving data to a register.

open 1. Accessible for user modification. 2. Conforming to well-established, nonproprietary standards or protocols. 3. To read a file into the computer's memory.

open architecture A system in which all the system specifications are made public so that other companies will develop add-on products, such as adapters for the system. See *open bus system*.

open bus system A design in which the computer's expansion bus contains receptacles that readily accept adapters. An open-architecture system generally has an open bus, but not all systems with open buses have open architectures; the Macintosh is an example of the latter.

OpenDoc   A compound document architecture similar to Microsoft's object linking and embedding (OLE) standard that functions in a cross-platform computing environment. Developed by IBM, Apple, and others, OpenDoc enables users to embed features from one or more applications into a single document.

OpenGL   An application programming interface (API) for graphics applications, including games, that was initially developed by Silicon Graphics. Currently standardized by the OpenGL Architecture Review Board, an independent industry consortium, OpenGL is the leading API for 2-D and 3-D graphics applications and is implemented on all widely used computer platforms, including Unix, Linux, BeOS, Mac OS X, and Microsoft Windows. See *Direct3D, DirectX*.

open-loop actuator   An obsolete mechanism for moving the read/write head over the storage medium of a hard disk. Unlike closed-loop actuators, open-loop actuators provide no feedback about the head's position to the hard disk controller, therefore reducing the accuracy with which the controller can tightly pack data. Ultimately, open-loop actuators reduce areal density.

Open Shortest Path First   See *OSPF.*

Open Shortest-Path First Interior Gateway Protocol   See *OSPF.*

Open Software Foundation (OSF)   A consortium of computer companies that promotes standards and publishes specifications for programs operating on computers that run Unix. OSF is perhaps best known for designing OSF Motif, a graphical user interface (GUI) for Unix. OSF also developed the OSF Distributed Computing Environment (DCE) (a set of programs that supplements a vendor's operating system and that enables cross-platform network interoperability) and the OSF/1 operating system, a publicly available variant of Unix. See *proprietary.*

open source software (OSS)   Software that is distributed under licensing terms that make the underlying source code available to the licensee. Open source licenses, such as the Free Software Foundation (FSF) General Public License (GPL), generally grant licensees the right to create modified versions of the software and to distribute the source code to others, as long as such distributions extend similar liberties to subsequent recipients of the code. These restrictions are deliberately designed to prevent the commercial exploitation of OSS code. However, the term "open source software" was deliberately devised as an alternative to "free software," the term preferred by the FSF, as well as to the FSF's ideology, which is thought to alienate commercial interests that might otherwise see interests in common with OSS proponents. Nevertheless, the majority of open source software is free. See *copyleft, Free Software Foundation (FSF), General Public License (GPL).*

open standard   A set of rules and specifications that describes the design or operating characteristics of a program or device, published and made freely available to the technical community and (ideally) standardized by an independent international standards body. Open standards may contribute to rapid market growth if they encourage interoperability (the capability of a device made by one manufacturer to work with a device made by a different manufacturer) and cross-platform computing (use in a network with computers made by several different vendors and running different operating systems). The opposite of an open standard is a proprietary standard, which a company pushes in the hope that its standard, and no others, will come to dominate the market. See *de facto standard.*

Open Systems Interconnection (OSI) Protocol Suite   See *OSI Protocol Suite.*

Open Systems Interconnection (OSI) Reference Model   See *OSI Reference Model.*

open tag In markup languages such as SGML, XML, and HTML, the series of characters that demarcates the beginning of a markup element. In HTML, <blockquote> is the open tag for the blockquote element; </blockquote> is the closing tag. See *HTML, markup language, SGML, XML.*

OpenWindows A graphical user interface (GUI) developed by Sun Microsystems that is based on the X Window System standard for Unix computers. See *Motif.*

operand The argument that is appended to an operator, such as a spreadsheet program's built-in function. For example, in the Excel expression AVERAGE(D10:D24), the cell range D10 to D24 is the operand of the AVERAGE function.

operating environment The total context in which applications function, including the operating system and hardware platform.

Operating System/2 See *OS/2.*

operating system (OS) A master control program that manages the computer's internal functions, such as accepting keyboard input, and that provides a means to control the computer's operations and file system. Typically, a computer's operating system is automatically loaded into memory when the computer is powered on; this operation is called booting.

Most operating systems are designed to run on a specific hardware platform. Still, it is possible to write operating systems in such a way that they can be ported (translated) so that they run on different hardware platforms. This is done by creating the operating system in such a way that most of the components are designed to function at a level of abstraction beyond the hardware level. Although operating systems vary, almost all of the features that are today regarded as essential to an operating system have their origin in Unix, which was developed at AT&T's Bell Laboratories (and subsequently by university professors and graduate students) during the 1970s and 1980s, as well as its ill-fated predecessor, Multics, and certain other early systems. By the mid-1980s, Unix had successfully incorporated preemptive multitasking, multithreading, multiuser capabilities, interprocess communication, application programming interfaces (API), multiprocessing, and other key innovations. With these features, Unix enables two or more applications to run simultaneously without interfering with each other's use of the memory (preemptive multitasking), permits applications to run two or more of its tasks simultaneously (multithreading), enables two or more users to use the system as if each of them had sole control (multiuser capabilities), enable applications to exchange data and give each other instructions (interprocess communication), provides a standardized set of system calls by which programmers can access operating system functions (application programming interface), and exploits the capabilities of computer systems that have two or more CPUs (multiprocessing). Today, most leading operating systems emulate Unix's advanced features or directly incorporate Unix code; Mac OS X, for example, is built on BSD Unix; in addition, several versions of Microsoft's Windows NT-derived operating systems (including Windows 2000) are known to incorporate BSD code. Gaining market share more rapidly than any other operating system at this writing is Linux, a Unix-like operating system that is under development by a worldwide programming team.

Operating systems vary according to their intended function. Server operating systems (such as Unix, Unix-related operating systems such as Linux and FreeBSD, and Microsoft Windows XP Server) are designed to make data and applications available to other applications on a local area network or the Internet. Other operating systems (such as Microsoft Windows XP Home) are designed with the end user in mind, and do not burden the user with a server operating system's complexity. Still other operating systems, called embedded operating systems, are designed to be installed in small, dedicated devices, including cellular phones and personal digital assistants (PDAs). See *application programming interface (API), BSD Unix, interprocess communication (IPC), multiprocessing, multitasking, multithreading, Plan 9, preemptive multitasking.*

operating voltage   The electrical voltage at which a microprocessor operates. Most microprocessors have operating voltages of 5 volts—a mostly arbitrary specification decided upon when the transistor was invented—but some chips run at 3.3 volts to save electricity (a real concern in portable computers) and reduce heat output.

operator   In programming, a code name or symbol that is used to describe a command or function, such as multiplying or dividing.

optical character recognition   See *OCR.*

optical disc   A large-capacity data storage medium for computers on which information is stored at extremely high density in the form of tiny pits. The presence or absence of pits is read by a tightly focused laser beam. CD-ROMs and and DVDs offer an increasingly economical medium for storing data and programs. Write-once, read-many (WORM) drives enable organizations to create their own huge, in-house databases. Erasable optical disc drives combine good storage capacity with the convenience of removable CDs; howver, they are still more expensive and slower than hard drives. See *interactive videodisk.*

optical fiber   See *fiber optics.*

optical mouse   Instead of using a rubber ball to communicate its movement, an optical mouse shines a beam of light onto the surface beneath it and reads the changes in that surface when the mouse moves. An optical mouse is more convenient because it does not require cleaning.

optical resolution   A measure of the sharpness with which a scanner can digitize an image without help from software. The more charge-coupled devices (CCDs) in a scanner (1200 is about average, and 4800 is very good), the better its optical resolution. By means of software interpolation, output can be improved, but software interpolation is a poor substitute for high optical resolution.

optical scanner   See *scanner.*

optimal recalculation   In Lotus 1-2-3 and other advanced spreadsheet programs, a method that speeds automatic recalculation by recalculating only those cells that have changed since the last recalculation.

optimizing compiler   A compiler that translates source code into machine language optimized to run as efficiently as possible on a particular microprocessor. Optimizing compilers are virtually essential when preparing programs to run on any microprocessor equipped with superscalar architecture.

option button   See *radio button.*

OR   1. In programming, a Boolean function that returns an expression as true if any of its arguments are true. 2. In computer database searching, a Boolean operator that retrieves a document if it contains any of the specified search terms.

Oracle Corporation   The leading manufacturer of relational database management systems (RDMS) for multiuser enterprise computing, and the first major database firm to adopt SQL as its standard query language.

ORB   Acronym for object request broker. A standard for requesting services from objects in a distributed object architecture, a cross-platform computer network in which program modules can be written in any computer language but still supply needed functions to other applications. The standard is the work of the Object Management Group (OMG), an industry consortium that is developing standards for middleware based on distributed object architecture. See *CORBA*.

ordered list In Hypertext Markup Language (HTML), a numbered list, created with <OL> ... </OL> tags.

ordinal number A number that expresses the numerical rank or position of an item in a hierarchical series (such as first, second, third, and so on).

organization chart In presentation graphics, a text chart used to diagram the reporting structure of an organization, such as a corporation or a club.

Organizer See *personal information manager (PIM)*.

orientation See *landscape orientation, portrait orientation*.

original equipment manufacturer (OEM) The company that actually manufactures a given piece of hardware, unlike the value-added reseller (VAR), the company that changes, configures, repackages, and sells the hardware. For example, only a few companies, such as Canon, Toshiba, and Ricoh make the print engines used in laser printers. These engines are installed in housings with other components and are sold by VARs such as Hewlett-Packard.

originate To make a telephone call rather than receive one. In computers, the term usually applies to contacting another computer system via modem.

originate mode In modems, a mode in which the modem will originate calls but not receive them. See *auto-dial/auto-answer modem*.

orphan 1. In word processing, a formatting flaw in which the first line of a paragraph appears alone at the bottom of a page. Most word processing and page layout programs suppress widows and orphans; the better programs let a user switch widow/orphan control on and off and choose the number of lines for which the suppression feature is effective. 2. In Unix, a process that continues running even

though its parent has died, consuming CPU time needlessly.

OS See *operating system*.

OS/2 Acronym for Operating System/2. A multitasking operating system for IBM PC–compatible computers that was initially developed jointly by Microsoft Corporation and IBM. A 32-bit operating system, OS/2 was initially seen to be the successor to Microsoft Windows 3.1, but Microsoft decided to develop Microsoft Windows NT, leaving IBM as the sole proponent of OS/2, which was re-released under the name OS/2 Warp. Due to the success of Windows, OS/2 has few remaining users.

OSF See *Open Software Foundation*.

OSI Protocol Suite Abbreviation for Open Systems Interconnect Protocol Suite. A wide area network (WAN) architecture that was developed by the International Organization for Standardization (ISO), with heavy support from European state postal and telegraph organizations. The OSI protocol suite has proven to be unwieldy and brittle in practice, and would not pose a threat to the global dominance of the competing TCP/IP suite if not for the OSI's strong backing by European nations' postal and telegraph service bureaucracies. See *OSI Reference Model*.

OSI Reference Model Abbreviation for Open Systems Interconnect Reference Model. An international standard for conceptualizing the architecture of computer networks, established by the International Organization for Standardization (ISO) and the Institute of Electrical and Electronic Engineers (IEEE), that improves network flexibility. The OSI Reference Model employs a divide-and-conquer approach, in which network functions are divided into seven categories, called layers, and communication standards are established to handle the transfer of data from one layer to another. Within each layer, protocols are developed that focus on that layer's functions, and no others. Within a network-connected computer, outgoing messages move down a protocol stack, successively undergoing transformations until the data is ready to be sent out via the physical network. At the receiving end, the data moves up the stack, undergoing the mirror image of the transformation process until the data is ready to be displayed by an application. The OSI Reference Model calls for a total of seven layers. From the top of the stack to the bottom, they are: application layer, presentation layer, session layer, transport layer, network layer, data link layer, and physical layer. See *application layer, data link layer, network layer, physical layer, presentation layer, session layer, transport layer.*

OSPF Acronym for Open Shortest Path First. An improved version of the Internet Protocol (standard) that governs the exchange of data using TCP/IP within an internal network (an autonomous system). A router running OSPF compiles a database of its own current connections, as well as those OSPF-compatible routers to which it is connected, and then uses a routing algorithm to determine the shortest possible path for the data.

outline font Synonymous with scalable font and vector font. A printer font or screen font in which a mathematical formula generates each character, producing a graceful and undistorted outline of the character, which the printer then fills in. Mathematical formulas rather than bit maps produce the arcs and lines of outline characters. The printer can easily change the type size of an outline font without introducing the distortion common with bitmapped fonts. (It may be necessary to reduce the weight of small font sizes by using a process called hinting, which prevents the loss of fine detail.)

outline utility In some full-featured word processing programs, a mode that helps one plan and organize a document by using outline headings as document headings. The program lets a user view the document as an outline or as ordinary text.

out-of-memory error A error that occurs when a program requests more

memory than is currently available. Virtual memory systems reduce out-of-memory systems by making the computer's hard disk available as an extension of RAM memory. See *virtual memory.*

out-of-order execution In microprocessors, a speed-enhancing design in which instructions are processed out of their sequential order, if it is possible to do so. For example, some instructions require more time to execute than others. While such an instruction is executing, the microprocessor executes a subsequent instruction that is not directly dependent on the results of the current operation. To resolve the problems that would otherwise result when out-of-order execution occurs, a buffer (temporary memory area) stores the results so that they can be re-assembled in the correct order.

output The process of displaying or printing the results of processing operations. See *input.*

outsourcing The transfer of a project to an external contractor.

overclocking Resetting the computer so that the microprocessor runs at a speed exceeding its specified maximum. Although this is sometimes done by computer game players to extract the maximum performance from their systems, it is not recommended because it could make the system unstable.

OverDrive Upgrade microprocessors created by Intel that fit into special sockets (called an OverDrive socket) on Intel 486DX and Intel 486SX motherboards and that improve their performance to the level of Intel 486DX/2 central processing units (CPUs). The performance gain realized by installing an OverDrive chip is only about 20 percent, so installing one is not necessarily the most cost-effective upgrade route available. These are also available for some Pentium systems. See *Pentium OverDrive.*

OverDrive socket A special socket provided on OverDrive-compatible motherboards designed for the Intel 80486 microprocessor; the chip is designed for OverDrive upgrade processors.

overflow A condition in which a program tries to place more data in a memory area than the area can accommodate, resulting in an error. Well-designed programs trap these errors so that they do not result in the program's abnormal termination. On a network, untrapped overflow conditions pose a security risk; under certain circumstances, an intruder can gain full control of a computer's operating system after inducing an overflow condition. See *error, error trapping.*

overhead On a network, the additional information that must be added to a message to ensure its error-free transmission. In asynchronous communications, for example, a start bit and a stop bit must be added to every byte of transmitted data, producing a high, inefficient overhead of roughly 20 percent.

overlaid windows In a graphical user interface (GUI), a display mode in which windows are allowed to overlap each other. If the top window is maximized to full size, it completely hides the other windows. See *cascading windows, tiled windows.*

overlay See *program overlay.*

overlay chart In a business graphics program, a second type of chart that is overlaid on the main chart, such as a line chart on top of a bar chart. Synonymous with combination chart. See *mixed column/line graph.*

override To interrupt or terminate a command, task, or process, generally because it is producing erroneous output.

overrun error A serial port error in which a microprocessor sends data faster than the Universal Asynchronous Receiver/Transmitter (UART) can handle it. An overrun error results in lost data.

overscan A condition that exists when the image created on a cathode ray tube (CRT) display is larger than the visible portion of the display. Users can adjust this to bring the hidden portion into view on most monitors, but some monitors may fail to do so; for this reason, AV professionals try to avoid placing important detail in the outer 10 percent of the image area.

overstrike Creating a character not found in a printer's character set by placing one character on top of another, such as using O and / to create zeros that can be easily distinguished from an uppercase letter O. Today's graphics-based computer systems eliminate the need for this printing technique; however, users of character-based DOS programs still need it sometimes.

overtype mode An editing mode in word processing programs and other software that lets the user enter and edit text. In overtype mode, the characters typed erase existing characters, if any. In WordPerfect, the overtype mode is called typeover mode. See *insert mode.*

overvoltage Unusually high voltage, typically in the form of spikes or surges greater than 130 volts from a wall outlet. A surge protector provides overvoltage protection.

overwrite To write data on a storage medium (such as a hard drive or floppy disk) in the same area where other data is stored, thereby destroying the original data.

P2P Abbreviation for peer-to-peer. A family of technologies—especially those that work over the Internet—that enable users to share files and information by establishing transient, decentralized networks. Because there are no centralized servers, each P2P application must have the built in ability to locate other applications of the same type. See *peer-to-peer network*.

package **1.** A term used to describe a software product that includes related or ancillary software; for example, Adobe Acrobat includes a number of utilities (such as Adobe Distiller, which translates PostScript files into the Portable Document Format). **2.** More generally, any software product that is sold in shrink-wrapped packages. **3.** In semiconductor technology, a hard plastic case that protects the semiconductor chip from damage.

packaged software Application programs commercially marketed, unlike custom programs privately developed for a specific client.

packet In networking, a unit of data of a fixed size—not exceeding the network's maximum transmission unit (MTU) size—that has been prepared for transmission over a packet-switching network. Each packet contains a header that indicates its origin and its destination. Synonymous with datagram. See *packet-switching network*.

packet driver On a local area network (LAN), a program that divides data into packets (transmission units of fixed size) before sending them out on the network.

Packet Internet Groper See *ping*.

packet loss The percentage of packets lost during transmission over a computer network. The TCP/IP protocols include provisions for automatic packet resubmissions in the event of packet loss; however, packet loss percentages in excess of single digits may indicate a technical problem. Packet loss can be determined using most versions of the ping program. See *ping*, *TCP/IP*.

packet radio A method of exchanging TCP/IP data by means of VHF radio transmissions linking two or more computers. First developed for military applications during the development of ARPANET, packet radio is now most widely used among radio hobbyists. Packet radio transmissions are limited by line of sight (approximately 10 to 100 miles, barring obstructions).

packet sniffer A program designed to search the data packets coursing through an Internet line for some predetermined pattern, such as a password, Social Security number, or credit card number; these are often transmitted via the Internet in cleartext. The ability of computer criminals to intercept such data is a fundamental security shortcoming of the Internet and explains why use of the network is inherently insecure unless encryption is used.

packet switching See *packet-switching network*.

packet-switching network One of two fundamental architectures for the design of a computer network; the other is a circuit-switching network. In a packet-switching network such as the Internet, no effort is made to establish a single electrical circuit between two computing devices; for this reason, packet-switching networks are often called connectionless. Instead, the sending computer divides a message into a number of efficiently sized units called packets, each of which contains the address of the destination computer. These packets are simply dumped onto the network. They are intercepted by devices called routers, which read each packet's destination address and, based on that information, send the packets in the appropriate direction. Eventually, the packets arrive at their intended destination, although some may have actually traveled by different physical paths. The receiving computer assembles the packets, puts them in order, and delivers the received message to the appropriate application. Packet-switching networks are highly reliable and efficient; however, they introduce a delay called network lag. For this reason, they are not well suited to the delivery of real-time voice and video unless a streaming media protocol is employed that builds a buffer sizeable enough to disguise network lag. The Internet uses a packet-switching protocol called IP. See *circuit-switching network, Internet, packet, router, TCP/IP.*

padded string   A string (series of characters) to which spaces have been added so that each line conforms to a specified length.

page   **1.** A fixed-size block of random access memory (RAM). See *paging memory.* **2.** In word processing and desktop publishing, an onscreen representation of a printed page of text or graphics. **3.** A Web page. **4.** To scroll through a document. **5.** To swap a fixed-size block of data into and out of the memory. See *swap file.*

page break   In word processing, a mark that indicates where the printer will start a new page. Word processing programs insert page breaks automatically when a full page of text has been typed. The automatic page break is called a soft page break because the program may adjust its location if text is inserted or deleted above the break. Users can enter a hard page break, also called a forced page break, which forces the program to start a new page at the hard page break's location.

page description language (PDL)   A programming language that describes printer output in device-independent commands. Normally, a program's printer output includes printer control codes that vary from printer to printer. A program that generates output in a PDL, however, can drive any printer containing an interpreter for the PDL. PDLs also transfer the burden of processing the printer output to the printer. See *PostScript.*

paged memory   See *paging memory.*

paged memory management unit (PMMU)   In hardware, a chip or circuit that enables virtual memory. Virtual memory allows a computer to use space on a hard disk to expand the apparent amount of random access memory (RAM) in its system. With virtual memory, a computer with only 4MB of RAM can function as though it were equipped with 16MB or more of RAM, enabling a person to run several programs simultaneously.

page fault   In virtual memory, an unsuccessful attempt to retrieve a page of data from random access memory (RAM). When a page fault occurs, the operating system retrieves the data from the hard disk, which is slower.

page layout program   In desktop publishing, an application program that assembles text and graphics from various files. One can determine the precise placement, sizing, scaling, and cropping of material in accordance with the page design represented onscreen. Page layout programs such as PageMaker and FrameMaker display a graphic representation of the page, including nonprinting guides that define areas into which text and graphics can be inserted.

page-mode RAM   High-performance dynamic random access memory (DRAM) chips that include a buffer, called a column buffer, which stores data likely to be needed next by the central processing unit (CPU). Page-mode RAM chips store data in a matrix of rows and columns. When data is requested from page-mode RAM, the entire column, or page, of data is read into the buffer because the next piece of data requested likely will be in the same column. If so, the data is read from the buffer, which is faster than accessing the matrix again. Page-mode RAM is not the same as paging memory systems. Faster memory technologies are now available. See *FPM, EDO RAM, SDRAM.*

page orientation   See *landscape orientation, portrait orientation.*

page printer   A printer that develops an image of a printed page in its memory and then transfers that image to paper in one operation. Laser printers, liquid crystal shutter (LCS) printers, and light-emitting diode (LED) printers are page printers; inkjet and dot matrix printers, which print one line at a time, are not.

pages per minute (ppm)   A measurement of how many pages a printer can print in one minute. Manufacturers often inflate their printers' ppm rating, and the ratings are almost always inaccurate for print jobs that involve graphics or fonts other than the printer's resident fonts. Like automakers' gas-mileage figures, ppm ratings (although inflated) can serve as a point of comparison between models.

Page Up/Page Down keys   On IBM PC–compatible computer keyboards, the keys one presses to move the cursor to the preceding screen (Page Up) or the next screen (Page Down).

pagination   In word processing, the process of dividing a document into pages for printing. Today's advanced word processing programs use background pagination, in which pagination occurs after one stops typing or editing and the microprocessor has nothing else to do. See *page break*.

paging memory   A memory system in which the location of data is specified by the intersection of a column and a row on the memory page, rather than by the actual physical location of the data. This makes it possible to store memory pages wherever memory space of any type becomes available, including disk drives. Paging memory is used to implement virtual memory, in which a computer's hard drive functions as an extension of random access memory (RAM). A chip or circuit called a paged memory management unit manages the movement of pages of data in and out of the memory devices. See *paged memory management unit (PMMU)*.

paint file format   A bitmapped graphics file format found in graphics programs such as MacPaint and PC Paintbrush. See *paint program*.

paint program   A program that enables its user to create graphical images by specifying the color of the individual dots or pixels that make up a bitmapped screen display. Although paint programs can produce interesting effects, they are difficult to edit because it is not possible to select objects individually. See *draw program*.

paired bar graph   A bar graph with two different x-axes (categories axes). A paired bar graph is an excellent way to demonstrate the relationship between two data series that share the same y-axis values but require two different x-axis categories. Because the bars mirror each other, variations become obvious. See *dual y-axis graph*.

paired pie graph   A graphic containing two separate pie graphs. For example, a paired pie graph is appropriate for showing the breakdown of product sales in two different time periods. To show the difference in the size of the totals represented by each of the two pie graphs, a proportional pie graph is useful.

pair kerning   See *kerning*.

PAL   Acronym for Page Alternation Line. The analog television standard that is used throughout Europe and much of the rest of the world, with the exception of the United States and Japan, where the NTSC standard prevails. PAL provides somewhat higher resolution because the standard requires CRTs to scan horizontally 625 times to form the video image; NTSC scans only 525 times. See *NTSC*.

palette   In computer video displays, the colors that the system can display. Video Graphics Array (VGA) displays offer a palette of 262,144 colors, although each screen can display a maximum of 256 colors simultaneously. In paint and draw programs, an onscreen display of options such as colors and drawing tools. See *draw program*, *paint program*.

Palm A popular personal digital assistant (PDA), originally called Palm Pilot, that has played a key role in creating a market for handheld computer devices. The device uses handwriting recognition for control and data entry purposes. By means of serial, modem, infrared, or Internet connections, Palms can exchange data with Windows, Macintosh, or Linux-powered desktop computers.

Palm OS The operating system of Palm personal digital assistants (PDAs) and certain other brands that have obtained a license to use Palm OS. Because Palm and compatible PDAs do not have secondary storage systems, Palm OS retains all permanent information, including saved user configuration choices and stored user data, in a section of RAM called storage RAM that is set aside to function as if it were a secondary storage device. See *PDA, random access memory (RAM), secondary storage.*

palmtop A portable computer that is small and light enough to be held in one's palm, such as a personal digital assistant (PDA). See *PDA.*

Palo Alto Research Center (PARC) Formerly known as XeroxPARC, PARC is a research laboratory, located in Menlo Park, California, which is a wholly owned subsidiary of the Xerox Corporation. Beginning in the early 1970s and spanning approximately one decade, PARC hosted one of the most impressive stretches of technological creativity that has ever occurred. During this period, PARC scientists invented many of the technologies now used in everyday computing, including the mouse, the graphical user interface (including pull-down menus, check boxes, radio buttons, dialog boxes, and windows with sizing and zooming controls), laser printers, onscreen fonts, and Ethernet networking. In spite of these innovations, Xerox was unable to market this technology successfully. After a visit to PARC in the early 1980s, Steve Jobs of Apple Computer developed the Lisa, an ill-fated business computer system that implemented PARC technology; subsequently, Apple's successful 1984 release of the Macintosh brought PARC technology to the public's attention. See *Macintosh.*

pan 1. In multimedia, the capability of a synthesizer or sound board to alter the left and right channel volumes to create the illusion of movement of the source of the sound. 2. In a video card, a feature than enables the user to zoom in on the desktop and then scroll to view different parts of it.

Pantone Matching System (PMS) A device-independent system for describing and adjusting colors. When using PMS colors, one chooses the color he or she wants from a booklet, uses that color's code in the software, and prints to a specially calibrated printer. The output should closely match the color in the PMS book. See *device-dependent color.*

PAP Acronym for Password Authentication Protocol. An Internet standard providing a simple (and fundamentally insecure) method of authentication. The authenticating computer demands the user's login name and password, and keeps doing so until these are supplied correctly. Computer criminals who possess a known login name can gain unauthorized access by running password-guessing programs that supply a variety of known insecure passwords.

paperless office An office in which using paper for traditional purposes—such as sending messages, filling out forms, and maintaining records—has been reduced or eliminated.

paper-white monitor A monochrome monitor that displays black text and graphics on a white background. Paper-white monitors are preferred for word processing and desktop publishing because the display closely resembles the appearance of the printed page. However, some users do not like the glare of a large expanse of white background.

paradigm An established mode of thinking, consisting of a set of assumptions that, over time, come to be accepted without much reflection or examination. In the

Unix paradigm, for example, it is assumed that the best programs are small ones that users can combine into useful applications. This assumption may be true for experienced programmers, but not for end users.

paradox In logic, a self-contradicting statement (for example, "I am lying now"); they are much beloved to computer programmers, who tend to find them humorous. See *recursive acronym*.

Paradox A sophisticated relational database management system (RDBMS), comparable to Microsoft Access, that is designed for Intel-powered systems. Originally developed by Borland, Paradox is now offered by Corel. See *Corel, Microsoft Access, relational database management system (RDBMS)*.

parallel computer See *parallel processing*.

parallel interface See *parallel port*.

parallel port A connection for the synchronous, high-speed flow of data along parallel lines to a device, usually a parallel printer. Parallel ports negotiate with peripheral devices to determine whether they are ready to receive data, and the ports report error messages if a device is not ready. More recent versions of parallel ports enable bidirectional communication between the computer and the printer. See *ECP, EPP*.

parallel printer A printer designed to be connected to the computer's parallel port.

parallel processing In a multiprocessor computer, the use of specially adapted hardware and software to run two or more tasks simultaneously. Parallel processing is distinguished from multiprocessing, in which a single computer equipped with two or more CPUs executes programs that are not modified (or are only superficially modified) to run on a multi-CPU system. Parallel processing employs operating systems that are specifically designed to take a processor-intensive problem, break it down into components that can be simultaneously executed, and assign these components to

multiple CPUs. See *massively parallel processing (MPP), parallel programming, symmetric multiprocessing (SMP)*.

parallel programming A branch of programming that designs operating systems and applications for systems that implement parallel processing. Unlike ordinary programs, which assume that only one processor is available, programs designed for parallel processing systems can execute multiple simultaneous tasks. As a result, parallel programming languages must be equipped with concurrency capabilities; one approach is to equip the language with control structures specifically designed so that a given module's task is assigned to its own, separate processor. See *massively parallel processing (MPP), parallel programming language*.

parallel programming language A programming language designed for use on massively parallel processing-based computers. See *Occam*.

parameter 1. A configuration variable that can be altered by the user. 2. A value or option that one adds or alters when giving a command so that the command accomplishes its task in the desired way. If a parameter is not stated, the program uses a default setting. 3. In programming, a value passed to a function by the code that calls the function. In the following function, "name" is a parameter:

A = Nice to meet you, "name"!

If we pass the value "Christine" to the "name" parameter, then A will equal the following:

Nice to meet you, Christine!.

See *actual parameter, function, function call, parameter passing convention*.

parameter passing convention In a programming language, the method used to pass one or more values (called actual parameters) to a function by means of a function call, such as the following:

square(2);

This function call launches a function that squares the supplied parameter (2), returning 4.

One fundamental difference among programming languages concerns what is done with the returned value. In a call-by-value convention, the function places the returned value in a new memory location and leaves the original actual parameter intact. In a call-by-reference convention, the function replaces the actual parameter (2) with the returned value (4) at the function call's location. The call-by-value convention is more efficient, but pointers are difficult to program and often result in program faults.

Most programming languages employ one of these conventions by default but allow programmers to use the other. In C++, for example, function calls use call-by-value by default; however, the returned value can be accessed by means of a pointer (a reference to a specific location in memory where a value is stored). See *function, function call, parameter.*

parameter RAM In the Macintosh environment, a small bank of battery-powered memory that stores configuration choices after the power is switched off.

PARC See *Palo Alto Research Center (PARC).*

parent In a hierarchical organization of data, a superordinate level that may contain one or more subordinate units (each unit is called a child). Levels in the hierarchy are named parent or child in relation to each other; for example, a child may be the parent of several children.

parent directory In DOS directories, the directory above the current subdirectory in the tree structure. One can move quickly to the parent directory by typing CD and pressing Enter.

parent process In multitasking operating systems such as Unix or Linux, a process (executing program) that spawns (initiates) and controls one or more subordinate processes (called child processes). See *Linux, multitasking, spawn, Unix.*

parity The quality of oddness or evenness. In comparing two numbers, parity exists if both are odd or both are even; no parity exists if one is even and one is odd.

parity bit In asynchronous communications and primary storage, an extra bit added to a data word for parity checking.

parity checking A technique used to detect memory or data communication errors. The computer adds up the number of bits in a 1-byte data item, and if the parity bit setting disagrees with the sum of the other bits, the computer reports an error. Parity-checking schemes work by storing a 1-bit digit (0 or 1) that indicates whether the sum of the bits in a data item is odd or even. When the data item is read from memory or received by another computer, a parity check occurs. If the parity check reveals that the parity bit is incorrect, the computer displays an error message. See *even parity, odd parity.*

parity error An error that a computer reports when parity checking reveals that one or more parity bits are incorrect, indicating a probable error in data processing or data transmission.

park To position a hard drive's read/write heads over the landing zone so that the disk is not damaged by jostling during transport. Most hard drives now do this automatically when they are turned off.

parse To break down into components. For example, spreadsheet programs often have parsing features that will break ASCII data into parts that will fit into cells.

parser 1. A program that breaks large units of data into smaller, more easily interpreted pieces. 2. In SGML, a program that reads a data file and determines whether the document's markup conforms to the document type definition (DTD).

partial-response maximum-likelihood (PRML) read-channel technology See *PRML read-channel technology.*

partition A section of the storage area of a hard disk created for organizational purposes or to separate different operating systems. A partition is created during initial preparation of the hard disk, before the disk is formatted. See *logical drives.*

Pascal A high-level, procedural language that encourages programmers to write well-structured, modular programs that take advantage of modern control structures and lack spaghetti code. Pascal has gained wide acceptance as a teaching and application-development language, although most professional programmers prefer C or C++. Pascal is available in interpreted and compiled versions.

passive attack In computer security, an attack on a computer system that is based on obtaining (but not altering) existing information. See *active attack.*

passive matrix display In notebook computers, a LCD (liquid crystal display) in which a single transistor controls an entire column or row of the display's tiny electrodes. Passive matrix displays are cheaper than active matrix displays (also called dual-scan displays) but offer lower resolution and contrast. See *active matrix display.*

passive termination Like active termination and forced-perfect termination, a way of ending a chain of SCSI devices. Passive termination is the simplest termination method and works best on daisy chains of four or fewer devices.

passphrase A lengthy password of up to 100 characters that is used to encrypt or decrypt secret messages. The use of a lengthy password renders password guessing computationally infeasible.

password An authentication tool used to identify authorized users of a program or network and to define their privileges, such as read-only, reading and writing, or file copying. Passwords are easily guessed or stolen, acquired through social engineering, or intercepted by packet sniffers as they are uploaded in cleartext to the authenticating network computer; therefore, this poses one of the greatest challenges to computer network security. One-time passwords and

digital signatures provide more secure means of authentication.

password aging In a computer network, a feature of the network operating system (NOS) that keeps track of the last time a user changed his or her password.

Password Authentication Protocol See *PAP.*

password guessing In computer security, a method of defeating password authentication by simply guessing common passwords, such as personal names, obscene words, and the word *password.*

password protection A method of limiting access to a program, file, computer, or network by requiring a person to enter a password. Some programs enable a user to password-protect his or her files so they cannot be read or altered by others.

paste In text editing, inserting at the location of the cursor text or graphics that have been cut or copied from another location. In Windows and Macintosh systems, a temporary storage area called the Clipboard stores the cut or copied material while the user moves to the material's new location. In pasting, the material is copied from the Clipboard to its new location. See *block move.*

patch 1. A quick fix, in the form of programming code, added to a piece of software to correct bugs or enhance its capabilities. 2. An executable program that repairs a defective program. 3. To fix a program by replacing one or more lines of code.

patent A form of intellectual property (IP) protection that is designed to protect inventions; creative works (such as books and musical recordings) are protected by copyright. U.S. patents protect inventors for a period of 20 years, during which time the patent holder—not necessarily the same person as the inventor—can exclude others from making use of the technology that the patent protects. Patent applications are subject to an examination, in which patent examiners attempt to determine whether the invention is truly novel (that is, whether it is an attempt to patent existing technology, called prior art) and whether the invention's novelty, if it exists, is sufficiently significant to warrant the patent's issuance. The patent holder may make use of this period to gain an exclusive foothold in an emerging market; more commonly, patent rights are licensed to others in return for financial and other considerations. In the United States, controversial court decisions have extended patent protection to computer software algorithms and business processes that involve the use of the computer. See *copyright, business process patent, patentable subject matter, software patent, trade secret.*

patentable subject matter In intellectual property (IP) law, a list of types of inventions that are legitimately held to be subject to patent protection, including compositions of matter (such as chemical compounds), methods and processes of the manufacturer, machines, and new and useful improvements to any of these. Not subject to patent is any form of knowledge that is essential to the growth of science and a flourishing economy, such as scientific knowledge, mathematical formulas, mental reasoning steps, or business processes. In the United States, the scope of patentable subject matter has been widened considerably in the past 25 years and now includes computerized business processes and software algorithms. See *business process patent, patent, software patent.*

path In a hierarchical file system such as Unix or Windows, the route the operating system must follow to find an executable program stored in a subdirectory.

path name In a hierarchical file system such as Unix or Windows, a statement that indicates the name of a file and precisely where it is located on a hard disk. When opening or saving a file with most applications, one must specify the full pathname to retrieve or store the file in a directory other than the current directory. For example, C:\My Documents\Reports\.

pathname separator The character that is used to differentiate the various directory names in a pathname. In Unix and the World Wide Web (WWW), the pathname separator is a forward slash (/); in Windows and MS-DOS, it is a backward slash (\).

path statement In DOS, an entry in the AUTOEXEC.BAT file that lists the directories in which executable programs are listed. See *path.*

pattern recognition In artificial intelligence, the provision of computers with the capability to identify objects or shapes within the stream of incoming visual data.

PC **1.** Abbreviation for personal computer. In practice, this abbreviation usually refers to IBM or IBM-compatible personal computers, as opposed to Macintoshes. **2.** Abbreviation for printed circuit board.

PC100 A type of synchronous DRAM (SDRAM) memory chip that is capable of working with 100 MHz motherboards. These chips produce a maximum data transfer rate of 800 Mbps. See *SDRAM.*

PC133 A type of synchronous DRAM (SDRAM) memory chip that is capable of working with 133 MHz motherboards. These chips produce a maximum data transfer rate of 1 GBps. See *SDRAM.*

PC150 A type of synchronous DRAM (SDRAM) memory chip that is capable of working with 150 MHz motherboards. These chips produce a maximum data transfer rate of 1.2 GBps. See *SDRAM.*

PC200 A type of double-data rate synchronous DRAM (DDR) memory chip that is used to assemble PC-1600 memory modules. See *DDR-SDRAM, PC-1600, SDRAM.*

PC266 A type of double-data rate synchronous DRAM (DDR) memory chip that is used to assemble PC-2100 memory modules. See *DDR-SDRAM, PC-1600, SDRAM.*

PC600 A type of Rambus DRAM memory chip that is capable of operating at a double-pumped rate of 532MHz. These chips produce a maximum data transfer rate of 1 GBps. See *Rambus DRAM*.

PC700 A type of Rambus DRAM memory chip that is capable of operating at a double-pumped rate of 712MHz. These chips produce a maximum data transfer rate of 1.4 GBps. See *Rambus DRAM*.

PC800 A type of Rambus DRAM memory chip that is capable of operating at a double-pumped rate of 800MHz. These chips produce a maximum data transfer rate of 1.6 GBps. See *Rambus DRAM*.

PC1600 A DDR-SDRAM memory module, composed of PC-200 memory chips, that can operate at a double-pumped rate of 200MHz (and with a maximum data transfer rate of 1.6 GBps).

PC2100 A DDR-SDRAM memory module, composed of PC-266 memory chips, that is capable of operating at a double-pumped rate of 266 MHz (and with a maximum data transfer rate of 2.1 GBps).

PC2600 A DDR-SDRAM memory module that is capable of running at a double-pumped rate of 333MHz (and with a maximum data transfer rate of 2.6 GBps).

PC card Formerly known as the PCMCIA card. A credit card-sized peripheral, such as a network card or modem, that is designed to connect to a PC card slot, usually in a portable computer. The PC card standard is regulated by the Personal Computer Memory Card International Association (PCMCIA). PC cards fall into three categories of varying thickness, called Type I (thin, used for memory cards), Type II (medium thickness, used for modems and other adapters), and Type III (thick, used for hard drives).

PC-DOS The version of the MS-DOS operating system released by IBM. PC-DOS is functionally identical to MS-DOS. See *MS-DOS*.

PCI Abbreviation for Peripheral Component Interface. A 32-bit expansion bus specification in wide use today and used on both PC-compatible and Macintosh computers. Intel Corporation released the PCI in 1992 to work with its Pentium microprocessor, but the design is flexible and works with today's 64-bit microprocessors as well. PCI has displaced the VESA local bus standard from the market and will likely soon do the same with the ISA expansion bus, although most motherboards still include a few ISA slots for downward compatibility. PCI supports Plug and Play, which likely will help cement its hold on the expansion bus market for the next several years. The original PCI specification called for a bus speed of 66 MHz, which is insufficient for today's microprocessors; for this reason, a new version of the standard, called PCI-X, has been developed. See *expansion bus*, *PCI-X*, *Plug and Play (PnP)*.

PCI slot A socket for adapters in a motherboard equipped with a PCI bus. The 32-bit PCI slots are preferred to VESA local bus slots and ISA slots because of their superior speed. See *PCI*.

PCI-X Acronym for Peripheral Component Interconnect (PCI) Extended. An updated version of the PCI expansion bus specification that increases the internal bus speed from 66 MHz to 133 MHz. PCI-X expansion busses are downwardly compatible with PCI adapters.

PCL See *printer control language*.

PCL3 The original, now-obsolete version of Hewlett-Packard's Printer Control Language (PCL). PCL3 supports only cartridge fonts and restricts users to only one font per page.

PCL4 An improved and widely used version of Hewlett-Packard's Printer Control Language (PCL) that supports downloadable fonts and multiple fonts on single pages.

PCL5 A version of Hewlett-Packard's Printer Control Language (PCL) that supports vector graphics and scalable fonts. PCL5 was first used on HP LaserJet III printers.

PCL5e A version of Hewlett-Packard's Printer Control Language (PCL), used on HP LaserJet printers, that supports bidirectional communication between printer and computer.

PCL6 An improved version of Hewlett-Packard's Printer Control Language that features a new, comprehensively modularized design and significantly increased performance. Although backwardly compatible with previous PCL specifications, PCL6 introduces a new command set.

PCM See *pulse code modulation.*

PCMCIA Acronym for Personal Computer Memory Card International Association, the organization that sets standards for the PCMCIA cards (now called PC cards) used mostly in notebook computers. See *PC card.*

PCMCIA card See *PC card.*

PCMCIA slot A slot (usually in a portable computer) designed to accept a PC card. See *PC card.*

p-code Synonymous with bytecode.

p-code compiler A type of interpreter that generates machine language from the incoming stream of bytecode, which is an intermediary between source code and compiled object code. The p-code compilers execute faster than source code interpreters, but they do not run as quickly as executable programs that have been compiled using a native compiler. See *Java.*

PCS Acronym for personal communications service. A U.S. standard for digital wireless telephony operating at 1900 MHz that makes a variety of services available, including paging, text-based Internet access by means of the Wireless Applications Protocol (WAP), and voice mail. Compared to analog cellular services operating at 800 MHz, PCS offers significantly improved battery life, lower noise, less interference, and freedom from eavesdropping. PCS is implemented in the U.S. by means of digital cellular telephony standards called CDMA and TDMA. Because PCS is a digital service, it is suitable (if far from ideal) for mobile wireless computing; for point-to-point (circuit-switched) connections, PCS offers data transfer rates of 14.4 Kbps. Emerging PCS standards for packet-switched data transfers will enable speeds of up to 384 Kbps for downloads. See *analog cellular phone, CDMA, circuit-switching network, packet-switching network, TDMA, WAP.*

PD See *public domain.*

PDA Acronym for personal digital assistant. A small, hand-held computer capable of accepting input that the user writes onscreen with a stylus. PDAs are designed to provide all the tools an individual would need for day-to-day organization. Such tools include an appointment calendar, an address book, a notepad, and a fax modem. See *Newton, Palm, pen computer, transceiver.*

PDF Acronym for Portable Document Format. A document file format created by Adobe Systems that makes extensive use of the PostScript printer description language; PDF is designed so that richly formatted documents (including fonts, graphics, and layout) can be viewed on any format capable of executing a PDF-compatible reader, such as Adobe Acrobat. Although Adobe claims a copyright in PDF's data structures, operators, and specifications, numerous open source implementations of PDF have emerged, to the point that PDF is well on its way to achieving world predominance as a means of presenting richly formatted content in the context of a cross-platform, international Internet.

PDL See *page description language.*

PDLC Acronym for program development life cycle. A step-by-step procedure used to develop software for information systems.

PDN See *public data network.*

PDS See *portable document software.*

peek In the various versions of the BASIC programming language, a statement that returns the value stored in a specific memory location. See *poke.*

peer-to-peer file transfer A file-sharing technique for local area networks (LANs) in which each user has access to the public files located on the workstation of any other network user. Each user determines which files, if any, he wants to make public for network access.

peer-to-peer network Any network without a central file server and in which all computers in the network have access to the public files located on all other workstations. See *client/server, P2P, peer-to-peer file transfer.*

pel Abbreviation for pixel.

PEM See *Privacy Enhanced Mail.*

pen computer A computer equipped with pattern-recognition circuitry so that it can recognize human handwriting as a form of data input. Some personal digital assistants (PDAs) use pen technology, but the high error rate has given handwriting recognition a poor reputation among users.

Pentium An Intel microprocessor, introduced in 1993, that introduced RISC-influenced design features to the Intel processor architecture, including pipelining and superscalar architecture. These innovations enabled the original Pentium chip to execute instructions at least 100% faster than a 486 chip operating at the same clock speed. The name "Pentium" was chosen in preference to "586," a name that, however logical in view of Intel's previous processor nomenclature, the company could not trademark. See *emulation, RISC.*

Pentium Classic A marketing term developed by Intel to refer to the second (P54C) version of the original Pentium microprocessor. See *Pentium.*

Pentium II A version of the sixth-generation Pentium Pro microprocessor, released in 1997, that runs 16-bit applications in an emulation mode (but more speedily than the widely criticized Pentium Pro); the processor is designed to run 32-bit applications natively. The Pentium II can be seen as an improved version of the Pentium Pro that includes the consumer-oriented innovations pioneered in the Pentium MMX. The processor was attached to the motherboard by means of a Single-Edge Concact Cartridge (SECC), which contained the L2 cache as well as the CPU. Best defined as a family of closely related processors, the Pentium II provided the basis for a range of products, including the Pentium II Xeon, the Celeron, the Pentium III, and the Pentium III Xeon. See *Intel Celeron, Intel Xeon, Pentium III.*

Pentium III The successor to Intel's sixth-generation Pentium II microprocessor; introduced in 1999, this chip is an improved version of its predecessor (the Pentium II) rather than a breakthrough in its own right; however, the improvements continued during the product's life. The earliest Pentium III chips incorporated an on-die L2 cache operating at full CPU speed, and used more advanced cache and buffering technology. For consumers, a key Pentium III innovation is Streaming SIMD Extensions (SIMD), which supports streaming video, engineering applications, speech recognition, and audio. The release of the Pentium III was shrouded in controversy when it was revealed that the chip contains a software-detectable processor serial number (PSN), which could disclose a user's identity to Web sites; PSN was removed from the third-generation Tualatin core. See *frontside bus, Pentium II, PSN, Streaming SIMD Extensions (SSE).*

Pentium 4 The successor to Intel's sixth-generation processors, including the Pentium II and Pentium III, this chip heralds the seventh generation of Intel processor technology. What is revolutionary about the Pentium 4 is its deep pipelining architecture; it is implemented in 20 stages (compared to 10 in the Pentium III). This enables the chip to run at significantly higher clock speeds than the Pentium III, which could not be pushed beyond 1.2 GHz. A tradeoff of this design is that the chip completes fewer executions per clock cycle. For this reason, early Pentium 4s were outperformed by Pentium III and Athlon processors running at lower clock speeds. Still, the Pentium 4's design enables Intel engineers to keep increasing the chip's clock speed to the point that this design tradeoff will become moot; experts believe that Intel will be able to push the Pentium 4's clock speed to as much as 15 GHz. Other improvements include system data bus speeds of up to 533 MHz when used with Rambus RDRAM memory, improved branch prediction, two arithmetic-logic units (ALU) that run at twice the chip's clock speed, and an expanded set of Streaming SIMD Extensions (SSE). See *arithmetic-logic unit (ALU), Athlon, clock speed, Pentium III, Rambus DRAM, Streaming SIMD Extensions (SSE)*.

Pentium MMX   An improved version of the original Pentium microprocessor, released in 1997, that included a set of multimedia extensions called MMX. These instructions were designed to run multimedia applications faster. The chip used a 4.1-million-transistor core and offered clock speeds of up to 300 MHz. When used with MMX-aware applications, these innovations increased the Pentium MMX's performance by as much as 60 percent over its predecessor. See *MMX, Pentium, SIMD*.

Pentium Pro   A 32-bit microprocessor designed and manufactured by Intel and introduced in 1996 that is specifically designed and optimized for executing 32-bit software. The first sixth-generation processor, the Pentium Pro implemented a radically new RISC-based architecture that ran 16-bit MS-DOS and Windows 3.1 applications through emulation; the result was that the Pentium Pro executed native 32-bit applications twice as fast as the original Pentium, but executed 16-bit applications more slowly. Code-named P6 during its development, the Pentium Pro incorporated sophisticated features of RISC design philosophy that enabled the processor to anticipate and schedule the future direction of program flow. See *branch prediction, DIB, Pentium, RISC, speculative execution*.

performance animation   See *motion capture*.

peripheral   A device such as a printer or disk drive connected to and controlled by a computer but external to the computer's central processing unit (CPU).

Peripheral Component Interconnect (PCI) Extended   See *PCI-X*.

Peripheral Component Interface   See *PCI*.

Perl   Acronym for Practical Extraction and Report Language. An interpreted scripting language that is specifically designed for scanning text files, extracting information from these files, and preparing reports summarizing this information. Written by Larry Wall, Perl is widely used to create Common Gateway Interface (CGI) scripts that handle the output of HTML forms. See *CGI, HTML, interpreter*.

permanent font   A Hewlett-Packard term for a font that, when downloaded to a laser printer, stays in the printer's memory until the printer is shut off. See *downloadable font, temporary font*.

permanent virtual circuit (PVC)   In telecommunications, a frame relay network configuration that creates the logical equivalent of a permanent leased line, but at a lower cost. Savings are introduced because frame relay enables service providers to combine multiple PVCs on a single circuit, using a technique called multiplexing.

permissions   See *file permissions*.

persistence   **1.** In hardware, a quality of the phosphor that coats the interior of a cathode ray tube (CRT) display. Persistence ensures that after being struck by the beam from an electron gun, a phosphor will continue to glow until the electron beam strikes it again. Persistence ensures that displays appear uniformly bright to human eyes. **2.** In object-oriented programming, one of the seven fundamental principles of the object model; the persistence principle states that an object should remain available even if its creator no longer exists or the object has been moved to a new location. See *object, object model, object-oriented programming.*

persistent connection In Microsoft Windows 95/98, a network connection that lasts longer than a single working session. A modem call to CompuServe is usually not a persistent connection, while an Ethernet connection to a network laser printer is. Windows 95/98 tries to establish persistent connections every time it starts.

personal area network (PAN) A computer network that is designed to serve the needs of an individual rather than a group. PANs are designed to integrate an individual's devices, including desktops computer, notebook computers, personal digital assistants (PDA), and digital cellular phones. Typically covering an area of only several dozen square feet, PANs can employ a variety of short-range physical media (including Bluetooth and 802.11 wireless radio LANs and IrDA infrared connectivity) in addition to the well-established Ethernet standard. See *Bluetooth, Ethernet, IEEE 802.11, IrDA.*

personal certificate A digital certificate attesting that a given individual who is trying to log on to an authenticated server really is the individual he claims to be. Personal certificates are issued by certificate authorities (CA).

personal communications service See *PCS.*

personal computer (PC) A small computer equipped with all the system, utility, and application software, as well as the input/output devices and other peripherals, that an individual needs to perform one or more tasks. The acronym PC is often used as a shorthand reference to the Intel-based IBM PC, the descendents of which account for between 80 and 90 percent of all personal computers sold.

Personal Computer Memory Card International Association (PCMCIA) See *PC card.*

personal digital assistant See *PDA.*

personal finance program A special-purpose application program that manages financial information. The best personal finance programs manage many types of information, including checking accounts, savings and investment plans, and credit card debt.

personal information manager (PIM) An application that stores and retrieves a variety of personal information, including notes, memos, names and addresses, and appointments. Unlike a database management program, a PIM is optimized for the storage and retrieval of a variety of personal information. One can switch among different views of his or her notes, such as people, to-do items, and expenses. PIM functionality has become part of PDAs (such as the Palm) and software such as Microsoft Outlook.

personal laser printer A laser printer designed to serve the printing needs of only one person, as opposed to a departmental laser printer that is designed to serve many people. Personal laser printers have monthly duty cycles of a few hundred pages.

personal productivity program Application software, such as word processing software or a spreadsheet program, that assists individuals in doing their work more effectively and efficiently.

petabyte (PB) A measurement unit of data storage capacity that is approximately equal to one quadrillion (10^{15}) bytes; it is exactly equal to 1,125,899,906,842,624 (2^{50}) bytes or 1,024 terabytes. One petabyte is approximately equal to the amount of information contained in leading U.S. research libraries. See *data storage capacity.*

petaflop A unit of measurement of computer performance that is equal to 1,000,000,000,000,000 (10^{15}) floating point operations per second (FLOPS). See *FLOP.*

p-frame In digital video formats that use interframe compression, such as MPEG video, a frame that is generated based on the source information provided by the i-frame that precedes it. See *b-frame*, *frame*, *i-frame*, *MPEG*.

PGA See *pin grid array*, *Professional Graphics Array.*

PGP See *Pretty Good Privacy.*

PgUp/PgDn keys See *Page Up/Page Down keys.*

phase In analog technologies, the displacement of a wave forward or backward from a specific point in the circuit. An example from human experience is jet lag, which shifts sleep cycles forward or backward from their usual schedule.

phono plug A connector with a short stem used to connect home audio devices. In computers, phono plugs are used for audio and composite monitor output ports. Synonymous with RCA plug.

phosphor An electrofluorescent material used to coat the inside face of a cathode ray tube (CRT). After being energized by the electron beam that is directed to the inside face of the tube, the phosphors glow for a fraction of a second, long enough to make the display appear uniformly bright to human eyes. The beam refreshes the phosphor many times per second to produce a consistent illumination. See *raster.*

Photo CD A standard for encoding photographs taken with ordinary 35-millimeter cameras and film onto CD-ROMs. Although PhotoCD technology has not become a big consumer hit, it is popular among publishers and some photographers.

PhotoGrade An Apple resolution-enhancement scheme that improves the appearance of grayscale images, such as photographs, when they are printed on a laser printer.

photo paper See *coated paper.*

photorealistic Of photographic quality. Printer output is said to be photorealistic when its colors are well-saturated and blend smoothly with one another.

photorealistic output printer Output that matches the quality of a chemically printed photograph. Thermal dye sublimation printers can generate photorealistic output with continuous tones, but they are very expensive, and the cost per page exceeds $3 because they require special coated paper.

PhotoShop See *image-editing software.*

phototypesetter See *imagesetter.*

PHP Acronym for PHP Hypertext Processor. A server-side, cross-platform scripting language that is designed to exploit the full potential of the most widely used Web server software, Apache. PHP scripts are embedded in HTML pages. When a Web browser accesses a PHP page, the Web server interprets the PHP script, constructs an HTML page on-the-fly based on the script's instructions, and provides the constructed page to the browser. PHP is derived from an older scripting language called Personal Home Page created by Rasmus Lerdorf in 1995; subsequently, an international team developed PHP 3.0, a complete rewrite. See *Apache*, *Web server.*

phrase search In a database program or Web search engine, a keyword search in which the search terms are surrounded by special markers (generally, quotation marks) to show that they form a phrase. The software returns only those items in which these words appear next to each other, and in exactly the same order as the supplied phrase. For example, an AltaVista search for "pipeline burst cache" returns only those Web pages that contain this exact phrase.

phreaking An illegal form of recreation that involves using one's knowledge of telephone system technology to make long-distance calls for free.

physical address The actual place in the computer's memory where data is stored, in contrast to a logical address; logical addresses are used in virtual memory systems, which are able to extend the computer's apparent memory capacity by using portions of the system's hard disk. See *virtual memory.*

physical drive   The disk drive actually performing the current read/write operation, as opposed to a logical drive, the existence of which is apparent only to the user of the system. A hard disk can be formatted into partitions, sections, and directories that have all the characteristics of a separate disk drive but are logical drives. The data, however, is actually encoded on the surface of a disk in either a floppy drive or a hard disk drive, which is referred to as the physical drive. See *floppy disk, secondary storage.*

physical format   See *low-level format.*

physical layer   In the OSI Reference Model of computer network architecture, the last of seven layers, in which the data is transformed into the electrical signals appropriate for the specific type of physical medium to which the computer is connected.

physical medium   In a computer network, the cabling through which network data travels. See *coaxial cable, fiber optics, T1, T3.*

physical memory   The actual random access memory (RAM) circuits in which data is stored, as opposed to virtual memory, the apparent RAM that results from using the computer's hard disk as an extension of physical memory. See *random access memory (RAM), virtual memory.*

physical network   The actual hardware (for example, NICs, cables, and routers) and software that form the network; as opposed to a logical network, the network that users perceive when they use their workstations. At the University of Virginia, for example, there are several physical networks made by a number of different LAN hardware manufacturers. However, the differences among these networks are not apparent or even discoverable by the students, faculty, and staff who log on to these networks; as far as they are concerned, there is a single logical network that makes all the university's

computer resources available and a broader global network (the Internet) that makes even more resources available. See *LAN, logical network.*

pica   **1.** In typography, a unit of measure equal to approximately ⅙ inch, or 12 points. Picas are used to describe horizontal and vertical measurements on the page, with the exception of type sizes, which are expressed in points. **2.** In formal typography, one pica is 0.166 of an inch, but in the interest of simplification, many word processing and page layout programs define one pica as ⅙ inch. **3.** In typewriting and letter-quality printing, pica is a 12-point monospace font that prints at a pitch of 10 characters per inch (cpi).

pico   Metric prefix for one-trillionth (10^{12}). Abbreviated p.

picosecond   One-trillionth (10^{12}) of a second.

PICS   Acronym for Platform for Internet Content Selection. A content description language, developed by the World Wide Web Consortium (W3C), that can be used to specify the appropriateness of a Web page's content for children.

PICT   A Macintosh graphics file format originally developed for the MacDraw program. An object-oriented graphics format, PICT files consist of separate graphics objects, such as lines, arcs, ovals, and rectangles, each of which can be independently edited, sized, moved, or colored. (PICT files also can store bitmapped graphics.) Some Windows graphics applications can read PICT files.

picture element   See *pixel.*

picture tube   See *cathode ray tube (CRT).*

pie graph   In presentation graphics, a graph that displays a data series as a circle to emphasize the relative contribution of each data item to the whole. Each slice of the pie appears in shades of gray or a distinctive pattern. Patterns can produce moiré distortions if one juxtaposes too many patterns. Some programs can produce paired pie graphs that display two data series. For presentations, exploding a slice from the whole is a useful technique to add emphasis. *See exploded pie graph, linked pie/column graph, moiré effect, proportional pie graph.*

pif Acronym for Program Information File. A file extension used to enable Microsoft Windows 95/98/ME to run older, 16-bit applications.

PIM See *personal information manager.*

pin **1.** A short wire that is employed to conduct current from a socket into an integrated circuit package. **2.** Acronym for personal identification number, a unique number that is used as a password for ATM and other electronic transactions.

pin-compatible Capable of fitting and operating in the same socket as another chip, especially one made by another manufacturer. See *Zero-Insertion Force (ZIF) socket.*

pincushion The bowing in of the sides of an image displayed on a computer monitor (the opposite effect, in which the sides bow out, is called barreling). Most monitors have a pincushion control that enables the user to correct this distortion.

pin feed See *tractor feed.*

ping **1.** Acronym for Packet Internet Groper. A diagnostic program that is commonly used to determine whether a computer is properly connected to the Internet; it is launched by issuing a textual command (ping) within the operating system's shell. The ping command is issued with an Internet address; the program attempts to contact the specified address. If it is successful, the program returns information concerning the time required for a round-trip transmission and the percentage of packets lost in the transmission. See *packet loss, shell.* **2.** Slang for contacting someone, as in "Ping Roxanne and ask her what she's doing for dinner."

pingable Capable of responding to PING; an Internet site that is "alive" and

should be capable of responding to Internet tools such as FTP and Gopher.

pin grid array (PGA) A rectangular or square package for a complex integrated circuit that connects to its socket by means of dozens of protruding pins, which are arranged in a grid. Because PGA packages have so many pins, they are usually inserted by means of a Zero-Insertion Force (ZIF) socket mechanisms, which keeps the pins from bending as the packet is inserted into the socket. See *Zero-Insertion Force (ZIF) socket.*

pin-out A table listing the functions assigned to electronic connectors.

PIO Acronym for Programmed Input/Output. A hard disk interface standard for transferring data from a hard disk. PIO employs the computer's CPU as part of the data path. An improved hard disk interface, Direct Memory Access (DMA), removes the CPU from the data path by enabling bus mastering, in which the hard disk takes over the task of controlling data transfers through the DMA interface. See *bus master, DMA.*

pipe In MS-DOS and Unix, an interprocess communication method in which the output of one command is sent to another command, rather than to the display. In the following example, the pipe (represented by the | symbol) tells DOS to send the output of the TREE command to the MORE command; the MORE command then displays the TREE result page by page onscreen:<C:\>TREE C:\ | MORE. See *filter, input/output (I/O) redirection.*

pipeline In computer processor design, an "assembly line" in the processor that dramatically speeds the processing of instructions through retrieval, execution, and writing data back to the memory. Within the pipeline, each step constitutes a functional unit that is optimally designed to perform one task, such as fetching instructions, decoding instructions, fetching arguments, performing arithmetic operations, or storing results. Because each of the pipeline's functional unit can work simultaneously, a processor can, in effect, process more than one instruction at a time. A microprocessor with two or more pipelines is said to employ superscalar architecture. Pipelines are one of several design characteristics of the reduced instruction set computer (RISC) architecture. See *pipeline stall, RISC, superscalar architecture.*

pipeline break See *pipeline stall.*

pipeline burst cache A secondary cache (also known as the L2 cache) that enables fast data transfer rates by spreading data fetches from memory over three clock cycles. This results in a slight delay initially, but it enables the cache to place requests in a queue so that subsequent fetches follow in just one clock cycle. Pipeline burst caches require synchronous SDRAM (chips that can synchronize with the microprocessor's clock). In addition, pipeline burst caches support burst mode transfers in which the SDRAM chips can deliver an entire line of cache contents when the processor requests just the first word in the line. See *SDRAM, secondary cache.*

pipeline stall A type of error in a RISC or RISC-influenced processor that delays the processing of an instruction. The error is an unavoidable result of the processor's design. RISC-based processors typically employ pipelines, in which instructions must be processed in a precise order. A problem arises when a program issues a branch instruction; in such cases, it is likely that the instructions that are just beginning to work their way through the pipeline will have to be discarded, generating a delay. Various techniques have been developed to reduce or eliminate delays, including branch prediction and out-of-order execution. Synonymous with pipeline break. See *branch prediction, out-of-order execution, pipeline, RISC.*

pipelining The use of pipelines in processor design. See *pipeline.*

piracy See *software piracy.*

Piranha A library of Linux software designed to facilitate clustering. See *Beowulf, clustering, Linux.*

pitch A horizontal measurement of the number of characters per linear inch in a monospace font, such as those used with typewriters, dot matrix printers, and daisy-wheel printers. By convention, pica pitch (not to be confused with the printer's measurement of approximately ⅙ inch) is equal to 10 characters per inch, and elite pitch is equal to 12 characters per inch. See *point.*

pixel Short for PICture ELement. A single point in a graphics image. The smallest element (a picture element) that a device can display and out of which the displayed image is constructed. See *bitmapped graphic.*

pixellation The out-of-focus, unattractive distortion that occurs when a bit-mapped graphic is enlarged too much. See *aliasing.*

PKCS Acronym for Public Key Cryptography Standards. A set of standards developed and maintained by a security industry consortium that defines a public key infrastructure (PKI) for encrypted data exchange on the Internet. The standards call for the use of the RSA encryption algorithm for digital certificates and secure e-mail. See *certificate, RSA encryption algorithm.*

PL/1 A high-level programming language, introduced in 1984 by IBM as part of its broader System 360 development effort. Like the System 360 computer series, PL/1 was designed to integrate the business and scientific sides of the computer industry; previous languages had appealed to business users (COBOL) or scientific users (FORTRAN), but not both. Although the PL/1 project was completed and the language has been used for mainframe software development, it was not considered to be successful; like other attempts to create comprehensive, "one-size-fits-all" programming languages, PL/1 was too complex for most programmers. See *COBOL, FORTRAN, high-level programming language.*

plain ASCII A text format that includes nothing but the basic set of ASCII characters. Synonymous with plain text.

Plain Old Telephone Service See *POTS*.

plain text A text format that contains nothing but the basic set of ASCII characters. Synonymous with plain ASCII.

plain vanilla Slang term for a simple computer or program that offers only the minimal or standard features. See *bells and whistles*.

Plan 9 An advanced operating system under development at Bell Laboratories that typifies the direction of operating system research: it moves the operating system from individual systems to the network. In so doing, it makes all network resources available to users in a seamless presentation; there is no obvious difference, for example, between local files and files on the network. See *distributed operating system, operating system (OS)*.

planar board See *motherboard*.

planar clock speed The clock speed at which the motherboard operates. This speed may differ from the clock speed of the microprocessor, which may be two or more times faster.

plan file A file in a Unix user's home directory that was originally intended to display a colleague's schedule and work plans for the future when accessed with the finger utility. It is more often used for compiling humorous quotations or other informal uses.

plasma display A display technology used with high-end laptop computers. The display is produced by energizing ionized gas held between two transparent panels. Synonymous with gas plasma display.

platen In dot matrix and letter-quality impact printers, the cylinder that guides paper through the printer and provides a backing surface for the paper when images are impressed onto the page.

platform A type of computer system defined by the type of hardware and operating system used. An example of a platform is the category of "Wintel" computers that have an Intel or Intel-compatible processor and are equipped with Microsoft Windows.

platform-dependent Not capable of functioning in a cross-platform environment; requiring a specific brand of computer or operating system to function. ActiveX controls are platform-dependent because they cannot run on any computer unless its operating system supports Microsoft-originated object linking and embedding (OLE).

Platform for Internet Content Selection See *PICS*.

platform-independent Capable of functioning in a computing network environment that connects computers made by several different manufacturers and running different operating systems. Java is platform-independent because it will execute on any computer system that is capable of running a Java interpreter.

plating A means of coating a hard disk platter with a thin-film magnetic medium. By submerging an electrically charged bare platter in a liquid containing oppositely charged molecules of the recording medium, the platter is evenly coated with the medium. See *sputtering*.

plot To construct an image by drawing lines.

plotter A printer that produces high-quality graphical output by moving ink pens over the surface of the paper. The printer moves the pens under the direction of the computer so that printing is automatic. Plotters are commonly used for computer-aided design (CAD) and presentation graphics.

plotter font In Microsoft Windows, a vector font designed to be used with a plotter. The font composes characters by generating dots connected by lines.

Plug and Play (PnP) A Microsoft-developed hardware standard for add-in hardware that enables the operating system to identify new hardware and locate the required software support. The standard has been succeeded by an Internet-capable standard called Universal Plug and Play (UPnP). See *Universal Plug and Play (UPnP).*

Plug and Play BIOS (PnP BIOS) A basic input-output system (BIOS) compatible with the Plug and Play standard that, when used in conjunction with a Plug and Play–compatible operating system (such as Microsoft Windows) and Plug and Play–compatible adapters, enables one to install adapters in the expansion bus without creating interrupt request (IRQ) conflicts or port conflicts. Note that a "plug and play" BIOS is not necessarily the same as a "Plug and Play" (capital letters) BIOS, which precisely conforms to the Plug and Play standard. See *BIOS, IRQ, Plug and Play (PnP), Universal Plug and Play (UPnP).*

Plug and Play object See *device node.*

Plug and Print A standard designed to improve the way printers and computers communicate. Developed by the Desktop Management Task Force (DMTF), Plug and Print creates a Management Information Base (MIB) or Management Information File (MIF) that contains details about a printer's operation. Plug and Print, an open standard, competes with Microsoft at Work, a standard designed to be used only by systems running Microsoft Windows. Synonymous with MIB/MI.

plug-compatible See *pin-compatible.*

plug-in A program module that is designed to directly interface with and give additional capability to a proprietary application, such as Adobe PhotoShop or Netscape Navigator. After installing the plug-in, the program takes on additional capabilities, which may be reflected in the appearance of new commands in the original application's menu system.

PMJI In online communications, shorthand for "pardon me for jumping in."

PMMU See *paged memory management unit.*

PMS See *Pantone Matching System.*

PNG Acronym for Portable Network Graphics. A bitmapped graphics format, similar to GIF, that does not use a patented compression algorithm. A major motivation for developing PNG is Unisys's actions in collecting licensing fees from software publishers for the use of GIF's LZW compression algorithm. The use of PNG graphics is expected to increase rapidly once the major browsers support it.

PnP See *Plug and Play.*

PnP BIOS See *Plug and Play BIOS.*

pocket modem An external modem about the size of a pack of cigarettes, designed for use with portable computers. Pocket modems have been largely replaced by PCMCIA modems.

point 1. To move the mouse pointer onscreen without clicking the button. 2. In typography, a fundamental unit of measurement (72 points equal approximately 1 inch). Computer programs usually ignore this slight discrepancy, making a point exactly equal to $\frac{1}{72}$ inch. See *pica, pitch.*

pointer 1. In a graphical user interface (GUI), an onscreen symbol (usually an arrow) that shows the current position of the mouse. 2. In database management programs, a record number in an index that stores the actual physical location of the data record. 3. In programming, a variable that contains directions to (points to) another variable. Pointers enable programmers to set many variables equal to one another without lots of assignment statements.

pointing device An input device such as a mouse, trackball, or graphics tablet used to manipulate a pointer onscreen.

pointing stick A pencil eraser-sized, rubberized device in the center of the keyboard, which is moved with the fingertip to relocate the cursor onscreen. Although pointing sticks originated in portable computers and are often used in them, pointing sticks appear on some desktop computers as well.

point of presence (POP) In a wide area network (WAN), a locality in which it is possible to obtain dial-up access to the network by means of a local telephone call. Internet service providers (ISP) provide POPs in towns and cities, but many rural areas are without local POPs.

point-of-sale software A program such as a bar code reader that automatically makes adjustments to accounting and inventory databases as a business sells merchandise.

Point-to-Point Protocol See *PPP.*

Point-to-Point Tunneling Protocol See *PPTP.*

poke In the various versions of the BASIC programming language, a statement that places a value in a specific memory location. See *peek.*

polarity **1.** In electronics, the negative or positive property of a charge. **2.** In graphics, the tonal relationship between foreground and background elements. Positive polarity is the printing of black or dark characters on a white or light background; negative polarity is the printing of white or light characters on a black or dark background.

polarization A physical phenomenon, in which light waves vibrate in a single plane, that is part of the foundation of magneto-optical (MO) disc drive technology. Along with the Kerr effect, polarization is at the core of how MO drives read and write data.

Polish notation See *Reverse Polish Notation (RPN).*

poll To request status information concerning a peripheral or remote data service to determine whether a connection is possible.

polling In local area networks (LANs), a method for controlling channel access in which the central computer continuously asks or polls the workstations to determine whether they have information to send. With polling channel access, one can specify how often and for how long the central computer polls the workstations. Unlike CSMA/CD and token-ring channel-access methods, the network manager can give some nodes more access to the network than others. See *CSMA/CD, token ring network.*

polyline In graphics, a drawing tool used to create a multisided, enclosed shape. To use the tool, draw a straight line to a point, and then continue the line in a different direction to a point. By continuing this operation until returning to the starting point, one can create a complex object of his or her own design. The result is a graphics primitive, which the program treats as a single object. Like the more familiar primitives (squares or circles), the polyline object can be independently edited, sized, moved, or colored. Some programs call this tool a polygon. See *vector graphics.*

polyphony In sound boards, the reproduction of multiple sounds at one time. High-end sound boards can put out 20 or more sounds at once.

POP See *point of presence, POP-3.*

POP-3 Also spelled POP3. Acronym for Post Office Protocol. An Internet e-mail standard that specifies how an Internet-connected computer can function as a mail-handling agent; the current version is called POP-3. Messages arrive at a user's electronic mailbox, which is housed on the service provider's computer. From this central storage point, one can access his or her mail from different computers, a networked workstation in the office, as well as a PC at home. In either case, a POP-compatible e-mail program, which runs on a workstation or PC, establishes a connection with the POP server and detects that new mail has arrived. One can then download the mail to his or her workstation or computer and reply to it, print it, or store it. POP does not send mail; that job is handled by SMTP. An alternative protocol is IMAP, in which all of a user's mail is stored at a central location rather than downloaded. IMAP is significantly more convenient for mobile users than POP-3. See *e-mail, IMAP.*

pop-up menu A menu that appears when a certain onscreen item is selected, such as text, a scroll bar, or a dialog box option. The name does not truly reflect a direction. If a pop-up menu appears too close to the top of the screen, it pops down. Microsoft Windows makes extensive use of pop-up menus, both for editing and for tutorial tasks. See *pull-down menu.*

port 1. An interface that governs and synchronizes the flow of data between the central processing unit (CPU) and external devices such as printers and modems. See *parallel port, serial port.* **2.** On the Internet, a logical channel through which a certain type of application data is routed to decode incoming data and route it to the correct destination. Each type of Internet service, such as FTP or IRC, has a certain port number associated with it. Port number assignments are controlled by the Internet Assigned Numbers Authority (IANA). **3.** To modify or translate a program so that it will run on a different computer.

portability A measure of the ease with which a given program can be made to function in a different computing environment, such as a different brand of computer or operating system. Programs written in C are said to be highly portable because only a small portion of the code needs to be written with the specifics of a particular computer in mind.

portable Capable of working on a variety of hardware platforms or working with differing applications. Unix and Unix-like operating systems such as Linux are examples of portable operating systems. Most operating systems are designed around the specific electronic capabilities of a given central processing unit (CPU). In contrast, a portable operating system such as Unix is designed with a predetermined, overall structure. Specific machine instructions are embedded within a program module that allows it to function on a given CPU. See *Linux, operating system (OS), Unix.*

portable computer A computer with a screen and keyboard built in and designed to be transported easily from one location to another. The first portable personal computers, such as the Osborne I and Compaq II, are best described as "luggables." These computers weighed in at more than 25 pounds and could not be carried comfortably for more than a short distance. Today's battery-powered laptop and notebook computers are much smaller and lighter. See *laptop computer, notebook computer, palmtop, PDA.*

portable document A richly formatted document, which may contain graphics as well as text, that can be transferred to another type of computer system without losing the formatting. To create portable documents, one needs portable document software (PDS), such as Adobe Acrobat, that is designed to save the formatting information to a file that can be easily transferred to a different type of computer system. To read the document, one needs a file viewer program that is specifically designed to work on the type of computer one is using. For example, one can create an Adobe Acrobat document on a Macintosh and give the file to somebody using a Sun workstation. To read the file, the Sun user needs a copy of the Adobe Acrobat reader program. See *PDF.*

Portable Document Format See *PDF.*

portable document software (PDS) A category of applications that can create portable documents, which can be transferred to different types of computer systems without losing their rich formatting and graphics. Two types of software are required: the document publishing program and a file viewer. The document publishing program creates a coded ASCII file that retains fonts, graphics, and layout information. This file can be distributed electronically by means of online services such as CompuServe or the Internet. File viewers, which are designed to run on a specific type of computer, enable users to read these files and to see a replica of the original document's fonts, graphics, and layout. The most popular PDS is Adobe Acrobat, thanks to the widespread Internet availability of free file viewers for a wide variety of computer systems.

Portable Network Graphics See *PNG*.

Portable Operating System Interface See *POSIX*.

portal On the Web, a page that attempts to provide an attractive starting point for Web sessions. Typically included are links to breaking news, weather forecasts, stock quotes, free e-mail service, sports scores, and a subject guide to information available on the Web. Leading portals include Netscape's NetCenter (www.Netcenter.com), Yahoo! (www.yahoo.com), and Snap (www.snap.com).

port conflict An error that occurs when two devices, such as a mouse and a modem, try to access the same serial port at one time. If possible, a user should set his or her mouse to serial port COM1 and his or her modem to serial port COM2, and disable all other serial ports because using them may cause problems.

port number A number that identifies the location of a particular Internet application, such as FTP, a World Wide Web (WWW) server, or Gopher, on a computer that is directly connected to the Internet. Regulated by the Internet Assigned Numbers Authority (IANA), port numbers are included in the headers of every Internet packet; the numbers tell the receiving software where to deliver the incoming data. See *well-known port number*.

portrait font A font oriented toward the short edges of a page. This book is printed with a portrait font.

portrait monitor See *full-page display*.

portrait orientation The default printing orientation for a page of text in which

the height of the page is greater than the width. See *landscape orientation*.

port replicator A hardware device containing standard parallel ports and serial ports that is designed to plug into a special receptacle in a notebook computer. The purpose of the replicator is to enable notebook users to plug in a printer and monitor quickly and easily.

POSIX Acronym for Portable Operating System Interface. A set of standards, developed by the IEEE in 1985, that defines how programs can be written so that they will run correctly on any POSIX-compatible version of Unix. The POSIX standard is proprietary and the standards documents are expensive. In addition, it is considered out of date. For this reason, operating system developers prefer to use the Single UNIX Specification standard, which was developed by the Open Group.

post **1.** In a newsgroup, to send a message so that it can be read by everyone who accesses the group. **2.** In database management, to add data to a data record.

POST See *Power-On Self-Test*.

postcardware A type of freeware save in which the author requests that those who wish to continue to use the program send the author a postcard.

postcondition In computer programming, a sanity check that is performed when a function or subroutine finishes running; the postcondition (such as *copies <100*) makes sure that the returned value does not exceed a stated range of acceptable values. See *function, subroutine*.

postfix notation See *Reverse Polish Notation (RPN)*.

postmaster In a network, the human administrator who configures the e-mail manager and handles problems that arise.

post-mortem debugger A type of bug-checking program that comes into play after a program has crashed. An example is the Dr. Watson utility that is included with

Microsoft Windows. Many programs are designed to keep an error log, which may contain information that explains the program's abnormal termination.

Post Office Protocol See *POP-3.*

post-processing Modification of data after it has been captured, generated, or recorded. For example, photo-editing programs incorporate post-processing utilities that enable digital camera users to eliminate or reduce the "red eye" artifacts in portraits taken with an electronic flash.

postprocessor A program that performs a final, automatic processing operation after a person finishes working with a file. Postprocessors include text formatters that prepare a document for printing and page description languages that convert an onscreen document into a set of commands that the printer's interpreter can recognize and use to print the document.

post-production In digital video, the final stage in the preparation of a finished video, in which the video is edited, assembled, and titled.

PostScript A sophisticated page description language (PDL), developed by Adobe Systems, Incorporated, that is used for high-quality printing on laser printers and other high-resolution printing devices. PostScript is capable of describing the entire appearance of a richly formatted page, including layout, fonts, graphics, and scanned images. Although PostScript is a programming language and one can learn to write page descriptions in it, programs generate PostScript code on-the-fly; the code goes to a display device (such as a printer, slide recorder, imagesetter, screen display, or PostScript printer), where a PostScript interpreter follows the coded instructions to generate an image of the page precisely according to these instructions. A major benefit of PostScript is its device-independence; one can print the PostScript code generated by an application on any printer with a PostScript interpreter. One can take PostScript files generated on his or her PC to a service bureau, which can print the document using expensive typesetting machines called imagesetters with resolutions of up to 2,400 dots per inch (dpi). See *page description language (PDL), PostScript font, PostScript printer.*

PostScript font A scalable outline font that conforms to Adobe Software's specifications for Type 1 fonts, which require a PostScript printer. Unlike bitmapped fonts, which often print with crude edges and curves, PostScript's outline font technology produces smooth letters that a printer renders at its maximum possible resolution. A PostScript font comes with a screen font, which simulates the font's appearance onscreen, and a printer font, which must either be built into a printer or be downloaded to the printer before printing. Note that the type may look jagged onscreen unless one buys Adobe Type Manager, which brings PostScript scalable font technology to the display screen.

PostScript Level 2 An improved version of PostScript that is faster and that supports color printing and file compression.

PostScript Level 3 The latest version of PostScript, which includes further color optimization as well as support for network and Web publishing.

PostScript printer A printer, generally a laser printer, that includes the processing circuitry needed to decode and interpret printing instructions phrased in PostScript, a page description language (PDL) widely used in desktop publishing. Because PostScript printers require their own microprocessor circuitry and at least 1MB of random access memory (RAM) to image each page, they are more expensive than non-PostScript printers. However, they can print text or graphics in subtle gradations of gray. They can also use Encapsulated PostScript (EPS) graphics and outline fonts, both of which can be sized and scaled without introducing distortions.

posture The slant of the characters in a font. Italic characters slant to the right, but the term italic is reserved by conservative typographers for custom-designed (as opposed to electronically produced) serif typefaces.

POTS Acronym for Plain Old Telephone Service. The traditional analog telephone system, which is adequate for voice communication and slow data communication with modems, but that lacks sufficient bandwidth to handle high-speed digital communications. Telephone companies must upgrade some of their equipment before they can offer faster Internet access, such as ADSL.Alternatives to telephone-based Internet access include cable modems and Digital Broadcast Satellite (DBS).

pound sign The "#" character on the standard keyboard. Also called hash.

power down To turn off a device.

power line filter An electrical device that smoothes out the peaks and valleys of the voltage delivered at the wall socket. Every electrical circuit is subject to voltage fluctuations; if these are extreme, they may cause computer errors and failures. If using a computer in a circuit shared by heavy appliances, one may need a power line filter to ensure error-free operation. See *surge protector.*

Power Macintosh A line of Apple Macintosh computers that use PowerPC (RISC-based) microprocessors. Power Macs, introduced in 1994, perform best when using native PowerPC applications; they run software written for previous Macintoshes (based on the Motorola 680x0 architecture) only by means of emulation. See *PowerPC.*

power management A microprocessor feature that reduces a computer's consumption of electricity by turning off peripherals such as monitors and hard disks during periods of nonuse. Although power management features are not part of all microprocessors, they are commonly found in chips used in portable computers because energy savings equates to longer battery life in those machines. See *green PC, sleep mode.*

Power-On Self-Test (POST) Internal testing performed when starting or resetting a computer. Encoded in read-only memory (ROM), the POST program first checks the microprocessor by having it perform a few simple operations. Then it reads the CMOS ROM, which stores the amount of memory and type of disk drives in a system. Next, the POST writes and then reads various data patterns to each byte of memory (one can watch the bytes count off onscreen and often end the test with a keystroke). Finally, the POST communicates with every device; one sees the keyboard and drive lights flash, and the printer resets, for example. The BIOS continues with hardware testing and then looks in drive A for an operating system; if drive A is not found, it looks in drive C. See *BIOS, boot sector.*

power outage A sudden loss of electrical power, causing all unsaved information on a computer to be lost.

PowerPC A reduced instruction set computer (RISC) microprocessor jointly developed by Apple Computer, IBM, and Motorola. Power PC chips provide the processing capabilities for Apple Computer's Power Macintosh system. The most recent PowerPC chips, which Apple called the G3 and G4, have helped Apple reverse its declining market share. See *G3, G4, Macintosh.*

PowerPC 601 The first of the PowerPC microprocessors jointly developed by IBM, Apple, and Motorola. The PowerPC 601 is a 32-bit microprocessor that employs superscalar architecture and a portion of reduced instruction set computer (RISC) technology. The PowerPC 601 was used in the first Power Macintoshes. The 601 chip runs at 80 MHz.

PowerPC 601v A version of the PowerPC 601 that uses 0.5-micron technology and an increased clock speed of 100 MHz to improve performance and reduce power consumption.

PowerPC 602 A 32-bit microprocessor designed for budget-minded computer users. The PowerPC 602 runs at a clock speed of 66 MHz and uses reduced instruction set computer (RISC) technology. See *PowerPC 601*.

PowerPC 603 A 32-bit microprocessor, similar in performance to the PowerPC 601, designed for situations such as portable computing in which power conservation is key. Available with clock speeds of 66 MHz and 80 MHz, the PowerPC 603 has a smaller internal cache than the PowerPC 601, but it uses 0.5-micron technology to reduce its power demand to only 2 watts. See *PowerPC 601, PowerPC 603e*.

PowerPC 603e A version of the PowerPC 603 that includes even more power-management features. Versions are available with clock speeds of up to 300 MHz.

PowerPC 604 A 64-bit microprocessor that incorporates reduced instruction set computing (RISC) technology and branch prediction techniques to achieve a CINT92 score of 160. The PowerPC 604, which runs at a clock speed of 100 MHz, is faster than the PowerPC 601 but considerably slower than the PowerPC 620. See *PowerPC 601*.

PowerPC 620 Designed for servers in local area networks (LANs), the PowerPC 620 is twice as fast as the PowerPC 604 thanks to a pre-decode step in the pipeline, a large internal cache, and excellent branch prediction capabilities. A 64-bit microprocessor that employs reduced instruction set computer (RISC) technology, the PowerPC 620 runs at 133 MHz and, due in part to its use of 0.5-micron technology, draws only 3.3 volts. See *PowerPC 601*.

PowerPC 750 Designed for consumer and notebook computers, this is the same microprocessor described as the G3 in Apple Computer's marketing. With clock speeds of 400 MHz and higher and an onboard L2 cache controller, the G3 offers performance that exceeds that of a comparable Pentium II processor running at the same clock speed. See *G3*.

PowerPC 74xx The family of microprocessors which are the successors to the PowerPC 750, this microprocessor is pin-compatible with its predecessor but offers faster clock speeds (well past the 1 GHz mark) and faster multimedia processing. Apple Computer uses the term G4 for these chips. See *G4*.

power save mode In a portable computer, an operating mode in which the system automatically switches into a power-conserving state after a specified period of inactivity. Typically, the computer shuts down the display and disk drive. These are automatically reactivated when the user presses a key or moves the pointing device.

power supply A device that provides the power to electronic equipment. In a computer system, the power supply converts standard AC current to the lower voltage DC current used by the computer.

power surge See *surge*.

power up To turn on a device.

power user A computer user who has gone beyond the beginning and intermediate stages of computer use. Such a person uses the advanced features of application programs, such as software command languages and macros, and can learn new application programs quickly. See *naive user*.

PPC See *PowerPC*.

ppm See *pages per minute*.

PPP Acronym for Point-to-Point Protocol. One of the two standards for directly connecting computers to the Internet via dial-up telephone connections (the other is SLIP). Unlike the older SLIP protocol, PPP incorporates superior data negotiation, compression, and error correction. However, these features add overhead to data transmission and are unnecessary when both the sending and receiving modems offer hardware error correction and on-the-fly data compression. See *SLIP*.

PPPoE Acronym for PPP Over Ethernet. A proposed standard for implementing virtual Point-to-Point Protocol (PPP) connections over broadband networks, such as cable Internet access and DSL, that present themselves to clients as if they were Ethernet networks. PPPoE enables PC users and Internet service providers alike to use familiar techniques, such as establishing connections by a process identical to dialing an ISP with a modem. See *cable modem, DSL, Ethernet, PPP.*

PPP Over Ethernet   See *PPPoE.*

PPTP   Acronym for Point-to-Point Tunneling Protocol. An extension of PPP that enables remote users of a corporate local area network (LAN) to access the internal network by means of protocol tunneling, in which the LAN data is encapsulated within TCP/IP and encrypted for secure, confidential transmission via the Internet. In effect, PPTP enables companies to create virtual private networks (VPNs), which employ inexpensive Internet connections as a communications medium rather than pricey private data networks (PDNs). Developed jointly by Microsoft Corporation and modem makers, the protocol enables companies to extend their LANs securely to remote users without posing a serious security risk. The protocol has been submitted to the Internet Engineering Task Force (IETF) for ratification as an Internet standard but is currently supported only by Microsoft Windows NT Server.

Practical Extraction and Report Language   See *Perl.*

PRAM   See *parameter RAM.*

precedence   The order in which a program performs the operations in a formula. Typically, the program performs exponentiation (such as squaring a number) before multiplication and division and then performs addition and subtraction.

precision   The number of digits past the decimal that are used to express a quantity. See *accuracy.*

pre-decode stage   In microprocessors that employ superscalar architectures, a step in the processing of instructions in which the microprocessor determines what resources, such as registers, will be needed to process a particular instruction. A pre-decode stage allows instructions to move through a pipeline faster.

preemptive multitasking   In an operating system, a means of running more than one task (executing process) at a time. In preemptive multitasking, the operating system uses a task scheduling algorithm to decide which task should receive the processor's attention; if necessary, the processor can preempt a process's access to the CPU. In contrast to cooperative multitasking, in which a busy application could monopolize the computer for as much as several minutes, a computer with a preemptive multitasking system seems much more responsive to user commands. Operating systems that employ preemptive multitasking (including Linux, Mac OS X, Microsoft Windows NT, Microsoft Windows 2000, Microsoft Windows XP, and Unix) can prevent tasks from invading each other's memory space, so they are considerably more stable than operating systems (such as Microsoft Windows 3.1) that cannot provide this protection (called protected memory). See *cooperative multitasking, task, task scheduling algorithm.*

prefix notation   In a programming language, a method of ordering operators and operands such that the operator precedes all the operands. In prefix notation, the asterisk (*) operator, symbolizing multiplication, precedes the numbers to be multiplied, as in the following example: * 2 4. This operation yields 8. See *infix notation, Reverse Polish Notation (RPN).*

presentation   In a markup language, the appearance of the document (including formatting), as opposed to the structure of the document (the components of the document, such as titles, headings, and lists). Markup language theory calls for a clear distinction between presentation and structural markup; the markup language should handle structure only, while separate style sheet languages (such as CSS) are used for presentation purposes.

presentation graphics The branch of the graphics profession that is concerned with the preparation of slides, transparencies, and handouts for use in business presentations. Ideally, presentation graphics combines artistry with practical psychology and good taste; color, form, and emphasis are used intelligently to convey the presentation's most significant points to the audience. See *analytical graphics.*

presentation graphics program An application designed to create and enhance charts and graphs so that they are visually appealing and easily understood by an audience. A full-featured presentation graphics package such as Lotus Freelance Graphics or Microsoft PowerPoint includes facilities for making a wide variety of charts and graphs and for adding titles, legends, and explanatory text anywhere in the chart or graph. A presentation graphics program also typically includes a library of clip art so that one can enliven charts and graphs by adding a picture related to the subject matter — for example, an airplane for a chart of earnings in the aerospace industry. One can print output, direct output to a film recorder, or display output onscreen as a computer slide show. See *Microsoft PowerPoint.*

presentation layer In the OSI Reference Model of computer network architecture, the second of seven layers, in which data passed down the protocol stack from the top-most layer (the application layer) is reorganized so that it conforms to international standards for the coding of data types. (The term "presentation" is somewhat misleading, in that it implies that the data is being prepared for presentation to the user; that is the function of the application layer.) See *OSI Reference Model.*

Pretty Good Privacy (PGP) A comprehensive cryptosystem for private e-mail created by Phil Zimmerman. PGP uses a public-key encryption algorithm for initial key exchange and employs the International Data Encryption Algorithm (IDEA) to encrypt data after keys have been exchanged. A unique feature of the PGP mail model is the use of circles of trust for authenticating the sender of a message; instead of validating digital signatures by means of a certificate authority (CA), PGP enables users to digitally sign other peoples' certificates, attesting that they know them personally and can vouch that the signature in question really came from that person and no other. See *encryption.*

PRI An ISDN standard that is designed to meet the needs of a small- to medium-sized business. The service provides 23 B channels that can transfer data at 56 or 64 Kbps, as well as one signaling channel.

primary cache Cache memory built into the microprocessor, instead of located on the motherboard like secondary cache memory, which is also called L2 cache. Primary cache is synonymous with internal cache, L1 cache, and onboard cache. See *secondary cache.*

primary domain controller See *domain controller.*

primary key In a database sort, a data field that is selected as the means by which all the data is to be sorted or alphabetized. For example, if a database user wishes to sort a lengthy list of names and addresses by ZIP code, the ZIP code is the primary key. Additional keys (the secondary key, the tertiary key, and so on) are used to order the data at subsequent levels; for example, after all the names and addresses from the ZIP code 22901 have been grouped together, they can be sorted secondarily by street address or name.

Primary Rate Interface (PRI) A high-capacity ISDN service that provides twenty-three 64 Kbps channels and one channel for carrying control information. PRI is designed for business use.

primary storage The computer's main memory, which consists of the random access memory (RAM) and the read-only memory (ROM) that is directly accessible to the central processing unit (CPU).

primitive A command or operator that is considered so basic in its utility that it is embedded within the basic functionality of the operating system or a programming language; an example is the standard set of arithmetic functions (addition, subtraction, multiplication, and division).

printed circuit board A thin plastic sheet, coated with a copper sheet, in which the connections between electronic devices have been created by the use of a photo-resist mask and acid etching. Printed circuit boards can be mass-produced at low cost.

print engine In a laser printer, the mechanism that uses a laser to create an electrostatic image of a page and fuse that image to a sheet of paper. One can distinguish print engines by their resolution, print quality, longevity, paper-handling features, and speed.

printer A computer peripheral designed to print computer-generated text or graphics on paper or other physical media. See *dot-matrix printer, inkjet printer, laser printer, letter-quality printer, thermal printer.*

printer control language A set of commands that tells a printer and printer driver how to print a document. Printer control languages are usually proprietary—Hewlett-Packard's Printer Control Language (note the capital letters) for laser printers is a very common example—and are different from page description languages (PDLs), such as PostScript, which are somewhat limited programming languages recognized by many manufacturers. See *PCL3, PCL4, PCL5, PCL5e.*

Printer Control Language (PCL) The printer control language used by Hewlett-Packard laser printers. See *PCL3, PCL4, PCL5e.*

printer driver A file that contains the information a program needs to print work with a given brand and model of printer. A major difference between the DOS environment and the Macintosh/Windows environments is the way printer drivers are handled. In the MS-DOS environment, printer drivers are the responsibility of application programs. Each program must come equipped with its own printer drivers for the many dozens of printers available; if a program does not include a driver for a printer, the user may be out of luck. The Microsoft Windows and Macintosh operating environments, on the other hand, provide printer drivers for all Windows applications, freeing application software from that responsibility.

printer emulation The capability of a printer to recognize the printer control language of a different printer. Widely emulated are Epson and Hewlett-Packard printers.

printer font A font that does not appear onscreen and that is available for use only by the printer. When using a printer font, one sees a generic screen font onscreen; he or she must wait until printing is complete to see his or her document's fonts. Ideally, screen and printer fonts should be identical; only then can a computer system claim to offer what-you-see-is-what-you-get (WYSIWYG) text processing. Character-based programs, such as WordPerfect 5.1, running under DOS cannot display typefaces other than those built into the computer's ROM. With Microsoft Windows and Macintosh systems, one can use TrueType or Adobe Type Manager (ATM) outline (scalable) fonts, which appear onscreen the way they appear when printed. See *outline font.*

printer maintenance Regular procedures, such as cleaning, that keep a printer operating without problems. Laser printers require periodic cleaning of their rollers, corona wires, and lenses.

printer port See *parallel port, serial port.*

print head   The mechanism that actually does the printing in a printer. There are several kinds of print head technologies, including impact (found in impact printers), thermal (found in thermal printers), inkjet (found in inkjet printers), and electrostatic (found in laser printers).

print queue   A list of files that a print spooler prints in the background while the computer performs other tasks in the foreground.

Print Screen (PrtScr)   On IBM PC–compatible keyboards, a key one can use to print an image of the screen display.

print server   In a local area network (LAN), a PC that has been dedicated to receiving and temporarily storing files to be printed, which are then doled out one by one to a printer. The print server, accessible to all the workstations in the network, runs print spooler software to manage a print queue.

print spooler   A utility program that temporarily stores files to be printed in a print queue and then doles them out one by one to the printer. See *background printing, print server.*

priority   An index of the precedence given to an operation that is competing for access to a shared resource, such as a printer, a network connection, or the CPU. Operations that are assigned low priority can run in the background, becoming active only when the system has been idle for a given period. Operations that are assigned high priority take precedence over those with lower priority. In multitasking operating systems that enable priority scheduling (including Linux, Mac OS X, Microsoft Windows 2000, Microsoft Windows XP, and Unix), users may alter the priority assigned to executing tasks. See *multitasking, priority scheduling, task.*

priority scheduling   In multitasking operating systems, a task scheduling algorithm that assigns default priorities to tasks competing for usage of the CPU. High priority tasks take precedence over low priority tasks. Users may alter the priorities given to executing tasks. See *multitasking, priority, task, task scheduling algorithm.*

privacy   On a network, a presumed right that one's disk storage area, e-mail, and files will not be scrutinized by persons to whom he or she has not given permission. However, privacy on a computer network does not exist. Although the federal Electronic Communications Privacy Act (1986) prohibits federal agencies from accessing e-mail while it is in transit or temporary storage, no federal law prevents employers or other persons from doing so. Many employers believe that they can read employees' mail with impunity; after all, employees are using the employer's equipment. One can protect his or her privacy by encrypting his or her messages. See *encryption, Privacy Enhanced Mail (PEM).*

Privacy Enhanced Mail (PEM)   An Internet standard that ensures the privacy of e-mail. PEM uses public key encryption techniques to ensure that only the intended recipient of the message will be able to read it. PEM is little used because the encryption algorithm PEM employs is patented; the MIME/S protocol, implemented in the e-mail utilities of Microsoft Internet Explorer and Netscape Navigator (beginning with Version 4.0 of the two products) is the preferred protocol for private e-mail on the Internet.

PRML read-channel technology   Abbreviation for partial-response maximum-likelihood read-channel technology. A design philosophy for hard disks that improves throughput and a real density. Typically used with magneto-resistive heads, PRML read-channel technology is very expensive and is found only on a few high-end hard disks for network servers.

problem user   In a computer network, a user that violates the network's acceptable use policies (AUP), such as by mailing unsolicited advertising, harassing other users, or attempting to gain unauthorized access to other computer systems.

procedural programming language
A programming language such as BASIC or Pascal that requires the programmer to specify the procedure the computer must follow to accomplish the task. See *declarative programming language*.

process   In operating systems designed for server applications (including Windows 2000, Unix, and Linux), an executing program or service. A parent process may have one or more child processes that perform additional tasks.

process color   One of the four colors—cyan, magenta, yellow, and black—that are mixed to create other colors. See *CMYK color model, color model, spot color.*

processing   The execution of program instructions by the computer's central processing unit (CPU) that in some way transforms data, such as sorting it, selecting some of it according to specified criteria, or performing mathematical computations on it.

processor   See *microprocessor*.

processor serial number   See *PSN*.

processor upgrade   A chip designed to replace or complement a microprocessor and provide improved performance. Intel's OverDrive chip is a processor upgrade for the Intel 80486. Also, the act of installing such a chip.

production   In digital video, the phase in which the raw footage is shot. See *post-production*.

Professional Graphics Array (PGA)
An early video adapter for IBM personal computers that was designed for computer-assisted design (CAD) applications. The adapter displays 256 colors with a resolution of 640 × 480.

professional workstation   A high-performance personal computer optimized for professional applications in fields such as digital circuit design, architecture, and technical drawing. Professional workstations typically offer excellent screen resolution, fast and powerful microprocessors, and lots of memory. Examples include the workstations made by Sun Microsystems and NeXT, Inc. Professional workstations are more expensive than personal computers and typically use the Unix operating system. The boundary between high-end personal computers and professional workstations, however, is eroding as personal computers become more powerful.

program   A list of instructions, written in a programming language, that a computer can execute so that the machine acts in a predetermined way. Synonymous with software. See *compiler, executable program, high-level programming language, machine language, source code.*

program development life cycle   See *PDLC*.

program generator   A program that creates the program code automatically from a description of the application. In database management programs, for example, one can use simple program-generation techniques to describe the format he or she wants graphically. The program generator then uses the input as a set of parameters by which to build the output program code.

Program Information File   See *pif*.

programmable   Capable of being controlled through instructions that can be varied to suit the user's needs.

programmable read-only memory
See *PROM*.

programmer   A person who designs, codes, tests, debugs, and documents a computer program. Professional programmers often hold bachelor of science or master of science degrees in computer science, but a great deal of programming (professional and otherwise) is done by individuals with little or no formal training. More than half the readers of a popular personal computer magazine, for example, stated in a survey that they regularly programmed their personal computers using languages such as BASIC, Pascal, and assembly language.

programmer/analyst　A person who performs system analysis and design functions as well as programming activities. See *programmer.*

programmer's switch　A plastic accessory included with pre-1991 Macintosh computers that, when installed on the side of the computer, enables one to perform a hardware reset and access the computer's built-in debugger.

programming　The process of providing instructions to the computer that tells the microprocessor what to do. Stages in programming include design, or making decisions about what the program should accomplish; coding, or using a programming language to express the program's logic in computer-readable form and entering internal documentation for the commands; testing and debugging, in which the program's flaws are discovered and corrected; and documentation, in which an instructional manual for the program is created, either in print or onscreen.

programming environment　A set of tools for programming that is commonly provided with a computer's operating system. Minimally, the tools include a line editor, a debugger, and an assembler to compile assembly language programs. These tools usually are not sufficient for professional program development, however, and often are replaced by an application development system.

programming language　An artificial language consisting of a fixed vocabulary and a set of rules (called syntax) that programmers use to write computer programs, which tell the computer what to do. Programming languages are differentiated according to their level of abstraction from machine code (low-level and high-level languages), their focus (procedural steps, object manipulation, or data relationships), the method used to transform the programmer's notations into executable code (interpreted or compiled), and the prominence of data typing (strongly typed, weakly typed, typeless). See *declarative programming language, high-level programming language, low-level programming language, object-oriented programming, procedural programming language.*

program overlay　A portion of a program kept on disk and called into memory only as required.

progressive JPEG　A type of JPEG graphic in which a low-resolution version of the entire image appears onscreen almost immediately and becomes sharper as additional information is downloaded.

project management program　Software that tracks individual tasks that make up an entire job and enables project managers to discern the critical path, the sequence of activities that must be completed in a timely fashion if the entire project is to be completed on time.

PROLOG　A high-level, fourth generation programming language used in artificial intelligence research and applications, particularly expert systems. PROLOG, short for PROgramming in LOGic, is a declarative language; rather than tell the computer what procedure to follow to solve a problem, the programmer describes the problem to be solved. The language resembles the query language of a database management system such as Standard Query Language (SQL) in that one can use PROLOG to ask a question such as, "Is Foster City in California?" But an important difference exists between PROLOG and a database management system (DBMS). A database contains retrievable information; in contrast, a PROLOG program contains knowledge, from which the program can draw inferences about what is true or false.

PROM　Acronym for programmable read-only memory. A read-only memory (ROM) chip programmed at the factory for use with a given computer. Unlike standard ROM chips, which have their programming included in the internal design of the chip circuits, programmable ROM chips are easy to modify. Although programmable

ROM chips can be programmed (burned) just once, after which the programming becomes permanent, it is easier to change the way the chips are programmed than to change their internal design. See *EPROM*.

prompt   A symbol or phrase that appears onscreen to inform the user that the computer is ready to accept input.

property   **1.** A characteristic or attribute of an object or resource made available by a computer program. In Microsoft Word, for example, a document's properties include its title and author. An object's properties are contained in its property sheet. **2.** In object-oriented programming, a variable that is declared in a class so that it is available to all the objects created with the class. See *method, object, object-oriented programming.*

property sheet   In application software, a dialog box, often displayed with index tabs, that stores all the properties associated with an object that the program makes available. In many applications, a given object's property sheet can be viewed by right-clicking the object and choosing Properties from the pop-up menu.

proportional pie graph   In presentation graphics, a paired pie graph in which the size of each pie is in proportion to the amount of data the pie represents. Proportional pie graphs are useful for comparing two pies when one is significantly larger than the other.

proportional spacing   In typefaces, setting the width of a character in proportion to the character shape so that a narrow character such as *i* receives less space than a wide character such as *m*. The text used in this dictionary entry uses proportional spacing. See *kerning, monospace.*

proprietary   Privately owned; based on trade secrets, privately developed technology, or specifications that the owner refuses to divulge, thus preventing others from duplicating a product or program unless an explicit license is purchased. Although there

are now a few carefully selected makers of Macintosh clones, the Macintosh system architecture is proprietary. The opposite of proprietary is open (privately developed but publicly published and available for emulation by others). With the exception of the basic input-output system (BIOS), the IBM PC system is open. From the user's perspective, proprietary designs or formats entail risk. If the company prospers and the design or format is widely emulated or accepted, the user benefits. But if the company does not prosper or fails, the user could be stuck with a computer system or with data that cannot be upgraded or exchanged with others. See *proprietary file format.*

proprietary file format   A file format developed by a firm for storing data created by its products. In word processing, proprietary file formats are needed to handle formatting choices, which are not represented using the standard ASCII characters. A proprietary file format usually is unreadable by other companies' application programs without the assistance of a file conversion utility. The popular programs typically include the utilities to convert the files of several other file formats.

proprietary local bus   A local bus standard developed by one company for use on only its machines. A proprietary bus requires adapter cards specifically designed for use on this bus, and there may be fewer of these than cards developed for open architectures. See *Micro Channel Architecture (MCA).*

proprietary protocol   An unpublished and nonpublic communications protocol developed by a company to enable its products to communicate with each other. The use of a proprietary communications protocol veils a not-so-subtle strategy to force users of one product to adopt other products made by the same company. The use of an open protocol, on the other hand, encourages the connection of the device with products made by other companies. See *connector conspiracy.*

proprietary standard An unpublished and sometimes secret design or specification for a device or program. The company that owns the standard refuses to permit other firms to emulate it, in the hope that the standard will eclipse all others and become the industry norm. Taken to the extreme, the use of a proprietary standard could force users to buy not just one, but a whole series of the firm's products (because nothing else will work with them). This strategy is often self-defeating in that it retards the development of a market. Users do not like to be forced into buying products from a single manufacturer. Open standards promote a growing market, thus benefiting all the corporate participants and other users by encouraging competition and interoperability.

protected memory In an operating system capable of preemptive multitasking, the random access memory (RAM) of the computer, in which programs are allotted memory space in such a way that it is not possible for other programs to invade this space and cause the computer to crash.

protected mode In Intel 80286 and later microprocessors, one of two operating modes (the other is called real mode). In real mode, memory addresses are directly mapped using the original IBM PC memory-addressing scheme. In effect, this limits the total amount of system memory to 640MB. In protected mode, real mode's limited memory registers contain pointers to additional registers, effectively breaking the 640K memory limitation. In addition, the pointers contain memory protection information, which enables the processor to protect the referenced memory from invasion by other programs—hence the term "protected mode." With operating system support, this enables preemptive multitasking, in which programs can safely coexist in the same memory space. In 80386 and later Intel processors, a page mode memory unit (PMMU) provides further memory-mapping functions, enabling virtual memory and faster processing. See *real mode.*

protocol In data communications and networking, a standard that specifies the format of data as well as the rules to be followed in transmitting it. Networks could not be easily or efficiently designed or maintained without protocols; a protocol specifies how a program should prepare data so that it can be sent on to the next stage in the communication process. For example, e-mail programs prepare messages so that they conform to prevailing Internet mail standards, which are recognized by every program that is involved in the transmission of mail over the network. See *protocol stack, protocol suite.*

protocol stack In a computer connected to a network, the vertical stack of protocols, ranging from the lowest-level protocols (the ones that handle the electrical connection to the network's physical media) to the highest-level protocols (the ones that prepare the data for presentation to the user). The OSI Reference Model conceptualizes seven distinct layers, each of which is governed by its own protocol. At each layer, a protocol provides services to the layers above and below.

protocol suite In a network, a set of related standards that, taken together, defines the architecture of the network. For example, the Internet is based on the TCP/IP protocol suite, a collection of more than 100 standards that are all designed to work smoothly together.

protocol switching See *automatic network switching.*

protocol tunneling The encapsulation of data packets conforming to one network's protocols within the packets of another network's protocols. By means of protocol tunneling, for example, an external workstation that uses local area network (LAN) protocols (such as IPX/SPX or NetBEUI) can employ the Internet (which packages data according to the TCP/IP protocols) to exchange data with internal LAN servers. See *PPTP, virtual private network (VPN).*

prototype A demonstration version of a proposed program or hardware device. In software, a prototype is usually a mock-up of a program's user interface, without much back-end code to support it. In hardware, a prototype is usually a cumbersome device with lots of wires and components that, if the prototype is mass produced, will be replaced by circuit boards and integrated circuits.

prototyping In information system development, the creation of a working system model that is functional enough to draw feedback from users. Also called joint application development (JAD).

proximity operator In database and Web searching, an operator (such as NEAR or WITH) that tells the search software to retrieve an item only if the words linked by the operator occur within a predetermined number of words of each other (such as 5 or 10 words). The use of a proximity operator is one way to narrow the focus of a search; if the specified words occur close together, it is more likely that the document pertains to the searcher's interests.

proxy server 1. Also called proxy. A program that stands between an internal network and the external Internet, intercepting requests for information. A proxy is generally part of a broader solution to internal network security called a firewall. The purpose of a proxy is to prevent external users from directly accessing resources inside the internal network or knowing precisely where those resources are located. The proxy intercepts an external request for information, determines whether the request can be fulfilled, and passes on the request to an internal server, the address of which is not disclosed to the external client. By disguising the real location of the server that actually houses the requested information, the proxy makes it much more difficult for computer criminals to exploit potential security holes in servers and related applications, which might enable them to gain unauthorized access to the internal network. This protection from outside

attack comes at the price of imposing inconveniences (including configuration hassles and slower performance) on internal users who want to access the external Internet. See *firewall.* **2.** In an online service, such as America Online, a server that has been configured to store Web pages that are frequently accessed by the service's members. When members request these pages, the server provides the copy it has stored rather than requesting the page from the external Internet. Members see Web pages more quickly and the network experiences a lighter load, but these benefits come at a price: The displayed page may be out-of-date.

PrtScr See *Print Screen.*

PS/2 mouse A mouse with a special connector that fits into a mouse port. PS/2 mouse devices, or mouse devices equipped with PS/2 connectors, do not require a serial port to operate and are much simpler to install.

PS/2 mouse port A mouse port on the back of the computer's case that enables the user to connect any mouse with a PS/2 mouse connector. This port enables users to connect a mouse without using a serial port or having to deal with the port conflict issues that such a connection might cause.

pseudoanonymous remailer In the Internet, an e-mail forwarding service that enables Internet users to send anonymous e-mail or to post anonymously to Usenet. These services maintain records that preserve the sender's true identity, so they are not truly anonymous. See *anonymous remailer.*

pseudocode An algorithm expressed in English to conceptualize a program before coding it in a programming language. Pseudocode cannot be compiled; it is for human use only.

PSN Acronym for processor serial number. A unique serial number assigned to Intel Pentium III microprocessors in such a way that software can detect and record this number. Web sitescould use the PSN to determine which computer is accessing the site; if this number were matched with an individual's name, it would be possible to track an individual's Web usage with precision. In response to criticism from privacy advocates, Intel shipped Pentium IIIs with PSN switched off. However, the function can be switched back on by programs that evade user monitoring. See *GUID*.

PSTN Acronym for public switched telephone network. The worldwide network of switched telephone interconnections, enabling hundreds of millions of telephones worldwide to establish direct connections. Originating in 1876 with Alexander Graham Bell's patent, the PSTN began with a number of local, manually switched analog networks, which were gradually interconnected as standards emerged. By the 1950s and 1960s, most local switching networks had made the transition from manual switching, which requires a human operator, to electronic switching, which enables direct dialing. In the industrialized nations today, much of the switching network employs digital technology, with the exception of the local loop, which is still primarily analog due to the antiquated wiring found in older homes. ISDN provides an international standard for the extension of digital telephony to homes and offices. Worldwide telephone standards are governed by the International Telecommunications Union (ITU), a division of the United Nations.

public data network (PDN) A wide area network (WAN) that makes long-distance data communication services available to organizations and individuals. PDNs are extensively used by corporations to enable secure communication with branch officers, field agents, and suppliers, as well as to implement Electronic Data Interchange (EDI) transaction processing. PDNs set up custom, dedicated connections, called leased lines, which are much more secure than the Internet because they are not used by anyone other than the network's authorized corporate users. There

are two kinds of PDNs: circuit-switched PDNs, which use telephone switching equipment to set up dedicated connections; and packet-switched PDNs, which are packet-switching networks based on the X.25 protocol. In the future, PDNs may face competition from virtual private networks (VPNs), which employ the Internet and ensure security by means of encryption and protocol tunneling.

public domain Intellectual property that has been expressly released for unconditional use, including for-profit distribution or modification, by any party under any circumstances whatsoever. According to international copyright law, no work should be considered public domain, even in the absence of an explicit copyright notice, unless the author of the work has clearly stated that the work is intended for the public domain and that all claims to the work are relinquished. By this definition, virtually all the ostensibly "public domain" software that is widely distributed by computer bulletin board systems (BBS) and FTP sites should not be regarded to be in the public domain, but rather as freeware, and should not be modified, sold, or reused without the author's explicit permission.

public domain program A program that has been distributed with an explicit notification from the program's author that the work is in the public domain. Very few publicly distributed programs meet this criterion. See *free software, freeware, General Public License (GPL), open source software (OSS), postcardware, shareware.*

public key cryptography In cryptography, a revolutionary new method of encryption that does not require the message's receiver to have received the decoding key in a separate transmission. The need to send the key, which is required to decode the message, is the chief vulnerability of previous encryption techniques. In public key cryptography, there are two keys: a public one and a private one. The public key is used for encryption, and the private key is used for decryption. If John wants to receive a private message from Alice, John sends his public key to Alice; Alice then uses the key to encrypt the message. Alice sends the message to John. Anyone trying to intercept the message en route would find that it is mere gibberish. When John receives the message, he uses his private key to decode it. Because John never sends his private key anywhere or gives it to anyone, he can be certain that the message is secure. Public key cryptography places into the hands of individuals a level of security that was formerly available only to the top levels of government security agencies. Also called asymmetric key cryptography.

Public Key Cryptography System See *PKCS*.

public key encryption The use of public key cryptography to encrypt messages for secret transmission. Because public key encryption techniques consume enormous amounts of computer processing overhead, they are generally used only for the initial phase of a connection between the sender and receiver of a secret message. In this phase, the users establish their identities by means of digital signatures and exchange the keys that will be used for symmetric key encryption using an encryption algorithm such as DES.

public key encryption algorithm Synonymous with asymmetric encryption algorithm. A step-by-step procedure for encrypting messages using the techniques of public-key cryptography. Popular public key encryption algorithms include El Gamal and the RSA encryption algorithm. Because public key encryption algorithms are as much as 100 times slower than symmetric key encryption algorithms, they are often used to establish an initial, encrypted communication channel, which can then be used to transmit a symmetric encryption key. See *symmetric key encryptional algorithm*.

public switched telephone network See *PSTN*.

pull-down menu In the Macintosh environment, an onscreen menu of command options that appears after the user uses the mouse to click on the menu name and drags down to display the menu. In Microsoft Windows, the user need only click the menu name to display the menu; it is not necessary to keep depressing the mouse button or to drag down to display the menu.

pull media On the Internet, the traditional Internet services (such as FTP and the World Wide Web), in which users do not obtain information unless they expressly and deliberately originate a request for it. To attract users (and therefore justify advertising), content providers must "pull" users to the site. See *push media*.

pull quote In desktop publishing, a quotation extracted from the copy of a newsletter or magazine article and printed in larger type in the column, often blocked off with ruled lines and sometimes shaded.

pulse code modulation (PCM) A technique used to transform an incoming analog signal into a noise-free, digital equivalent. In multimedia, PCM is used to sample sounds digitally.

punched card An obsolete method of data and program input in which data is represented by means of holes physically punched through a stiff piece of cardboard. Punched cards originated in the early twentieth century as a means of representing data for processing with mechanical tabulating machines.

purge To remove unwanted or outdated information, usually from the hard drive, in a systematic and ideally automatic manner. Also, in systems using a form of delete protection, purge refers to deleting protected files so that they no longer can be undeleted. See *undelete utility*.

pushbutton In industry-standard and graphical user interfaces (GUIs), a large button in a dialog box that initiates actions after one chooses an option. Most dialog boxes contain an OK button, which confirms choices and carries out the command, and a Cancel button, which cancels choices and closes the dialog box. The button representing the option one is most likely to choose, called the default button, is highlighted.

push media   In the Internet, a series of new content-delivery mechanisms, in which users subscribe to what amounts to a broadcasting service, which subsequently delivers content to the user's computer without the user having to make further requests for information. In contrast to pull media, which must attract the user to the site, push media can guarantee advertisers that subscribers will continue to receive updates and view advertising banners. Among the various push media models that have been developed are applications such as PointCast that deliver news, weather, and sports scores to the user's screen saver, and services such as Castanet, which employ a radio metaphor: The user tunes to a channel, and content is delivered to the user whenever updates are available. The delivered content may appear in a special window that appears on the user's desktop. Castanet can also automatically deliver software and updates to software, and thus creates a new and potentially significant model for software distribution and maintenance. The ultimate push medium is e-mail spamming, in which e-mail advertisers send unsolicited e-mail advertisements to as many as millions of e-mail addresses. See *pull media*.

PVC   See *permanent virtual circuit*.

Python   An interpreted, object-oriented programming (OOP) scripting language that is widely used to create scripts (short programs) for system administration, network administration, and Web content delivery. In contrast to its older competitors, Perl and Tcl, Python offers superior readability and simpler syntax. In consequence, Python is considerably easier to learn than Perl or Tcl. In addition, Python is highly portable; interpreters are available for a variety of platforms, including Unix, Linux, MS-DOS, Microsoft Windows, OS/2, and Mac OS. See *object-oriented programming, Perl, scripting language, Tcl*.

Q

QA See *quality assurance.*

QAM See *Quadrature Amplitude Modulation* or *Quality Assurance Management.*

QBE See *query by example.*

QEMM 386 A memory-management program by Quarterdeck Office Systems that moves network drivers, disk-cache programs, device drivers, and terminate-and-stay-resident (TSR) programs to the upper memory area, thus freeing conventional memory for DOS programs.

QIC See *quarter-inch cartridge.*

QIC-wide A variation on quarter-inch cartridge (QIC) technology that uses tape 0.32 inches wide instead of 0.25 inches wide to increase data capacity.

QNX Neutrino A Unix-like, real-time operating system that is designed for use in embedded systems. Developed by QNX Systems, QNX employs a microkernel design that keeps the operating system quite small (it will fit on a single floppy disk) and enables it to function at high speeds. QNX offers an embedded graphical user interface (called QNX Photon microGUI), networking capabilities, Java support, file system support, and other capabilities designed to optimize the operating system's use in a real-time, embedded environment. See *microkernel, real-time operating system (RTOS).*

QoS Acronym for quality of service. In a network, the guaranteed data transfer rate. A major drawback of the Internet for real-time voice and video, as well as for time-sensitive data communication, is the fact that quality of service cannot be assured. Network congestion can delay the arrival of data. Also used more generically to define a host of minimum network performance requirements, such as availability (how much of the time the network is running and usable).

quad density See *high density.*

quad-issue processor A microprocessor with a dual-pipeline superscalar architecture that can begin handling four instructions at the same time.

Quadrature Amplitude Modulation (QAM) A modulation protocol that employs four distinct areas of signal amplitude and phase variation to codify sixteen four-bit units of data. QAM is employed in fax machines and wireless devices.

quadrature modulation A group coding technique used in modems to modulate the carrier. Modems that use quadrature modulation can exchange data at 2400 bps. Trellis-code modulation enables higher data transfer rates.

quality In technology, the totality of characteristics of a system or a device such that it dependably satisfies the needs for which it was developed. See *ISO 9000, quality assurance.*

quality assurance In software engineering, a process that is designed to assure that the development process results in high-quality software; that is, it dependably satisfies the needs for which it was developed. Software engineering experience shows that one major obstacle to software quality lies in the generally poor communication between clients (who are often unable to express their needs fully and coherently) and developers (who are oriented to technology, not communication). A comprehensive quality assurance program addresses all the potential flaws of software development processes by means of explicit, formal processes, including frequent prototyping and repeated technical reviews, standards compliance measurements, documentation standards conformance, task fulfillment measurements, and formal reporting mechanisms. See *quality, software development life cycle (SDLC).*

Quality Assurance Management (QAM) In software engineering, a methodology for assuring the timely delivery of software that meets exceptionally high quality standards. QAM involves several process areas, including requirements management, project planning, project tracking, project oversight, quality assurance, product engineering, and intergroup coordination. Examples of QAM methodologies are the Capability Maturity Model (CMM) and ISO 9000. See *ISO 9000.*

quantization General term for numerous analog-to-digital conversion methods, all of which involve translating variations in analog signal amplitudes into binary data. See *analog-to-digital conversion.*

quantization noise Spurious binary data that results from errors in analog-to-digital conversion. See *analog-to-digital conversion, quantization.*

quantum computer A computing technology, currently at the theoretical stage, that employs the various states of atoms (such as spin direction) to represent and process digital data.

quantum leap A major development or gain that results from what appears to be a disproportionately small improvement. For example, the microprocessor's development is said to have brought about a "quantum leap" in computing. The term is derived from the behavior of subatomic particles, which do not move smoothly from one state to another when subjected to small increases in energy; instead, they abruptly "leap" to a new state.

QuarkXPress See *desktop publishing software.*

quarter-inch cartridge (QIC) A tape cartridge using quarter-inch-wide magnetic tape widely used for backup operations. Standards for QIC devices are maintained by the Quarter-Inch Drives Standards Association, Inc.

Quartz The imaging engine that generates the user interface for Apple's Mac OS X operating system. Quartz relies on the OpenGL graphics standard to render 2D and 3D graphics, and anti-aliased fonts in an environment capable of transparency and shadowing; it uses the Portable Document Format (PDF) standard as the basis of its imaging model. See *Mac OS X, PDF.*

queing Placing units of data (such as packets, print jobs, messages, or tasks) in a waiting area (such as a buffer or temporary file) until they can be processed. See *queue, queue management.*

query In database management, a search question that tells the program what kind of data should be retrieved from the database. An effective database management system lets a person retrieve only the information he or she needs for a specific purpose. A query specifies the characteristics (criteria) used to guide the computer to the required information. See *data independence, declarative programming language, query language, SQL.*

query by example (QBE) In database management programs, a query technique (developed by IBM for use in the QBE program) that prompts one to type the search criteria into a template resembling the data record.

query language In database management programs, a retrieval and data-editing language one uses to specify what information to retrieve and how to arrange the retrieved information onscreen or when printing. See *query, SQL.*

question mark (?) The wildcard symbol that stands for a single character at a specific location, unlike the asterisk (*), which can stand for one or more characters. In AB?DE, for example, only file names or character strings that are five characters long—with AB as the first two characters and DE as the last two characters—are selected.

queue In computing, a stream or list of tasks, packets, bits, messages, or some other unit of data that is waiting to be processed. See *job queue, print queue, queue management.*

queue management A procedure for managing a queue so that the waiting items are processed as quickly as possible and in a prioritized order that takes system and user needs into account. See *queue.*

QuickDraw The object-oriented graphics and text-display technology stored in every Macintosh's read-only memory (ROM). When creating Macintosh programs, programmers achieve a common look by drawing on the QuickDraw resources to create onscreen windows, dialog boxes, menus, and shapes.

Quicken A personal finance program developed by Intuit that features integrated online banking, credit card tracking, investment management, and a variety of analytical tools. See *Microsoft Money, personal finance program.*

QuickTime An extension to the Macintosh System software that allows applications that support QuickTime to display animated or video sequences precisely synchronized with high-quality digital sound. In a training document, for instance, one can click an icon to see a QuickTime video sequence (a "movie") that visually shows a specific technique or procedure. QuickTime software is available for several operating systems, including Windows.

quit To exit a program properly so that all configuration choices and data are properly saved.

QWERTY (Pronounced *kwer-tee.*) The standard typewriter keyboard layout, also used for computer keyboards. The keyboard name comes from the six keys on the left end of the top row of letter keys. Alternative keyboard layouts, such as the Dvorak keyboard, are said to speed typing by placing the most commonly used letters on the home row.

RAD Acronym for rapid application development. In object-oriented programming, a method of program development in which a programmer works with a library of prebuilt objects, allowing him to build programs much more quickly.

radio button In a graphical user interface (GUI), the round option buttons that appear in dialog boxes. Unlike check boxes, radio buttons are mutually exclusive; selecting one radio button option within a group deselects the other options.

radio frequency interference (RFI) The radio noise generated by computers and other electronic and electromechanical devices. Excessive RFI generated by computers can disrupt the reception of radio and television signals. See *FCC certification*.

radix The number of digits available for use in a given numbering system. Binary numbers, which are a base 2 numbering system, employ only two digits, 0 and 1. Synonymous with base.

RAID Acronym for Redundant Array of Inexpensive Disks or Redundant Array of Independent Disks. A group of drives under the control of array-management software that work together to improve performance and decrease the odds of losing data due to mechanical or electronic failure by using such techniques as data striping. Because of their complexity and cost, RAID implementations are most often used on network servers. Several RAID levels exist, each with advantages and disadvantages. RAID arrays are generally used for high-volume servers. See *RAID 0, RAID 1, RAID 2, RAID 5, RAID 10*.

RAID 0 A type of RAID storage device that combines two or more hard disks into a single logical drive. The technique used is called disk striping; data is written in blocks to each drive in a sequence, producing very fast performance. However, RAID 0

devices do not provide data redundancy and are therefore unsuitable for applications involving mission-critical data. See *RAID*.

RAID 1 A type of RAID storage device that combines two or more hard disks into a single logical drive, but—in contrast to RAID 0—in a way that backs up the data so that nothing is lost if one of the drives should fail. Performance is sacrificed for the sake of data integrity. See *RAID*.

RAID 2 A type of RAID storage device that combines two or more hard disks into a single logical drive. Like RAID 0, RAID 2 provides fast performance but does not provide data protection in case of a drive failure. However, it does provide a means of verifying whether write operations were performed correctly, so it is suitable for backup operations. See *RAID*.

RAID 5 A type of RAID storage device that combines three or more hard disks into a single logical drive. Like RAID 0, RAID 5 provides high write speed, but the striping technique used creates sufficient redundant information that all the data can be reconstructed if one of the drives should fail. See *RAID*.

RAID 10 Also known as RAID 1 + 0. A type of RAID storage device that combines the benefits of RAID 0 (high speed) with RAID 1 (data integrity). Although this approach requires twice as many drives as any of the other RAID standards, it offers the best combination of performance and data integrity. See *RAID*.

RAM See *random access memory (RAM)*.

Rambus DRAM See *RDRAM*.

Rambus Inline Memory Module See *RIMM*.

RAM cache See *cache memory*.

RAMDAC Acronym for random access memory digital-to-analog converter. A chip in the video adapter that converts three digital signals (one for each primary color) into one analog signal that is sent to the monitor. RAMDACs use onboard random access memory (RAM) to store information before processing it.

RAM disk   An area of random access memory (RAM) configured by a utility program to emulate a hard drive. Data stored in a RAM disk can be accessed more quickly than data stored on a disk drive, but this data is erased whenever one turns off or reboots the computer. See *configuration file, device driver, RAMDRIVE.SYS.*

RAMDRIVE.SYS   In MS-DOS, a configuration file provided with the operating system that sets aside part of a computer's random access memory (RAM) as a RAM disk, which is treated by MS-DOS as though it were a hard disk drive. RAMDRIVE.SYS is a device driver that must be loaded using a DEVICE or DEVICE-HIGH statement in the CONFIG.SYS file.

random access   An information storage and retrieval technique in which the computer can access information directly, without having to go through a sequence of locations. A better term is direct access, but the term "random" access has become enshrined in the acronym random access memory (RAM). To understand the distinction between random and sequential access, compare a cassette tape (sequential access) with a vinyl record (random access). See *sequential access.*

random access memory (RAM)   The computer's primary working memory, in which program instructions and data are stored so that they can be accessed directly by the central processing unit (CPU) via the processor's high-speed external data bus. RAM often is called read/write memory to distinguish it from read-only memory (ROM), the other component of a personal computer's primary storage. In RAM, the CPU can write and read data. Most programs set aside a portion of RAM as a temporary workspace for data so that one can modify (rewrite) as needed until the data is ready for printing or storage on secondary storage media, such as a hard or floppy disk. RAM does not retain its contents when the power to the computer is switched off, so one should save his or her work frequently. See *read-only memory (ROM).*

random access memory digital-to-analog converter   See *RAMDAC.*

random number   A number generated by a computer program that simulates a number generated by a random process, such as drawing a card from a shuffled deck. See *random number generator.*

random number generator   A program that generates a simulated random number (also called a pseudo-random number). The number is not truly random since the program begins with a constant, called a seed, and follows a predictable sequence to generate the simulated random number from the seed. To produce true random numbers, some random number generators use seeds drawn from more random processes, such as the timing variations of user-entered keystrokes during a timing period. See *random number.*

range   In a spreadsheet program, a cell or a rectangular group of adjacent cells. Valid ranges include a single cell, part of a column, part of a row, and a block spanning several columns and several rows. Ranges allow one to perform operations, such as formatting, on groups of cells. See *range expression, range name.*

range expression   In a spreadsheet program, an expression that describes a range by defining the cells in opposing corners of a rectangle. In Microsoft Excel, for example, one writes a range expression by typing the beginning cell address, a colon, and the ending cell address: A9:B12, for example. See *range name.*

range format   In a spreadsheet program, a numeric format or label alignment format that applies only to a range of cells and that overrides the global format.

range name   In a spreadsheet program, a title the user assigns to a range of cells. A range name, such as "Total Rainfall," is easier to remember than a range expression.

rapid application development See *RAD*.

rapid prototyping In the software development life cycle (SDLC), a reality check procedure that involves creating a highly simplified version of the program under development (or some feature of the program under development). The prototype is shown to clients, enabling developers to more clearly understand their clients' needs. Several such prototypes may be developed and progressively refined during the development process. See *RAD*, *software development life cycle (SDLC)*.

RARP Acronym for Reverse Address Resolution Protocol. An Internet standard (protocol) that enables diskless workstations to obtain an IP address so that they can fully function as Internet hosts. See *BOOTP*.

raster On a monitor or television screen, the horizontal pattern of lines that forms the image. Within each line are dots, called pixels, that can be illuminated individually.

raster font See *bitmapped font*.

raster graphics See *bitmapped graphic*.

raster image processor (RIP) A device that converts object-oriented graphics into raster graphics before printing to output devices. See *vector-to-raster conversion program*.

rave To carry on an argument in support of a position beyond all bounds of reason and sensitivity. On e-mail and newsgroups, a rave is annoying but is not considered to be worthy of a flame unless the argument is couched in offensive terms.

raw data Unprocessed or unformatted data that has not been arranged, edited, or represented in a form for easy retrieval and analysis.

raw footage In digital video, the original video as it was shot, prior to editing or other postproduction operations.

ray tracing In computer graphics, a computationally intensive technique for rendering three-dimensional objects by introducing variations in color and shading produced by specific light rays falling upon the object. To create a ray-traced graphic, the designer begins by specifying the source and intensity of the light source.

RBOC See *Regional Bell Operating Companies*.

RC4 A widely used symmetric key encryption algorithm developed by RSA Data Security, Inc. The algorithm's vulnerability to cryptanalysis (code-breaking) is highly dependent on the length of the key; a key of 40 characters or less can be easily broken, even by amateur cryptanalysts. This is the encryption method that is used by the Secure Sockets Layer (SSL) standard. U.S. government export restrictions prevent the use of RC4 keys greater than 40 characters for exported products, which essentially means that supposedly secure programs based on 40-key RC4 encryption are, in fact, quite insecure and vulnerable to interception and decoding while they are being transmitted via the network. See *symmetric key encryption algorithm*.

RCA plug See *phono plug*.

RDBMS See *relational database management system*.

RDF Acronym for Resource Description Framework. A specification for developing logical resource classification systems. Developed by the World Wide Web Consortium, RDF enables programmers to create classification systems for a variety of Web-accessible resources. RDF has been used to create classification schemes to rate sites' suitability for children, for example. See *PICS*.

RDRAM Also called Direct Rambus DRAM and Rambus DRAM. A high-performance random access memory (RAM) design that is capable of data transfer rates of up to 2.6 GBps (PC-2600). In contrast to SDRAM, which uses a wider but slower bus to connect to the microprocessor, Rambus DRAM uses a narrow but very fast bus and, in the end, achieves better throughput. Like DDR-SDRAM, Rambus DRAM can send and receive data within one clock cycle. Directly competing with DDR-SDRAM, Rambus DRAM is Intel's choice for high-performance PCs; however, DDR-SDRAM has been more widely adopted. See *DDR-SDRAM, PC-600, PC-700, PC-800, PC-1600, PC-2100, PC-2600, RIMM*.

read To retrieve data or program instructions from a device such as a hard or floppy disk, and place the data into the computer's random access memory (RAM).

read buffering A method of increasing the apparent speed of disk access by storing frequently accessed program instructions or data in memory chips, which operate more quickly than disks. See *buffer.*

README file A text file, often included on the installation disk of application programs, that contains last-minute information not contained in the program's documentation. Typical README file names are README.1ST, README.TXT, and READ.ME.

read-only Capable of being displayed or used, but not deleted. If a display of read-only data can be edited, formatted, or otherwise modified, it cannot be saved under the same file name. See *file attribute, locked file, read/write.*

read-only attribute In operating systems such as MS-DOS and Microsoft Windows, a file attribute stored with a file's directory entry that indicates whether the file can be changed or deleted. When the read-only attribute is on, the user can display the file, but cannot modify or erase it. When the read-only attribute is off, the user can modify or delete the file.

read-only memory (ROM) The portion of a computer's primary storage that does not lose its contents when one switches off the power. ROM contains essential system programs that neither the user nor the computer can erase. Because the computer's internal memory is blank at powerup, the computer can perform no functions unless given startup instructions. These instructions are stored in ROM. A growing trend is toward including substantial portions of the operating system on ROM chips instead of on disk. See *EPROM, PROM.*

read/write The capability of a primary or secondary storage device to record data (write) and to play back data previously recorded or saved (read).

read/write file A file whose read-only file attribute is set so that the file can be deleted and modified. See *locked file.*

read/write head In a hard disk or floppy disk, the magnetic recording and playback device that travels back and forth across the surface of the disk, storing and retrieving data.

read/write memory See *random access memory (RAM).*

RealAudio A proprietary streaming audio technology developed by RealNetworks, which enables Internet users to begin hearing an audio file moments after they start downloading the file. Quality varies according to the speed of the user's Internet connection, and ranges from the quality of an AM radio broadcast to the quality of an FM radio broadcast under ideal conditions. See *streaming audio.*

real mode In Intel microprocessors, an operating mode in which memory locations are directly mapped by a limited set of registers, producing a total maximum memory size of 1MB (and, in practice, 640K, due to the allocation of some of the memory for the use of peripheral devices). Processors prior to the 80286 could work only in real mode; the 80286 and higher processors can be switched into protected mode, which enables them to address much larger amounts of memory and to support the reliable execution of two or more programs simultaneously. See *multitasking.*

real time A timing constraint imposed on a computer system that originates from the "real world" outside the computer instead of the computer's internal timing mechanisms. Examples include the immediate processing of point-of-sale transactions in a busy department store or data acquired by an analog laboratory device.

real-time clock A battery-powered clock contained in the computer's internal circuitry. The real-time clock keeps track of the time of day even when the computer is switched off. This clock should be distinguished from the system clock that governs the microprocessor's cycles.

real-time operating system (RTOS) An operating system that is optimized to respond to externally generated events. Such operating systems are commonly used in embedded devices, such as anesthesia monitors, automobile navigation devices, pay telephones, and test equipment. See *QNX Neutrino* .

reboot To restart. Rebooting is often necessary after installing new software or after a system crash occurs. In most cases, one can restart the system from the keyboard, but especially severe crashes may require the user to push the reset button or, if no such button exists, turn off the computer and turn it on again. See *programmer's switch*.

rec A new top-level domain (TLD) name for the Internet, added in 1998, that is designed for Web sites providing recreational information. See *domain name, gTLD-MoU, top-level domain (TLD)*.

recalculation method In a spreadsheet program, the way the program recalculates cell values after the user changes the contents of a cell. See *automatic recalculation, manual recalculation, recalculation order*.

recalculation order In a spreadsheet program, the sequence in which calculations are performed when one enters new values, labels, or formulas. Options for recalculation order usually include column-wise recalculation, row-wise recalculation, and natural recalculation. See *optimal recalculation*.

recall In database searching, a measure of how successfully the search retrieves records that are pertinent to the search subject. In a search with poor recall, many relevant records exist, but they are not retrieved.

rec hierarchy One of the seven standard newsgroup hierarchies in Usenet. This category includes newsgroups relating to recreational interests, such as movies, comics, science fiction, or audio systems. See *Usenet*.

record See *data record*.

record locking In a multiuser relational database management system (RDMS) program, a feature that enables a user to protect a data record from alteration by other users while the user is actively updating this record. See *data record, relational database management system (RDMS)*.

record-oriented database management program A database management program that displays data records as the result of query operations, unlike a relational database management program, in which the result of all data query operations is a table. See *database management system (DBMS), data retrieval, SQL*.

record pointer In a database management program, an onscreen status message that states the number of the data record now visible (or in which the cursor is positioned).

recover To bring a computer system back to a previous stable operating state, or to restore erased or misdirected data. Recovery is needed after a system or user error occurs, such as telling the system to write data to a drive that does not contain a disk. See *undelete utility*.

recoverable error An error that does not cause the program or system to crash or to erase data irretrievably.

recto In desktop publishing, the right (odd-numbered) page in facing pages. In a book or magazine, the recto page is the right, odd-numbered page. See *verso*.

recursion In programming, a program module or subroutine that calls itself in order to perform an iterative operation; in other words, a simple expression repeats itself in order to perform a much more complex operation.

The principle of recursion is illustrated by Fibonacci numbers, a number series in which the first two terms are 1; successive terms are given by summing the two previous terms (1, 1, 2, 3, 5, 8, 13, 21, 34, 55, 89, 144, etc.). Fibonacci numbers can be generated by the following equation, as long as n is greater than 2:

$$\text{Fibonacci } (n) = \text{Fibonacci } (n - 1) + \text{Fibonacci } (n - 2).$$

Recursive algorithms should be used with caution; in general, iterative solutions are better, even when a recursive algorithm is known. The reason is that recursive algorithms can lead to exponentially expanding calculations; for example, in order to solve for the 45th Fibonacci number, more than one billion calculations are required. Through the use of a loop control structure in which the two previous values are readily stored and readily accessible, a simple iterative algorithm can find fibonacci(45) about ten million times faster than the recursive algorithm.

recursive acronym An acronym that, when expanded, turns out to contain the same acronym. Such acronyms exemplify the principle of recursion and are greatly esteemed by programmers. The canonical example is GNU, the GNU Project's version of the Unix operating system. The acronym stands for GNU's Not Unix. See *recursion*.

recycle bin In Microsoft Windows, an onscreen icon in which deleted files are stored. From the recycle bin, one can restore deleted files or discard them permanently.

Red Book An International Standards Organization (ISO) standard (number 10149) that describes the way in which music is recorded on Compact Disc–Digital Audio (CD-DA) disks.

Red Hat Linux A popular and well supported commercial version of Linux distributed by Red Hat Software. In the U.S., it is the de facto standard. See *Linux, Linux distribution*.

Red Hat Package Manager See *RPM*.

redirection See *input/output (I/O) redirection*.

redirection operator In operating system shells such as Unix or MS-DOS, a symbol that routes the results of a command from or to a device other than the keyboard and video display (console), such as a file or a printer. See *input/output (I/O) redirection*.

redlining In word processing, a display attribute (such as reverse video or double underlining) that marks the text that co-authors have added to a document. The redlined text is highlighted so that other authors or editors know exactly what has been added to or deleted from the document.

reduced instruction set computer See *RISC*.

Redundant Array of Inexpensive Disks See *RAID*.

reengineering In software engineering, a method of development that involves changing the way physical work is done in the "real world" as well as creating the software required to support the altered work patterns. Reengineering stems from the ample evidence that computerization of a "real world" work process does not automatically make it more efficient. To realize productivity gains, developers and clients may attempt to redesign the way physical work is done and alter the process to be more efficient. In many companies, for example, after the credit department grants credit, the receiving department receives goods and the accounting department writes checks. The reengineering strategy for this kind of setting may be to put computers in the receiving department so that the receiving staff can confirm what has been received and then write the checks on the spot. Experience in industry suggests that reengineering may fail if management ignores the need to enlist employee support for the significant and often threatening changes reengineering entails. See *software engineering*.

reflective liquid crystal display An LCD (liquid crystal display) with no edge-lighting or backlighting to enhance readability in bright-light conditions. Reflective LCDs are generally unsuitable for outdoor use.

reformat In operating systems, to repeat a formatting operation on a floppy or hard disk. In word processing or page layout programs, to change the arrangement of text elements on the page.

refresh To repeat the display or storage of data to keep it from fading or becoming lost. The monitor and random access memory (RAM) must be refreshed constantly.

refresh rate See *vertical refresh rate*.

REGEDIT A Microsoft Windows utility that enables knowledgeable users to edit the Registry directly. This should not be attempted by novices.

regexp See *regular expression*.

Regional Bell Operating Companies (RBOC) The regional telephone companies (Baby Bells) that were created as a result of the 1982 breakup of AT&T, which forced the former telephone monopoly to leave the local and regional telephone business.

register A memory location within a microprocessor, used to store values and external memory addresses while the microprocessor performs logical and arith-

metic operations on them. A larger number of registers enables a microprocessor to handle more information at one time.

register renaming A means of enabling software designed to run on x86 microprocessors, which can recognize only 8 registers, to use the 32 or more registers available in more advanced microprocessors with superscalar architecture. A microprocessor capable of register renaming differentiates between the registers an x86 program can address and the actual number of registers available, and will divert information sent to an occupied register to one that is not in use.

registration fee An amount of money that must be paid to the author of a piece of shareware to continue using it beyond the duration of the evaluation period.

Registry In Microsoft Windows, a hierarchically-structured database that provides programs a way to store configuration data, program file locations, and other information that is needed for the programs to execute correctly. The Registry replaces the text-based *.INI files used with Windows 3.1 applications. It is contained in two vital system files (user.dat and system.dat); if these files become corrupted and backups are not available, reinstallation is required. See *REGEDIT*.

regular expression (regexp) A notation system for describing text patterns in search and search-and-replace procedures. Originally developed for the text-processing tools included with the Unix operating system (such as awk and sed), regular expressions are now supported by numerous programming languages and applications. Although the notation is difficult to learn, it is much more powerful than the text searching options normally supplied with end-user applications or operating systems.

A regular expression contains ordinary characters as well as metacharacters, which have special meaning. The following lists commonly used metacharacters:

.	Matches any single character.
$	Matches the end of a line.
^	Matches the beginning of a line.
*	Matches zero or more repeated occurrences of the preceding character.
[ ]	Signals a bracketed expression, which matches any one of the characters within the brackets.
( )	Signals a grouped expression (block).
|	Inserts a logical OR operator.
+	Matches one or more occurrences of the preceding character or block.
?	Matches 0 or 1 occurrences of the preceding character or block.

Examples:

[a-z]	Matches any lower case letter.
[A-Z]	Matches any uppercase letter.
[a-c]	Matches *a* or *c*.
[warm|cool]	Matches *warm* or *cool*.
[ch]?at	Matches *at*, *cat*, and *hat*.

Regular expressions are derived from various strands of mathematical theory, including automata and formal language theory. In the 1950s, mathematician Stephen Kleene formalized regular expression theory in a mathematical notation called regular sets. Unix co-author Ken Thompson incorporated this theory into several Unix utilities (most notably grep).

Reiser file system   A journal file system for Linux that offers faster system starts, more efficient disk usage than the ext2 file system, faster access and retrieval times, and better recovery from system failures. See *ext2, journaled file system (JFS)*.

relational database   A type of database constructed of multiple tables of data that are inter-related. Complex searches can be performed to view the data in many different ways. Opposite of flat file database. See *join, relational database management*.

relational database management   An approach to database management, employed by Microsoft Access and other database management programs, in which data that is stored in two-dimensional data tables of columns and rows can be related if the tables have a common column or field. The term "relational" suggests the capability of this type of database software to relate two tables on the basis of this common field and to construct a new third table based on this relation. For example, suppose that a bookstore's database program stores one table listing customer names and customer numbers, and a second table listing customer numbers and the subjects of the books purchased by the customer with this number. By formulating a query, a user could produce a third, new table that lists the customer name and the subjects of the books purchased by this customer. The customer number provides the common field by which the two original tables can be related. See *join, relational database management system (RDBMS)*.

relational database management system (RDBMS)   A relational database application, especially one that comes with all the necessary support programs, programming tools, and documentation needed to create, install, and maintain custom database applications.

relational operator   A symbol used to specify the relationship between two numeric values. The result of a calculation using a relational operator is either true or false. In query languages, relational operators often are used in specifying search criteria. For example, a video store manager may want to tell the computer, "Show me all the telephone numbers of customers with overdue tapes that are due on a date less than or equal to May 7, 2003." In spreadsheets, for example, relational operators are used in @IF formulas to perform tests on data so that different values are displayed, depending on whether the result of the test is true or false.

relationship   In a relational database program, a link between two tables by a common field. See *join*.

relative addressing   In a program, specifying a random access memory (RAM) location using an expression so that the address can be calculated instead of using an absolute address.

relative cell reference   In a formula in a spreadsheet program, a reference to the contents of a cell that is adjusted by the program when one copies the formula to another cell or range of cells. To understand what happens when one copies a relative cell reference, it is important to know how a spreadsheet program actually records a cell reference. If one were to type the formula @SUM(C6:C8) in cell C10, the program would record a code that means, "Add all the values in the cells positioned in the second, third, and fourth rows up from the current cell." When the user copies this formula to the next four cells to the right (D10:G10), it still reads, "Add all the values in the cells positioned in the second, third, and fourth rows up from the current cell," and sums each column correctly. See *absolute cell reference, mixed cell reference.*

relative path   In a hierarchical file system, a pathname expression that does not specify the exact location of a directory, but instead specifies its relative position (up or down) from the current directory. In Unix and Unix-related file systems, the expression "./index.html" refers to a file named index.html that is located one directory above the current directory.

relative URL (RELURL)   One of two basic kinds of uniform resource identifiers (URIs), a string of characters that gives a resource's file name (such as merlot.html) but does not specify its type or exact location. Parsers (such as Web browsers) will assume that the resource is located in the same directory that contains the RELURL. See *URI.*

release number   See *version.*

relevance feedback   In search engines, a quantitative measurement, usually expressed as a percentage, of the likelihood that a given document is relevant to the search questions. The higher the percentage, the greater the chance that the document is indeed relevant.

reliability   The capability of hardware or software to perform as the user expects and to do so consistently throughout a specified system lifetime, without failures or erratic behavior. Reliability may be compromised by a failure (the system no longer meets its design specifications), an error (an inherent flaw in the system that produces incorrect results), a fault (erratic or erroneous behavior caused by a system state that designers failed to anticipate), or human error. Reliability and safety must be clearly distinguished; a reliable system is still unsafe if it the system's use involves a hazard (a condition in which a mishap could occur) and no provisions are made in the event of its failure, however unlikely. Reliability should also be distinguished from availability. In Bhopal, India, chemical plant engineers disabled plant safety systems to increase the availability of processing systems; the result was a catastrophic loss of life. See *error.*

reliable connection   See *reliable link.*

reliable link   An error-free connection established via the telephone system (despite its high line noise and low bandwidth) by two modems that use error-correction protocols.

RELURL See *relative URL*.

REM Short for remark. In batch files such as AUTOEXEC.BAT, it is common to add REM before a command that needs to be deactivated rather than deleting it. That way, if the command later needs to be reinstated, the REM can be removed.

remark In a batch file, macro, or source code, explanatory text that is ignored when the computer executes the commands. See *REM*.

remote access In a local area network (LAN), a means by which mobile users can gain authenticated access to internal network resources, preferably without posing a security risk to valuable assets within the network. The simplest but most expensive means of remote access is a direct long-distance call to a modem within the network, but this method of access is risky without some means of strong authentication. Medium- to large-scale corporations provide remote access to branch offices and business allies by means of private data networks (PDNs); new developments in this area include extranets and virtual private networks (VPNs), which make use of Internet connections.

remote control program A utility program that lets one link two computers so that he or she can use one to control the other.

remote login See *remote access*.

remote management A feature of newer departmental laser printers that transmits information about toner level, paper supply, and mechanical problems across a network to the person responsible for maintaining the printer.

remote procedure call (RPC) In local area networks (LANs), a data exchange protocol that enables one program to issue a request for data; the request is addressed, and the data is returned, by a program

running on another. See *Common Internet File System (CIFS)*, *NFS*, *Server Message Block (SMB Protocol)*.

remote system The computer or network to which a computer is connected by a modem and a telephone line.

remote terminal See *terminal*.

REM out See *comment out*.

removable hard disk A hard disk that employs a data cartridge that can be removed for storage and replaced with another.

removable mass storage A high-capacity data storage device (such as a magneto-optical drive or tape drive) in which the disk or tape is encased in a plastic cartridge or cassette so that it can be removed from the drive for safekeeping.

removable storage media See *removable mass storage*.

rendering In computer graphics, a process in which a vector graphic representation is transformed into a richly detailed bitmapped image containing color, shading, and other realistic features. Rendering is a computationally intensive process that requires a high-end processor or a multiprocessor system. See *bitmapped graphic*, *ray tracing*, *vector graphics*.

repagination See *pagination*.

repeater In a local area network (LAN), a device that amplifies network signals so that they can traverse greater distances. Synonymous with active hub. See *bridge*, *intelligent hub*.

repeating field In database design, a data field in which the user must type the same few data items, such as suppliers' names and addresses, thus creating many possibilities for errors due to typos or misspellings. See *data integrity*, *data redundancy*.

repeating label In a spreadsheet program, a character preceded by a label prefix that causes the character to be repeated across a cell. For example, Lotus 1-2-3 uses "\" to repeat one or more characters across a cell. The entry \= would produce a line of equal signs across the cell.

repeat key   A key that continues to enter the same character as long as one holds it down.

repetition control structure   In structured programming, a logical construction of commands that is repeated over and over. Also called a looping or iteration control structure.

repetitive strain injury   See *repetitive stress injury (RSI)*.

repetitive stress injury (RSI)   Also called repetitive strain injury and cumulative trauma disorder (CTD). A serious and potentially debilitating occupational illness caused by prolonged repetitive hand and arm movements that can damage, inflame, or kill nerves in the hands, arms, shoulders, or neck. RSI occurs when constantly repeated motions strain tendons and ligaments, resulting in scar tissue that squeezes nerves and eventually may kill them. With the proliferation of computer keyboards, RSI is increasingly noted among office workers and poses a genuine threat to personal computer users who work long hours at the keyboard. Specific RSI disorders include carpal tunnel syndrome (CTS).

replace   Also called search and replace or find and replace. In word processing programs, a feature that searches for a string and replaces it with another string.

replaceable parameter   In MS-DOS, a symbol used in a batch file that MS-DOS replaces with information a user types. The symbol consists of a percent sign and a number from 1 through 9, such as %1.

replication   1. In general, the reproduction of a complete set of data in another location. 2. In a spreadsheet program, the copying of a formula down a column or across a row; the program automatically adjusts the cell references so that the formulas function correctly relative to their new location. See *spreadsheet*. 3. In a client/server network, the reproduction of

a complete set of data to another computer for backup or security purposes. **4.** In database management software, the reproduction of a complete set of data to another server; used to decrease access time on highly trafficked servers and to make data available in remote locations.

report   In database management, printed output that usually is formatted with page numbers and headings. With most programs, reports can include calculated fields, showing subtotals, totals, averages, and other figures computed from the data.

report generator   A program or function that allows a nonprogrammer to request printed output from a database.

Report Program Generator (RPG)   An innovative programming language, created by IBM in 1965, that enabled programmers to write programs capable of generating formatted reports (printouts) of transaction data. The latest version of RPG is part of IBM's Websphere development tools.

repository   A database that is designed to store all the data related to a development project, including items such as the following: source code, compiled code, code libraries, reports, white papers, documentation, related multimedia, contact information, and download libraries; the database automatically tracks version information using a version control system. See *version control system*.

Request for Comments   See *RFC*.

requirements analysis   In the software life cycle, a phase of development that focuses on the formal description of an organization's processes that enables system analysts to state the functional requirements of the envisioned software correctly. See *software development life cycle (SDLC)*.

research network   A computer network, such as ARPANET or NSFnet, developed and funded by a governmental agency to improve research productivity in areas of national interest.

ResEdit   A Macintosh utility program, available free from Apple Computer dealers, that lets the user edit (and copy to other programs) many program features, such as menu text, icons, and dialog boxes.

reserved memory   In the original IBM PC memory architecture, the memory locations between the maximum 640K available for user programs and the 1024K maximum memory that is defined by the real mode of Intel microprocessors. Within this range, certain portions of the memory are reserved for the basic input/output system (BIOS) and video cards. Memory that is not utilized cannot be made available to user programs without the use of a memory management utility. See *upper memory area (UMA), upper memory block (UMB)*.

reserved word   In a programming language or operating system, a word (also called a keyword) that has a fixed function and cannot be used for any other purpose. In Java, for example, the word public is reserved to indicate that a variable can be accessed from anywhere in the program. One can use a reserved word only for its intended purpose; one cannot use the word for naming files, variables, or other user-named objects.

reset button   A button, usually mounted on the system unit's front panel, that allows one to perform a warm boot if the reset key does not work. On older Macintoshes, the reset button is part of the programmer's switch. Synonymous with hardware reset switch.

reset key   A key combination that restarts the computer when pressed. This key combination (Ctrl+Alt+Del on IBM-compatible machines) provides an alternative to switching the power off and on after a crash so severe that the keyboard does not respond. See *hardware reset, programmer's switch, warm boot*.

resident font   As opposed to a downloadable font or a cartridge font, a font that is present in a printer's memory whenever it is turned on.

resident program   See *terminate-and-stay-resident (TSR) program*.

resolution   The quality of a computer-represented image or sound, especially with respect to its capability to trick the eye (or ear) into perceiving it as a convincing duplicate of the original. In printers, resolution quality is expressed in linear dots per inch (dpi). In sound boards, resolution is expressed by means of the number of bits used to encode sounds. Resolution determines the number of sound levels with which recorded sounds must be represented. Higher resolutions ensure greater fidelity to the original sound. Though a resolution of 8 bits is minimally acceptable for voice reproduction, 16-bit resolution is required to reproduce the range of sounds in complex pieces of music. In graphics, resolution is measured by means of dots per inch (dpi) and color depth (the number of colors that make up the image). In monitors, resolution is expressed as the number of pixels horizontally and lines vertically onscreen. For example, a color graphics array (CGA) monitor displays fewer lines than a video graphics array (VGA) monitor; therefore, a CGA image appears more jagged than a VGA image.

resolution enhancement technology   A way of reducing aliasing and smoothing the curves in laser printer output. Resolution enhancement technology, which inserts small dots between large ones, increases effective resolution.

Resource Description Framework   See *RDF*.

resource fork   In the Macintosh file system, one of two portions of a file (the other is the data fork). The resource fork is used to store information about the file, such as the code number of the application that created it and the icon that the Finder should display.

response time   The time a computer needs to carry out a request. Response time is a better measurement of system performance than access time because it more fairly states the system's throughput.

retina scan   A type of biometric authentication that uses computer-based pattern recognition to recognize unique capillary patterns in each individual's eyes. Although retina scans provide much greater security than other authentication schemes, it is sufficiently intrusive that its use is restricted to high-security systems, such as those employed in intelligence agencies. See *authentication, biometric authentication.*

retrieval   All the procedures involved in finding, summarizing, organizing, displaying, or printing information from a computer system in a form useful for the user.

Return   See *Enter/Return.*

return on investment (ROI)   A calculation that considers the projected economic benefits of an investment as a percentage of the investment cost; for example, if a company invests $10,000 in a new computer system and can document $20,000 in future savings due to the installation of the system, the return on investment is 100 percent.

reusability   In computer programming, a measurement of the likelihood that a given unit of code can be successfully incorporated into another program. Computer programming languages offer varying degrees of reusability. In structured programming languages, programmers develop code libraries that contain frequently used routines, such as those related to opening a window and displaying it onscreen.

To make use of a library routine, the programmer writes a statement that calls the routine. Although this procedure sounds simple in practice, the programmer must know a great deal about the routine and must call the routine according to the routine's precise (and often complex) rules. Object-oriented programming languages attempt to simplify code re-use by means of their object-orientation; that is, programmers focus on creating objects, which contain procedural instructions (methods) as well as the data that these instructions are designed to modify. Methods are available to other objects by means of a simple, standardized interface, which can be used without knowing anything about how the hidden methods actually work (or, at the extreme, the programming language in which they were written). See *library, library routine, object, object-oriented programming, structured programming.*

reusable object   In object-oriented programming (OOP), an object that has been designed with such generality and customizability that it can be quickly and easily incorporated into new programs. For example, a programmer may develop a single object to support the creation of an onscreen window; when this is done, the object can be used in any program. The reuse of objects in this way saves enormous amounts of programming time and increases programming efficiency accordingly.

Reverse Address Resolution Protocol   See *RARP.*

reverse engineering   The process of systematically taking apart a chip or application program to discover how it works, with the aim of imitating or duplicating some or all of its functions. In the U.S., courts have held that reverse engineering is right guaranteed under the First Amendment; as one of the enumerated rights in the Constitution, it is therefore superior to trade secret law. It is therefore held by some legal experts that a company is within the law if it employs reverse engineering to learn a competitor's trade secrets, but numerous current court challenges may alter this picture. See *trade secret.*

Reverse Polish Notation (RPN)   A means of describing mathematical operations that makes calculations easier for computers. Many compilers convert arithmetic expressions into RPN. In RPN, the expression "a b +" adds the variables a and b, and would be written as "a + b" in standard notation. Synonymous with Polish notation and postfix notation. See *infix notation, prefix notation.*

reverse slash   See *backslash.*

reverse video In monochrome monitors, a means of highlighting text on the display so that normally dark characters are displayed as bright characters on a dark background, or normally bright characters are displayed as dark characters on a bright background.

rewrite Synonymous with overwrite.

RFC Acronym for Request for Comments. An Internet publication that constitutes the chief means by which standards are promulgated (although not all RFCs contain new standards). More than 1,000 RFCs are accessible from network information centers (NIC). The publication of RFCs is currently controlled by the Internet Architecture Board (IAB).

RFI See *radio frequency interference.*

RGB color model Acronym for red-green-blue color model. A color model (a means by which colors can be mathematically described) in which a given color is specified by the relative amounts of the three primary colors. The amount of each color is specified by a number from 0 to 255; 0,0,0 is black, while 255,255,255 is white.

RGB monitor A color digital monitor that accepts separate inputs for red, green, and blue and then produces a much sharper image than composite color monitors.

Rich Text Format (RTF) A text formatting standard developed by Microsoft Corporation that allows a word processing program to create a file encoded with all the document's formatting instructions, but without using any special hidden codes. An RTF-encoded document can be transmitted over telecommunications links or can be read by another RTF-compatible word processing program, without loss of the formatting.

right justification See *justification.*

RIMM A trademark of Rambus, Inc., which is commonly (but inaccurately) said to be an acronym for Rambus Inline Memory Module. A memory module used to package between 8 and 16 Rambus DRAM chips. The module is pin-compatible with SDRAM DIMM memory modules, but the motherboard must support RIMM in order for the Rambus DRAM chips to function. See *DIMM, Rambus DRAM, random access memory (RAM), SDRAM.*

ring network In local area networks (LANs), a decentralized network topology in which a number of nodes (including workstations, shared peripherals, and file servers) are arranged around a closed loop cable. Like a bus network, a ring network's workstations can send messages to all other workstations. Each node in the ring has a unique address, and its reception circuitry constantly monitors the bus to determine whether a message is being sent. The failure of a single node can disrupt the entire network; however, fault-tolerance schemes have been devised that allow ring networks to continue to function even if one or more nodes fail. See *token ring network.*

RIP Acronym for Router Information Protocol. An Internet protocol that routes data within an internal TCP/IP-based network based on a table of distances. A more recent and sophisticated version of this protocol is the OSPF Interior Gateway Protocol.

ripper A program that can extract audio tracks from audio CDs and write them to the computer's hard disk, generally to WAV files. Also called CD ripper.

ripple-through effect In a spreadsheet program, the sudden appearance of ERR values throughout the cells after the user make a change that breaks a link among formulas. If this happens, the user may think that he or she has ruined the entire spreadsheet, but after locating and repairing the problem, all the affected formulas are restored.

RISC Acronym for reduced instruction set computer. A central processing unit (CPU) architecture in which the number of instructions the microprocessor can execute is kept to a minimum to increase processing speed. The idea of RISC architecture is to reduce the instruction set to the bare minimum, emphasizing the instructions used most of the time and optimizing them for the fastest possible execution. A RISC processor ostensibly runs faster than its CISC counterpart, but CISC manufacturers (such as Intel) have substantially narrowed the performance gap by including many of the design features found in CISC architectures. See *complex instruction set computer (CISC), central processing unit (CPU)*.

riser   In the LPX and NLX form factors, a board mounted perpendicular to the motherboard plane that is designed to accommodate expansion boards.

risk   A condition or state in which the use of a system could result in potentially devastating consequences, such as injury or death to humans, catastrophic financial losses, or environmental devastation. Risk is highest when unsafe use of a system is hazardous, the system is complex, unusual performance conditions are likely, and safe operation may push human operators beyond their educational, psychological, performance, or training limitations. Increasingly, risk arises from the actions of human attackers (or their automated agents); attacks may originate from sophisticated intruders (also called crackers), unsophisticated intruders ("script kiddies") who use "cookbook" methods to gain unauthorized entry; automated attacks orchestrated by widely distributed Trojan horses, viruses, and other rogue programs; disgruntled employees and ex-employees; competitors and foreign governments that engage in espionage to gain competitive advantage; contractors attempting to discover information that will enable them to negotiate more effectively; managers and executives who believe they can conceal fraudulent acts or embezzlement; the forces of nature (wind storms, floods, hurricanes, tornados, or forest fires; and electrical phenomena (such as power outages or brownouts). See *script kiddies, security*.

river   In desktop publishing (DTP), a formatting flaw that results in the accidental alignment of white space between words in sequential lines of text, encouraging the eye to follow the flow down three or more lines. Rivers injure what typographers refer to as the color of the page.

RJ-11   Standardized name for the four-wire modular connector used for telephone and modem connections. See *modular jack*.

RJ-45   Standardized name for the eight-pin connector used in 10Base-T and 100Base-T network connections.

RLE   See *Run-Length Encoding*.

RLL   See *Run-Length Limited*.

rlogin   A Unix utility that enables users of one machine to log in to other Unix systems via a network. Because rlogin uses plain text passwords, it is not widely used due to the possibility that such passwords could be intercepted en route and used to gain unauthorized entry to the system. See *Telnet*.

robot   A computerized device that is capable of moving mechanical parts under the computer's direction and control.

robust   Capable of surviving exceptional conditions and unpredicted errors; relatively free from bugs and fault-tolerant.

ROI   See *return on investment*.

rollout   A marketing technique in which a new product or product theme is announced in a series of staged events, which are designed to attract publicity and consumer interest.

rollover   In Web publishing, an effect triggered when the user moves the mouse pointer over an object depicted on a Web page. The object can change color, blink, or display other effects.

ROM   See *read-only memory*.

Roman   In typography, an upright serif typeface of medium weight. In proofreading, opposite of italic.

root In a hierarchically organized classification system, the top-level category.

root directory In a secondary storage device's file system, the top-level directory, which is symbolized with a forward slash (/) in Unix and Unix-related operating systems, or a backward slash (\) in Microsoft operating systems. See *parent directory*, *subdirectory*.

root name The first, mandatory part of an MS-DOS file name, using from one to eight characters.

root user In Unix, an administrative account that enables the account holder to override file permissions and to browse freely through the computer's file directories. A fundamental objective of system intruders is to gain root user status, which enables the user to obtain the encrypted password file; this file can be analyzed by password-guessing programs, which may succeed in decrypting user passwords and destroying the system's security. Synonymous with superuser. See *cracker*, *script kiddies*.

rot-13 In Usenet newsgroups, a simple encryption technique that offsets each character by 13 places (so that an *e* becomes an *r*, for example).

rotated type In a graphics, word processing, or desktop publishing (DTP) program, text that has been turned vertically from its normal, horizontal position on the page. The best graphics programs, such as CorelDRAW, allow the user to edit the type even after rotating it.

rotational speed In a hard drive, the number of revolutions the disk makes in 1 minute (RPM). Rotational speed is the largest single factor in determining drive speed. Currently, hard drives have rotational speeds as high as 10,000 RPM.

rotation tool In a graphics or desktop publishing (DTP) program, a command option (represented by an icon) that the user can use to rotate type from its normal, horizontal position. See *rotated type*.

roughs In desktop publishing (DTP), the preliminary page layouts that the designer creates using rough sketches to represent page design ideas. Synonymous with thumbnail.

rounding error A calculation error that occurs by rounding quantities at one or more intermediate steps in a calculation, so that the result varies from that obtained by exact calculations. In computer programs, rounding errors can be iterative and can accumulate, with potentially catastrophic results. After 22 months, an index designed to track the performance of the Vancouver stock exchange resulted in an undervaluation approaching 50 percent. In the Gulf War, a rounding error rendered the Patriot missile system ineffective and may have been responsible for the deaths of 26 people.

router In a local area network (LAN) or any other network based on packet switching technology, an intelligent hub (connecting device) that examines each packet of data it receives and then decides which way to send it onward toward its destination. See *bridge*, *intelligent hub*, *switch*.

Router Information Protocol See *RIP*.

routine A program module that carries out a well-defined task. Synonymous with subroutine.

row In a spreadsheet program, a block of cells running horizontally across the spreadsheet. In a database, a row is the same as a record or a data record.

row-wise recalculation In spreadsheet programs, an order that calculates the values in row 1 before moving to row 2, and so on. See *column-wise recalculation*, *optimal recalculation*.

RPC See *remote procedure call*.

RPG See *Report Program Generator*.

RPM Acronym for Red Hat Package Manager. A software installation utility developed by Red Hat, Inc., the distributors of Red Hat Linux, that enables users of Red

Hat Linux and related operating systems to install binary software without having to go through the tedious and error-prone process of compiling source code on their systems. RPM is released according to the GNU Project's General Public License (GPL). See *Red Hat Linux*.

RPN   See *Reverse Polish Notation*.

RS-232C   A standard recommended by the Electronic Industries Association concerning the transmission of data between computers using serial ports. Most personal computers have an RS-232-compatible serial port, which one can use for external modems, printers, scanners, and other peripheral devices.

RS-232C port   See *serial port*.

RS-422   A standard recommended by the Electronic Industries Association (EIA) and used as the serial port standard for Macintosh computers. RS-422 governs the asynchronous transmission of computer data at speeds of up to 920,000 bps.

RSA Data Security, Inc.   The leading cryptography software publisher. The company holds patents on a number of widely used encryption algorithms, including the RSA public key encryption algorithm, the de facto world standard, and several symmetric key encryption algorithms, including RC4, which is part of the Secure Sockets Layer (SSL) standard.

RSA encryption algorithm   The most popular algorithm for public key encryption and a de facto world standard. RSA Data Security, Inc., held a patent on this algorithm that expired in 2000. The RSA encryption algorithm is employed in a number of encryption products, including the commercial versions of Pretty Good Privacy (PGP). See *Diffie-Hellman encryption algorithm*.

RSI   See *repetitive stress injury*.

RTF   See *Rich Text Format*.

RTFM   Acronym for Read the "Frigging" Manual.

rule   In graphics and desktop publishing (DTP), a thin horizontal or vertical line.

ruler   In many word processing and desktop publishing (DTP) programs, an onscreen bar that measures the page horizontally, showing the current margins, tab stops, and paragraph indents.

run   To execute a program.

Run-Length Encoding (RLE)   A data compression algorithm that looks for commonly occurring sequences of data and replaces them with a much shorter code. RLE is a lossless compression technique because the original data can be totally restored by reversing the encoding process.

Run-Length Limited (RLL)   A method of storing and retrieving information on a hard disk that, compared to double-density techniques, increases by at least 50 percent the amount of data a hard disk can store. The improvement in storage density is achieved by translating the data into a digital format that can be written more compactly to the disk. See *Advanced Run-Length Limited (ARLL)*, *MFM*.

running head   See *header*.

runtime   The period during which a program is executing and under the user's control.

runtime environment   The setting in which a program executes when it is launched by a user, including operating version, data storage format, processor speed, hardware configuration, and many other variables. Failure to predict and handle runtime environment variations accurately is a major cause of software failure.

runtime error   An error that occurs while the program is executing (in contrast to a compile time error, in which the error is noted by the compiler). Runtime errors may include errors in program semantics, which are difficult to catch prior to the program's actual execution. See *compiler*, *semantics*.

runtime library In an interpreted programming language, a code library that must be present so that the interpreter can execute the program code. For example, a runtime library called VBRUN.DLL must be present in order to run interpreted Visual Basic programs. See *interpreted programming language, interpreter, library, Visual Basic.*

runtime version A limited version of an application program that enables the program's data files to be viewed even on a computer that does not have the full application program installed. For example, Microsoft PowerPoint users can save their files in a runtime version so that their presentations can be viewed on a computer that does not have PowerPoint installed.

r/w A common abbreviation for read/write, indicating that the file or device is configured so that one can write data to it as well as read data from it. See *read/write file.*

SAA See *Systems Application Architecture.*

safe format A disk formatting method that does not destroy the data on the disk, so one can use an undelete utility to recover the data if it is subsequently discovered that a disk containing valuable data was erroneously formatted. See *undelete utility.*

safe mode In the various versions of Microsoft Windows, a mode in which the operating system starts without loading user-added extensions, including drivers for peripherals. This mode enables the user to determine which of the recently added programs are causing problems. See *Microsoft Windows.*

safety In computer systems, a measurement of the system's ability to avoid unwanted harm, loss, injury, or damage. Safety is of major concern when the system's use involves a hazard (the likelihood of injury, damage, loss, or death if the system is operated in an unsafe manner), and is a fundamental characteristic of safety-critical systems. Safety is one of four aspects of system dependability; the other three are availability, reliability, and security. A safe system is not necessarily highly available; safety systems can degrade system performance to the point that irresponsible operators may attempt to disable them. In addition, a safe system is not necessarily reliable; in radiation therapy, safety concerns warrant that the device should shut down rather than administer potential lethal radiation doses. Finally, a safe system is not necessarily secure; a space agency's satellite positioning system may be vulnerable to unauthorized intrusion (and may become unsafe if intruders compromise the system in dangerous ways). See *availability, hazard, reliability, safety-critical system, security.*

safety-critical system A safety-critical system is one that must function correctly in order to avoid human injury, human death, damage to property, financial loss, damage to the natural environment, or devastating systemic effects (such as a catastrophic drop in stock market prices). A system is judged to be safety-critical when its use involves risk (a potential that a mishap could occur, with severe consequences). Most safety-critical systems are designed to assure the safe use of systems involving a hazard, a state or condition in which unsafe use of the system will inevitably result in a mishap; for example, a train moving at high speed poses a hazard. Most hazards are caused by the use of potentially dangerous or lethal amounts of energy, such as the potential kinetic energy of a train moving at high speed. A train's safety system is designed to ensure that operators obey safety signals, thus avoiding the potentially lethal release of kinetic energy. See *availability, fault tolerance, hazard, mishap, risk.*

salami shaving A computer crime in which a program is altered so that it transfers a small amount of money from a large number of accounts to make a large profit.

Samba An open source networking protocol and associated software that implements the Common Internet File System (CIFS) standard, which is the current version of the Windows networking protocol, called Server Message Block (SMB) Protocol. Samba enables Unix and Linux servers to network with Microsoft Windows workstations and to emulate the server capabilities of Microsoft Windows NT and Microsoft Windows 2000 Server. See *Common Internet File System (CIFS), open source software (OSS), Server Message Block (SMB) Protocol.*

sample **1.** In analog-to-digital conversion, a measurement of the magnitude of an analog signal at a particular moment in time that results in a digital representation. See *analog-to-digital conversion.* **2.** In musical composition, the use of a short recorded excerpt as an element in a broader, new composition. Synonymous with needle drop.

sampling In analog-to-digital conversion, a process in which samples of analog signal levels are taken at frequent intervals in order to create an accurate digital representation; the more frequently the samples are taken, the more accurate the representation. See *analog-to-digital conversion, sample, sampling rate.*

sampling rate In analog-to-digital conversion, the frequency with which samples of an analog signal's magnitude are converted into digital representations. Accurate representation of complex analog signals, such as the sound produced by a symphony orchestra, requires frequent sampling; audio CDs contain the results of a 44.1 Khz sampling rate. See *sample, sampling.*

sandbox In Java, a safe area created by the Java virtual machine for the execution of applets; applets in the sandbox cannot get access to the computer's file system. See *Java.*

sanity check In programming or systems analysis, an interim, low-accuracy check that is performed to ensure that the results obtained thus far are not wildly outside system development goals. For example, a programmer may show a user interface prototype to a client to make sure that the client has successfully explained the system's intended uses to the programmer.

sans serif A typeface that lacks serifs, the ornamental straight or curved lines across the ends of the main strokes of a character. Helvetica and Arial are two readily available sans serif fonts. Sans serif typefaces are preferable for display type but, when used for body type, are harder to read than serif typefaces such as Times Roman. See *serif.*

SAP A business application software firm that leads the market for enterprise resource planning (ERP) software, such as programs that synchronize the various aspects of industrial production. See *ERP.*

SAPI Acronym for Speech Application Progamming Interface. A Microsoft-developed standard application programming interface that supports speech recognition and speech synthesis on systems running

Microsoft Windows. See *speech recognition, speech synthesis.*

SASI See *Shugart Associates Standard Interface.*

SATAN A network security diagnostic tool that exhaustively examines a network and reveals security holes. SATAN is a two-edged sword: In the hands of network administrators, it is a valuable tool for detecting and closing security loopholes. In the hands of intruders, it is an equally valuable tool for exposing remaining loopholes and gaining unauthorized access to a network. See *security.*

satellite **1.** In a multiuser system, a terminal or workstation linked to a centralized host computer. **2.** In the output of inkjet and laser printers, an extraneous spot of ink in the area around characters in which no ink should be present. **3.** In telecommunications, a wireless relaying station that is placed in orbit around the Earth. See *geostationary satellite, low Earth orbit (LEO) satellite.*

saturation **1.** In a charge-coupled device (CCD), the degree to which pixels can hold a charge and therefore sustain the appearance of even color in the display. See *charge-coupled device (CCD).* **2.** In monitors, the degree to which the display can differentiate among colors and display each color accurately, throughout the screen area.

save To transfer data from the computer's volatile random access memory (RAM), where the data is vulnerable to erasure, to an auxiliary storage medium such as a disk drive; when data has been saved, the computer system can be switched off without loss of data. Because computer systems vary in their dependability and because failure-inducing power anomalies (including outages and low voltage) are common, users are strongly advised to save data frequently. See *save as.*

save as A command available within most applications that enables the user to save data using a different file name, different directly location, or both. The previously-saved document remains unaltered. See *save.*

sawtooth distortion   See *aliasing*.

scalability   The ability of a system to accommodate increasing numbers of users without unacceptable levels of performance degradation. A server that can accommodate a dozen users may fail catastrophically when the number of users expands to 1,000. A scalable system includes an upgrade path that enables administrators to add extra capacity as needed so that overall system performance is not degraded in the slightest. Scalability differs from expandability, which refers to a system's capacity to accept add-on components. See *expandability*.

scalable font   A screen font or printer font that one can enlarge or reduce to any size, within a specified range, without introducing unattractive distortions. Outline font technology is most commonly used to provide scalable fonts, but other technologies—including stroke fonts, which form characters from a matrix of lines—are sometimes used. The most popular scalable fonts for Macintosh and Microsoft Windows systems are PostScript and TrueType fonts. See *bitmapped font*.

scalar   A quantity that is measured by magnitude alone; in contrast, a vector is measured by direction as well as magnitude. See *vector*.

scalar architecture   The design of a microprocessor with only one pipeline. Microprocessors with multiple pipelines have superscalar architecture. See *superscalar architecture*.

scalar data type   In a high-level programming language, a class of data types that store only one value at a time (compound data types can contain more than one value at a time). Examples of scalar data types are integers, floating-point numbers, strings, and Boolean (yes/no) data. See *Boolean data type, compound data type, data type, floating point notation, integer, string, typing, value, variable*.

scale-up problem   In a network, a technical problem caused by the system expanding far beyond its projected maxi-

mum size. For example, every computer connected to the Internet must have its own unique address, called an IP address. However, the Internet's designers, never guessing how popular the Internet would become, did not allow for a sufficient number of IP addresses. The network will have to be redesigned from the ground up—that is, with a new IP protocol (called IPv6) to cope with the problem.

scale well   To handle very large increases in size or scope of usage without performance degradation or other problems (for example, the sales department may say, "This technology scales well."). This is a matter to be measured, not asserted. See *scalability*.

scaling   **1.** In graphics, the resizing of an image. **2.** In presentation graphics, the adjustment of the y-axis (values), chosen arbitrarily by the program, to make differences in the data more apparent. Most presentation graphics programs scale the y-axis, but the programs' scaling choice can be unsatisfactory. Manually adjusting the scaling often produces better results.

Scandisk   A Microsoft Windows utility that checks magnetic disks (floppy disks and hard drives) for errors, such as lost clusters and file system irregularities. The program can correct most of these errors and should be run periodically to ensure data integrity.

scanner   A peripheral device that digitizes artwork or photographs and stores the image as a computer file that can be edited or printed. See *flatbed scanner, hand-held scanner, OCR, sheet-feed scanner*.

scan rate   See *vertical refresh rate*.

scatter diagram   An analytical graphic that plots data items as points on two numeric axes; also called a scattergram. Scatter diagrams show clustering relationships in numeric data. Computer magazines often use a scatter diagram to compare similarly configured computer systems, with price on one axis and the result of performance testing on the other axis to draw the reader's attention to slow, expensive computers and fast, inexpensive computers. See *analytical graphics*.

scatter plot   See *scatter diagram*.

scheduler   **1.** In computer operating systems or applications, a procedure or utility that automatically initiates a process at a given time, date, or both. **2.** A stand-alone utility, or a component in a personal information management (PIM) program, that enables the user to schedule appointments.

scheduling algorithm   See *task scheduling algorithm*.

schema   **1.** In XML, a statement of the XML tags that are preferred in a specific subject area or discipline; a schema encourages XML authors to write document type definitions (DTD) that conform to the schema's standards. See *DTD, XML*. **2.** In relational databases, a table that describes the table's underlying structure (a list of each field's structural definition, including data type and index order). See *relational database, table, XML*.

Scheme   A simplified version of the Lisp programming language that was originally developed for instructional purposes but is now sometimes used for application development. See *GUILE*.

scientific notation   A method for expressing very large or very small numbers as powers of 10, such as 7.24×10^{23}. In computer programs and programming languages, scientific notation often employs the symbol E, which stands for exponent, as in the following example: 7.24E23 (equivalent to 7.24×10^{23}) .

sci hierarchy   In Usenet's standard newsgroup hierarchy, a category of newsgroups devoted to topics in the sciences. The category includes newsgroups that cover astronomy, biology, engineering, geology, mathematics, psychology, and statistics. See *standard newsgroup hierarchy, Usenet*.

scissoring   In graphics editing, a deletion technique in which an image is cropped to a size determined by a superimposed frame.

scope   In computer programming, an area within a program's code in which a variable and its associated value are retained and recognized. In structured programming, variables generally have local scope when they are included in a subroutine; if the programmer wishes the variable and its value to be available throughout the program, it must be declared to be a global variable. See *global variable, variable, value*.

scramble   To encrypt a message so that it can be understood only by its intended recipient, who possesses the information or device necessary to decode the message. See *encryption*.

scratch pad   A temporary storage or memory area where an application stores intermediate values or other temporary information.

screen capture   A copy of a screen display that is saved as a text or graphics file on disk. Screen captures can then be printed in books or reports to show how a computer screen looks at a certain point in a program. Synonymous with screen dump in most cases; however, the term screen capture implies some attempt to exclude irrelevant portions of the captured image. See *screen dump*.

screen dump   A printout of the screen's current contents, with little or no attempt made to format the printed data aesthetically or eliminate irrelevant portions of the screen. See *Print Screen (PrtScr), screen capture*.

screen flicker   See *flicker*.

screen font   A bitmapped font designed to mimic the appearance of printer fonts when displayed on medium-resolution monitors. Modern laser printers can print text with a resolution of 4800 dots per inch (dpi) or more, but except for the most expensive professional units, video displays lack such high resolution and cannot display typefaces with such precision. What one sees onscreen usually is not as good as what one gets from the printer. Adobe International's Adobe Type Manager (ATM), the TrueType standard jointly developed by

Apple and Microsoft, and Microsoft's ClearType technology provide screen fonts that closely mimic printer fonts. See *bitmapped font, ClearType, outline font*.

screening In computer graphics, the process by which an image is converted to a grid of colored dots so that it can be reproduced by standard printing processes. See *halftone*.

screen memory See *video memory*.

screen pitch See *dot pitch*.

screen saver A utility program that changes the screen display—to an aquarium scene or a variable pattern of lines, for example—while one is away from his or her computer. In the past, screen savers were needed to prevent "burn-in," which could damage a monitor by recording a permanent "ghost" image of a frequently viewed screen display in the screen's phosphors. Today's advanced phosphors are not as susceptible to burn-in, so the use of screen savers is not required for system maintenance. Some screen savers come with password utilities, so they become very useful for providing a measure of security when users are away from their desks. See *phosphor*.

script A series of instructions, expressed in a scripting language, that instructs the computer to perform a specific procedure, such as logging on to an e-mail system. Most operating systems are equipped with shell scripting languages that enable a skilled operator to write scripts to perform common system maintenance tasks; these scripts can be stored in files and executed as if they were executable programs. Typically, scripts are interpreted rather than compiled, relatively short, and relatively easy to write. Some scripting languages (such as PHP) are designed to generate Web content from information stored in databases. Others, such as JavaScript, are included in Web pages and provide Web pages with features that do not require the Web browser to obtain additional information from the server. Still others are provided with applications and enable users

to automate a program's functionality. See *scripting language*.

scripting language A simple programming language designed to enable computer users to write useful programs quickly. Examples of scripting languages are JavaScript, a scripting language that adds active content to downloaded Web pages, and Perl, which is widely used to write Common Gateway Interface (CGI) scripts for World Wide Web (WWW) forms processing. Typically, scripting languages are used to assemble or "glue" resources, such as objects within the Document Object Model (DOM); for this reason, a scripting language's variables may refer (for example) to units of code, objects, or files as well as standard data types (such as integers or strings). To facilitate resource gluing, most scripting languages are typeless, which means that errors may not be detected until the code is actually executed. Most scripting languages are designed to be translated into executable code by an interpreter; however, some can also be compiled. See *CGI, compiler, DOM, interpreted programming language, interpreter, JavaScript, Jscript, Perl, PHP, Python, Tcl*.

script kiddies Derogatory slang term for youthful crackers who run automated scripts enabling them to detect the presence of a poorly secured computer on the Internet. When such a computer is detected, these unskilled crackers use a variety of well-known, simple techniques to gain superuser status on the targeted computer; they may subsequently destroy data, steal passwords, or install Trojan horse programs. Script kiddies may lack technical expertise, but they nevertheless pose a major threat to the security of computer systems worldwide; their scripts are constantly hunting for poorly secured systems. Synonymous with kidiot. See *cracker, superuser, Trojan horse*.

scroll To move a window horizontally or vertically so that its position over a document or worksheet changes. In some programs, scrolling is clearly distinguished from cursor movement; when one scrolls, the cursor stays put. In other programs, however, scrolling the screen also moves the cursor.

scroll arrow   In a graphical user interface (GUI), an arrow (pointing up, down, left, or right) that one can click to scroll the screen in the desired direction. The scroll arrows are located at the ends of scroll bars. See *graphical user interface (GUI)*.

scroll bar/scroll box   A graphical user interface (GUI) feature that enables the user to scroll horizontally and vertically using rectangular scrolling areas on the right and bottom borders of the window. One scrolls the document horizontally or vertically by clicking the scroll bars (or scroll arrows) or by dragging the scroll boxes. See *graphical user interface (GUI)*.

Scroll Lock key   On IBM PC–compatible keyboards, a toggle key that, in some programs, switches the cursor-movement keys between two different modes. The exact function of this key varies among programs. See *toggle key*.

SCSI   (Pronounced *skuh-zee*.) Acronym for Small Computer System Interface. An interface amounting to a complete expansion bus in which one can plug devices such as hard disk drives, CD-ROM drives, scanners, and laser printers. The most common SCSI device in use is the SCSI hard disk, which contains most of the controller circuitry, leaving the SCSI interface free to communicate with other peripherals. One can daisy-chain as many as seven SCSI devices to a single SCSI port. Confusing to consumers is the profusion of SCSI standards with their varying combinations of data transfer rates (from 5 to 640 Mbps) and bus widths (8 or 16 bits). Although SCSI continues to play an important role in the high-end hard disk drive market, FireWire (IEEE 1394) and USB 2.0 are increasingly preferred for other types of peripherals, such as digital cameras. See *Fast SCSI, Fast/Wide SCSI, SCSI-1, SCSI-2, SCSI-3, Ultra SCSI, Ultra/Wide SSCI, Ultra-3 SCSI, Ultra 320 SCSI, Ultra 640 SCSI*.

SCSI-1   Commonly used name for the original SCSI, which enables data transfer rates of up to 5 Mbps using an 8-bit bus.

SCSI-2   An improved version of the SCSI-1 interface that reduces the number of conflicts among devices in a daisy chain and includes a common command set to enable different types of devices (such as scanners, CD-ROM drives, and tape back-up drives) to work together smoothly. SCSI-2 defines a Fast SCSI mode (with a data transfer rate of up to 10 Mbps) as well as an Ultra SCSI mode (with data transfer rates of up to 20 Mbps). Both standards call for an 8-bit bus. More recent versions of these standards use a 16-bit bus: Fast/Wide SCSI transfers data at 20 Mbps, while Ultra/Wide SCSI transfers data at speeds up to 40 Mbps.

SCSI-3   See Ultra-3 SCSI.

SD Card   Abbreviation for Secure Digital Card. A flash memory storage device, about the size of a postage stamp, that is used to provide auxiliary storage for digital cameras and other small computer peripherals. The SD Card format is backed by a broad industry consortium that does not include Sony. See *CompactFlash (CF)*.

SDH   Acronym for Synchronous Digital Hierarchy, the international name for SONET.

SDLC   See *software development life cycle (SDLC)*.

SDMI   Acronym for Secure Music Digital Initiative. A standard for music playback devices that imposes after-sale restrictions (called digital rights management) on the uses that can be made of a lawfully purchased musical recording, such as the number of times that the recording can be copied. Supported by a consortium of recording industry firms and copyright holders, SDMI represents a response to the widespread Internet sharing of MP3 files. In response to an SDMI-issued challenge, a group of French hackers quickly defeated the "unbreakable" SDMI encryption scheme; subsequently, the initiative lost momentum and is, at this writing, said to be in "hiatus." Meanwhile, the MP3 format continues to proliferate, even though it includes no provisions for digital rights management. See *copyright, digital rights management (DRM), first sale, MP3.*

SDRAM Acronym for synchronous dynamic random access memory. A high-speed random access memory (RAM) technology that can synchronize itself with the clock speed of the microprocessor's data bus. SDRAM is available to suit a variety of motherboard data bus speeds, ranging from 66MHz (PC66) to 150 MHz (PC150). Faster than EDO RAM and other asynchronous DRAM technologies, PC133 SDRAM is the memory technology of choice for most systems at this book's writing; however, DDR-SDRAM, found in high-end systems, is expected to replace SDRAM in most systems, including entry-level systems, in the coming years. See *DDR-SDRAM, PC100, PC133, PC150, random access memory (RAM), RDRAM.*

SDRAM II See *DDR-SDRAM.*

SDSL Acronym for symmetric digital subscriber line. A Digital Subscriber Line (DSL) standard that provides the same data transfer rates in both directions (upstream and downstream), with speeds up to 2.3 Mbps. Like other DSL standards, SDSL works with standard, twisted-pair telephone lines. See *DSL.*

SD slot A receptacle designed to accept a variety of devices that conform to the Secure Digital Card specification. These devices are not limited to flash memory cards; the standard supports a variety of adapters, including wireless LAN adapters. See *SD Card.*

search and replace See *replace.*

search engine 1. Any program that locates needed information in a database. **2.** An Internet search service that enables a person to search for information on the Internet. To use a search engine, the user types one or more keywords; the result is a list of documents or files that contain one or

more of these words in their titles, descriptions, or text. Consistently popular is the Google service; following in popularity are the default search services of the leading Web portals (Yahoo, MSN, and AOL).

SEC See *single edge contact.*

SECC See *single edge contact cartridge.*

secondary cache Cache memory that is on the motherboard rather than inside a microprocessor. Also called L2 cache memory, secondary cache memory dramatically improves system performance and is essential to every computer system. Several kinds of secondary cache memory are available, ranging from the slow but inexpensive direct-map cache to fast and expensive four-way set-associative cache. Write-back secondary cache memory is better than write-through secondary cache memory. See *full-associative cache, L3 cache.*

secondary key In a sorting operation performed on a database, the second key that is used to order the data within sub-groupings after an initial grouping has been performed by the primary key. For example, a user may want to sort a mailing list by ZIP code (the primary key); within a given ZIP code, a secondary sort organizes the records by last name.

secondary storage A nonvolatile storage medium, such as a disk drive, that stores program instructions and data even after one switches off the power. Synonymous with auxiliary storage. See *primary storage.*

secondary user rights In a software license, a contract clause that enables the user to install an additional copy of the licensed program on the user's second computer, such as a notebook computer. Most End User License Agreements (EULA) no longer grant secondary user rights. See *commercial software, EULA, software license.*

second-generation computer An early type of computer, built during the 1950s and early 1960s, that was constructed out of hand-wired transistors rather than vacuum tubes.

second-generation programming language The first programming language, called assembly language, that enabled programmers to work at one level of abstraction higher than machine language.

second-person virtual reality A virtual reality (VR) system that presents the user with a high-definition video screen and a cockpit with navigation controls, as in a flight simulator program. This type of virtual reality is less engaging than computer-generated worlds that can be explored through the use of goggles and sensor gloves (hence the term "second person").

sector A segment of one of the concentric tracks encoded on a floppy or hard disk during a low-level format. In IBM PC–compatible computing, a sector usually contains 512 bytes of information. See *cluster.*

sector interleave See *interleaving.*

sector interleave factor See *interleave factor.*

Secure Electronic Transactions See *SET.*

Secure Hypertext Transport Protocol See *S-HTTP.*

Secure Sockets Layer See *SSL.*

security A general term that encompasses all aspects of the measures taken to safeguard computer systems and the data they contain from losses attributable to any kind of attack, whether initiated by people or natural elements. A given system's security boils down to a calculated assessment of the risks entailed by losses, the costs imposed by security measures, and the likelihood that the system will be subjected to attack. A secure computer system, therefore, is a dependable system that offers its users a desirable level of performance and protection against loss while, at the same time, raises the costs, difficulty, and risks of attack to a level that discourages all or nearly all intrusions.

A system's security is dependent on five fundamental measures: authentication (users cannot access the system without proving their identity), access control (users are assigned varying levels of access permissions and cannot access those resources that are denied to them); confidentiality (data is protected from unauthorized disclosure); availability (the system is protected from attacks intended to make the system unavailable for its intended use); integrity (data and software are protected from unauthorized modification); non-repudiation (users who initiate messages or transactions cannot deny that they did so); and privacy (users retain control over the use and dissemination of personal or other confidential information they supply to the system). All of the following steps must be taken to assure a desirable level of security: risk avoidance (avoiding unnecessary computer or Internet uses that pose unacceptable risks); deterrence (making the consequences of security intrusions clear to would-be offenders); prevention (employing every possible technical means to prevent attempts to compromise a system's security, such as firewalls); detection (using every possible technical means to determine whether a system has been compromised); and recovery (protecting valuable systems and resources by keeping complete backups and establishing a disaster recovery plan). Security can also be conceptualized as involving several discrete levels or domains, including the physical level (losses attributable to physical phenomena such as leaks, flooding, electrical surges, etc.); operational level (losses attributable to inadequate organization of personnel); employee level (losses attributable to inadequate screening of new hires, inadequate supervision of current employees, and inadequate protections against actions that may be undertaken by ex-employees); system/network component level (losses attributable to theft or sabotage of equipment, unprotected systems in open offices or employee eavesdropping). See *access control, authentication, availability, confidentiality, firewall, integrity non-repudiation, privacy, risk, social engineering.*

seek To locate a specific region of a disk and to position the read/write head so that the computer can retrieve data or program instructions.

seek time   In a secondary storage device, the time that it takes the read/write head to reach the correct location on the disk. See *access time.*

segmented memory architecture   A computer memory design in which specified regions of physical random access memory (RAM) can be reserved for portions of a program's executing code. Intel's original x86 architecture is based on segmented memory principles. Although this design is intended to enhance system stability by preventing one program from invading another's memory space, today's operating systems provide this protection without imposing the overhead and other constraints imposed by a segmented memory architecture. See *operating system (OS), overhead, random access memory (RAM).*

select   To highlight part of a document so that the program can identify the material on which one wants to perform the next operation. In addition to selecting text, one can highlight or select an item from a list box or select a check box item to toggle it on or off.

selection   **1.** A portion of a document's text or graphics that has been highlighted in reverse video for formatting or editing purposes. **2.** In programming, a branch or conditional control structure. **3.** In database management programs, the retrieval of records by using a query. See *branch control structure.*

selection control structure   In structured programming, a method of handling a program branch by using an IF-THEN-ELSE structure. This is much more efficient than using a GOTO statement. Also called a conditional or branch control structure.

selection handle   In a graphics program, a box or dot that, when dragged, moves or alters the selection.

self-extracting archive   A compressed file that contains the software needed to decompress itself. Double-clicking a self-extracting archive launches the decompression portion of the program and decompresses the files.

Self-Monitoring Analysis and Reporting Technology   See *SMART.*

semantic net   In hypertext theory, a set of connections among the ideas in a web. In principle, the sum total of hyperlinks within the web exploit every possible connection with every document in the web; in practice, only a few of the possible links are implemented. See *hyperlink, hypertext, web.*

semantics   In computer programming, the behaviors resulting from the program's execution (in contrast to its syntax, the form in which the program is expressed). In general, syntax is easier to check than semantics; it is exceptionally difficult (and, in practice, prohibitively expensive) to test all of the conditions under which all of a program's behaviors might occur. The difficulty and expense of testing program semantics explains the high frequency of program faults and errors; when faults and errors occur in safety-critical systems and are not handled by redundant systems or other measures, mishaps (accidents) may occur. See *error, fault tolerance, mishap, safety-critical system, syntax.*

semiconductor   A material such as silicon or germanium that is less electrically conductive than excellent electrical conductors, such as copper, and insulating materials. Semiconductor wafers or chips of varying resistance can be assembled to create a variety of electronic devices.. Historically, semiconductor technology developed through a series of stages, conventionally called large scale integration (LSI, capable of integrating up to 100,000 transistors on a single chip) and very large scale integration (VLSI, capable of integrating more than 100,000). These terms are quaint in light of contemporary semiconductor technology; for example, the Pentium 4 contains the equivalent of more than 55 million transistors. See *large-scale integration (LSI), very large scale integration (VLSI).*

sendmail An e-mail message transfer agent (MTA) that is in widespread use on UNIX and Unix-like operating systems, including Linux. The program sends and receives mail over TCP/IP networks (including the Internet) in accordance with the Simple Mail Transport Protocol (SMTP). Widely available in freely redistributable open source code, sendmail is also available in a commercial version maintained by Sendmail, Inc., a company founded by sendmail's original author. Although sendmail still handles most of the mail conveyed via the Internet, the open source version of the program is exceptionally difficult to install, configure, and secure; furthermore, a continuing series of newly discovered security vulnerabilities has diminished the program's reputation. A competing, well-regarded program called qmail is steadily taking market share away from sendmail. See *message transfer agent (MTA), SMTP.*

send statement In a SLIP or PPP dialer program's script language, a statement that tells the program to send certain characters. Send statements follow expect statements, which tell the program to wait until the service provider's computer sends certain characters to a computer.

sensor glove In virtual reality (VR) systems, an interface that is worn on a hand and that enables the user to manipulate and move virtual objects in a virtual reality environment. See *head-mounted display (HMD).*

separator A character that is used to divide units of data so that they can be differentiated by a program or procedure. See *terminator.*

sequence control structure A control structure that tells the computer to execute program statements in the order in which the statements were written. One of three fundamental control structures that govern the order in which program statements are executed, the sequence control structure is the default in all programming languages. One can use loops and branch control structures to alter the sequence.

sequential access An information storage and retrieval technique in which the computer must move through a sequence of stored data items to reach the desired one. Sequential access media, such as cassette tapes, are much slower than random access media, such as hard disk drives.

serial See *asynchronous communication, multitasking, parallel port, serial communication, serial port.*

Serial ATA (SATA) A family of high-speed specifications for hard drive interfaces that can transfer data at speeds ranging from 100 Mbps to 4.5 Gbps; the hot-swappable SATA interface is expected to replace IDE and to compete effectively against SCSI drives, which currently dominate the high-end disk drive market. Using a high-speed serial interface instead of the IDE/ATA parallel interface, Serial ATA simplifies computer wiring (only 7 wires are required instead of the 80 needed by IDE/ATA). During the transition from IDE to SATA, motherboards will support both standards in order to ensure compatibility. See *hot-swapping, IDE, SCSI.*

serial communication A type of electronic communication that, unlike parallel communication, requires that data bits be sent one after the other rather than several at once. Modems rely on serial communication to send data over telephone lines. See *serial port.*

Serial Line Internet Protocol See *SLIP.*

serial mouse A mouse designed to be connected directly to one of the computer's serial ports. See *bus mouse.*

serial port A port that synchronizes and manages asynchronous communication between the computer and devices such as serial printers, modems, and other computers. The serial port not only sends and receives asynchronous data in a one-bit-after-the-other stream, but it also negotiates with the receiving device to ensure that no data is lost when it is sent or received. The negotiation occurs through hardware or software handshaking. See *FireWire, RS-232C, UART.*

Serial Presence Detect (SPD)   A feature found on high-end motherboards that enables the system to detect and save information about the type of SDRAM memory modules installed in the system. See *SDRAM.*

serial printer   A printer designed to be connected to a computer's serial port. Due to the inherent difficulty of configuring serial printers, most printers are now designed to use the computer's parallel or USB ports.

serif   The fine, ornamental cross-strokes across the ends of the main strokes of a character. Serif fonts are easier to read for body type, but most designers prefer to use sans serif typefaces for display type. See *sans serif.*

server   **1.** In a client/server network, a computer or program that is dedicated to providing information in response to external requests. See *client/server, file server, print server.* **2.** On the Internet, a program that supplies information when it receives external requests via Internet connections. See *Web server.*

server application   In object linking and embedding (OLE), the program that creates a source document. Data from a source document is linked or embedded in one or more destination documents created by client applications. See *OLE.*

server-based application   A network version of a program stored on a network's file server and available to more than one user at a time. See *client application.*

server farm   Slang expression for a group of computers that are used to provide network services. Load balancing techniques are used to spread the access demand evenly among the available systems.

Server Message Block (SMB) Protocol   The native Microsoft Windows networking protocol, developed jointly by Microsoft, IBM, and Intel in the late 1980s. SMB enables simple peer-to-peer networks to be created with two or more Windows workstations, all of which function as clients; because clients advertise their presence on SMB networks, all the linked workstations in a workgroup (a defined network segment) will appear in each other's Network Neighborhood windows and, provided users set sharing permissions correctly, they can exchange files. SMB also enables network administrators to set up servers, which can implement a variety of functions, including centrally administered network logon authentication. An open source project called Samba is developing SMB-compatible networking software for Unix and Linux systems, enabling them to function as clients and servers in networks that include Windows-based systems. The most recent version of SMB, called Common Internet File System (CIFS), has been proposed as an Internet standard. See *Common Internet File System (CIFS), Samba.*

server-side include (SSI)   In an HTML document, a statement that tells the Web server to include information on-the-fly, such as the date of the file's last modification.

service bureau   A business that provides a variety of publication services such as graphics file format conversion, optical scanning of graphics, and typesetting on high-resolution imagesetters such as Linotronics and Varitypes.

Service Protocol Identifier   See *SPID.*

service provider   See *ISP, Internet access provider (IAP).*

servo-controlled DC motor   An electric motor used to turn the spindle of a hard disk. Unlike synchronous motors, servo-controlled DC motors are inexpensive and can operate at whatever speed the disk's designers want because the motor's rotation speed is independent of the frequency of the wall outlet's current.

servo-voice coil actuator   The most popular kind of head actuator used in modern hard disks. Servo-voice coil actuators are closed-loop actuators that operate by using an electromagnet to pull the read/write head against tension created by a spring. See *head actuator.*

session layer In the OSI Reference Model of computer network architecture, the third of seven layers, in which a virtual connection is established with a corresponding service at the same layer on another computer. (The connection is virtual because the link to the destination computer at this level is only apparent; the actual connection requires passing the data down the protocol stack all the way to the physical layer, where the data is sent out over the network.) Protocols at the session layer govern this virtual connection. See *OSI Reference Model.*

SET An Internet security standard developed by major credit-card firms that is intended to prevent credit-card fraud. The SET standard works with established Internet encryption standards, such as SSL. To prevent fraud, the SET standard calls for shoppers to identify themselves using personal certificates. In addition, the customer's credit card information is never seen by employees; SET technology relays the encrypted credit card information to the bank, which responds with an authorization code.

SETI@home A scientific experiment that makes use of underutilized home computers to assist in the search for extraterrestrial civilizations. To assist the Search for Extraterrestrial Intelligence (SETI) project, volunteers download the SETI@home application. After SETI@home is installed, the software contacts the SETI server at the University of California, Berkeley, and receives a chunk of unanalyzed data gathered by the Arecibo radio telescope in Puerto Rico. During periods in which the computer is idle, the SETI@home software processes the data, and relays the results to SETI's server. More than 3.5 million computer users are using SETI@home; thanks to their efforts, SETI researchers have identified more than one thousand signals that do not appear to be the product of terrestrial radio interference, at least initially; most (if not all) of these will turn out to be spurious. SETI scientists are attempting to determine the 25 most likely candidates for further investigation.

set-associative cache A type of cache memory used in random access memory (RAM) and processors A set-associative cache divides the cache into two to eight sets, or areas. Data stored in the cache is distributed in bits to each set in sequence. In most instances, data from each set in the cache is read sequentially. Therefore, the set just read or written to can prepare to be read or written to again while data is being read from or written to the next set. The set-associative cache design enables the microprocessor to complete an instruction in one clock cycle. A four-way set-associative cache provides the best compromise between cost and performance. See *cache memory.*

setup parameters Information about a computer system encoded as part of the basic input-output system (BIOS). Setup parameters include the amount of random access memory (RAM) in the computer, the type of keyboard used, and the hard disk's geometry. To change the setup parameters, use the setup program.

setup program A program recorded as part of the basic input-output system (BIOS) that changes the setup options. To run the setup program, one presses a special key combination (usually shown onscreen) as the computer boots up.

setup string A series of characters that a program conveys to a printer so that the printer operates in a specified mode.

setup switches Dual in-line package (DIP) switches in older modems that enabled one to set certain options, such as whether to answer incoming calls. Modern modems have no setup switches; instead, the communications program handles the setup.

set user ID See *SUID.*

SFX A power supply that is designed for use with the small motherboard form factors, such as microATX or its more recent derivative, flexATX. Found on low-end systems, the SFX power supply is not suitable for high-end systems that incorporate numerous system upgrades. See *flexATX, microATX.*

SGML Acronym for Standard Generalized Markup Language. A means of describing markup languages, such as the Hypertext Markup Language (HTML), which is widely used on the World Wide Web (WWW). SGML can be used to define a document type definition (DTD), which defines the elements of a specific type of document and the tags that can be used to display these elements with distinctive formats. A program called a parser is needed to read the tags and display the text appropriately. SGML is an open, international standard defined by the International Organization for Standards (ISO). See *DTD, HTML, ISO, markup language.*

SGRAM Acronym for Synchronous Graphics Random Access Memory. A type of synchronous DRAM (SDRAM) chip that supports memory writing methods specifically optimized for graphics and multimedia applications.. Formerly a feature of high-end video adapters, the chip has been supplanted by the significantly faster DDR-SDRM, which can transfer data on both the rising and falling edge of the clock cycle. See *clock cycle, DDR-SDRAM, SDRAM, video adapter.*

sh An, early, text-mode command shell for Unix and Unix-like operating systems that does not offer command-line editing capabilities. Synonymous with Bourne Shell. Much more widely used is the bash (Bourne-Again) shell, which is the default shell on Linux systems. See *bash, csh, shell.*

shadowing Copying the information stored in system or video adapterROM into RAM)so that the microprocessor can access this information more quickly. See *shadow RAM.*

shadow mask A metal screen located just inside the display of a cathode ray tube (CRT) that prevents electron beams from striking phosphors that glow in the incorrect color. The shadow mask, which is very carefully aligned with the electron guns and the phosphors on the inside of the display, causes the red electron gun to strike only red phosphors and the blue electron gun to strike only blue phosphors, for example. See *cathode ray tube (CRT).*

shadow RAM In Intel-based PCs, a portion of the upper memory area between 640K and 1MB set aside for programs ordinarily retrieved from read-only memory (ROM). Random access memory (RAM) is faster than ROM, so shadow RAM increases performance.

shared memory multiprocessing In a computer with two or more processors that function simultaneously, a method of linking the CPUs by means of a single, shared memory space. An example of shared memory multiprocessing approaches is the symmetric multiprocessing (SMP) capabilities offered by Unix and Unix-like operating systems as well as the current server versions of Microsoft Windows, such as Microsoft Windows XP Server. See *multiprocessing, symmetric multiprocessing (SMP).*

shareware Copyrighted programs made available free of charge on a trial basis. If users like a shareware program and decide to use it, they are expected to pay a fee to the program's author. Some shareware programs, called nagware, introduce increasingly disruptive or delaying reminders once the registration deadline has passed; others stop working entirely. See *nagware, open source software (OSS), public domain program.*

sheet-fed scanner A type of flatbed scanner that can automatically load a series of documents for scanning. Sheet-fed scanners are useful for optical character recognition (OCR) work. See *flatbed scanner, OCR.*

sheet feeder See *cut-sheet feeder.*

shell In computer operating systems, a text-mode command interface that enables users to communicate directly with the kernel, the heart of the operating system. In Unix and Unix-like operating systems, the shell is an independent layer, and users can choose among a variety of available shells. See *bash, csh, kernel, ksh.*

shell account An inexpensive but limited type of Internet dial-up access. A shell account does not directly connect a computer to the Internet. Instead, users employ a communications program to access a Unix host computer, After logging on to this computer, users get limited, text-only access to this Unix computer's operating system (its shell). From the shell, one can run the text-mode Internet tools that are available on the service provider's computer, such as a text-only Usenet newsreader or Web browser. See *communications program, Lynx, shell.*

shell script A script written in a scripting language such as Perl that enables programmers to automate certain functions of a shell (a command interface to the operating system). Shell scripting capabilities are an important component of system administration expertise on UNIX and Unix-related operating systems, including Linux. See *Perl, scripting language, shell, system administration.*

shielded speaker An auxiliary speaker designed to protect the monitor and other computer components from the magnetic field that generates sounds. If unshielded, magnetic fields can distort a monitor's image or even erase data on disks.

Shift+click A mouse maneuver accomplished by holding down the Shift key while clicking the mouse. Applications implement Shift+clicking differently, but in most applications, the action extends a selection.

Shift key The key one presses to enter uppercase letters or punctuation marks. Early IBM keyboards labeled the Shift key only with an up-pointing arrow. More modern keyboards label this key with the word *Shift*. See *Caps Lock key.*

shop A new top-level domain (TLD) name for the Internet, added in 1998, that is designed for the firms offering goods for sale online (as opposed to corporate home pages, which should be named using the firm TLD). See *domain name, gTLD-MoU, top-level domain (TLD).*

shopping basket In Internet shopping, a method of implementing an online store in which users can select items and add them to a virtual shopping basket; when shopping is done, users then see all the items they have selected on an order page. Shopping baskets require cookies to function.

shortcut In Microsoft Windows, an icon that provides fast access to a program. After creating the shortcut, one sees the program's icon on the desktop, where he or she can start it quickly by double-clicking the icon.

shortcut key A key combination that provides quick access to a command or dialog box, bypassing any intermediate menus. See *hot key.*

shoulder surfing In computer security, a method of defeating password authentication by peeking over a user's shoulder and watching the keyboard as that person inputs a password. See *social engineering.*

shrink-wrap license A software license containing language asserting that the end user in effect agrees to the license's terms by breaking the shrink wrap and opening the package. Whether such licenses are legally enforceable remains a matter of legal debate. Unlike software purchased during the early years of computing, in which customers and software publishers directly negotiated with each other to determine license provisions, most software is today purchased "off the shelf" at third-party retail outlets. Because the consumer may be unaware of the contract's terms and is in no position to negotiate with the publisher concerning the terms of the agreement, a software license could be viewed as an unconscionable contract of adhesion (a "take-it-or-leave-it" contract that is so one-sided that it is legally unenforceable). In the U.S., shrink-wrap licenses conflict with

Federal copyright law, which enables purchasers of copyrighted works to sell them (but not to republish them), and state commerce laws, which require licenses to be made available to customers prior to purchase. See *commercial software, secondary user rights, site license, volume purchasing agreement.*

S-HTTP Acronym for Secure Hypertext Transport Protocol. An extension of the World Wide Web's Hypertext Transport Protocol (HTTP) that supports secure commercial transactions on the Web. Secure HTTP provides this support in two ways: by assuring vendors that the customers attempting to buy the vendors' wares are who they say they are (authentication) and by encrypting sensitive information (such as credit card numbers) so that it cannot be intercepted while en route. Secure HTTP was developed by Enterprise Integration Technology (EIT) and the National Center for Supercomputer Applications (NCSA), with subsequent commercial development by Terisa Systems. Netscape Communications developed a competing security technology, the Secure Sockets Layer (SSL) protocol. Although S-HTTP is still used by some Web servers, SSL has emerged as the clear de facto standard. for good reason. S-HTTP is an application-layer protocol, which means that it cannot support secure, encrypted exchange of other types of data, including FTP or NNTP resources.

sig Common abbreviation for signature.

SIG See *special interest group.*

signal The portion of a transmission that coherently represents information, unlike the random and meaningless line noise that occurs in the transmission channel. See *noise.*

signal-to-noise ratio **1.** In online text chatting, the ratio between meaningful content and noise (ranting, raving, and flaming). A good newsgroup or chat room has a high signal-to-noise ratio. A major advantage of moderated online meeting places is that the moderator's activities (including removing obnoxious users) ensure a high signal-to-noise ratio. **2.** In engineering, the ratio of meaningful information to background noise in an electronic circuit.

signature **1.** In e-mail, a brief file (of approximately three or four lines) that contains the message sender's name, organization, address, e-mail address, and (optionally) telephone numbers. One can configure most systems to add this file automatically at the end of each message he or she sends. **2.** In virus-protection utilities, a segment of program code identifiable as belonging to a known virus. See *antivirus program.*

signature capture A computer system that captures a customer's signature digitally so that the store can prove that a purchase was made. Signature capture systems are increasingly common in point of sale (POS) and parcel delivery services. Although consumers worry that they will be exposed to risk if their stored signatures are misused, vendors and adopting companies say that the technology significantly reduces credit card fraud (in part because the system does not produce waste paper containing credit card information).

silicon chip See *chip.*

silicon on insulator (SOI) An IBM-developed chip fabrication technique that employs a thin layer of pure silicon bonded to an insulating substrate. Unlike complementary metal-oxide semiconductor (CMOS) technology, SOI does not employ a "doping" process to introduce impurities. In CMOS chips, these impurities are alternately charged and discharged in order to create the chip's electronic characteristics, but this process releases heat—and the faster the clock speed, the more heat is released. CMOS heat production places an upper limit on the processor clock speed that can be achieved with this technology. SOI fabrication eliminates this roadblock by eliminating the heat-producing impurities. The result is that SOI-based chips are as much as 30 percent faster, and consume 80 percent less power, than comparable CMOS chips. See *CMOS.*

Silicon Valley An area in California's Santa Clara Valley with one of the largest concentrations of high-technology businesses in the world. The word *silicon* suggests the area's prominence in chip design and manufacturing.

SIM See *Society for Information Management.*

SIMD Acronym for Single Instruction Multiple Data. A type of instruction used in microprocessors that can perform operations over multiple additional instructions. SIMD instructions are used to speed three-dimensional graphics processing.

SIMM Acronym for Single In-Line Memory Module. A plug-in memory unit that contains multiple DRAM chips. SIMMs use two form factors: a 30-pin module (used in early systems such as 286- and 386-powered computers) and a 72-pin module (used in 486s and Pentiums before the use of DIMMs became widespread. See *DDR-SDRAM, DIMM, DRAM, SDRAM.*

simple list text chart In presentation graphics, a text chart used to display items in no particular order, with each item given equal emphasis.

Simple Mail Transport Protocol See *SMTP.*

Simple Network Management Protocol (SNMP) A method for keeping track of various hardware devices, such as printers, connected to a network. An SNMP-enabled device, such as a network printer, can automatically send messages to the network administrator when it is low on paper or toner, or when a paper jam has occurred. SNMP seems destined to be replaced by the Microsoft at Work standard or the Desktop Management Interface (DMI) standard.

Simple Object Access Protocol See *SOAP.*

simulation An analytical technique in which an analyst investigates an item's properties by creating a model of the item and exploring the model's behavior. Aeronautical engineers, for example, use computer simulation techniques to design and test thousands of alternative aircraft models quickly, pushing the wind tunnel toward obsolescence in modern aerospace firms. Simulation is also applied in education (to perform virtual science experiments) and in business (to perform financial what-if analyses). As with any model, however, a simulation is only as good as its underlying assumptions. If these assumptions are not correct, the model does not accurately mimic the behavior of the real-world system being simulated.

single density A magnetic recording scheme for digital data that uses a technique called frequency modulation (FM) recording. Single-density disks, common in early personal computing, use large-grained magnetic particles. Such disks have low storage capacity, such as 90K per disk, and are rarely used today. They have been superseded by double-density disks with finer-grained partitions, and high-density disks with even finer partitions. See *MFM.*

single edge contact See *Single Edge Contact Cartridge (SECC).*

Single Edge Contact Cartridge (SECC) SThe physical and electrical specification for the connector used by certain early versions of the Pentium II; the processor and secondary cache are contained within a bulky module with a 242-lead edge-connector; this connector is pressed into a corresponding slot on the motherboard.

Single In-line Memory Module See *SIMM.*

single in-line package (SIP) A set of random access memory (RAM) chips encased in hard plastic and attached to the motherboard with pins. Modern computers have replaced SIPs with single in-line memory modules (SIMMs).

single in-line pinned packages (SIPPs) Synonymous with single in-line package (SIP).

single-pass scanner Any scanner that scans a document in one scanning pass, but especially a color scanner that does so. Single-pass color scanners collect data about all three primary colors on a single trip, unlike triple-pass scanners, which require three trips. Single-pass scanners are not necessarily faster than triple-pass scanners, however.

single-sided disk A floppy disk designed so that only one side of the disk can be used for read/write operations. See *single density.*

single-user mode In Linux, a startup mode that starts the operating system with a minimum of features so that the system administrator can identify and solve problems. Analogous to safe mode in Windows 98.

SIP See *single in-line package.*

site license An agreement between a software publisher and a buyer that permits the buyer to make copies of specific software for internal use. Often a company using a local area network (LAN) buys a site license for a program so that all the users on the LAN can access the program. Most site licenses limit the number of copies that the purchasing organization can make. The cost per copy is much less than that of individually purchased copies. See *commercial software, software license, volume purchasing agreement.*

site registration On the World Wide Web, a process used to gain entry to a Web site that requires one to provide his or her name, e-mail address, and other personal information, which may be disclosed to marketing firms.

skin A configuration file that can be used to change the look of a program. A popular MP3 player, WinAmp, works with thousands of available skins, which can be downloaded from the Internet.

skip factor In a presentation graphics program, an increment that specifies how many data items the program should skip when it labels a chart or graph. Use a skip factor when the category axis is too crowded with headings. If labeling an axis with months, for example, a skip factor of 3 displays the name of every third month.

Skipjack A public key encryption algorithm, reportedly closely related to the Diffie-Hellman public key encryption algorithm, that the U.S. National Security Agency wants American citizens and others to use when they encrypt their Internet transactions. The algorithm contains a key recover scheme that would enable government investigators to obtain the decoding key from a (supposedly) independent authority, but only when public safety or national security is at stake. The algorithm has been ignored by the cryptographic industry because the government has refused to enable cryptographers to examine the algorithm, which some suspect to contain deliberate built-in weaknesses that would aid government surveillance of encrypted communications.

SKU Acronym for stock keeping unit. In conventional but computerized retail businesses as well as e-commerce sites, a unique number that is associated with a specific product. The SKU number is encoded on a bar code attached to or printed on the product, and is used to track inventory and shipment. See *bar code, e-commerce.*

slave 1. The second hard drive in a series of two connected to a single IDE channel on the motherboard. When two hard disks are connected to the same cable, one must be the master and the other must be the slave. The first disk in the series, the master disk, does not control the disk, but it decodes instructions from the host adapter before sending them to the slave. The master hard drive on the first IDE channel is drive that is first searched when the system attempts to boot. See *IDE, master.* **2.** In database replication, a secondary server used to archive data or as a live backup for the master server

sleep mode In computers equipped with power-management features, a state in which the microprocessor shuts down nonessential components during periods of disuse. Often, computers in sleep mode write the contents of their random access memory (RAM) to a hard disk to save the energy required to refresh memory chips. See *display power management signaling (DPMS)*, *green PC*.

slide In a presentation graphics program, an onscreen image that is sized in proportion to a 35-mm slide.

slider See *write-protect tab*.

slide show In presentation graphics, a predetermined list of charts and graphs displayed one after the other.

slide sorter view In a presentation graphics program, a view of a presentation in which all slides are represented by small thumbnail graphics. One can restructure a presentation by dragging a slide to a new location.

SLIP Acronym for Serial Line Internet Protocol. The earliest of two Internet standards specifying how a workstation or personal computer can link to the Internet by means of a dial-up connection (the other standard is PPP). SLIP defines the transport of data packets through an asynchronous telephone line. Therefore, SLIP enables computers not directly connected to local area networks (LANs) to be fully connected to the Internet. This mode of connectivity is far superior to a shell account (a dial-up, text-only account on a Unix computer) because it enables the user to use the Internet tools of his or her choice (such as a graphical Web browser) to run more than one Internet application at a time and to download data directly to his or her computer, with no intermediate storage required.

SLIP/PPP A commonly used abbreviation for the two types of dial-up Internet access that directly integrate a computer with the Internet: SLIP and PPP. See *shell account*.

slot See *expansion slot*.

Slot 1 An Intel-developed receptacle standard for attaching microprocessors to motherboards. Intended as a replacement for the Zero-Insertion Force (ZIF) socket used with earlier Pentium processors, Slot 1 accepts processors packed in a Single Edge Cartridge (SEC) and enables an external secondary cache unit (called a backside cache) to be installed in close physical proximity to the processor. Slot 1-compatible processors include the Pentium II. See *backside cache*, *secondary cache*, *single edge contact cartridge*, *socket 370*, *Zero-Insertion Force (ZIF) socket*.

Slot 2 An enlarged version of the Slot 1 receptacle standard for microprocessors which provides additional room for secondary cache memory. Intel's Xeon requires a motherboard with Slot 2.

slot pitch The distance between the wires of a Trinitron-type monitor's aperture grille. Although slot pitch is an important specification for Trinitron-type monitors, screen pitch is even more important.

slow mail A polite term for the postal service. See *snail mail*.

slug In word processing and desktop publishing (DTP), a code inserted in headers or footers to generate page numbers when the document is printed.

Small Computer System Interface See *SCSI*.

small office/home office See *SoHo*.

small scale integration (SSI) The first generation of semiconductor technology, developed during the 1950s, in which it was possible to fabricate devices, with between 2 and 100 devices positioned on each individual flake of silicon.

SmallTalk A high-level, declarative programming language and programming environment that treat computations as objects that send messages to one another. SmallTalk encourages the programmer to define objects in terms relevant to the intended application. The language is highly extensible because it enables one to create objects, which can be reused, quite easily. SmallTalk inspired HyperTalk, the software command language of Hyper-Card, an application provided with every Macintosh produced since 1987. In this new guise, SmallTalk fulfills its goal of making programming more accessible; tens of thousands of Macintosh users have learned how to program in HyperTalk. See *object-oriented programming*.

SMART Acronym for Self-Monitoring Analysis and Reporting Technology (also spelled S.M.A.R.T.). A feature of the Enhanced IDE (EIDE) hard drive specification that enables the operating system to query the drive's self-analysis system. If the self-analysis reveals a potential problem, users see a message warning of possible future drive failure.

smart card A credit card-sized token that contains a microprocessor and memory circuits used for authenticating a user of computer, banking, or transportation services. When used for authentication purposes, a smart card is often paired with a personal identification number (PIN); the combination between what one has (the token) and what one knows (the PIN) is considered to establish strong authentication.

SMARTDRV In MS-DOS and Microsoft Windows, a disk cache program that substantially speeds apparent disk access times by caching frequently accessed program code.

smart machine Any device containing microprocessor-based electronics that enables the device either to branch to alternative operating sequences depending on external conditions, to repeat operations until a condition is fulfilled, or to execute a series of instructions repetitively. Microprocessors are so inexpensive that they can be embedded in even the most prosaic of everyday devices, such as toasters, coffeemakers, and ovens.

SmartMedia In digital cameras and other devices, a removable, reusable flash memory card for storing data. See *ATA flash memory*, *CompactFlash (CF)*.

smart terminal In a multiuser system, a terminal that contains its own processing circuitry so that it not only retrieves data from the host computer but also carries out additional processing operations and runs host-delivered programs.

SMB See *Samba*, *Server Message Block Protocol*.

SMIL Acronym for Synchronized Multimedia Integration Language. A scripting language designed to enhance Web browsers with multimedia capabilities without the use of plug-in programs.

smiley In e-mail and newsgroups, a sideways face made of ASCII characters that puts a message into context and compensates for the lack of verbal inflections and body language that plagues electronic communication. with emoticon. See *ASCII art*.

S/MIME Abbreviation for Secure Multipurpose Internet Mail Extensions. An addition to the MIME protocol that supports the exchange of encrypted e-mail via the Internet. S/MIME uses RSA's public key encryption algorithm for the initial authentication (which makes use of certificates); after the secure connection is established, an exchange of symmetric encryption algorithm keys occurs.

SMP See *symmetric multiprocessing*.

SMPTE timecode In digital video, a method of synchronizing multiple video input streams using a four-part, colon-separated time expression that denotes hours, minutes, seconds, and frames.

SMTP Acronym for Simple Mail Transport Protocol. An Internet protocol that governs the transmission of e-mail over computer networks. SMTP is simple indeed; it does not provide any support for the transmission of data other than plain text. For this reason, the Multipurpose Internet Mail Extensions (MIME) provides support for binary files of many types, and S/MIME provides support for encrypted e-mail.

smurf A denial-of-service attack that exploits weaknesses in the Internet Control Message Protocol (ICMP). Using a technique (called spoofing) that forges the origin of packets, the attack causes a server to be flooded with responses to ping messages.

snaf The messy strips of wastepaper that litter the office after one removes the perforated edge from continuous, tractor-fed printer paper. The term snaf was the winning entry in a contest sponsored by National Public Radio's *All Things Considered*. The runner-up, perfory, is worthy of mention.

snail mail A derogatory term for the postal service. In an e-mail message, one might say "I'm sending the article to you by snail mail."

snaking columns See *newspaper columns*.

snap-on pointing device In portable computers, a pointing device that snaps onto the side of the computer's case in a special port. No serial port or mouse port cable is required. Snap-on pointing devices are convenient because they save one from having to connect the serial or mouse port cable every time that he or she wants to use the computer. Instead, one simply snaps the trackball into its receptacle. See *built-in pointing device, clip-on pointing device*.

snapshot See *Print Screen (PrtScr), screen capture*.

snapshot printer A thermal transfer printer designed to print the output of digital cameras as a maximum size of 4 by 6 inches. Snapshot printers are less expensive than other thermal transfer printers.

sneakernet A network architecture in which a person physically carries a data-laden floppy disk or tape from one computer to another. Although sneakernets usually are small, they sometimes involve transcontinental air travel.

sniffer A program that intercepts routed Internet data and examines each packet in search of specified information, such as passwords transmitted in cleartext. Synonymous with packet sniffer.

SNOBOL Acronym for String-Oriented Symbolic Language. A high-level programming language designed for text-processing applications. SNOBOL has particularly strong text pattern-matching capabilities and has been used for research work in fields such as language translation, the generation of indexes or concordances to literary works, and text reformatting. However, SNOBOL tends to generate inefficient, hard-to-read source code, and thus is rarely used. See *BASIC, FORTRAN*.

snow See *video noise*.

SOAP Acronym for Simple Object Access Protocol. An object request protocol developed by Microsoft Corporation that relies on widely implemented communications and Internet protocols, including HTTP and XML. Like other object request protocols, SOAP enables programmers to write code that requests network-accessible objects, but it does so without introducing the overhead and additional software needed to support competing object request protocols such as CORBA. See *CORBA, HTTP, .NET, object, ORB, protocol, XML*.

soc hierarchy In Usenet, one of the standard newsgroup hierarchies. The soc newsgroups deal with social issues, social groups, and world cultures.

social engineering Psychological, non-technical methods used by computer intruders to obtain passwords for unauthorized access. Typically, this involves calling an authorized user of a computer system and posing as a network administrator. The caller says, "We've run into a serious problem and we can't access your mailbox. If you give me your password, there's a chance we can save your mail."

Society for Information Management (SIM) A professional society for executives in information-systems fields that has branches in many cities. The SIM was formerly called the Society for Management Information Systems (SMIS).

Society for Management Information Systems (SMIS) See *Society for Information Management (SIM)*.

socket On a TCP/IP network, a virtual port that enables client applications to connect to the appropriate server. To achieve a connection, a client needs to specify both the IP address and the port number of the server application. See *IP address, TCP/IP*.

Socket 7 A processor socket developed by Intel for the original Pentium microprocessor and widely emulated by Intel's competitors.

Socket 8 A processor module socket developed by Intel for the Pentium Pro; the processor module includes secondary cache memory mounted on a backside bus.

Socket 370 A microprocessor socket, originally designed for Intel Celeron processors, that enables the technician to install a compatibly designed microprocessor by inserting the chip into the socket and closing a locking lever. See *Slot 1*.

soft Temporary or changeable, as opposed to hard (permanently wired, physically fixed, or inflexible). Compare to software, soft return, and a page break inserted by a word processing program and subject to change if one adds or deletes text to hardware, a hard return, and a page break that one inserts manually and that remains fixed in place despite further editing.

soft boot A system restart that does not involve switching the power off and on (a hard boot).

soft cell boundary In a spreadsheet program, a feature of cells that enables one to enter labels that are longer than the cell's width (unless the adjacent cells are occupied).

soft copy A temporary form of output, as in a monitor display.

soft font See *downloadable font*.

soft hyphen A hyphen formatted so that it does not take effect unless the word that contains the hyphen otherwise wraps to the next line. In that event, the word is hyphenated to improve the kerning of the line. See *hard hyphen*.

soft page break In a word processing program, a page break that the program inserts based on the current format of the text. This page break could move up or down if one inserts or deletes text or change margins, page size, or fonts. See *forced page break*.

soft return In a word processing program, a line break that the program inserts to maintain the margins. The location of soft returns changes automatically if one changes the margins or inserts or deletes text. See *hard return, word wrap*.

soft-sectored disk A disk that, when new, contains no fixed magnetic patterns of tracks or sectors. Tracks and sectors are created during formatting.

soft start See *warm boot*.

software A computer program or programs, in contrast to the physical equipment on which programs run (hardware). Simultaneously singular and plural, the word compels some speakers to add the redundant "software program" or "software programs" in an attempt to clarify the noun's number. Software is conventionally divided into two categories: system software (programs needed to operate the computer) and application programs (programs that enable users to perform tasks using the computer). See *firmware, hardware*.

software cache A large area of random access memory (RAM) that a program, such as SMARTDRV.EXE, sets aside to store frequently accessed data and program instructions. A 1MB to 2MB software cache can speed up disk-intensive applications such as database management programs.

software compatibility The capability of a computer system to run a specific type of software. The Commodore 64, for example, is not software-compatible with software written for the Apple II, even though both computers use the MOS Technology 6502 microprocessor.

software development life cycle (SDLC) In software engineering, the phases that a large-scale software system goes through from the time it is initially conceived until the time it is discarded. The phases are given varying names, but the following are typical: requirements analysis (also called specification), design, construction (also called manufacturing), validation (also called testing), installation, operation, maintenance, and retirement. See *software engineering*.

software engineering The use of a systematic, disciplined, and quantifiable approach to the development of large-scale software systems; in other words, the application of engineering principles to software development. Software engineering directly addresses the problems that too often arise in large-scale software development. According to a 1994 IBM study of 24 companies that attempted to develop large-scale software systems, 55% had cost overruns, 68% had schedule overruns, and 88% of the systems had to be redesigned before they could be used. The study concluded that, by any standard, the record of achievement was abysmal: three-quarters of all large-scale software systems must be considered operational failures: they do not function as intended or proved so unworkable that they were abandoned. A major reason: such systems were created by developers using idiosyncratic techniques that they could neither measure nor repeat. To improve this dismal performance record, software engineering offers a process model that brings engineering methodologies to the various phases of the software development life cycle (SDLC). The resulting software should be maintainable (easily modified to meet changing requirements; dependable (sufficiently stable to avoid losses attributable to system failure); efficient (does not waste system resources); and usable (includes a well-designed user interface and documentation). See *software development life cycle (SDLC)*.

software error control An error-correction protocol that resides partly or entirely in a communications program rather than in modem hardware. Software error control makes modems cheaper but also taxes the rest of the computer system and is supported by very few communications programs. For these reasons, one should avoid software error control.

software handshaking A method of flow control that ensures that the data that a modem sends does not overwhelm the modem with which it is communicating. In a software handshaking scheme, such as XON/XOFF handshaking, modems exchange special codes when they are ready to send and receive data.

software interpolation In scanners, a method of improving the scanner's true optical resolution by using computer algorithms to guess how the image would appear at a higher resolution.

software license A contractual agreement between software purchasers and the software publisher that specifies what the purchaser may and may not do with the software. Typically, such licenses include clauses that deny that any sale of goods has taken place; what is being sold is not the software itself, the ownership of which is retained by the software publisher, but rather specific rights to use the software, as detailed in the license; for end-user software sold in the mass market, such rights are typically limited to installing and using the software on one computer only. Additional license provisions typically absolve the publisher of all liability in case of losses attributable to software flaws and forbid the user to engage in any of the following actions: making additional, unauthorized copies; decompiling or reverse engineering the software; and giving, selling, or renting the software to others. Since most commercial software is sold as if it were an ordinary packaged good, the publisher cannot readily obtain the purchaser's signature on the license contract; in consequence, the license generally includes a provision that equates the user's opening of the package (breaking the seal on the package's shrink wrap) or installation of the software with acceptance of the license's contractual terms. Because the enforceability of these so-called "shrink-wrap licenses" is questionable, software publishers are pushing for the passage of the Uniform Computer Information Transactions Act (UCITA), which—if enacted by U.S. state legislatures—affirms the enforceability of software licenses, including those that the user is unable to read prior to engaging in an action that constitutes assent to the license's provisions. See *EULA, shrink-wrap license, site license, UCITA, volume purchasing agreement.*

software package   A program delivered to the user in a complete and ready-to-run form, including all necessary utility programs and documentation. See *application software.*

software patent   In the United States and certain other countries (including Japan), a form of patent protection that is extended to software algorithms, the underlying step-by-step process by which a computer program accomplishes its intended objectives. Many countries do not include software algorithms in the list of patentable subject matter due to the belief that such algorithms are the "stock in trade" of computer programmers, and that economic development would suffer if programmers were required to obtain licenses for algorithms that may well have been in widespread use prior to the issuance of a software patent. See *intellectual property (IP), patent, patentable subject matter.*

software piracy   The illegal duplication of copyrighted software without the permission of the software publisher.

software protection   See *copy protection.*

software suite   A collection of programs, which are generally also for sale individually, that, taken together, provide what is intended to be a comprehensive solution for the customer.

SoHo   Abbreviation for small office/home office, a growing and important market for computers and computer software.

Solaris   A version of the Unix operating system developed by Sun Microsystems. Solaris includes OpenWindows, an X Windows-based graphical user interface (GUI).

SONET   Acronym for Synchronous Optical Network. An emerging standard for high-speed networks based on fiber-optic cable. The basic data transfer rate is 51.8 Mbps, which is more than 50 times the data capacity (bandwidth) of the T1 lines that carry much of the data traffic in industrialized nations. Bandwidth can be increased in multiples of 51.8 Mbps, up to a maximum of 48 Gbps. Synonymous with Synchronous Digital Hierarchy (SDH), the non-U.S. name for this standard.

sort   An operation that rearranges data so that it is in a specified ascending or descending order, usually alphabetical or numerical.

sort key   In sort operations, the data that determines the order in which the operation arranges data records. A database sort key is the data field by which to sort; in a spreadsheet, the sort key is the column or row used to arrange the data in alphabetical or numerical order. In a word processing program, the sort key is a word, but the word can be in any position. See *primary key, secondary key.*

sort order   The order, such as ascending and descending, in which a program arranges data when performing a sort. Most programs also sort data in the standard order of ASCII characters. Synonymous with collating sequence. See *ASCII sort order, collate, dictionary sort.*

sound board   See *sound card.*

sound card   An expansion card that can process and play the two basic types of digital audio: waveform sound (a digitized recording of analog audio) and MIDI (a standard for writing instructions that tell a synthesizer how to mimic music and sound effects). The cheapest sound cards offer only three basic connectors (microphone in, line in, and speaker out), while high-end cards include game ports, connectors for

MP3 devices, and an S/PDIF jack for connecting digital recording devices. Older, inexpensive sound cards used FM synthesis to play MIDI sounds; today, low-end sound cards use wavetable synthesis, while the best use waveguide synthesis. On some systems, sound circuitry is incorporated into the motherboard. See *FM synthesis, MIDI, waveform, waveguide synthesis, wave table synthesis.*

soundex An algorithm for retrieving records from a database that can retrieve items that are homonyms of the search terms. A soundex search will retrieve "Woulthers" as well as "Walters."

sound format A specification of how a sound should be digitally represented. Sound formats usually include some type of data compression to reduce the size of sound files.

source The record, file, document, or disk from which information is taken or moved, as opposed to the destination.

source code In a high-level programming language, the typed program instructions that programmers write before the program is compiled or interpreted into machine language instructions the computer can execute.

source document In dynamic data exchange (DDE) and object linking and embedding (OLE), the document that contains data linked to copies of that data in other documents, called destination documents.

source file In many MS-DOS commands, the file from which data or program instructions are copied. See *destination file.*

source worksheet In Microsoft Excel, a worksheet containing a cell or range linked to one or more dependent worksheets. The dependent worksheets reflect the changes that one makes to the source worksheet.

SPA See *Association for Systems Management (ASM).*

spaghetti code A poorly organized program that is almost impossible to read and debug. The cure is to use a well-structured

programming language (such as C, or Pascal) that offers a full set of control structures. See *structured programming.*

spam 1. Unsolicited and unwanted advertising in a Usenet newsgroup or e-mail. The term is apparently derived from a Monty Python skit. **2.** To subject one or more persons with unwanted e-mail.

spamdexing In Web publishing, the inclusion of large numbers of subject words, often in a hidden area of the document, that are unrelated to the subjects actually covered in the document. Spamdexing is undertaken in the hope that a search engine user will see a link to the document after performing a search using one or more of the subject words and will click the link out of curiosity.

SPARC Acronym for Scalable Processor Architecture. An open standard for a RISC microprocessor. Sun Microsystems manufactures a series of workstations based on the SPARC architecture called SPARCstations.

SPARCstation See *SPARC.*

spawn In Unix, to initiate a child process for accomplishing further processing tasks. See *parent process, process, Unix.*

S/PDIF Acronym for Sony-Philips Digital Interface. A standard for connecting digital audio devices via fiber optic cable. Found in high-end sound cards, the S/PDIF connector enables accessory components (such as digital audio recorders) to be connected to the sound card without requiring the output to be converted to analog. See *sound card.*

SPEC See *Standard Performance Evaluation Corporation.*

special interest group (SIG) A subgroup of an organization or network, consisting of members who share a common interest. Common SIG topics include software, hobbies, sports, and literary genres such as mystery or science fiction. See *user group.*

specification In software engineering, one of the phases of the software life cycle.

speculative execution A method of analyzing instructions entering a microprocessor with superscalar architecture and determining how to route the instructions through the pipelines as efficiently as possible. Speculative execution, supposedly employed on Intel's P6 microprocessor, greatly increases a microprocessor's throughput.

Speech Application Progamming Interface See *SAPI.*

speech recognition The decoding of human speech into transcribed text by means of a computer program. To recognize spoken words, the program must transcribe the incoming sound signal into a digitized representation, which must then be compared to an enormous database of digitized representations of spoken words. To transcribe speech with any tolerable degree of accuracy, users must speak each word independently, with a pause between each word. This substantially slows the speed of speech-recognition systems and calls their utility into question, except in the case of physical disabilities that would prevent input by other means. Dragon Software, a leader in the speech recognition field, has announced a new speech recognition technology that the company claims is capable of recognizing continuous speech. This and other improvements in speech-recognition algorithms, coupled with impressive increases in computing horsepower, will eventually relegate the keyboard and mouse—and the repetitive stress injuries (RSI) that they cause—to the technological dustbin. See *discrete speech recognition.*

speech synthesis Computer production of audio output that resembles human speech. Such output is particularly useful to visually impaired computer users. Unlike speech recognition, speech synthesis technology is well developed. Existing speech synthesis boards are inexpensive and can do an impressive job of reading virtually any file containing English sentences in ASCII script—although, to some listeners, the English sounds as though it is being spoken with a Czech accent.

spell-checker A program, often a feature of word processing programs, that checks for the correct spelling of words in a document by comparing each word against a file of correctly spelled words. A good spell-checker displays suggestions for the correct spelling of a word and enables one to replace the misspelled word with the correct one. Words can usually be added to the spell-checker's dictionary.

SPID Acronym for Service Protocol Identifier. In ISDN, a unique number assigned to a B-channel that enables the service provider's ISDN switching system to identify a specific client. See *ISDN.*

spider A program that prowls the Internet, attempting to locate new, publicly accessible resources such as World Wide Web (WWW) documents, files available in public File Transfer Protocol (FTP) archives, and Gopher documents. Also called wanderers or robots, spiders contribute their discoveries to a database, which Internet users can search by using an Internet-accessible search engine (such as Lycos or WebCrawler). Spiders are necessary because the rate at which people are creating new Internet documents greatly exceeds manual indexing capacity.

spike See *surge.*

spindle The axle on which a hard or floppy disk turns. The spindle, which is turned by a spindle motor, is not permanently attached to a floppy disk but is permanently attached at the center of a hard disk platter.

spindle motor The electric motor—either a synchronous motor or a servo-controlled DC motor—that turns hard and floppy disks. Floppy-disk spindle motors turn only when one is writing data to a disk in his or her drive, but hard disk spindle motors turn whenever a computer is on.

split bar In a graphical user interface (GUI) such as Microsoft Windows or the Macintosh Finder, a bar that one can drag to split the window horizontally or vertically.

split screen A display technique that divides the screen into two or more windows. In word processing programs that have split-screen capabilities, one can usually display two parts of the same document independently or display more than one document. Splitting the screen is useful when a person wants to refer to one document, or part of a document, while writing in another. The technique also facilitates cut-and-paste editing.

spoiler In a Usenet newsgroup, a message that contains the ending of a novel, movie, or television program, or the solution to a computer or video game. Network etiquette (or netiquette) requires that one encrypt such messages so that users cannot read them unless they choose to do so. In Usenet newsgroups, the encryption technique is called rot-13.

spoof To deceive or to fake, especially with the intention of gaining unauthorized access to computer resources.

spoofing **1.** A method of increasing the apparent speed of a network by configuring routers so that they send faked conformation signals in response to a workstation's polling signals, which attempt to confirm that a distant server is still connected. Polling signals consume a great deal of network bandwidth, but this is unnecessary in today's more reliable network environment. Spoofing enables network administrators to cut down on network overhead while still retaining an acceptable level of service. **2.** A method of falsifying the IP address of an Internet server by altering the IP address recorded in the transmitted packets. The fact that spoofing is possible reflects an underlying security hole of prodigious magnitude in the current Internet protocol suite: The headers of data packets are transmitted in cleartext with no network-level support for authenticating their true origin.

spooler A utility program, often included with an operating system, that routes printer commands to a file on disk or in random access memory (RAM) rather than to the printer, and then doles out the printer commands when the central processing unit (CPU) is idle. A print spooler provides background printing; a program thinks that it is printing to a super-fast printer, but the spooler is actually directing the printer output to RAM or a disk file. One can continue working with his or her program, and the spooler guides the printer data to the printer whenever the CPU is not busy handling the work.

spot color A color defined by the Pantone Matching System (PMS). Spot color is a form of device-independent color.

spreadsheet In a spreadsheet application, a graphics representation of an accountant's worksheet, replete with rows and columns for recording labels (headings and subheadings) and values. A spreadsheet is a matrix of columns (usually assigned alphabetical letters) and rows (usually numbered) that form individual cells. Each cell has a distinct cell address, such as B4 or D19. Into each cell one can place a value, which is a number or a hidden formula that performs a calculation; or a label, which is a heading or explanatory text. A formula can contain constants, such as 2+2, but the most useful formulas contain cell references, such as D9+D10. By placing formulas in a spreadsheet's cells, one can create a complex network of links among the parts of a spreadsheet. After embedding formulas, one can adjust constants—such as the tax rate or acceleration due to gravity—to see how the bottom line changes.

spreadsheet program An application that simulates an accountant's worksheet onscreen and lets one embed hidden formulas that perform calculations on the visible data. Many spreadsheet programs also include powerful graphics and presentation capabilities to create attractive products. See *spreadsheet*.

sputtering Like plating, a means of coating hard disk substrate with thin-film magnetic media. Sputtering uses heat and the attraction of oppositely charged particles to coat the platters evenly.

SQL (Often pronounced *sequel*.) Acronym for Structured Query Language. In database management systems, an IBM-developed query language that has become the de facto standard for querying databases in a client/server network. The four basic commands (SELECT, UPDATE, DELETE, and INSERT) correspond to the four basic functions of data manipulation (data retrieval, data modification, data deletion, and data insertion, respectively). SQL queries approximate the structure of an English natural-language query. A data table consisting of columns (corresponding to data fields) and rows (corresponding to data records) displays a query's results. See *database management system (DBMS), ODBC, query, query language.*

squelch In a network, to suspend or cancel a problem user's access privileges. A network might squelch such privileges after a user repeatedly violates the terms under which the account was created.

SRAM Acronym for static random access memory. A type of random access memory (RAM) chip that holds its contents without constant refreshing from the central processing unit (CPU). Although as volatile as dynamic random access memory (DRAM) chips, SRAM does not require the CPU to refresh its contents several hundred times per second. These chips are substantially faster but also are significantly more expensive than DRAM chips and, therefore, are most often used for RAM caches. Two types of SRAM are available: asynchronous and synchronous. Unlike asynchronous SRAM, synchronous SRAM is significantly faster because it is capable of synchronizing with the microprocessor's clock speed, enabling it to perform operations that are timed by the system clock;. See *cache memory, DRAM, SDRAM.*

S register A special unit of memory inside a modem that contains alterations to the AT command set, such as the number of rings to wait before answering a call or the time to wait for the carrier to be established.

SSE See *streaming SIMD extensions.*

SSL Acronym for Secure Sockets Layer. An Internet security standard that is widely supported by leading Web browsers and Web servers. Unlike its chief competition, S-HTTP, SSL is application-independent—it works with all Internet tools, not just the World Wide Web (WWW). This is because SSL functions at the network layer rather than the application layer and is thus available to any SSL-ready Internet application, including newsreaders. Applications that use SSL use RSA public key encryption and RSA certificates and digital signatures to establish the identities of parties to the transaction; after the link is established, a key exchange takes place, and RSA's RC4 encryption technology (a symmetric key encryption algorithm) is used to secure the transaction. With the 128-bit keys used for SSL communication within the United States, the encrypted transaction would be computationally infeasible to decode, so it is safe from snoopers and criminals. (The 40-bit version used in export versions of popular browsers, however, is not secure and should be avoided for commercial transactions.)

ST-506/ST-412 A hard disk interface standard once widely used in IBM and IBM-compatible computers. These drives, virtually unavailable today, are slower and cheaper than drives that use more recent interface standards, such as Enhanced System Device Interface (ESDI), Integrated Drive Electronics (IDE), and Small Computer System Interface (SCSI). The ST-506/ST-412 interface uses the Modified Frequency Modulation (MFM) and Run-Length Limited (RLL) standards.

stack In programming, a data structure in which the first items inserted are the last ones removed. Programs that use control structures use the Last In First Out (LIFO) data structure. A stack enables the computer to track what it was doing when it branched or jumped to a procedure. In HyperCard, the term refers to a file that contains one or more cards that share a common background.

stacked column graph A column graph that displays two or more data series on top of one another. See *histogram*.

staggered windows See *cascading windows*.

stale Out-of-date; no longer accurate.

stale link In the World Wide Web (WWW), a hyperlink to a document that has been erased or moved.

standalone Self-sufficient; not requiring any additional component or service.

standalone computer A computer system dedicated to meeting all the computing needs of an individual user. The user chooses just the software needed for daily tasks. Links with other computers, if any, are incidental to the system's chief purpose. See *distributed processing system, multiuser system, professional workstation*.

standalone program An application that is sold individually. See *suite*.

standalone server In a client/server network, a server that maintains its own authentication and user accounting services. Although this is convenient for a small network, it quickly becomes a liability in a larger network, in which users may have to access several servers to get the data they need. If each of these servers is a standalone server, users will have to supply multiple login names and passwords. As an additional liability, each server represents a different point of vulnerability to intrusion by unauthorized users. In networks with several servers, a better solution is to move authentication and user accounting to the network level. See *DCE speed, Kerberos*.

standard In computing, a set of rules or specifications that, taken together, define the architecture of a hardware device, program, or operating system. Standards are often maintained by an independent standard body, such as the American National Standards Association (ANSI). See *de facto standard, open standard, proprietary standard*.

Standard Generalized Markup Language See *SGML*.

standard newsgroup hierarchy In Usenet, a collection of categories that every Usenet site is expected to carry, if sufficient storage room exists. The standard newsgroup hierarchy includes the following newsgroup categories: comp.★, misc.★, news.★, rec.★, sci.★, soc.★, and talk★. A voting process creates new newsgroups within the standard newsgroup hierarchies. See *Call for Votes (CFV)*.

Standard Performance Evaluation Corporation (SPEC) A consortium of computer-industry companies, founded in 1988, that works to establish fair benchmark tests for evaluating computers. SPEC has developed numerous tests that are suited to varying applications; for example, the SPECapc benchmark tests system performance while using graphics-intensive applications. Other SPEC benchmarks are designed to establish comparison baselines for floating-point calculations, high-demand server performance, Java performance, and many more.

standby UPS An uninterruptible power supply (UPS) that protects against complete power failure but does not protect against reductions in line voltage (brownouts). Standby units are less expensive than line interactive UPS devices, but their incapability of protecting against brownouts might render them generally useless. See *surge protector*.

star network In local area networks (LANs), a centralized network topology with a physical layout that resembles a star. At the center is a central network processor or wiring concentrator; the nodes are arranged around and connected directly to the central point. A star network's wiring costs are considerably higher than those of other network topologies because each workstation requires a cable that links the workstation directly to the central processor. See *bus network, LAN, ring network, topology*.

start bit In serial communications, a bit inserted into the data stream to inform the receiving computer that a byte of data is to follow. See *asynchronous communication, stop bit*.

starting point   In the World Wide Web (WWW), a Web document that contains useful starting points for Web navigation, such as introductions to the Internet and to the Web, subject trees, search engines, and interesting Web sites.

start page   In a Web browser, the page that appears when the user launches the program (or clicks the Home button on the toolbar). By default, this is generally the browser publisher's home page; both Netscape Navigator and Microsoft Internet Explorer enable users to customize the start page.

startup disk   The disk that a person normally uses to boot his or her computer. The disk (often a hard disk) contains portions of the operating system. Synonymous with boot disk and system disk.

startup screen   A text or graphics display at the beginning of a program. Usually, the startup screen includes the program name and version and often contains a distinctive program logo.

statement   In a high-level programming language, an expression that can generate machine language instructions when the program is interpreted or compiled.

state-of-the-art   Technically sophisticated, representing the highest level of technical achievement.

static object   A document or portion of a document pasted into a destination document using standard copy-and-paste techniques. The object does not change if one make changes to the source document. To update the information in the object, one makes changes to the source document and copy from it again. See *embedded object, linked object, OLE.*

static random access memory   See *SRAM.*

station   See *workstation.*

statistical software   An application program that makes conducting statistical tests and measurements easier.

status bar   In a graphical user interface (GUI), a bar across the bottom of the window that displays information about the program.

status line   A line of an application program's display screen, usually at the bottom, that describes the state of the program. The information presented in the status line often includes the name of the file that a person is modifying, the cursor location, and the name of any toggle keys that he or she has pressed, such as Num Lock or Caps Lock.

stem   In typography, the main vertical stroke of a character.

stepper motor   A motor that makes a precise fraction of a turn each time that it receives an electrical impulse. Stepping motors are used as part of head actuator mechanisms in floppy disk and hard drives.

stepping motor   See *stepper motor.*

stereoscopy   A technology that presents two pictures taken from slightly different perspectives that, when viewed together using a stereoscope, creates a profound illusion of three-dimensional space. Stereoscopic viewers were popular in the last century, and the technology lives on today as one of the foundations of virtual reality (VR). See *head-mounted display (HMD).*

stickup initial   See *initial.*

stop bit   In serial communications, a bit inserted into the data stream to inform the receiving computer that the transmission of a byte of data is complete. See *asynchronous communication, start bit.*

storage   The retention of program instructions and data within the computer so that this information is available for processing purposes. See *primary storage, secondary storage.*

storage device   Any optical or magnetic device capable of information storage functions in a computer system. See *secondary storage.*

storage medium

356

storage medium In a storage device, the material that retains the stored information (such as the magnetic material on the surface of a hard drive).

store-and-forward network A wide area network (WAN) created by means of the telephone system. Each computer in the network stores messages received during the day. At night, when telephone rates are low, the computer's automatic software dials a central distribution site. The computer uploads those messages addressed to other computers on the system and downloads messages from other computers. Store-and-forward technology is the basis of the Unix-to-Unix Copy Program (UUCP), a Unix network, and FidoNet, one of several wide area networks that link computer bulletin board systems (BBS).

stored program concept The idea, which underlies the architecture of all modern computers, that programs should be stored in memory with data. This concept suggests that a program can jump back and forth through instructions instead of executing them sequentially. This insight launched virtually the entire world of modern computing, but it also introduced a known limitation. See *parallel processing*, *von Neumann bottleneck*.

storefront In the World Wide Web (WWW), a Web document that establishes a commercial enterprise's presence on the Web. Typically, a storefront does not attempt to provide a complete catalog, but instead illustrates a few items or services that typify what the firm has to offer. Web marketing experience demonstrates that the most successful storefronts are those that offer some interesting freebies, such as information or downloadable software. As security protocols become more widely used, customers will be able to use their credit cards safely to place orders. See *S-HTTP*, *SSL*.

stream A continuous flow of data through a channel, in contrast to data delivery by means of packets (fixed, numbered, and addressed units of data that may arrive out of order).

streaming audio On a computer network, a method of sending audio data as a continuous, compressed stream that is played back on-the-fly. In contrast to downloaded sounds, which may not begin playing for several minutes, streaming audio begins almost immediately. There is no universally supported streaming audio standard; the de facto standard is Real-Audio.

Streaming SIMD Extensions (SSE) A set of 3D graphics instructions incorporated into Intel microprocessors, beginning with the Pentium III. Also known as Katmai New Instructions (KNI). See *SIMD*.

streaming tape drive A secondary storage device that uses continuous tape, contained in a cartridge, for backup purposes.

streaming video On a computer network, a method of sending video data as a continuous, compressed stream that is played back on-the-fly. Like streaming audio, streaming videos begin playing almost immediately.

stress test An alpha test procedure in which the manufacturer tries to determine how a program will behave under heavy demands. By pushing lots of data into a program, a manufacturer can determine whether, when, and how the program will fail under real-life conditions.

strikeout See *strikethrough*.

strikethrough A font attribute in which text is struck through with a hyphen, as in strikethrough formatting. Strikethrough is often used to mark text to be deleted from a co-authored document so that the other author can see changes easily. Also called strikeout. See *redlining*.

string 1. In programming, a series of alphanumeric characters or a unit of data other than a numeric value. 2. A keyword in a database search.

string formula In a spreadsheet program, a formula that performs a string operation, such as changing a label to uppercase or lowercase.

string operation A computation performed on alphanumeric characters. Computers cannot understand the meaning of words and therefore cannot process them like people do; however, computers can perform simple processing operations on textual data, such as comparing two strings to see whether they are the same, calculating the number of characters in a string, and arranging strings in ASCII order.

String-Oriented Symbolic Language See *SNOBOL*.

stroke weight The width of the lines that make up a character. Light, medium, and bold are designators of stroke weight for fonts.

strong AI In artificial intelligence, a research focus based on the conviction that computers will achieve the ultimate goal of artificial intelligence, namely, the creation of machines rivaling the intelligence of humans.

strong authentication In computer security, the use of authentication measures that go beyond supplying a reusable password. Strong authentication techniques include the use of digital signatures and certificates, tokens, and smart cards.

strong typing A class of programming languages that employs type checking to ensure that the programmer has associated the correct data type with each variable. For example, suppose a programmer declares *a* an integer variable; if this variable is later used to store a date, the language's compiler or interpreter will generate an error when type checking occurs. Typically, strongly typed languages execute faster and are less prone to errors than weakly typed or typeless languages. See *compiler, data type, declaration, interpreter, type checking, typeless, variable, weak typing.*

structural analysis and design tools Methods of graphical analysis that system analysts can use to convey a description of an information system to managers, programmers, and users.

structural sabotage In information warfare, attacks on the information systems that support major transportation, finance, energy, and telecommunications.

structural unemployment A type of unemployment created by a mismatch between employee skills and employer needs. Structural unemployment is often caused by technological change. For example, more than 100,000 Appalachian coal miners lost their jobs between 1945 and 1968 because coal lost ground to other sources of heat (oil, gas, and electricity). In the 1970s, fear was widespread that microprocessor technology would replace millions of workers because computers would enable one worker to do the jobs formerly done by four people; however, this trend did not materialize. According to numerous studies, computers do not improve productivity dramatically; some studies have found that productivity actually declines after computers are adopted.

structured programming A set of quality standards that make programs more verbose but more readable, reliable, and easily maintained. The goal of structured programming is to avoid spaghetti code caused by over-reliance on programming techniques like GOTO statements, a problem often found in BASIC and FORTRAN programs. Structured programming—such as that promoted by C, Pascal, Modula-2, and the dBASE software command language—insists that the overall program structure reflect what the program is supposed to do, beginning with the first task and proceeding logically. Indentations help make the logic clear, and the programmer is encouraged to use loops and branch control structures and named procedures rather than GOTO statements.

Structured Query Language See *SQL*.

style **1.** In fonts, a defining characteristic such as italics, underlining, or boldface. **2.** In word processing, a saved definition consisting of formatting commands that one regularly applies to specific kinds of text, such as main headings. Styles can include alignment, font, line spacing, and any other text-formatting features. After creating and saving a style, one can quickly apply it to the text by using one or two keystrokes. See *style sheet*.

style sheet   In some word processing and page layout programs, a collection of styles frequently used in a specific type of document, such as newsletters, that are saved together. Synonymous with style library.

stylus   A pen-shaped instrument used to select menu options on a monitor screen or to draw line art on a graphics tablet.

subdirectory   In a hierarchical file system, a directory structure created in another directory. A subdirectory can contain files and additional subdirectories. When a hard disk is formatted, a fixed-size root directory area is created that is only large enough to contain the information for 512 files. To add more files to the hard drive, one creates subdirectories in which he or she can store other files. By using subdirectories, one can create a treelike, hierarchical structure of nested directories so that he or she can group programs and files and organize his or her data to suit his or her needs. Subdirectories can be created within subdirectories, up to a maximum of nine levels. See *hierarchical file system*.

subdomain   In the Internet's domain name system (DNS), a domain that is subordinate to a domain name; for example, in the Web address www.virginia.edu/tcc, www.virginia.edu is the domain and tcc is the subdomain. See *domain name system (DNS)*.

subject drift   In Usenet newsgroups, the tendency of the subject lines of follow-up posts to become increasingly irrelevant to the articles' contents. Subject drift is an unintended consequence of newsreader software, which automatically echoes the original article's subject (a brief one-line description) when one writes a follow-up post. As the discussion progresses into new territory, newsreaders keep echoing the same subject line, even though it soon becomes irrelevant to the subject actually being discussed.

subject tree   In the World Wide Web (WWW), a guide to the Web that organizes Web sites by subject; the example *par excellence* is Yahoo! (the name of which was originally an acronym for "Yet Another Hierarchically Officious Oracle"). The term originates from many of the subject classifications (such as Environment or Music) having branches, or subcategories. At the lowest level of the tree, one finds hyperlinks, which he or she can click to display the cited Web document. See *search engine*.

submenu   A subordinate menu that may appear when one chooses a command from a pull-down menu. The submenu lists further choices. Not all menu commands display submenus. Some carry out an action directly; others display dialog boxes (these options are shown with ellipses [. . .]).

submicron technology   A semiconductor chip-fabricating process that is capable of creating components that are less than one micron (one millionth of a meter) in width.

subnet   In the Internet, a segment of an Internet-connected local area network (LAN) that is differentiated from other segments by using an operation (called a subnet mask) that is performed on the network's IP address. Subnets share a common IP address with the rest of the network of which they are a part, but they can function autonomously. A subnet is a virtual unit identified conceptually by using the addressing methodology, and it is generally created to reflect valid organizational distinctions, even if the members of an organizational unit are, in fact, using two or more physically dissimilar portions of the network. For example, in a university, a single academic department can be assigned a subnet, even though some of the faculty connect to the Internet by using a high-speed Ethernet and others by using an AppleTalk network. See *IP address, LAN*.

subnet mask   A transformation performed on an organization's IP address that enables the network administrators to create subnets, which are virtual subunits of the organization's physical network. See *IP address, subnet*.

subnotebook　A portable computer that omits some components (such as a CD-ROM drive) to cut down on weight and size.

subroutine　A section of a computer program that is designed to perform a specific task. Set aside from the rest of the code, the subroutine can be used (called) from one or more sections of the main part of the program, as needed.

subscribe　In Usenet, to add a newsgroup to the list of groups that one reads regularly. Subscribed newsgroups appear in the newsgroup selector, enabling the subscriber to choose them easily. If one stops reading a newsgroup, he or she can unsubscribe to remove the newsgroup name from his or her subscription list.

subscript　In word processing, a number or letter printed slightly below the typing line, as in the following example: n_1. See *superscript*.

substitutional compression algorithm　A compression algorithm that searches for lengthy but repeated data patterns and replaces them with shorter codes; when decompression occurs, each code is replaced with its corresponding unit of lengthy data. The result is significant data compression without loss of data. The most widely used substitutional compression algorithm is based on the Lempel-Ziv compression algorithm that was first proposed in 1977. See *compression, Lempel-Ziv compression algorithm, Lempel-Ziv-Welch (LZW) compression algorithm, lossless compression, LZ78*.

substrate　The material to which the recording medium of a hard or floppy disk is affixed. Floppy disks usually have plastic substrates, which are coated with a mixture of recording medium and binder; hard disks have aluminum or glass substrates that, by plating or sputtering, are coated with thin-film magnetic media.

SUID　In Unix and Unix-like operating systems such as Linux, a file attribute of executable files that gives any user executing the file the privileges of the file's owner. If the owner is the root user, SUID gives any user the privileges of the system administrator, which is a known security risk. See *GUID*.

suitcase　In the Macintosh environment, an icon containing a screen font or desk accessory (DA) not yet installed in the System Folder.

suite　A group of applications programs, sold in a single package, that are designed to work well together. Suites (such as Microsoft Office Standard and Corel WordPerfect Suite) usually include a word processing program, a spreadsheet, and an e-mail program. High-end suites (such as Corel Office Suite, Microsoft Office Professional, and Lotus SmartSuite) include database management programs. Suites cost less than the individual applications would if one purchased them separately.

Sun Microsystems　The world's leading manufacturer of Unix-based workstations, with an estimated one-third of the market. Based in Mountain View, California, the company manufactures products that include the Solaris operating system, as well as workstations (SPARCstation) and servers (SPARCserver) based on the high-performance SPARC and UltraSPARC microprocessors, which are based on reduced instruction set computer (RISC) principles. A major new Sun initiative is the Java programming language, which is capable of producing computer programs that can run on any computer.

supercomputer　A sophisticated, expensive computer designed to execute complex calculations at the maximum speed permitted by state-of-the-art technology. Supercomputers are used for scientific research, especially for modeling complex, dynamic systems, such as the world's weather, the U.S. economy, or the motions of a galaxy's spiral arms. The Cray-MP is an example of a supercomputer.

SuperDisk A removable 3.5-inch storage technology developed by Imation Corporation that can store up to 120MB of data. SuperDisk drives are downwardly compatible with 3.5-inch disks.

SuperDrive An innovative 3.5-inch floppy disk drive now standard on Macintosh computers. SuperDrives can read all Macintosh formats (400K, 800K, and 1.4MB). With the aid of Apple's Apple File Exchange software, included with all Macintosh system software, the drive also can read and write to 720K and 1.44MB MS-DOS disks. SuperDrives also can format disks in the MS-DOS format.

superpipelining A method of extending pipelining, in which the microprocessor begins executing a new instruction before the previous instruction's execution is complete so that as many as four or five instructions are being executed simultaneously. Intel's Pentium Pro microprocessor employs superpipelining.

superscalar architecture A design that enables the microprocessor to take a sequential instruction and send several instructions at a time to separate execution units so that the processor can execute multiple instructions per clock cycle. The architecture includes a built-in scheduler, which looks ahead in the instruction queue, identifies a group of instructions that do not conflict with one another or that require simultaneous use of a particular service, and passes the group along for execution. The two pipelines available in the Pentium chip enable the processor to execute two instructions per clock cycle. The PowerPC, with three execution units, can handle three instructions simultaneously. See *pipelining*.

superscript A number or letter printed slightly above the typing line, as in the following example: a². See *subscript*.

superuser In multiuser operating systems, a type of user who possesses the ability to access and modify virtually any file on a given computer. If intruders obtain superuser status, they can obtain the passwords of everyone who uses the system and can erase valuable files. Synonymous with root user. See *cracker, root user, script kiddies*.

Super VGA See *SVGA*.

support **1.** To be capable of working with a device, file format, or program. For example, Netscape Navigator supports a variety of plug-ins. **2.** To provide human assistance with computer problems. See *technical support*.

surf To explore the World Wide Web serendipitously by following hyperlinks that seem interesting.

surfing Exploring the Web by following interesting links—to some, a monumental waste of time; to others, a joy.

surge A momentary and sometimes destructive increase in the amount of voltage delivered through a power line. A surge is caused by a brief and often very large increase in line voltage resulting from appliances being turned off, lightning striking, or power being re-established after a power outage. See *power line filter, surge protector*.

surge protector An inexpensive electrical device that prevents high-voltage surges from reaching a computer and damaging its circuitry. See *power line filter*.

SVGA Acronym for Super Video Graphics Array. An enhancement of the Video Graphics Array (VGA) display standard. Super VGA can display at least 800 pixels horizontally and 600 lines vertically, and up to 1,280 pixels by 768 lines with 16 colors, 256 colors, or 16.7 million colors simultaneously displayed. The amount of video memory required to display 16 colors is nominal, but as much as 3.9MB of video memory is required to display 16.7 million colors. See *VGA, video standard*.

S-video A component video transmission format that splits video information into two separate channels: one for chrominance (hue and saturation) and one for luminance (brightness). A consumer version of S-Video is S-VHS (Super VHS).

swap file   A large, hidden system file that stores program instructions and data that do not fit in the computer's random access memory (RAM). Swap files can be created and used by applications. Operating systems use swap files to deal with situations in which physical memory is exhausted. See *virtual memory.*

swash   A character that sweeps over or under adjacent characters with a curvilinear flourish.

switch   An addition to an MS-DOS command that modifies the way that the command performs its function. The switch symbol is a forward slash (/), which is followed by a letter. For example, the command DIR /p displays a directory listing one page at a time.

switchable power supply   A power supply that lets one use both U.S. and European electrical power to run the computer. Unlike cheap travel converters, which can ruin a PC's electronics, switchable power supplies enable a computer to use either 115-volt 60 Hz U.S. electricity, or 230-volt 50 Hz European electricity.

SXGA   Acronym for Super Extended Graphics Array. Originally an extension to IBM's Extended Graphics Array (XGA) video standard, this term in practice refers to a display with a resolution of 1400 x 1050 pixels on notebook LCDs and LCD projection devices.

Sybase, Inc.   A major publisher of Unix-based relational database management systems (RDMS) for client/server computing in multiuser enterprise contexts. Based in Emeryville, California, Sybase offers extensive consulting and system integration services to corporations that need sophisticated database management systems.

Symantec   The leading publisher of utility software for Macintosh and Microsoft Windows computers, including the well-known Norton AntiVirus and Norton Utilities. Based in Cupertino, California, the company also publishes a number of popular application programs, including Act! (a contact management program), WinFax (a fax program for Microsoft Windows), and pcANYWHERE (a remote control program).

symbolic coding   Expressing an algorithm in coded form by using symbols and numbers that people can understand (rather than the binary numbers that computers use). All modern programming languages use symbolic coding.

symmetric digital subscriber line   See *SDSL.*

symmetric key encryption algorithm   An encryption algorithm that uses the same key to encode and decode messages. Symmetric key algorithms have many advantages: They require relatively small amounts of computer overhead, and when used with keys of sufficient length, they produce virtually uncrackable ciphertext. However, it is necessary to convey the key to the message's receiver by some secure means. In Internet security services, this is typically done by means of public key encryption algorithms, which are used initially to authenticate the two parties to the transaction and to manage the initial exchange of symmetric keys; subsequent communication between the two parties uses the symmetric key algorithm. See *SSL.*

symmetric multiprocessing (SMP)   In a computer with more than one central processing unit (CPU), a type of multiprocessing architecture in which each processor has equal access to the system's memory and I/O devices. The processors are connected by a high-speed bus. Processing tasks are parceled out by the operating system (OS), usually in fairly straightforward ways, such as assigning printing or communication tasks to one processor while assigning data processing tasks to another. Alternatively, the processor can parcel out a single application's threads among the available processors. Microsoft Windows NT and Linux (with kernel version 2.4 or higher) support symmetric multiprocessing. See *parallel processing.*

sync   See *synchronization.*

synchronization   **1.** A procedure that adjusts the timing of two or more data streams so that they occur simultaneously. **2.** A procedure that updates a file archive to make sure that the archive contains the most recent version of the files. Synchronization superficially resembles a backup procedure; however, synchronization does not alter the files' archive bit and may not provide a reliable means of restoring lost data after a catastrophic data loss. See *archive bit, backup, one-way synchronization, synchronize.*

synchronization utility   A utility that is designed to compare the date and time file attributes of files in two directories; if discrepancies are found, the files can be synchronized so that one or both directories contain the newest versions of the files. Synchronization utilities should not be confused with backup programs; they are intended to help users maintain mirror-image directories of working documents on two separate computer systems, and provide no facilities for restoring data in the event of catastrophic data loss. Synchronization utilities can perform one-way synchronizations (in which the newer files in one directory are copied to a second directory) or two-way synchronization (in which both directories are updated so that they both contain the newest files). See *backup, synchronization.*

synchronize   **1.** In multimedia, to modify the timing of two or more independent multimedia content streams so that the streams are synchronous (that is, events in the various streams occur at the same time). **2.** In computer file systems, to update archived files so that that archive contains the most recent versions of these files.

Synchronized Multimedia Integration Language   See *SMIL.*

synchronous   Occurring together, due to regular pulses received by some type of timing device. See *asynchronous.*

synchronous   communication   Sending data at very high speeds by using circuits in which electronic clock signals synchronize the data transfer. Computers in high-speed mainframe computer networks use synchronous communication. See *asynchronous communication.*

Synchronous Digital Hierarchy (SDH)   See *SONET.*

Synchronous   Dynamic   Random Access Memory   See *SDRAM.*

Synchronous   Graphics   Random Access Memory   See *SGRAM.*

synchronous motor   An obsolete kind of electric motor that some hard disks once used as a spindle motor. Now replaced by the servo-controlled DC motor, synchronous motors ran on high-voltage alternating current and could not be designed to run at different speeds.

Synchronous Optical Network   See *SONET.*

syntax   The rules that govern the structure of commands, statements, or instructions in a computer programming or scripting language.

syntax error   An error resulting from stating a command in a way that violates a program's syntax rules.

synthesizer   An audio component that uses frequency modulation (FM), wavetable, or waveguide technology to create sounds imitative of actual musical instruments. See *sound board.*

SyQuest drive   A type of removable hard disk that is compatible with the SCSI standard and that is very popular among both Macintosh and IBM PC–compatible computer users. In addition to the traditional 44MB and 88MB cartridges, new storage formats include 135MB, 230MB, and 270MB cartridges, but these are not backward-compatible with previous SyQuest drives.

sysop   Abbreviation for system operator. A person who runs a bulletin board system (BBS).

system   **1.** An organized collection of components that have been optimized to work together in a functional whole. **2.** The entire computer system, including peripheral devices. See *computer.*

System/360   A line of mainframe computers introduced by IBM in 1964 that was responsible for a series of key technological innovations, including the use of integrated circuits, software compatibility across an entire series of computers, input/output (I/O) channels with interrupt requests, and microprogramming. Developed with a bet-the-company investment of $5 billion, an astronomical sum in 1960s, System/360 was as much a marketing as a technological innovation: it was designed to provide a stable upgrade path by which a customer could begin with one of the smaller, less expensive systems, and upgrade smoothly to more powerful models as the business grew. Although System/360 development was plagued by delays and cost overruns, the new line of computers was so successful that it relegated all of IBM's competitors to the status of bit players.

system administration   Collectively, all the tasks related to running a multiuser computer system safely and efficiently while, at the same time, keeping users happy; since these two jobs conflict, system administration is often cited as the canonical thankless job. Typical system administration tasks include managing users, maintaining printers, backup up data, providing user support, monitoring system activity, plugging security holes, ensuring adequate disk space, solving network problems, and installing new equipment.

system administrator   The person responsible for system administration duties in an organization's multiuser computer system. See *system administration.*

system board   IBM's term for motherboard.

system call   An application's request for services from the computer's operating system, such as a request to open a file. The syntax for writing system calls is specified by the operating system's application programming interface (API).

system clock   A timer circuit on the motherboard that emits a synchronizing pulse at a regular interval, such as 33,000,000 times per second on a 33 MHz motherboard. The pulses of the system clock help synchronize processing operations. See *clock cycle.*

system date   The calendar date that a computer system maintains even when the power is switched off, thanks to a battery inside the computer's case.

system disk   A disk that contains the operating system files necessary to start the computer. Hard disk users normally configure a hard disk to serve as the system disk.

system error   In a computer system, an inherent flaw in the system that produces incorrect, erroneous, or misleading results. System errors compromise system reliability. See *reliability.*

system file   A program or data file that contains information that the operating system needs; distinguished from the program or data files that the application programs use.

System Folder   A folder in the Macintosh desktop environment that contains the System and Finder files, the two components of the Mac's operating system. In addition to the System and Finder files, the System Folder also contains all the desk accessories (DAs), INITs, control panel devices (CDEVs), screen fonts, downloadable printer fonts, and printer drivers available during an operating session. See *blessed folder, downloadable font.*

system integrator   An individual or company that provides value-added reseller (VAR) services by combining various components and programs into a functioning system, customized for a particular customer's needs.

System Management Mode (SMM)
In Intel microprocessors, a low power-consumption state that can be switched on to conserve battery power. All recent Intel microprocessors are equipped with SMM circuitry and, therefore, are suitable for use in notebook computers.

system prompt In a command-line operating system, the text that indicates that the operating system is available for tasks such as copying files, formatting disks, and loading programs. In MS-DOS, the system prompt (a letter designating the disk drive, followed by a greater-than symbol) shows the current drive. When one sees the prompt C>, for example, drive C is the current drive, and DOS is ready to accept instructions. One can customize the system prompt by using the PROMPT command.

systems analysis A professional specialty that involves determining an organization's computing needs and designing computer systems to fit those needs. Systems analysis is less structured than programming or other aspects of computer science because it is often difficult to determine whether the analyst has found the best system for an organization or even whether the analyst has completely solved an organization's computing problems.

Systems and Procedures Association (SPA) See *Association for Systems Management (ASM)*.

Systems Application Architecture (SAA) A set of standards for communication among various types of IBM computers, from personal computers to mainframes. Announced in 1987, SAA was IBM's response to criticisms that its products did not work well together, and to the competitive pressure exerted by Digital Electronic Corporation (DEC), which claimed that it had optimized its products for easy interconnection. SAA calls for a consistent user interface and consistent system terminology across all environments. The standard influenced the design of Presentation Manager, the windowing environment jointly developed by Microsoft and IBM for OS/2. See *windowing environment*.

systems development life cycle See *SDLC*.

system software All the software used to operate and maintain a computer system, including the operating system and utility program; distinguished from application programs.

system time The time of day maintained by the computer system even when the power is off, thanks to a battery inside the computer's case.

system unit The case that houses the computer's internal processing circuitry, including the power supply, motherboard, disk drives, plug-in boards, and speaker. The case often is called the central processing unit (CPU), but this usage is inaccurate. Properly, the CPU consists of the computer's microprocessor and memory (usually housed on the motherboard), but not peripherals such as disk drives.

T1   A high-bandwidth telephone trunk line that is capable of transferring 1.544 Mbps of data. See *physical medium, T3.*

T3   A very high-bandwidth telephone trunk line that is capable of transferring 44.7 Mbps of computer data. See *physical medium, T1.*

TA   See *terminal adapter.*

tab-delimited   See *tab separated.*

Tab key   A key used to move a fixed number of spaces or to the next tab stop in a document. The Tab key often is used to guide the cursor in on-screen command menus.

table   **1.** In a relational database management system, the fundamental structure of data storage and the display in which data items are linked by the relations formed by placing the items in rows and columns. The rows correspond to the data records of record-oriented database management programs, and the columns correspond to data fields. **2.** In a word processing program, a matrix of columns and rows, usually created using a table utility. **3.** In HTML, a matrix of rows and columns that appears on a Web page, if the user is browsing with a table-capable browser (such as Netscape Navigator).

table of authorities   A table of legal citations generated by a word processing program from references that have been marked in a document.

table utility   In a word processing program, a utility that makes the typing of tables easier by creating a spreadsheet-like matrix of rows and columns, into which one can insert text without forcing word wrapping.

tabloid printer   See *B-size printer.*

tab separated   Separated by tab characters. Tab-separated values can be easily imported into most spreadsheet and database programs. See *comma-separated.*

tab-separated file   A text file containing values that are delimited by tab characters. Such files are commonly created so that the data can be imported into a spreadsheet or database program. See *comma-separated values (CSV).*

tab stop   The place where the cursor stops after one presses the Tab key. Most word processing programs set default tab stops every ½ inch, but one can set tabs individually anywhere he or she wants, or can redefine the default tab width.

tactile display   A display that stimulates the sense of touch using vibration, pressure, and temperature changes.

tactile feedback   Any information gained through the sense of touch. Typically, tactile feedback applies to the way a keyboard's keys feel to a typist, but the term also applies to mouse and joystick design and a variety of virtual reality applications.

tag   In HTML, a code that identifies an element (a certain part of a document, such as a heading or list) so that a Web browser can tell how to display it. Tags are enclosed by beginning and ending delimiters (angle brackets). Most tags begin with a start tag (delimited with <>), followed by the content and an end tag (delimited with </>), as in the following example: <H1> Welcome to my home page</H1>. See *HTML.*

Tagged Image File Format (TIFF)   A bitmapped graphics format for scanned images with resolutions of up to 300 dots per inch (dpi). TIFF simulates grayscale shading.

tail recursion   In programming, a type of recursion in which the recursive instruction is the last statement in a function. In tail recursion, the function terminates when the recursive call has been completed. Functions employing tail recursion can be easily translated into iterative functions that use a FOR... NEXT loop control structure; iterative functions are preferred over tail recursion because they do not lead to an exponential explosion of calculations as input values increase. See *recursion*.

talk A utility often installed in Unix and Unix-like operating systems that enables users to engage in a typed, real-time conversations with other system users while they are online.

talk hierarchy In Usenet, one of the seven standard newsgroup hierarchies. The talk newsgroups are expressly devoted to controversial topics and are often characterized by acrimonious debate. Topics covered include abortion, drugs, and gun control. See *Usenet*.

tape A strip of thin plastic coated with a magnetically sensitive recording medium. In mainframe computing and minicomputing, tape is widely used as a backup medium. Thanks to a dramatic price drop in cartridge tape backup units, tape has become increasingly common in personal computing for backing up entire hard drives. See *backup utility, quarter-inch cartridge (QIC), random access, sequential access, tape backup unit*.

tape archive In a large organization, a collection of magnetic tapes that store information that is important, but not currently needed.

tape backup A process in which the contents of a hard disk are copied to backup tapes so that the system can be restored in the event of a hard disk failure. In large-scale, multiuser computer systems, tape backups are automatically performed at frequent intervals by tape drives mounted on servers.

tape backup unit A device that reads and writes data on a magnetically sensitive tape. Tape backup units are useful for performing backups on hard disks—thus protecting data from loss by accidental erasure—and for storing important but rarely needed data that would otherwise take up space on a hard disk. Quarter-inch cartridge (QIC) tape drives are the most common tape backup units for personal computers.

tape drive See *tape backup unit*.

TAPI Acronym for Telephony Application Programming Interface. Microsoft's telephony interface for Microsoft Windows. The interface provides connectivity for modems and voice mail.

tar A standard file archive utility in Unix and Unix-like operating systems (including Linux)that does not offer compression services. After they are created, tar archives are generally compressed using the Unix compress (.Z extension) or gzip (.gz extension) utilities, resulting in compound extensions such as tar.Z or tar.gz. See *archive, compression, gzip*.

Targa A graphics file format developed by Truevision for Targa and Vista graphics products, and now widely used as a standard file format for high-end graphics output (such as rendering and ray tracing). Targa files, with the extension .TGA, can have a color depth of up to 32 bits for certain purposes, although the most common color depth is 24 bits, providing more than 16 million colors.

task An executing process that, in a multitasking operating system, can appear to run simultaneously with other tasks. Each task is given its own system resources, including memory. To create the appearance of simultaneous execution, the operating sytem switches among tasks so rapidly that users believe they are actually running at the same time. Tasks are assigned a default priority, which governs the order of precedence that the operating system assigns to them as the various tasks compete for system resources. Users with advanced knowledge of the operating system can raise or lower a task's priority. When two or more tasks are running, it is crucial that they do not invade each other's memory space and cause each other to crash. See *cooperative multitasking, multitasking, preemptive multitasking*.

taskbar In Microsoft Windows, an application launcher and task switcher that (by default) remains visible at the bottom of the screen. After launching a program with the

Start menu, the program's task button appears on the taskbar, allowing the user to switch to it by clicking the button.

task button In Microsoft Windows, a button that appears on the taskbar after an application program is launched. The user can switch to the application by clicking the task button.

task scheduling algorithm In operating systems, an approach to implementing multitasking on a single-processor computer. To provide the illusion that tasks are executing simultaneously, multitasking rapidly switches among executing tasks. The task scheduling algorithm establishes the order of precedence in which tasks are given control of the CPU. The most widely used task scheduling algorithm is called priority scheduling, in which tasks are assigned a default priority. See *preemptive multitasking, priority, priority scheduling, task.*

TB See *terabyte.*

Tcl (Pronounced *tickle*) An interpreted scripting language that is now maintained by Sun Microsystems. Used primarily on Unix and Linux systems, Tcl includes a graphical user interface toolkit that enables developers to create simple GUI applications in short order. See *Perl, Python, scripting language.*

TCM See *trellis-code modulation.*

TCO **1.** Acronym for Tjaünstemaünnens Centralorganisation, the Swedish Confederation of Professional Employees (Sweden's largest white-collar labor union). In monitors, TCO is known for its very stringent regulations regarding electromagnetic radiation—even stricter than MPR II rules. Not many TCO-certified monitors are available in the United States, but the TCO standards are the toughest in the world. **2.** Acronym for Total Cost of Ownership. See *Total Cost of Ownership (TCO).*

TCP Acronym for Transmission Control Protocol. On the Internet, the protocol (standard) that permits two Internet-connected computers to establish a reliable connection. TCP ensures reliable data delivery with a method known as positive acknowledgment with retransmission (PAR). The computer that sends the data continues to do so until it receives a confirmation from the receiving computer that the data has been received intact. See *Internet Protocol (IP), TCP/IP.*

TCP/IP Abbreviation for Transmission Control Protocol/Internet Protocol (TCP/IP), and a commonly used phrase to refer to the entire Internet protocol suite. By far the most widely used suite of networking protocols, TCP/IP provides the technical foundation for the public Internet as well as for large numbers of private networks (called internets with a small "i" to distinguish them from the public Internet) that are not linked to the public Internet. The key achievement of TCP/IP is its flexibility with respect to lower-level protocols, which—in contrast to the design philosophy expressed in the OSI Reference Model—are not defined. As a result, TCP/IP can work with a wide variety of physical media, including local area networks (LANs) such as Ethernets, frame relay, digital T1 and T3 backbones, fiber optic, packet radio, and many more. Although more than 100 protocols make up the entire TCP/IP protocol suite, the two most important of these (TCP and IP) sum up the network's character; the Internet Protocol (IP) is a highly efficient connectionless, packet-switching protocol that defines the format used for transmitting data. Transmission Control Protocol (TCP) is a connection-oriented protocol that defines how to computers establish communication ,exchange data, and verify that data is received in the proper order. See *connectionless protocol, connection-oriented protocol, Ethernet, internet, Internet, Internet Protocol (IP), OSI Reference Model, TCP.*

TCP/IP network A network that uses Internet technology and the TCP/IP protocols, whether or not it is connected to the external Internet. The public Internet is indicated by spelling "Internet" with a capital I; private, TCP/IP-based networks may also be called internets, but with a small initial "i." See *Internet, TCP/IP.*

TDMA Acronym for Time Division Multiple Access. One of two major protocols (the other is CDMA) for digital cellular telephony. TDMA enables multiple callers to share the same channel by giving each phone a specified time slot in which it may transmit or receive. TDMA operates at 800 MHz or 1900 MHz; when operating at the higher frequency, it enables Personal Communication Services (PCS) such as paging, text-based Internet access by means of the Wireless Applications Protocol (WAP), and voice mail. TDMA enables data communications at a transfer rate of 14.4 Kbps. U.S. TDMA service providers include AT&T Wireless and Nextel. A narrowband version of the TDMA standard called Global System for Mobile Communications (GSM) is the *de facto* cellular telephony standard in Europe and Asia, but it is not widely available in the U.S. GSM enables data communications at a transfer rate of 9.6 Kbps. See *CDMA, digital cellular phone, GSM.*

techie An often derogatory term for a programmer or other computer expert. Like "bit twiddler," "computer jock," and "computer nerd," the term sometimes connotes a lack of interpersonal skills. Like all thoughtless stereotypes, this one may be unfair and inaccurate when applied to individuals.

technical support Providing technical advice and problem-solving expertise to registered users of a hardware device or program.

technobabble Technical jargon, especially when it is used excessively or vaguely for marketing purposes ("The new application supports enterprise-wide object integration") or used metaphorically in noncomputer contexts ("The President is getting input from his advisors").

technocentrism An overidentification with computer technology, often associated with a preference for factual thinking,

denial of emotions, a lack of empathy for other people, and a low tolerance for human ambiguity. First noted by the psychotherapist Craig Brod, technocentrism stems from the stress that individuals encounter as they try to adapt to a computer-driven society.

technological innovation The process by which an invention is made available for use and begins to impact its broader environment. See *invention.*

technology **1.** In the general sense, a complex human enterprise that integrates numerous resources (including skills, scientific knowledge, technical expertise, experience, and imagination) into a going enterprise with multiple stakeholders, including sources of capital, executives, managers, professional staff such as engineers, workers, competing firms, users and non-users, and the impact environment (social, economic, cultural, and environmental). **2.** A specific line of technological development, such as cellular phone technology. See *invention, technological innovation.*

technology transfer A process in which a technology moves from one socially and economically embedded context to another; the context in question could be companies, states, regions, or nations. Because technology is a highly complex enterprise (see the definition of *technology*), technology transfer is not, as Houston Advanced Technology Research Center director W. Arthur Porter notes, a "plug-and-play enterprise." For example, numerous attempts have been made to replicate research corridors such as California's Silicon Valley or North Carolina's Research Triangle Park; some have met with limited success, but it is now generally recognized that research corridors result from a long development process that may take three to five decades to come to fruition. See *invention, technology, Silicon Valley, technological innovation.*

telco Abbreviation for telephone company.

telecommunications **1.** In a strict sense, the transmission of computer data via the public switched telephone network (PSTN). **2.** More broadly, the transmission of any type of information over public or private networks.

Telecommunications Act of 1996 A U.S. federal legislative act, signed into law in 1996, that opened local telephone systems to competition. The Communications Decency Act (CDA) was attached to this bill and signed into law by President Clinton; key provisions of the CDA that attempted to regulate indecent speech online were subsequently overturned by U.S. courts. See *Communications Decency Act (CDA).*

telecommuting Performing work at home while linked to the office by means of a telecommunications-equipped computer system.

telemedicine The provision of high-quality, up-to-date medical information to medical practitioners. In rural areas and community health centers, doctors who are out of touch with the latest knowledge may make faulty diagnoses or prescribe an out-of-date therapy. A telemedicine system that can provide these practitioners with high-quality information could indeed save lives.

Telephony Application Programming Interface See *TAPI.*

telepresence A psychological sensation of being immersed in a virtual reality that is persuasive and convincing enough to pass for the real world.

teletype (TTY) display A method of displaying characters on a monitor in which characters are generated and sent, one by one, to the video display; as the characters are received, the screen fills, line by line. When full, the screen scrolls up to accommodate the new lines of characters appearing at the bottom of the screen. See *character-mapped display.*

Telnet An Internet protocol that enables Internet users to log on to another computer linked to the Internet, including those that cannot directly communicate with the Internet's TCP/IP protocols. Telnet establishes a plain vanilla computer terminal called a network virtual terminal. By means of this simulated terminal screen, users can interact with the remote computer as if they were sitting before its screen and keyboard.

temp Abbreviation of temporary; for example, "temp file" means "temporary file."

template In a program, a document or worksheet that includes the text or formulas needed to create standardized documents. The template can be used to automate the creation of these documents in the future. In word processing, templates frequently are used for letterheads; the template version of the file contains the corporate logo, the company's address, and all the formats necessary to write the letter, but no text. One uses the template by opening it, adding text to it, and printing. In spreadsheet programs, templates are available for repetitive tasks such as calculating and printing a mortgage amortization schedule.

temporary directory **1.** A directory created by a program for temporary use; normally, it is deleted after the use is complete. For example, the popular compression and archiving utility WinZip creates temporary directories to store intermediate files generated during its operations. **2.** A permanent directory that the operating system uses to store temporary files (such as Windows/Temp in Microsoft Windows systems or /tmp in Linux or Unix systems).

temporary file A file created by an executing program to store working or intermediate data, such as the information required to reconstruct previous document states when the Undo command is chosen. Normally, these files are deleted when the application is closed, but some applications are not well-mannered in this respect. In addition, crashed applications may leave numerous temporary files in their wake. Periodically, it is wise to search for temporary files and delete those that are more than several days old. Applications use various file extensions for these files, but many are given the *.tmp extension on Windows systems.

temporary font A font that, when downloaded to a laser printer, stays in the printer's memory only until the printer is reset. See *downloadable font, permanent font*.

tensioning wire A very thin wire that stretches across an aperture grille perpendicular to the other wires to keep them steady. Sometimes tensioning wires cast shadows on the display. The shadows are most visible in solid white images.

tera- Metric prefix indicating one trillion (10^{12}).

terabyte (TB) A unit for measuring data storage capacity that is equal to approximately one trillion (10^{12}) bytes; it is exactly equal to 1,099,511,627,776 (2^{40}) bytes or 1,024 gigabytes. One terabyte is approximately equal to the total amount of information contained in printed paper made from 50,000 trees. See *data storage capacity*.

teraflop A measurement of computer processor speed that is equal to one trillion 10^{12} floating point operations per second. See *floating–point notation, FLOP, gigaflop, megaflop*.

terminal An input/output device, consisting of a keyboard and a monitor, commonly used with multiuser systems. A terminal lacking its own central processing unit (CPU) and disk drives is called a dumb terminal and is restricted to interacting with a distant multiuser computer, such as a mainframe. A smart terminal, on the other hand, has some processing circuitry and, in some cases, a disk drive so that one can download information and display it later. A personal computer is a terminal when it is connected to a network, by either a cable or a modem. See *terminal emulation*.

terminal adapter (TA) A device that is functionally equivalent to a modem and that connects a computer or fax machine to an ISDN system. TAs typically plug into the expansion bus like other adapters, although external versions exist. See *ISDN*.

terminal emulation The use of a communications program to transform a computer into a terminal for the purpose of data communication.

terminal mode A state of a communications program in which the computer on which it is running becomes a remote terminal of another computer, to which it is linked by modem.

terminate **1.** To close an application so that it stops running. **2.** To cap off the ends of an electronic circuit to prevent signal reflection. **3.** In programming, to demarcate the end of a procedure or function by inserting a closing bracket or some other terminating symbol.

terminate-and-stay-resident (TSR) program An accessory or utility program designed to remain in random access memory (RAM) at all times so that one can activate it quickly, even if another program also is in memory.

terminator A small electronic device that is applied to the end of a SCSI or Ethernet cable so that signals are not reflected back into the circuit. See *Ethernet, SCSI*.

tessellation In computer graphics, a translation process in which a two-dimensional object is broken down into a collection of polygons. The result is a wireframe graphic.

test driver A program that tests another program, often as part of an alpha test. Test drivers typically send every conceivable input to a program and monitor the results.

test message In Usenet, a message that is posted just to see whether one's newsreader software and Usenet connection are really working.

TeX   A page description language (PDL) for professional typesetting created by noted computer scientist and programming expert Donald Knuth. It is often used in the computer science community, in part out of homage to Knuth and in part because TeX contains a number of interesting programming features that are in themselves illustrative of the didactic points that Knuth makes in his multivolume *Art of Computer Programming*. TeX is not widely used outside computer science circles.

Texas Instruments Graphics Architecture (TIGA)   An obsolete high-resolution graphics standard for PCs. TIGA boards and monitors display 1,024 pixels horizontally by 786 lines vertically with 256 simultaneous colors. See *Super VGA*.

text   Data composed only of standard ASCII characters, without any formatting codes.

text chart   In presentation graphics, a slide, transparency, or handout that contains text, such as a bulleted list. See *column text chart, free-form text chart, organization chart, simple list text chart*.

text editor   A program designed for writing and editing text, but without the features of a full-fledged word processing program. Text editors are used for writing source code as well as creating basic text documents.

text file   A file consisting of nothing but standard ASCII characters (with no control codes or characters from the extended character set).

text mode   An operating mode of IBM PC–compatible video boards in which the computer displays images constructed using the built-in 256-character ASCII character set. Text mode is synonymous with character mode and is the opposite of graphics mode. Because the character set includes several graphics characters, text mode can display graphic images such as boxes and lines. Also, text can be displayed in bold and reverse video. Text mode is much faster than graphics mode.

text-oriented database   A flat file database program that is designed to facilitate the storage, retrieval, and maintenance of textual data. See *database management program, flat file database management program*.

TFT   See *thin-film transistor*.

TFTP   Acronym for Trivial File Transfer Protocol. A TCP/IP network file transfer protocol that is specifically designed for downloading programs onto diskless workstations. See *diskless workstation, file transfer protocol (ftp), TCP/IP*.

thermal dye-sublimation printer   A high-end color printer capable of generating photorealistic output, but at a very high price. By focusing a precisely controllable heat source on a special ribbon containing dyes, the dyes can be transferred to the special coated paper that thermal dye-sublimation printers require. Thermal dye-sublimation printers have very good color saturation but can cost more than $15,000, plus a cost per page of $3 or more.

TGA   See *Targa*.

thermal fusion printer   A printer that melts dye from a special ribbon onto plain paper to form sharp text. Thermal fusion printers are often designed to be portable.

thermal printer   A nonimpact printer that forms an image by moving heated styluses over specially treated paper. Although quiet and fast, thermal printers have one disadvantage: Most of them require specially treated paper that smells odd and has an unpleasant, waxy feel.

thermal wax-transfer printer   A printer that heats wax-based dyes and deposits them on the page in a very dense pattern. Although thermal wax-transfer printers cannot generate photorealistic output, as thermal dye sublimation printers can, they produce excellent saturation and output that is nearly photorealistic. Thermal wax-transfer printers are much less expensive than thermal dye sublimation printers—they can be had for less than $1,000. The cost per page is lower, too—about 50 cents. See *thermal dye-sublimation printer.*

thin client In a client/server network, a client that occupies relatively little memory or disk storage space and that leaves most of the processing to the server. Advocates of thin clients point to the exceptionally high cost of training employees to use fat clients, which are full-featured application programs running on the user's desktop systems; to access needed external data, users would typically have to learn how to use several fat clients, each with its own proprietary commands and menu structure. The thin client par excellence is the Web browser, which can access Web pages configured to display data from virtually any service an enterprise can make available.

thin-film magnetic medium A recording medium used in hard disks that is not composed of tiny bits of metal oxide, but instead is made up of thin layers of special metal alloys. Thin-film magnetic media, applied to disk substrates by plating or sputtering, allow higher areal densities and increased coercivities than oxide-based media.

thin-film transistor (TFT) A type of active matrix display that is in widespread use in notebook computers, desktop flat-panel displays, and high-definition televisions (HDTV). In contrast to passive-matrix displays, TFT displays offer a superior viewing angle (at least 170 degrees). The best TFT displays use new technologies called In-Plane Switching (IPS) or Multi-Domain Vertical Alignment (MDVA or MVA). See *active matrix display.*

third-generation computer A mid-1960s-era computer based on small-scale integrated circuits and, generally, the use of semiconductors for main memory. This period in the computer's development saw the rise of multiuser systems and minicomputers. See *first-generation computer, fourth-generation computer, second-generation computer.*

third-generation programming language A high-level programming language that enables programmers to write programs in a language that is easier for humans to understand than second-generation programming languages (that is, assembly language) or first-generation programming languages (machine code).

third-party DMA An older Direct Memory Access (DMA) bus standard that requires the intervention of a DMA controller in order to function. Third-party DMA is closely associated with the ISA bus and, like the ISA bus, has fallen into disuse in newer Intel-based computer systems. See *DMA, first-party DMA, ISA bus.*

third-party vendor A firm that markets an accessory hardware product for a given brand of computer equipment. Many companies act as third-party vendors of Macintosh accessories.

thread **1.** In a Usenet newsgroup, a chain of postings on a single subject. Most newsreaders include a command that allows a user to follow the thread (that is, jump to the next message on the topic rather than display each message in sequence). **2.** A portion of a program that can operate independently. In a multithreaded application, a running program may have two or more threads running at the same time. The operating system decides which of these threads should receive the processor's attention. In this way, an operation such as printing or downloading a file can occur in the background, without tying up other threads or other applications. This is called preemptive multitasking. See *cooperative multitasking.*

threaded newsreader A Usenet newsreader program that can group articles by topic of discussion and then show where a given article stands in the chain of discussion. Often, this is done using indentation. See *thread selector.*

thread selector In a Usenet newsreader, a program mode in which one sees articles sorted by threads. Many newsreaders use indentation to indicate that the indented article is a response to the one positioned above it. See *threaded newsreader.*

three-dimensional graph   See *3-D graph*.

three-dimensional spreadsheet   A spreadsheet program that can create a workbook file made up of multiple stacked pages, with each page resembling a separate worksheet.

three-gun tube   A color cathode ray tube (CRT). Each of the three electron guns emits electrons that paint one of the primary colors on the display. So-called one-gun tubes in color monitors really have three guns, but the three guns are assembled into one unit. A monochrome monitor truly has only one gun.

throughput   **1.** A measure of a computer's overall performance, as measured by its capability to send data through all components of the system, including data storage devices such as disk drives. Throughput is a much more meaningful indication of system performance than some of the benchmark speeds commonly reported in computer advertising. **2.** In modems, the rate at which data moves from one modem to another, including the effects of data-compression and error-correction protocols.

thumbnail   A small version of a graphic, large enough to show what is in the full-sized version but small enough to be opened (or transmitted via a network) without making inordinate demands on the system. On a Web page, users can click on a thumbnail to see a larger version of the graphic.

Thunderbird   A version of the Athlon microprocessor, manufactured by AMD, that incorporates a secondary cache within the chip, thus offering superior performance. See *Athlon*.

thunking   The means by which a hybrid 32-bit operating system that is capable of working with 16-bit applications such as Microsoft Windows 95/98/Me, communicates with 16-bit code. A computer system slows significantly when it must pause to perform this communication.

.TIF   The extension usually attached to a file containing graphics in Tagged Image File Format (TIFF). TIF files often are used to hold scanned photographic images. See *Tagged Image File Format*.

TIFF   See *Tagged Image File Format*.

tilde   Pronounced till-duh (properly, till-day). **1.** In Spanish, a mark placed over the consonant *n* to indicate that a *y* sound follows and becomes an integral part of the *n* sound, for example, señor (senyor). **2.** In Unix and Unix-related operating systems, as well as HTTPD-descended Web servers such as Apache, a symbol that stands for the user's home directory. **3.** In file directory listings, a prefix that is sometimes used to indicate a temporary file. **4.** ASCII character 124. See *Apache, home directory, Hypertext Transfer Protocol Daemon (HTTPD), Unix*.

tiled windows   In a graphical user interface (GUI), a display mode in which all windows occupy an equal portion of screen space. If one opens additional windows, the others are automatically sized so that he or she still sees all of them. See *cascading windows, overlaid windows*.

time bomb   A program, either existing independently or built into a larger program, that waits until a specific day and time to come out of hiding and be disruptive. The famous Michelangelo virus activated itself on the birthday of the artist Michelangelo. See *Trojan horse*.

timecode editing   In digital video, an editing method that relies on timecodes, such as MIDI or STPME timecodes, to synchronize editing events and multiple input streams. See *control track editing, MIDI timecode, SMPTE timecode*.

timed backup   A desirable application program feature that saves work at a specified interval, such as every 5 minutes. Synonymous with automatic backup. If a power outage or system crash occurs and a timed backup of one's work has been performed, he or she will be notified when next starting the program that a timed backup is available, and will be asked whether he or she want to keep it. The best word processing programs include timed backup features that allow one to specify the interval.

Time Division Multiple Access See *TDMA*.

time out An interruption, resulting in a frozen keyboard, that occurs while the computer tries to access a device (or a remote computer) that is not responding as it should. The computer keeps trying for a predetermined time and then gives up, returning control to the user.

time sharing A technique for sharing a multiuser system's resources in which each user has the illusion that he is the only person using the system. In the largest mainframe systems, hundreds or even thousands of people can use the system simultaneously without realizing that others are doing so. At times of peak usage, however, system response time tends to increase noticeably.

title bar In graphical user interfaces (GUIs) such as Windows, a bar that stretches across the top of a window, indicating the name of the document displayed in that window. The color of the title bar indicates whether the window is active.

toggle To switch back and forth between two modes or states. On the IBM PC–compatible keyboard, for example, the Caps Lock key is a toggle key. When one presses the key the first time, he or she switches the keyboard into a capitals-only mode. When he or she presses the key the second time, the keyboard is switched back to the normal mode, in which one must press the Shift key to type capital letters.

toggle key A key that switches back and forth between two modes. See *Caps Lock key, Num Lock key, Scroll Lock key, toggle*.

token **1.** In authentication systems, some type of physical device (such as a card impregnated with a magnetic stripe, a smart card, or a calculator-like device that generates a password) that must be in the individual's possession to grant access to a network. The token itself is not sufficient; the user must also be able to supply something memorized, such as a personal identification number (PIN). Combining "something you have" with "something you know," tokens provide strong authentication. See *authentication*. **2.** In token-ring networks, a bit configuration that is circulated among workstations; workstations cannot broadcast data to the network unless they possess the token. See *token ring network*.

token passing In local area networks (LANs), a network protocol in which a special bit configuration, called a token, is circulated among the workstations. A node can send information across the network only if the node can obtain an available token, in which case the node converts the token into a data frame containing a network message. Nodes constantly monitor the network to catch tokens addressed to them. Because token-passing rules out the data collisions that occur when two devices begin transmitting at the same time, this channel access method is preferred for large, high-volume networks. See *contention, CSMA/CD, LAN, polling*.

token ring network A local area network (LAN) architecture that combines token passing with a hybrid star/ring topology. Developed by IBM and announced in 1986, the IBM Token Ring Network uses a Multistation Access Unit at its hub. This unit is wired with twisted-pair cable in a star configuration with up to 255 workstations, but the resulting network is actually a decentralized ring network.

toner The electrically charged ink used in laser printers and photocopying machines. To form the image, toner is applied to an electrostatically charged drum and is fused to the paper by a heating element. See *toner cartridge*.

toner cartridge In laser printers, a cartridge containing the toner that the printer fuses to the page.

toolbar   A bar across the top of a window containing buttons, each with a distinctive icon and sometimes some explanatory text. These icons represent frequently accessed commands. Synonymous with icon bar.

toolbox   **1.** A set of programs that helps programmers develop software without having to create basic routines from scratch. Some software publishers call these sets developer's toolkits. **2.** In programs such as drawing and presentation graphics applications, the on-screen icon bar of drawing tools is called the toolbox.

toolkit   See *toolbox*.

top-down programming   A method of program design and development in which the design process begins with a statement (in English) of the program's fundamental purpose. This purpose is broken into a set of subcategories that describe aspects of the program's anticipated functions. Each subcategory corresponds to a specific program module that can be coded independently. Structured programming languages (such as Pascal, C, and Modula-2) and object-oriented programming languages (such as C++) are especially amenable to the top-down approach. See *structured programming*.

topic drift   See *subject drift*.

top-level domain (TLD)   An Internet naming convention for domain names that specifies the legal usages for top-level domain names. A top-level domain is the last of the names in the sequence of dot-separated names, such as "com" in yahoo.com. Top-level domains include the traditional top-level domains (com, gov, edu, org, mil, and net), as well as country-specific domains (such as ca [Canada], uk [United Kingdom], and it [Italy]). In 1998, new top-level domains were added (arts, firm, info, nom, rec, shop, web) under the supervision of the Generic Top Level Domain Memorandum of Understanding (gTLD-MoU). See *arts, domain name, firm, gTLD-MoU, info, nom, rec, shop, web*.

topology   See *network topology*.

Total Cost of Ownership (TCO)   An estimate of the costs of computer system ownership that takes into account hidden costs. Failure to take these costs into account can prove devastating because these costs can easily exceed the cost of the physical system. TCO includes not only the cost of purchasing and installing a computer system, but some or all of the following: strategic planning to ensure the correct technology is chosen, staff training, technical support, software maintenance, software upgrades, hardware upgrades, hardware replacement, work hours lost dealing with system problems or upgrades, and the cost of consumables (printer cartridges, storage media, etc.).

touch screen   See *touch-sensitive display*.

touch-sensitive display   A display designed with a pressure-sensitive panel mounted in front of the screen. One selects options by pressing the screen at the appropriate place. Touch-sensitive displays are typically used for public-access information purposes in such settings as museums, supermarkets, and airports. Synonymous with touch screen.

tower case   A system unit case designed to stand vertically on the floor rather than sit horizontally on a desk. Tower cases usually have much more room for accessories than desktop cases and permit one to move noisy components, including cooling fans and hard disks, away from the immediate work area.

tpi   See *tracks per inch*.

TPS   Acronym for transaction processing system. A system that handles the day-to-day operations of a company; examples include sales, purchases, orders, and returns.

track   On a floppy or hard disk, one of many concentric rings that are encoded on the disk during the low-level format and that define distinct areas of data storage on the disk. See *cluster, sector*.

trackball   An input device, designed as an alternative to the mouse, that moves the mouse pointer on-screen as one uses his or her thumb or fingers to rotate a ball embedded in the keyboard or in a case near the keyboard. Unlike a mouse, a trackball does not require a flat, clean surface to operate; as a result, trackballs are often used with portable or notebook computers. See *built-in pointing device, clip-on pointing device, freestanding pointing device, snap-on pointing device*.

track buffering A hard disk design feature in which the entire contents of a hard disk track are read into a memory area, regardless of how much of the information on the track is requested by the hard disk controller and host adapter. Track buffering eliminates the need for interleaving, so all track-buffered disks (all modern hard disks and most Enhanced Small Device Interface [EDSI] drives are track-buffered) should have interleave factors of 1.

trackpad A pointing device that enables a person to move the mouse pointer by sliding a finger around on a touch-sensitive surface. To click, one taps his or her finger on the surface or press a button.

tracks per inch (tpi) A measurement of the data-storage density of magnetic disks, such as floppy disks. The greater the tpi, the more data the disk can hold. In DOS, double-density 5.25-inch floppy disks are formatted with 48 tpi, and high-density 5.25-inch disks are formatted with 96 tpi. High-density 3.5-inch floppy disks are formatted with 135 tpi.

track-to-track seek time The time a hard or floppy disk drive requires to move the read/write head from one track to the next. Track-to-track seek time is much less important than access time in comparing disk drives.

tractor feed A printer paper-feed mechanism in which continuous paper is pulled (or pushed) into and through the printer with a sprocket wheel. The sprockets fit into prepunched holes on the left and right edges of the paper. Dot-matrix printers normally come with tractor-feed mechanisms.

Tractor-feed printers require one to spend time carefully separating the pages after printing.

trademark A form of intellectual property (IP) protection that is granted to a word, phrase, symbols, or designs, or combinations of these that uniquely identify the source of goods from competitors. (A similar form of protection, called a service mark, is available to companies that provide services rather than goods.) A firm that first uses a trademark possesses the right to register it with a national trademark office; once registration is in hand, the firm can more easily prevent its competitors from emulating the protected trademark. Unlike copyrights and patents, trademarks are granted in perpetuity as long as they are in continued use. See *copyright, intellectual property (IP), patent, trade secret*.

trade secret A form of intellectual property (IP) protection that enables firms to protect knowledge or techniques that are essential to their capability to compete effectively. Unlike patents, trade secrets are not subject to time limitations, and the underlying knowledge or technology need not be disclosed in a formal application. However, trade secret protection ceases to exist the moment the secret is made public, even by illegal means. In the United States, trade secret protection is governed by state rather than federal law and is subject to certain restrictions, such as the right of users to reverse-engineer a product to gain access to knowledge that is not subject to trade secret protection. See *intellectual property (IP), patent, reverse engineering*.

traffic The volume of messages sent over a network.

transactional application In a local area network (LAN), a program that creates and maintains a master record of all the transactions in which network participants engage, such as filling out invoices or time-billing forms. If a system crash results in the loss of data, this record can be used to restore data files to an earlier state. See *nontransactional application*.

transaction processing system See *TPS*.

transceiver Concatenation of transmitter and receiver. **1.** In local area networks (LANs), an adapter that enables a workstation to connect to the network cabling. **2.** In wireless wide area networks (WANs), a modem that can send and receive data via radio frequencies. See *PDA*.

transducer A device that converts a detectable physical phenomenon, such as sound, pressure, or light, into electronic signals that can be processed by a computer.

transfer rate The number of bytes of data that can be transferred per second from a disk to the microprocessor after the read/write head reaches the data. The maximum transfer rate is limited by how fast the disk rotates and the areal density of the data on the disk (or how fast data passes under the drive head). These inflexible hardware limitations can be overcome by caching disk information. See *access time*, *ESDI*, *hardware cache*, *SCSI*.

transform and lighting processing (T & L) In 3-D gaming adapters, a hardware capability that dramatically improves three-dimensional processing performance by taking over display tasks that would otherwise have to be performed by the computer's CPU.

transient See *surge*.

transient command See *external command*.

transistor An electronic device with three connectors that can be used for switching or amplification. Invented at Bell Laboratories in 1947, transistors are simple semiconductor devices that provide an inexpensive, low-power replacement for the bulky, power-consuming, and unreliable vacuum tubes that were used previously for amplification and switching purposes in electronic circuits.

transistor-transistor logic (TTL) monitor An obsolete type of monochrome monitor that accepts digital video signals.

TTL monitors work only with Hercules and MDA video adapters; they have been replaced by monitors that conform to Video Graphics Array (VGA) and Super VGA display standards.

transition effect In multimedia production, an effect that is added to add visual interest to a transition between content segments. Examples of transition effects include fade-outs, barn doors, wipes, and left-to-right slide-ins.

translate To convert a data file from one file format to another, or to convert a program from one programming language or operating system to another.

Transmission Control Protocol See *TCP*.

Transmission Control Protocol/Internet Protocol See *TCP/IP*.

transmitter In push media, a program that sends updated information to subscribers. An example is Castanet's Transmitter, which automatically downloads updates to Java programs installed on subscribers' computers.

transparency A see-through piece of acetate that can be displayed during presentations by overhead projection. Laser and inkjet printers can both print transparencies, but be sure to get the right kind of transparency material—inkjet transparency material will melt inside a laser printer.

transparency adapter A scanner attachment that allows one to scan slides and transparencies.

transparent A computer operation or entity that programmers have made invisible so that it does not have to be dealt with. A transparent computer function is present, but cannot be seen; a virtual computer function is not present, but can be seen. Microsoft Word, for example, inserts formatting codes in a document, but they are transparent—one sees only his or her formatted text. A random access memory (RAM) disk drive, in contrast, is not a disk drive at all; it is just part of a computer's memory, set aside to act like a disk drive. See *virtual*.

transparent GIF A GIF graphics file conforming to the GIF-89a specification and configured so that the graphic's background color matches the color of the surrounding surface on which it is positioned (such as a Web page or the computer's desktop). See *GIF*.

transport layer In the OSI Reference Model of computer network architecture, the fourth of seven layers, in which the data is broken up into discrete units, called packets, each of which is addressed to the destination computer and numbered so that the destination computer can reassemble them on receipt. The protocols on this level govern the precise format for the data packets as well as the procedures to be followed for dividing the data packets on transmission and reassembling them on reception. See *OSI Reference Model*.

transpose To change the order in which characters, words, or sentences are displayed. Some word processing programs include commands that transpose text.

trap In programming, an exception to program execution that enables the program to recover from an unanticipated or unusual situation. See *error trapping*.

trap door 1. In computer networks, a built-in entry point that enables an employee or ex-employee to gain access to the network without authentication. 2. In programming, a function that takes input values and produces a series of output values with very little computational effort; however, it is impossible (in practice) to derive the original input values from an examination of the output values. Trap doors have important applications in strong authentication and cryptography. See *hash function*.

trapping See *error trapping*.

trash can In the MacOS, an icon that can be used to dispose of unwanted files. The files are not actually erased unless the

user chooses Empty Trash from the Special menu.

tree A conceptual or graphical representation of data organized into a tree structure.

tree structure A way of organizing information into a hierarchical structure with one root and several branches, much like a family tree or genealogy chart. There is only one possible route between any two data items in a tree structure. See *directory*, *subdirectory*.

trellis-code modulation (TCM) A group coding modulation technique employed by high-speed modems. By enabling a modem to alter the carrier in a variety of ways, TCM enables modems to communicate at data transfer rates of 9,600 bps or faster.

trigger In a computer program, an event (such as a mouse click) that automatically initiates a procedure.

Trinitron A cathode ray tube (CRT) design that, instead of a shadow mask, has an aperture grill to ensure that electrons from the electron guns hit the proper pixels on the display. An invention of Sony, Trinitron monitors are uniformly bright all over the display, unlike other monitor designs that are less bright around the edges. On the down side, Trinitron monitors have two thin tensioning wires that sometimes cast shadows on the display.

Triple DES In cryptography, an encryption method that involves encrypting the same data three times with the DES encryption algorithm. The result is a form of very strong encryption that is computationally infeasible to decode without possessing the key. See *DES*.

triple-pass scanner A color scanner that gathers data about one of the primary colors on each of three scanning passes. Triple-pass scanners are not necessarily slower than single-pass scanners, but the extra scanning passes can put extra wear on the scanning mechanism.

Triton A chip set for IBM and IBM-compatible Pentium-based computers that (in the most recent versions) provides support for EDO RAM and SDRAM memory chips, Plug and Play (PnP) adapters, ECC bidirectional printer ports, and high-speed IDE hard disk interfaces.

Trivial File Transfer Protocol See *TFTP.*

trn A Usenet newsreader for Unix computer systems. A threaded newsreader that can show the chain of discussion in a newsgroup, trn is a successor to the widely used rn. Somewhat difficult to learn and use, trn is a powerful program that offers many advanced features (such as the capability to decode binary postings).

troff In Unix and Unix-like operating systems, a scriptable typesetting program that, in the days prior to PostScript, TeX, and desktop publishing software, was extensively used to prepare programming documentation for output to typesetting devices. See *desktop publishing, TeX, Unix.*

Trojan horse A program that appears to perform a valid function but that contains, hidden in its code, instructions that cause damage (sometimes severe) to the systems on which it runs. Unlike computer viruses, Trojan horses cannot replicate themselves, but that may be small consolation to someone who has just lost days or weeks of work.

troll In Usenet, a facetious message containing an obvious exaggeration or factual error. The troller hopes to trick a gullible person into posting a follow-up post pointing out the error.

troubleshooting The process of determining why a computer system or specific hardware device is malfunctioning. When a computer fails, most people panic and assume that a huge bill is on the way. Most likely, however, the problem is a minor one, such as a loose connection. One should turn off the power and carefully inspect all the cables and connections, then remove the case lid, and press down on the adapters to make sure that they are well seated in the expansion slots. One also should check connections at peripheral devices.

True BASIC A modern, structured version of the BASIC programming language developed by its originators, John Kemeny and Thomas Kurtz, in response to criticism of earlier versions of BASIC. With modern control structures and optional line numbers, True BASIC is a well-structured language used to teach the principles of structured programming. The language, which is interpreted rather than compiled, is not frequently used for professional programming purposes.

true color The display of on-screen colors with a depth of 24 bits, which enables more than 16 million colors. See *24-bit color, color depth.*

TrueType An outline font standard and font engine technology, originally developed by Apple and subsequently adopted by Microsoft, that was designed to compete with Adobe's Type 1 fonts for on-screen display and printing. TrueType offers a cost-effective alternative to PostScript font technology. TrueType fonts are displayed on-screen (and prepared for printing) by means of a bytecode interpreter, which constructs the fonts on-the-fly. See *bytecode font engine, Freetype, interpreter, outline font, Type 1 font.*

truncate To cut off part of a number or character string.

truncation error A rounding error that occurs when part of a number is omitted from storage because it exceeds the capacity of the memory set aside for number storage.

trusted system A hardware device, such as a computer or home entertainment center, that is equipped with digital rights management (DRM) software. DRM software controls the uses that can be made of copyrighted material in the secondary (after sale) market, in violation of established U.S. principles of copyright law; however, copyright law restrictions are evaded by software licenses denying that a sale has taken place. Software for such systems specifies transport rights (permission to copy the media, loan it to another user, or transfer the license to another user), rendering rights (permission to view or listen to the content), and derivative-work rights (permission to extract and reuse content from the protected work). In the U.S. and countries that acquiesce to U.S. intellectual property laws, users who attempt to circumvent DRM systems violate provisions of the Digital Millennium Copyright Act (DMCA), even if the circumvention is not followed by any act that violates the copyright holder's exclusive rights (such as copying or distribution); penalties approach those of second degree murder in most U.S. states. See *copyright, Digital Millennium Copyright Act (DMCA), digital rights management (DRM), first sale.*

truth table   In logic, a table that is formed to show all the possible permutations when two propositions are connected by a Boolean operator. For example, consider two propositions, P and Q. Either could be true or false. If the two propositions are joined by the AND operator, the resulting compound proposition is true only if both P and Q are true. The resulting truth table lists four options: P is true and Q is true (therefore, P AND Q is true); P is true and Q is false (therefore, P AND Q is false); P is false and Q is true (therefore, P AND Q is false); and P is false and Q is false (therefore, P AND Q is false). Truth tables are extensively used in programming and computer system design.

TSR   See *terminate-and-stay-resident (TSR) program.*

TTL Monitor   See *transistor-transistor logic (TTL) monitor.*

TTY   See *teletype (TTY) display.*

tuple   In computer programming, a set of values, generally separated by commas, that are passed from one program to another.

Turbo Pascal   A high-performance compiler developed by Borland International for Pascal. The compiler comes with a full-screen text editor and creates executable programs (object code). Outperforming compilers that cost 10 times as much, Turbo Pascal took the world of DOS programming by storm when released in 1984; it is now used in hobby and academic environments, and some professional programmers use Turbo Pascal to prepare short- to medium-sized programs. See *interpreter.*

Turing Test   An experiment developed by Alan Turing and used to determine whether a computer could be called intelligent. In a Turing Test, judges are asked to determine whether the output they see on computer displays is produced by a computer or a human being. If a computer program succeeds in tricking the judges into believing that only a human could have generated that output, the program is said to have passed the Turing Test.

turnkey system   A computer system developed for a specific application, such as a point-of-sale terminal, and delivered ready to run, with all the necessary application programs and peripherals.

tutorial   A form of instruction in which the student is guided step by step through the application of a program to a specific task, such as developing a budget or writing a business letter. Some programs come with on-screen tutorials.

tweak   To adjust a program or computer system slightly to improve performance. For example, an unethical researcher might alter an underlying variable slightly so that program output is more in line with what is expected.

tweening   See *key frame interpolation.*

twisted pair   An improved physical medium for local area networks (LANs) and telephone service to homes and offices. Twisted-pair wiring consists of two insulated copper cables that are twisted together like a braid, thus randomizing interference from other electrical circuits. Unlike the plain copper cable used in pre-1970 telephone installations, twisted-pair wiring can handle computer data and is sufficient for Basic Rate Interface (BRI). See *ISDN.*

two-way set-associative cache   A secondary cache memory design that is faster than the direct-map cache design but less expensive than the four-way set-associative cache, which is the fastest of the three.

.TXT The MS-DOS file extension usually attached to a file containing ASCII text.

type **1.** In mathematics, a set of objects that all share the same syntactical properties. Type definition has many advantages, including classification of functions according to their behavior, avoidance of error, and convenience. **2.** In computer programming languages, a class of data in which all the data stored in this class share a fundamental syntactical characteristic; for example, they are all integers. Synonymous with data type. See *dynamic typing, strong typing, typeless, weak typing.*

Type 1 font A PostScript-compatible font that includes Adobe Systems' proprietary font-scaling technology, which improves type legibility at low resolutions and small type sizes. See *PostScript font.*

type checking In a high-level programming language, a process that checks to make sure that each variable contains the correct data type. For example, if a variable is declared to be an integer, it cannot contain a string. Type checking occurs when the program is compiled (static checking) or interpreted (dynamic checking). See *compiler, data type, dynamic checking, interpreter, strong typing, typeless, weak typing.*

typeface The distinctive design of a set of type, distinguished from its weight (such as bold), posture (such as italic), and type size. Many laser printers come with 100 or more typefaces available in the printer's read-only memory (ROM), and literally thousands more can be downloaded. Notice that professional graphic artists rarely use more than two typefaces in one document: They choose one typeface for display type and a second for body type. See *font, font family.*

typeless A class of high-level programming languages that lack any concept of data types. In such a language, there is essentially only one data type, so that a variable can store any type of data (and the type of data stored in a variable can change as the program executes). A typeless programming language (such as JavaScript) is ideal for scripting, in which variables may stand for computer system resources or components in addition to the data types normally found in strongly or weakly typed programming languages. A typeless language allows for rapid program development and maximum flexibility, but no type checking is performed; for this reason, errors may not be detected until the code is executed. See *data type, JavaScript, scripting language, strong typing, type, type checking, weak typing.*

typeover See *overtype mode.*

typeover mode See *overtype mode.*

typesetter See *imagesetter.*

typesetting The production of camera-ready copy on a high-end imagesetter, such as a Linotronic or Varityper. The current crop of office-quality PostScript laser printers can produce 1,200 dots per inch (dpi) output, which is considered crude by professional typesetting standards but which may be acceptable for applications such as newsletters, textbooks, instructional manuals, brochures, and proposals. See *resolution.*

type size The size of a font, measured in points (approximately ½ inch) from the top of the tallest ascender to the bottom of the lowest descender. See *pitch.*

type style The weight (such as bold) or posture (such as italic) of a font, distinguished from a font's typeface design and type size. See *attribute, emphasis.*

typing **1.** In computer programming languages, the strictness with which the consistent use of data types is enforced. See *data type, strong typing, typeless, weak typing.* **2.** In object-oriented programming, one of the seven fundamental principles of the object model. The typing principle states that objects must be clearly differentiated by class so that the differences between objects are unmistakable. See *class, object, object model, object-oriented programming.*

typography The science and art of designing aesthetically pleasing and readable typefaces.

U A standard unit of measurement, equal to 1.75 inches, for computer cases and enclosures.

UART Acronym for Universal Asynchronous Receiver/Transmitter. An integrated circuit that transforms the parallel data stream within the computer to the serial, one-after-the-other data stream used in asynchronous communications. In addition to the UART, serial communication requires a serial port and a modem. See *modem, motherboard, serial port.*

ubiquitous computing A scenario for future computing in which computers are so numerous that they fade into the background, providing intelligence for virtually every aspect of daily life.

UCITA Acronym for Uniform Computer Information Transactions Act. Model legislation proposed for adoption by all 50 U.S. states. The legislation directly addresses characteristics of software licenses that courts have often refused to uphold, such as prohibitions on reverse engineering, blanket liability disclaimers, the validity of a contract that the software purchaser is not able to read prior to undertaking actions (such as opening the package or installing the software) that constitute acceptance of the contract, and the prohibition of the purchaser's transfer of a license to a third party without the vendor's permission. The proposed legislation would also enable vendors to disable software remotely if an infringement was detected. See *EULA, shrink-wrap license.*

UCS Acronym for Univeral Character Set. A character set, developed and maintained by the International Organization for Standards (ISO), which is believed to be capable of representing all or nearly all known writing systems. Initiated in 1983 and faced with seemingly intractable representation problems that had to be solved, UCS was so slow to develop that a computer industry consortium created a competing project, called the Unicode Consortium, to ensure that their products would be marketable in China, Korea, Japan, India, and other countries where non-Roman scripts are in widespread use. The two projects now cooperate; still, the UCS project is more concerned with solving the theoretical issues involved in representing all possible scripts, while the Unicode Consortium is more concerned with bringing an acceptable product to large markets where non-Roman scripts predominate. See *ISO 10646, Unicode.*

UDDI Acronym for Universal Description, Discovery, and Integration. An XML-based service launched by an industry consortium that seeks to provide a business registry service for companies that are willing to work together to make their systems compatible for e-commerce. See *XML.*

UDP Acronym for User Datagram Protocol. One of the fundamental Internet protocols, collectively known as TCP/IP. UDP operates at the same level as the Transmission Control Protocol (TCP) but has much lower overhead and is not reliable; however, the latter quality is intentional. Unlike TCP, UDP does not attempt to establish a connection with the remote computer; it simply hands the data down to the connectionless IP protocol. UDP comes into play when a connection is not needed and would consume network bandwidth needlessly (for example, when responding to a ping request). See *TCP, TCP/IP.*

ULSI See *ultra-large scale integration (ULSI).*

Ultra-2 SCSI A SCSI standard that employs an 8-bit bus and delivers data transfer rates of up to 20 Mbps. See *SCSI.*

Ultra-2 Wide SCSI A SCSI standard that employs an 8-bit bus and delivers data transfer rates of up to 80 Mbps. See *SCSI.*

Ultra-3 SCSI A SCSI standard that employs a 16-bit data bus and delivers data transfer rates of up to 160 Mbps. Synonymous with Ultra 160 SCSI. See *SCSI.*

Ultra 160 SCSI See *Ultra-3 SCSI.*

Ultra 320 SCSI A SCSI standard that employs a 16-bit bus and delivers data transfer rates of up to 320 Mbps. See *SCSI.*

Ultra 640 SCSI A SCSI standard that employs a 16-bit bus and delivers data transfer rates of up to 640 Mbps. See *SCSI.*

Ultra ATA A hard drive interface standard for Integrated Drive Electronics (IDE)–compatible drives that is based on Ultra DMA. See *IDE, Ultra DMA.*

Ultra ATA/66 A hard drive interface standard for Integrated Drive Electronics (IDE)–compatible drives that enables communication speeds of up to 66 MHz, twice that of the original Ultra DMA standard (now called Ultra DMA/33). Ultra ATA/66 drives require a special 80-conductor cable as well as explicit Ultra ATA/66 motherboard or controller support. Also called Ultra DMA/66. See *IDE.*

Ultra ATA/100 A hard drive interface standard for Integrated Drive Electronics (IDE)–compatible drives that enables communication speeds of up to 100 MHz, three times that of the original ATA standard (now called Ultra DMA/33). Ultra ATA/ 100 drives require a special 80-conductor cable as well as explicit Ultra ATA/100 motherboard or controller support. Ultra ATA/100 appears to be the last ATA standard that will use a parallel connector; the next IDE standard, called Serial ATA, will use a high-speed serial cable. See *IDE, Serial ATA, Ultra DMA.*

Ultra DMA A Direct Memory Access (DMA) bus standard that provides Integrated Drive Electronics (IDE) drives with direct, fast access to the computer's memory. Because this standard is specified in an AT Attachment (ATA) hard drive interface standard called Ultra ATA, it is often thought that Ultra DMA and Ultra ATA are synonymous; however, Ultra DMA refers to a DMA bus standard, while Ultra ATA refers to a hard disk interface standard that incorporates the Ultra DMA specification. See *DMA, IDE.*

Ultra DMA/66 See *Ultra ATA/66.*

Ultra DMA/100 See *Ultra ATA/100.*

ultra-large scale integration (ULSI) In integrated circuit technology, the fabrication of a chip containing more than 1 million transistors. The Pentium chip, for example, includes more than 3 million transistors.

Ultra SCSI A SCSI standard that employs an 8-bit data bus to provide data transfer rates of up to 20 Mbps.

Ultra/Wide SCSI A SCSI standard that employs a 16-bit data bus to provide data transfer rates of up to 40 Mbps. See *SCSI-2.*

UMA See *upper memory area (UMA).*

UMB See *upper memory block (UMB).*

unauthorized access A computer break-in, done by a computer cracker for criminal or ego-boosting purposes. Unauthorized access is a crime in most states.

UNC See *Universal Naming Convention (UNC).*

undelete utility A utility program that can restore a file that was accidentally deleted from a disk.

Undernet One of several international Internet Relay Chat (IRC) networks, independent of other IRC networks.

underscore The underline character on the standard keyboard, which is often used to connect the words in a phrase when a program cannot tolerate spaces in a string ("This_is_a_phrase").

undo A command that restores a program and the user's data to the stage they were in just before the last command was given or the last action was initiated. Undo commands let the user reverse the often catastrophic effects of giving the wrong command.

undocumented call In operating systems, a system call that is not disclosed in the documentation available to programmers and users. Often, such calls are undocumented because they contain unresolved bugs. Microsoft Corporation has been accused of concealing operational calls within Microsoft Windows that enable Microsoft's application programmers to obtain better performance than competing programs. See *operating system (OS)*, *system call*.

undocumented feature A program feature that is present in the software but not discussed in the user documentation, and one that is not accessible by means of program menus because testing revealed that the feature's behavior was unsatisfactory or erratic for some reason.

unformatted text file See *plain text*.

unformat utility A utility program that can restore the data on an inadvertently formatted disk.

unicast To send a signal to a single, specific receiver. See *anycast*, *broadcast*, *multicast*.

Unicode A replacement for ASCII, Unicode is a 16-bit character set that is capable of representing many of the world's written languages, including Cyrillic, Greek, Japanese (hirigana and katakana), Chinese, Korean, Devanagri (Hindi), and Tamil. Developed by an industry consortium called the Unicode Project, Unicode is a stop-gap measure that can represent many of the written languages in areas where the market for computer equipment is large. A more scientific (but slower) project, the Universal Character Set (UCS), is working with the Unicode Project but strives to develop a 32-bit character set capable of encoding all written languages. See *UCS*.

Unified Modeling Language (UML) In software engineering, a notational language used for describing, specifying, and visualizing large-scale information systems in organizations. Incorporating the best software engineering practices available, UML is a tool that helps programmers implement the philosophy of object-oriented programming in the development of very large, complex software projects. UML diagrams are visual representations of how the components of a piece of software will relate to and interact with each other. The UML standard, maintained by the Object Management Group (OMG), was developed by a consortium of industry partners when it became apparent that the lack of a standard modeling language was delaying the use of object-oriented approaches in information system development. See *Object Management Group (OMG)*, *object-oriented programming*, *software development life cycle (SDLC)*, *software engineering*.

Uniform Computer Information Transactions Act See *UCITA*.

uniform resource identifier See *URI*.

uniform resource locator See *URL*.

uninstall To remove a program from a computer system by using a special utility designed specifically for that purpose.

uninterruptible power supply (UPS) A battery that can supply continuous power to a computer system in the event of a power failure. The battery, which is charged while a computer is switched on, kicks in if the power fails and provides power for 10 minutes or more, during which time one can save files and shut down the computer to preserve the integrity of crucial data.

Universal ADSL See *G.Lite*.

Universal Asynchronous Receiver/ Transmitter See *UART*.

Universal Character Set See *UCS*.

Universal Description, Discovery, and Integration See *UDDI*.

Universal Naming Convention (UNC)
A network resource naming convention
developed by Microsoft for Windows networking. UNC names conform to the
following template:

>//server name/share name/path/file

In the previous example, "share name"
refers to the shared resource that is made
available on the server, such as a directory.
The following is an example of a valid
UNC expression:

>//lothlorien/My Documents/templates/
>template1.dot

See *Common Internet File System (CIFS),
Samba, Server Message Blocks (SMB) Protocol.*

Universal Plug and Play (UPnP) A
network-based implementation of Plug-
and-Play services that enables compatible
devices to be connected to a computer network and to be automatically recognized by
all the systems connected to the network.
Developed by Microsoft and now supported
by hundreds of vendors, UPnP is primarily
aimed at home and small office users who
need to network a range of network-
capable devices, including personal digital
assistants (PDA) and digital cameras.

Universal Serial Bus See *USB.*

Unix (Pronounced *YEW-nicks.*) A 32-bit
multitasking and multiuser operating system that originated at AT&T's Bell
Laboratories and is now used on a wide
variety of computers, from mainframes to
personal digital assistants (PDA). With its
support for preemptive multitasking, multiple users, long file names, symmetric
multiprocessing, and 32-bit applications,
Unix has defined the state of the art in
operating system design for the past two
decades; 64-bit versions of Unix have been
developed and provide operating system
support for some of the most powerful
server systems now available. See *multitasking, symmetric multiprocessing (SMP).*

Unix-like operating system An oper-
ating system that is functionally identical to
Unix in the sense that it can compile and
run Unix software but does not use the
Unix name (which is trademarked by
X/Open). Examples of Unix-like operating
systems are FreeBSD and Linux. See
FreeBSD, Linux.

Unix-to-Unix Copy Program See
UUCP.

unmoderated newsgroup In a distributed bulletin board system (BBS) such as
EchoMail (FidoNet) or Usenet (Internet), a
topical discussion group in which postings
are not subject to review before distribution. Unmoderated newsgroups are
characterized by spontaneity, but some
postings may be inflammatory or inconsid-
erate, and flame wars may erupt. See
moderated newsgroup, newsgroup.

unordered list In HTML, a bulleted list
created with <UL></UL> tags. Text
tagged as an unordered list often appears
bulleted.

unsolicited commercial e-mail (UCE)
Unwanted and unrequested e-mail (spam)
that is sent by vendors or advertising firms.
Defended by direct marketing advocates,
UCE is regarded by many Internet users as
the use of privately funded resources (such
as a user's contract with an Internet service
provider) to send unsolicited advertising.
The costs to businesses and consumers are
far from trivial; Internet service providers
must constantly upgrade their bandwidth
to keep up with the swelling volume of
UCE, and they pass on the costs—
estimated to be nearly $9 billion a year
worldwide—to consumers. According to a
recent study, consumers will receive more
than 200 billion UCE mailings by 2006;
each received e-mail is estimated to cost
about $1 in lost productivity. See *spam.*

unsubscribe In Usenet, to remove a
newsgroup from a subscription list so that it
does not appear on the list of newsgroups
one is actively following. It is also possible to
unsubscribe from a mailing list. See *subscribe.*

update In database management, a fundamental data manipulation that involves adding, modifying, or deleting data records so that data is brought up-to-date. See *database management*.

upgrade To install a new release or version of a program, or a more recent or more powerful version of a microprocessor or peripheral.

upgrade processor A microprocessor specifically defined to upgrade older systems.

upgrade socket A receptacle on a motherboard specially designed for an upgrade processor.

upload To send a file to another computer on the network. See *download*.

UPnP See *Universal Plug and Play*.

upper memory area (UMA) In an IBM PC–compatible computer running MS-DOS, the memory between the 640K limit of conventional memory and 1,024K. In the original PC system design, some of the memory in this area was reserved for system use, but most was actually unused. Memory management programs (as well as HIMEM.SYS, available with MS-DOS 6.2) can configure the upper memory area so that it is available for system utilities and application programs. The upper memory area is distinguished from the high memory area (HMA), which is the first 64K of extended memory.

upper memory block (UMB) A collection of noncontiguous memory locations in the upper memory area (UMA) that can be combined to provide MS-DOS programs with additional memory. The portions of this memory that cannot be assigned to user programs have been reserved for system functions.

UPS See *uninterruptible power supply*.

upward compatibility Software that functions without modification on later or more powerful versions of a computer system.

urban legend A type of folklore that is distributed by contemporary communications technologies rather than word of mouth. The Internet presents a fertile environment for the propagation of urban legends. Many are hoaxes with cruel intent; for example, a widely circulated but false rumor states that some 4,000 Israeli workers at the World Trade Center were told to stay home from work on 9/11/2001.

URI Abbreviation for uniform resource identifier. In the Hypertext Transfer Protocol (HTTP), a string of characters that identifies an Internet resource, including the type of resource and its location. There are two types of URIs: uniform resource locators (URLs) and relative URLs. See *HTTP, URL*.

URL Acronym for uniform resource locator. On the World Wide Web, one of two basic kinds of Universal Resource Identifiers (URI), a string of characters that precisely identifies an Internet resource's type and location. For example, the following fictitious URL identifies a World Wide Web document (http://), indicates the domain name of the computer on which it is stored (www.wolverine.virginia.edu), fully describes the document's location within the directory structure (~toros/winerefs/), and includes the document's name and extension (merlot.html):

http://www.wolverine.virginia.edu/~toros/winerefs/merlot.

See *relative URL (RELURL)*.

USB Abbreviation for Universal Serial Bus. An interface standard that enables computer peripherals, such as keyboards, mice, printers, digital cameras, backup storage devices, and Ethernet ports, to be connected to a USB-compatible computer by means of an inexpensive cable. Capable of transferring data at a rate of 12 Mbps, USB represents an advance over the sluggish RS-232 serial ports built into most computers, but USB's speed is itself considered sluggish when compared to IEEE 1394 (also called FireWire), which enables data transfer rates of up to 400 Mbps. Some

USB peripherals can be connected or disconnected without shutting down the computer, in an operation called hot swapping. See *hot swapping, IEEE 1394, Plug and Play (PnP), USB 2.0.*

USB 2.0 An upgraded USB standard that enables USB peripherals to compete with IEEE 1394 (FireWire) devices. It enables data transfer speeds of up to 480 Mbps while retaining downward compatibility with the initial USB standard (12 Mbps). See *downward-compatible, IEEE 1394, USB.*

Usenet A worldwide computer-based discussion system that uses the Internet and other networks for transmission media. Discussion is channeled into more than 30,000 topically named newsgroups, which contain original contributions called articles, as well as commentaries on these articles called follow-up posts. As follow-up posts continue to appear on a given subject, a thread of discussion emerges; a threaded newsreader collates these articles together so that readers can see the flow of the discussion. Usenet is accessed daily by more than 15 million people in more than 100 countries. See *Network News Transfer Protocol (NNTP).*

Usenet site A computer system—one with lots of disk storage—that receives a news feed and enables dozens or hundreds of people to participate in Usenet. Currently, approximately 120,000 Usenet sites exist, providing an estimated 4 million people with access to Usenet newsgroups.

user See *end user.*

user agent (UA) In the terminology established by the OSI Reference Model, a client e-mail program that runs on the user's machine and assists in contacting a server. See *OSI Reference Model.*

User Datagram Protocol See *UDP.*

user default A user-defined program operating preference, such as the default margins for every new document that a word processing program creates. Also

called preferences, options, or setup in various applications.

user-defined Selected or chosen by the user of the computer system.

user-friendly A program or computer system designed so that individuals who lack extensive computer experience or training can use the system without becoming confused or frustrated.

user group A voluntary association of users of a specific computer system or program who meet regularly to exchange tips and techniques, hear presentations by computer experts, and obtain public domain software and shareware.

user interface All the features of a program or computer that govern the way people interact with the computer. See *command-driven program, graphical user interface (GUI).*

UTC Abbreviation for Universal Coordinated Time. Formerly known as Greenwich Mean Time (GMT), UTC is a standard time at the Earth's prime meridian (0° longitude).

utility program A program that assists in maintaining and improving the efficiency of a computer system.

UUCP Acronym for Unix-to-Unix Copy Program. A network based on long-distance telephone uploads and downloads. UUCP allows Unix users to exchange files, e-mail, and Usenet articles. In the 1980s, when Internet connectivity was hard to come by, UUCP played an important role in providing support for the Unix operating system.

uudecode A Unix utility program that decodes a uuencoded ASCII file, restoring the original binary file (such as a program or graphic). A uudecode utility is needed to decode the binary files posted to Usenet. Most newsreading programs incorporate such a utility. See *newsreader, Usenet, uuencode.*

uuencode A Unix utility program that transforms a binary file, such as a program or graphic, into coded ASCII text. This text can be transferred by using the Internet, or it can be posted to a Usenet newsgroup. At the receiving end, the uudecode utility decodes the message and restores the binary file. See *Usenet, uudecode.*

UXGA An improvement on the SXGA standard that allows monitor and projector resolutions of 1600x1200.

V.17 An ITU-TSS modulation protocol for transmitting and receiving faxes at speeds up to 14,400 bps. See *ITU-TSS, modulation protocol*.

V.21 An ITU-TSS modulation protocol for modems transmitting and receiving data at 300 bps. V.21 conflicts with the Bell 103A standard once widely used in the United States and Canada. See *ITU-TSS, modem, modulation protocol*.

V.22 An ITU-TSS modulation protocol for modems transmitting and receiving data at 1200 bps. V.22 conflicts with the Bell 212A standard once widely used in the United States and Canada. See *ITU-TSS, modem, modulation protocol*.

V.22bis An ITU-TSS modulation protocol for modems transmitting and receiving data at 2400 bps. See *ITU-TSS, modem, modulation protocol*.

V.27ter An ITU-TSS modulation protocol for fax modems and fax machines transmitting and receiving fax information at 4800 bps. V.27ter modems can fall back to 2400 bps, if necessary. See *fax modem, ITU-TSS, modem, modulation protocol*.

V.29 An ITU-TSS modulation protocol for fax modems and fax machines transmitting and receiving data at 9600 bps. V.29 modems can fall back to 7200 bps if necessary, to link with slower devices or to accommodate line noise. See *ITU-TSS, modem, modulation protocol*.

V.32 An ITU-TSS modulation protocol for modems transmitting and receiving data at 9600 bps. Modems compliant with the V.32 standard can fall back to 4800 bps, if necessary, to link with slower devices or to accommodate line noise. See *ITU-TSS, modem, modulation protocol*.

V.32bis An ITU-TSS modulation protocol for modems transmitting and receiving data at 14,400 bps. Modems that use the V.32bis standard can transfer data at slower speeds, if necessary, to link with slower devices or to accommodate line noise. See *ITU-TSS, modem, modulation protocol*.

V.32terbo A proprietary modulation protocol developed by AT&T to regulate modems transmitting and receiving data at 19,200 bps. If needed, these modems fall back to the data transfer rates supported by the V.32bis standard. Despite its apparently official name, V.32terbo is not recognized by the ITU-TSS. The V.34 standard has replaced V.32 terbo. See *modem, modulation protocol*.

V.34 An ITU-TSS modulation protocol for modems transmitting and receiving data at 28,800 bps. V.34 modems adjust to changing line conditions to avoid having to fall back to a lower data transfer rate. A recent addition to the protocol enables transmission rates of up to 33.6 Kbps. See *ITU-TSS, modem, modulation protocol*.

V.42 An ITU-TSS error-correction protocol designed to counter the effects of line noise. A pair of V.42-compliant modems check each transmitted piece of data to make sure they arrive error-free and then retransmit any faulty data. The V.42 standard uses the Link Access Protocol for Modems (LAPM) as its default error-correction method but will switch to MNP4, if needed. See *error correction, ITU-TSS, Link Access Protocol for Modems (LAPM), MNP-4*.

V.42bis An ITU-TSS compression protocol that increases the throughput of modems. V.42bis is an on-the-fly compression technique that reduces the amount of data a modem needs to transmit. See *compression, ITU-TSS, modem*.

V.90 An ITU-TSS modulation protocol for modems transmitting and receiving data at 56 Kbps. The V.90 standard replaces two proprietary standards, called X2 and K56flex, that were widely used prior to the publication of V.90. Some X2 and K56flex modems can be upgraded so that they support the new standard protocol. See *ITU-TSS, modem, modulation protocol, x2.*

V.92 An ITU-TSS modulation protocol that is intended to replace V.90. It offers faster upstream data transfers, the ability to pause transfers so that a telephone call can be taken or made on the same line, and quick-connect features that reduce connection time when calls from previously connected modems are made. See *ITU-TSS, modem, modulation protocol, V.90.*

vaccine A program designed to offer protection against viruses. By adding a small amount of code to files, an alert sounds when a virus tries to change the file. Vaccines are also called immunizing programs. See *virus.*

validation **1.** A process that ensures the data entered into a database form, a Web form, or a computer program conforms to the correct data type. See *data type, mask.* **2.** In programming, the final phase in the software life cycle. The program is tested to see if it conforms to specifications. See *software development life cycle (SDLC).*

value **1.** In programming, the data stored in a variable or constant. In most programming languages, the data must conform to a specified data type. See *constant, data type, variable.* **2.** In a spreadsheet program, a numeric cell entry. Two kinds of values exist. The first, called a constant, is a value one types directly into a cell. The second kind of value looks like a constant but is produced by a formula placed into a cell. Be careful not to confuse the two and type a constant over a formula. See *cell protection, label.*

value-added network (VAN) A public data network (PDN) that provides value-added services for corporate customers, including end-to-end dedicated lines with guaranteed security. See *public data network (PDN).*

value-added reseller (VAR) A business that repackages and improves hardware manufactured by an original equipment manufacturer (OEM). A value-added reseller typically improves the original equipment by adding superior documentation, packaging, system integration, and exterior finish. Some VARs, however, do little more than put their name on a device. See *original equipment manufacturer (OEM).*

vampire tap Slang expression for a network connection made by drilling through the outer shield of a coaxial cable.

VAN See *value-added network (VAN).*

vanilla Plain and unadorned, without bells, whistles, or advanced features, as in, "I'm using a plain vanilla text processor." See *bells and whistles.*

vaporware A program that is heavily marketed even though it is still under development, or, at the extreme, does not even exist. Vaporware marketing may reflect unwarranted optimism, but it may also reflect a firm's desire to demoralize competitors. A famous example is Ovation, an integrated program that was announced in 1983 with saturation advertising; however, the product never shipped.

VAR See *value-added reseller (VAR).*

variable In a high-level programming language, a storage location in the computer's memory that contains a variable name and the value currently associated with the variable name. The value can change as the program executes. Variables must be declared. See *constant, declaration, variable name.*

variable bit rate An asynchronous communication mode in which maximum and minimum bandwidth requirements can be stated. See *asynchronous communication.*

variable length record In a database management program, a record that can expand or contract, as needed, to accommodate large units of data (such as text or graphics). See *database management.*

variable name In a high-level programming language, a name associated with a variable stored in memory. The variable name must be typed according to the language's syntax rules, which may include an identifying symbol (such as $), case sensitivity ($total and $Total may represent different variables), and other restrictions; for example, the syntax rules may require that the variable name start with an alphanumeric character, not a number. See *syntax, value, variable.*

variant   In programming, a data type that, when assigned to a variable, allows the programmer to assign numerical or string values to the variable. The compiler or interpreter discriminates between the two by examining the context of the variant's use. See *data type, value, variable.*

VBA   See *Visual Basic for Applications.*

VBScript   A scripting language, developed by Microsoft, that is used to write short programs (scripts) that can be embedded in Web pages. VBScript is a simplified version of Visual Basic. See *Active Server Page (ASP), Visual Basic.*

vCard   A communications protocol for exchanging the type of information normally found on business cards, such as name, address, company name, telephone numbers, and e-mail address. Most recent e-mail programs support vCard, which enables e-mail users to distribute their business card information automatically in all outgoing messages.

Very High Data Rate Digital Subscriber Line   See *VDSL.*

VDSL   Acronym for Very High Data Rate Digital Subscriber Line. A standard for Digital Subscriber Line (DSL) service at downstream speeds of up to 55 Mbps using standard, twisted-pair telephone lines. The operating range of VDSL is sharply limited; subscribers must be positioned within 1 mile of the central office (CO). See *CO, DSL.*

VDT   Acronym for video display terminal. Synonymous with monitor.

VDT radiation   See *cathode ray tube (CRT), extremely low-frequency (ELF) emission.*

VDU   Abbreviation for video display unit. Synonymous with monitor.

vector   **1.** In computer graphics, a shape defined by the coordinates of its beginning, intermediate, and end points; in contrast to a bitmapped graphic, such a shape is susceptible to manual and automatic manipulation. **2.** The memory address of an executable program; the program can be activated by addressing its vector. **3.** A quantity that is measured by direction as well as by magnitude.

vector font   See *outline font.*

vector graphics   The formation of an image made of independent objects, each of which can be individually selected, sized, moved, and otherwise manipulated. The image's objects are formed by geometrical calculations, rather than permanently "painting" the color of each bit in the image, as in a bitmapped graphic. Vector graphics are much easier to edit than bitmapped graphics and are preferred for professional illustration purposes. See *illustration software.*

vector-to-raster conversion program   A utility program available with many professional illustration programs, such as CorelDRAW, that transforms object-oriented (vector) graphics into bitmapped (raster) graphic images. See *object-oriented graphic.*

vendor   A seller or supplier of computer systems, peripherals, or computer-related services.

Vendor Independent Messaging (VIM)   In e-mail programs, an application program interface (API) that lets e-mail programs from different manufacturers exchange mail with one another. The consortium of developers that designed VIM did not include Microsoft Corporation, which uses the Messaging Application Program Interface (MAPI). A VIM-to-MAPI dynamic link library (DLL) file makes it possible for the two interfaces to exchange messages.

verify To determine the accuracy and completion of a computer operation.

Veronica In Gopher, a search service that scans a database of Gopher directory titles and resources (such as documents, graphics, movies, and sounds) and generates a new Gopher menu containing the results of the search.

version A specific release of a software or hardware product that is identified by a version number or a date (such as 2003). A larger version number indicates a more recent product release. For example, Internet Explorer 6 is a more recent product than Internet Explorer 5. In many cases, version numbers are skipped, such as Windows 3.1 to Windows 95. Revisions that repair minor bugs, called bug fixes or maintenance releases, often have small intermediate numbers such as 1.02 or 1.2a. It should be noted that software publishers are under no obligation to state version numbers accurately; for example, to compete effectively with a competitor whose product is numbered 8.0, a version that should have received a version number representing an incremental increase, such as 7.1, may be moved to the next higher integer. A more accurate version number is the software publisher's build number. See *build number.*

version control system A component employed in a repository that automatically affixes version numbers to any type of data submitted to the repository. Previous versions are available in the repository, enabling project participants to see how the project has evolved. See *repository.*

verso In printing, the left-side, even-numbered page in a two-page spread. See *recto.*

vertical application An application program created for a narrowly defined market, such as the members of a profession or a specific type of retail store. A vertical application is usually designed to provide complete management functions such as scheduling, billing, inventory control, and purchasing.

vertical centering The automatic centering of graphics or text vertically on the page. For example, WordPerfect includes a Center Top to Bottom command that centers text vertically.

vertical frequency See *vertical refresh rate.*

vertical justification The alignment of newspaper columns by means of feathering (adding vertical space) so that all columns end evenly at the bottom margin. A page layout program capable of vertical justification inserts white space between frame borders and text, between paragraphs, and between lines to even the columns at the bottom margin.

vertically flat A monitor design used in Trinitron-type and other monitors that somewhat reduces image distortion. Vertically flat displays are curved like cylinders, instead of like spheres, as most cathode ray tubes (CRTs) are. See *flat-square monitor, flat tension-mask monitor.*

vertical market A market that is limited to a particular industry or industry sector, such as banking and finance. See *horizontal market, vertical application.*

vertical refresh rate The rate at which a monitor and video adapter pass the electron guns of a cathode ray tube (CRT) from the top of the display to the bottom. Measured in Hertz (Hz), the refresh rate determines whether a display appears to flicker. At a resolution of 1,280 pixels by 1,024 lines, a refresh rate of 72 Hz or more will eliminate visible flicker.

vertical retrace The process of the electron beam in a cathode ray tube (CRT) being directed by the yoke from the end of one vertical scan to the beginning of the next. Video adapters must allow time for vertical retrace in preparing the video signal. During vertical retrace, blanking is in effect.

very high-level language (VHL) A declarative language that is used to solve a particular kind of problem. VHLs, nearly all of which are proprietary, are used to generate reports in spreadsheets and database management programs.

very large scale integration (VLSI) A level of technological sophistication in the manufacturing of semiconductor chips that allows the equivalent of more than 100,000 (and up to 1 million) transistors to be placed on one chip.

VESA Acronym for Video Electronics Standards Association. See *VESA local bus, video standard.*

VESA bus See *local bus, VESA local bus.*

VESA local bus A local bus architecture created to work with the Intel 80486 and provide a standard to compete with incompatible proprietary local buses. VESA local bus adapters typically are used to connect video adapters and network adapters to the expansion bus. See *local bus.*

VESA local bus slot A socket for adapters found on expansion buses compatible with the VESA local bus standard. VESA local bus slots provide 32-bit communication between the microprocessor and adapters, and were common in computers based on various versions of the 486-class microprocessor. However, PCI slots are much more flexible than VESA local bus slots and are expected to be the standard used for several more years. See *AGP, ISA, ISA slot.*

V.FC See *V.Fast Class.*

V.Fast Class (V.FC) A proprietary modulation protocol used by several modem manufacturers before the V.34 standard was published. Most V.FC modems can be upgraded to comply fully with V.34.

VGA Acronym for Video Graphics Array. A color bitmapped graphics display standard introduced by IBM in 1987 with its PS/2 computers. VGA video adapters and analog monitors display as many as 256 continuously variable colors simultaneously, with a resolution of 640 pixels horizontally by 480 lines vertically. VGA circuitry is downwardly compatible with all previous display standards, including Color Graphics Adapter (CGA), monochrome display adapter (MDA), and Enhanced Graphics Adapter (EGA). Although the VGA standard has been surpassed by more recent standards that offer higher resolution and greater color depth, it is still the default resolution for most operating systems (including Microsoft Windows) because almost any video adapter can display it. See *video standard.*

VHL See *very high-level language.*

vi A text editor that is configured to be the default editor on many Unix systems. Notoriously difficult to learn, vi has little in common with Macintosh and Microsoft Windows 95/98 word processing programs. To avoid vi, many Unix users prefer to use applications that have their own built-in text editors, such as the e-mail program pine. See *emacs.*

video accelerator See *graphics accelerator board.*

video adapter The card in a computer that generates the output required to display text and graphics on a monitor.

video amplifier Part of the monitor circuitry that increases the weak signal received from the video adapter to a level high enough to drive the electron guns. Monochrome monitors have one video amplifier, while color monitors have three that are carefully tuned to work together.

video board See *video adapter.*

video capture board An adapter that plugs into the computer's expansion bus and that enables a person to control a television, video camera, videocassette recorder (VCR), or CD/DVD and manipulate its output. Video capture cards usually compress the video input to a manageable size and are useful for developing multimedia presentations.

video card See *graphics accelerator board.*

videoconferencing The use of a computer network to enable real-time remote conferencing with live sound and video. A popular videoconferencing application for Internet use is CU-SeeMe.

video controller A microprocessor on the video adapter that reads the information in video memory, arranges it into a continuous stream, and sends it to the monitor.

videodisk See *interactive videodisk*.

video driver A program that tells other programs how to work with a particular video adapter and monitor. Video drivers often have user-accessible controls that determine resolution, refresh rate, and color depth.

Video Electronics Standards Association See *VESA*.

Video Graphics Array See *VGA*.

video memory A set of memory chips to which the central processing unit (CPU) writes display information, and from which the video controller reads data prior to sending it to the monitor. Video memory often uses inexpensive dynamic random access memory (DRAM) chips, but high-end video adapters use much faster DDR-SDRAM memory.

video monitor See *monitor*.

video noise Random dots of interference on a display. Synonymous with snow. Video noise is rarely a problem in modern displays, but it caused problems for users of Color Graphics Array (CGA) video adapters and monitors.

video RAM (VRAM) Specially designed dynamic random access memory (DRAM) chips that maximize the performance of video adapters. The central processing unit (CPU) loads display information into VRAM, which is then read by the video system. High-end VRAM, called dual-ported VRAM, allows simultaneous reading and writing of data. Replaced by DDR-SDRAM. See *DDR-SDRAM, random access memory (RAM), video adapter.*

video standard A standard for video display adapters developed so that software developers can anticipate how their programs will appear onscreen. Video standards are defined by industry groups and specify maximum screen resolution, which is measured by the number of pixels that can be displayed horizontally and the number of lines that can be displayed vertically; for example, the VGA standard defines a horizontal resolution of 640 pixels by 480 lines (640 × 480). Video display standards also specify the adapter's maximum color depth, which is determined by the bit length of the information used to represent distinct colors; a color depth of 8 bits yields 256

Video Standard	Resolution	
	Horizontal	Vertical
VGA	640	480
SVGA	800	600
SXGA	1280	1024
SXGA+	1400	1024
SXGA-Wide	1600	1024
UXGA	1600	1200
HDTV	1920	1080
UXGA-Wide	1920	1200
QXGA	2056	1536

colors, a depth of 16 bits yields 65,536 colors, and a depth of 24 bits yields 16,777,216 colors. Although the various video standards originally defined additional electronic characteristics of video adapters, such as video interlacing, they are now used to indicate an adapter or display's maximum resolution. See *color depth, eXtended Graphics Array (XGA), HDTV, MCGA, resolution, SVGA, SXGA, VGA.*

videotext   The transmission of information (such as news headlines, stock quotes, and movie reviews) through a cable television system.

view   **1.** In database management programs, an onscreen display of the information in a database that meets the criteria specified in a query. With most database management programs, views can be saved; the best programs update each view every time one adds or edits data records. See *database management program.* **2.** In application software, to display an image or a document in a different view mode; for example, most applications enable users to view the document as it will appear when printed. **3.** In Web site management, a fundamental usage measurement equal to one display of a specific page on the site. See *visit.*

viral marketing   A marketing method that uses the Internet and its various services, especially e-mail, to distribute advertising using the activities and resources of others. For example, the free e-mail service Hotmail originated this concept by including advertising in messages sent by its users. More recently, attempts have been made to create "word of mouse" campaigns in which users would spread the word by forwarding messages to their friends, family, and co-workers. In 1999, the makers of the hit film *Blair Witch Project* gained considerable word of mouse by disseminating e-mail containing a rumor that the film was actually about a true incident.

virtual   Not real; a computer representation of something that is real.

Virtual 8086 mode   A mode available with 80386 and higher microprocessors, in which the chip simulates an almost unlimited number of Intel 8086 machines.

virtual community   A group of people who, although they may have never met, share interests and concerns, and communicate with each other via e-mail and newsgroups. The people who see themselves as members of such communities feel a sense of belonging and develop deep emotional ties with other participants, even though the relationships that develop are mediated by the computer and may never involve face-to-face interaction.

virtual corporation   A means of organizing a business in which the various units are geographically dispersed but are actively and fruitfully linked by the Internet or some other wide area network (WAN).

virtual device   The simulation of a computer device or peripheral, such as a hard disk drive or printer, that does not exist—at least, not nearby. In a local area network (LAN), a computer may appear to have an additional enormous hard disk, but it is really located on the file server.

Virtual Device Driver (VxD)   In Microsoft Windows 95/98, a 32-bit program that manages a specific system resource, such as a sound card or printer. Unlike the device drivers used in Windows 3.1, Virtual Device Drivers run in the processor's protected mode, where they are less likely to conflict with other applications and cause system crashes. The abbreviation VxD covers a range of devices, including virtual printer devices (VPD), virtual display devices (VDD), and virtual timing devices (VTD).

Virtual Library   In the World Wide Web (WWW), a Web subject guide in which volunteers take on the responsibility of maintaining the portion of the tree that is devoted to a specific subject, such as astronomy or zoology. The Virtual Library, headquartered at www.vlib.org, is a good place to look for academically oriented information on the Web. See *subject tree.*

virtual machine **1.** In 80386 and higher microprocessors, a protected memory space created by the microprocessor's hardware capabilities. Each virtual machine can run its own programs, completely isolated from other machines. The virtual machines can also access the keyboard, printer, and other devices without conflicts. Virtual machines are made possible by a computer with the necessary processing circuitry and a lot of random access memory (RAM). See *Virtual 8086 mode.* **2.** In Java, a protected memory space in which a Java applet can execute safely, without any access to the computer's file system. Synonymous with sandbox.

virtual memory A method of extending the apparent size of random access memory (RAM) by using part of the hard disk as an extension of RAM. Many application programs—and most modern operating systems, such as Windows—routinely use the disk instead of memory to store some data or program instructions while one runs the program. See *virtual memory management.*

virtual memory management The management of virtual memory operations at the operating system level rather than the application program level. An advantage to implementing virtual memory at the operating system level rather than the application level is that any program can take advantage of the virtual memory, with the result that memory extends seamlessly from random access memory (RAM) to the computer's secondary storage. Microsoft Windows 95/98/2000/ME/XP and Linux users can take full advantage of the virtual memory capabilities of their system's microprocessors. In the Macintosh world, MacOS makes virtual memory management available for users of Power Macintoshes.

virtual private network (VPN) A highly secure network for transmitting sensitive data (including electronic commerce transactions) that uses the public Internet as its transmission medium. To ensure data confidentiality and integrity, VPNs use encryption and protocol tunneling.

Businesses often use VPNs to enable employees to access the corporate network from a remote location. See *PPTP.*

virtual reality (VR) A computer-generated illusion of three-dimensional space. On the Web, virtual reality sites enable Web users to explore three-dimensional virtual reality "worlds" by means of VR plug-in programs. These programs enable a person to walk or fly through the three-dimensional space that these worlds offer. In advanced VR, the user wears a head-mounted display (HMD), which displays a stereoscopic image, and wears a sensor glove, which permits the user to manipulate objects in the virtual environment. See *cyberspace, electrocutaneous feedback, second-person virtual reality, sensor glove, stereoscopy.*

Virtual Reality Modeling Language See *VRML.*

virus A program that replicates itself, and in so doing resembles a biological virus, by attaching to other programs and carrying out unwanted and sometimes damaging operations. Although some viruses are relatively benign and are little more than pranks, most are written with malicious intent; at the extreme, they can wipe out all the contents on a computer's hard disk.

Viruses fall into three general categories: boot sector viruses, file viruses, and macro viruses. Boot sector viruses attach themselves to the hidden boot sector of floppy or hard disks so that they can enter the computer's memory when the system is started. File viruses attach themselves to executable files so that they can spread when the infected program is launched. Macro viruses take advantage of the scripting languages built into popular applications, especially Microsoft Office.

Early viruses propagated by means of floppy disks, which users often exchanged in order to share data or software. Today, the Internet provides the means of choice for virus propagation. Most are spread by means of e-mail attachments. To safeguard one's system from viruses attached to e-mail messages, it is necessary to refrain from opening or executing any attachment of unknown origin; in addition, all users should install and run anti-virus software. See *boot sector virus, macro virus, Trojan horse.*

visit In Web site management, a basic measurement of site popularity that is equal to one session initiated from an external IP address. See *view.*

Visual Basic An object-oriented, visual programming language for developing applications designed to run in Microsoft Windows that derives from BASIC, an easy-to-use programming language originally designed for teaching purposes. Using Visual Basic, the programmer uses a screen designer to set up the contents of a window, selecting control objects (pushbuttons, list boxes, and so on) from an onscreen toolbox and placing them in a person's design. The programmer then writes procedures for the objects using a modern version of BASIC. Visual Basic enables programmers to develop functional applications in short order and is widely used to develop custom software. See *visual programming language.*

Visual Basic for Applications (VBA) A version of the Visual Basic programming language included with Microsoft Windows applications, such as Microsoft Excel; also called Visual Basic Programming System, Applications Edition. Visual Basic for Applications is used to create procedures as simple as basic macros and as complex as custom application programs, complete with dialog boxes, menus, pushbuttons, and unique commands.

Visual C++ An object-oriented, visual programming language and comprehensive development environment developed by Microsoft, for C++ programming.

visual programmi.ng language A programming language that is equipped with a comprehensive development environment, which includes tools for constructing a program's user interface without programming. Elements of the user interface can then be associated with

code to make a functional application. See *Visual Basic, Visual C++.*

VL–Bus See *VESA local bus.*

VLSI See *very large scale integration (VLSI).*

VML Acronym for Vector Markup Language. A declarative markup language that extends the functionality of XML by enabling programmers to represent vector graphics on Web pages. The VML standard is maintained by the World Wide Web Consortium (W3C). See *vector graphics, World Wide Web Consortium (W3C), XML.*

voice actuation Computer recognition and acceptance of spoken commands as instructions to be processed. See *speech recognition.*

voice-capable modem A modem that, like a fax switch, can distinguish fax transmissions, data transmissions, and voice telephone calls, and then route each to the proper device. Voice-capable modems can serve as voice mail systems for small offices.

voice coil actuator See *servo-voice coil actuator.*

voice mail In office automation, a communications system in which voice messages are transformed into digital form and are stored on a network. When the person to whom the message is directed logs on to the system and discovers that a message is waiting, the system plays the message. Synonymous with voice store and forward.

Voice Over IP See *VoIP.*

voice portal A Web site that enables users to interact by means of voice-related technologies, including text-to-speech synthesis, and speech recognition. To interact with such a site, the user's computer must be equipped with a microphone and speakers.

voice recognition See *speech recognition.*

voice store and forward See *voice mail.*

voice synthesis The audible output of computer-based text in the form of synthesized speech that people can recognize and understand. Voice synthesis is much easier to achieve than voice recognition; one can equip virtually any personal computer to read ASCII text aloud with few errors. This capability has helped blind people gain increased access to written works not recorded on cassette tape. See *speech recognition*.

VoIP Acronym for Voice Over IP. The use of TCP/IP-based packet switching technology to transmit voice calls over long-distance trunk lines. Because packet-switching networks can carry more calls over a transmission channel of given bandwidth than circuit-switching networks, VOIP has an inherent economic advantage in that long-distance carriers using VOIP can offer lower long-distance rates. However, the quality of service (QoS) may be lower than that offered by traditional long-distance carriers. See *QoS*.

volatility The susceptibility of a computer's random access memory (RAM) to the complete loss of stored information if power is interrupted.

volume A unit of storage that is normally the same as a disk (floppy or hard); however, it is possible to map volumes to more than one disk, and a disk can likewise contain two more volumes.

volume label An identifying name assigned to a disk and displayed on the first line of a directory. The name can be no longer than 11 characters and is assigned when one formats the disk.

volume purchasing agreement A contract between a software publisher and a purchaser (such as a company or university) that enables the purchaser to receive a significant discount as long as a large number of copies of a program are ordered. See *commercial software, site license, software license*.

von Neumann bottleneck The limitation on processing speed imposed by computer architectures linking a single microprocessor with memory. John von Neumann discovered that a program will spend more time retrieving data from memory than it spends actually processing it. One proposed solution to the von Neumann bottleneck is parallel processing, in which a program's tasks are divided between two or more microprocessors. Existing programming languages and techniques, however, cannot handle parallel processing very well. The Pentium microprocessor minimizes the von Neumann bottleneck by incorporating separate caches for data and instructions. See *stored program concept*.

VR See *virtual reality*.

VRAM See *video RAM*.

VRML Acronym for Virtual Reality Modeling Language. A scripting language that enables programmers to specify the characteristics of a three-dimensional world that is accessible on the Internet. VRML worlds can contain sounds, hyperlinks, videos, and animations as well as three-dimensional spaces, which can be explored by using a VRML plug-in.

W

W3C See *World Wide Web Consortium (W3C).*

wafer A thin disk of semiconductor material, generally four or five inches in diameter, that is cut into smaller sections to make chips. See *chip, semiconductor.*

WAI See *Web Accessibility Initiative (WAI).*

wait state A microprocessor clock cycle in which nothing occurs. A wait state is programmed into a computer system to allow other components, such as random access memory (RAM), to catch up with the central processing unit (CPU). The number of wait states depends on the speed of the processor in relation to the speed of memory. Wait states can be eliminated—resulting in a "zero wait state" machine—by using fast (but expensive) cache memory, interleaved memory, page-mode RAM, or static RAM chips. See *cache memory, interleaved memory, page-mode RAM, SRAM.*

Wake on LAN (WOL) A technology jointly developed by Intel and IBM that enables compatible devices to "wake up" from a standby mode after receiving a signal from an Ethernet network. Using remote network management software, a network administrator can program this software to "wake up" computers when they are not likely to be in use (for example, at 3 a.m.) so that routine system administration tasks can be performed, such as installing security upgrades. To take advantage of this technology, the networked computers must use Wake on LAN-compatible Ethernet adapters and computers. See *Ethernet.*

walled garden A Web site that is configured so that, once users access the site, they are restricted to certain resources and find it difficult or impossible to access other Web resources. Walled gardens are created to trap unwary consumers so that they can be repeatedly subjected to controlled advertising or to prevent them from accessing content unacceptable for certain devices, such as Web-enabled phones. Within a walled garden, visitors find that the costs of leaving the site are higher than the costs of remaining within it. For example, a user who attempts to leave the site by clicking a hyperlink may discover that the linked page, even though it resides on a site with no relation to the walled garden, appears within a frame in which the walled garden's banner—and advertising — continues to appear. Most users lack the technical expertise to escape from walled gardens. The European-based Opera Web browser is one of the few that enables such an escape by means of a context menu, which enables users to maximize the frame containing the external page.

wallpaper A digitized graphic that is large enough to cover the entire desktop without distortion. Most operating systems enable users to choose a wallpaper graphic. Utilities are available that change wallpaper at specified intervals. See *desktop pattern.*

wall time An elapsed time as measured by a clock or chronometer.

WAN Acronym for wide area network. A data network that provides data communications services for businesses and government agencies. Most WANs use the X.25 protocols, which are designed to overcome problems related to noisy analog telephone lines. See *LAN.*

WAP Acronym for Wireless Application Protocol. A digital cellular phone standard, part of the second-generation digital cellular service known in the U.S. as Personal Communication Service (PCS), that enables servers to deliver Web content to remote wireless devices such as digital cellular phones and personal digital assistants (PDAs). The data is distributed in the Wireless Markup Language (WML), which enables Web content to be displayed on remote devices with small screens and limited memory. See *digital cellular phone, PCS, PDA, WML.*

war dialer A computer program, employed by computer intruders, that can enable them to gain access to poorly secured computer systems. The program randomly dials telephone numbers, looking for a number that is connected to a modem. It then attempts to gain entry using a lengthy list of commonly chosen passwords. Successful use of such a program constitutes unauthorized computer access, which is illegal in the U.S. and most foreign countries.

war driving An attempt to gain illegal, unauthorized access to wireless local area networks (wireless LANs) by driving around with a notebook computer, a wireless Ethernet adapter set to promiscuous mode, and an antenna. In promiscuous mode, the adapter attempts to find any available byte that has been transmitted, even if it cannot detect the entire message. When wireless data is discovered, the intruder moves closer to the data source and attempts to break into the network. Many wireless LANs are poorly secured, leaving them open to such attacks.

warez (Pronounced *wares*.) Slang term for commercial software that has been made available for downloading on the Internet, in violation of international copyright law.

warm boot A system restart performed after the system has been powered and operating. A warm boot is performed by using a special key combination or by pressing a reset button, while a cold boot involves actually turning the big red switch off and on. See *programmer's switch*.

warm link In object linking and embedding (OLE) and dynamic data exchange (DDE), a dynamic link that is updated only when one explicitly requests the update by choosing an update link command. Warm links have also been available in Lotus 1-2-3 since Release 2.2 and in Corel Quattro Pro since Version 1.0. See *hot link*.

Warnock's dilemma In online text chatting, mailing lists, and Weblogging, a creative incapacity induced when one's favorite chat sites are so full of brilliant commentary that there is nothing to say, or to the contrary, so full of stupidity that one would lower oneself by joining the discussion. The dilemma's name is said to be that of a mailing list participant who first described the phenomenon.

waterfall model A processual model of software development that moves in a series of fixed stages: requirements specification, design, implementation, testing, and installation. The model works well for small-scale development, but it is too rigid for large-scale system development. For example, clients are rarely able to explain their functional requirements fully at the beginning of the project; they may realize what they want only after they are able to see the system in operation. But the waterfall model delays system implementation until relatively late in the project, when it is too late to change the software. For this reason, software engineers prefer to use process models that emphasize an incremental, iterative approach, in which a small, working version of the system is constructed at an early date and improved by increments as the project moves on. See *incremental development, iterative development, software development life cycle (SDLC), software engineering.*

watermark A hidden code or identifier that a copyright holder places within a computer program, Web page, graphic, or multimedia file. It is invisible to the user. In copyright infringement cases, the watermark enables plaintiffs to identify infringing copies of a work with ease.

WAV A sound file format jointly developed by Microsoft and IBM. The format's specification calls for both 8-bit and 16-bit storage formats, in both monaural and stereo. Although sound quality of a WAV-encoded file can be excellent, uncompressed WAV files can be quite large; for this reason most users prefer to store lengthy sound files in a format that enables higher compression ratios, such as MP3. See *compression, MP3.*

waveform   A type of digitized audio format used to record live sounds or music.

waveform audio   See *waveform sound.*

waveform sound   Like MIDI sound, a type of digitized audio information. Especially when recorded with 16-bit resolution, waveform sound can produce startlingly good fidelity, but it takes up voluminous amounts of storage space. For example, each minute of sound recorded in the WAV format takes up 27MB. For peer-to-peer (p2p) or other network file exchange purposes, compressed file formats such as MP3 are preferred; they can reduce the size of a recorded waveform audio file by 70 percent or more. See *MP3, p2p, WAV.*

waveguide synthesis   A method of generating and reproducing musical sounds in a sound card. Waveguide synthesis simulates what happens when a real musical instrument produces a sound. Waveguide synthesis is superior to wave table and FM synthesis. See *FM synthesis, wave table synthesis.*

wave sound   A digitized recording of the sound waves captured by a microphone. Wave sound file formats include AU, AIFF, MP3, and WAV.

wave table synthesis   A method far superior to FM synthesis for generating and reproducing music in a sound board. Wave table synthesis uses a prerecorded sample of dozens of orchestral instruments to determine how particular notes played on those instruments should sound.

WAX   Acronym for Wireless Abstract eXtensible Markup Language. A markup language developed by Kargo, Inc. as an integral part of its Morphis platform, a Java-based system for wireless application development. See *Java, markup language.*

Wayback Machine   A Web site (located at http://web.archive.org) that stores a series of "snapshots" of the Web dating back to 1996. The site uses sophisticated database technology to retrieve archived Web pages from more than 100 terabytes of stored data, containing approximately 10 billion Web pages. See *terabyte.*

WCDMA   Acronym for Wideband CDMA. An international third-generation (3G) mobile wireless technology that supports digital data transmission at 2 Mbps locally or 345 Kbps in a wider area. See *3G, CDMA.*

weak typing   In a programming language, a design philosophy that strictly enforces the use of explicit data types (such as Boolean, integer, or string), but provides for certain explicit exceptions or offers a mechanism for overriding typing rules. See *data type.*

web   **1.** A new top-level domain (TLD) name for the Internet, added in 1998, that is designed for the organizations or individuals discussing Web-based material, such as Web technologies, changes to the Web infrastructure, and Web standards. See *domain name, gTLD-MoU, top-level domain (TLD).* **2.** A hypertext. See *hypertext.*

Web   See *World Wide Web (WWW).*

Web Accessibility Initiative (WAI)   A comprehensive program, including specifications, tools, research and development, and education, that is designed to make the Web more accessible to people with limited vision, hearing, or dexterity. The program is sponsored by the World Wide Web Consortium (W3C). See *World Wide Web Consortium (W3C).*

Web-based Training (WBT)   The use of the Web to deliver instructional materials to Web users. When Web-based Training is used to extend the geographic reach of instructional services, it is often called distance learning. See *distance learning.*

Web browser   A client program that runs on an Internet-connected computer and uses the Hypertext Transport Protocol (HTTP) to connect with Web servers. Web browsers are of two kinds: text-only browsers and graphical Web browsers. The two most popular graphical browsers are

Microsoft Internet Explorer and Netscape Navigator. All Web browsers can decode Web pages that have been marked with the Hypertext Markup Language (HTML); graphical browsers can also read and display graphics (including GIF and JPEG graphics). Graphical browsers can also read formatting information encoded according to the Cascading Style Sheet (CSS) standard, interpret embedded JavaScript programs, run Java applets, play multimedia objects (such as sounds and videos), and set up secure communications for financial transactions. Graphical browsers are preferable because the user can see in-line graphics, fonts, and document layouts; however, text-only browsers may be preferred by people with limited vision, who can link text-only browsers to speech synthesis devices. See *applet, CSS, HTML, HTTP, JavaScript, Web server.*

Web bug A Web user monitoring trick that works through the simple expedient of embedding an invisible, 1-pixed graphic image, linked to a server other than the one the user is accessing, within a Web page. A Web site can employ Web bugs to determine the user's Internet address, the time the Web page was accessed, and identification that may have been previously stored on the user's computer for identification purposes.

webcam A low-cost video camera used for low-resolution videoconferencing on the Internet. Thousands of Web sites offer periodically updated live webcam images of such vistas as street scenes, beaches, fish tanks, and traffic conditions.

webcasting The real-time delivery of streaming audio or streaming video, or both, by means of the Web. See *real time, streaming audio, streaming video.*

Web crawler See *spider.*

Web hosting A Web-based service that rents Web server space to its customers. Web hosting services typically offer a range of services, including domain name registration,

database software for automation of Web pages, and Web page design.

Web integration A variety of techniques used to make information stored in databases available via Internet or intranet connections.

Weblog A Web publishing program that is specifically designed to enable an individual to publish a daily commentary. Thousands of Web sites offer Weblogs; their fame—or infamy, as the case may be—travels by an electronic version of word-of-mouth. As a result, a previously obscure Weblog may be "discovered," and the site will get pelted with hundreds of thousands of hits. Soon, interest drops off. The Weblog phenomenon seems to confirm artist Andy Warhol's prediction that, in the future, everyone will be famous for 15 minutes. Synonymous with blog.

Webmaster or **Webmistress** A person who is designated to be responsible for maintaining a Web page and dealing with user feedback.

Web of Trust In public key cryptography, a means of confirming the validity of a given user's digital certificate that relies on the affirmation of known associates rather than a central distribution center. Popular among computer enthusiasts and cryptographers, this certificate verification model has received little support from the private sector; corporations using certificates for internal purposes need to control certificate validity as employees come and go, while the firms attempting to build a certificate infrastructure, such as VeriSign, hope to make money by selling valid certificates to the public. See *public key cryptography.*

Web portal A Web site that offers so many free and useful features that many Web users configure their browsers so that the portal appears when they click the Home button. One of the most popular Web portals is www.yahoo.com. Among the features offered are Web searches, free e-mail, stock quotes, sports scores, news stories, columns, and chat rooms. The companies that offer Web portals hope to keep users within the portal so that they can be repeatedly subjected to advertising, which supplies most of the portal's revenue. To make sure users stay within the portal, developers may create a walled garden,

Web ring A group of Web sites that have agreed to facilitate user navigation to sites on a similar subject. Each site administrator must insert a navigation code, usually at the bottom of the site's home page, which enables users to visit the next site in the ring, the previous site, view a list of sites, or return to the ring's home page. A significant drawback of current Web ring technology is the lack of any means to update these links automatically; on many Web ring sites, the links point to sites that no longer exist.

Web server In the World Wide Web (WWW), a program that accepts requests for information framed according to the Hypertext Transport Protocol (HTTP). The server processes these requests and sends the requested document. See *Apache, HTTP, Hypertext Transfer Protocol Daemon (httpd).*

Web server farm See *server farm.*

Web Services A repertoire of Web-based data and procedural resources made available by a resource description language, the Web Services Description Language (WSDL). Each described service is conceptualized as a point-to-point communication channel in which XML-based messages are exchanged. Independent of messaging protocols, Web Services can be implemented using HTTP and SOAP. See *HTTP, SOAP, WSDL, XML.*

Web Services Description Language See *WSDL.*

Web site **1.** In common but technically inaccurate usage, a Web page. **2.** In technically correct usage, one or more computers that are associated with a fully qualified domain name and make content available on the Web. See *fully qualified domain name (FQDN).*

Web site hosting See *Web hosting.*

Web Standards Project A volunteer, non-profit organization of programmers and Web users who pressure browser publishers to conform to the standards published by the World Wide Web Consortium (W3C). Both Netscape/AOL and Microsoft have added proprietary features to open standards (such as HTML). In consequence, Web developers must write voluminous code to detect the type of browser that is accessing their sites, so that a version of a given Web page can be displayed properly on the user's browser. Despite arduous efforts and publicity campaigns, the Web Standards Project has met with only limited success in its attempt to pressure companies to adhere to Web standards. See *Microsoft Internet Explorer, Mozilla, Netscape Navigator.*

Web surfing Serendipitous (and often inordinately time-consuming) exploration of the World Wide Web, in which a browser user follows a previously unknown link trail to unknown destinations.

Web TV A set-top appliance that enables users to connect to the Internet and display Web sites and e-mail on the TV screen. Web TV units include a built-in modem, a processor, memory, and storage. The newer Web TV Plus standard enables viewers to enhance their TV experience by consulting onscreen TV schedules and accessing Web pages related to shows they are viewing.

weight The overall lightness or darkness of a typeface design, or the gradations of lightness to darkness within a font family. A type style can be light or dark. Within a type style, several gradations of weight are visible: extra light, light, semi-light, regular, medium, semi-bold, bold, extra bold, and ultra-bold. See *book weight.*

welcome page In the Web, a Web-accessible document that is meant to be the point of entry to a series of related documents, called a web. For example, a company's welcome page typically includes the company's logo, a brief description of the web's purpose, and links to the additional documents available at that site. Welcome pages are also called home pages because they are the home page (the top-level document) of the series of related documents that makes up the web.

well-known port number An Internet port address that has been permanently linked with a certain application by the Internet Assigned Numbers Authority (IANA). A port address enables the TCP/IP software to direct incoming data to a certain application. The port address 80, for example, directs the incoming data to a Web server. Because IANA fixes port numbers for frequently used Internet applications (such as Telnet, File Transfer Protocol [FTP], and the World Wide Web [WWW]), it is not generally necessary to include port numbers when attempting to locate data on the Internet because Web browsers, FTP programs, and other Web clients, as well as Web servers, are designed to default to the well-known port numbers. See *Internet Assigned Numbers Authority (IANA), port number.*

well-structured programming language A programming language that encourages programmers to create logically organized programs that are easy to read, debug, and update. Poorly structured programming languages allow programmers to create illogically organized programs, based on spaghetti code, that are almost impossible to debug or alter. Modular programming languages encourage structured programming—clear, logical code—by allowing the programmer to break down the program into separate modules, each of which accomplishes just one function. More recently, object-oriented programming (OOP) languages (such as SmallTalk and C++) have introduced another approach to modularity. The languages are structured by a hierarchy of objects, such as option buttons, dialog boxes, and windows. See *object-oriented programming, structured programming.*

WEP Acronym for Wired Equivalent Privacy. A privacy protection protocol for IEEE 802.11 wireless services that is designed to prevent unauthorized users from eavesdropping on wireless data transfers. The protocol has been sharply criticized for employing an inadequate key length and an authentication mechanism that is vulnerable to forgery. See *IEEE 802.11.*

wetware Among programmers, a slang expression for human intelligence, or lack thereof.

wetware exploit A computer system intrusion facilitated by exploiting human gullibility, naivety, or incompetence. For example, an intruder may obtain a password by calling a service center and convincing the attendant that the caller is indeed a valid user who has lost the password. Synonymous with social engineering.

whack-a-mole Slang expression used to describe an unscrupulous trick used by overly aggressive Web sites. When the site is accessed, the user is confronted by a series of additional windows popping up so rapidly that, in the end, the user's only recourse is to shut down the browser or switch off the computer. This trick has its origins in the economic structure of Web pornography sites, which sometimes offer to pay other sites a small fee when users are referred to them.

what-if analysis In spreadsheet programs, an important form of data exploration in which one changes key variables to see the effect on the results of the computation. What-if analysis provides business people and professionals with an effective vehicle for exploring the effect of alternative strategies.

what-if scenario In business, an experiment using make-believe data to see how it impacts outcome, such as sales volume.

what-you-see-is-what-you-get (WYSIWYG) A design philosophy for word processing programs in which formatting commands directly affect the text onscreen so that the screen shows the appearance of the printed text. See *embedded formatting command*.

White Book A standards specification issued jointly by Sony and Philips in 1994 that brings the CD-ROM standard into closer compatibility with the ISO 9660 logical data format, an international standard. See *CD-ROM*.

white hat A computer enthusiast who possesses the knowledge needed to gain unauthorized entry into computer systems or sabotage them, but chooses instead to help computer users and organizations identify and close security holes.

white pages A computer version of the white pages section of a telephone book. White pages services are set up by organizations (such as corporations or universities) to provide computer assistance to people looking for a person's phone number or e-mail address. Many white pages services are accessible via the Internet. See *LDAP*, *X.500*.

white paper Originally an objective, scientific analysis of a new technology. More commonly, now, white papers are subjective advertisements written by marketing departments.

white space The portion of the page not printed. Good page design involves the use of white space to balance the areas that receive text and graphics, and also to improve the readability of the document.

white-write technique See *print engine*.

whois A utility commonly found on Unix and Unix-like operating systems (such as Linux) that enables users to view information about other users who are logged on to the same system.

wide area network See *WAN*.

Wideband CDMA See *WCDMA*.

Wideband Code-Division Multiple Access See *WCDMA*.

wide SCSI A SCSI-2 specification that enables the use of a 16-bit data bus, doubling the data transfer rate of SCSI drives and devices. See *SCSI*.

widow A formatting flaw in which the last line of a paragraph appears alone at the top of a new column or page. Most word processing and page layout programs suppress widows and orphans; better programs allow one to switch widow/orphan control on and off, and to choose the number of lines at the beginning or end of the paragraph that he or she wants kept together.

Wi-Fi A marketing term created by the Wi-Fi Alliance to describe the IEEE 802.11a and IEEE 802.11b wireless LAN protocols. See *IEEE 802.11a, IEEE 802.11b*.

Wi-Fi Alliance A non-profit industry consortium that tests products for compliance to IEEE Wireless LAN standards. See *IEEE, IEEE 802.11a, IEEE 802.11b, IEEE 802.11g*.

Wiki A Web-enabled collaboration system based on the principle that any user, including unregistered or unauthenticated users, can obtain full read/write access to all or most of the available pages in the Wiki. The system is designed to minimize the amount of learning necessary to use the system. For example, to create a hyperlink to another page within the Wiki, the user need only type the page name as a compound without spaces (for example, WelcomeToWiki). Although some Wikis are available to the public, this collaboration system is rapidly gaining users within large, complex organizations; for example, a geographically separated team of co-workers can use the wide-open read/write capabilities of a Wiki to collaboratively develop and maintain specifications, documents, manuals, and other material. All that is required to use the Wiki is a Web browser.

wildcard A character (such as an asterisk or question mark) that stands for any other character, or series of any other characters, that may appear in the same place. Two commonly used wildcards are the asterisk (*), which stands for zero or more character or characters, and the question mark (?), which stands for any single character.

Winchester drive   See *hard disk*.

window   A rectangular, onscreen frame through which one can view a document, worksheet, database, drawing, or application program. This window functions as a frame through which users can view their work onscreen. A window generally has a control menu and control buttons, which enable the user to minimize the window to an icon, to maximize (zoom) the window so that it occupies the whole screen, or to restore the previous window size. Windows can be moved by dragging on the title bar, and sized by dragging window edges or corners. Scroll bars, scroll boxes, and scroll arrows are generally provided to enable the user to view documents that are larger than the available display space. In Microsoft Windows, each application window contains the application's command menu; in Mac OS, an application's command menu appears at the top of the screen, independent of the application's windows. See *control menu, maximize, minimize, scroll arrow, scroll bar/scroll box, title bar.*

windowing environment   An application program interface (API) that provides the features commonly associated with a graphical user interface (GUI) (such as windows, pull-down menus, onscreen fonts, and scroll bars or scroll boxes). A windowing environment makes these features available to programmers of application packages. Consumer operating systems such as MacOS and Microsoft Windows combine a windowing environment with the features of a desktop environment, but the two areas are separated in Unix and Unix-like operating systems, such as Linux, in which the X Window System provides the windowing environment. Users can dispense with a desktop environment, if they want, or can choose from two competing alternatives (KDE and GNOME). See

GNOME, graphical user interface (GUI), Linux, Unix, X Window System.

window manager   In the X Window System, a special type of client that enables users to select from a variety of window display options, such as window border color, menu font, and window controls location. In keeping with the X Window System philosophy, users are free to select their preferred window manager. Although it is clearly desirable to give users the opportunity to choose their preferred window manager, the lack of such standards discourages programmers from including features in their software that might not function if a given window manager feature is absent. To correct this situation, two competing desktop environment projects—KDE and GNOME—are attempting to provide a predictable programming environment by requiring the use of a predetermined or compatible window manager. See *desktop environment, GNOME, KDE, X Window System.*

window menu   In Microsoft Windows, a synonym for control menu. See *control menu.*

Windows   Generic term for any of Microsoft's 16/32-bit or 32-bit operating systems that employ its familiar graphical user interface. See *Microsoft Windows 3.1, Microsoft Windows 95, Microsoft Windows 98, Microsoft Windows Millennium Edition (ME), Microsoft Windows NT, Microsoft Windows Server 2003, Microsoft Windows XP.*

Windows 3.1   See *Microsoft Windows 3.1.*

Windows 95/98   Commonly used (but unofficial) expression for Microsoft's hybrid 16/32-bit code base, which provides the foundation for Microsoft Windows 95, Microsoft Windows 98, and Microsoft Windows Millennium Edition (ME). This expression, sometimes updated to include Me (Windows 95/98/ME), is often used to describe the operating system compatibility of programs that require the 16/32-bit codebase, as in "this program will run on Windows 95/98"; such a program will *not* run on Microsoft Windows NT or

Microsoft Windows 2000, which are true 32-bit operating systems. See *32-bit operating system, Microsoft Windows 95, Microsoft Windows 98, Microsoft Windows 2000, Microsoft Windows Millennium Edition (ME), Microsoft Windows NT.*

Windows 95   See *Microsoft Windows 95.*

Windows 98   See *Microsoft Windows 98.*

Windows 2000   See *Microsoft Windows 2000.*

Windows accelerator   See *graphics accelerator board.*

Windows application   An application that can run only within the Microsoft Windows windowing environment, taking full advantage of Windows' application program interface (API), its capability to display fonts and graphics onscreen, and its capability to exchange data dynamically between applications. See *non-Windows application.*

Windows Explorer   In Microsoft Windows, a file management program that enables users to perform file copying, moving, deletion, and other tasks with an easy-to-use, drag-and-drop interface.

Windows File Protection   A service introduced in Microsoft Windows 2000 that prevents unauthorized programs from altering or deleting important system files. This gives Windows 2000 systems a degree of protection from computer viruses or other rogue software that attempts to replace one or more system files with copies containing destructive code.

Windows Internet Naming Service (WINS)   A network directory service that enables Windows-based workstations to locate and exchange data with each other without requiring each workstation to keep a record of the exact physical addresses of other network resources.

Windows keyboard   A keyboard that contains special keys that activate certain

menus and commands in Microsoft Windows, in addition to all the normal computer keyboard keys.

Windows Me   See *Microsoft Windows Millennium Edition (ME).*

Windows Media Audio (WMA)   See *WMA.*

Windows Media Player (WMP)   An audio and video player distributed with all recent versions of Microsoft Windows. Microsoft developed WMP to counter the growing popularity of the Real audio and video player by providing streaming audio and video services. Unlike MP3 files, which contain no copyright management features, WMP and its proprietary file format, WMA, contain features that will enable Microsoft to enable a Digital Rights Management (DRM) infrastructure for the distribution of commercial digital content via the Internet; users will not be able to copy such content, or indeed to access the content, without payment and subsequent authorization. To discourage the use of MP3s, the latest versions of WMP contain only limited support for such files, and MP3 support may be eliminated entirely in future versions of the program. When copyright holder industries are ready to start selling audio and video content over the Internet, WMP is likely to become their platform of choice. Such an outcome may raise concerns that, in the U.S. market, Microsoft could be accused once again of violating U.S. antitrust law. See *antitrust, Digital Rights Management (DRM), monopoly, MP3, trusted system, WMA.*

Windows Metafile Format (WMF)   An object-oriented (vector) graphics file format for Microsoft Windows applications. All Windows applications that support object-oriented graphics can read graphics files saved with the WMF format.

Windows NT   See *Microsoft Windows NT.*

Windows printer   See *Graphical Device Interface (GDI) printer.*

Windows Scripting Host (WSH) In Microsoft Windows 95 and subsequent versions of the operating system, a utility that enables programmers to write Visual Basic or JScript programs that are tightly linked to Microsoft applications, such as Microsoft Outlook. In 2000, a rapidly propagating worm called VBS/Love Letter demonstrated the danger in linking system-wide scripting capabilities so closely to the operating system's messaging protocol. Many Windows users who attempted to cope with this security risk discovered that WSH may not appear on the Add/Remove Programs control panel; in many cases, WSH could be removed only by locating WSH (wscript.exe) and deleting it manually. See *worm*.

Windows XP See *Microsoft Windows XP.*

WINS See *Windows Internet Naming Service (WINS).*

Winsock An open standard that specifies how a dynamic link library (DLL) should be written to provide TCP/IP support for Microsoft Windows 95/98 systems. An outgrowth of a "birds of a feather" session at a Unix conference, the Winsock standard (currently in Version 2.0) is actively supported by Microsoft Corporation.

Winstone A benchmark test developed by Ziff-Davis Publishing's PC Labs that attempts to simulate real-world conditions and test all aspects of a system's performance. By making a computer system execute scripts in more than a dozen popular application programs, the Winstone gives an idea of how well a system performs.

Wintel Slang expression for computers equipped with the Microsoft Windows operating system and Intel microprocessors. Wintel systems overwhelmingly dominate the personal computer market.

WinZip A popular compression/decompression program for Microsoft Windows created by Niko Mak Computing, Inc., that is ideal for decompressing software downloaded from the Internet. WinZip supports all major compression schemes used on the Internet, including Unix compression and archiving formats such as TAR, gzip, and compress. Its native compression scheme is derived from the Lempel-Ziv algorithm. WinZip combines file compression and file archiving functions; that is, a compressed WinZip file may contain more than one file. The archived files can be stored with path information. See *compression, Lempel-Ziv compression algorithm.*

Wired Equivalent Privacy See *WEP.*

wire frame graphic A graphic image rendered as a collection of polygons that can be manipulated; for example, a two-dimensional wire frame graphic can be made to appear three-dimensional through a process called rendering. See *rendering, tessellation.*

Wireless Abstract eXtensible Markup Language See *WAX.*

Wireless Application Protocol See *WAP.*

wireless communication A means of linking computers using infrared or radio signals.

wireless LAN A local area network (LAN) that uses infrared or radio signals to free mobile users from fixed cable connections. Wireless LANs are increasingly used in hospitals to monitor patients as they are moved from place to place. See *IEEE 802.11, LAN.*

Wireless Local Loop See *WLL.*

Wireless Markup Language See *WML.*

wizard An interactive help utility originally developed by Microsoft for its Windows applications (and now widely imitated). The wizard guides the user through each step of a multistep operation, offering helpful information and explaining options along the way.

WLL Acronym for Wireless Local Loop. In a local telecommunications utility, a means of providing "last mile" (local loop) connections by means of digital radio.

Because they do not require the costly excavation required to install conventional wires and cables, Wireless Local Loops are much less expensive than conventional local loop technology. In the U.S., they are often used by Competitive Local Exchange Carriers (CLEC) that compete with former telephone monopolies under terms established by the Telecommunications Act of 1996; in developing countries, they are used to reduce the cost of providing more widespread telephone service. See *CLEC*, *local loop*.

WMA   Acronym for Windows Media Audio. An audio file format developed by Microsoft Corporation that offers compression ratios and audio quality comparable to the popular MP3 file format; however, WMA includes support for a digital rights management (DRM) architecture, which can prevent users from making unauthorized copies or accessing the file without authorization. See *Digital Rights Management (DRM)*, *Windows Media Player (WMP)*.

WMF   A file name extension indicating that the file contains a graphic saved in the Windows Metafile Format (WMF).

WML   Acronym for Wireless Markup Language, formerly known as HDML. A declarative markup language, similar to HTML, that is suitable for coding text-only Web content so that it can be correctly displayed by wireless devices such as personal digital assistants (PDA) and Personal Communication Service (PCS) digital cellular phones. See *HTML*, *PCS*, *PDA*, *WAP*.

WOL   See *Wake on LAN (WOL)*.

word   A unit of information composed of characters, bits, or bytes that is treated as an entity and that can be stored in one location. In word processing programs, a word is defined as including the space, if any, at the end of the characters.

Word   See *Microsoft Word*.

WordPerfect   A word processing program, initially developed by Utah-based WordPerfect Corporation, that dominated the market prior to the widespread adoption of Microsoft Office. Now the property of Corel, WordPerfect is available for the Windows and Linux operating systems, but it possesses only a small percentage of a market overwhelmingly dominated by Microsoft Office (which includes Microsoft Word). WordPerfect still has many ardent defenders in niche markets, including law offices, where its features are still judged superior to those offered by competitors. See *Microsoft Office*, *Microsoft Word*.

word processing   The use of a computer to create, edit, proofread, format, and print documents. By a wide margin, word processing is the most popular computer application and is partly responsible for the dramatic growth of the personal computer industry. Unlike typewriters, computer word processing programs allow users to change text before printing it and provide powerful editing tools.

word processing program   A program that transforms a computer into a tool for creating, editing, proofreading, formatting, and printing documents, such as Microsoft Word and WordPerfect. Popular word processing programs include many features to make writers' and editors' jobs easier. Search-and-replace features help ease revising documents, while spell-checkers and thesauruses ensure clean, readable output. Various formatting tools make words graphically appealing. With the rise of the graphical user interface (GUI), word processing programs acquired the capability to display fonts and font size choices onscreen precisely as they will appear when printed. Today's word processing software can take on light desktop publishing duties, such as newsletter production. See *what-you-see-is-what-you-get (WYSIWYG)*.

word size   The number of bits a computer's central processing unit (CPU) can work with at one time.

WordStar   The first mass-market word processing program with a WYSIWYG (what-you-see-is-what-you-get) interface. Other pioneering innovations included cut-and-paste and mail merge commands. The program relied on a unique set of keyboard commands that were memorized by millions of users and continued to affect keyboard shortcut layouts well into the 1980s. (The lingering influence of this keyboard command set is attested by the continued availability of a Microsoft Word add-on program that emulates WordStar keyboard commands.) Released in 1978 for the CP/M operating system, WordStar was made available in an MS-DOS version in 1982; however, the program met stiff competition from WordPerfect, which quickly dominated the market. A 16-bit version was made available for Microsoft Windows 3.0 in 1991, but the program failed to keep pace with its competitors. Rights to the WordStar code and various offshoots have been purchased and are still owned by a variety of companies, including Corel and The Learning Company, but the program is not expected to return to the market.

word wrap   A feature of word processing programs, and other programs that include text-editing features, that wraps words down to the beginning of the next line if they go beyond the right margin.

workaround   A way of circumventing a bug without actually fixing it. Workarounds may be desirable when time is short or programmers are unavailable.

workbook   In a spreadsheet program, a collection of related worksheets kept in a single file. Workbooks make it easy to create hot links among worksheets.

workflow   The precise, person-to-person or department-to-department path that a given type of work follows as it moves through an organization. For example, an order begins in sales, and successively moves through accounting, shipping, and inventory. See *workflow automation*.

workflow automation   An information system in which documents are automatically sent to the people who need to see them.

workgroup   **1.** A small group of employees assigned to work together on a specific project. Much of the work accomplished in large businesses is done in workgroups. If this work is to be done well and quickly, the workgroup needs to communicate effectively and share resources. Especially when linked in a local area network (LAN), personal computer technology is thought to enhance workgroup productivity by giving the group additional communication channels (in the form of e-mail), facilities for the group editing of documents (such as redlining and strikethrough), and shared access to a common database. **2.** The default name Microsoft Windows assigns to a peer-to-peer workgroup in a Windows networking setting. See *LAN*.

working directory   See *current directory*.

working model   See *crippled version*.

worksheet   In spreadsheet programs, the two-dimensional matrix of rows and columns within which one enters headings, values, and formulas. The worksheet resembles the ledger sheet used in accounting. Synonymous with spreadsheet. See *spreadsheet program*.

worksheet window   In spreadsheet programs, the portion of the worksheet visible onscreen. With up to 8,192 rows and 256 columns, modern electronic spreadsheets are larger than a two-car garage in size. The worksheet window displays only a small portion of the total area potentially available.

workstation   In a local area network (LAN), a desktop computer that runs application programs and serves as an access point to the network. See *file server, personal computer (PC), professional workstation*.

World Wide Web (WWW)   A global hypertext system that uses the Internet as its transport mechanism; the communication between Web clients (browsers) and Web servers is defined by the Hypertext Transport Protocol (HTTP). In a hypertext system, users navigate by clicking a hyperlink embedded in the current document;

this action displays a second document in the same or a separate browser window. Web documents are created using HTML, a declarative markup language; advanced formatting is possible through the use of Cascading Style Sheets (CSS), while interactivity can be achieved through the use of embedded scripts written in scripting languages such as JavaScript. Incorporating hypermedia (graphics, sounds, animations, and video), the Web has become the ideal medium for publishing information on the Internet and serves as the platform for the emerging electronic economy. See *CSS, HTML, HTTP, hypermedia, hypertext, JavaScript, Web browser, Web server.*

World Wide Web Consortium (W3C) An independent standards body composed of university researchers and industry practitioners that is devoted to setting effective standards to promote the orderly growth of the World Wide Web. Housed at the Massachusetts Institute of Technology (MIT), W3C sets key Web standards such as Hypertext Markup Language (HTML), the Hypertext Transport Protocol (HTTP), Cascading Style Sheets (CSS), Extensible Markup Language (XML), and many other aspects of Web usage. See *CSS, HTML, HTTP, XML.*

worm A program that propagates itself over a computer network by making copies of itself and sending them on to additional networked workstations. The canonical example is the Internet Worm, developed by Cornell University graduate student Robert T. Morris. Described by Morris as an "experiment," the program proved to contain bugs that, after its release, overloaded servers to the extent that widespread Internet service outages occurred. Morris was subsequently convicted, fined $10,000, and sentenced to community service. Note that worms are not viruses or Trojan Horses. See *Trojan Horse, virus.*

WORM See *write-once, read-many.*

wrap-around type Type contoured so that it surrounds a graphic. Because wraparound type is harder to read than noncontoured type, use wrap-around type sparingly.

wrapper In computer programming, a script that precedes some other function and serves to limit or circumscribe its activity.

write A fundamental processing operation in which the central processing unit (CPU) records information to the computer's random access memory (RAM) or to the computer's secondary storage media, such as disk drives. In personal computing, the term most often refers to storing information on floppy or hard disks, removable storage media, CD-ROM and other optical media, or any other write-enabled secondary storage medium.

write-back One of four basic operations carried out by the control unit of a microprocessor. The write-back operation involves writing the results of previous operations to an internal register.

write-back cache A type of cache memory that stores information written to memory as well as information read from memory. Write-back caches, particularly those used in secondary caches, are considered to be technically superior to write-through caches.

write-black engine See *print engine.*

write-enabled Able to record new data. When used to refer to a storage medium, this term is synonymous with read/write.

write head See *read/write head.*

write-once, read-many (WORM) An optical disc drive with storage capacities of up to 1TB. After one writes data to the disk, it becomes a read-only storage medium. WORM drives can store huge amounts of information and have been touted as an excellent technology for organizations that need to publish large databases internally (such as collections of engineering drawings or technical documentation). The advent of fully read/write-capable optical disc drives, however, has greatly diminished the appeal of WORM technology. See *CD-ROM, erasable optical disc drive.*

write permission In Unix and Unix-like operating systems such as Linux, a permission level that enables the file owner, the group owner, or others to create new files, alter existing files, or delete existing files.

write precompensation A hard disk's upward adjustment of the magnetic field that the read/write head uses to record data near the spindle, where data must be closely packed. The disk geometry includes the cylinder at which write precompensation begins.

write-protect To modify a file or disk so that no one can edit or erase its data.

write-protect notch On a 5.25-inch floppy disk, a small notch cut out of the disk's protective jacket that, when covered by a piece of tape, prevents the disk drive from performing erasures or write operations to the disk. See *floppy disk.*

write-protect tab On a 3.25-inch floppy disk, a tab located in the disk's upper-left corner as one holds the disk with the label facing away from him or her. When one slides the tab up to open the hole, he or she has write-protected the disk. See *floppy disk.*

write-through cache A cache memory scheme in which memory read operations are cached, but not memory write operations. Write operations are cached in random access memory (RAM), which is much slower than cache memory. Experts consider write-through caches to be inferior to write-back caches, which record both read and write operations. See *cache.*

write-white engine See *print engine.*

WSDL Acronym for Web Services Description Language. An XML-based messaging protocol, developed by the World Wide Web Consortium (W3C), which is intended to enable an organization to unify a wide variety of network resources (including procedural code as well as data) through the use of an overarching, XML-based messaging system. WSDL enables point-to-point Web services to be described in a formal, XML-based nomenclature that is independent of the messaging protocol actually in use, such as HTTP or SOAP. See *HTTP, SOAP, World Wide Web Consortium (W3C), XML.*

WSH See *Windows Scripting Host (WSH).*

WWW See *World Wide Web.*

WYSIWYG (Pronounced *wiz-zee-wig.*) Acronym for what-you-see-is-what-you-get.

WYSIWYG HTML editor A Web page production program that enables users to view the page as it will appear in a Web browser. WYSIWYG HTML editors are easy to use because they disguise the underlying HTML code. The leading programs, such as ColdFusion, Dreamweaver, and Microsoft FrontPage, include advanced features for site automation and management. See *HTML, HTML editor.*

X Commonly used abbreviation for X Window System. See *X Window System*.

x2 An unratified, proprietary modulation protocol for modems transferring data at 56.6 Kbps. This protocol has been replaced by the official ITU-TSS standard, called V.90, and is no longer in widespread use. See *V.90*.

X-10 A standard for computer-controlled home automation devices.

X.25 An international standard for a packet-switching network that is widely used in public data networks (PDNs). See *public data network, WAN.*

x86 Shorthand expression for Intel's processor architecture in the broadest possible sense of the term; that is, it refers to older, 8-bit processors such as the 8086 as well as the latest Pentium chips. See *Intel 8086 x386, x586.*

x386 Shorthand expression for Intel's 32-bit processor architecture, beginning with the 80386 and including the latest Pentiums. See *Intel 80386. x386, x586.*

X.400 An international standard maintained by the ITU-TSS for e-mail and fax transmissions.

X.500 An international standard for e-mail directories maintained by ITU-TSS that can be maintained by organizations to facilitate looking up users' e-mail addresses. See *LDAP, white pages.*

X.509 An international standard for digital certificates maintained by ITU-TSS that can be used for strong authentication. The latest version, X.509V3, helps to ensure interoperability among software employing certificates.

x586 Shorthand expression for Intel's Pentium processor architecture. See *Pentium, x86, x386.*

XAG Acronym for XML Accessibility Guidelines (XAG). Developed by the World Wide Web Consortium (W3C), these guidelines are designed to enable XML authors to make their XML-driven Web pages more accessible for people with limited vision, dexterity, or hearing. Its principles and standards are adopted from the Web Accessibility Initiative (WAI). See *Web Accessibility Initiative (WAI), XML.*

Xanadu A proposed global hypertext system that was described by computer visionary Ted Nelson in his 1987 book titled *Literary Machines.* Xanadu differs from the World Wide Web, although both use hypertext principles. In contrast to the Web, Xanadu hyperlinks would incorporate the linked data where a hyperlink is inserted, creating the impression of a seamless document. To make sure all authors received recognition and some compensation for the incorporation of their work in others' documents, Xanadu would track all such incorporations and, if the author desired, charge a tiny fee for them. In addition, the system would assure that no broken links existed (this is a major problem on the Web). Despite considerable funding and development sponsored by CAD software maker Autodesk in the late 1980s and early 1990s, Nelson has not been able to bring his concept to market. The code has since been released on an open source model in the hope that volunteer programmers will help Nelson carry the project forward.

x-axis In a graph, the categories axis, which usually is the horizontal axis. See *bar graph, column graph, y-axis, z-axis.*

Xbase A generic term denoting any of the programming environments derived from the original dBASE programming language created by Ashton-Tate, Inc. Because the word dBASE is a registered trademark, the term Xbase has come to be used as a description for any programming language based on the dBASE programming language. See *dBASE.*

X-Box A console game-playing machine developed by Microsoft Corporation that is intended to be connected to a television. Unlike previous console devices, X-Box more closely resembles a computer than a game-playing machine; the initial offering included a Pentium III processor running at 733 MHz, a hard disk, a high-speed video card, and an Ethernet port for multiple player gaming. Options include a kit to enable DVD movies to be played on the machine.

XCFN   See *external function*.

X client   In the X Window System, an application that requests services from an X server. The client can be any X-compatible application running on the same or a networked computer. A special kind of client, called the window manager, makes configuration options available to the user. Note that the use of the term "client" in the X Window System should be differentiated from the use of the same term in the client/server model; in X, the server resides on each user's workstation, while clients may include programs running elsewhere on the network. See *client/server*, *X Protocol*, *X server*, *X Window System*.

XCMD   See *eXternal CoMmanD*.

xDSL   Abbreviation that refers to several Digital Subscriber Line (DSL) technologies, including asymmetric digital subscriber line (ADSL). Capable of bringing high-bandwidth data communications to homes and offices using standard twisted-pair wiring, DSL connections can achieve a data transfer rate of 1.5 Mbps. See *DSL*.

XENIX   A Unix-like operating system originally developed by Microsoft Corporation and currently incorporated into Santa Cruz Operation's SCO Unix. See *Unix*.

Xeon   See *Intel Xeon, Intel Xeon MP*.

Xerox Corporation Palo Alto Research Center   See *Palo Alto Research Center (Parc)*.

XeroxPARC   See *Palo Alto Research Center (Parc)*.

XForms   An xHTML application, developed by the World Wide Web Consortium (W3C), that is designed to solve many of the problems caused by HTML tables. XForms separates content from presentation, and includes features that reduce the number of queries to the Web server. See *HTML, World Wide Web Consortium (W3C), xHTML*.

XFree86   An open source version of the X Window System. Originally developed for Intel-based PCs, XFree86 is now available for other platforms, including the DEC Alpha and PowerPC. XFree86 is included with Linux distributions. See *Linux, Linux distribution, X Window System*.

XGA   See *eXtended Graphics Array*.

X-height   In typography, the height of a font's lowercase letters, measured from the baseline up. Because many fonts have unusually long or short ascenders and descenders, the x-height is a better measurement of the actual size of a font than the type size, measured in points. Synonymous with Z-Height. See *ascender, descender*.

xHTML   A version of HTML 4.0 that has been expressed as an eXtended Markup Language (XML) document type definition (DTD). Unlike HTML, XHTML enables developers to extend the HTML tag set without requiring specific support from browser publishers. XML-capable software is required to display code marked up in XHTML. See *DTD, HTML, markup language, XML*.

Xlink   Abbreviation for XML Linking Language. The portion of the XML standard, created and maintained by the World Wide Web Consortium (W3C), that defines the basic, HTML-like hyperlinking capabilities of XML, as well as much more advanced capabilities (such as bidirectional linking and links that embed the requested resource at the link's location). See *HTML, hyperlink, World Wide Web Consortium (W3C), XML*.

XML Abbreviation for eXtensible Markup Language. XML is not a declarative markup language like HTML; rather, it is a language for *creating* markup languages. XML is maintained by the World Wide Web Consortium (W3C). A slimmed-down version of SGML, XML enables Web authors to create and name their own tags so that they can more accurately capture the structure of their data. In a well-structured XML document that complies with XML syntax rules, the user-created tag hierarchy can be read and processed by an XML-aware browser, even if it has never encountered the specific tag set before. XML authors can state their document's structure more formally by means of a Document Type Definition (DTD), which specifies the rules for using each tag correctly. By means of the XPointer language, XML also enables more sophisticated hyperlinks than HTML, including links which point to multiple documents or retrieve material that is dynamically incorporated into the linking page. The complete XML specification actually consists of four related standards, beginning with the XML language specification and continuing with the following: XML Pointer Language (XPointer), XML Linking Language (XLink), and XML Namespaces. XML data can be formatted for presentation purposes using Cascading Style Sheets (CSS) or the eXtensible Style Language (XSL). Development of XML is ongoing and includes a query language for extracting data from XML documents (XML Query) and a specification for machine-readable Document Type Definitions (DTD) called XML Schema. See *CSS, XLink, XML Namespaces, XML Query Language, XMLP, XPointer, XSL.*

XML Accessibility Guidelines (XAG) See *XAG.*

XML Key Management Specification (XKMS) A standard for XML-based public encryption key distribution and registration developed by the World Wide Web Consortium (W3C). See *public key encryption, World Wide Web Consortium (W3C), XML*

XML Linking Language See *Xlink.*

XML Namespaces A proposed World Wide Web Consortium (W3C) standard that describes a technique to use the element names defined in an XML document type definition (DTD), even if that DTD is not incorporated into local documents. The XML namespace proposal would encourage XML authors to develop a consistent nomenclature for frequently used elements, such as <title>, <author>, and <publisher> in bibliographic markup. See *XML Schema.*

XMLP Acronym for XML Protocol. A network protocol, developed and maintained by the World Wide Web Consortium (W3C), which enables devices in a peer-to-peer network to communicate by using XML as an encapsulation medium. See *peer-to-peer network, World Wide Web Consortium (W3C), XML.*

XML Path Language (XPATH) A syntax and semantics specification, developed by the World Wide Web Consortium (W3C), for describing the location of a specific element within an XML tree-based data structure. XPATH is analogous to the path specifications used to describe file locations, except that it operates on the logical structure of an XML document instead of physical data. See *path, World Wide Web Consortium (W3C), XML.*

XML Pointer Language See *XPointer.*

XML Protocol See *XMLP.*

XML Query Language (XQL) A query language, developed and maintained by the World Wide Web Consortium (W3C), that specifies how users or programs can extract data from XML-encoded databases. See *query language, World Wide Web Consortium (W3C), XML.*

XML Schema A standard developed and maintained by the World Wide Web Consortium (W3C) that specifies how the rules of XML markup can be expressed in a form that can be processed without human intervention. In contrast, a Document Type Definition (DTD) specifies human-readable markup rules. See *DTD*, *World Wide Web Consortium (W3C)*, *XML*.

XMODEM An asynchronous File Transfer Protocol (FTP) for personal computers that makes the error-free transmission of files through the telephone system easier. Developed by Ward Christiansen for 8-bit computers running Control Program for Microprocessors (CP/M) and placed in the public domain, the XMODEM protocol is included in most personal computer communications programs and commonly is used to download files from bulletin board systems (BBSs).

XMODEM-1K A data transmission protocol that retains XMODEM/CRC's error-checking capabilities but with higher throughput. By performing a cyclic redundancy check (CRC) only on 1,024-byte blocks of data, transmission overhead is reduced. See *YMODEM*, *ZMODEM*.

XMODEM/CRC A version of the XMODEM data transmission protocol that reduces throughput but also reduces errors. XMODEM/CRC performs a cyclic redundancy check (CRC) on every 2 bytes transmitted, a more reliable scheme than the checksum technique employed by XMODEM. See *XMODEM-1K*, *YMODEM*, *ZMODEM*.

XMS See *eXtended Memory Specification*.

XON/XOFF handshaking See *handshaking*.

XOR One of seven fundamental logical operations that, when electronically implemented as logic gates, are used to construct electronic digital computing equipment. The XOR gate does not allow data to pass through the gate unless either of two inputs are true, but not both. See *logic gate*.

XPointer Abbreviation for XML Pointer Language. The portion of the complete XML specification, developed and maintained by the World Wide Web Consortium (W3C), that deals with XML fragment identifiers. A fragment identifier is a hyperlink that points to a certain position within the linked document. XPointer enables XML authors to use simple fragment identifiers such as those used in XML, as well as much more sophisticated pointers that incorporate a query language. XPointer capabilities thus go far beyond the page linking capabilities of HTML, which can deliver the reader to a predetermined location within a Web page only if the page's author has deliberately embedded a named anchor at that point and the link incorporates a reference to the anchor. See *anchor*, *HTML*, *hyperlink*, *World Wide Web Consortium (W3C)*, *XML*.

X Protocol A client-server protocol that specifies how X Window System clients and servers can exchange messages. X clients use the protocol to tell the X server how to display an application's window onscreen; X servers use the protocol to convey keystrokes, mouse movements and clicks, menu choices, and additional information to the X client. See *X client*, *X server*, *X Window System*.

XQL See *XML Query Language*.

XrML Acronym for eXtensible Rights Markup Language. A markup language for digital rights management developed by Content Guard, Inc., using patented technology from Xerox's Palo Alto Research Center (PARC). See *digital rights management (DRM)*.

X server In the X Window System, a program that runs on a specific computer and that is configured to work with this computer's video card, monitor, and keyboard. X clients request windowing services from the X server using a generalized, hardware-independent protocol called the X protocol. Because the X server takes over the job of knowing precisely how to display images on a particular computer's video hardware, X-compatible applications do not have to include hardware-specific information concerning the video display. Note that the use of the term "server" in the X Window System should be differentiated from the use of the same term in the client/server model; in X, the server resides on each user's workstation, while clients may include programs running elsewhere on the network. See *client/server, X Window System*.

XSL Acronym for eXtensible Style Language. A style sheet language, developed by the World Wide Web Consortium (W3C), that goes far beyond the static style markup made possible by Cascading Style Sheets (CSS). Unlike CSS, XSL is a true programming language that will enable XML authors to implement dynamic operations, such as page numbering. See *CSS, style sheet, World Wide Web Consortium (W3C), XML*.

XSLT Acronym for XSL Transformations. A specification, developed by the World Wide Web Consortium (W3C), that specifies how data may be extracted from a tree-like XML data structure and, on the fly, formatted with XSL for onscreen display. *World Wide Web Consortium (W3C), XML, XSL*.

XSL Transformations See *XSLT*.

X Window System A graphical, network-based windowing environment originally developed for Unix and Unix-like operating systems (and since made available for other platforms) at the Massachusetts Institute of Technology; currently, it is under continued development as an open source program by the Open Group, a Unix industry consortium. X (as the X Window System is known to Unix users) provides the basic windowing services, including fonts and pull-down menus, for graphical Unix applications. X is designed to function in a network environment. Thanks to its client-server architecture, X can display the graphical interface of an application running on some other computer on the network. One drawback of X is that it does not supply (or does not consistently supply) many of the services (such as drag-and-drop across applications and desktop utilities) that are familiar to users of consumer operating systems; for this reason, desktop environments such as GNOME or KDE have been developed to supply the X Window System with these features. A version of X under independent development, called XFree86, was initially designed to run on Intel-based hardware; it is included in most Linux distributions. See *desktop environment, GNOME, KDE, Unix, Unix-like operating system, windowing environment, window manager, X client, X Protocol, X server*.

x-y graph See *scatter diagram*.

y Abbreviation for year.

Y2K Abbreviation for Year 2000. The turn of the century posed problems for computer-users because many older computers and programs were designed to store information about dates by using only two characters for the year. As a result, some computer systems were not capable of telling the difference between the year 1900 and the year 2000. Although predictions were made of devastating breakdowns in financial and transportation systems due to the "Y2K bug," most computer-using organizations remedied the problem by revising existing code or replacing legacy systems, and relatively few problems were reported.

Y2K-compliant Able to work with four-digit year data. See *Y2K*.

Yahoo! Abbreviation for Yet Another Hierarchically Officious Oracle. A Web directory that was initiated in the early 1990s by two Stanford graduate students, David Filo and Jerry Yang. Yahoo! has since expanded into a full-featured Web portal offering a Web subject directory, Web search, discussion groups, free e-mail, instant messaging (IM) software, and much more. Today, Yahoo! consistently ranks among the most oft-visited sites on the Web. See *Web portal*.

y-axis In a graph, the values axis which normally is vertical. See *bar graph*, *column graph*, *x-axis*, *z-axis*.

Year 2000 See *Y2K*.

Yellow Book A 1983 specification manual published by Sony and Philips that defines the data format for CD-ROM disks. See *CD-ROM*.

Yellow Pages See *Network Information Services (NIS)*

yet another... Among programmers, the first two words that are humorously applied to a new program that has a great deal of competition, such as the following (imaginary) example: Yet Another Web Browser (YAWB).

YMCK See *CMYK color model*.

YMMV In text chatting, an abbreviation for "your mileage may vary." In other words, "Don't blame me if what I've suggested doesn't work out for you."

YMODEM A file transfer protocol that is an improved version of XMODEM-1K. YMODEM transfers data in 1,024-byte blocks and performs a cyclic redundancy check (CRC) on each frame. YMODEM also supports sending more than one file in sequence. See *XMODEM-1K*, *YMODEM-g*, *ZMODEM*.

YMODEM-g A file transfer protocol that leaves error-checking to protocols encoded on modem hardware, such as V.42 and MNP4, and that is best used with high-speed modems in low line noise conditions. ZMODEM is usually a better choice than YMODEM-g.

yoke The collection of electromagnets precisely arrayed around the outside of a cathode ray tube (CRT). The yoke, which is controlled by the monitor circuitry and video adapter, steers electrons from the electron guns to the proper pixels on the display. If the yoke gets out of alignment, the monitor is useless.

yottabyte (YB) A very large unit of computer data that is equal to 2^{80} (1,208,925,819,614,629,174,706,176 bytes) or 1024 zettabytes. See *exabyte (EB)*, *zettabyte (ZB)*.

Yourdon diagram A data flow diagram for use by programmers that was invented by Edward Yourdon in the 1970s. The diagram enables programmers to visualize the flow of data through a program. See *data flow diagram*.

YTD   Acronym for Year to Date, a term used in accounting to specify the total amount that has accumulated since the start of the calendar or financial year.

yy   Abbreviation for display of a year with two digits, such as "05."

yyyy   Abbreviation for display of a year with four digits, such as "2005."

Z In Unix and Unix-like operating systems such as Linux, a file extension used to indicate that the file was compressed with the Unix compress program. Use of the compress program is deprecated because it relies on a patented compression algorithm. See *compress, compression algorithm, deprecate.*

Z39.50 A protocol for the network retrieval of bibliographic data that was developed by the National Information Standards Organization (NISO), a unit of the American National Standards Institute (ANSI). Using a Z39.50-compatible application, a user can frame a query that can be processed on any other computer attached to a network, even if it is made by a different manufacturer. The protocol precisely specifies the format of the query in a way that is ideal for searching bibliographic databases, such as library card catalogues. Z39.50 applications are being developed to allow Internet applications to retrieve data from databases stored on IBM mainframe computers, which house most of the online library catalogues currently in existence.

zap **1.** To ruin a sensitive electronic circuit by exposing it to static electricity or excessive voltage. **2.** To apply a program patch or some other quick fix that corrects a program error.

Zapf Dingbats A professionally designed font consisting of symbols, called dingbats, instead of alphanumeric characters. By switching to this font while typing, an author can include such symbols in a document. . The font is named for its creator, Hermann Zapf (b. 1918), who also created Palatino, a font that is widely used on today's computer systems. See *dingbats.*

z-axis In a three-dimensional graphic image, the third dimension, usually depth . See *3-D graph, x-axis, y-axis, Z-buffer.*

Z-buffer In computer graphics, a method of storing Z-axis (depth) data in a rapidly updatable memory buffer so that the Z-axis quantity can be rapidly updated. Z-buffering enables the apparent depth of onscreen objects to be altered so that they still look realistic if the screen's point of view changes. See *z-axis.*

ZCAV Acronym for Zoned Constant Angular Velocity. See *multiple zone recording (MZR).*

zero **1.** The number zero, which so closely resembles the capitalized form of the English letter "O" that the two are easily confused. In some computer systems, zeroes are displayed with a center dot or slash in an attempt to distinguish the two. **2.** To reduce to zero. **3.** To disable a variable by making sure that its contents are set to zero throughout a program's execution.

Zero-Insertion Force (ZIF) socket An easy-to-use socket designed to accept chips conforming to the Pin Grid Array (PGA) standard. The socket enables installers to easily insert or remove the processor without bending pins. By raising a lever at the side of the ZIF package, the pins are released and the chip may be easily removed. When another chip is installed, the lever may be moved back to clamp the pins in place again. See *pin grid array (PGA), Slot 1, socket 370.*

zero-latency read In a hard disk drive, an improved read operation in which the drive begins transferring data as soon as any portion of the requested data becomes available. Drives lacking this feature must wait until the first portion of the data is accessed. See *hard disk, latency.*

zero-slot LAN A local area network (LAN) designed to use a computer's serial port rather than requiring the user to buy a network interface card. See *LAN.*

zero wait state computer An Intel-powered computer with memory speed optimized by using a scheme such as cache memory, interleaved memory, page-mode (RAM), or SRAM chips so that the microprocessor does not have to wait (enter a wait state) for the memory to catch up with processing operations. See *cache memory, interleaved memory, page-mode RAM, SRAM.*

zettabyte (ZB)   A very large unit of computer data that is equal to 2^{70} (1,180,591,620,717,411,303,424) or 1024 exabytes. See *exabyte (EB), yottabyte (YB).*

Z-force   In touch-screen displays, the amount of force required to trigger the screen's response. See *touch-sensitive display.*

Z-height   In a font, the height of a lowercase letter's body (not including the ascender or descender). Synonymous with X-height.

ZIF socket   See *Zero-Insertion Force (ZIF) socket.*

Zilog Z-80   An early 8-bit microprocessor first released by Zilog Corp. in 1976. With an 8-bit data bus and 16-bit address bus, the Zilog Z-80 had a clock speed of 2.5 MHz and was employed in several of the earliest microcomputers to become publicly available. See *8-bit microprocessor, address bus, data bus.*

zine   An electronically distributed magazine. Synonymous with e-zine and digizine.

zip   **1.** The file extension used for files compressed by a program, such as the popular WinZip, that employs the Lempel-Ziv compression or similar algorithms. **2.** To compress a file using compression software that employs the Lempel-Ziv compression algorithm or related algorithms. See *Lempel-Ziv compression algorithm, WinZip.* **3.** See *Zone Information Protocol (ZIP).*

Zip drive   A popular removable storage medium created by Iomega Corporation that provides 100MB to 250MB of storage on relatively inexpensive portable disks. Zip drives are included with some computers; other manufacturers make Zip drives available as an option. Still, their use is declining due to the rise of competing storage media

(such as CD-RW and DVD-RW discs and drives) that offer considerably more storage space.

zip file   A file compressed with compression software that employs the Lempel-Ziv compression algorithm or related algorithms. Lempel-Ziv compression algorithm, WinZip.

ZMODEM   An asynchronous file transfer protocol that enables the error-free transmission of computer files with a modem. It is fast and enables file transfers to be resumed after an interruption. See *XMODEM, YMODEM.*

zombie   A Trojan Horse program that an intruder deposits on a computer system after gaining unauthorized entry. The program alerts that intruder that it has been successfully installed. It can then join with hundreds or thousands of similar zombies and mount a distributed denial of service attack. See denial of service (DOS) attack, distributed denial of service attack.

zombie process   In Unix and Unix-like operating systems such as Linux, a child process that continues to be listed among running processes even though its parent process has exited. In such cases, the parent process probably stopped executing after an error was encountered. Therefore, a zombie process may indicate a bug in the parent program or a configuration error. See *child process, Linux, parent process, Unix.*

zone   In an AppleTalk network, a logical group of resources (such as workstations or printers) that have been grouped together by an administrator. This logical grouping is not necessarily the same as the way resources are grouped physically by means of hubs or routers. See *AppleTalk, Zone Information Protocol (ZIP).*

zone-bit recording (ZBR)   In hard disk drives, a method to increase the drive's storage capacity by defining additional sectors on the outer portion of the drive. See *hard disk, sector.*

Zoned Constant Angular Velocity (ZCAV) See *multiple zone recording (MZR)*.

Zone Information Protocol (ZIP) In an AppleTalk network, the protocol that enables powered-down resources, including computers and printers, to rejoin the network automatically when they are switched on again. See *AppleTalk, zone, zone information table*.

zone information table In an AppleTalk network, a data table that lists the zone's logical resources and indicates where they are physically located. This table propagates throughout the network and is dynamically updated. The zone information enables routers, workstations, and other devices to locate other resources. See *AppleTalk, zone, Zone Information Protocol (ZIP)*.

zoom 1. To increase or decrease the apparent magnification of a window's contents so that more or less of these contents are visible. Typically, zoom values are expressed in percentages of expansion or contraction (for example, a zoom value of 125% magnifies the contents; a value of 75% reduces the magnification). **2.** To maximize a window by clicking the zoom box so that it fills available screen space. See *zoom box*.

zoom box In a graphical user interface (GUI), a window control that enlarges a given window so that it fills all available space on the screen. See *maximize*.

Zoomed Video Port (ZV) In portable notebook computers, a video camera port and associated circuitry that handles MPEG decompression without placing a load on the computer's main processor. See *MPEG*.

Zope Abbreviation for Z Object Publishing Environment. An open-source platform for Web application development that conceptualizes the contents of a Web page as objects, each of which contains all the code necessary to make use of the object as well as specific data. Its proponents believe that, due to its commitment to object-oriented programming, it is technically superior and more versatile than competing Web application development platforms, such as Macromedia's Cold-Fusion. See *object-oriented programming*.

zorch To propel data through a computer system or network at astonishing and unprecedented speed.

Zork A text-based adventure game developed at MIT during the 1970s in which the gamer must navigate through an underground dungeon and overcome its dangers. It was subsequently released commercially by InfoCom as the Zork Trilogy. The game continues to influence computer gaming, as evidenced by the many popular games (such as Doom) that involve subterranean horrors.

zsh In Unix and Unix-like operating systems such as Linux, a command shell that is based on the Bourne Shell (sh) but incorporates features useful to programmers, such as database integration and list processing. Synonymous with Z-Shell. See *sh, shell*.

Z-time Abbreviation for Zulu time (Universal Coordinated Time). See *UTC*.

Zulu time Shorthand expression for Universal Coordinated Time (UTC). See *UTC*.